Bridging the Gap

Bridging the Gap

College Reading

Sixth Edition

Brenda D. Smith

Georgia State University

LONGMAN

An imprint of Addison Wesley Longman, Inc.

New York • Reading, Massachusetts • Menlo Park, California • Harlow, England
Don Mills, Ontario • Sydney • Mexico City • Madrid • Amsterdam

Acquisitions Editor: *Steven Rigolosi*
Development Manager: *Arlene Bessenoff*
Development Editor: *Susan Moss*
Technical Reviewer: *Jacqueline Stahlecker*
Marketing Manager: *Sue Westmoreland*
Supplements Editor: *Donna Campion*
Electronic Page Makeup: *York Production Services*
Project Coordination and Text Design: *York Production Services*
Full Service Production Manager: *Joseph Vella*
Cover Designer/Manager: *Nancy Danahy*
Cover Illustration: *Copyright © Paul Woods*
Photo Researcher: *Photosearch, Inc.*
Senior Print Buyer: *Hugh Crawford*
Printer and Binder: *Von Hoffman Press, Inc.*
Cover Printer: *The Lehigh Press, Inc.*

Library of Congress Cataloging-in-Publication Data
Smith, Brenda D., 1944–
 Bridging the gap : college reading / Brenda D. Smith.—6th ed.
  p.   cm.
 Includes bibliographical references and index.
 ISBN 0-321-04590-4
  1. Reading (Higher education)   2. Study skills   I. Title.
 II. Title: College reading.
 LB2395.3.S64   2000
 428.4'071'1—dc21   99-24053
                                                          CIP

Please visit our Website at http://www.awlonline.com

ISBN 0-321-04590-4 (Student edition)
ISBN 0-321-04591-2 (Instructor's annotated edition)

2345678910—VH—02010099

To
My Mother and Father

Brief Contents

Detailed Contents   ix

Preface   xix

Paired Readings   xxvi

Representative Features in This Edition of *Bridging the Gap*   xxviii

1 Active Learning   1

2 Vocabulary   43

3 Reading and Study Strategies   71

4 Main Idea   121

5 Organizing Textbook Information   187

6 Inference   233

7 Point of View   281

8 Critical Thinking   325

9 Graphic Illustrations   367

10 Rate Flexibility   395

11 Test Taking   423

12 Textbook Application   451

Glossary   479

Credits   483

Index   489

Paired Readings in *Bridging the Gap*, 6th Edition   494

Contents

Preface   *xix*

Paired Readings   *xxvi*

Representative Features in This Edition of **Bridging the Gap**   *xxviii*

Chapter 1   **Active Learning   1**

What Is Active Learning?   2

What is Cognitive Psychology?   2

How Does the Brain Screen Messages?   2

Is Divided Attention Effective?   4

Can Tasks Become Automatic?   4

   Automatic Aspects of Reading   4

Cognitive Styles   5

What Is Concentration?   6

Poor Concentration: Causes and Cures   7

   External Distractions   7

   Internal Distractions   9

   Reader's Tip: Improving Concentration   12

Focusing on Successful Academic Behaviors   13

Selection 1: Computer Science   19

Contemporary Focus: "Net Addiction" from *Oracle Service Humor Mailing List*   19

"The Internet" by H. L. Capron   20

Searching the Net   27

   Secrets of a Successful Search   28

   Make a Plan   28

   Reader's Tip: Popular College Databases   29

   Search and Search Again   30

   Reader's Tip: Manipulating the Search   30

   Read Selectively   30

   Record as You Go   31

   Consider the Source   31

Selection 2: Psychology   33
Contemporary Focus: "Maternal Instincts" by Daniel J. Cox   33
"Critical-Period Hypothesis" by James V. McConnell   34

Reader's Journal   42

Chapter 2   Vocabulary   43

Remembering New Words   44
Using Context Clues   46
    Definition   46
    Elaborating Details   46
    Examples   47
    Comparison   47
    Contrast   48
    Limitations of Context Clues   48
    Multiple Meanings of a Word   52
Understanding the Structure of Words   53
Using a Dictionary   57
Word Origins   60
Using a Glossary   61
Using a Thesaurus   62
Using Analogies   64
    Reader's Tip: Categories of Analogy Relationships   64
Easily Confused Words   65
Recognizing Acronyms   66
Recognizing Transitional Words   67
    Reader's Tip: Signals for Transition   67
Reader's Journal   70

Chapter 3   Reading and Study Strategies   71

What Is a Study System?   72
Why Use a Study System?   73
Stage 1: Previewing   73
    Signposts for Answering Preview Questions   73
    Reader's Tip: Asking Questions Before Reading   74
    Preview to Activate Schemata   76
Stage 2: Integrating Knowledge While Reading   77
    Expanding Knowledge   78
    Integrating Ideas: How Do Good Readers Think?   78

Metacognition   78
Reader's Tip: Using Thinking Strategies While Reading   79
Reader's Tip: Developing a Metacognitive
   Sense for Reading   81
Stage 3: Recalling for Self-Testing   84
 Recall by Writing   84
 Reader's Tip: Recalling After Reading   85
 How to Recall   85

Selection 1: Psychology   89
Contemporary Focus: "Finding the Flow" by Mihaly Csikszentmihalyi
 89
"Expressing Emotion" by David Myers   91

Selection 2: Business   100
Contemporary Focus: "Motorcyclists in Cross-Hairs" by Jim Jensen
 100
"The Story of Harley-Davidson Motorcycles" by Thomas C. Kinnear,
 Kenneth Bernhardt, and Kathleen Krentler   101

Selection 3: Sociology   110
Contemporary Focus: "It's What You Say and Do" by Marcia Pounds
 110
"Unity in Diversity" by Donald Light, Jr. and Suzanne Keller   111

Reader's Journal   120

Chapter 4 **Main Idea   121**

What Is a Main Idea?   122
 Labels for Main Idea   122
Importance of Prior Knowledge in Main Idea   122
Main Idea Strategies   123
 "Informed" Expert Readers   123
 "Uninformed" Expert Readers   123
What Is a Topic?   124
How Do Topics and Main Ideas Differ?   124
Questioning for the Main Idea   126
 Reader's Tip: Finding the Main Idea   127
What Do Details Do?   128
 Reader's Tip: Signals for Significance   130
Stated and Unstated Main Ideas   130
 Examples of Stated Main Idea   133
 Examples of Unstated Main Idea   139

Interpreting Longer Selections   143
   Reader's Tip: Getting the Main Idea of Longer Selections   143
Patterns of Organization   144
   Simple Listing   144
   Definition   145
   Description   146
   Time Order or Sequence   146
   Comparison-Contrast   147
   Cause and Effect   147
Summary Writing: A Main Idea Skill   151
   Why Summarize?   152
   Reader's Tip: How to Summarize   152

Selection 1: Psychology   157
Contemporary Focus: "Building a Better Mouse" by Dennis Meredith   157
"Monkey Love" by James V. McConnell   158

Selection 2: History   167
Contemporary Focus: "Black Entrepreneurs Face a Perplexing Issue: How to Pitch to Whites" by Angelo B. Henderson   167
"Heroes for Civil Rights" by James Martin et al.   168

Selection 3: Biology   176
Contemporary Focus: "Death in Venison" by Geoffrey Norman   176
"Nile Perch and Rabbits and Kudzu, Oh My!" by Cecie Starr and Ralph Taggart   177

Reader's Journal   186

Chapter 5   Organizing Textbook Information   187

The Demands of College Study   188
Building Knowledge Networks   188
Methods of Organizing Textbook Information   189
Annotating   190
   Why Annotate?   191
   When to Annotate   191
   Reader's Tip: How to Annotate   192
Notetaking   196
   Why Take Textbook Notes?   196
   Reader's Tip: How to Take Notes   196
Outlining   199
   Why Outline?   199

How to Outline   200
Reader's Tip: Avoiding Pitfalls in Outlining   200
Mapping   204
Why Map?   204
Reader's Tip: How to Map   206

Selection 1: Biology   207
Contemporary Focus: "Umbilical Cord Blood Helps Fight Cancer"
by Renee Twombly   207
"Pregnancy and Birth" by Robert Wallace   208

Selection 2: History   214
Contemporary Focus: "Evita Stylish, Thieving Diva of Cult Politics"
by Jim Pinkerton   214
"Women in History" by Leonard Pitt   216

Selection 3: Allied Health   222
Contemporary Focus: "Best and Worst Cafeteria Foods" by
Lisa M. Flores   222
"Nutrition, Health, and Stress" by Barbara Brehm   223

Reader's Journal   232

Chapter 6 **Inference   233**

What Is an Inference?   234
Connotation of Words   235
Figurative Language   238
Idioms   238
Similes   239
Metaphors   239
Personification   239
Verbal Irony   239
Implied Meaning   241
Prior Knowledge and Implied Meaning   244
Expanding Prior Knowledge   246
Drawing Conclusions   247
Reader's Tip: Making Inferences   250

Selection 1: Literature   253
Contemporary Focus: "To Make a Drama Out of Trauma"
by Fokko De Vries   253
"Mother Savage" by Guy de Maupassant   254

Selection 2: Essay   **263**

Contemporary Focus: "Language in the Dumps" by John Leo   263

"Doubts about Douplespeak" by William Lutz   264

Selection 3: Essay   **268**

Contemporary Focus: "If Only We All Spoke Two Languages"
by Ariel Dorfman   268

"Bilingual Education" by Richard Rodriguez   269

Reader's Journal   279

Chapter 7   Point of View   281

Is a Textbook Influenced by the Author's Point of View?   282

What Is the Author's Point of View?   282

What Is the Reader's Point of View?   285

What Is a Fact and What Is an Opinion?   289

   Reader's Tip: Questioning to Uncover Bias   289

What Is the Author's Purpose?   292

What Is the Author's Tone?   295

Editorial Cartoons   299

Selection 1: Essay   **303**

Contemporary Focus: "The New Family Dinner" by Carol Wallace   303

"Elderly Parents" A Cultural Duty" by Ta Thuc Phu   304

Selection 2: Literature   **308**

Contemporary Focus: "San Antonio Journal: Novelist's Purple Palette
Is Not to Everyone's Taste" by Sara Rimer   308

"Only Daughter" by Sandra Cisneros   309

Selection 3: Business   **314**

Contemporary Focus: "Tort Reform: Excessive Litigation by Trial
Lawyers" by William S. Stavropoulos   314

"Understanding the Legal Context of Business" by Ricky Griffin and
Ronald Ebert   315

Reader's Journal   323

Chapter 8   Critical Thinking   325

What Is Critical Thinking?   326

Applying Skills to Meet College Goals   326

   Reader's Tip: How to Think Critically   327

   Barriers to Critical Thinking   327

Power of Critical Thinking   328
   Courtroom Analogy   329
Recognizing an Argument   329
Steps in Critical Thinking   330
   Step 1: Identify the Issue   330
   Step 2: Identify Support for the Argument   333
   Reader's Tip: Categories of Support for Arguments   335
   Step 3: Evaluate the Support   335
   Step 4: Evaluate the Argument   340
Inductive and Deductive Reasoning   341
   Applying the Critical Thinking Steps 1–4: An Example   342
   Explanation of the Steps   343
Creative and Critical Thinking   348

Selection 1: Psychology   351
Contemporary Focus: "Screen: End of the Word?" by Colin MacCabe   351
"Has Television Killed Off Reading—and If So, So What?" by Carole Wade and Carol Tavris   352

Selection 2: Editorial Essay   356
Contemporary Focus: "The Sound and Fury of Ignorance" by Peter Cochrane   356
"Students Led to Believe Opinions More Important than Knowledge" by Thomas Sowell   357

Selection 3: Editorial Essay   361
Contemporary Focus: "Should You Carry a Gun?" by Romesh Patnesar   361
"Shooting Holes in Gun Laws" by Mike Royko   362

Reader's Journal   366

Chapter 9   **Graphic Illustrations   367**

What Graphics Do   368
   Reader's Tip: How to Read Graphic Material   370
   Geographic Review   373

Selection 1: Allied Health   381
Contemporary Focus: "Higher Education: Crocked on Campus" by Christine Gorman   381
"Alcohol and Nutrition" by Eva May Nunnelley Hamilton et al.   382

Reader's Journal   394

Chapter 10 **Rate Flexibility   395**

Why Is Rate Important?   396

What Is Your Reading Rate?   396

How Fast Should You Read?   399

    Rate Varies According to Prior Knowledge   400

Techniques for Faster Reading   400

    Concentrate   400

    Stop Regressing   401

    Expand Fixations   401

    Monitor Subvocalization   402

    Preview   402

    Use Your Pen as a Pacer   403

    Push and Pace   404

Skimming   409

Scanning   409

    Reader's Tip: Techniques for Skimming   410

    Reader's Tip: Techniques for Scanning   411

Selection 1: Allied Health   412

"Passive Smoking" by Curtis Byer and Louis Shainberg   412

Selection 2: Business   415

"The Baby Boomers and the Generation Xers" by Philip Kotler and
    Gary Armstrong   415

Selection 3: Essay   418

"The Sanctuary of School" by Lynda Barry   418

Reader's Journal   422

Chapter 11 **Test Taking   423**

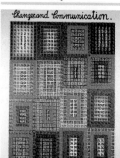

Can Testwiseness Help?   424

Strategies for Mental and Physical Awareness   424

    Before Taking a Test   424

    During the Test   425

    Reader's Tip: Preparing for a Test   426

    After the Test   427

Strategies for Standardized Reading Tests   428

    Read to Comprehend the Passage as a Whole   428

    Anticipate What Is Coming Next   428

    Read Rapidly, But Don't Allow Yourself to Feel Rushed   429

    Read with Involvement to Learn and Enjoy   429

Self-Test for the Main Idea   429
Recognizing the Major Question Types   431
   Main Idea   431
   Details   432
   Implied Meaning   432
   Purpose   433
   Vocabulary   434
Strategies for Multiple-Choice Items   434
   Consider All Alternatives Before Choosing an Answer   434
   Anticipate the Answer and Look for Something Close to It   435
   Avoid Answers with 100 Percent Words   435
   Consider Answers with Qualifying Words   435
   Choose the Intended Answer Without Overanalyzing   436
   True Statements Must Be True Without Exception   436
   If Two Options Are Synonymous, Eliminate Both   436
   Study Similar Options to Determine the Differences   437
   Use Logical Reasoning If Two Answers Are Correct   437
   Look Suspiciously at Directly Quoted Pompous Phrases   437
   Simplify Double Negatives by Canceling Out Both   438
   Use Can't-Tell Responses If Clues Are Insufficient   438
   Validate True Responses on "All of the Following Except"   438
   Note Oversights on Hastily Constructed Tests   439
Strategies for Content Area Exams   442
   Multiple-Choice Items   442
   Short-Answer Items   443
   Essay Questions   443
   Reader's Tip: Key Words in Essay Questions   447
Locus of Control   448
Reader's Journal   450

Chapter 12   **Textbook Application   451**

Meeting the Challenge   452
   Reader's Tip: Organizing Your Study   452

Chapter Selection: Sociology   453
Contemporary Focus: "A No-Fault Holocaust" by John Leo   453
"Race and Ethnicity" by Alex Thio   454

Glossary   *479*

Credits   *483*

Index   *489*

Paired Readings in Bridging the Gap, *6th Edition*   **494**

Preface

With *Bridging the Gap*, my objective has always been for students to become capable readers and thinkers who take ownership of their learning. More than ever, this sixth edition focuses on developing schema by connecting textbook reading to real-world issues. In an exciting new feature called *Contemporary Focus*, excerpts from recent magazine and newspaper articles are paired with the longer end-of-chapter textbook reading selections. The purpose of these brief and engaging articles is to increase interest in reading, to activate the reader's schema by linking a current issue to a concept within the longer textbook selections, to stimulate classroom discussion, and to promote critical thinking. This sixth edition contains nineteen of these new introductory articles.

Another new sixth edition feature focusing on making connections is the *Search the Net* activity that follows each longer textbook reading selection. Electronic reading skills are becoming essential for college students. To support this need, the first *Search the Net* activity in Chapter 1 begins with an explanation of how to plan and conduct an effective Internet search. Subsequent activities pose questions that connect Internet exploration with the textbook topics in each longer reading selection. In many cases, relevant URLs are suggested to help launch the student's search.

The new *Reader's Tip* boxes in this edition give easy-to-access advice by condensing techniques for improving reading into practical hints for quick reference. Each chapter in this edition contains at least one (and usually several) of these key concepts boxes. New to the sixth edition, vocabulary development is presented in a complete chapter early in the book (Chapter 2). This edition also continues to include vocabulary words in context after most of the longer reading selections. In addition to the nineteen new *Contemporary Focus* articles, this edition contains eleven new longer end-of-chapter reading selections, including a piece about the Internet and a work by acclaimed author Sandra Cisneros.

The intent of the sixth edition, as with previous editions, is to personally involve the reader, to build and enrich the knowledge networks for academic reading, to stimulate engaging class discussion, and to foster independent learning and thinking. I hope students enjoy learning from this colorful new edition.

CONTENT AND ORGANIZATION

The sixth edition continues the tradition of previous editions by using actual college textbook material for teaching and practice. Designed for an upper-level course in college reading, each chapter introduces a new skill, provides short practice exercises to teach the skill, and then offers practice through longer textbook selections.

Presentation of skills in the text moves from the general to the specific. Initial chapters discuss active learning, vocabulary, study strategies, main idea, and organization, while later chapters teach inference, point of view, critical thinking, graphic illustrations and rate flexibility. The reading and study skills discussions in the first portion of the book stress the need to construct the main idea of a passage and to select significant supporting details. Exercises encourage "engaged thinking" before reading, while reading, and after reading. Four different methods of organizing textbook information for later study are explained.

The critical thinking chapter is a culmination and application of main-idea, inference, and point-of-view skills. The chapter on test taking is designed to help students gain insights into text construction and the testing situation. The book concludes with an opportunity to apply all the skills to an actual chapter from a college textbook.

SPECIAL FEATURES OF THE SIXTH EDITION

- **Contemporary Focus** articles linked to the longer textbook readings are included to stimulate cognitive connections and to promote group discussion. Each Contemporary Focus article is drawn from a popular source, such as a magazine or newspaper, to demonstrate the textbook readings relevant to the "real world."

- **Contemporary Link** questions promote critical thinking by demonstrating the relevance of the introductory articles to the textbook selections that they accompany. A list of textbook readings, along with their accompanying Contemporary Focus features, follows the Preface.

- **Search the Net** activities encourage students to amplify textbook study through Internet research. Instructions on how to use the Internet are presented in the first chapter. A book-specific Longman website is also available: **http://www.awlonline.com/SmithBTG.**

- **Reader's Tip** boxes give easy-to-access advice for readers, condensing strategies for improving reading into practical hints for quick reference.

- **Eleven new longer reading selections** are included.

- A broad range of **vocabulary development** topics and corresponding exercises are presented in a separate chapter early in the book.

- For the instructor's convenience, **critical thinking and collaborative study** opportunities are signaled throughout by means of decorative marginal icons.

CONTINUING FEATURES

Other classroom-tested features of the book include the following:

- Actual **textbook selections** are used for practice exercises.
- **Many academic disciplines** are represented throughout, including psychology, history, business, allied health, biology, sociology, nutrition, computer science, and English literature.
- Each longer textbook selection has both **explicit and inferential questions.**
- Selections include essay questions that elicit an organized **written response.**
- **Vocabulary is presented in context,** and exercises on prefixes, suffixes, and roots are included in each chapter.
- Although skills build and overlap, **each chapter can be taught as a separate unit** to fit individual class or student needs.
- **Pages are perforated** so that students can tear out and hand in assignments.
- A **Reader's Journal** activity appears at the end of each chapter so that students can learn about themselves, reflect on their strengths and weaknesses, and monitor their progress as learners.
- Discussion and practice exercises on **barriers to critical thinking** are included that include cultural conditioning, self-deception, and oversimplification.
- Practice is offered in **identifying fallacies** in critical thinking and in **evaluating arguments.**
- At the end of the text, a **chapter-length reading selection,** "Racial and Ethnic Minorities" explores the history of ethnic groups in America. Taken from a freshman sociology textbook, this longer selection provides the opportunity to practice the transfer of skills while still including study questions and strategy suggestions. Both multiple-choice and essay questions are provided.

THE TEACHING AND LEARNING PACKAGE

Each component of the teaching and learning package has been crafted to ensure that the course is a rewarding experience for both instructors and students.

The **Annotated Instructor's Edition** is an exact replica of the student edition, but includes all answers printed directly on the fill-in lines provided in the text. (0-321-04591-2)

The **Instructor's Manual** contains overhead transparency masters and additional vocabulary and comprehension questions for each reading selection. The true-false, vocabulary, and comprehension quizzes can be used as prereading quizzes to stimulate interest or as evaluation quizzes after reading. For the sixth edition, a new vocabulary-in-context exercise has been added to reinforce the words in the longer textbook selections. To receive an examination copy of the Instructor's Manual, please contact your Addison Wesley Longman sales representative. You may also request an exam copy by calling 1-800-552-2499, or by sending your request via e-mail to exam@awl.com (0-321-04450-9)

The **Test Bank** includes additional reading selections, chapter tests, vocabulary tests, and midterm and final exams. To receive an examination copy of the Test Bank, please contact your Addison Wesley Longman sales representative. You may also request an exam copy by calling 1-800-552-2499, or by sending your request via e-mail to exam@awl.com (0-321-04593-9)

In addition to the book-specific supplements discussed above, a series of other skills-based supplements are available for both instructors and students. All of these supplements are available either free or at greatly reduced prices.

Electronic and Online Offerings

Reading Road Trip **Multimedia Software.** This innovative and exciting multimedia reading software package takes students on a tour of 15 cities and landmarks throughout the United States. Each of the 15 modules corresponds to a reading or study skill (for example, finding the main idea, understanding patterns of organization, and thinking critically). All modules contain a tour of the location, instruction and tutorial, exercises, interactive feedback, and mastery tests. The *Reading Road Trip* is packaged free with this textbook.

Bridging the Gap **Text-Specific Website.** Free to adopters, this book specific Website offers chapter summaries, additional quizzes, and Internet activities and resources for students. In addition, it offers instructor ancillaries, a syllabus manager, and interactive chat. **http://longman.awl.com/smithBTG.**

The Longman English Pages Web Site. Both students and instructors can visit our free content-rich Web site for additional reading selections and writing exercises. From the Longman English pages, visitors can conduct a simulated Web search, learn how to write a resume and cover letter, or try their hand at poetry writing. Stop by and visit us at http://longman.awl.com/englishpages.

The Basic Skills Electronic Newsletter—Twice a month during the spring and fall, instructors who have subscribed receive a free copy of the Longman Basic Skills Newsletter in their e-mailbox. Written by experienced classroom instructors, the newsletter offers teaching tips, classroom activities, book reviews, and more. To subscribe, visit the Longman Basic Skills Web site at **http://longman.awl.com/basicskills,** or send an e-mail to **Basic Skills@awl.com.**

Teaching Online: Internet Research, Conversation and Composition, Second Edition. Ideal for instructors who have never surfed the Net, this easy-to-follow guide offers basic definitions, numerous examples, and step-by-step information about finding and using Internet sources. Free to adopters. 0-321-01957-1

Researching Online, Third Edition. A perfect companion for a new age, this indispensable new supplement helps students navigate the Internet. Adapted from *Teaching Online,* the instructor's Internet guide, *Researching Online* speaks directly to students, giving them detailed, step-by-step instructions for performing electronic searches. Paperback version available free to students when the instructor adopts *Bridging the Gap.* 0-321-05802-X.

For Additional Reading and Reference

The Longman Textbook Reader. This reader offers five complete chapters from freshman-level textbooks in the following disciplines: computer science, biology, psychology, communications, and business. Each chapter includes all the original features from the text, as well as additional comprehension quizzes, critical thinking questions, and group activities. Available free to students when instructors adopt *Bridging the Gap.* 0-321-04617-X

The Dictionary Deal. Two dictionaries can be shrinkwrapped with any Longman Basic Skills title at a nominal fee. *The New American Webster Handy College Dictionary* (0-451-18166-2) is a paperback reference text with more than 100,000 entries. *Merriam Webster's Collegiate Dictionary,* tenth edition (0-87779-709-9), is a hardback reference with a citation file of more than 14.5 million examples of English words drawn from actual use.

Penguin Quality Paperback Titles. A series of Penguin paperbacks is available at a significant discount when shrinkwrapped with any Longman Basic Skills title. Some titles available are: Toni Morrison's *Beloved* (0-452-26446-4), Julia Alvarez's *How the Garcia Girls Lost Their Accents* (0-452-26806-0), Mark Twain's *Huckleberry Finn* (0-451-52650-3), *Narrative of the Life of Frederick Douglass* (0-451-52673-2), Harriet Beecher Stowe's *Uncle Tom's Cabin* (0-451-52302-4), Dr. Martin Luther King, Jr.'s *Why We Can't Wait* (0-451-62754-7), and plays by Shakespeare, Miller, and Albee. For a complete list of titles or more information, please contact your Addison Wesley Longman sales consultant.

80 Readings, Second Edition. This inexpensive volume contains 80 brief readings (1–3 pages each) on a variety of themes: writers on writing, nature, women and men, customs and habits, politics, rights and obligations, and coming of age. Also included is an alternate rhetorical table of contents. 0-321-01648-3.

Newsweek **Alliance & Interactive Guide to** *Newsweek.* Instructors may choose to shrinkwrap a 12-week subscription to *Newsweek* with this text. The price of the subscription is greatly discounted from the cover price. Available with the subscription is a free *Interactive Guide to Newsweek*—a workbook for students who are using the text. In addition, *Newsweek* provides a wide variety of instructor supplements free to teachers, including maps, Skills Builders, and weekly quizzes. *Newsweek* subscription card: 0-321-04759-1. Interactive Guide to *Newsweek*: 0-321-05528-4.

For Instructors

CLAST Test Package, Fourth Edition. These two 40-item objective tests evaluate students' readiness for the CLAST exams. Strategies for teaching CLAST preparedness are included. Free to instructors. Reproducible sheets: 0-321-01950-4 Computerized IBM version: 0-321-01982-2 Computerized Mac version: 0-321-01983-0

TASP Test Package, Third Edition. These 12 practice pre-tests and post-tests assess the same reading and writing skills covered in the TASP examination. Free to instructors. Reproducible sheets: 0-321-01959-8 Computerized IBM version: 0-321-02623-3 Computerized Mac version: 0-321-02622-5

Reading Critically: Texts, Charts, and Graphs, Second Edition. For instructors who would like to emphasize critical thinking in their courses, this brief book (65 pages) provides additional critical thinking material to supplement coverage in the text. Free to instructors. 0-673-97365-4

For Students

Learning Together. This brief guide to the fundamentals of collaborative learning teaches students how to work effectively in groups, how to revise with peer response, and how to co-author a paper or report. Shrinkwrapped free with any Longman Basic Skills text. 0-673-46848-8

ACKNOWLEDGMENTS

© 2000 Addison-Wesley Educational Publishers, Inc.

I am extremely happy to have worked on this sixth edition with Basic Skills Editor Steven Rigolosi. Steve has the creative vision to see new possibilities and the organizational skills to implement ideas. He is responsible for the new *Contemporary Focus* feature, the addition of four-color printing, and the *Annotated Instructor's Edition.*

I continue to appreciate the opportunity to work with Developmental Editor Susan Moss. In fact, I have come to believe that I could not do a book without Sue. She is intuitive about the needs of students and teachers, and I value her insights and opinions.

In this edition Karen Oates assisted with the instructions for using the Internet and the related exercises. Michelle Elbe helped locate many of the *Contemporary Focus* articles, and Chris LaBudda researched many of the *Search the Net* exercises. Both Kelly Daniels and Julie Smith assisted as researchers. Jackie Stahlecker served as technical reviewer. The book benefited from their excellent contributions.

Again, I feel extremely privileged to have received advice from so many learned colleagues in the college reading profession. The book is strengthened by their insightful, sincere, and constructive comments. Their students are lucky to have these knowledgeable and concerned instructors:

Hilda Barrow, Pitt Community College
Dina Beeghly, West Chester University
Paul Beran, St. Louis Community College, Meramec Campus
Dianne Cates, Central Piedmont Community College
Marva Cromer, DeKalb College
Kathleen Engstrom, Fullerton College
Karen Foley, Angelina College
Barbara J. Grossman, Essex County College
Susie Khirallah-Johnston, Tyler Junior College
Jane Killman, Davenport College of Business
Karen L. Reinhart, Spokane Community College
Patricia Rottmund, Harrisburg Area Community College
Mary Sue Scott, Tyler Junior College
Pam Smith, Pellissippi State Technical College
Diane Starke, El Paso Community College
Shirley Wachtel, Middlesex County College

Brenda D. Smith
Atlanta, Georgia

PAIRED READINGS IN *BRIDGING THE GAP*, 6TH EDITION

This edition of *Bridging the Gap* features paired readings at the end of most chapters. Each reading selection begins with a "Contemporary Focus" reading drawn from a popular source, such as a newspaper or magazine, that demonstrates the relevance of the following textbook selection to the world beyond college. A complete listing of the longer end-of-chapter academic readings, along with their accompanying Contemporary Focus articles, appears below.

	Title/Source of End-of-Chapter Textbook or Academic Selection	**Title/Source of Accompanying Contemporary Focus Article**
Chapter 1 Active Learning	"The Internet," by H. L. Capron, *Computers: Tools for an Information Age*	"Net Addiction," from *Oracle Service: Humor Mailing List* (oracle-humor-subscribe@lyris.oraclehumor.com)
	"Critical-Period Hypothesis," by James V. McConnell, *Understanding Human Behavior*	"Maternal Instincts," by Daniel J. Cox, *Life*
Chapter 3 Reading and Study Strategies	"Expressing Emotion," by David Myers, *Psychology, fifth edition*	"Finding the Flow," by Mihaly Csikszentmihalyi, *Psychology Today*
	"The Story of Harley-Davidson Motorcycles," from Thomas C. Kinnear et al., *Principles of Marketing*	"Motorcyclists in Cross-Hairs," by Jim Jensen, *Rocky Mountain News*
	"Unity in Diversity," by Donald Light, Jr., and Suzanne Keller, *Sociology, fourth edition*	"It's What You Say and Do," by Marcia Pounds, *Sun Sentinel*
Chapter 4 Main Idea	"Monkey Love," by James V. McConnell, *Understanding Human Behavior*	"Building a Better Mouse," by Dennis Meredith, *Meridian: Midway Airlines*
	"Heroes for Civil Rights," by James Martin et al., *America and Its People*	"Black Entrepreneurs Face a Perplexing Issue: How to Pitch to Whites," by Angelo B. Henderson, *The Wall Street Journal*
	"Nile Perch and Rabbits and Kudzu, Oh My!" by Cecie Starr and Ralph Taggart, *Biology: The Unity and Diversity of Life, eighth edition*	"Death in Venison," by Geoffrey Norman, *The American Spectator*
Chapter 5 Organizing Textbook Information	"Pregnancy and Birth," by Robert Wallace, *Biology: The World of Life*	"Umbilical Cord Blood Helps Fight Cancer," by Renee Twombly, *Duke Comprehensive Cancer Center Notes*
	"Women in History," by Leonard Pitt, *We Americans*	"Evita Stylish, Thieving Diva of Cult Politics," by Jim Pinkerton, *USA Today*
	"Nutrition, Health, and Stress," by Barbara Brehm, *Stress Management*	"Best and Worst Cafeteria Foods," by Lisa M. Flores, *Muscle & Fitness*

	Title/Source of End-of-Chapter Textbook or Academic Selection	Title/Source of Accompanying Contemporary Focus Article
Chapter 6 **Inference**	"Mother Savage," by Guy de Maupassant, *Mademoiselle Fifi and Other Stories*	"To Make a Drama Out of Trauma," by Fokko De Vries, *Lancet*
	"Doubts about Doublespeak," by William Lutz, from Gary Goshgarian, *Exploring Language, eighth edition*	"Language in the Dumps," by John Leo, *U.S. News and World Report*
	"Bilingual Education," by Richard Rodriguez, *Hunger of Memory*	"If Only We All Spoke Two Languages," by Ariel Dorfman, *The New York Times*
Chapter 7 **Point of View**	"Elderly Parents: A Cultural Duty," by Ta Thuc Phu, *The Orlando Sentinel*	"The New Family Dinner," by Carol Wallace, *Parents*
	"Only Daughter," by Sandra Cisneros, *Women's Voices From Borderlands*	"San Antonio Journal: Novelist's Purple Palette Is Not to Everyone's Taste," by Sara Rimer, *The New York Times*
	"Understanding the Legal Context of Business," by Ricky Griffin and Ronald Ebert, *Business, fourth edition*	"Tort Reform: Excessive Litigation by Trial Lawyers," by William S. Stavropoulos
Chapter 8 **Critical Thinking**	"Has Television Killed Off Reading— and If So, So What?" by Carole Wade and Carol Tavris, *Psychology, fifth edition*	"Screen: End of the Word?" by Colin MacCabe, *The Guardian*
	"Students Led to Believe Opinions More Important than Knowledge," by Thomas Sowell, *The Arizona Republic*	"The Sound and Fury of Ignorance," by Peter Cochrane, *The Daily Telegraph*
	"Shooting Holes in Gun Laws," by Mike Royko, *Tribune Media Services*	"Should You Carry A Gun?" by Romesh Patnesar, *Time*
Chapter 9 **Graphic Illustrations**	"Alcohol and Nutrition," by Eva May Nunnelley Hamilton et al., *Nutrition*	"Higher Education: Crocked on Campus," by Christine Gorman, *Time*
Chapter 10 **Rate Flexibility**	"Passive Smoking," by Curtis Byer and Louis Shainberg, *Living Well*	(No Contemporary Focus readings in this chapter.)
	"The Baby Boomers and the Generation Xers," by Philip Kotler and Gary Armstrong, *Principles of Marketing*	
	"The Sanctuary of School," by Lynda Barry, *The New York Times*	
Chapter 12 **Textbook Application**	"Race and Ethnicity," by Alex Thio, *Sociology: A Brief Introduction*	"A No-Fault Holocaust," by John Leo, *U.S. News and World Report*

Representative Features in *Bridging the Gap, 6th Edition*

	Reading or Study Skills	Reader's Tip Boxes	Critical Thinking Topics	Internet Search Topics
Chapter 1 Active Learning	• Accumulating and Interpreting Information, *2* • Understanding Cognitive Processes, *2* • Assessing Your Learning Style, *5* • Improving Concentration, *7* • Motivating Yourself, *10* • Focusing on Successful Academic Behaviors, *13* • Using a Syllabus, *15*	• Improving Concentration, *12* • Popular College Databases, *29* • Manipulating the Internet Search, *30*	• Internet Access From the Workplace: Ethical Issues, *24* • Critical Future Steps in Internet Development, *24* • Proving the Existence of a Critical Period in An Organism's Life, *38* • Manipulating Maternal Instincts, *38*	• Pivotal Historic Figures and Events in Internet Evolution, *32* • Survival Value of Unusual Maternal Instinct in Birds, *41*
Chapter 2 Vocabulary	• Remembering New Words, *44* • Using Context Clues, *46* • Distinguishing Multiple Meanings, *52* • Understanding Word Structure, *53* • Using a Dictionary, *57* • Understanding Word Origins, *60* • Using a Glossary, *61* • Using a Thesaurus, *62* • Using Analogies, *64*	(None included given nature of chapter)	(None included given nature of chapter)	• Vocabulary-building Websites, *69*

© 2000 Addison-Wesley Educational Publishers, Inc.

	Reading or Study Skills	Reader's Tip Boxes	Critical Thinking Topics	Internet Search Topics
	• Identifying Easily Confused Words, 65 • Recognizing Acronyms, 66 • Recognizing Transitional Words, 67			
Chapter 3 **Reading and Study Strategies**	• Developing a Study System, 73 • Previewing, 73 • Integrating Knowledge, 77 • Understanding Metacognition, 80 • Recalling for Self-Testing, 84	• Asking Questions Before Reading, 74 • Using Thinking Strategies While Reading, 79 • Developing a Metacognitive Sense for Reading, 81 • Recalling After Reading, 85	• Controlling Fear, Reducing Anger, and Promoting Happiness, 96 • Real-World Examples of Csikszentmihalyi's "Flow," 97 • Harley-Davidson's Success in Three Business Development Stages, 105 • Transformation of a Dangerous Machine into a Lucrative Product, 106 • Cultural Universals and Ethnocentrism in Our Society, 115 • Importance of Knowledge of Values and Norms in the Corporate World, 116	• More About the Research of Csikszentmihalyi, 99 • Riding Tips and the Harley-Davidson "Attitude," 109 • Intercultural Communication Training, 118
Chapter 4 **Main Idea**	• Identifying Main Idea, 122 • Recognizing Importance of Prior Knowledge, 122	• Finding the Main Idea, 127 • Signals for Significance, 130	• Applicability of Harlow's Findings to Human Infants, 163	• Causes of and Risk Factors for Child Abuse, 166 • Museums Related to the Civil Rights Movement, 175

Reading or Study Skills	Reader's Tip Boxes	Critical Thinking Topics	Internet Search Topics
• Differentiating Topic, Main Idea, and Supporting Details, *124* • Recognizing Stated and Unstated Main Ideas, *130* • Interpreting Longer Selections, *143* • Identifying Patterns of Organization, *144* • Summary Writing, *151*	• Getting the Main Idea of Longer Selections, *143* • How to Summarize, *152*	• Medical Research on Mice vs. Psychological Research on Monkeys, *163* • Cause-and-Effect Significance of Historical Figures and Events, *172* • Historical Heroes vs. Contemporary Entrepreneurs: Philosophical Differences, *172* • Predicting Ecological Events, *181* • Comparing and Contrasting Solutions to the Endangered Species Problem, *181*	• Exotic Species and Their Environmental Impact, *184*
***Chapter 5* Organizing Textbook Information**	• Building Knowledge Networks, *188* • Annotating, *190* • Notetaking, *196* • Outlining, *199* • Mapping, *204*	• How to Annotate, *192* • How to Take Notes *196* • Avoiding Pitfalls in Outlining, *200* • How to Map, *206*	• Importance of Medical Self-Care, *212* • Ethics of Donation or Sale of Umbilical Cord Blood, *213* • Impact of Early feminists on Stereotypical Thinking, *218* • Evita Peron and Sojourner Truth: Contrasting Sources of Power, *218*	• Birth Defects and Preventive Measures, *213* • More on Sojourner Truth, *221* • Creating the Optimal Diet and Exercise Plan for You, *230*

	Reading or Study Skills	Reader's Tip Boxes	Critical Thinking Topics	Internet Search Topics
			• Using Nutritional Knowledge to Enhance Mental Performance During Exam Week, *227*	
			• Avoiding the "Freshman 15,"*228*	
Chapter 6 Inference	• Understanding the Inferential Level of Reading, *234*	• Making Inferences, *250*	• Rationale for Mother Savage's Behavior, *259*	• French Frustration Under Prussian Occupation as Reflected in the Work of Guy deMaupassant, *262*
	• Distinguishing Connotation and Denotation, *235*		• Modern Psychological Interpretation of Mother Savage's Circumstances, *259*	• Doublespeak in the Political Arena, *267*
	• Recognizing Figurative Language, *238*		• Societal Factors That Promote Doublespeak, *266*	• *Hunger of Memory* via Online Bookstore, *278*
	• Interpreting Implied Meaning Through Inferences, *241*		• Comparing Two Authors' Attitudes about Linguistic Changes, *266*	
	• Prior Knowledge and Implied Meaning, *244*		• Bilingual Education: Rodriguez's Position vs. Your Position, *274*	
	• Drawing Conclusions, *247*		• Language Instruction: Bilingual Approach vs. Immersion Method, *275*	
Chapter 7 Point of View	• Recognizing the Author's Point of View, *282*	• Questioning to Uncover Bias, *292*	• Family Traditions and Care of Elderly Parents: Your View, *306*	• Value of the Internet as a Resource for Elderly People, *307*

	Reading or Study Skills	Reader's Tip Boxes	Critical Thinking Topics	Internet Search Topics
	• Prior Knowledge and the Reader's Point of View, 285		• Care of Elderly: Cultural Differences, 306	• More about Sandra Cisneros and other Female Hispanic Authors, 313
	• Differentiating Facts and Opinions, 289		• Interpreting Mexican-American Pride Through the Work of Sandra Cisneros, 312	• Finding an Attorney Online, 322
	• Determining the Author's Purpose, 292			
	• Determining the Author's Tone, 295		• Advantages and Disadvantages of Tort Laws, 319	
	• Interpreting Editorial Cartoons, 299		• Stavropoulos' View of the Contract with America: Your Prediction, 319	
Chapter 8 Critical Thinking	• Applying Skills to Meet College Goals, 326	• How to Think Critically, 327	• Misuse of Television by College Students and Ideas for Improved Programming, 354	• Effect of Television on Childhood Reading, 355
	• Identifying Barriers to Critical Thinking, 327	• Categories of Support for Arguments, 335	• Editorials Based on Inadequate Knowledge, 359	• More About Thomas Sowell, 360
	• Recognizing an Argument, 329			• Arguments For Or Against Gun Control, 365
	• Identifying the Issue, 330		• Evaluating Effectiveness of Two Articles Advocating Concealed Weapons, 364	
	• Identifying Support for the Argument, 333			
	• Evaluating the Support, 335			
	• Evaluating the Argument, 340			
	• Distinguishing Inductive and Deductive Reasoning, 341			
	• Distinguishing Vertical and Lateral Thinking, 349			

	Reading or Study Skills	Reader's Tip Boxes	Critical Thinking Topics	Internet Search Topics
Chapter 9 **Graphic Illustrations**	• Understanding What Graphics Do, 368 • Reading a Diagram, 368 • Reading a Table, 369 • Reading a Map, 372 • Reading a Pie Graph, 375 • Reading a Bar Graph, 376 • Reading a Line Graph, 377 • Reading a Flowchart, 378	• How to Read Graphic Material, 370	• Danger of Driving After Drinking, 390 • Binge Drinking: Why It Can Be Fatal, 390	• Fetal Alcohol Syndrome: Support Groups and Associations, 393
Chapter 10 **Rate Flexibility**	• Assessing Reading Rate, 396 • Techniques for Faster Reading, 400 • Differentiating Skimming and Previewing, 409 • When to Scan, 409	• Techniques for Skimming, 410 • Techniques for Scanning, 411	• Asserting Nonsmoking Rights—Why Important, 414 • Baby Boomers vs. Generation Xers: Differences in Goal-Seeking, 417 • Accounting for Shrinking Number of Potential Teachers, 421	• (None included given nature of chapter)
Chapter 11 **Test Taking**	• Strategies for Mental and Physical Awareness, 424 • Strategies for Standardized Reading Tests, 428 • How to Recognize Major Question Types, 431	• Preparing for a Test, 426 • Key Words in Essay Questions, 447	• (None included given nature of chapter)	• (None included given nature of chapter)

	Reading or Study Skills	Reader's Tip Boxes	Critical Thinking Topics	Internet Search Topics
	• Strategies for Multiple-Choice Items, *434*			
	• Strategies for Content Area Exams, *442*			
	• Locus of Control, *448*			
Chapter 12 **Textbook Application**	• Study Strategies, *476*	• Organizing Your Study, *452*	• Recognizing Problems Among Ethnic Groups, *476*	• International Organizations Opposing Racial Violence and Genocide, *477*

Active Learning

- What is active learning?
- How does the brain "pay attention"?
- Can you do two things at once?
- How can you improve your concentration?
- What are common internal and external distractors and cures?
- Why is your syllabus important?

Ed Malitsky/Liaison Agency Inc.

WHAT IS ACTIVE LEARNING?

Rather than being a single task, active learning is a *project with multiple components*. You, your instructor, your textbook, and your fellow learners are all components in the project. All contribute to your ability to accumulate and interpret new information, to connect and arrange the information into your own unique knowledge networks, and to retain and recall that information. As an active learner, you are thoughtfully and intellectually involved in each of the components in the project of learning.

Active learning requires alertness, concentration, and attention to details beyond the pages of a textbook. Because it is a project, active learning also requires that you learn to manage yourself, manage the assignment or learning task, and manage others who can contribute to or detract from your success. In this chapter we will discuss many factors that contribute to your ability to become an effective active learner. First, however, let's consider what psychologists have to say about thinking and learning.

WHAT IS COGNITIVE PSYCHOLOGY?

Cognitive psychology is the body of knowledge that describes how the mind works, or at least how experts think the mind works. Fortunately or unfortunately, the activity of the brain in concentration, reading, and remembering cannot be observed directly. These cognitive processes are invisible, just as thinking and problem solving are also invisible.

Since so little is actually known about thinking, the ideas of cognitive psychologists are frequently described as *models* or designs of something else we understand. For the last thirty years, for example, the central processing unit of a computer has been a popular model for describing how the brain processes information. The human brain is more complex than a computer, but the analogy provides a comparison that can help us understand.

HOW DOES THE BRAIN SCREEN MESSAGES?

Cognitive psychologists use the word **attention** to describe a student's uninterrupted mental focus. Thinking and learning, they say, begin with attention. During every minute of the day the brain is bombarded with millions of sensory messages. How does the brain decide which messages to pay attention to and which to overlook? At this moment, are you thinking about the temperature of the room, outdoor noises, or what you are reading? Since all of this information is available to you, how are you able to set priorities?

The brain relies on a dual command center to screen out one message and attend to another. According to a researcher at UCLA, receptor cells send millions of messages per minute to your brain.[1] Your reticular activating system (RAS), a network of cells at the top of the spinal cord that runs to the brain, tells the cortex in the brain not to bother with most of the sensory input. Your RAS knows that most sensory inputs do not need attention. For example, you are probably not aware at this moment of your back pressing against your chair or your clothes pulling on your body. Your RAS has decided not to clutter the brain with such irrelevant information unless there is an extreme problem, like your foot going to sleep because you are sitting on it.

The cortex can also make attention decisions. When you decide to concentrate your attention on a task, like reading your history assignment, your cortex tells your RAS not to bother it with trivial information. While you focus on learning, your RAS follows orders and "holds" the messages as if you were on an important long-distance call. The cortex and the RAS cooperate in helping you block out distractions and concentrate on learning.

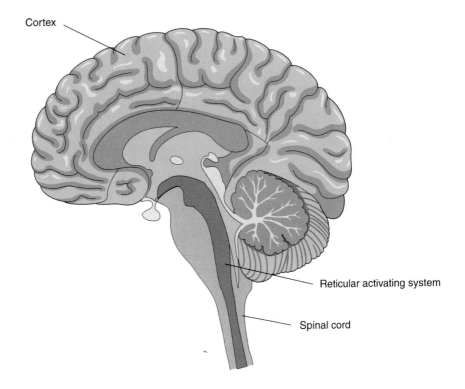

Cortex

Reticular activating system

Spinal cord

[1]H. W. Magoun, *The Waking Brain*, 2nd ed. (Springfield, IL: Charles C. Thomas, 1963).

IS DIVIDED ATTENTION EFFECTIVE?

Students often ask if it is possible to do two things at once, such as watching television and doing homework. Most psychologists agree that you can attend to only one thing at a time. An early researcher used a "switch model" to describe his belief, saying that attention operates like the on-off switch of a light fixture in that only one channel is "on" at a time.[2] The "cocktail party effect" illustrates this model. At a party with many available conversations within your listening range, you would probably attend to only one at a time. If your name were spoken in a nearby group, however, your attention would be diverted. You would probably "switch" your attention to the nearby group to seek more information on such a fascinating topic while only pretending to listen to the original conversation. According to Broadbent's model, you would not be able to listen intently to both conversations at the same time.

Two later researchers conducted an experiment to test the effectiveness of divided attention.[3] They asked participants to watch two televised sports events with one superimposed over the other. When instructed to attend to only one of the games, they did an excellent job of screening out the other and answering questions accurately. When asked to attend to both games simultaneously, however, they made eight times more mistakes than when focusing on only one game. This research seems to confirm the old adage, "You can't do two things at once and do them well."

CAN TASKS BECOME AUTOMATIC?

How can you walk and chew gum at the same time? Does every simple activity require your undivided attention? Many tasks—walking, tying shoelaces, and driving a car, for example—begin under controlled processing, which means that they are deliberate and require concentrated mental effort. After much practice, however, such tasks become automatic. Driving a car is an overlearned behavior that researchers would say becomes an automatic process after thousands of hours of experience. You can probably drive, change radio stations, and talk at the same time. Driving no longer requires your full cognitive capacity unless conditions are hazardous. Similarly, a skilled athlete can dribble a basketball automatically while also attending to strategy and position. Attention is actually not divided because it can shift away from tasks that have become automatic.

Automatic Aspects of Reading

The idea of doing some things automatically is especially significant in reading. As a first-grade reader, you had to concentrate on recognizing let-

---

[2]D. E. Broadbent, *Perception and Communication* (London: Pergamon Press, 1958).
[3]U. Neisser and R. Becklen, "Selective Looking: Attending to Visually Significant Events," *Cognitive Psychology* 7 (1975): 480–494.

ters, words, and sentences, as well as trying to construct meaning. After years of practice and overlearning, much of the recognition aspect of reading has become automatic. You no longer stop laboriously to decode each word or each letter. For example, why can you look at the word *child* without processing the meaning? It is because you automatically think the meaning. Thus, you can focus your mental resources on understanding the *message* in which the word appears, rather than on understanding the word itself.

College textbooks tend to contain many unfamiliar words and complex concepts that are not automatically processed. Attention to the message can be interrupted by the need to attend to an individual unit of thought. Such breaks are to be expected in college reading because of the newness of the material. You can become caught in the dilemma of trying to do two things at once—that is, trying to figure out word meaning as well as trying to understand the message. When this happens, your attention shifts to defining and then returns to comprehending. After such a break, you can regain your concentration, and little harm is done if the breaks are infrequent. However, frequent breaks in this automatic aspect of reading can undermine your ability to concentrate on the message.

COGNITIVE STYLES

Many psychologists believe that people develop a preference for a particular style or manner of learning at an early age and that these preferences affect concentration and learning. For example, some people learn easily by reading, but others benefit more readily from a demonstration or a diagram. Similarly, engineers like to work with details whereas politicians prefer broad generalizations. Cognitive style theorists focus on strengths and assert that there is no right or wrong way. These researchers believe that instruction is best when it matches the learner's particular preference.

Although knowing your preferences may not affect how your classes are taught, such knowledge can improve your attitude about yourself as a learner and your ability to focus by enabling you to build on your strengths.

Cognitive Style Preferences. One popular measure of individual cognitive style preferences is the Myers-Briggs Type Indicator (MBTI). Based on psychologist Carl Jung's theory of personality types, it measures individual cognitive style preferences in four categories. The inventory must be administered by a licensed specialist and is frequently given to entering freshmen. The following description of its four categories gives an idea of the kinds of issues that its proponents consider significant.

1. *Extroverted—Introverted*
   Extroverts prefer to talk with others and learn through experience, whereas introverts prefer to think alone about ideas.

2. *Sensing—Intuitive*

Sensing types prefer working with concrete details and tend to be patient, practical, and realistic. Intuitive types like abstractions and are creative, impatient, and theory oriented.

3. *Thinking—Feeling*

Thinking types tend to base decisions on objective criteria and logical principles. Feeling types are subjective and consider the impact of the decision on other people.

4. *Judging—Perceiving*

Judging types are time-oriented and structured, whereas perceivers are spontaneous and flexible.

Another test that uses the same type indicators as the Myers-Briggs is the Keirsey Temperament Sorter II. This 70-item online personality inventory gives an extensive printout, but experts do not consider it to have passed the same rigorous standards for validation and reliability as the Myers-Briggs. The Keirsey home page has background information about the test, begins with a brief questionnaire, and then has a link to the longer 70-item Keirsey Temperament Sorter II. The Website is http://www.keirsey.com

Right- Versus Left-Brain Dominance. Another popular cognitive style theory is concerned with right- or left-brain dominance. Proponents of this theory believe that left-brain dominant people are analytical and logical and excel in verbal skills. Right-brain people, on the other hand, are intuitive, creative, and emotional, and tend to think in symbols. Albert Einstein, for example, said that he rarely thought in words, but that his concepts appeared in symbols and images.

Cognitive style theorists offer another way of looking at attention and learning by encouraging us to recognize and appreciate our strengths and differences. If you are "turned off" by an assignment, try to translate it into activities and ideas that are more compatible with your learning preferences. For example, if you prefer right-brain activities, use maps, charts, and drawings to help you concentrate while studying. Acknowledge your strengths and use them to enhance your concentration.

WHAT IS CONCENTRATION?

Concentration is a skill that is developed through self-discipline and practice—not a mystical power, a hereditary gift, or an extra gene. It is a **habit** that requires time and effort to develop for consistent success. Athletes have it, surgeons have it, and successful college students must have it. *Concentration is essential for active learning.*

Concentration is no more than *paying attention*—that is, focusing your full attention on the task at hand. Someone once said that the mark of a genius is the ability to concentrate completely on one thing at a time. This is easy if the task is fun and exciting, but it becomes more difficult when you are required to read something that is not very interesting to you. At this point your mind begins to wander, and the words on the page remain just words for the eyes to see rather than becoming meaningful thoughts to connect and remember.

POOR CONCENTRATION: CAUSES AND CURES

The type of intense concentration that forces the RAS and cortex to close out the rest of the world is the state we would all like to achieve each time we sit down with a textbook. Too often, however, our attention becomes divided.

Students frequently ask, *How can I keep my mind on what I'm doing?* or they say, *I finished the assignment, but I don't know a thing I read.* The solution is not a simple mental trick to fool the brain; rather, it involves a series of practical short- and long-range planning strategies targeted at reducing external and internal distractions.

External Distractions

External distractions are the temptations of the physical world that divert your attention away from your work. They are the people in the room, the noise in the background, the time of day, or your place for studying. To control these external distractions, create an environment that says, "Now this is the place and the time for me to get my work done."

Create a Place for Studying. Start by establishing your own private study cubicle; it may be in the library, on the dining room table, or in your bedroom. Wherever it is, choose a straight chair and face the wall. Get rid of gadgets, magazines, and other temptations that trigger the mind to think of *play*. Stay away from the bed because it triggers *sleep*. Spread out your papers, books, and other symbols of studying and create an atmosphere in which the visual stimuli signal *work*. Be consistent by trying to study in the same place at the same time.

Use a Pocket Calendar or Assignment Book. At the beginning of the quarter or semester record dates for tests, term papers, and special projects on a calendar that you can keep with your books. Use the planner to organize all course assignments. A look at the calendar will remind you of the need for both short- and long-term planning. Assigned tests, papers, and projects will be due whether you are ready or not. Your first job is to devise a plan for getting ready.

Schedule Weekly Activities. Successful people do not let their time slip away; they manage time, rather than letting time manage them. Plan realistically and then follow your plan.

Time	Monday	Tuesday	Wednesday	Thursday	Friday	Saturday	Sunday
7:00–8:00							
8:00–9:00							
9:00–10:00							
10:00–11:00							
11:00–12:00							
12:00–1:00							
1:00–2:00							
2:00–3:00							
3:00–4:00							
4:00–5:00							
5:00–6:00							
6:00–7:00							
7:00–8:00							
8:00–9:00							
9:00–10:00							
10:00–11:00							
11:00–12:00							

A model of a weekly activity chart appears above. Analyze your responsibilities and in the squares on the chart write your fixed activities such as class hours, work time, mealtime, and bedtime. Next, think about how much time you plan to spend studying and how much on recreation, and plug those into the chart. For studying, indicate the specific subject and exact place involved.

Make a fresh chart at the beginning of each week since responsibilities and assignments vary. Learn to estimate the time usually needed for typical assignments. Include time for a regular review of lecture notes.

Examinations require special planning. Many students do not realize how much time it takes to study for a major exam. Spread your study out over several days and avoid last-minute cramming sessions late at night. Plan additional time for special projects and term papers to avoid deadline crises.

Plan Breaks. Even though it is not necessary to write this on the chart, remember that you need short breaks. Few students can study uninterrupted for two hours without becoming fatigued and losing concentration. Try the *50:10 ratio*—study hard for fifty minutes, take a ten-minute break, and then promptly go back to the books for another fifty minutes.

Internal Distractions

Internal distractions are the concerns that come repeatedly into your mind as you try to keep your attention focused on an assignment. Rather than the noise or the conversations in a room, they are the nagging worries or doubts in your mind that disrupt your work.

Unfortunately, students, just like everyone else, have to run errands, pick up laundry, make telephone calls, and pay bills. The world does not stop just because George has to read four chapters for a test in "Western Civ." by Wednesday. Consequently, when George sits down to read, he worries about getting an inspection sticker for his car or about picking up tickets for Saturday's ball game rather than concentrating completely on the assignment.

Make a List. For the most part, the interferences that pop into the mind and break reading concentration are minor concerns rather than major problems. To gain control over these mental disruptions, make a list of what is on your mind that is keeping you from concentrating on your studies. Jot down on a piece of paper each mental distraction and then analyze each to determine if immediate action is possible. If so, get up and take action. Make that phone call, write that letter, or finish that chore. Maybe it will take a few minutes or maybe half an hour, but the investment will have been worthwhile if the quality of your study time—your concentration power—has improved. Taking action is the first step in getting something off your mind.

For a big problem that you can't tackle immediately, ask yourself, "Is it worth the amount of brain time I'm dedicating to it?" Take a few minutes to think and make notes on possible solutions. Jotting down necessary future action and forming a plan of attack will help relieve the worry and clear the mind for studying.

Right now, list five things that are on your mind that you need to remember to do. Alan Lakein, a specialist in time management, calls this a **to-do list.**

In his book, *How to Get Control of Your Time and Your Life*,[4] Lakein claims that successful business executives start each day with such a list. Rank the activities on your list in order of priority and then do the most important things first.

To-Do List	Sample
1.	*1. Get hair cut*
2.	*2. Do my book report*
3.	*3. Buy stamps*
4.	*4. Call power co.*
5.	*5. Pay phone bill*

Increase Your Self-Confidence. Saying "I'll never pass this course" or "I can't get in the mood to study" is the first step to failure. Concentration requires self-confidence. If you didn't think you could do it, you would not be in a college class reading this book. Getting a college degree is not a short-term goal. Your enrollment indicates that you have made a commitment to a long-term goal. Ask yourself the question, "Who do I want to be in five years?" In the following space, describe how you view yourself, both professionally and personally, five years from now.

Five years from now I hope to be _____

_____

_____

Sometimes identifying the traits you admire in others can give you further insight into your own values and desires. Think about the traits you respect in others and your own definition of success. Answer the two questions that follow and consider how your responses mirror your own aspirations and goals.

Who is the person that you admire the most? _____

Why do you admire this person? _____

_____

_____

_____

[4]A. Lakein, *How to Get Control of Your Time and Your Life* (New York: Signet, 1974).

Improve Your Self-Concept. Have faith in yourself and in your ability to be what you want to be. How many people do you know who have passed the particular course that is worrying you? Are they smarter than you? Probably not. Can you do as well as they did? Turn your negative feeling into a positive attitude. What are some of your positive traits? Are you a hard worker, an honest person, a loyal friend? Take a few minutes to pat yourself on the back. Think about your good points and, in the following spaces, list five positive traits that you believe you possess.

Positive Traits

1. _____
2. _____
3. _____
4. _____
5. _____

What have you already accomplished? Did you participate in athletics in high school, win any contests, or master any difficult skills? Recall your previous achievements, and in the following spaces, list three accomplishments that you view with pride.

Accomplishments

1. _____
2. _____
3. _____

Reduce Anxiety. Have you ever heard people say, "I work better under pressure?" This statement contains a degree of truth. A small amount of tension can help you to force yourself to direct full attention on an immediate task. For example, concentrated study for an exam is usually more intense two nights before, rather than two weeks before, the test.

Yet too much anxiety can cause nervous tension and discomfort, which interfere with the ability to concentrate. Students operating under too much tension sometimes "freeze up" mentally and experience nervous physical reactions. The causes can range from fear of failure to lack of organization and preparation; the problem is not easily solved.

As an immediate, short-term response to tension, try muscle relaxation and visualization. For example, if you are reading a particularly difficult section in a chemistry book and are becoming frustrated to the point that you can no longer concentrate, stop your reading and take several deep breaths. Use your imagination to visualize a peaceful setting in which you are calm and relaxed. Imagine yourself rocking back and forth in a hammock or lying on a beach listening to the surf. Use the image you created and the deep breathing to help relax your muscles and regain control. Take several deep breaths and allow your body to release the tension so that you can resume reading and concentrate on your work.

As a long-term solution, nothing works better than success. Just as failure fuels tension, success tends to weaken it. Each successful experience helps to diminish feelings of inadequacy. Early success in a course can make a big psychological difference.

Spark an Interest. Approaching potentially dull material, like meeting reputedly dull people, can benefit from background work. Ask some questions, get some ideas, and do some thinking before starting to read. If the material was assigned, it must have merit, and finding it will make your job easier. Make a conscious effort to stimulate your curiosity before reading, even if in a contrived manner. Make yourself want to learn something. First look over the assigned reading for words or phrases that attract your attention, glance at the pictures, check the number of pages, and then ask yourself the following question: What do *I* want to learn about this?

With practice, this method of thinking before reading can create a spark of enthusiasm that will make the actual reading more purposeful and make concentration more direct and intense.

Set a Time Goal. An additional trick to spark your enthusiasm is to set a time goal. Study time is not infinite and short-term goals create a self-imposed pressure to pay attention, speed up, and get the job done. After looking over the material, project the amount of time you will need to finish it. Estimate a reasonable completion time and then push yourself to meet the goal. The purpose of a time goal is not to "speed read" the assignment, but rather to be realistic about the amount of time to spend on a task and to learn how to estimate future study time.

► READER'S TIP   **Improving Concentration**

- ► Create an environment that says, *study.*
- ► Use a calendar/assignment book for short- and long-term planning.
- ► Keep a daily *To-Do* List.
- ► Visualize yourself as a successful graduate.
- ► Reduce anxiety by passing the first test.
- ► Set time goals for completing daily assignments.

FOCUSING ON SUCCESSFUL ACADEMIC BEHAVIORS

Good concentration geared toward college success involves more than the ability to comprehend reading assignments. College success demands concentrated study, self-discipline, and the demonstration of learning. If the "focused athlete" can be successful, so can the "focused student." Begin to evaluate and eliminate behaviors that waste your time and divert you from your goals. Direct your energy toward activities that will enhance your chances for success. Adopt the following behaviors of successful students.

Attend Class. At the beginning of the quarter or semester, most college professors have an outline of what they plan to cover during each class period. Although they may not always check class attendance, the organization of the daily course work assumes perfect attendance. College professors *expect* you to attend class, and they usually do not repeat lecture notes or give makeup lessons for those who are absent. Be responsible and set yourself up for success by coming to class. You paid for it!

Be on Time. Professors usually overview the day's work at the beginning of each class, as well as answer questions and clarify assignments. Arriving late puts you at an immediate disadvantage. You are likely to miss important "class business" information. In addition, tardy students distract both the professor and other students. Put on a watch and get yourself moving.

Be Aware of Essential Class Sessions. Every class session is important, but never *ever* miss the last class before a major test. Usually students will ask questions about the exam that will stimulate your thinking. In reviewing, answering questions, and rushing to finish uncovered material, the professor will often drop important clues to exam items. Unless you are critically ill, take tests on time because makeups are usually more difficult, and be in class when the exams are returned to hear the professor's description of an excellent answer.

Read Assignments Before Class. Activate your knowledge on the subject before class by reading homework assignments. The lecture and class discussion can thus be used to build your knowledge network rather than create it. Jot down several questions that you would like to ask the professor about the reading.

Review Lecture Notes Before Class. Always review your lecture notes before the next class period, preferably within twenty-four hours after the class. Review your notes during a break or when on the phone with another classmate. Fill in gaps and make notations to ask questions to resolve confusion.

Consider Using a Tape Recorder. If you are having difficulty concentrating, with the professor's permission tape-record the lecture. Take notes at the same time as you record, and you can review your notes while listening to the recording.

Pass the First Test. Stress interferes with concentration. Do yourself a favor and over-study for the first exam. Passing the first exam will help you avoid a lot of tension while studying for the second one.

Predict the Exam Questions. Never go to an exam without first predicting test items. Turn chapter titles, subheadings, and boldface print into questions, and then brainstorm the answers. Feeling prepared boosts self-confidence.

Network with Other Students. You are not in this alone; you have lots of potential buddies who can offer mutual support. Collect the names and phone numbers of two classmates who are willing to help you if you do not understand the homework, miss a day of class, or need help on an assignment. Be prepared to help your classmates in return for their support.

Classmate_____ Phone_____

Classmate_____ Phone_____

Form a Study Group. Research experiments involving college students have shown that study groups can be very effective. Studying with others is not cheating; it is a wise use of available resources. In many colleges such groups have become so popular that counselors assist students in finding study partners. If asked, many professors will assist networking efforts by distributing copies of the class roll on which willing participants have provided phone numbers. A junior on the dean's list explained, "I call my study buddy when I have a problem. One time I called about an English paper because I couldn't think of my thesis. She asked what it was about. I told her and she said, 'That's your thesis.' I just couldn't see it as clearly as she did."

Learn from Other Student Papers. Talking about an excellent paper is one thing but actually reading one is another. In each discipline we need models of excellence. Always read an "A" paper. Don't be shy. Ask the "A" students (who should be proud and flattered to share their brilliance) or ask the professor. Don't miss this important step in becoming a successful student.

Collaborate. When participating in group learning activities, set expectations for group study so that each member contributes, and try to keep the studying on target. As a group activity, ask several classmates to join you in discovering the resources that are available for students on your campus. First, brainstorm with the group to record answers that are known to be true. Next, divide responsibilities among group members to seek information to answer unknown items. Reconvene the group to complete the responses.

> **EXERCISE 1.1**   *Campus Facts*

Form a collaborative study group to answer the following questions.

1. Where are the academic advisors located?_____

   _____

2. Where is the learning lab, and what kind of help is offered?

   _____

3. When does the college offer free study skills workshops?

   _____

4. Where can you use a word processor and check your E-mail?

   _____

5. Where do you get an identification number for the Internet?

   _____

6. Where is your professor's office, and what is the phone number?

   _____

7. What kind of financial aid is available, and where can you find this information? _____

   _____

8. What services does the dean's office offer to students?

   _____

9. How late is the library open on weekends?

   _____

10. What free services does the counseling center offer?

   _____

Use the Syllabus. The syllabus is a general outline of the goals, objectives,
and assignments for the entire course. The syllabus includes examination
dates, course requirements, and an explanation of the grading system. Most
professors distribute and explain the syllabus on the first day of class.

   Ask questions to help you understand the "rules and regulations" in the
syllabus. Keep it handy as a ready reference and use it as a plan for learning.
Devise your own daily calendar for completing weekly reading and writing
assignments.

   The following is a syllabus for Psychology 101. Study the course syllabus
and answer the questions that follow.

INTRODUCTION TO PSYCHOLOGY

Class: 9:00—10:00 a.m. daily   Dr. Julie Wakefield
10-week quarter   Office: 718 Park Place
Office hours: 10:00—12:00 daily Telephone: 651—3361
                                 E-mail: JuWake@ABC.edu

Required Texts
Psychology: An Introduction by Josh R. Gerow
Paperback: Select one book from the attached list for a report.

Course Content
The purpose of Psychology 101 is to overview the general areas of study in the field of psychology. An understanding of psychology gives valuable insights into your choices and behaviors and those of others. The course will also give you a foundation for later psychology courses.

Methods of Teaching
Thematic lectures will follow the topics listed in the textbook assignments. You are expected to read and master the factual material in the text as well as take careful notes in class. Tests will cover both class lectures and textbook readings.

Research Participation
All students are required to participate in one psychological experiment. Details and dates are listed on a separate handout.

Grading
Grades will be determined in the following manner:
Tests (4 tests at 15% each)   60%
Final exam   25%
Written report   10%
Research participation   5%

Tests
Tests will consist of both multiple-choice and identification items as well as two essay questions.

Important Dates
Test 1: 1/13
Test 2: 1/29
Test 3: 2/10
Test 4: 2/24
Written report: 3/5
Final exam: 3/16

Written Report
Your written report should answer one of three designated questions and reflect your reading of a book from the list. Each book is approximately 200 pages long. Your re-

port should be at least eight typed pages. More information to follow.

Assignments
Week 1: Ch. 1 (pp. 1–37), Ch. 2 (pp. 41–75)
Week 2: Ch. 3 (pp. 79–116)
   Test 1: Chapters 1–3
Week 3: Ch. 4 (pp. 121–162), Ch. 5 (pp. 165–181)
Week 4: Ch. 5 (pp. 184–207), Ch. 6 (pp. 211–246)
   Test 2: Chapters 4–6
Week 5: Ch. 7 (pp. 253–288), Ch. 8 (pp. 293–339)
Week 6: Ch. 9 (pp. 345–393)
   Test 3: Chapters 7–9
Week 7: Ch. 10 (pp. 339–441), Ch. 11 (pp. 447–471)
Week 8: Ch. 11 (pp. 476–491), Ch. 12 (pp. 497–533)
   Test 4: Chapters 10–12
Week 9: Ch. 13 (pp. 539–577), Ch. 14 (pp. 581–598)
   Written Report
Week 10: Ch. 14 (pp. 602–618), Ch. 15 (pp. 621–658)
   Final exam: Chapters 1–15

EXERCISE 1.2   *Review the Syllabus*

Refer to the syllabus to answer the following items with *T* (true) or *F* (false).

_____ 1. Pop quizzes count 5 percent of the final grade.
_____ 2. The written report is due more than a week before the final exam.
_____ 3. The professor is not in her office on Thursdays.
_____ 4. Each of the four tests covers two weeks of work.
_____ 5. Two books are required for the course.

EXERCISE 1.3   *Review Your Own Course Syllabus*

Examine your syllabus for this college reading course and answer the following questions.

1. How many weeks are in your quarter or semester?

_____

2. When is your next test and how much does it count?

_____

3. Will your next major exam have a multiple-choice or essay format?

_____

4. What is the professor's policy about absences?

_____

5. Which test or assignment constitutes the largest portion of your final grade?

_____

Explain. _____

6. Do you have questions that have not been answered on your syllabus?

Name two issues that you would like the professor to clarify.

_____

_____

Summary Points

■ **What is active learning?**

Active learning is your own intellectual involvement with the teacher, the textbook, and fellow learners in the process of aggressively accumulating, interpreting, assimilating, and retaining new information.

■ **How does the brain "pay attention"?**

Research indicates that the brain has two cooperating systems, the RAS and the cortex, that allow it to selectively attend to certain inputs and to block out others.

■ **Can you do two things at once?**

The ability to do several tasks at once depends on the amount of cognitive resources required for each.

■ **How can you improve your concentration?**

Concentration requires self-confidence, self-discipline, and persistence. Adopt successful academic behaviors, including networking with other students and collaborating on assignments, to focus your energy and enhance your chances for success. Use your syllabus as a guide for learning.

■ **What are common internal and external distractors and cures?**

External distractions are physical temptations that divert your attention. You can manipulate your environment to remove these distractions. Internal distractions are mental wanderings that vie for your attention. You can learn to control these by organizing your daily activities, planning for academic success, and striving to meet your goals for the completion of assignments.

■ **Why is your syllabus important?**

Your syllabus is the learning guide designed by the instructor to document the goals and requirements of the course.

CONTEMPORARY FOCUS

New technology brings a sequence of challenges. First, it is "Please use it," and later it's "Let's not abuse it." How is the Internet, with its short history, already positively and negatively affecting your life?

NET ADDICTION

Sky: Delta Air Lines, July 1998, p. 57
Oracle Service Humor Mailing List (oracle-humor-subscribe @lyris.oraclehumor.com)(Website: www.oraclehumor.com)
Compiled by Sarah Lindsay and Mickey McLean

You know you are addicted to the Internet when . . .

. . . all of your friends have an @ in their names.

. . . your dog has his own home page.

. . . you can't call your mother because she doesn't have a modem.

. . . you check your E-mail, and it says "no new messages," so you check it again.

. . . you wake up at 3 A.M. to go to the bathroom and stop and check your E-mail on the way back to bed.

. . . you never have to deal with busy signals because you never log off.

. . . your car crashes through the guardrail on a mountain road and your first instinct is to search for the "back" button.

Collaborate on responses to the following questions:

■ What do you find addictive about the Internet?

■ What are the advantages and disadvantages of E-mail as opposed to telephone calls?

■ Why will people who would not say "Hello" to a neighbor interact with others in chat rooms?

SKILL DEVELOPMENT: ACTIVE LEARNING

Before reading the following selection, take a few minutes to analyze your active learning potential and answer the following questions.

1. **Physical Environment** Where are you and what time is it? _____

_____

What are your external distractions? _____

_____

2. **Internal Distractions** What is popping into your mind and interfering with your concentration? _____

_____

3. **Spark Interest** Glance at the selection and predict what it will cover. What about it will be of interest to you? _____

4. **Set Time Goals** How long will it take you to read the selection? _____ minutes. To answer the questions? _____ minutes

Word Knowledge

What do you know about these words?

comprehensive   reconstituted   protocol   pivotal   parlance
domain   spectrum   inaccessible surveillance dissemination

Your instructor may give a true-false vocabulary review before or after reading.

Time Goal

Record your starting time for reading. _____:_____

The Internet expands the walls of the workplace.

THE INTERNET

From H. L. Capron, *Computers: Tools for an Information Age*

The **Internet,** sometimes called simply "the 'Net," is the largest and most far-flung network system of them all, connecting users worldwide. Surprisingly, the Internet is not really a network at all but a loosely organized collection of about 25,000 networks. Many people
5 are astonished to discover that no one owns the Internet; it is run by volunteers. It has no central headquarters, no centrally offered services, and no comprehensive index to tell you what information is available.

To many people who are recent users, it seems as if the Internet sprang up overnight. That, of course, is not true, but its popularity caught a lot of peo-
10 ple by surprise. A look at its history explains why.

Don't Know Much About History

The history of the Internet bears telling. It is mercifully short. The reason that there is little to say is that it slumbered and stuttered for approximately twenty-

five years before the general public even knew it existed. The 'Net was started
by obscure military and university people as a vehicle for their own purposes.
15 They never in their wildest dreams thought it would become the international
giant it is today. Let us look back briefly, to understand their point of view.

First Stirrings at the Department of Defense

Ever heard of a fallout shelter? In the Cold War of the 1950s, people worried
about "the bomb," a nuclear attack whose radiation aftereffects—fallout—would
be devastating. Some people built underground shelters, usually under their own
20 houses, to protect themselves. It was in this climate of fear that the United States
Department of Defense became concerned that a single bomb could wipe out its
computing capabilities.

Working with the RAND Corporation, they decided to rely on not one but several computers, geographically dispersed. No one computer would be in charge.
25 A message to be sent to another computer would be divided up into *packets*, each labeled with its destination address. Each packet would wind its way
individually through the network, probably taking different routes, but each
heading in the direction of its destination and eventually being reconstituted
into the original message at the end of the journey. The idea was that even if
30 one computer was knocked out, the others could still carry on by using alternative routes. A packet can travel a variety of paths; the chosen path does not
matter as long as the packet reaches its destination. The software that took
care of the packets was Transmission Control Protocol/Internet Protocol
(TCP/IP), a universal standard. TCP does the packeting and reassembling of
35 the message. The IP part of the protocol handles the addressing, seeing to it
that packets are routed across multiple computers.

They called the new set of connections **ARPANet,** an acronym that stands for
Advanced Research Projects Agency Network. The year was 1969. Before long,
computers from research universities and defense contractors joined the network.
40 But the network was limited to people who had some technical expertise—a major reason why it was not yet of particular interest to the general public.

Tim and Marc

Tim Berners-Lee is arguably the pivotal figure in the surging popularity of the
Internet: He made it easy. In 1990, Dr. Berners-Lee, a physicist at a laboratory for particle physics in Geneva, Switzerland, perceived that his work
45 would be easier if he and his far-flung colleagues could easily link to one another's computers. He saw the set of links from computer to computer to
computer as a spider's web; hence the name **Web.** The *CERN site*, the name
of the particle physics laboratory where Dr. Berners-Lee worked, is considered the birthplace of the *World Wide Web.*

50 A *link* on a web site is easy to see: it is either colored text called *hypertext* or
an icon or image called a **hyperregion.** A mouse click on the link appears to
transport the user to the site represented by the link, and in common parlance
one speaks of moving or transferring to the new site; actually, data from the
new site is transferred to the user's computer.

55   **Marc Andreessen** was only a student when, in 1993, he led a team that invented the *browser*, software used to explore the Internet. The browser featured a graphical interface, so that users could see and click on pictures as well as text. That first browser was named *Mosaic,* and it made web page multimedia possible. For the viewing public, the 'Net now offered both easy
60   movement with Dr. Berners-Lee's links and attractive images and a graphical interface provided by the browser. Today there are many competitive browsers, one of which is Netscape Navigator, produced by a company founded by Marc Andreessen and others.

The Internet Surges Ahead

TCP/IP is software in the public domain. Since no one was really in charge of
65   the network, there was no one to stop others from just barging in and linking up wherever they could. The network became steadily more valuable as it embraced more and more networks.

A new name, taken from the name of the TCP/IP protocol, evolved: the Internet. The original ARPANet eventually disappeared altogether.

Your Own Home Page

70   If you want to have your own site on the Web, commonly called a "home page" because it is often a single page, you must have a service provider that will store it for you and let it be accessible to other people. You also must have some software with which to write it, and you must know how to use that software. In an academic environment, you may be permitted to keep your
75   work on the school's computer, at least temporarily, and you can probably find a class that teaches you how to create a home page. You could even teach yourself. Ready to get started? Not by a long shot. What most page makers fail to understand is that they need to have *something to say*. A page that describes yourself ("I'm cool"), your pet ("So cute!"), and your hobbies ("I like jazz and
80   collecting barbecue recipes") will not make a contribution to the Internet.

Useless, Overburdened, and Misinformed

Some people consider some home pages useless. In fact, there is a site called Useless Pages that maintains a listing of pages the site manager deems useless. However, many people are willing to pay for the connection to a web server in order to promote a home page they fancy, whatever anyone else may think.
85   Others put out birth or wedding announcements, complete with photos. One useless page does nothing except count the number of times the page is accessed. At the other end of the spectrum are sites that, apparently, have so much value that their popularity renders them mostly inaccessible. Any list of "cool" sites, a favorite Web word, is likely to be crowded.
90   There are no guarantees. The Internet is full of misinformation. Just because something is on the Internet does not mean it is true. If someone steps up to announce that the government uses black helicopters to spy on us or that tapes sound better if you soak them in water first, you need not accept such information as fact. It's not that people intend to be wrong, it's just that

95 they sometimes are. If you are doing serious research on the Internet, be sure to back it up with other sources, especially non-Internet sources.

The Internet: Security and Privacy Problems

Networks, whether connected to the Internet or not, pose unique security and privacy problems. Many people have access to the system, often from remote locations. Clearly, questions arise: If it is so easy for authorized people
100 to get data, what is to stop unauthorized people from tapping it? Organizations must be concerned about unauthorized people intercepting data in transit, whether hackers or thieves or industrial spies.

Privacy Problems for Networked Employees

Although employees do not have expectations of total privacy at the office, they are often shocked when they discover that the boss has been spying on
105 them via the network, even their comings and goings on the Internet. The boss, of course, is not spying at all, merely "monitoring." This debate has been heightened by the advent of software that lets managers check up on networked employees without their ever knowing that they are under surveillance. With a flick of a mouse button, the boss can silently pull up an em-
110 ployee's current computer screen.

Surveillance software is not limited to checking screens. It can also check on E-mail, count the number of keystrokes per minute, note the length of a worker's breaks, and monitor what computer files are used and for how long.

Junk E-mail

Privacy invasion in the form of junk E-mail has become, unfortunately, a
115 common event. Furthermore, it promises to get worse. The volume of junk E-mail will only soar as marketers discover how cheap it is. A postal mailing to a million people costs about $800,000, including postage and printing. Internet marketers can reach the same number of people by making a phone call and paying a few hundred dollars for time spent online. The software that
120 makes mass advertising—called **spamming**—possible both gathers E-mail addresses and sends E-mail messages for marketers—thousands and thousands every day. One of the most annoying aspects of E-mail is that, unlike postal junk mail, which at least arrives at no cost to you, a user who pays for online usage may be paying for part of the cost of junk E-mail delivery.

Ethics and Privacy

125 Snooping did not begin with computers. Neither did improper dissemination of personal information. But computers have elevated those problems to a much more serious level. As we have already noted, just about everything there is to know about you is already on a computer file, more likely several computer files. The thorny issues center around appropriate ethical treatment
130 of that data by those who control it or merely have access to it.

Time Goals

Record your finishing time. _____:_____

Calculate your total reading time. _____

Rate your concentration as high _____ medium _____ or low. _____

Recall what you have read, and review what you have learned.
Your instructor may choose to give a true-false comprehension review.

Thinking About   ## THE INTERNET

What controversial ethical issues do you foresee emerging between employers and employees over Internet access from the workplace?
Response Suggestion: Blend the text ideas with your own thoughts and form a list of four or five controversial issues. Explain and give examples of each.

Contemporary Link

Reflect on your own use of the Internet. What do you believe are the next critical steps in its development? If Congress put you in charge of an improvement or wish list, what would be your top five priorities? List each and explain why.

COMPREHENSION QUESTIONS

After reading the selection, answer the following questions with *a, b, c,* or *d.* In order to help you analyze your strengths and weaknesses, the question types are indicated.

Main Idea   _____ 1. The best statement of the main idea is
   a. the history of the Internet shows what direction it will go in the future.
   b. useless home pages, unreliable information, and junk E-mail flaw the Internet.
   c. the Internet was originally intended for popular use, and it is beset with many problems.
   d. the Internet started as a military system, and continues to evolve to be used by the mainstream of society.

Inference   _____ 2. In the statement, "The boss, of course, is not spying at all, merely 'monitoring' . . . ," the author suggests that
   a. the boss is actually spying.
   b. there is a vast difference between spying and monitoring.
   c. a boss has no right or reason to monitor an employee.
   d. the boss is not spying.

Inference _____ 3. The author suggests that home pages
   a. are useless.
   b. are an appropriate way to announce weddings and births.
   c. often have nothing to say.
   d. are "cool" and accessible.

Detail _____ 4. The Internet is owned and maintained by
   a. the Department of Defense.
   b. the RAND Corporation.
   c. volunteers.
   d. Tim Berners-Lee.

Inference _____ 5. The author believes that all of the following are problems with the Internet except
   a. home pages that say nothing.
   b. ethical concerns regarding privacy.
   c. the lack of a central ownership.
   d. crowded Websites cause networks to run too slowly to be useful.

Detail _____ 6. According to the author, the initial popularity of the Internet began because
   a. icons, rather than text, appealed to the public.
   b. Tim Berners-Lee made it easy to use by developing the World Wide Web.
   c. the speed of new modems made it efficient to access information.
   d. Marc Andreessen invented the browser, which allowed the general public to "surf" the net with ease.

Inference _____ 7. The author suggests that researchers who use the Internet should
   a. only use Web pages of acknowledged authorities.
   b. be skeptical and include other sources.
   c. trust Internet sources.
   d. feel confident with multiple Internet sources.

Inference _____ 8. The author's attitude toward software designed to allow bosses to check up on networked employees is that
   a. it is unethical and should be banned.
   b. the Defense Department should encourage such use under certain circumstances.
   c. it is a human problem rather than a technological problem.
   d. it can be motivational to employees and beneficial to businesses.

Detail   _____ 9. When the Internet was created, no one computer was in charge because
   a. the U.S. Department of Defense was concerned that a bomb would wipe out a single computer.
   b. no one computer is powerful enough to maintain 25,000 networks.
   c. the cost to the RAND Corporation of building one super computer was more than that of building several smaller computers.
   d. several computers were geographically dispersed to encourage strategic competition.

Inference   _____ 10. All of the following can be concluded from this selection except
   a. the Internet was never intended for its current use.
   b. because of the Internet's short history, many of the problems have not been solved.
   c. the original developers of the Internet had no way to anticipate the number of users online today.
   d. tools of war do not have peacetime applications.

Answer the following with *T* (true) or *F* (false).

Detail   _____ 11. Hypertext refers to icons.

Inference   _____ 12. The author would be more likely to compare the ownership of the Internet to the ownership of air than to the ownership of an automobile.

Detail   _____ 13. The Internet was created because of the threat of nuclear warfare.

Detail   _____ 14. The main purpose of TCP/IP software is to disassemble and reassemble packets of information in a network.

Inference   _____ 15. The author implies that junk E-mail and privacy issues will lead to a gradual decline of Internet popularity.

VOCABULARY

According to the way the italicized word was used in the selection, select *a*, *b*, *c*, or *d* for the word or phase that gives the best definition. The number in parentheses indicates the line of the passage in which the word is located.

_____ 1. "no *comprehensive* index" (7)
   a. all inclusive
   b. limited
   c. restricted
   d. similar

_____ 2. "*reconstituted* into the original" (28–29)
   a. dispatched
   b. reassembled
   c. monitored
   d. dissected

_____ 3. "part of the *protocol*" (35)
   a. procedure
   b. circuit
   c. management
   d. function

_____ 4. "the *pivotal* figure" (42)
   a. mobile
   b. secondary
   c. original
   d. crucial

_____ 5. "in common *parlance*" (52)
   a. knowledge
   b. participation
   c. speech
   d. times

_____ 6. "the public *domain*" (64)
   a. territory
   b. picture
   c. consciousness
   d. goal

_____ 7. "the other end of the *spectrum*" (87)
   a. computer chip
   b. difficult situation
   c. entire range
   d. operating rules

_____ 8. "mostly *inaccessible*" (88)
   a. confusing
   b. unreachable
   c. prohibited
   d. devalued

_____ 9. "they are under *surveillance*" (108–109)
   a. guidance
   b. close observation
   c. pressure
   d. collaboration

_____ 10. "improper *dissemination*" (125)
   a. production
   b. preservation
   c. security
   d. distribution

SKILL DEVELOPMENT

Record your time for answering the questions. _____:_____

Calculate your total time for reading and answering the questions. _____

What changes would you make to enhance your concentration on the new selection? _____

_____

SEARCHING THE NET

Each of the reading selections in this text will be followed by an Internet exercise to challenge your computer skills, your research skills, and your critical thinking skills. You will be asked to use the Internet, also known as the

World Wide Web (WWW) or "Web," to research a question and find information at different Websites. Some of these Websites will be suggested and others you may discover on your own. You will then blend or synthesize the new information with your own thoughts to produce a written response. These Internet exercises can be done individually or as group activities. To help you get started, read the following suggestions for successful Internet searches.

Secrets of a Successful Search

Searching for information on the Internet can be both rewarding and frustrating. The key to avoiding frustration, or at least reducing it to a bare minimum, is organization. Organization requires a plan, an ongoing search strategy, and good record keeping. A successful Internet search consists of the following five steps:

1. Make a plan.
2. Search and search again.
3. Read selectively.
4. Record as you go.
5. Consider the source.

1. Make a Plan

Locating information on the Web requires the use of a search engine such as Alta Vista, Excite, Infoseek, or Lycos. Once you have selected a search engine, enter a search term or phrase, which may consist of one or more words, a phrase, or a name. The search engine will search the Internet for sites that contain your search term or phrase, count them, and display the first ten to twenty-five sites (called "hits") on the computer screen. Successful searches are dependent on which terms are chosen and how they are entered.

Experts recommend using a notebook to organize your search strategy. Using a two-column format, begin by writing down your general research topic and related questions. Next, jot down all of the key terms that you can think of that relate to your topic and create additional questions if necessary. At this beginning point, prior knowledge of the topic is extremely helpful. If your knowledge of the topic is limited, however, perform a quick search to select and read a few of the sites on the topic in order to become familiar with related terminology, names, and events.

Decide on a few key words that you believe will help you locate the information you want and use them as search terms. In your notebook, list each search term on the left side of the paper and allow room on the right side for writing the locations of Websites and comments about the site. For example, if your research topic is the history of the Internet, your list of search terms may include Internet history, ARPANet, TCP/IP, and the history of TCP/IP. A sample search notebook page is illustrated on the opposite page.

Check with your college library on how to gain access to online databases containing online journals, collections, and other resources that can provide a wealth of information.

Sample Search Notebook Page

Research topic	*Growth of the Internet*
Research questions	*What are the major events in the history of the Internet?*
	What is the future of the Internet?
What I already know	*Tim Berners-Lee—birth of the Web*
	Marc Andreessen's team—invented browser software
	ARPANet—small network for researchers/beginning of the Internet
	TCP/IP—public domain software that routes messages from one computer to another

Search Terms	**Notes and Websites**
✓*History of the Internet*	*good history, timeline graph (http://www.isoc.org/internet-history/brief.html)*
	brief history (http://www.delphi.com/navnet/faq/history.html)
	really detailed timeline, starting from 700 BC with homing pigeons (http://www.geocities.com/~anderberg/ant/history/)
✓*ARPANet*	*good overview (http://clavin.music.uiuc.edu/sean/internet_history.html)*
✓*TCP/IP*	*summary (http://pclt.cis.yale.edu/pclt/comm/tcpip.htm)*
✓*History of TCP/IP*	*not much luck—couldn't connect to possible site, check back later*
✓*Future of the Internet*	*talks about bandwidth, (http://www.uvc.com/gbell/4transcript.html)*
	biography of Tim Berners-Lee, (http://www.w3.org/People/Berners-Lee/)
	history/future, etc site maintained by Tim Berners-Lee, (http://www.w3.org/Talks/CompSem93/FutureText.html)

▶ **READER'S TIP**   **Popular College Databases**

- ▶ Galileo
- ▶ Periodical abstracts
- ▶ Newspaper abstracts
- ▶ Lexis-Nexis Academic Universe
- ▶ MLA Bibliography
- ▶ ABI Inform
- ▶ Psyc FIRST
- ▶ Social Science abstracts
- ▶ ERIC
- ▶ MEDLINE

2. Search and Search Again

One of the most important tasks in conducting a successful search is to enter search terms that will produce the information that you want. Search terms that are too *narrow* may bring thousands of hits. Some researchers suggest beginning with a *broad* search (a single term) and then narrowing the search, whereas others suggest beginning with a narrow search (multiple terms) and broadening it later. Both methods are acceptable, and you can experiment to discover which method works best for you. Be flexible in trying new terms and different combinations. In the previous example, searching for *history* or *Internet* alone will bring a multitude of hits. Narrowing your search by typing in *history of the Internet* should produce sites more attuned to your research. Entering too many terms, however, may result in no hits or only limited information. Searches also provide additional terms to pursue.

> ▶ **READER'S TIP**   **Manipulating the Search**
>
> In our sample case, by entering *future of the Internet* in the search term box, you will receive all sites that contain either *future, Internet,* or *future of the Internet.* Placing quotation marks around a phrase or the term—that is, *"future of the Internet"*—will pull up only those sites containing the full term. Other ways to find suitable sites is to add an AND, +, OR, or NOT in the phrase.

At some point you may need to find the home page of a particular company—for example, Harley-Davidson. If your search does not produce the home page of the company, try to guess or work out the company's URL, or Uniform Resource Locator. Remember that a simple URL is composed of four or five parts. The first part is usually *http://. Http* is a protocol or mechanism used by browsers to communicate with Websites. The second part is *www* for the World Wide Web. The third part is usually the name of a company, product, institution, or its abbreviation. The fourth part is the site's designation or type such as *http://www.cnn.com* for the CNN News Corporation and *http://www.whitehouse.gov* for the White House.

The three-letter designation at the end of the URL, sometimes called the *domain,* depends on the type of site. For example, *gov* is for government, *org* is for organization, *com* is for commercial site, and *edu* is for education. Some URLs have a fifth part; they end in a two-letter code to signify a country. For example, *uk* means *United Kingdom* in the Website for the British monarchy, which is *http://www.royal.gov.uk* (see the diagram on the opposite page).

3. Read Selectively

The amount of information on the Internet can be overwhelming. Rarely, however, is it desirable or practical to read all the available information on a

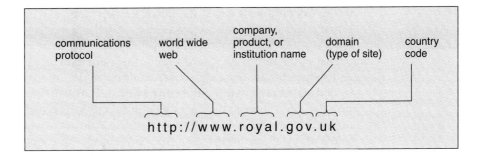

subject. Read selectively to narrow the scope of your research. After entering a search term and receiving a list of possible sites, scan the list of hits to look for key words relating to your search needs. The sites that contain the most information are usually listed first. Some search engines such as Excite and Infoseek will place a percent value next to the site link indicating the likelihood that the information being sought is located at that site. In addition, a summary of the site may also be included.

After selecting a Website or link that appears to have the information you need, study the table of contents or outline and move around the site to determine its layout or structure. Check secondary links that look promising. Skim definitions, statements, quotes, and other text, while asking yourself, "Is this the information I am looking for?" Web pages follow some uniform patterns, but styles vary because there are no requirements for a standard format. Most Websites, however, contain a title, subtitles, links, a table of contents, and an outline or introductory paragraph.

4. Record as You Go

As you discover sites, make sure to record them in your notebook. Once you have searched a term, check it off on your term list. Also, note the results of the search next to the term. This will help you avoid searching for the same term a second time. Include the site location (the URL), particularly if you would like to return to the site or include it as a reference. If you are trying to locate a specific URL, such as a Website listed in this textbook, do not be surprised if the URL has changed. Unfortunately, site locations may change without notice, thus making mastery of the steps in the search process even more important.

There are three ways of noting the site: (1) by recording the URL in your notebook next to the term, (2) by printing out the site material, since the URL is usually listed at the top of the printout, or (3) by bookmarking or saving a site so that you may return to it at a later date. If you are using a computer in a location that you may not again have access to, save your bookmarks to disk.

5. Consider the Source

Information on the Internet, although abundant, may not be accurate. In 1998 a U.S. congressman saw an obituary for a prominent entertainer posted on the Web and announced the death to the Congress. As it turned out, the obituary had been posted by accident, and the entertainer, comedian Bob Hope, was quite alive and hitting golf balls.

One of the best ways to avoid collecting poor data on the Internet is to use good judgment. In the case above, confirming the information would have avoided embarrassment for the congressman. In other instances, information posted on the Web can be misleading, unfounded, or based on personal opinions and beliefs rather than facts.

When reviewing information from a Website, ask yourself, "What person, company, or agency is providing the information?" and "Is this a reliable source?" Reliable information usually comes from reliable sources. Information gathered from sites such as news stations, libraries, city newspapers, and government databases is probably more reliable than that from obscure sites with no obvious signs of credibility.

SEARCH THE NET

For the first activity, your search has already been started for you in the previous illustration on the history of the Internet. Use the Websites listed in the Sample Search Notebook Page (see page 29) to respond to the following questions:

■ What are the two historic computer visionaries, Tim Berners-Lee and Marc Andreessen, doing now? Begin by trying:

http://www.w3.org/People/Berners-Lee/

■ Explore a timeline of the Internet and describe three other people or events that were influential in the evolution of the Internet. Begin by trying:

http://www.pbs.org/internet/timeline/index.html

Organize your approach and use your own notebook to record information. In your response, list the Websites from which you took information as references.

CONTEMPORARY FOCUS

Animals have instinctive behaviors that enhance their own survival and the survival of the species. Notice how widely instincts vary among different animal species, as well as between the male and female within the species.

MATERNAL INSTINCTS

Daniel J. Cox

"Maternal Instincts," *Life*, June 1998, p. 105

I was photographing at Cape Churchill in Manitoba, Canada, a popular gathering place for polar bears. They wait there until Hudson Bay freezes, so they can go out on the ice to hunt seals. I had been watching a female bear with two cubs for several days when I noticed that one of the little bears was in trouble. Much as it tried to follow in the footsteps of its mother and sibling, it couldn't keep pace. The next day, I noticed blood on the cub's fur, as well as on the snow. The cub was obviously very sick, and although its mother and sibling took care to walk more slowly, it kept lagging behind. On the third day, I found the bears huddled on a snow-bank, where the mother tried many times to coax the sick cub to its feet. At one point she even pulled it out from beneath the snow by grasping its head in her mouth. But the cub was too weak to move on its own, so the female and her other cub snuggled near it and waited. On the fourth day, the cub was almost entirely covered by snow. It was dead. Still the mother tried lifting it; still she waited. But when I returned the next day, the female and her healthy cub were gone. In their place was a male bear feeding on the corpse. It wasn't easy to watch the cub die, yet we have to remember that this is sometimes the way nature works.

Collaborative Activity

Collaborate on responses to the following questions:

- What is an instinct?
- What are some maternal instincts in animals?
- Which animals have paternal instincts?

SKILL DEVELOPMENT: ACTIVE LEARNING

Before reading the following selection, take a few minutes to analyze your active learning potential and answer the following questions.

1. **Physical Environment**

   Where are you and what time is it? _____

   _____

What are your external distractions? _____

_____

_____

2. **Internal Distractions**

   What is popping into your mind and interfering with your concentration?

   _____

   _____

3. **Spark Interest**

   Glance at the selection and predict what it will cover. What about it will be of interest to you? _____

4. **Set Time Goals**

   How long will it take you to read the selection? _____ minutes

   To answer the questions? _____ minutes

Word Knowledge

What do you know about these words?

hypothesis	incubator	genetic	instinctive	sustain
restrained	inseminate	disrupted	irreversible	coax

Your instructor may give a true-false vocabulary review before or after reading.

Time Goal

Record your starting time for reading. _____:_____

Lorenz swims with the goslings who have imprinted on him.

CRITICAL-PERIOD HYPOTHESIS

From James V. McConnell, *Understanding Human Behavior*

There is some evidence that the best time for a child to learn a given skill is at the time the child's body is just mature enough to allow mastery of the behavior in question. This belief is often called the *critical-period hypothesis*—that is, the belief that an or-
5 ganism must have certain experiences at a *particular time* in its developmental sequence if it is to reach its mature state.

© 2000 Addison-Wesley Educational Publishers, Inc.

There are many studies from animal literature supporting the critical-period hypothesis. For instance, German scientist Konrad Lorenz discovered many years ago that birds, such as ducks and geese, will follow the first mov-
10 ing object they see after they are hatched. Usually the first thing they see is their mother, of course, who has been sitting on the eggs when they are hatched. However, Lorenz showed that if he took goose eggs away from the mother and hatched them in an incubator, the fresh-hatched *goslings* would follow him around instead.

15 After the goslings had waddled along behind Lorenz for a few hours, they acted as if they thought he was their mother and that they were humans, not geese. When Lorenz returned the goslings to their real mother, they ignored her. Whenever Lorenz appeared, however, they became very excited and flocked to him for protection and affection. It was as if the visual image of the
20 first object they saw moving had become so strongly *imprinted* on their consciousness that, forever after, that object was "mother."

During the past 20 years or so, scientists have spent a great deal of time studying *imprinting* as it now is called. The effect occurs in many but not in all types of birds, and it also seems to occur in mammals such as sheep and
25 seals. Whether it occurs in humans is a matter for debate. Imprinting is very strong in ducks and geese, however, and they have most often been the subjects for study.

The urge to imprint typically reaches its strongest peak 16 to 24 hours after the baby goose is hatched. During this period, the baby bird has an innate
30 tendency to follow anything that moves, and will chase after its mother (if she is around), or a human, a bouncing football or a brightly painted tin can that the experimenter dangles in front of the gosling. The more the baby bird struggles to follow after this moving object, the more strongly the young animal becomes imprinted to the object. Once the goose has been imprinted,
35 this very special form of learning cannot easily be reversed. For example, the geese that first followed Lorenz could not readily be trained to follow their mother instead; indeed, when these geese were grown and sexually mature, they showed no romantic interest in other geese. Instead, they attempted to court and mate with humans.

40 If a goose is hatched in a dark incubator and is not allowed to see the world until two or three days later, imprinting often does not occur. At first it was thought that the "critical period" had passed and hence the bird could never become imprinted to anything. Now we know differently. The innate urge to follow moving objects does appear to reach a peak in geese 24 hours
45 after they are hatched, but it does not decline thereafter. Rather, a second innate urge—that of fearing and avoiding new objects—begins to develop, and within 48 hours after hatching typically overwhelms the prior tendency the bird had to follow after anything that moves. To use a human term, the goose's *attitude* toward strong things is controlled by its genetic blueprint—at
50 first it is attracted to, then it becomes afraid of, new objects in its environment. As we will see in a moment, these conflicting "attitudes" may explain much of the data on "critical periods" in both animals and humans.

*How might these two apparently conflicting
behavioral tendencies help a baby goose survive
in its usual or natural environment?*

In other experiments, baby chickens have been hatched and raised in the
dark for the first several days of their lives. Chicks have an innate tendency to
55 peck at small objects soon after they are hatched—an instinctive behavior pattern that helps them get food as soon as they are born. In the dark, of course,
they cannot see grain lying on the ground and hence do not peck (they must be
hand-fed in the dark during this period of time). Once brought into the light,
these chicks do begin to peck, but they do so clumsily and ineffectively, as if
60 their "critical period" for learning the pecking skill had passed. Birds such as
robins and blue jays learn to fly at about the time their wings are mature
enough to sustain flight (their parents often push them from the nest as a means
of encouraging them to take off on their own). If these young birds are restrained and not allowed to fly until much later, their flight patterns are often
65 clumsy and they do not usually gain the necessary skills to become good fliers.

The "Maternal Instinct" in Rats

Suppose we take a baby female rat from its mother at the moment of its birth and
raise the rat pup "by bottle" until it is sexually mature. Since it has never seen
other rats during its entire life (its eyes do not open until several days after birth),
any sexual or maternal behavior that it shows will presumably be due to the nat-
70 ural unfolding of its genetic blueprint—and not due to learning or imitation.
Now, suppose we inseminate this hand-raised female rat artificially—to make
certain that she continues to have no contact with other rats. Will she build a nest
for her babies before they are born, following the usual pattern of female rats, and
will she clean and take care of them during and after the birth itself?

75 The answer to that question is *yes—if*. If, when the young female rat was
growing up, there were objects such as sticks and sawdust and string and
small blocks of wood in her cage, and which she played with. Then, when in-
seminated, the pregnant rat will use these "toys" to build a nest. If the rat
grows up in a bare cage, she won't build a nest *even though we give her the ma-*
80 *terials to do so once she is impregnated*. If this same rat is forced to wear a stiff
rubber collar around her neck when she is growing up—so that she cannot
clean her sex organs, as rats normally do—she will not usually lick her newborn babies clean *even though we take off the rubber collar a day or so before she*
gives birth. The genetic blueprint always operates best within a particular en-
85 vironmental setting. If an organism's early environment is abnormal or particularly unusual, later "innate" behavior patterns may be disrupted.

Overcoming the "Critical Period"

All of these examples may appear to support the "critical-period" hypothesis—that there is one time in an organism's life when it is best suited to
learn a particular skill. These studies might also seem to violate the general

90 rule that an organism can "catch up" if its development has been delayed. However, the truth is more complicated (as always) than it might seem from the experiments we have cited so far.

Baby geese will normally not imprint if we restrict their visual experiences for the first 48 hours of their lives—their fear of strange objects is by then too 95 great. However, if we give the geese tranquilizing drugs to help overcome their fear, they can be imprinted a week or more after hatching. Once imprinting has taken place, it may seem to be irreversible. But we can occasionally get a bird imprinted on a human to accept a goose as its mother, if we coax it enough and give it massive rewards for approaching or following its 100 natural mother. Chicks raised in darkness become clumsy eaters—but what do you think would happen if we gave them special training in how to peck, rather than simply leaving the matter to chance? Birds restrained in the nest too long apparently learn other ways of getting along and soon come to fear heights; what do you think would happen if we gave these birds tranquilizers 105 and rewarded each tiny approximation to flapping their wings properly?

There is not much scientific evidence that human infants have the same types of "critical periods" that birds and rats do. By being born without strong innate behavior patterns (such as imprinting), we seem to be better able to adjust and survive in the wide variety of social environments human babies 110 are born into. Like many other organisms, however, children do appear to have an inborn tendency to imitate the behavior of other organisms around them. A young rat will learn to press a lever in a Skinner box much faster if it is first allowed to watch an adult rat get food by pressing the lever. This learning is even quicker if the adult rat happens to be the young animal's 115 mother. Different species of birds have characteristic songs or calls. A European thrush, for example, has a song pattern fairly similar to a thrush in the United States, but both sound quite different from blue jays. There are *local dialects* among songbirds, however, and these are learned through imitation. If a baby thrush is isolated from its parents and exposed to blue jay calls 120 when it is very young, the thrush will sound a little like a blue jay but a lot like other thrushes when it grows up. And parrots, of course, pick up very human-sounding speech patterns if they are raised with humans rather than with other parrots.

Time Goals

Record your finishing time. _____:_____ Calculate your total reading time. _____

Rate your concentration as high _____ medium _____ or low._____

Recall what you have read, and review what you have learned.
    Your instructor may choose to give you a true-false comprehension review.

CRITICAL-PERIOD HYPOTHESIS

Provide proof that a critical period exists during which an organism must have certain experiences in order to reach its normal mature state.

Response Suggestion: Review the selection and number the experiments that provide proof of the hypothesis. Define the hypothesis and describe three to five supporting examples from the text.

Contemporary Link

Why does it seem logical that altering the maternal instinct of a bear caring for her sick cub would be much more difficult than preventing the development of the maternal instincts of rats building nests and cleaning their young?

COMPREHENSION QUESTIONS

After reading the selection, answer the following questions with *a, b, c,* or *d.*

Main Idea _____ 1. The best statement of the main idea of this selection is
   a. studies show that goslings can be imprinted on humans.
   b. a particular few days of an animal's life can be a crucial time for developing long-lasting "natural" behavior.
   c. imprinting seems to occur in mammals but is very strong in ducks and geese.
   d. the "crucial period" of imprinting is important but can be overcome with drugs.

Detail _____ 2. The critical-period hypothesis is the belief that
   a. there is a "prime time" to develop certain skills.
   b. most learning occurs during the first few days of life.
   c. fear can inhibit early learning.
   d. the "maternal instinct" is not innate but is learned.

Detail _____ 3. In Lorenz's studies, after the goslings imprinted on him, they would do all of the following except
   a. follow him around.
   b. flock to him for protection.
   c. return to their real mother for affection.
   d. become excited when Lorenz appeared.

Detail _____ 4. The author points out that in Lorenz's studies the early imprinting of geese with humans
   a. was easily reversed with training.
   b. caused the geese to be poor mothers.
   c. produced later sexually abnormal behavior in the geese.
   d. made it difficult for the goslings to learn to feed themselves.

Inference _____ 5. The author suggests that after 24 hours the innate urge to imprint in geese is
    a. decreased significantly.
    b. increased.
    c. overwhelmed by the avoidance urge.
    d. none of the above.

Inference _____ 6. In a small gosling's natural environment, the purpose of the avoidance urge that develops within 48 hours of hatching might primarily be to help it
    a. learn only the behavior of its species.
    b. follow only one mother.
    c. escape its genetic blueprint.
    d. stay away from predators.

Inference _____ 7. The author suggests that there is a critical period for developing all of the following except
    a. desire to eat.
    b. pecking.
    c. flying.
    d. cleaning the young.

Inference _____ 8. The studies with rats suggest that nest building and cleaning behavior are
    a. totally innate behaviors.
    b. totally learned behaviors.
    c. a combination of innate and learned behaviors.
    d. neither innate nor learned behaviors.

Detail _____ 9. Abnormal imprinting during the critical period can later be overcome by using all of the following except
    a. tranquilizing drugs.
    b. natural tendencies.
    c. special training.
    d. massive reward.

Inference _____ 10. Because humans do not seem to have strong innate behavior patterns, the author suggests that humans
    a. are better able to adapt to changing environments.
    b. have more difficulty learning early motor skills.
    c. find adjustment to change more difficult than animals.
    d. need more mothering than animals.

Answer the following with *T* (true) or *F* (false).

Detail _____ 11. The author states that whether imprinting occurs in humans is a matter of debate.

Inference _____ 12. The author implies that a goose can be imprinted on a painted tin can.

Inference _____ 13. In the author's opinion, studies show that organisms can catch up adequately without special training when skill development has been delayed past the critical period.

Inference _____ 14. If an abandoned bird egg is hatched and raised solely by a human, the author suggests that the bird will be abnormal.

Inference _____ 15. The author suggests that the urge to imitate is innate in both humans and animals.

VOCABULARY

According to the way the italicized word was used in the selection, select *a, b, c,* or *d* for the word or phrase that gives the best definition.

_____ 1. "The critical-period *hypothesis*" (4)
  a.   association
  b.   tentative assumption
  c.   law
  d.   dilemma

_____ 2. "in an *incubator*" (13)
  a.   cage
  b.   electric enlarger
  c.   nest
  d.   artificial hatching apparatus

_____ 3. "its *genetic* blueprint" (49)
  a.   sexual
  b.   emotional
  c.   hereditary
  d.   earned

_____ 4. "an *instinctive* behavior pattern" (55)
  a.   desirable
  b.   innate
  c.   early
  d.   newly acquired

_____ 5. "to *sustain* flight" (62)
  a.   support
  b.   imitate
  c.   begin
  d.   imagine

_____ 6. "birds are *restrained*" (63–64)
  a.   pressured
  b.   pushed
  c.   held back
  d.   attacked

_____ 7. "suppose we *inseminate*" (71)
  a.   imprison
  b.   artificially impregnate
  c.   injure
  d.   frighten

_____ 8. "may be *disrupted*" (86)
  a.   thrown into disorder
  b.   repeated
  c.   lost
  d.   destroyed

_____ 9. "seem to be *irreversible*" (97)
  a.   temporary
  b.   changeable
  c.   frequent
  d.   permanent

_____ 10. "*coax* it enough" (99)
  a.   encourage fondly
  b.   punish
  c.   feed
  d.   drill

Time Goals

Record your time for answering the questions. _____:_____

Calculate your total time for reading and answering the questions. _____

What changes would you make to enhance your concentration on the new selection? _____

SEARCH THE NET

Animals have many unusual instincts that are beneficial to their survival. Conduct a search to discover an unusual maternal instinct of birds. Write a paragraph describing the unusual instinct and its value for survival. Use the following notebook format to plan your search and record your findings.

Sample Search Notebook Page

Research topic:	*Maternal instincts of birds*
Research questions:	*What are some unusual maternal instincts of birds?*
	How do these instincts aid in the survival of the species?
What I already know:	*Birds and other animals have some unusual instincts such as imprinting. Imprinting is the process where attachments are formed by young birds on the first social objects they encounter. Konrad Lorenz led the research on imprinting using goslings.*

Search Terms	**Notes and Websites**
✓ *Bird behavior*	*poor results—sites are related to pet bird behaviors*
✓ *Maternal instincts*	*only found instincts on cows, pigs, and sheep*
✓ *Bird instincts*	*host-parasite conflict (http://birding.miningco.com/library/weekly/aa060797.htm)*
✓ *Maternal instincts of birds*	*killdeer, mother feigns broken wing (http://www.birdwatching.com/stories/killdeer.html)*
✓ *Killdeer*	*personal report (http://www.newton.dep.anl.gov/natbltn/400-499/nb482.htm)*
	very brief description (http://www.baylink.org/wpc/killdeer.html)

Go Electronic!

For additional readings, exercises, and Internet activities, visit this book's Website at:
http://www.awlonline.com/smithBTG

For even more activities, visit the Longman English pages at:
http://longman.awl.com/englishpages

If you need a user name and password, please see your instructor.

Take a Road Trip to Mt. Rushmore! Be sure to visit the Memorization and Concentration module in your Reading Road Trip CD-ROM for multimedia tutorials, exercises, and tests.

READER'S JOURNAL

Name _____ Date _____

Chapter 1

To improve your skills, you must seriously reflect on the daily choices you make and your progress as a learner. Be your own best teacher by questioning your academic behaviors, your understanding of the material, and your academic performance. Take ownership of new ideas and strategies by finding a way to make them a part of you.

Many experts believe that writing is a mode of learning. In other words, writing about something helps a person understand it. With that purpose in mind, record a response to the following questions to communicate to yourself and your instructor. Learn about yourself through your journal writing. Use the perforations to tear the assignment out for your instructor.

1. Where have you decided to do most of your studying? Why?

   _____

2. If the telephone is a distraction, how are you managing your calls?

   _____

3. Which television programs do you plan to watch on a regular basis?

   _____

   _____

4. When and where do you tend to waste time? _____

   _____

5. When do you write your *To-Do* list for the day? _____

6. Which classmates would you feel comfortable calling about an assignment?

   _____

7. Have some of your classmates been late for class? How were these tardy students put at a disadvantage? _____

   _____

8. What two "success behaviors" have you observed in fellow classmates that you would like to copy? _____

   _____

Vocabulary

- How do you remember new words?
- What are context clues?
- Why learn prefixes, roots, and suffixes?
- What will you find in a dictionary?
- What is a glossary?
- What is a thesaurus?
- What are analogies?
- What are acronyms?
- How are transitional words used?

Mark Wallinger, Q3, 1994. Acrylic on canvas. Private collection. © Mark Wallinger, courtesy Anthony Reynolds Gallery, London.

REMEMBERING NEW WORDS

Have you ever made lists of unknown words that you wanted to remember? Did you dutifully write down the word, a colon, and a definition, and promise to review the list at night before going to bed? Did it work? Probably not! Memorization can be an effective cramming strategy, but it does not seem to produce long-term results. Recording only the word and definition does not establish the associations necessary for long-term memory.

The best way to expand your vocabulary is to place yourself in an environment where challenging words are used. As you repeatedly hear the words, you begin to understand and remember them. Books also can offer a rich verbal environment. Books both introduce and reinforce new words. The more you read, the more you will notice new words. With a little effort, these "new" words will gradually become "old." Once you start noticing words, you will probably be surprised at how often they recur. The following suggestions can help you make new words into old friends.

Associate Words in Phrases. Never record a word in isolation. Think of the word and record it in a phrase that suggests its meaning. The phrase may be part of the sentence in which you first encountered the word, or it may be a vivid creation of your own imagination. Such a phrase provides a setting for the word and enriches the links to your long-term memory.

For example, the word *caravel* means a "small sailing ship." Record the word in a phrase that creates a memorable setting, like "a caravan of gliding caravels on the horizon of the sea."

Associate Words in Families. Words, like people, have families that share the same names. In the case of words, the names are called *prefixes, roots,* and *suffixes*. A basic knowledge of word parts can help you unlock the meaning to thousands of associated family members.

The prefix *ambi* means "both," as in the word *ambivert*, which means being both introverted and extroverted. Although this word is seldom used, it can be easily remembered because of its association with the other two more common words. A useful transfer occurs, however, when the knowledge of *ambi* is applied to new family members like *ambidextrous, ambiguous,* and *ambivalence*.

Associate Words in Images. Expand the phrase chosen for learning the word into a vivid mental image. Create a situation or an episode for the word. Further, enrich your memory link by drawing a picture of your mental image.

For example, the word *candid* means frank and truthful. Imagine a friend asking your opinion on an unattractive outfit. A suggestive phrase for learning the word might be "My candid reply might have hurt her feelings."

Seek Reinforcement. Look and listen for your new words. As suggested previously, you will probably discover that they are used more frequently than you ever thought. Notice them, welcome them, and congratulate yourself on your newfound wisdom.

Create Concept Cards. The illustrations shown here represent the front and back of index cards for recording information on new words. Each word is already presented in a phrase on the front of the card, along with a notation of where the word was encountered. On the back of each card, write an appropriate definition, use the word in a new sentence, and draw an image illustrating the word. Review the cards to reinforce the words and quiz yourself.

Front   *Back*

"gliding caravels on the horizon of the sea"
From BTG vocab. chapter

small sailing boats
The caravels sailed off into the sunset.

"candid reply might have hurt her feelings"
From BTG vocab. chapter

frank and truthful
Please give me your candid opinion about my new dress. (Ugh!)

"birds are restrained"
from "Critical Period"

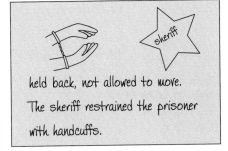
held back, not allowed to move.
The sheriff restrained the prisoner with handcuffs.

USING CONTEXT CLUES

Context clues are the most common method of unlocking the meaning of unknown words. The *context* of a word refers to the sentence or paragraph in which it appears. Readers use several types of context clues. In some cases, words are defined directly in the sentences in which they appear; in other instances, the sentence offers clues or hints that enable the reader to arrive indirectly at the meaning of the word. The following are examples of how each type of clue can be used to figure out word meaning in textbooks.

Definition

Complex scientific material has a heavy load of specialized vocabulary. Fortunately, new words are often directly defined as they are introduced in the text. Do you know the meaning of *erythrocytes* and *oxyhemoglobin?* Read the following textbook sentence in which these two words appear, and then select the correct definition for each word.

EXAMPLE

When oxygen diffuses into the blood in external respiration, most of it enters the red blood cells, or erythrocytes, and unites with the hemoglobin in these cells, forming a compound called oxyhemoglobin.

Willis H. Johnson et al., *Essentials of Biology*

_____ *Erythrocytes* means
a. diffused oxygen.
b. red blood cells.
c. respiration process.

_____ *Oxyhemoglobin* means
a. hemoglobin without oxygen.
b. dominant oxygen cells.
c. combination of oxygen and hemoglobin.

EXPLANATION The answers are *b* and *c*. Notice that the first word is used as a synonym to follow the words that define it, and the second is part of the explanation of the sentence.

Elaborating Details

In political science you will come across the term *confederation*. Keep reading and see if you can figure out the meaning from the hints in the following sentence.

EXAMPLE

There is a third form of governmental structure, a *confederation*. The United States began as such, under the Articles of Confederation. In a confederation, the national government is weak and most or all the

© 2000 Addison-Wesley Educational Publishers, Inc.

power is in the hands of its components, for example, the individual states. Today, confederations are rare except in international organizations such as the United Nations.

Robert Lineberry, *Government in America*

_____ A *confederation* is a governmental structure with
a. strong federal power.
b. weak federal power.
c. weak state power.
d. equal federal and state power.

EXPLANATION The answer is *b* and can be figured out from the details.

Examples

In psychology you will frequently encounter a complicated word describing something you have often thought about but not named. Read the following sentence to find out what *psychokinesis* means.

EXAMPLE Another psychic phenomenon is *psychokinesis,* the ability to affect physical events without physical intervention. You can test your powers of psychokinesis by trying to influence the fall of dice from a mechanical shaker. Are you able to have the dice come up a certain number with a greater frequency than would occur by chance?

Douglas W. Matheson, *Introductory Psychology: The Modern View*

_____ *Psychokinesis* means
a. extrasensory perception.
b. an influence on happenings without physical tampering.
c. physical intervention affecting physical change.

EXPLANATION The answer is *b*. Here the word is first directly defined in a complicated manner and then the definition is clarified by a simple example.

Comparison

Economics uses many complex concepts that are difficult to understand. The use of a familiar term in a comparison can help the reader relate to a new idea. Can you explain a *trade deficit?* The following comparison will help.

EXAMPLE When the United States imports more than it exports, we have a trade deficit rather than a trade balance or surplus. Similarly, a store manager who buys more than she sells will create a financial deficit for the company.

_____ A *trade deficit* means that the nation
a. sells more than it buys.
b. buys more than it sells.
c. sells what it buys.

EXPLANATION The answer is *b*. The comparison explains the definition by creating a more understandable situation.

Contrast

Can you explain what *transsexuals* are and how they differ from *homosexuals?* The following sentences will give you some clues.

EXAMPLE Transsexuals are people (usually males) who feel that they were born into the wrong body. They are not homosexuals in the usual sense. Most homosexuals are satisfied with their anatomy and think of themselves as appropriately male or female; they simply prefer members of their own sex. Transsexuals, in contrast, think of themselves as members of the opposite sex (often from early childhood) and may be so desperately unhappy with their physical appearance that they request hormonal and surgical treatment to change their genitals and secondary sex characteristics.

Rita Atkinson et al., *Introduction to Psychology*

_____ A *transsexual* is a person who thinks of himself/herself as
a. a homosexual.
b. a heterosexual.
c. a member of the opposite sex.
d. a person without sex drive.

EXPLANATION The answer is *c*. By comparing homosexual and transsexual, the reader is better able to understand the latter and distinguish between the two.

Limitations of Context Clues

Although the clues in the sentence in which an unknown word appears are certainly helpful in deriving the meaning of a word, these clues will not always give a complete and accurate definition. To understand totally the meaning of a word, take some time after your reading is completed to look the word up in a glossary or a dictionary. Context clues operate just as the name suggests; they are hints and not necessarily complete definitions.

▶ EXERCISE 2.1   *The Power of Context Clues*

How can context clues assist you in clarifying or unlocking the meaning of unknown words? For each of the following vocabulary items, make two responses. First, without reading the sentence containing the unknown word, select *a*, *b*, *c*, or *d* for the definition that you feel best fits each italicized word. Then, read the material in which the word is used in context and answer again. Compare your answers. Did reading the word in context help? Were you uncertain of any word as it appeared on the list, but then able to figure out the meaning after reading it in a sentence?

_____ 1. *usurped*
    a. shortened
    b. acknowledged
    c. aggravated
    d. seized

> _____ Henry, to the end of his life, thought of himself as a pious and orthodox Catholic who had restored the independent authority of the Church of England *usurped* centuries before by the Bishop of Rome.
>
> Shepard B. Clough et al., *A History of the Western World*

_____ 2. *assimilationist*
    a. one who adopts the habits of a larger cultural group
    b. a machinist
    c. typist
    d. one who files correspondence

> _____ When members of a minority group wish to give up what is distinctive about them and become just like the majority, they take an *assimilationist* position. An example is the Urban League.
>
> Reece McGee et al., *Sociology: An Introduction*

_____ 3. *dyad*
    a. star
    b. two-member group
    c. opposing factor
    d. leader

> _____ George Simmel was one of the first sociologists to suggest that the number of members in a group radically transforms its properties. He began with an analysis of what happens when a *dyad*, a two-member group, becomes a triad, a three-member group.
>
> *Ibid.*

_____ 4. *anticoagulants*
    a. demonstrators
    b. substances against clotting
    c. coal-mining disease agents
    d. germs

_____ The body can produce some natural *anticoagulants* such as heparin or dicumarol, which are formed in the liver. Also, some animals that depend on blood for nutrition—such as fleas and leeches—secrete substances to inhibit clotting.

Willis H. Johnson et al., *Essentials of Biology*

_____ 5. *expropriated*
   a. taken from its owners
   b. industrialized
   c. approximated
   d. increased in size

_____ Under a decree of September 1952, the government *expropriated* several hundred thousand acres from large landholders and redistributed this land among the peasants.

Jesse H. Wheeler, Jr., et al., *Regional Geography of the World*

_____ 6. *adherents*
   a. children
   b. followers
   c. instigators
   d. detractors

_____ One of the fundamental features of Hinduism has been the division of its *adherents* into the most elaborate caste system ever known.

Ibid.

_____ 7. *stimulus*
   a. writing implement
   b. distinguishing mark
   c. something that incites action
   d. result

_____ While we are sleeping, for example, we are hardly aware of what is happening around us, but we are aware to some degree. Any loud noise or other abrupt *stimulus* will almost certainly awaken us.

Gardner Lindzey et al., *Psychology*

_____ 8. *debilitating*
   a. weakening
   b. reinforcing
   c. exciting
   d. enjoyable

_____ However, anyone who has passed through several time zones while flying east or west knows how difficult it can be to change from one sleep schedule to another. This "jet lag" can be so *debilitating* that many corporations will not allow their executives to enter negotiations for at least two days after such a trip.

Ibid.

_____ 9. *autocratic*
   a. automatic
   b. democratic
   c. self-starting
   d. dictatorial

_____ Autocratic leadership can be extremely effective if the people wielding it have enough power to enforce their decisions and if their followers know that they have it. It is especially useful in military situations where speed of decision is critical. Among its disadvantages are the lack of objectivity and the disregard for opinions of subordinates.

David J. Rachman and Michael Mescon, *Business Today*

_____ 14. *disseminated*
   a. dissolved
   b. spread
   c. destroyed
   d. originated

_____ Disseminated Magmatic Deposits are the simplest of the magmatic deposits. The valuable mineral is *disseminated* or scattered throughout the igneous body. In the diamond deposits of South Africa, for example, the diamonds are disseminated in unusual rock, somewhat similar to peridotite.

Robert J. Foster, *Physical Geology*

EXERCISE 2.2   Context Clues in Academic Reading

Use the context clues of the sentence to write the meaning of each of the following italicized words.

1. Andrew was a thin old man despite his toughness, and soon he was in danger. Fortunately, friends formed a cordon and managed to *extricate* him through a rear door.

John Garraty, *The American Nation*

Extricate means _____

2. But they were unfamiliar with the *regenerative* powers of the starfish. The central disk merely grows new arms, and a single arm can form a new animal.

Robert Wallace, *Biology: The World of Life*

Regenerative means _____

3. To our delight, the *planarians* that had eaten educated victims learned much faster than did the worms that had consumed their untrained brethren.

Ibid.

Planarians are _____

4. Belle Starr, the *moniker* of one Myra Belle Shirley, was immortalized as "the bandit queen," as pure in heart as Jesse James was socially conscious.

Ibid.

Moniker means _____

5. Calamity Jane (Martha Cannary), later said to have been Wild Bill's *paramour*, wrote her own romantic autobiography in order to support a drinking problem.

Ibid.

A *paramour* is _____◀

Multiple Meanings of a Word

Many words, particularly short ones, can be confusing because they have more than one meaning. The word *bank*, for example, can be used as a noun to refer to *a financial institution, the ground rising from a river*, or a *mass of clouds. Bank* as a verb can mean *to laterally incline an airplane, to accumulate,* or *to drive a billiard ball into a cushion.* Thus the meaning of the word depends on the sentence and paragraph in which the word is used. Be alert to context clues that indicate an unfamiliar use of a seemingly familiar word.

▶ EXERCISE 2.3   *Multiple Meanings*

The boldface words in the following sentences have multiple meanings. Write the definition of each boldface word as it is used in the sentence.

1. For a foreign film, the movie had an unprecedented **run** at the box office.

_____

2. As a team player for IBM, she demonstrated **industry** and intelligence in accomplishing the goals. _____

_____

3. The technician used the new idea to **land** a contract for computer programs.

_____

4. Volunteers signed up for different shifts to **man** the ticket booth.

_____

5. The insect did not **light** long enough to be caught.

_____

UNDERSTANDING THE STRUCTURE OF WORDS

What is the longest word in the English language and what does it mean? Maxwell Nurnberg and Morris Rosenblum in _How to Build a Better Vocabulary_ (Prentice-Hall, 1949) say that at one time the longest word in _Webster's New International Dictionary_ was

pneumonoultramicroscopicsilicovolcanokoniosis

Look at the word again and notice the smaller and more familiar word parts. Do you know enough of the smaller parts to figure out the meaning of the word? Nurnberg and Rosenblum unlock the meaning as follows:

pneumono: pertaining to the lungs, as in _pneu_monia

ultra: beyond, as in _ultra_violet rays

micro: small, as in _micro_scope

scopic: from the root of Greek verb _skopein_, to view or look at

silico: from the element _silicon_, found in quartz, flint, and sand

volcano: the meaning of this is obvious

koni: the principal root, from a Greek word for dust

osis: a suffix indicating illness, as trichin_osis_

Now, putting the parts together again, we deduce that _pneumonoultramicroscopicsilicovolcanokoniosis_ is a disease of the lungs caused by extremely small particles of volcanic ash and dust.

This dramatic example demonstrates how an extremely long and technical word can become more manageable by breaking it into smaller parts. The same is true for many of the smaller words that we use every day. A knowledge of word parts will help you unlock the meaning of literally thousands of words. One vocabulary expert identified a list of thirty prefixes, roots, and suffixes and claims that knowing these thirty word parts will help unlock the meaning of 14,000 words.

Words, like people, have families and, in some cases, an abundance of close relations. Clusters, or what might be called *word families*, are composed of words with the same base or root. For example, *bio* is a root meaning *life*. If you know that *biology* means *the study of life*, it becomes easy to figure out the definition of a word like *biochemistry*. Word parts form new words as follows:

prefix + root   root + suffix   prefix + root + suffix

Prefixes and suffixes are added to root words to change the meaning. A prefix is added to the beginning of a word and a suffix is added to the end. For example, the prefix *il* means *not*. When added to the word *legal*, the resulting word, *illegal*, becomes the opposite of the original. Suffixes can change the meaning or change the way the word can be used in a sentence. The suffix *cide* means to *kill*. When added to *frater*, which means *brother*, the resulting word, *fratricide*, means to *kill one's brother*. Adding *ity* or *ize* to *frater* changes both the meaning and the way the word can be used grammatically in a sentence.

EXAMPLE   To demonstrate how prefixes, roots, and suffixes overlap and make families, start with the root *gamy*, meaning *marriage*, and ask some questions.

1. What is the state of having only one wife called?   _____
   (*mono* means *one*)

2. What is a man who has two wives called?   _____
   (*bi* means *two* and *ist* means *one who*)

3. What is a man who has many wives called? _____
   (*poly* means *many*)

4. What is a woman who has many husbands called? _____
   (*andry* means *man*)

5. What is a hater of marriage called?   _____
   (*miso* means *hater of*)

EXPLANATION   The answers are (1) monogamy, (2) bigamist, (3) polygamist, (4) polyandrist, and (5) misogamist. Note that in several of the *gamy* examples, the letters change slightly to accommodate language sounds. Such variations of a letter or two are typical when working with word parts. Letters are often dropped or added to maintain the rhythm of the language, but the meaning of the word part remains the same regardless of the change in spelling. For example, the prefix *con* means *with* or *together* as in *conduct*. This same prefix is used with variations in many other words:

cooperate   *collection*   *correlate*   *communicate*   *connect*

Thus, *con, co, col, cor,* and *com* are all forms of the prefix that means *with* or *together*.

▶ **EXERCISE 2.4**   *Word Families*

Create your own word families from the word parts that are supplied. For each of the following definitions, supply a prefix, root, or suffix to make the appropriate word.

Prefix: *bi* means *two*

1. able to speak two languages: bi ____ _____

2. having two feet, like humans: bi _____

3. representing two political parties: bi _____

4. occurring at two-year intervals: bi _____

5. having two lenses on one glass: bi _____

6. cut into two parts: bi _____

7. mathematics expression with two terms: bi _____

8. instrument with two eyes: bi _____

9. tooth with two points: bi _____

10. coming twice a year: bi _____

Root: *vert* means *to turn*

1. to change one's beliefs: _____ vert

2. to go back to old ways again: _____ vert

3. a car with a removable top: _____ vert _____

4. to change the direction of a stream: _____ vert

5. activities intended to undermine or destroy: _____ vers _____

6. an outgoing, gregarious person: _____ vert

7. a quiet, introspective, shy person: _____ vert

8. conditions that are turned against you; misfortune: _____ vers _____

9. one who deviates from normal behavior, especially sexual: _____ vert

10. one who is sometimes introspective and sometimes gregarious: _____ vert

Suffix: *ism* means *doctrine, condition,* or *characteristic*

1. addiction to alcoholic drink: _____ ism

2. a brave and courageous manner of acting: _____ ism

3. doctrine of the fascists of Germany: _____ ism _____

4. doctrine concerned only with fact and reality: _____ ism

5. system using terror to intimidate: _____ ism

6. using someone's words as your own: _____ ism

7. driving out an evil spirit: _____ ism

8. purification to join the church: _____ ism

9. informal style of speech using slang: _____ ism

10. characteristic of one region of the country: _____ ism

EXERCISE 2.5   *Prefixes, Roots, and Suffixes*

Using the prefix, root, or suffix provided, write the words that best fit the following definitions.

1. *con* means *with*
   infectious or catching: con _____

2. *contra* means *against*
   to speak against another's statement: contra _____

3. *post* means *after*
   to delay or set back: post _____

4. *psych* means *mind*
   a physician who studies the mind: psych _____

5. *pel* means *drive* or *push*
   to push out of school: _____ pel

6. *thermo* means *heat*
   device for regulating furnace heat: therm _____

7. *ven* means *come*
   a meeting for people to come together: _____ ven _____

8. *rupt* means *break* or *burst*
   a volcanic explosion: _____ rupt _____

9. *meter* means *measure*
   instrument to measure pressure: _____ meter

10. *naut* means *voyager*
    voyager in the sea: _____ naut

USING A DICTIONARY

Do you have an excellent collegiate dictionary such as *Merriam-Webster's New Collegiate Dictionary?* Every college student needs two dictionaries: a small one for class and a large one to keep at home. In class you may use a small paperback dictionary for quick spelling or word meaning checks. The paperback is easy to carry but does not provide the depth of information needed for college study that is found in the larger collegiate editions. Good dictionaries contain not only the definitions of words, but also provide the following additional information for each word.

Guide Words. The two words at the top of each dictionary page are the first and last entries on the page. They help guide your search for a particular entry by indicating what is covered on that page.

In the sample below, *flagrante delicto* is the first entry on the page of the dictionary on which *flamingo* appears, and *flappy* is the last entry. Note that the pronunciation of the word *flamingo* is followed by part of speech (n), plural spellings, and the origin of the word.

flagrante delicto ● flappy

fla·min·go \flə-'miŋ-(ˌ)gō\ *n, pl* **-gos** *also* **-goes** [obs. Sp *flamengo* (now *flamenco*), lit., Fleming, German (conventionally thought of as ruddy-complexioned)] (1565) : any of several large aquatic birds (family Phoenicopteridae) with long legs and neck, webbed feet, a broad lamellate bill resembling that of a duck but abruptly bent downward, and usu. rosy-white plumage with scarlet wing coverts and black wing quills

flamingo

\ə\ abut \ᵊ\ kitten, F table \ər\ **further** \a\ **ash** \ā\ **ace** \ä\ mop, mar
\aù\ **out** \ch\ **chin** \e\ bet \ē\ **easy** \g\ go \i\ hit \ī\ ice \j\ job
\ŋ\ **sing** \ō\ go \ò\ **law** \òi\ boy \th\ **thin** \th̲\ **the** \ü\ loot \ù\ foot
\y\ **yet** \zh\ **vision** \ȧ, k̲, ⁿ, œ, œ̄, ᵫ, ᵫ̄, ᵊ\ *see* Guide to Pronunciation

By permission. From Merriam-Webster's Collegiate ® Dictionary, Tenth Edition; © 1998 by Merriam-Webster, Incorporated.

Pronunciation. The boldface main entry divides the word into sounds, using a dot between each syllable. In parentheses after the entry, letters and symbols show the pronunciation. A diacritical mark (´) at the end of a syllable indicates stress on that syllable. A heavy mark means major stress; a lighter one shows minor stress.

As shown in the illustration above, a key explaining the symbols and letters appears at the bottom of the dictionary page. For example, a word like *ragweed* (rag´ w-d) would be pronounced with a short *a* as in *ash* and a long *e* as in *easy*.

666 lemma • leopard frog

²lemma *n* [Gk, husk, fr. *lepein* to peel — more at LEPER] (1906) : the lower of the two bracts enclosing the flower in the spikelet of grasses
lem·ming \ˈle-miŋ\ *n* [Norw] (1713) : any of various small short-tailed furry-footed rodents (as genera *Lemmus* and *Dicrostonyx*) of circumpolar distribution that are notable for the recurrent mass migrations of a European form (*L. lemmus*) which often continue into the sea where vast numbers are drowned — **lem·ming·like** \-ˌlīk\ *adj*
lem·nis·cate \lem-ˈnis-kət\ *n* [NL *lemniscata*, fr. fem. of L *lemniscatus* with hanging ribbons, fr. *lemniscus*] (ca. 1781) : a figure-eight shaped curve whose equation in polar coordinates is $\rho^2 = a^2 \cos 2\theta$ or $\rho^2 = a^2 \sin 2\theta$
lem·nis·cus \lem-ˈnis-kəs\ *n, pl* **-nis·ci** \-ˈnis-ˌkī, -ˌkē; -ˈni-ˌsī\ [NL, fr. L, ribbon, fr. Gk *lēmniskos*] (ca. 1905) : a band of fibers and esp. nerve fibers — **lem·nis·cal** \-kəl\ *adj*
¹lem·on \ˈle-mən\ *n* [ME *lymon*, fr. MF *limon*, fr. ML *limon-*, *limo*, fr. Ar *laymūn*] (15c) **1 a :** an acid fruit that is botanically a many-seeded pale yellow oblong berry and is produced by a small thorny tree (*Citrus limon*) **b :** a tree that bears lemons **2 :** one (as an automobile) that is unsatisfactory or defective — **lem·ony** \ˈle-mə-nē\ *adj*
²lemon *adj* (1598) **1 :** of the color lemon yellow **2 a :** containing lemon **b :** having the flavor or scent of lemon
lem·on·ade \ˌle-mə-ˈnād\ *n* (1604) : a beverage of sweetened lemon juice mixed with water

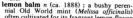

lemon 1: branch with fruit and flowers

lemon balm *n* (ca. 1888) : a bushy perennial Old World mint (*Melissa officinalis*) often cultivated for its fragrant lemon-flavored leaves
lem·on·grass \ˈle-mən-ˌgras\ *n* (1801) : a grass (*Cymbopogon citratus*) of robust habit that grows in tropical regions, is used as an herb, and is the source of an essential oil with an odor of lemon or verbena
lemon law *n* (1982) : a law offering car buyers relief (as by repair, replacement, or refund) for defects detected during a specified period after purchase
lemon shark *n* (1942) : a medium-sized requiem shark (*Negaprion brevirostris*) of the warm Atlantic that is yellowish brown to gray above with yellow or greenish sides
lemon sole *n* (1876) : any of several flatfishes and esp. flounders: as **a :** a bottom-dwelling flounder (*Microstomus kitt*) of the northeastern Atlantic that is an important food fish **b :** WINTER FLOUNDER
lemon yellow *n* (1807) : a brilliant greenish yellow color
lem·pi·ra \lem-ˈpir-ə\ *n* [AmerSp, fr. *Lempira*, 16th cent. Indian chief] (ca. 1934) — see MONEY table
le·mur \ˈlē-mər\ *n* [NL, fr. L *lemures*, pl., ghosts] (1795) : any of various arboreal chiefly nocturnal mammals that were formerly widespread but are now largely confined to Madagascar, are related to the monkeys but are usu. regarded as constituting a distinct superfamily (Lemuroidea), and usu. have a muzzle like a fox, large eyes, very soft woolly fur, and a long furry tail
le·mu·res \ˈle-mə-ˌrās, ˈlem-yə-ˌrēz\ *n pl* [L] (1555) : spirits of the unburied dead exorcised from homes in early Roman religious rites

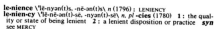

lemur

lend \ˈlend\ *vb* **lent** \ˈlent\; **lend·ing** [ME *lenen*, *lenden*, fr. OE *lǣnan*, fr. *lǣn* loan — more at LOAN] *vt* (bef. 12c) **1 a :** to give for temporary use on condition that the same or its equivalent be returned **b :** to let out (money) for temporary use on condition of repayment with interest **2 a :** to give the assistance or support of : AFFORD, FURNISH ⟨a dispassionate and scholarly manner which ~s great force to his criticisms —*Times Lit. Supp.*⟩ **b :** to adapt or apply (oneself) readily : ACCOMMODATE ⟨a topic that ~s itself admirably to class discussion⟩ ~ *vi* : to make a loan ***usage*** see LOAN — **lend·able** \ˈlen-də-bəl\ *adj* — **lend·er** *n*
lending library *n* (1708) : a library from which materials are lent; *esp* : RENTAL LIBRARY
lend–lease \ˈlend-ˈlēs\ *n* [U.S. *Lend-Lease* Act (1941)] (1941) : the transfer of goods and services to an ally to aid in a common cause with payment made by a return of the original items or their use in the cause or by a similar transfer of other goods and services — **lend–lease** *vt*
length \ˈleŋ(k)th, ˈlen(t)th\ *n, pl* **lengths** \ˈleŋ(k)ths, ˈlen(t)ths, ˈleŋ(k)s\ [ME *lengthe*, fr. OE *lengthu*, fr. *lang* long] (bef. 12c) **1 a :** the longer or longest dimension of an object **b :** a measured distance or dimension ⟨10 feet in ~⟩ — see METRIC SYSTEM table, WEIGHT table **c :** the quality or state of being long **2 a :** duration or extent in time **b :** relative duration or stress of a sound **3 a :** distance or extent in space **b :** the length of something taken as a unit of measure ⟨his horse led by a ~⟩ **4 :** the degree to which something (as a course of action or a line of thought) is carried — often used in pl. ⟨went to great ~s to learn the truth⟩ **5 a :** a long expanse or stretch **b :** a piece constituting or usable as part of a whole or of a connected series : SECTION ⟨a ~ of pipe⟩ **6 :** a vertical dimension of an article of clothing — **at length 1 :** FULLY, COMPREHENSIVELY **2 :** at last : FINALLY
length·en \ˈleŋ(k)-thən, ˈlen(t)-\ *vb* **length·ened; length·en·ing** \ˈleŋ(k)th-niŋ, ˈlen(t)th-; ˈleŋ(k)-thə-, ˈlen(t)-\ *vt* (14c) : to make longer ~ *vi* : to grow longer ***syn*** see EXTEND — **length·en·er** \ˈleŋ(k)th-nər, ˈlen(t)th-; ˈleŋ(k)-thə-, ˈlen(t)-\ *n*
length·ways \ˈleŋ(k)th-ˌwāz, ˈlen(t)th-\ *adv* (1599) : LENGTHWISE
length·wise \-ˌwīz\ *adv* (ca. 1580) : in the direction of the length : LONGITUDINALLY — **lengthwise** *adj*
lengthy \ˈleŋ(k)-thē, ˈlen(t)-\ *adj* **length·i·er; -est** (1689) **1 :** protracted excessively : OVERLONG **2 :** EXTENDED, LONG — **length·i·ly** \-thə-lē\ *adv* — **length·i·ness** \-thē-nəs\ *n*
le·nience \ˈlē-nyən(t)s, -nē-ən(t)s\ *n* (1796) : LENIENCY
le·nien·cy \ˈlē-nē-ən(t)-sē, -nyən(t)-sē\ *n, pl* **-cies** (1780) **1 :** the quality or state of being lenient **2 :** a lenient disposition or practice ***syn*** see MERCY
le·nient \ˈlē-nē-ənt, -nyənt\ *adj* [L *lenient-*, *leniens*, prp. of *lenire* to soften, soothe, fr. *lenis* soft, mild; prob. akin to Lith *lėnas* tranquil — more at LET] (1652) **1 :** exerting a soothing or easing influence : relieving pain or stress **2 :** of mild and tolerant disposition; *esp* : INDULGENT — **le·nient·ly** *adv*
Leni–Len·a·pe *or* **Len·ni–Len·a·pe** \ˌle-nē-ˈle-nə-pē, -lə-ˈnä-pē\ *n* [Delaware (Unami dialects) *lə̀ni-lənáp·e*] (ca. 1782) : DELAWARE 1
Le·nin·ism \ˈle-nə-ˌni-zəm\ *n* (1918) : the political, economic, and social principles and policies advocated by Lenin; *esp* : the theory and practice of communism developed by or associated with Lenin — **Le·nin·ist** \-nist\ *n or adj* — **Le·nin·ite** \-ˌnīt\ *n or adj*
le·nis \ˈlē-nəs, ˈlā-\ *adj* [NL, fr. L, mild, smooth] (ca. 1897) : produced with an articulation that is lax in relation to another speech sound ⟨\t\ in *gutter* is ~, \t\ in *toe* is fortis⟩
len·i·tion \lə-ˈni-shən\ *n* [L *lenire*] (1912) : the change from fortis to lenis articulation
len·i·tive \ˈle-nə-tiv\ *adj* [ME *lenitif*, fr. MF, fr. ML *lenitivus*, fr. L *lenitus*, pp. of *lenire*] (15c) : alleviating pain or harshness : SOOTHING — **lenitive** *n* — **len·i·tive·ly** *adv*
len·i·ty \ˈle-nə-tē\ *n* (1548) : the quality or state of being lenient : CLEMENCY
le·no \ˈlē-(ˌ)nō\ *n* [perh. fr. F *linon* linen fabric, lawn, fr. MF *lin* flax, linen, fr. L *linum* flax] (1821) **1 :** an open weave in which pairs of warp yarns cross one another and thereby lock the filling yarn in position **2 :** a fabric made with a leno weave
¹lens *also* **lense** \ˈlenz\ *n* [NL *lent-*, *lens*, fr. L, lentil; fr. its shape] (1693) **1 a :** a piece of transparent material (as glass) that has two opposite regular surfaces either both curved or one curved and the other plane and that is used either singly or combined in an optical instrument for forming an image by focusing rays of light **b :** a combination of two or more simple lenses **c :** a piece of glass or plastic used (as in safety goggles or sunglasses) to protect the eye **2 :** a device for directing or focusing radiation other than light (as sound waves, radio microwaves, or electrons) **3 :** something shaped like a double-convex optical lens ⟨~ of sandstone⟩ **4 :** a highly transparent biconvex lens-shaped or nearly spherical body in the eye that focuses light rays (as upon the retina) — see EYE illustration **5 :** something that facilitates and influences perception, comprehension, or evaluation ⟨the author's own ~ seems blurred by bias —Seymour Topping⟩ — **lensed** \ˈlenzd\ *adj* — **lens·less** \ˈlenz-ləs\ *adj*
²lens *vt* (1942) : to make a motion picture of : FILM
lens·man \-mən, -ˌman\ *n* (1938) : PHOTOGRAPHER
Lent \ˈlent\ *n* [ME *lente* springtime, Lent, fr. OE *lencten*; akin to OHG *lenzin* spring] (13c) : the 40 weekdays from Ash Wednesday to Easter observed by the Roman Catholic, Eastern, and some Protestant churches as a period of penitence and fasting
len·ta·men·te \ˌlen-tə-ˈmen-(ˌ)tā\ *adv or adj* [It, fr. *lento* slow] (1724) : LENTO
len·tan·do \len-ˈtän-(ˌ)dō\ *adv or adj* [It] (ca. 1847) : becoming slower — used as a direction in music
Lent·en \ˈlen-tᵊn\ *adj* (bef. 12c) : of, relating to, or suitable for Lent; *esp* : MEAGER ⟨~ fare⟩
len·tic \ˈlen-tik\ *adj* [L *lentus* sluggish] (ca. 1938) : of, relating to, or living in still waters (as lakes, ponds, or swamps) — compare LOTIC
len·ti·cel \ˈlen-tə-ˌsel\ *n* [NL *lenticella*, dim. of L *lent-*, *lens* lentil] (ca. 1864) : a loose aggregation of cells which penetrates the surface (as of a stem) of a woody plant and through which gases are exchanged between the atmosphere and the underlying tissues
len·tic·u·lar \len-ˈti-kyə-lər\ *adj* [ME, fr. L *lenticularis* lentil-shaped, fr. *lenticula* lentil] (15c) **1 :** having the shape of a double-convex lens **2 :** of or relating to a lens **3 :** provided with or utilizing lenticules ⟨a ~ screen⟩
len·ti·cule \ˈlen-tə-ˌkyü(ə)l\ *n* [L *lenticula*] (1942) **1 :** any of the minute lenses on the base side of a film used in stereoscopic or color photography **2 :** any of the tiny corrugations or grooves molded or embossed into the surface of a projection screen
len·til \ˈlen-tᵊl\ *n* [ME, fr. OF *lentille*, fr. L *lenticula*, dim. of *lent-*, *lens*] (13c) **1 :** a widely cultivated Eurasian annual leguminous plant (*Lens culinaris*) with flattened edible seeds and leafy stalks used as fodder **2 :** the seed of the lentil
len·tis·si·mo \len-ˈti-sə-ˌmō\ *adv or adj* [It, superl. of *lento*] (ca. 1903) : at a very slow tempo — used as a direction in music
len·ti·vi·rus \ˌlen-tə-ˈvī-rəs\ *n* [NL, fr. L *lentus* slow + NL *virus*] (1982) : any of a group of retroviruses that cause slowly progressive often fatal animal diseases
len·to \ˈlen-(ˌ)tō\ *adv or adj* [It, fr. *lento*, adj., slow, fr. L *lentus* pliant, sluggish, slow — more at LITHE] (ca. 1724) : at a slow tempo — used esp. as a direction in music
Leo \ˈlē-(ˌ)ō\ *n* [L (gen. *Leonis*), lit., lion — more at LION] **1 :** a northern constellation east of Cancer **2 a :** the 5th sign of the zodiac in astrology — see ZODIAC table **b :** one born under this sign — **Le·o·nine** \ˈlē-ə-ˌnīn\ *adj*
le·one \lē-ˈōn\ *n, pl* **leones** *or* **leone** [*Sierra Leone*] (1964) — see MONEY table
Le·o·nid \ˈlē-ə-nid\ *n, pl* **Leonids** *or* **Le·on·i·des** \lē-ˈä-nə-ˌdēz\ [L *Leon-*, *Leo*; fr. their appearing to radiate from a point in Leo] (1876) : any of the meteors in a meteor shower occurring every year about November 14
le·o·nine \ˈlē-ə-ˌnīn\ *adj* [ME, fr. L *leoninus*, fr. *leon-*, *leo*] (14c) : of, relating to, suggestive of, or resembling a lion
leop·ard \ˈle-pərd\ *n* [ME, fr. OF *leupart*, fr. LL *leopardus*, fr. Gk *leopardos*, fr. *leōn* lion + *pardos* leopard] (13c) **1 :** a large strong cat (*Panthera pardus*) of southern Asia and Africa that is adept at climbing and is usu. tawny or buff with black spots arranged in rosettes — called also *panther* **2 :** a heraldic representation of a lion passant guardant — **leop·ard·ess** \-pər-dəs\ *n*
leopard frog *n* (1839) : a common No. American frog (*Rana pipiens*) that is bright green or brown with large black white-margined blotches on the back; *also* : a similar frog (*R. sphenocephala*) of the southeastern U.S.

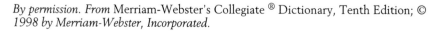

By permission. From Merriam-Webster's Collegiate ® Dictionary, Tenth Edition; © *1998 by Merriam-Webster, Incorporated.*

The *a* in *flamingo* sounds like the *a* in *abut*, and the final *o* has a long sound as in *go*. The stress is on the first syllable.

Part of Speech. The part of speech is indicated in an abbreviation for each meaning of a word. A single word, for example, may be a noun with one definition and a verb with another. The noun *flamingo* can be used as only one part of speech, but *sideline* can be both a noun and a verb (see the entry below).

Spellings. Spellings are given for the plural of the word and for special forms. This is particularly useful in determining whether letters are added or dropped to form the new words. The plural of *flamingo* can be spelled correctly in two different ways. Both *flamingos* and *flamingoes* are acceptable.

Origin. For many entries, the foreign word and language from which the word was derived will appear after the pronunciation. For example, *L* stands for a Latin origin and G for Greek. A key for the many dictionary abbreviations usually appears at the beginning of the book.

The word *flamingo* has a rich history. It is Portuguese (*Pg*) and comes from the Spanish (*fr Sp*) word *flamenco*. It is derived ultimately from the Old Provençal (*fr OProv*) *flamenc*, from *flama* for *flame*, which comes from the Latin (*fr L*) word *flamma*.

Multiple Meanings. A single word can have many shades of meaning or several completely different meanings. Different meanings are numbered.

The word *flamingo* has only one meaning. The word *sideline*, however, has several, as shown in the entry below.

A sideline can be a business, a product, or a designated area. In addition, it can mean to move something out of the action.

¹**side·line** \-ˌlin\ *n* (1862) **1** : a line at right angles to a goal line or end line and marking a side of a court or field of play for athletic games **2**
a : a line of goods sold in addition to one's principal line **b** : a business or activity pursued in addition to one's regular occupation **3 a**
: the space immediately outside the lines along either side of an athletic field or court **b** : a sphere of little or no participation or activity —
usu. used in pl.
²**sideline** *vt* (1943) : to put out of action : put on the sidelines

By permission. From Merriam-Webster's Collegiate ® Dictionary, Tenth Edition; © *1998 by Merriam-Webster, Incorporated.*

> **EXERCISE 2.6**   *Using the Dictionary*

Answer the following questions, using the page from *Merriam-Webster's Collegiate Dictionary* reproduced on page 58, with *T* (true), *F* (false), and *CT* (can't tell).

_____ 1. *Lent* is eight weekends before Easter.

_____ 2. *Lentils* can be eaten.

_____ 3. The word *lemming* is derived from the Greek word *lemmus*, which means to drown.

_____ 4. A convex *lens* lets in more light than a concave lens.

_____ 5. *Lenient* can be both an adjective and a noun.

_____ 6. The plural of *leone* can be either *leones* or *leone*.

_____ 7. One of the origins of *lemur* is the Latin word *lemures*, meaning *ghosts*.

_____ 8. The word *lemures* can be correctly pronounced in two different ways.

_____ 9. When the words *lend* and *lease* are used together to mean a transfer of goods, no hyphen is required.

_____ 10. A legitimate word can be formed by adding the suffix *-esque* to the first part of Leonardo da Vinci's name.

WORD ORIGINS

The study of word origins is called *etymology*. Not only is it fascinating to trace a word back to its earliest recorded appearance, but your knowledge of the word's origin can strengthen your memory for the word. For example, the word *narcissistic* means *egotistically in love with yourself*. Its origin is a Greek myth in which a beautiful youth named Narcissus falls in love with his own reflection; he is punished for his vanity by being turned into a flower. Thus, the myth creates an intriguing image that can enhance your memory link for the word.

The amount of information on word origins varies with the type of dictionary. Because of its size, a small paperback dictionary such as the *American Heritage Dictionary* usually contains very little information on word origins, whereas a textbook-size edition of the *Webster's Collegiate Dictionary* offers more. For the most information on word origins, visit the reference room in your college library and use an unabridged dictionary such as *Webster's Third New International Dictionary*, *Random House Dictionary of the English Language*, or *American Heritage Dictionary of the English Language*.

▶ **EXERCISE 2.7**   *Word Origins*

Read the following dictionary entries and answer the questions about the words and their origins.

> ¹**bribe** \'brib\ *n* [ME, something stolen, fr. MF, bread given to a beggar] (15c)   **1** : money or favor given or promised in order to influence the judgment or conduct of a person in a position of trust   **2** : something that serves to induce or influence
> ²**bribe** *vb* **bribed; brib·ing** *vt* (1528) : to induce or influence by or as if by bribery ~ *vi* : to practice bribery — **brib·able** \'bri-bə-bəl\ *adj* —

By permission. From Merriam-Webster's Collegiate ® Dictionary, Tenth Edition; © *1998 by Merriam-Webster, Incorporated.*

1. *Bribe* means _____

2. Explain the origin _____

¹scape·goat \'skāp-ˌgōt\ *n* [¹*scape;* intended as trans. of Heb *'azāzēl* (prob. name of a demon), as if *'ēz 'ōzēl* goat that departs—Lev 16:8 (AV)] (1530)   **1 :** a goat upon whose head are symbolically placed the sins of the people after which he is sent into the wilderness in the biblical ceremony for Yom Kippur   **2   a :** one that bears the blame for others   **b :** one that is the object of irrational hostility
²scapegoat *vt* (1943) : to make a scapegoat of — **scape·goat·ism** \-ˌgō-ˌti-zəm\ *n*

3. *Scapegoat* means _____

4. Explain the origin _____

mar·a·thon \'mar-ə-ˌthän\ *n, often attrib* [*Marathon,* Greece, site of a victory of Greeks over Persians in 490 B.C., the news of which was carried to Athens by a long-distance runner] (1896)   **1 :** a long-distance race: **a :** a footrace run on an open course usu. of 26 miles 385 yards (42.2 kilometers)   **b :** a race other than a footrace marked esp. by great length   **2   a :** an endurance contest   **b :** something (as an event, activity, or session) characterized by great length or concentrated effort

5. *Marathon* means _____

6. Explain the origin _____

_____

bon·fire \'bän-ˌfīr\ *n* [ME *bonefire* a fire of bones, fr. *bon* bone + *fire*] (15c) : a large fire built in the open air

7. *Bonfire* means _____

8. Explain the origin _____

van·dal \'van-d²l\ *n* [L *Vandalii* (pl.), of Gmc origin] (1555)   **1** *cap* **:** a member of a Germanic people who lived in the area south of the Baltic between the Vistula and the Oder, overran Gaul, Spain, and northern Africa in the 4th and 5th centuries A.D. and in 455 sacked Rome   **2** : one who willfully or ignorantly destroys, damages, or defaces property belonging to another or to the public — **vandal** *adj, often cap* —

9. *Vandal* means _____

10. Explain the origin _____

By permission. From Merriam-Webster's Collegiate ® Dictionary, *Tenth Edition; © 1998 by Merriam-Webster, Incorporated.*

USING A GLOSSARY

When you begin studying a new subject area, like sociology or geology, the first shock is the vocabulary. Each subject seems to have a language, or jargon, of its own. For example, words like *sociocultural* or *socioeconomic* crop up again and again in a sociology text. In truth, these words are somewhat unique to the subject-matter area—they are *invented* words to describe sociological phenomena. The best explanation of such words and their relation to the subject area can usually be found in the textbook itself rather than in a dictionary. Often, textbooks have definitions displayed in *the margins* of a page, or more frequently, in a glossary of terms at the end of the book or at the end of a chapter. The glossary defines the words as they are used in the textbook.

Notice the following examples from the glossary of a psychology text. The terms using "learning" are part of the jargon of psychology and would probably not be found in the dictionary.

latent learning   Hidden learning that is not demonstrated in performance until that performance is reinforced

learned helplessness   A condition in which a subject does not attempt to escape from a painful or noxious situation after learning in a previous, similar situation that escape is not possible

learning   A relatively permanent change in behavior that occurs as the result of practice or experience

learning set   An acquired strategy for learning or problem solving; learning to learn

---

▶ **EXERCISE 2.8**   *Using Your Glossary*

Turn to the glossary at the end of this book for help in defining the following terms. Write a definition for each in your own words.

1. schema _____

_____

2. bias _____

_____

3. context clues _____

_____

4. metacognition _____

_____

5. inference _____

_____

USING A THESAURUS

The first thesaurus was compiled by Dr. Peter Mark Roget, an English physician, who collected lists of synonyms as a hobby. The book, called *Roget's Thesaurus*, focuses mainly on suggested synonyms for commonly used words, but it also includes antonyms. Since its publication in 1852, the book has been updated many times, and Roget's thesaurus has been copied by others.

A thesaurus is a writer's tool. It is not a dictionary, and it does not include all words. Use a thesaurus to add variety to your writing and avoid repetitious wording. For example, if you find yourself repeating the word *guilt* in a research paper in sociology, consult a thesaurus for substitutes. *Roget's 21st Century Thesaurus* suggests synonyms such as *delinquency, fault, misconduct, shame,* or *transgression:*

> **guilt** [*n*] *blame; bad conscience over responsibility*
> answerability, blameworthiness, contrition, crime, criminality, culpability, delinquency, dereliction, disgrace, dishonor, error, failing, fault, indiscretion, infamy, iniquity, lapse, liability, malefaction, malfeasance, malpractice, misbehavior, misconduct, misstep, offense, onus, peccability, penitence, regret, remorse, responsibility, self-condemnation, self-reproach, shame, sin, sinfulness, slip, solecism, stigma, transgression, wickedness, wrong; SEE CONCEPTS *101,532, 645,690*

At the end of the entry, inclusion of the words SEE CONCEPTS (printed in capitals and followed by numbers) indicates that you can find additional synonyms under these numbers at the end of the book.

Most word-processing programs have an electronic thesaurus. Usually it is located near the Spell Check or in the "Tools" pull-down menu. Use your cursor to highlight (select) the word for which you want alternatives, and then click on the thesaurus. Consider the context of your sentence in choosing from the array of words that appear. A thesaurus in book form will offer more choices than the one offered by your word processing program.

▶ EXERCISE 2.9   *Thesaurus*

Use the following entries for *edge* in *Roget's 21st Century Thesaurus* to select an alternative word that fits the meaning of edge in the sentences.

> **edge** [*n1*] *border, outline*
> bend, berm, bound, boundary, brim, brink, butt, circumference, contour, corner, crook, crust, curb, end, extremity, frame, fringe, frontier, hem, hook, ledge, limb, limit, line, lip, margin, molding, mouth, outskirt, peak, perimeter, periphery, point, portal, rim, ring, shore, side, skirt, split, strand, term, threshold, tip, trimming, turn, verge; SEE CONCEPTS *484,513*
> **edge** [*n2*] *advantage*
> allowance, ascendancy, bulge, dominance, draw, handicap, head start, lead, odds, start, superiority, upper hand*, vantage; SEE CONCEPT *712*
> **edge** [*v1*] *border, trim*
> bind, bound, decorate, fringe, hem, margin, outline, rim, shape, skirt, surround, verge; SEE CONCEPTS *751,758*
> **edge** [*v2*] *defeat narrowly*
> creep, ease, inch, infiltrate, nose out*, sidle, slip by, slip past, squeeze by*, squeeze past*, steal, worm*; SEE CONCEPT *95*
> **edge** [*v3*] *sharpen*
> file, grind, hone, polish, sharpen, strop, whet; SEE CONCEPTS *137,250*

1. On the tenth hole the least experienced golfer took the *edge* with a long

   putt. _____

2. The new software company is on the *edge* of bankruptcy. _____

3. Disruptive children can reach the *edge* of a parent's patience. _____

4. The decorator wanted to *edge* the blue fabric with a yellow one. _____

5. The baseball player's face was shaded by the *edge* of his hat. _____

USING ANALOGIES

Analogies are comparisons that measure not only your word knowledge, but your ability to see relationships. They can be difficult, frustrating, and challenging. Use logical thinking and problem-solving skills to first pinpoint the initial relationship and then to establish a similar relationship with two other words.

> ▶ **READER'S TIP**   **Categories of Analogy Relationships**
>
> ▶ **Synonyms:** similar in meaning
> *Find* is to *locate* as *hope* is to *wish*.
>
> ▶ **Antonyms:** Opposite in meaning
> *Accept* is to *reject* as *rude* is to *polite*.
>
> ▶ **Function, use, or purpose:** Identifies what something does; watch for the object (noun) and then the action (verb)
> *Pool* is to *swim* as *blanket* is to *warm*.
>
> ▶ **Classification:** Identifies the larger group association
> *Sandal* is to *shoe* as *sourdough* is to *bread*.
>
> ▶ **Characteristics and descriptions:** Shows qualities or traits
> *Nocturnal* is to *raccoon* as *humid* is to *rainforest*.
>
> ▶ **Degree:** shows variations of intensity
> *Fear* is to *terror* as *dislike* is to *hate*.
>
> ▶ **Part to whole:** shows the larger group
> *Page* is to *book* as *caboose* is to *train*.
>
> ▶ **Cause and effect:** Shows the reason (cause) and result (effect)
> *Study* is to *graduation* as *caffeine* is to *insomnia*.

▶ **EXERCISE 2.10**   *Analogies*

Study the analogies that follow to establish the relationship of the first two words. Record that relationship, using the categories outlined above. Then choose the word that duplicates that relationship to finish the analogy.

1. *Trash* is to *refuse* as *soil* is to _____.

   Relationship _____
   a. earthworms
   b. dirt
   c. minerals
   d. growing

2. *Cappuccino* is to *coffee* as *jazz* is to _____

   Relationship _____
   a. singer
   b. opera
   c. rock
   d. music

3. *Fork* is to *eat* as *television* is to _____

   Relationship _____
   a. video
   b. actor
   c. entertain
   d. produce

4. *Smart* is to *genius* as *rigid* is to _____

   Relationship _____
   a. steel
   b. comedy
   c. angle
   d. focus

5. *Recklessness* is to *accident* as *laziness* is to _____

   Relationship _____
   a. work
   b. money
   c. failure
   d. ability

EASILY CONFUSED WORDS

Pairs or groups of words may cause confusion because they sound exactly alike or almost alike, but are spelled and used differently. *Stationary* and *stationery* are examples of this confusion. You ride a stationary bike to work out and you write a business letter on your office stationery. For a memory link, associate the *e* in *letter* with the *e* in *stationery*. Students frequently confuse *your* and *you're*: *your* shows possession, and *you're* is a contraction for *you are*. To differentiate confusing words, create associations and memorize them.

> **EXERCISE 2.11**   *Confusing Words*

Study the following easily confused words, and then circle the one that is correct in each sentence.

> **accept:** receive
> **except:** all but

1. When children reach adolescence, they begin to (**accept, except**) the values of their peers.

> **to:** a preposition
> **too:** additionally
> **two:** the number

2. Entrapment is used as an excuse from criminal liability in (**to, too, two**) many undercover drug cases.

> **thorough:** careful
> **threw:** tossed
> **through:** by means of

3. A (**thorough,   threw, through**) investigation can help reveal whether the murder was premeditated.

> **consul:** foreign representative
> **council:** elected officials
> **counsel:** give advice

4. The court will appoint (**consul, council, counsel**) for an armed robbery defendant who has no money to pay for a lawyer.

> **site:** place
> **cite:** quote
> **sight:** vision

5. Attorneys need to (**site, cite, sight**) references from previous trials to support their interpretation of the law.

RECOGNIZING ACRONYMS

An *acronym* is an abbreviation that is pronounced as a word. An acronym can thus be considered invented words that are often thoughtfully contrived to simplify a lengthy name and gain quick recognition for an organization or agency. For example, *UNICEF* is the abbreviation for the United Nations International

Children's Emergency Fund. The arrangement of consonants and vowels formed by the first letter of each word in the title creates an invented term that we can easily pronounce and quickly recognize. When names are created for new organizations, clever organizers thoughtfully consider the choice and sequence of words in order to engineer a catchy acronym. In some cases, acronyms have become so ingrained in our language that the abbreviations have become accepted as words with lowercase letters. An example of this is the word *radar*, which is a combination of the initial letters of the phrase *radio detecting and ranging*.

▶**EXERCISE 2.12**   *Acronyms*

The following letters are abbreviations. Write an A beside those that are pronounced as words and thus are considered acronyms.

_____ 1. CNN
_____ 2. NAFTA
_____ 3. MP3
_____ 4. NASA
_____ 5. IRS
_____ 6. CD
_____ 7. UNESCO
_____ 8. OSHA
_____ 9. MCI
_____ 10. NASDAQ

RECOGNIZING TRANSITIONAL WORDS

Transitional words are connecting words that signal the direction of the writer's thought. They are single words or short phrases that lead the reader to anticipate a continuation or a change in thought. For example, the phrase *in addition* signals a continuation, whereas *but* or *however* signal a change.

▶**READER'S TIP**   **Signals for Transition**

▶ **For addition:** in addition   furthermore   moreover

▶ **For examples:** for example   for instance   to illustrate   such as

▶ **For time:** first   secondly   finally   last   afterward

▶ **For comparison:** similarly   likewise   in the same manner

▶ **For contrast:** however   but   nevertheless   whereas
on the contrary   conversely   in contrast

▶ **For cause and effect:** thus   consequently   therefore   as a result

▶ **EXERCISE 2.13**   *Transitions*

Read to understand the direction of the author's thought and then choose a signal word from the boxed lists to complete the following sentences.

furthermore	similarly	consequently	however	for example

1. The Internet is a valuable research tool; _____ it can be frustrating.

2. Ragweed causes allergies; _____ mildew and dust mites also stimulate allergic reactions.

3. The chemist walked to class yesterday in the rain and _____ has a cold today.

4. Papers are due at the beginning of the period, and _____ they should be put on my desk when you first enter the classroom.

5. Runners train for many different events. _____, the Boston Marathon attracts thousands of athletes.

Summary Points

■ **How do you remember new words?**

To remember new words, associate words in phrases, in families, and in images. Use concept cards to record a new word's definition with a phrase and an image that suggest the meaning.

■ **What are context clues?**

The context clues in a sentence or paragraph can help unlock the meaning of unknown words. These can be definitions, details, examples, and comparisons or contrasts.

■ **Why learn prefixes, roots, and suffixes?**

A knowledge of prefixes, suffixes, and roots can reveal smaller and more familiar word parts in unknown words.

■ **What will you find in a dictionary?**

A collegiate dictionary contains definitions, word origins, pronunciations, and spellings.

■ **What is a glossary?**

A glossary defines words that are unique to a subject matter area.

■ **What is a thesaurus?**

A thesaurus contains synonyms for frequently used words to add variety to writing.

■ **What are analogies?**

Analogies are comparisons that fall into different categories of relationships.

■ **What are acronyms?**

Acronyms are abbreviations that are pronounced as words.

■ **How are transitional words used?**

Transitional words are used to connect words that signal the writer's thought.

SEARCH THE NET

Locate a site on the Internet designed for vocabulary building. Describe what the site offers and how it could be used to enhance your vocabulary. Reference your Websites.

Go Electronic!
For additional readings, exercises, and Internet activities, visit this book's Website at:
http://www.awlonline.com/smithBTG

For even more activities, visit the Longman English pages at:
http://longman.awl.com/englishpages

If you need a user name and password, please see your instructor.

Take a Road Trip to the Library of Congress! Be sure to visit the Vocabulary module in your Reading Road Trip CD-ROM for multimedia tutorials, exercises, and tests.

READER'S JOURNAL

Name _____ Date _____

Chapter 2

Answer the following questions to reflect on your own learning and progress. Use the perforations to tear the assignment out for your instructor.

1. Name and evaluate the quality of the dictionary that you use. _____

    _____

    _____

2. What has been your experience with using a dictionary on the computer?

    _____

3. How does a thesaurus differ from a dictionary? _____

    _____

4. In the past, which techniques have you used effectively to remember new words? Which ones did not work? _____

    _____

5. Which techniques are you using to remember the new words that you encounter in this book? _____

    _____

6. Name a difficult word that you enjoy using that many of your friends might not understand. _____

    _____

7. Explain how you would teach someone the meaning of the word you named above._____

    _____

8. Why are the index cards suggested for remembering words called *concept cards?* _____

    _____

Reading and Study Strategies

■ What is a study strategy?

■ What are the three stages of reading?

■ What is previewing?

■ Why should you activate your schema?

■ What is metacognition?

■ Why recall or self-test what you have read?

Winslow Homer, 1836–1910, United States. Sunlight and Shadow, 1872. Oil on Canvas. Cooper-Hewitt, National Design Museum, Smithsonian Institution/Art Resource, NY. Gift of Charles Savage Homer, Jr., 1917-14-7. Cooper-Hewitt, National Design Museum, Smithsonian Institution/Art Resource, NY.

WHAT IS A STUDY SYSTEM?

In 1946, after years of working with college students at Ohio State University, Francis P. Robinson developed the textbook-study system called SQ3R. The system was designed to help students efficiently read and learn from textbooks and effectively recall relevant information for subsequent exams. The letters in Robinson's acronym, SQ3R, stand for the following five steps: survey, question, read, recite, and review.

Numerous variations have been developed since SQ3R was introduced. One researcher, Norman Stahl, analyzed sixty-five textbook study systems and concluded that there are more similarities than differences among the systems.[1] The commonalities in the systems include a previewing stage, a reading stage, and a final self-testing stage. In the *previewing* stage students ask questions, activate past knowledge, and establish a purpose for reading. During the *reading* stage, students answer questions and continually integrate old and new knowledge. The *self-testing* stage of reading involves review to improve recall, evaluation to accept or reject ideas, and integration to blend new information with existing knowledge networks. Strategies used in these stages are depicted in the chart shown here and are discussed in this chapter.

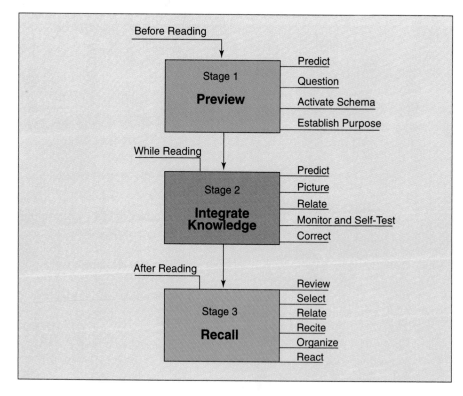

© 2000 Addison-Wesley Educational Publishers, Inc.

---

[1]N. A. Stahl, *Historical Analysis of Textbook Study Systems* (Ph.D. diss., University of Pittsburgh, 1983).

WHY USE A STUDY SYSTEM?

When a professor ends a class by saying "Read the assigned pages for your next class meeting," everyone knows that the real message is, "*Actively read, study, and remember* the assigned pages." Reading a textbook means "reading to learn." Rather than being a single task, it is a project that needs an organized approach. Unlike an adventure novel, each chapter—even each page—of a textbook contains new and complex ideas. To be a successful academic reader, you should systematically engage in predicting, summarizing, self-testing, and establishing relationships to prior knowledge. In other words, you need a study system to help you succeed.

STAGE 1: PREVIEWING

Previewing is a method of personally connecting with the material before you start to read. When you preview, you look over the material, predict what the material is probably about, ask yourself what you already know about the topic, decide what you will probably know after you read, and make a plan for reading. Does this process sound similar to the concentration technique of sparking an interest before reading? The difference is that with previewing, your questions are related more directly to your purpose for reading. Even though it may take a few extra minutes in the beginning, your increased involvement will mean increased comprehension.

To preview, look over the material, think, and ask questions. The process is similar to the concentration technique of sparking an interest before reading, except that in previewing, the questions are more directly related to the purpose. The focus is, "What do I already know, what do I need to know, and how do I go about finding it out?" (See the box on page 74.)

Signposts for Answering Preview Questions

A public speaking rule says, "Tell them what you are going to tell them, tell them, and then tell them what you told them." This same organizational pattern frequently applies to textbook material. Typically, a chapter begins with a brief overview of the topic. The ideas are then developed in paragraphs or sections. Concluding statements at the end summarize the important points the author wants the reader to remember. Although this pattern does not apply in every case, it can serve as a guide in determining what to read when previewing textbook material.

Previewing can be a hit-or-miss activity since there may or may not be an introductory or concluding statement. Because of differences in writing styles, no one set of rules will work for all materials. Consider the following signposts when previewing.

Title. Titles are designed to attract attention and reflect the contents of the material. The title of an article, a chapter, or a book is the first and

© 2000 Addison-Wesley Educational Publishers, Inc.

▶ READER'S TIP Asking Questions Before Reading

▶ **What is the topic of the material?**

What does the title suggest? What do the subheadings, italics, and summaries suggest?

▶ **What do I already know?**

What do I already know about this topic or a related topic? Is this new topic a small part of a larger idea or issue that I have thought about before?

▶ **What is my purpose for reading?**

What will I need to know when I finish?

▶ **How is the material organized?**

What is the general outline or framework of the material? Is the author listing reasons, explaining a process, or comparing a trend?

▶ **What will be my plan of attack?**

What parts of the textbook seem most important? Do I need to read everything with equal care? Can I skim some parts? Can I skip some sections completely?

most obvious clue to its content. Think about the title and turn it into a question. If the article is entitled "Acupuncture," a major concern in your reading would probably be to find out "What is acupuncture?" Learn the "five-*W* technique" that journalists often use in the first paragraphs of their articles when they ask *who, what, when, where,* and *why.*

Introductory Material. To get an overview of an entire book, refer to the table of contents and preface. Sophisticated students use the table of contents as a study guide, turning the chapter headings into possible exam items. Many textbooks open each chapter with an outline and preview questions. Italicized inserts, decorative symbols, and color type are also used to overview and highlight contents. In textbook chapters and articles, the first paragraph frequently introduces the topic to be covered and gives the reader a sense of perspective.

Subheadings. Subheadings are titles for sections within chapters. The subheadings, usually appearing in **boldface print** or *italics*, outline the main points of the author's message and thus give the reader an overview of the organization and the content. Turn these subheadings into questions that need to be answered as you read.

Italics, Boldface Print, and Numbers. Italics and boldface print are used to highlight words that merit special attention and emphasis. These are usually new words or key words that students should be prepared to define and remember. For example, a discussion of sterilization in a biology text might emphasize the words *vasectomy* and *tubal ligation* in italics or boldface print. Numbers usually signal a list of important details. In another book on the same subject, the two forms of sterilization might be emphasized with enumeration, by indicating (1) vasectomy and (2) tubal ligation.

Concluding Summary. Many textbooks include a summary at the end of each chapter to highlight the important points within the material. The summary can serve not only as a review to follow reading but also as an introduction for overviewing the chapter.

EXERCISE 3.1   *Previewing This Textbook for the Big Picture*

To get an overview of the scope of this textbook and its sequence of topics, look over the table of contents and preface. Think about how the different chapter topics fit into the goals of college reading. Glance at the chapters to get a sense of the overall organization, and then answer the following questions.

1. Who is the author? Is the author an instructor? _____

   _____

2. What seems to be the purpose of the numbered reading selections?_____

   _____

3. List six different college disciplines that are represented in the numbered

   reading selections.

   _____

4. What seems to be the purpose of the "Contemporary Focus" selections?

   _____

5. Does the text have any study aids such as an index, a glossary, or summaries?

   _____

6. Which reading selection do you think will be the most interesting? _____

   _____

EXERCISE 3.2   *Previewing This Chapter*

To get an overview of this chapter, look first at the table of contents at the beginning of the book and then read the list of questions at the beginning of the chapter. Read the chapter summary points. Use your previewing to answer the following questions.

1. What is a study system? _____

_____

2. What is a schema? _____

_____

3. What is metacognition? _____

_____

4. What is the purpose of a recall diagram? _____

_____

5. Which reading selection do you think will be most interesting? _____

_____

6. What are the five thinking strategies used by good readers? _____

_____

Use your answers to these questions to help establish a purpose for reading the chapter. Why is this chapter important, and what do you hope to gain from reading it?

Preview to Activate Schemata

Despite what you may sometimes think, you are not an empty bucket into which the professor is pouring information. You are a learner who already knows a lot, and you are actively selecting, connecting, and eliminating information.

What do you bring to the printed page? As a reader, you have a responsibility to think and interact before, during, and after reading. Your previewing of material helps you predict the topic. Then, as a further part of the prereading stage, you need to activate your schema for what you perceive the topic to be.

A **schema** is like a computer chip in your brain that holds all you know on a subject. Each time you learn something new, you pull out the computer chip on that subject, add the new information, and return the chip to storage. The depth of the schema or the amount of information on the chip varies according to previous experience. For example, a scientist would have a more detailed computer chip for DNA than would a freshman biology student.

All college students have a schema for Shakespeare. Suppose your previewing of a ten-page essay led you to predict that the discussion focused on the strength of the main characters in five of Shakespeare's plays. Next you would ask, "What existing knowledge do I have on the subject?" or "What is on my computer chip labeled 'Shakespeare'?" Most students would immediately think of *Macbeth* and *Hamlet*, both the characters and the plays. Others who have studied Shakespeare more might recall *King Lear*, the comedies, and a model of the Globe Theater. The richness of your background determines the amount you can activate. In general, the more you are able to activate, the more meaningful your reading will be.

STAGE 2: INTEGRATING KNOWLEDGE WHILE READING

Is it easier to understand a passage if you already know something about the topic? You already know that the answer is *yes*. Read the following paragraphs for a demonstration.

Passage A: Water Balance

Water may be the single most important nutrient for athletic performance. The body may be able to survive weeks or even months without certain vitamins and minerals, but without water, performance may be compromised in as little as 30 minutes. Our bodies are approximately 60% water, and our muscles are approximately 70%. For an athlete exercising vigorously, water's main function is to remove the heat (calories) generated by exercise. The body's metabolic rate may increase 20 to 25 times during intense exercise. The body gets rid of this heat by picking it up in the circulation and transporting it to the skin, where it is lost through evaporation.

S. Fike et al., "Fluid and Electrolyte Requirements of Exercise,"
Sports Nutrition, ed. by Dan Benardot

Passage B: Echinoderms (i kí nə dərms')

Echinoderms have protective skeletal elements embedded in their body walls. They also have an unusual feature called a water vascular system, which is used as a kind of hydraulic pump to extend the soft, pouchlike *tube feet*, with their terminal suckers. They are sluggish creatures with poorly developed nervous systems. However, they are tenacious foragers. Some species feed on shellfish, such as oysters. They wrap around their prey and pull relentlessly until the shells open just a bit. Then they evert their stomachs, squeezing them between the shells, and digest the flesh of the oysters on the spot.

Robert Wallace, *Biology: The Science of Life*

Even if you are a biology major, the first passage is probably easier to read than the second. People tend to be interested in the health of the human body. Thus, most people have greater prior knowledge of the water balance needs of the human body than those of echinoderms. This prior knowledge makes reading more interesting, easier to visualize, and therefore easier to understand. Linking the old with the new provides a schema on which to hang the new ideas.

Before and while reading, good readers ask, "What do I already know about this topic?" and "How does this new information relate to my previous knowledge?" Although textbook topics may at times seem totally unfamiliar, seldom are all of the ideas completely new. Usually there is a link, an old bit of knowledge that you can associate with the new ideas. For example, although you may not be familiar with the echinoderms described in Passage B, you probably know what an oyster looks like and can visualize the tenacity needed to open its shell.

On the other hand, your view of Passage A or B might have been different if you had known before reading that starfish are echinoderms. You might have found the description of mealtime downright exciting. Reread the second passage with this knowledge and visualize the gruesome drama.

Later in this chapter you will read another passage on echinoderms. Be ready to pull out your already developed "echinoderm knowledge network."

Expanding Knowledge

Most experts agree that the single best predictor of your reading comprehension is what you already know. In other words, the rich get richer. The good news about this conclusion is that once you have struggled and learned about a subject, the next time you encounter the subject, learning about it will be easier. Does this help to explain why some experts say that the freshman year is the hardest? Frequently, students who barely make C's in introductory courses end up making A's and B's during their junior and senior years. Their intellectual energies during their junior and senior years can go into assimilating and arranging new information into previously established frameworks rather than striving to build schemata. Be comforted to know that during that initial struggle with new subjects, you are building schemata that you will later reuse. Tell yourself, "The smart get smarter, and I'm getting smart!"

Integrating Ideas: How Do Good Readers Think?

Understanding and remembering complex material requires as much thinking as reading. Both consciously and subconsciously, the good reader is predicting, visualizing, and drawing comparisons in order to assimilate new knowledge. The list of suggestions shown in the box on the opposite page, which were devised by a reading researcher, represents the kind of thinking strategies good readers use.[2]

The first three thinking strategies used by good readers are perhaps the easiest to understand and the quickest to develop. Young readers quickly learn to predict actions and outcomes as the excitement of an adventure escalates. Vivid descriptions and engaging illustrations nurture the imagination to create exciting mental images triggering past experiences. When the ideas get more complicated, however, the last two thinking strategies become essential elements in the pursuit of meaning. College textbooks are tough and require constant use of the monitoring strategy and frequent use of the correction strategy.

These last two strategies involve a higher level of thinking than just picturing an oyster. They reflect a deeper understanding of the process of getting meaning and require a reader who both knows and controls. This ability to know and control is called *metacognition*.

Metacognition

When you look at the following words, what is your reaction?

feeet   thankz   supplyyied

Your reaction is probably, "The words don't look right. They are misspelled." The reason for your realizing the errors so quickly is that you have a global un-

---

[2]B. Davey, "Think Aloud—Modeling for Cognitive Processes of Reading Comprehension," *Journal of Reading* 27 (October 1983): 44–47.

▶ READER'S TIP   **Using Thinking Strategies While Reading**

▶ **Make predictions.** (Develop hypotheses.)

"From the title, I predict that this section will give another example of a critical time for rats to learn a behavior."

"In this next part, I think we'll find out why the ancient Greeks used mnemonic devices."

"I think this is a description of an acupuncture treatment."

▶ **Describe the picture you're forming in your head from the information.** (Develop images during reading.)

"I have a picture of this scene in my mind. My pet is lying on the table with acupuncture needles sticking out of its fur."

▶ **Share an analogy.** (Link prior knowledge with new information in text.) We call this the *"like-a" step.*

"This is like my remembering, 'In 1492 Columbus sailed the ocean blue.'"

▶ **Verbalize a confusing point.** (Monitor your ongoing comprehension.)

"This is confusing."

"This just doesn't make sense. How can redwoods and cypress trees both be part of the same family?"

"This is different from what I had expected."

▶ **Correct gaps in comprehension** (Use fix-up strategies.)

"I'd better reread."

"Maybe I'll read ahead to see if it gets clearer."

"I'd better change my picture of the story."

"This is a new word to me—I'd better check the context to figure it out."

derstanding of the manner in which letters can and cannot occur in the English language. You instantly recognize the errors, and immediately scan your knowledge of words and the rules of ordering letters. Through your efficient recognition and correction, you have used information that goes beyond knowing about each of the three individual words. You have demonstrated a metacognitive awareness and understanding of lettering in the English language.[3]

---

[3]The author is grateful to Professor Jane Thielemann, University of Houston (Downtown), for inspiring this paragraph.

The term **metacognition** is a coined word. *Cognition* refers to knowledge or skills that you possess. The Greek prefix *meta-* suggests an abstract level of understanding as if viewed from the outside. Thus, metacognition not only means having the knowledge but also refers to your own awareness and understanding of the thinking processes involved and your ability to regulate and direct these processes. If you know how to read, you are operating on a cognitive level. To operate on a metacognitive level, you must know the processes involved in reading and be able to regulate them.

Let's take a real-life example. If you are reading a chemistry assignment and failing to understand it, you must first recognize that you are not comprehending. Next you must identify what and why you don't understand. Remember, you will be able to do this because you understand the skills involved in the reading process. Finally, you try to figure out how to eliminate your confusion. You attempt a correction strategy. If it does not work, you try another and remain confident that you will succeed. The point is to understand how to get meaning, to know when you don't have it, and to know what to do about getting it. One researcher calls this "knowing about knowing."[4]

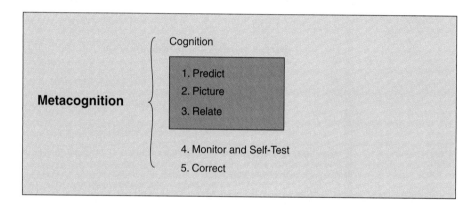

Comparing reading to a similar activity, do you know when you are really studying? Do you know the difference between really studying and simply going through the motions of studying? Sometimes you can study intensely for an hour and accomplish a phenomenal amount. Other times you can put in twice the time with books and notes but learn practically nothing. Do you know the difference and do you know what to do about it? Some students do not.

Poor readers see their failure to comprehend as a lack of ability and feel that nothing can be done about it. Successful readers see failure only as a need to reanalyze the task. They know they will eventually correct their problems and succeed.

---

[4]A. L. Brown, "The Development of Memory: Knowing, Knowing about Knowing, and Knowing How to Know," in H. W. Reese, ed., *Advances in Child Development and Behavior*, vol. 10 (New York: Academic Press 1975), pp. 104–146.

▶ **READER'S TIP**   **Developing a Metacognitive Sense for Reading**

With instruction and practice, you can improve your reading performance.

▶ *Know about reading.* Are you aware of the many strategies you use to comprehend? These include knowledge about words, main ideas, supporting details, and implied ideas. Also, think about the organization of the text and where meaning can be found.

▶ *Know how to monitor.* Monitor as an ongoing process throughout your reading. Use predicting and questioning to corroborate or discard ideas. Continually clarify and self-test to reinforce learning and pinpoint gaps in comprehension.

▶ *Know how to correct confusion.* Reread to reprocess a complex idea. Unravel a confusing writing style on a sentence level. Read ahead for ideas that unfold slowly. Consult a dictionary or other sources to fill in background knowledge you lack.

EXAMPLES   Use both your cognitive and metacognitive knowledge to answer the following test item. Interact with the material, monitor, and predict the ending phrase before reading the options. The highlighted handwriting models the thinking of an active reader.

Picture the comparison   *pollutes and kills*

What is euphemistically called an "oil spill" can very well become an oil

disaster for marine life. This is particularly true when refined or

wants to make more money

semirefined products are being transported. As the tankers get bigger, so

do the accidents, yet we continue to

key word

a. fight for clean water   c. use profits for cleanup

shows a parallel idea

b. search for more oil   d. build larger vessels

Robert Wallace, Biology: The Science of Life

The following passage illustrates the use of these thinking strategies with longer textbook material. Modeled thoughts of the reader are highlighted in handwriting. Keep in mind that each reader reacts differently to material, depending on background and individual differences. This example merely represents one reader's attempt to integrate knowledge.

What have I already read about this?

Dehydration and Fluid Replacement Guidelines

What's that in cups?

An athlete exercising under hot and humid conditions may lose more than 2 L of water per hour. Research has shown, under experimental conditions in subjects wearing football equipment, a loss of 1.8% of body

How much for a 150 lb guy?

weight in 30 minutes. Marathon runners have been shown to lose 6% to 10%

How much for a 130 lb girl?

of body weight during a race. A 2% loss of body weight by dehydration can impair the body's ability to dissipate heat, and a 4% loss can cause exhaustion. Besides impairing the body's thermoregulatory functions, dehydration can harm performance by causing reductions in strength, power, endurance, and aerobic capacity. Unreplaced fluid losses will

When do athletes replace fluids?

eventually raise the body's core temperature to the point of heat exhaustion or even life-threatening heat stroke.

Fortunately, most coaches and athletes now understand the importance of fluid replacement, and fluid restriction is seldom practiced. An exception

Why wrestling?

is in the sport of wrestling, where fluid restriction or voluntary dehydration still appears prominent. Although the importance of fluid intake may be understood, a recent survey reported that 53% of athletes did not know how

Do they get sick?

much fluid to drink. Thirst is not a reliable indicator of the need for fluid.

What is?

Individuals exercising in the heat who are given water ad libitum replace only about two thirds of their fluid losses. Exercise blunts the thirst mechanism. Consequently, the most reliable indicator for fluid needs is body weight.   *Is there a chart?*

S. Fike, et al., "Fluid and Electrolyte Requirements of Exercise," Sports Nutrition, *ed. by Dan Benardot*

EXPLANATION   The examples may be confusing to read because many of the thoughts that are highlighted normally occur on the subconscious level rather than the conscious level. Stopping to consciously analyze these reactions seems artificial and disruptive. It is important, however, to be aware that you are incorporating these thinking strategies into your reading. The following exercise is designed to heighten your awareness of this interaction.

EXERCISE 3.3   *Integrating Knowledge While Reading*

For the following passage, demonstrate with written notes the way you use the five thinking strategies as you read. The passage is double-spaced so that you can insert your thoughts and reactions between the lines. Make a conscious effort to experience all of the following strategies as you read:

1. Predict (develop hypotheses).
2. Picture (develop images during reading).
3. Relate (link prior knowledge with new ideas).
4. Clarify points (monitor your ongoing comprehension).
5. Correct gaps in comprehension (use correction strategies).

Sea Stars

Let's take a look at one class of echinoderms—the sea stars. Sea stars (starfish) are well known for their voracious appetite when it comes to gourmet foods, such as oysters and clams. Obviously, they are the sworn enemy of oystermen. But these same oystermen may have inadvertently helped the spread of the sea stars. At one time, when they caught a starfish, they chopped it apart and vengefully kicked the pieces overboard. But they were unfamiliar with the regenerative powers of the starfish. The central disk merely grows new arms, and a single arm can form a new animal.

Stars are slow-moving predators, so their prey, obviously, are even slower-moving or immobile. Their ability to open an oyster shell is a testimony to their persistence. When a sea star finds an oyster or clam, the prey clamps its shell together tightly, a tactic that discourages most would-be predators, but not the starfish. It bends its body over the oyster and attaches its tube feet to the shell, and then begins to pull. Tiring is no problem since it uses tube feet in relays. Finally, the oyster can no longer hold itself shut, and it opens gradually—only a tiny bit, but it is enough. The star then protrudes its stomach out through its mouth. The soft stomach slips into the slightly opened shell, surrounds the oyster, and digests it in its own shell.

Robert Wallace, *Biology: The Science of Life*

At first glance, you probably recognized *echinoderm* as an old friend and activated your newly acquired schema from a previous page. The description of the starfish lends itself to a vivid visualization. Were some of your predictions corroborated as you read the passage? Did you find yourself monitoring to reconcile new facts with old ideas? Did you need to use a correction strategy? Has your computer chip been expanded?

STAGE 3: RECALLING FOR SELF-TESTING

Recall does not have to be a formal process. It involves briefly telling yourself what you have learned, remembering, relating it to what you already know, and forming an opinion and reaction. Actually, all of this also occurs while reading, but an additional stop at the conclusion of an assignment helps you fill in any gaps and assimilate the many parts into an organized and meaningful whole. Improve your comprehension by taking those few extra minutes to digest what you have read; then, have a short conversation with yourself or a friend about the new material.

Recall also involves arranging new information into old schemata and creating new schemata. Not only are you recalling what you just read, but you are also recalling old knowledge and seeking to make connections. While "sorting through" ideas, you are accepting and rejecting information based on your opinions, making decisions about storage, rearranging old networks, and creating new ones. You are updating your computer chip. Good readers take the time to make these connections.

Recall by Writing

Good readers also benefit from taking the time to write about what they have read. Writing is a powerful learning tool that helps students translate and discover their own thinking. Experts define writing as a "mode of learning," which means that writing is a process that helps students blend, reconcile, and gain personal ownership of new knowledge. When you write about a subject, you not only discover how much you know and don't know, but you begin to make meaningful personal connections.

Writing requires an active commitment that goes beyond oral recall and class discussion. When you write, you have to actively wrestle with ideas. A humorous adage about the power of writing says, "How do I know what I think until I see what I say?" Writing can be hard work, but it helps you clarify and crystallize what you have learned. Answering multiple-choice questions after reading requires one type of mental processing, but writing about the reading requires another type of processing. Writing is another valuable resource in the learning process. Use its power to take your recall to a higher level.

> ▶ **READER'S TIP** | **Recalling After Reading**
>
> ▶ *Pinpoint the topic.* Sift through the generalities and the nonessentials to get focused on the subject. Use the title and the subheading to help you recognize and narrow down the topic.
>
> ▶ *Select the most important points.* Poor readers want to remember everything, thinking facts have equal importance. Good readers pull out the important issues and identify significant supporting information.
>
> ▶ *Relate the information.* Facts are difficult to learn in isolation. Many first-year college students have difficulty with history courses because they have limited schemata. Events appear to be isolated happenings rather than results of previous occurrences. Network your new knowledge to enhance memory.
>
> ▶ *React.* Evaluate and form opinions about the material and the author. Decide what you wish to accept and what you will reject. Blend old and new knowledge, and write about what you have read.

How to Recall

To recall, simply take a few minutes after reading to recap what you have learned. This can be done in your head or on paper. To visualize the main points graphically, make a recall diagram. On a straight line across the top, briefly state the topic, or what the selection seems to be mainly about. Indented underneath the topic, state the supporting details that seem to be most significant. Next, make a connection. What do you already know that seems to relate to this information? Your answer will be unique because you are connecting the material to your own knowledge networks. Draw a dotted line, your thought line, and recall a related idea, issue, or concern. Finally, react to the material. Formulate an opinion about the author and the message.

EXAMPLE

Autopsies

Today, many dead people receive some form of autopsy or postmortem examination. At least two main reasons for this are (1) the desire of the family to know the exact cause of death, and (2) the fact that increased medical knowledge results. Because of the important moral and legal restrictions on human experimentation, much of our knowledge of pathology comes from autopsies. This fact prompts many people to donate their bodies to medical schools and/or donate certain organs for possible transplantation.

John Cunningham, *Human Biology*

(Topic)	Why autopsies are done
(Significant details— examples, facts, or phrases)	To know exact cause of death
	To increase medical knowledge
	— thus donations
(Related idea)	Will this relieve the need for much animal research?
(Reaction— your opinions)	I would donate my organs but not my body to medical school.

EXPLANATION   Remember that the recall diagram is a temporary and artificial format. The diagram graphically demonstrates a process that you will learn to do in your head. Practice using the diagram will help you learn to organize and visualize your reading.

EXERCISE 3.4   *Recall Diagrams*

After reading each of the following passages, stop to recall what the passage contained. Use the recall diagrams to record what the passage seems to be mainly about, list significant supporting details, identify a related idea, issue, or concern to which you feel the information is connected, and react.

Passage A: Deborah Sampson

Assuming the name "Robert Shurtleff," this former indentured servant enlisted in the Continental Army in 1782 and became the only woman to serve formally in the Revolution. Fighting with the Fourth Massachusetts, she managed to maintain her disguise, although her fellow soldiers nicknamed her "Molly" because of her hairless face. A fever finally uncovered her true identity, and [Deborah] Sampson was discharged in 1783. She married the next year and received a small military pension. In 1802 she began a lecture tour, one of the first American women to do so, recounting her experiences as a soldier, a performance capped by her donning a soldier's uniform. Congress granted her heirs a full military pension in 1838.

Kenneth Davis, *Don't Know Much About History.*

(Topic) _____

(Significant
details)   _____
             _____
             _____

(Related idea) -

(Reaction) _____

Passage B: Kangaroos

Kangaroos and Australia are synonymous for most people, and the abundance of the large kangaroos has gone up since the British colonized Australia. The increase in kangaroo populations has occurred in spite of intensive shooting programs, since kangaroos are considered pests by ranchers and are harvested for meat and hides. The reason seems to be that ranchers have improved the habitat for the large kangaroos in three ways. First, in making water available for their sheep and cattle, the ranchers have also made it available for the kangaroos, removing the impact of water shortage for kangaroos in arid environments. Second, ranchers have cleared timber and produced grasslands for livestock. Kangaroos feed on grass, and so their food supply has been increased as well as the water supply. Third, ranchers have removed a major predator, the dingo. The dingo is a doglike predator, the largest carnivore in Australia. Because dingoes eat sheep, ranchers have built some 9,660 kilometers of fence in southern and eastern Australia to prevent dingoes from moving into sheep country. Intensive poisoning and shooting of dingoes in sheep country, coupled with the dingo fence that prevents recolonization, has produced a classic experiment in predator control.

Charles Krebs, *The Message of Ecology*

(Topic) _____

(Significant
details)   _____
             _____
             _____

(Related idea) -

(Reaction) _____

Summary Points

■ **What is a study strategy?**

All study systems include a previewing stage to ask questions and establish a purpose for reading, a reading stage to answer questions and integrate knowledge, and a final stage of self-testing and reviewing to improve recall.

■ **What are the three stages of reading?**

Reading is an active rather than a passive process. Good readers preview before reading, integrate knowledge while reading, and recall after reading.

■ **What is previewing?**

Previewing is a way to assess your needs before you start to read by deciding what the material is about, what needs to be done, and how to go about doing it.

■ **Why should you activate your schema?**

If you brainstorm to make a connection with your reading topic before you begin to read, the information will be more meaningful and memorable.

■ **What is metacognition?**

Good readers control and direct their thinking strategies as they read. They know about knowing.

■ **Why recall or self-test what you have read?**

Recalling what you have read immediately after reading forces you to select the most important points, to relate the supporting details, to connect new information into existing networks of knowledge, and to react.

CONTEMPORARY FOCUS

Are you more often happy when you are working intently or when you are playing? What does it take to make you happy? A scientific investigation of your happy moments might surprise you.

FINDING THE FLOW

Mihaly Csikszentmihalyi

Psychology Today, July/August 1997, pp. 46–48

The metaphor of flow is one that many people have used to describe the sense of effortless action they feel in moments that stand out as the best in their lives. Athletes refer to it as "being in the zone," religious mystics as being in "ecstasy," artists and musicians as "aesthetic rapture." It is the full involvement of flow, rather than happiness, that makes for excellence in life.

How often do people experience flow? If you ask a sample of typical Americans, "Do you ever get involved in something so deeply that nothing else seems to matter and you lose track of time?" roughly one in five will say that this happens to them as much as several times a day, whereas about 15 percent will say that this never happens to them.

Flow at Work

Although adults tend to be less happy than average while working, and their motivation is considerably below normal, ESM (Experimental Sampling Method) studies find more occasions of flow on the job than in free time. This finding is not that surprising: Work is much more like a game than most other things we do during the day. It usually has clear goals and rules of performance.

Flow at Play

In comparison to work, people often lack a clear purpose when spending time at home with the family or alone. The popular assumption is that no skills are involved in enjoying free time, and that anybody can do it. Yet the evidence suggests the opposite: Free time is more difficult to enjoy than work. Apparently, our nervous system has evolved to attend to external signals, but has not had time to adapt to long periods without obstacles and dangers. Unless one learns how to use this time effectively, having leisure at one's disposal does not improve the quality of life.

Leisure time in our society is occupied by three major sorts of activities: media consumption, conversation, and active leisure—such as hobbies, making music, going to restaurants and movies, sports, and exercise. Not all of these free-time activities are the same in their potential for flow. For example, U.S. teenagers experience flow about 13 percent of the time that they spend watching television, 34 percent of the time they do hobbies, and 44 percent of the time they are involved in sports and games. Yet these same teenagers spend at least four times more of their free hours watching TV than doing hobbies or sports. Similar ratios are true for adults.

Why would we spend four times more of our free time doing something that has less than half the chance of making us feel good? Each of the flow-producing activities requires an initial investment of attention before it begins to be enjoyable. If a person is too tired, anxious, or lacks the discipline to overcome that initial obstacle, he or she will have to settle for something that, although less enjoyable, is more accessible.

Collaborate on responses to the following questions:

■ What activities create the sense of flow for you that is described by the author?

■ What do you do in your leisure time that makes you happy?

■ How would you evaluate Csikszentmihalyi's theory of flow?

SKILL DEVELOPMENT—STAGE 1: PREVIEW

Preview the next selection to predict the purpose, organization, and your learning plan.

The author probably emphasizes positive ways to deal with anger.
Agree ☐   Disagree ☐

After reading this selection, I will need to know

_____

Activate Schema

Why are people afraid when they are alone in a house at night?

How does America's cultural acceptance of expressing anger harm our society?

Learning Strategy

Recall research findings that explain fear, anger, and happiness.

Word Knowledge

What do you know about these words?

induced	phenomenon	hostile	retaliate	escalating
preoccupy	amplify	trivial	perceive	consistent

Your instructor may give a true-false vocabulary review before or after reading.

STAGE 2: INTEGRATE KNOWLEDGE WHILE READING

Since each reader interacts with material in a unique manner, it is artificial to require certain thinking strategies to be used in certain places. In order to heighten awareness, however, several questions have been inserted within this selection. Briefly respond in the margin to the inserted comments or questions. In addition, make a note in the margin of at least one other instance when you used each of the following strategies:

Predict   Picture   Relate   Monitor   Correct

As people of differing cultures and races, do our faces speak differing languages? Which face expresses disgust? Anger? Fear? Happiness? Sadness? Surprise?

Answers: *(l. to r., top to bottom) happiness, surprise, disgust, anger, sadness, and fear*

EXPRESSING EMOTION

From David Myers, *Psychology*, Fifth ed.

The Effects of Facial Expressions

Expressions not only communicate emotion, they also amplify and regulate it. In his 1872 book, *The Expression of the Emotions in Man and Animals*, Darwin contended that "the free expression by outward signs of an emotion
5 intensifies it. . . . He who gives way to violent gestures will increase his rage."

Was Darwin right? I was driving in my car one day when the song "Put On a Happy Face" came on the radio. How phony, I thought. But I tested Darwin's hypothesis
10 anyway, as you can, too. Fake a big grin. Now scowl. Can you feel the difference?

The subjects in dozens of experiments have felt a difference. For example, James Laird and his colleagues subtly induced students to make a frowning expression
15 by asking them to "contract these muscles" and "pull your brows together" (supposedly to help the researchers attach facial electrodes). The results? The students reported feeling a little angry. Students similarly induced to smile felt happier, found cartoons more humorous, and recalled happier memories than did the frowners.

Try these expressions yourself.

20 Why might this be so? Paul Ekman and his colleagues designed an experiment to find out. Their subjects were professional actors trained in the Stanislavsky method, in which they physically (and psychologically) "become" the characters they are playing. The actors were asked to assume an expression and then hold it for 10 seconds while the researchers measured their
25 heart rates and finger temperatures. When they made a fearful expression, their heart rate increased some 8 beats per minute and finger temperature was steady. When making an angry expression, both heart rate and finger temperature increased as though the actor were indeed "hot-headed." Our facial expressions, it seems, send signals to our autonomic nervous system, which then
30 responds accordingly. This experiment also confirms that subtly different body states do underlie different emotions.

Sara Snodgrass and her associates observed the behavior feedback phenomenon with walking behavior. You can duplicate her subjects' experience: Walk for a few minutes while taking short, shuffling steps, keeping your eyes
35 downcast. Now walk around taking long strides, with your arms swinging and your eyes looking straight ahead. Can you feel your mood shift?

Try this to see if your mood shifts.

Experiencing Emotion

The ingredients of emotion include not only physiological arousal and expressive behavior but also our conscious experience. Consider three of the basic emotions: fear, anger, and happiness. What influences each?

Fear

Fear can be a poisonous emotion. It can torment us, rob us of sleep, and pre-
40 occupy our thinking. People can be literally scared to death. Fear can also be contagious. In 1903, someone yelled "Fire!" as a fire broke out in Chicago's Iroquois Theater. Eddie Foy, the comedian on stage at the time, tried to reassure the crowd by calling out, "Don't get excited. There's no danger. Take it easy!" Alas, the crowd panicked. During the 10 minutes it took the fire
45 department to arrive and quickly extinguish the flames, more than five hundred people perished, most of them trampled or smothered in a stampede. Bodies were piled 7 or 8 feet deep in the stairways, and many of the faces bore heel marks.

Picture what you might have done.

More often, fear is an adaptive response. Fear prepares our bodies to flee
50 danger. Fear of real or imagined enemies binds people together as families, tribes, and nations. Fear of injury protects us from harm. Fear of punishment or retaliation constrains us from harming one another. Fear triggers worry, which focuses the mind on a problem and rehearses coping strategies.

Psychologists note that we can learn to fear almost anything. As infants be-
55 come mobile they experience falls and near-falls—and become increasingly afraid of heights. Through such conditioning, the short list of naturally painful and frightening events can multiply into a long list of human fears—fear of driving or flying, fear of mice or cockroaches, fear of closed or open spaces, fear of failure, fear of another race or nation.

What fears have been conditioned in you?

Anger

60 Popular books and articles on aggression sometimes advise that even hostile outbursts can be better than keeping anger pent up. When irritated, should we go ahead and curse, tell a person off, or retaliate? Was Ann Landers right that "youngsters should be taught to vent their anger"?

Encouragement to vent your rage typifies individualized cultures, but it would
65 seldom be heard in cultures where people's identity is more group-centered. People who keenly sense their *inter*dependence see anger as a threat to group harmony. In Tahiti, for instance, people learn to be considerate and gentle. From infancy on in Japan, expressions of anger are less common than in Western cultures.

The "vent your anger" advice presumes that emotional expression provides
70 emotional release, or *catharsis*. The catharsis hypothesis maintains that we reduce anger by releasing it through aggressive action or fantasy. Experimenters report that this sometimes occurs. When people retaliate against someone who has provoked them, they may indeed calm down—*if* their counterattack

is directly against the provoker, *if* their retaliation seems justifiable, and *if*
75 their target is not intimidating. In short, expressing anger can be *temporarily*
calming *if* it does not leave us feeling guilty or anxious.

Despite the afterglow—people sometimes feel better for hours afterward—
catharsis usually fails to cleanse one's rage. More often, expressing anger breeds
more anger. For one thing, it may provoke retaliation, thus escalating a minor con-
80 flict into a major confrontation. For another, expressing anger can magnify anger.

Is expressing anger ultimately beneficial?

Thus, although "blowing off steam" may temporarily calm an angry person,
it may also amplify underlying hostility. When angry outbursts do calm us,
they may be reinforcing and therefore habit forming. If stressed managers can
drain off some of their tension by berating employees, then the next time
85 they feel tense with irritation they may be more likely to explode again. Similarly, the next time you are angry you are likely to do whatever has relieved
your anger in the past.

So what's the best way to handle anger? Experts have offered two suggestions. First, bring down the level of physiological arousal of anger by waiting.
90 "It is true of the body as of arrows," noted Carol Tavris. "What goes up must
come down. Any emotional arousal will simmer down if you just wait long
enough." Second, deal with anger in a way that involves neither being chronically angry over every little annoyance nor passively sulking, which is merely
rehearsing your reasons for anger. Don't be like those who, stifling their feel-
95 ings over a series of provocations, finally overreact to a single incident. Vent
the anger by exercising, playing an instrument, or confiding your feelings to a
friend or a diary.

Anger can benefit relationships when it expresses a grievance in ways that
promote reconciliation rather than retaliation. Civility means not only keep-
100 ing silent about trivial irritations but also communicating important ones
clearly and assertively. A nonaccusing statement of feeling—perhaps letting
one's housemate know that "I get irritated when you leave your dirty dishes
for me to clean up"—can help resolve the conflicts that cause anger.

Relate to your own experiences in controlling anger.

Happiness

People who are happy perceive the world as safer, make decisions more eas-
105 ily, rate job applicants more favorably, and report greater satisfaction with
their whole lives. When your mood is gloomy, life as a whole seems depress-
ing. Let your mood brighten, and suddenly your relationships, your self-image, and your hopes for the future all seem more promising.

Moreover—and this is one of psychology's most consistent findings—when
110 we feel happy we are more willing to help others. In study after study, a
mood-boosting experience (such as finding money, succeeding on a challenging task, or recalling a happy event) made people more likely to give money,

pick up someone's dropped papers, volunteer time, and so forth. It's called
115 the feel-good, do-good phenomenon.

Happiness Is Relative to Others' Attainments

Happiness is relative not only to our past experience, but also to our comparisons with others. We are always comparing ourselves with others. And whether we feel good or bad depends on who those others are. We are smart or agile only when others are slow-witted or clumsy.

120 Such comparisons help us understand why the middle- and upper-income people in a given country, who can compare themselves with the relatively poor, tend to be slightly more satisfied with life than their less fortunate compatriots. Nevertheless, once a person reaches a moderate income level, further increases do little to increase happiness. Why? Because as people climb the
125 ladder of success they mostly compare themselves with peers who are at or above their current level.

"Beggars do not envy millionaires, though of course they will envy other beggars who are more successful," noted Bertrand Russell. Thus "Napoleon envied Caesar, Caesar envied Alexander, and Alexander, I daresay, envied Hercules,
130 who never existed. You cannot, therefore, get away from envy by means of success alone, for there will always be in history or legend some person even more successful than you are."

By "counting our blessings" when we compare ourselves with those less fortunate, we can, however, increase our satisfaction. As comparing ourselves
135 with those who are better-off creates envy, so comparing ourselves with those less well-off boosts contentment. Marshall Dermer and his colleagues demon-

"I've got the bowl, the bone, the big yard. I know I should be happy."

©*The New Yorker Collection 1992, Mike Twohy from cartoonbank.com. All Rights Reserved.*

strated this by asking University of Wisconsin-Milwaukee women to study others' deprivation and suffering. After viewing vivid depictions of how grim life was in Milwaukee in 1900, or after imagining and then writing about var-
140 ious personal tragedies, such as being burned and disfigured, the women expressed greater satisfaction with their own lives. Similarly, when mildly depressed people read about someone who is even more depressed, they feel somewhat better.

What makes you feel happy?

Predictors of Happiness

If, as the adaptation-level phenomenon implies, our emotions tend to balance
145 around normal, then why do some people seem so filled with joy and others so gloomy day after day? What makes one person normally happy and another less so? Research reveals several predictors of happiness (see the table shown here).

What would you say predicts happiness?

Happiness Is. . .

Researchers Have Found That Happy People Tend to	However, Happiness Seems Not Much Related to Other Factors, Such as
Have high self-esteem	Age
Be optimistic and outgoing	Race
Have close friendships or a satisfying marriage	Gender (women are more often depressed, but also more often joyful)
Have work and leisure that engage their skills	Educational level
Have a meaningful religious faith	Parenthood (having children or not)
Sleep well and exercise	Physical attractiveness

Source: *Summarized from Myers (1993) and Myers & Diener (1995, 1996).*

Remember, though, that knowing that two variables correlate does not tell us
150 whether one causes the other. For example, many studies indicate that religiously active people tend to report greater happiness and life satisfaction. Is happiness conducive to faith? Or does faith enhance happiness?

Whether at work or leisure, most of us derive greatest enjoyment from engaging, challenging activities. Mihaly Csikszentmihalyi (pronounced chick-
155 SENT-me-hi, 1990) and his colleagues discovered this after giving research volunteers a pager. When beeped, the people would note what they were doing and how they were feeling. Usually, they felt happier if mentally engaged by work or active leisure than if passively vegetating. Ironically, the less expensive (and usually more involving) a leisure activity is, the more absorbed

160 and happy people are while doing it. People are happier when gardening than when sitting on a power boat. They're happier when talking to friends than when watching TV. Happy adolescents and young adults also are more likely to be focused on personal strivings and close relationships than on money and prestige. So, happy are those whose work and leisure, and friendships absorb

165 them, enabling them unself-consciously to "flow" in focused activity.

Satisfying tasks and relationships impact our happiness, but within limits imposed by our genetic leash. From their study of 254 identical and fraternal twins, David Lykken and Auke Tellegen estimated that 50 percent of the difference among people's happiness ratings is heritable. Even identical twins

170 raised apart often are similarly happy. Depending on our outlooks and recent experiences, our happiness fluctuates around our "happiness set point," which disposes some people to be ever upbeat, and others down.

STAGE 3: RECALL

Stop to self-test, relate, and react. Use the subheadings in the recall diagram to guide your thinking. For each subheading, jot down a key idea that you feel is important to remember.

Your instructor may choose to give you a true-false comprehension review.

Expressing Emotions

      Effects of Facial Expressions —

      Fear —

      Anger —

      Happiness —

Related idea -

Reaction

Thinking About **EXPRESSING EMOTION**

If you were a college counselor, what techniques would you suggest for controlling fear, reducing anger, and promoting happiness?

Response Suggestion: Describe each emotion and describe your specific suggestions.

Contemporary Link

Describe the characteristics of people intently at work and explain how these characteristics duplicate the "feelings of flow" described by Csikszentmihalyi?

COMPREHENSION QUESTIONS

After reading the selection, answer the following questions with *a, b, c,* or *d.*

Main Idea

_____ 1. The best statement of the main idea is

    a. anger and fear are adaptive responses that provide emotional releases.
    b. comparing your emotions with those of others who are less fortunate leads to happiness.
    c. physiological arousal, expressive behavior, and past experiences influence the manner in which people express and cope with emotions.
    d. the tendency to vent anger is characteristic of individualized cultures.

Detail

_____ 2. The author believes that you will feel happier if you
    a. fake a big grin.
    b. scowl and feel the difference.
    c. pull your brows together.
    d. give way to violent gestures.

Detail

_____ 3. Ekman's experiment with professional actors trained in the "Stanislavsky" method proved all of the following except
    a. acting fearful can increase the number of heart beats per minute.
    b. making an angry expression can raise body temperature.
    c. facial expressions signal the autonomic nervous system to make a specific response.
    d. the emotions expressed by actors alter their minds but not their bodies.

Inference

_____ 4. The author suggests that fear serves a positive purpose in influencing all of the following except
    a. social bonding.
    b. personal safety.
    c. deterring aggressive behavior.
    d. the multiplication of human fears through conditioning.

Detail _____ 5. The difference between the attitude toward expressing anger in individualized and group-centered cultures is
   a. group-centered cultures have more independence.
   b. individualized cultures are more tolerant of open displays of anger.
   c. individualized cultures have a stronger sense of interdependence.
   d. individual cultures see anger as a threat to group harmony.

Detail _____ 6. Retaliation can have a calming effect if all of the following exist except
   a. the counterattack is directly against the provoker.
   b. the retaliator seems justifiable.
   c. the target is intimidating.
   d. the retaliator does not feel guilty.

Inference _____ 7. Based on the author's description, the best definition of *catharsis* is
   a. a kind deed for a harmful act.
   b. a release from tensions by expressing emotions.
   c. a hypothesis stressing compromise as a means to emotional resolution.
   d. a fantasy to cope with feelings of guilt and anxiety.

Inference _____ 8. As a response to anger, the author would most likely suggest
   a. retaliation.
   b. the quoted advice of Ann Landers.
   c. the catharsis hypothesis.
   d. civility.

Detail _____ 9. According to the article, happy people are more likely than unhappy ones to do all of the following except
   a. make decisions more easily.
   b. earn more money.
   c. volunteer to help others.
   d. feel safe from harm.

Inference _____ 10. The author suggests that the term *happiness is relative* means that happiness can be enhanced by
   a. comparing yourself to others who are more fortunate.
   b. moving from a moderate income level to a higher one.
   c. considering the deprivation and suffering of others.
   d. using the catharsis hypothesis.

Answer the following with *T* (true) or *F* (false).

Inference _____ 11. According to Csikszentmihalyi's research study, most people would feel happier sitting by a swimming pool as opposed to fixing a child's toy while sitting by the pool.

Detail _____ 12. According to the passage, a person's "happiness set point" is 80 percent inherited.

Detail _____ 13. The example of the Chicago theater fire shows the destruction caused by the contagious nature of fear.

Inference _____ 14. The author feels that people should be encouraged to vent their anger.

Detail _____ 15. Research shows that physical attractiveness is related to happiness.

VOCABULARY

According to the way the italicized word was used in the selection, select *a*, *b*, *c*, or *d* for the word or phrase that gives the best definition.

_____ 1. "subtly *induced* students" (14)
   a. trained
   b. forced
   c. bribed
   d. persuaded

_____ 2. "behavioral feedback *phenomenon* (32–33)
   a. system
   b. model
   c. unusual occurrence
   d. illusion

_____ 3. "*preoccupy* our thinking" (39–40)
   a. engross
   b. strain
   c. negate
   d. paralyze

_____ 4. "*hostile* outbursts" (60–61)
   a. sudden
   b. quarrelsome
   c. foolish
   d. continuous

_____ 5. "When people *retaliate*" (72)
   a. seek revenge
   b. become aware
   c. find forgiveness
   d. reconcile

_____ 6. "*escalating* a minor conflict" (79–80)
   a. increasing
   b. preventing
   c. stopping
   d. discouraging

_____ 7. "*amplify* underlying hostility" (82)
   a. temper
   b. balance
   c. create
   d. increase

_____ 8. "*trivial* irritations" (100)
   a. important
   b. recent
   c. insignificant
   d. numerous

_____ 9. "*perceive* the world" (104)
   a. to mistake
   b. to see
   c. to confuse
   d. to desire

_____ 10. "most *consistent* findings" (109)
   a. constant
   b. unpredictable
   c. compatible
   d. inappropriate

SEARCH THE NET

Conduct a search to find out more about Csikszentmihalyi's research. List his eight components of enjoyment and describe the second component. Reference the Website.

CONTEMPORARY FOCUS

Few would disagree that motorcycling is dangerous. Yet, clever marketing and a well-developed product have made motorcycling glamorous. How can a business create an aura for a dangerous product?

MOTORCYCLISTS IN CROSS-HAIRS

Jim Jensen

Rocky Mountain News, 26 June 1998, p. 8.

If you ride a motorcycle, you sometimes get the feeling you either wear a cloak of invisibility or you have a bull's-eye painted on each side of your body. Wasn't it only yesterday you were cruising down Parker Road and a Suburban pulled over into your lane without so much as a courtesy turn signal? You knew, by way of your dagger-throwing glare, the driver of the 4-wheeled behemoth didn't have a clue you were there. They teach you in **motorcycle safety** courses to never ride in a vehicle's blind spot—but sometimes you just can't help it. Especially when you're in a 40-mph zone and the 20-foot-long vehicle is being navigated by a soccer mom with a cell phone glued to her ear. Hmmm, you think, maybe loud pipes do save lives!

The plight of a motorcyclist is only too well known to those of us who enjoy our two-wheeled beasts. Doctors call our bikes "donor cycles"; others refer to them as "murder cycles." Whoa! Where is all of this coming from? Now, all motorcycle operators realize the margin of error is greatly reduced because of the two-wheeled nature of our passion.

Road rage is a term we all learned as soon as we could keep two wheels and a motor upright on the street. The day-to-day battle for survival becomes a matter of habit for the motorcyclist.

Collaborate on responses to the following:

- Do you know someone who has been injured on a motorcycle?
- How do you feel about motorcycles on the highway?
- What is the meaning of *road rage*?

SKILL DEVELOPMENT—STAGE 1: PREVIEW

Preview the next selection to predict the purpose and organization and your learning plan.

The author probably emphasizes the accident rate and dangers of riding motorcycles. Agree ☐ Disagree ☐

After reading this selection, I will need to know

_____

Activate Schema

What is the average price of a motorcycle?

Why do you think Harley-Davidson is a popular motorcycle?

Learning Strategy

Explain how the Harley-Davidson company has become a successful business.

Word Knowledge

What do you know about these words?

crest	revenue	espouse	evolved	buoyed
termination	devastated	consummate	prominent	spectrum

Your instructor may give a true-false vocabulary review before or after reading.

STAGE 2: INTEGRATE KNOWLEDGE WHILE READING

Since each reader interacts with material in a unique manner, it is artificial to require that certain thinking strategies be used. In order to heighten awareness, however, several questions have been inserted within this selection. Briefly respond in the margin to the inserted questions. In addition, make a note in the margin of at least one other instance when you used each of the following strategies:

Predict   Picture   Relate   Monitor   Correct

Riders celebrate the 85th Harley-Davidson anniversary.

THE STORY OF HARLEY-DAVIDSON MOTORCYCLES

From Thomas C. Kinnear, Kenneth Bernhardt, and Kathleen Krentler, *Principles of Marketing*

Overview

Harley-Davidson, Incorporated, the only remaining major American manufacturer of motorcycles, is riding the crest of success as measured by consumer demand, revenue, and profits. The company produces motorcycles and related products that espouse a unique attitude and inspire power, excite-

5 ment, and individuality both in Harley-Davidson riders and in much of the nonriding public.

As a company, Harley-Davidson has evolved through stages of development that have affected business throughout the past century. When Harley first began to produce motorcycles in 1903, it entered the *produc-*
10 *tion concept* stage, during which a company presumes that supply will create its own demand for a product. During this stage, there was no conscious effort to increase mass market sales; Harley-Davidson's primary goal was simply to develop a technically superior motorcycle. However, as the firm's success became more evident, it moved into the *sales concept* stage,
15 during which improved manufacturing processes allowed supply to outpace demand. The natural response was to increase sales efforts, and at this time Harley-Davidson developed its worldwide dealership network.

Over the last two decades, Harley-Davidson has entered into the *marketing concept* stage, which involves a strong focus on consumer needs and has in-
20 cluded developing the Harley Owners Group (HOG), the world's largest organization of motorcycle enthusiasts.

*Can you visualize the activities of the company
during the three concept periods?*

How Did It Happen?

Harley-Davidson's success did not come overnight nor has it been sustained continuously. In the early 1900s, Harley-Davidson was one of more than 100 U.S. motorcycle manufacturers on the scene. However, when Ford Motor
25 Company first introduced its Model T car, the motorcycle market was devastated, and most of the companies folded by 1920. Harley-Davidson did well in the 1960s and early 1970s in selling to an often misunderstood market. However, the company went from claiming 100 percent of the U.S. heavyweight motorcycle market to less than 15 percent in the early 1980s, when
30 higher-quality and lower-priced Japanese offerings dominated.

At the time, Harley-Davidson maintained that Japanese manufacturers were producing motorcycles at record rates and flooding the U.S. market, despite the fact that a sharp decline in new motorcycle purchases had been occurring. As a result, dealers of imported motorcycles resorted to intense price
35 discounting to relieve their inventories, which created an unfair selling environment for Harley-Davidson. In late 1982, Harley-Davidson appealed to the International Trade Commission (ITC) to increase tariffs on imported heavyweight motorcycles to help support the company against Japanese competition. Based on the ITC's recommendations, in 1983 the United States im-
40 posed additional tariffs, effective for five years. Buoyed by the tariffs, Harley-Davidson had regained the top position in the U.S. heavyweight market by the end of 1986. On firm financial footing, Harley-Davidson felt confident enough to petition the ITC for early termination of the tariffs in 1987.

*What other major companies have received government
support to get on a firm financial footing?*

The Harley-Davidson Family

The first Harley-Davidson motorcycle was built in 1903 in Milwaukee, Wisconsin. There William Harley and the Davidson brothers (Walter, Arthur, and William) designed and built high-quality motorcycles from scratch. The reputation of the bikes spread, and throughout the 1920s and 1930s police department, postal workers, and even the U.S. military began to use the motorcycles. In World War II, all of Harley-Davidson's production (more than 90,000 units) was sold to the U.S. government for military use.

Why were motorcycles useful in World War II?

Primary Segments and Targets

As a result of good market analysis and customer research, Harley-Davidson was able to design and sell the right product to the right group. From 1983 to 1992 it increased its share in the heavyweight market from less than 15 percent to more than 60 percent.

The average Harley-Davidson buyer is male, 41.6 years old, and shares an average household income of about $45,000 per year. Aging baby boomers are the heavyweight motorcycle's future lifeblood. Sales figures show this group increasing at least until the year 2000. Interestingly, Harley-Davidson does not target women differently than it does men. Rather, it finds that rider characteristics are not gender-specific, and that women ride their motorcycles for basically the same reasons that men do. However, the company provides an extension line of women's apparel and also sponsors the Ladies of Harley organization of motorcycle enthusiasts.

Do you know women who ride motorcycles?

Harley-Davidson sells about 70 percent of its bikes in the United States and roughly 30 percent abroad. The company has a strong international reputation. Riders abroad are usually professionals who can afford to pay up to $25,000 for a motorcycle and who thrill to the classic American image. In fact, export sales in 1993 equaled $283 million (24 percent of sales, up from 14 percent in 1989).

What would you predict to be the targeted personality traits or "attitude" of Harley owners?

Product Considerations

The core strength of Harley-Davidson is its excellent product—one that many thousands of people want to buy, and others who can't buy, still want. When purchasing a Harley-Davidson, you are not just buying a motorcycle, but also the heritage, image, service, and attitude that come with it. In order to stress their commitment to service, employees and dealers strive to build long-term relationships with customers. Management makes it a policy to attend Harley-Davidson's frequent "Town Hall Meeting," where Harley Owners Groups (HOGs) meet and share Harley stories and ideas for improvements in products and services.

Why would the company promote HOG meetings?

Production Process

Today, demand for Harley-Davidson motorcycles exceeds the company's supply of bikes. This fact reflects well on the product, but puts pressure on
80 production to make more bikes more quickly. Under such circumstances, a keen eye must be kept on maintaining the high quality of the bikes. Harley-Davidson continues to invest millions of dollars in production to ensure quality and consistency in the end product.

Ancillary and Licensed Products

Licensing the trademark emblem and logos creates and increases an awareness
85 of the brand among the riding and nonriding public and reinforces the company's image with customers. Harley-Davidson motorcycles are complemented in the secondary market with licensing arrangements to create such products and services as T-shirts and other apparel, motorcycle collectibles, restaurants, and children's toys. These are target-specific; not all consumers
90 respond to each of these items. Harley-Davidson is regarded as a consummate promoter with an excellent product in high demand.

Which of these products have you seen?

Advertising

In 1993, Harley-Davidson was recognized for its creative ads by *Adweek* magazine. One example of the company's advertising is the following ad placed in a number of magazines to celebrate Harley-Davidson's 90th an-
95 niversary in 1993. The ad copy playfully expresses the attitude at the core of the Harley-Davidson mystique:

> We've survived four wars, a depression, a few recessions, 16 U.S. presidents, foreign and domestic competition, racetrack competition, and one Marlon Brando movie. Sounds like a party to us.

Why do you like or dislike the ad copy?

Public Relations

The patronage of famous personalities is usually a dependable boon to sales. Jay Leno of *The Tonight Show* rides a Harley-Davidson and has appeared at charitable benefits sponsored by the company. The late Malcolm Forbes,
100 owner and publisher of *Forbes* magazine, was a great lover of Harley-Davidson motorcycles. His trip on a Harley-Davidson through China with other prominent dignitaries was well publicized.

Can you name another celebrity who rides a Harley?

Sales

Much of Harley-Davidson's recent boost in sales is due to improved quality and manufacturing systems and increased employee involvement. However, 105 while quality and sales are up and production has nearly tripled in the past six years, the company has not been able to supply enough motorcycles to satisfy total demand in the marketplace. Because Harley-Davidson knows that reliability and service play a critical role in its competition advantage, it refuses to sacrifice quality for the sake of increased production and sales. Moreover, 110 Harley-Davidson has learned from experience about the cyclical nature of market and customers' demand. By keeping growth under control, Harley-Davidson carefully avoids overexpansion. Meanwhile, the company develops parts, services, and accessories to maintain sales volume and profits for dealers.

Why doesn't Harley build more motorcycles?

Premium Product at a Premium Price

Pricing is taken very seriously at Harley Davidson. Managers and employees 115 recognize that not everyone can afford the price of a Harley-Davidson motorcycle, which ranges from $5,600 to $16,000 (without accessories). The company knows it must produce such an excellent product that enough customers say the price is worth it. Harley-Davidson has been able to prove the worth of its bikes with more than 600,000 registered in the United States alone.

How do consumers react to a premium price?
Relate an example.

120   While Harley-Davidson management recognizes that its motorcycles occupy the high end of the price spectrum, it is continuously evaluating the possible development of smaller, entry-level-priced motorcycles. The hope is that these new bikes will attract more customers to the Harley-Davidson brand. Some of these new customers might eventually decide to buy a larger, 125 more traditional Harley-Davidson model.

STAGE 3: RECALL

Stop to self-test, relate, and react. Use the subheadings in the recall diagram on page 106 to guide your thinking. For each subheading, jot down a key idea that you feel is important to remember.

Your instructor may choose to give you a true-false comprehension review.

Thinking About   THE STORY OF HARLEY-DAVIDSON MOTORCYCLES

Describe how the Harley-Davidson company, as well as other successful companies, have "done right" in each of the three stages of business concept development?

Response Suggestion: Define each of the three stages and give company examples from the text and your own experience for each.

The Success of Harley-Davidson

How did it happen? —

Harley-Davidson family —

Primary segments and targets —

Product considerations —

Ancillary products —

Advertising —

Public relations —

Sales —

Premium product —

Related idea

Reaction

Contemporary Link

How has the Harley-Davidson company transformed a dangerous product into a lucrative product line with mainstream acceptance?

COMPREHENSION QUESTIONS

After reading the selection, answer the following questions with *a, b, c,* or *d.*

Main Idea _____ 1. The best statement of the main idea of this selection is
- a. Harley-Davidson is the only remaining major American motorcycle manufacturer.
- b. Harley-Davidson targets customers who are upscale and independent.
- c. Harley-Davidson increased profits by licensing the trademark and logo to ancillary products.
- d. Harley-Davidson's success is built on an excellent product and on marketing that inspires an attitude and excitement.

Detail   _____ 2. The product concept stage is a period during which
a. mass marketing efforts occur.
b. the goal is to create a superior product that wins sales.
c. the company develops a network of dealerships.
d. demand outstrips supply.

Detail   _____ 3. The stage of marketing when organizations focus on the needs and concerns of customers is called the
a. productions concept stage.
b. dealership network stage.
c. sales concept stage.
d. marketing concept stage.

Inference   _____ 4. The authors suggest that Harley-Davidson outdistanced the Japanese competition in the mid-1980s through
a. a faster rate of production.
b. intense discount pricing.
c. the protection provided by import tariffs on Japanese goods.
d. direct and unprotected market competition.

Detail   _____ 5. According to the authors, Harley-Davidson does not advertise differently for women and men because
a. women are motivated to buy for similar reasons as men.
b. women do not buy as many bikes as men.
c. women buy more apparel than men.
d. women and men customers are approximately the same age and income level.

Detail   _____ 6. In 1993 the percentage of total Harley-Davidson sales outside the United States was
a. 70 percent.
b. 50 percent.
c. 24 percent.
d. 14 percent.

Inference   _____ 7. The advertisement includes the reference to a Marlon Brando movie for the purpose of
a. humor.
b. clarity.
c. comparison.
d. identifying owners.

Inference   _____ 8. The authors suggest that the Harley-Davidson marketing image promotes all of the following except
a. status.
b. historical tradition.
c. speed.
d. membership in a group.

Inference _____ 9. The author suggests that Jay Leno and Malcolm Forbes
   a. were employed by Harley-Davidson.
   b. stimulated sales through their personal bike choices.
   c. sought avenues for promoting the motorcycles.
   d. advertised regularly for Harley-Davidson.

Inference _____ 10. The authors suggest that currently the Harley-Davidson motorcycle is
   a. overproduced.
   b. underproduced.
   c. sacrificing quality for quantity.
   d. overexpanding.

Answer the following with *T* (true) or *F* (false).

Detail _____ 11. The trade tariffs originally requested still remain on Japanese motorcycles.

Detail _____ 12. Harley and Davidson were the two brothers who designed and built the first Harley-Davidson motorcycle.

Inference _____ 13. The authors suggest that the company knowingly promotes an image of status.

Detail _____ 14. Currently the demand for Harley-Davidson motorcycles exceeds the supply.

Detail _____ 15. The average Harley-Davidson owner is a baby boomer born after 1945.

VOCABULARY

According to the way the italicized word was used in the selection, select *a, b, c,* or *d* for the word or phrase that gives the best definition.

_____ 1. "*crest* of success" (2)
   a. roar
   b. cost
   c. peak
   d. smell

_____ 2. "demand, *revenue,* and profits" (3)
   a. income
   b. tax
   c. pensions
   d. overhead

_____ 3. "*espouse* a unique attitude" (4)
   a. repeat
   b. demand
   c. buy
   d. support

_____ 4. "*evolved* through stages" (7)
   a. matured
   b. floundered
   c. held the market
   d. manipulated

_____ 5. "market was *devastated*"
(25–26)
    a. ruined
    b. tapped
    c. shot
    d. divided

_____ 6. "*Buoyed* by the tariffs" (40)
    a. bought out
    b. supported
    c. overwhelmed
    d. disregarded

_____ 7. "early *termination* of the tariffs"
(43)
    a. payout
    b. recognition
    c. resumption
    d. end

_____ 8. "a *consummate* promoter"
(90–91)
    a. authentic
    b. wealthy
    c. accomplished
    d. educated

_____ 9. "*prominent* dignitaries" (102)
    a. foreign
    b. well-known
    c. hard-working
    d. promising

_____10. "end of the price *spectrum*"
(121)
    a. array
    b. image
    c. ticket
    d. increase

SEARCH THE NET

Find the Website for the Harley-Davidson company. List five riding tips suggested by the company, and describe what the company promotes as the proper Harley-Davidson "attitude" about reaching a destination. Reference the Website.

Remember, if your search does not produce the home page of the company, try to guess or work out the company's URL as described in Chapter 1.

CONTEMPORARY FOCUS

Success in the international marketplace requires more than hard work, business competence, and appreciation of cultural differences. Such success requires specific knowledge of cultural habits that have evolved as part of the psyche of the society.

IT'S WHAT YOU SAY AND DO

Marcia Pounds

Sun Sentinel, March 14 and 21, 1997

Robin Adelman was making a point about ethnocentrism, the attitude that your culture is superior. It can be a defeating attitude if you want to do business with another country. Adelman was one of three experts who gave a free seminar on international cultural awareness, sponsored by Florida Atlantic University's Small Business Development Center.

In Asian cultures, the key words to remember are patience, face-saving and harmony, he said. When you bring business cards, bring enough for everybody. "Otherwise they lose face. If you hurt a member of the team, you might lose the sale," John Diep said. Business gifts should be given at the end of a meeting. And they should not be wrapped in white, or black and white; these are symbolic of death.

Establishing a relationship is important to business people in Latin America, said Horacio A. Agostinelli. Dinner usually starts late, 10 P.M. to 2 A.M., and in Buenos Aires, Argentina, expect to socialize into the wee hours. Because of the Latinos' survival of economic struggles, instabilities of government and war, they are particularly good at adapting to changing conditions. So, be prepared: "The Latino will either have in his mind an alternative solution or propose something that may not be standard but will be a benefit to everybody," Agostinelli said.

Collaborative Activity

Collaborate on responses to the following questions:

■ Do you believe it is wrong to start a business dinner at 2 A.M.? Why or why not?

■ Is it "right" for businesses in some cultures to close at noon and reopen until late at night?

■ What would an Asian executive or a Latino executive need to know about doing business in the United States?

SKILL DEVELOPMENT—STAGE 1: PREVIEW

Preview the next selection to predict the purpose, organization, and your learning plan.

The phrase "unity in diversity" is a paradox. What does it mean?

After reading this selection, I will need to know

_____

Activate Schema

Is it wrong for primitive tribal people to wear no clothes?

Does social status exist in primitive cultures?

Could you eat insects if doing so meant survival?

Learning Strategy

Define and use examples to explain cultural universals, adaptation, relativity, ethnocentrism, norms, and values.

Word Knowledge

What do you know about these words?

| curb | naiveté | adornments | articulate | bizarre |
| smirk | abstained | postpartum | agile | consign |

Your instructor may give a true-false vocabulary review before or after reading.

STAGE 2: INTEGRATE KNOWLEDGE WHILE READING

Since each reader interacts with material in a unique manner, it is artificial to require that certain thinking strategies be used. In order to heighten awareness, however, several questions have been inserted within this selection. Briefly respond in the margin to the inserted questions. In addition, make a note in the margin of at least one other instance when you used each of the following strategies:

Predict   Picture   Relate   Monitor   Correct

In a traditional Indian wedding ceremony the bride and groom pray at the altar.

Unity in Diversity

From Donald Light, Jr.,
and Suzanne Keller, *Sociology*[5]

Does this title make sense or are these words opposites?

What is more basic, more "natural" than love between a man and woman? Eskimo men offer their wives to guests and friends as a gesture of hospitality; both husband and

[5]From Donald Light, Jr., and Suzanne Keller, *Sociology*, 4th ed. (New York: McGraw-Hill, 1986), pp. 74–77. Reproduced by permission of McGraw-Hill, Inc.

wife feel extremely offended if the guest declines. The Banaro of New Guinea
5 believe it would be disastrous for a woman to conceive her first child by her
husband and not by one of her father's close friends, as is their custom.

> The real father is a close friend of the bride's father. . . . Nevertheless the first
> born child inherits the name and possessions of the husband. An American
> would deem such a custom immoral, but the Banaro tribesmen would be equally
> shocked to discover that the first born child of an American couple is the off-
> spring of the husband.

The Yanomamö of Northern Brazil, whom anthropologist Napoleon A.
Chagnon named "the fierce people," encourage what we would consider extreme
disrespect. Small boys are applauded for striking their mothers and fathers in the
10 face. Yanomamö parents would laugh at our efforts to curb aggression in children,
much as they laughed at Chagnon's naïveté when he first came to live with them.

What would your parents do if you slapped either of them in the face?

The variations among cultures are startling, yet all peoples have customs
and beliefs about marriage, the bearing and raising of children, sex, and hospitality—to name just a few of the universals anthropologists have discovered in
15 their cross-cultural explorations. But the *details* of cultures do indeed vary: in
this country, not so many years ago, when a girl was serious about a boy and
he about her, she wore his fraternity pin over her heart; in the Fiji Islands,
girls put hibiscus flowers behind their ears when they are in love. The specific
gestures are different but the impulse to symbolize feelings, to dress courtship
20 in ceremonies, is the same. How do we explain this unity in diversity?

Cultural Universals

Cultural universals are all of the behavior patterns and institutions that have
been found in all known cultures. Anthropologist George Peter Murdock
identified over sixty cultural universals, including a system of social status,
marriage, body adornments, dancing, myths and legends, cooking, incest
25 taboos, inheritance rules, puberty customs, and religious rituals.

The universals of culture may derive from the fact that all societies must perform the same essential functions if they are to survive—including organization,
motivation, communication, protection, the socialization of new members, and
the replacement of those who die. In meeting these prerequisites for group life,
30 people inevitably design similar—though not identical—patterns for living. As
Clyde Kluckhohn wrote, "All cultures constitute somewhat distinct answers to
essentially the same questions posed by human biology and by the generalities
of the human situation."

The way in which a people articulates cultural universals depends in large
35 part on their physical and social environment—that is, on the climate in
which they live, the materials they have at hand, and the peoples with whom
they establish contact. For example, the wheel has long been considered one
of humankind's greatest inventions, and anthropologists were baffled for a
long time by the fact that the great civilizations of South America never dis-

40 covered it. Then researchers uncovered a number of toys with wheels. Apparently the Aztecs and their neighbors did know about wheels; they simply didn't find them useful in their mountainous environment.

Describe your mental picture.

Adaptation, Relativity, and Ethnocentrism

Taken out of context, almost any custom will seem bizarre, perhaps cruel, or just plain ridiculous. To understand why the Yanomamö encourage aggressive
45 behavior in their sons, for example, you have to try to see things through their eyes. The Yanomamö live in a state of chronic warfare; they spend much of their time planning for and defending against raids with neighboring tribes. If Yanomamö parents did *not* encourage aggression in a boy, he would be ill equipped for life in their society. Socializing boys to be aggressive is *adaptive* for
50 the Yanomamö because it enhances their capacity for survival. "In general, culture is . . . adaptive because it often provides people with a means of adjusting to the physiological needs of their own bodies, to their physical-geographical environment and to their social environments as well."

In many tropical societies, there are strong taboos against a mother having
55 sexual intercourse with a man until her child is at least two years old. As a Hausa woman explains,

> A mother should not go to her husband while she has a child such is sucking . . . if she only sleeps with her husband and does not become pregnant, it will not hurt her child, it will not spoil her milk. But if another child enters in, her milk will make the first one ill. (Smith, in Whiting 1969, p. 518)

Undoubtedly, people would smirk at a woman who nursed a two-year-old child in our society and abstained from having sex with her husband. Why do Hausa women behave in a way that seems so overprotective and overindul-
60 gent to us? In tropical climates protein is scarce. If a mother were to nurse more than one child at a time, or if she were to wean a child before it reached the age of two, the youngster would be prone to *kwashiorkor*, an often fatal disease resulting from protein deficiency. Thus, long postpartum sex taboos are adaptive. In a tropical environment a postpartum sex taboo and a long pe-
65 riod of breast-feeding solve a serious problem.

No custom is good or bad, right or wrong in itself; each one must be examined in light of the culture as a whole and evaluated in terms of how it works in the context of the entire culture. Anthropologists and sociologists call this *cultural relativity*. Although this way of thinking about culture may seem self-
70 evident today, it is a lesson that anthropologists and the missionaries who often preceded them to remote areas learned the hard way, by observing the effects their best intentions had on peoples whose way of life was quite different from their own. In an article on the pitfalls of trying to "uplift" peoples whose ways seem backward and inefficient, Don Adams quotes an old Oriental story:

> Once upon a time there was a great flood, and involved in this flood were two creatures, a monkey and a fish. The monkey, being agile and experienced, was lucky enough to scramble up a tree and escape the raging waters. As he looked down from

his safe perch, he saw the poor fish struggling against the swift current. With the very best intentions, he reached down and lifted the fish from the water. The result was inevitable (1960, p. 22).

What is the difference between adaptation and relativity?

75   *Ethnocentrism* is the tendency to see one's own way of life, including behaviors, beliefs, values, and norms as the only right way of living. Robin Fox points out that "any human group is ever ready to consign another recognizably different human group to the other side of the boundary. It is not enough to possess culture to be fully human, you have to possess *our* culture."

Values and Norms

80 The Tangu, who live in a remote part of New Guinea, play a game called *taketak*, which in many ways resembles bowling. The game is played with a top that has been fashioned from a dried fruit and with two groups of coconut stakes that are driven into the ground (more or less like bowling pins). The players divide into two teams. Members of the first team take turns throwing
85 the top into the batch of stakes; every stake the top hits is removed. Then the second team steps to the line and tosses the top into their batch of stakes. The object of the game, surprisingly, is not to knock over as many stakes as possible. Rather, the game continues until both teams have removed the *same* number of stakes. Winning is completely irrelevant.

What will be covered in this next part?

90   In a sense games are practice for "real life"; they reflect the values of the culture in which they are played. *Values* are the criteria people use in assessing their daily lives, arranging their priorities, measuring their pleasures and pains, choosing between alternative courses of action. The Tangu value equivalence: the idea of one individual or group winning and another losing bothers them, for
95 they believe winning generates ill-will. In fact, when Europeans brought soccer to the Tangu, they altered the rules so that the object of the game was for two teams to score the same number of goals. Sometimes their soccer games went on for days! American games, in contrast, are highly competitive; there are *always* winners and losers. Many rule books include provisions for overtime and
100 "sudden death" to prevent ties, which leave Americans dissatisfied. World Series, Superbowls, championships in basketball and hockey, Olympic Gold Medals are front-page news in this country. In the words of the late football coach Vince Lombardi, "Winning isn't everything, it's the only thing."

     Norms, the rules that guide behavior in everyday situations, are derived
105 from values, but norms and values can conflict. You may recall a news item that appeared in American newspapers in December 1972, describing the discovery of survivors of a plane crash 12,000 feet in the Andes. The crash had occurred on October 13; sixteen of the passengers (a rugby team and their supporters) managed to survive for sixty-nine days in near-zero temperatures.
110 The story made headlines because, to stay alive, the survivors had eaten parts

of their dead companions. Officials, speaking for the group, stressed how valiantly the survivors had tried to save the lives of the injured people and how they had held religious services regularly. The survivors' explanations are quite interesting, for they reveal how important it is to people to justify their
115 actions, to resolve conflicts in norms and values (here, the positive value of survival vs. the taboo against cannibalism). Some of the survivors compared their action to a heart transplant, using parts of a dead person's body to save another person's life. Others equated their act with the sacrament of communion. In the words of one religious survivor, "If we would have died, it would
120 have been suicide, which is condemned by the Roman Catholic faith."

STAGE 3: RECALL

Stop to self-test, relate, and react. Use the subheadings in the recall diagram to guide your thinking. For each subheading, jot down a key idea that you feel is important to remember.

Your instructor may choose to give you a true-false comprehension review.

(Topic)	
(Significant details– examples, facts, or phrases)	
(Related idea)	
(Reaction)	

Thinking About   UNITY IN DIVERSITY

Define the following terms and describe two examples for each that are not mentioned in the selection:

cultural universals adaptation relativity ethnocentrism norms values

Response Suggestion: Define the cultural concepts in your own words and relate examples from today's society.

Contemporary Link

Of the terms defined in the passage, why would a knowledge of the values and norms of a culture be extremely important to a person who wants to conduct business in the country?

COMPREHENSION QUESTIONS

After reading the selection, answer the following questions with *a, b, c,* or *d.*

Main Idea

_____ 1. The best statement of the main idea of this selection is
   a. the variety of practices and customs in society show few threads of cultural unity.
   b. the unusual variations in societies gain acceptability because of the cultural universals in all known societies.
   c. a variety of cultural universals provides adaptive choices for specific societies.
   d. cultural universals are found in all known societies even though the details of the cultures may vary widely.

Inference

_____ 2. The author believes that the primary cultural universal addressed in the Eskimo custom of offering wives to guests is
   a. bearing and raising of children.
   b. social status.
   c. hospitality.
   d. incest taboos.

Detail

_____ 3. The custom of striking practiced by the Yanomamö serves the adaptive function of
   a. developing fierce warriors
   b. binding parent and child closer together.
   c. developing physical respect for parents.
   d. encouraging early independence from parental care.

Detail

_____ 4. *Cultural universals* might be defined as
   a. each culture in the universe.
   b. similar basic living patterns.
   c. the ability for cultures to live together in harmony.
   d. the differences among cultures.

Inference

_____ 5. The author implies that cultural universals exist because of
   a. a social desire to be more alike.
   b. the differences in cultural behavior patterns.
   c. the competition among societies.
   d. the needs of survival in group life.

Inference   _____   6. The author suggests that the wheel was not a part of the ancient Aztec civilization because the Aztecs
a. did not find wheels useful in their mountainous environment.
b. were not intelligent enough to invent wheels.
c. were baffled by inventions.
d. did not have the materials for development.

Inference   _____   7. The underlying reason for the postpartum sexual taboo of
the Hausa is
a. sexual.
b. nutritional.
c. moral.
d. religious.

Inference   _____   8. The term *cultural relativity* explains why a custom can be
considered
a. right or wrong regardless of culture.
b. right or wrong according to the number of people practicing it.
c. right in one culture and wrong in another.
d. wrong if in conflict with cultural universals.

Inference   _____   9. The author relates Don Adams's oriental story to show that
missionaries working in other cultures
a. should be sent back home.
b. can do more harm than good.
c. purposefully harm the culture to seek selfish ends.
d. usually do not have a genuine concern for the people.

Inference   _____ 10. The tendency of ethnocentrism would lead an American to
view the Eskimo practice of wife sharing as
a. right.
b. wrong.
c. right for Eskimos but wrong for Americans.
d. a custom about which an outsider should have no opinion.

Answer the following questions with *T* (true) or *F* (false).

Inference   _____ 11. An American's acceptance of the Banaro tribal custom of fa-
thering the firstborn is an example of an understanding by
cultural relativity.

Inference   _____ 12. The author feels that the need to symbolize feelings in
courtship is a cultural universal.

Inference   _____ 13. The author feels that culture is not affected by climate.

Detail   _____ 14. The author states that all societies must have a form of organization if they are to survive.

Inference   _____ 15. The author implies that the rugby team that crashed in the Andes could have survived without eating human flesh.

VOCABULARY

According to the way the italicized word was used in the selection, select *a*, *b*, *c*, or *d* for the word or phrase that gives the best definition.

_____ 1. "efforts to *curb* aggression" (10)
    a. stabilize
    b. release
    c. promote
    d. restrain

_____ 2. "at Chagnon's *naïveté*" (11)
    a. lack of knowledge
    b. gentle manner
    c. jolly nature
    d. clumsiness

_____ 3. "body *adornments*" (24)
    a. ailments
    b. treatments
    c. scars
    d. decorations

_____ 4. "*articulate* cultural universals" (34)
    a. remember
    b. design
    c. express clearly
    d. substitute

_____ 5. "will seem *bizarre*" (43)
    a. phony
    b. unjust
    c. grotesque
    d. unnecessary

_____ 6. "*smirk* at a woman" (57)
    a. refuse to tolerate
    b. smile conceitedly
    c. lash out
    d. acknowledge approvingly

_____ 7. "*abstained* from having sex" (58)
    a. matured
    b. regained
    c. refrained
    d. reluctantly returned

_____ 8. "long *postpartum* sex taboos" (63)
    a. after childbirth
    b. awaited
    c. subcultural
    d. complicated

_____ 9. "being *agile* and experienced" (quote bottom p. 113, line 2)
    a. eager
    b. nimble
    c. young
    d. knowledgeable

_____ 10. "ready to *consign*" (77)
    a. assign
    b. remove
    c. reorganize
    d. overlook

SEARCH THE NET

Intercultural communication has become a popular topic on college campuses. Conduct a search to define the term, and describe five aspects of communication, other than words, that are included in intercultural communication training. Plan your own search or begin by trying the following:

http://www.csudh.edu/global_options/Default.HTM

http://www2.soc.hawaii.edu/com/

Go Electronic!

For additional reading, exercises, and Internet activities, visit this book's Website at:

http://www.awlonline.com/smithBTG

For even more activities, visit the Longman English pages at:

http://longman.awl.com/ englishpages

If you need a user name and password, please see your instructor.

Take a Road Trip to New Orleans! Be sure to visit the Active Reading module in your Reading Road Trip CD-ROM for multimedia tutorials, exercises, and tests.

READER'S JOURNAL

Name _____ Date _____

Chapter 3

Answer the following questions to reflect on your own learning and progress. Use the perforations to tear the assignment out for your instructor.

1. What do you enjoy reading on a regular basis? Why?

   _____

2. How do you preview a book or magazine before purchasing it?

   _____

3. What do you plan to do to "train" yourself to use the Recall Stage?

   _____

4. Which of the five thinking strategies do you tend to use the most while reading? Explain.

   _____

5. What seems to be the main cause of confusion in your comprehension?

   _____

6. Compare your thinking when you are really studying and when you are just holding the book.

   _____

   _____

7. Reflect on the longer selections and review the 45 multiple-choice items. How many did you answer correctly? _____ What type of questions are you missing the most? _____

8. Identify the page and item numbers and explain the reasons for two of your comprehension errors in this chapter. _____

   _____

9. Which selection did you enjoy the most? Why?

   _____

   _____

Main Idea

- What is a topic?
- What is a main idea?
- What are significant details?
- What is an organizational pattern?
- What is a summary?

Georges Seurat,
Le Cirque,
1890–1891.
Oil on canvas.
Musée d'Orsay,
Paris. Erich
Lessing/Art
Resource, NY.

WHAT IS A MAIN IDEA?

The **main idea** of a passage is the central message that the author is trying to convey about the material. It is a sentence that condenses thoughts and details into a general, all-inclusive statement of the author's message.

Comprehending the main idea is crucial to your comprehension of text, and many experts believe that it is the most important reading skill. In fact, if all reading comprehension techniques were combined and reduced to one essential question, that question might be, "What is the main idea the author is trying to get across to the reader?" Whether you read a single paragraph, a chapter, or an entire book, your most important single task is to understand the main idea of what you read.

Labels for Main Idea

Reading specialists use various terms when referring to the main idea. In classroom discussions, all of the following words are sometimes used to help students understand the meaning of *main idea:*

main point

central focus

gist

controlling idea

central thought

thesis

The last word on the list, *thesis,* is a familiar word in English composition classes. Students usually have had practice in stating a thesis sentence for English essays, but they have not had as much practice in stating the main idea of a reading selection. Recognizing the similarity between a thesis and a main idea statement can help you understand the concept.

IMPORTANCE OF PRIOR KNOWLEDGE IN MAIN IDEA

Research has been done investigating the processes readers use to construct main ideas. One researcher, Peter Afflerbach, asked graduate students and university professors to "think aloud" as they read passages on both familiar and unfamiliar topics. These expert readers spoke their thoughts to the researcher before, during, and after reading. From these investigations, Afflerbach concluded that expert readers use different strategies for familiar and unfamiliar materials.

This research showed that *already knowing something about the topic is the key* to easy reading. When readers are familiar with the subject, constructing the main idea is effortless and, in many cases, automatic. These readers quickly assimilate the unfolding text into already well-developed knowledge networks. They seem to organize text into chunks for comprehension and later retrieval. These "informed" readers do not have to struggle with an information overload.

By contrast, expert readers with little prior knowledge of the subject are absorbed in trying to make meaning out of unfamiliar words and confusing sentences. Because they are struggling to recognize ideas, few mental resources remain for constructing a main idea. These "uninformed" experts were reluctant to guess at a main idea and to predict a topic. Instead, they preferred to read all the information before trying to make sense of it. Constructing the main idea was a difficult and deliberate task for these expert readers.

MAIN IDEA STRATEGIES

The following strategies for getting the main idea were reported by Afflerbach's expert readers. Can you see the differences in the thinking processes of the informed and uninformed experts?

"Informed" Expert Readers

Strategy 1: The informed expert readers skimmed the passage before reading and took a guess at the main idea. Then they read for corroboration.

Strategy 2: The informed experts automatically paused while reading to summarize or reduce information. They frequently stopped at natural breaks in the material to let ideas fall into place.

"Uninformed" Expert Readers

Strategy 1: Expert readers who did not know about the subject were unwilling to take a guess at the main idea. Instead they read the material, decided on a topic, and then looked back to pull together a main idea statement.

Strategy 2: The uninformed experts read the material and they reviewed it to find key terms and concepts. They tried to bring the key terms and concepts together into a main idea statement.

Strategy 3: The uninformed experts read the material and then proposed a main idea statement. They double-checked the passage to clarify or revise the main idea statement. What differences do you see in these two approaches?

Since introductory college textbooks address many topics that are new and unfamiliar, freshmen readers will frequently need to use the last three strategies listed on page 123 to comprehend the main ideas of their college texts. Until prior knowledge is built for the different college courses, main idea construction for course textbooks is likely to be a *conscious effort* rather than an automatic phenomenon.

WHAT IS A TOPIC?

The **topic** of a passage is like a title. It is a word or phrase that labels the subject but does not reveal the specific contents of the passage. The topic is a general, rather than specific, term and forms an umbrella under which the specific ideas or details in the passage can be grouped. For example, what general term would pull together and unify the following items?

Items: carrots
              lettuce
              onions   Topic? _____
              potatoes

EXERCISE 4.1   *Identifying Topics*

Each of the following lists includes four specific items or ideas that could relate to a single topic. At the end of each list, write a general topic that could form an umbrella under which the specific ideas can be grouped.

1. shirt	2. psychology	3. democracy	4. Bermuda	5. coffee
pants	history	autocracy	Cuba	tea
jacket	sociology	oligarchy	Haiti	cola
sweater	political science	monarchy	Tahiti	chocolate
_____	_____	_____	_____	_____

HOW DO TOPICS AND MAIN IDEAS DIFFER?

Topics are general categories, like titles, but they are not main ideas. In the previous list, caffeine is a general term or topic that unifies the items, *coffee, tea, cola,* and *chocolate.* If those items were used as details in a paragraph, the main idea could not be expressed by simply saying "caffeine." The word *caffeine* would answer the question, "What was the passage about?" but not the second question, "What is the author's main idea?"

A writer could actually devise several very different paragraphs about caffeine using the same four details as support. If you were assigned to write a paragraph about caffeine, using the four items as details, what would be the main idea or thesis of your paragraph?

Topic: Caffeine

Main idea or thesis: _____

Read the following examples of different main ideas that could be developed in a paragraph about caffeine.

1. Consumption of caffeine is not good for your health. (Details would enumerate health hazards associated with each item.)
2. Americans annually consume astonishing amounts of caffeine. (Details would describe amounts of each consumed annually.)
3. Caffeine can wake up an otherwise sluggish mind. (Details would explain the popular use of each item as a stimulant.)
4. Reduce caffeine consumption with the decaffeinated version of popular caffeinated beverages. (Details would promote the decaffeinated version of each item.)

EXAMPLE   Below are examples of a topic, main idea, and supporting detail.

Topic   **Early Cognitive Development**

Main Idea   Cognitive psychologists sometimes study young children to observe the very beginnings of cognitive activity. For example, when children first begin to utter words and sentences, they overgeneralize what they know and make language more consistent than it actually is.

Detail

Christopher Peterson, *Introduction to Psychology*

EXPLANATION   The topic pulls our attention to a general area, and the main idea provides the focus. The detail offers elaboration and support.

EXERCISE 4.2   *Differentiating Topic, Main Idea, and Details*

This exercise is designed to check your ability to differentiate statements of main idea from topic and specific supporting details. Compare the items within each group and indicate whether each one is a statement of main idea (*MI*), a topic (*T*), or a specific supporting detail (*D*).

Group 1

_____ a. In New Mexico, Governor Tony Anaya called himself the nation's highest elected Hispanic officer and worked to create a national "Hispanic force."

_____ b. Hispanics slowly extended their political gains

_____ c. Hispanic political progress

Gary B. Nash et al., *The American People*

Group 2

_____ a. For poor farm families, life on the plains meant a sod house or a dugout carved out of the hillside for protection from the winds.

_____ b. One door and usually no more than a single window provided light and air.

_____ c. Sod houses on the plains

James W. Davidson et al., *Nation of Nations*

Group 3

_____ a. The daughter of English poet Lord Byron and of a mother who was a gifted mathematician, Ada helped develop the instructions for doing computations on Babbage's analytical engine.

_____ b. Babbage and the Countess

_____ c. If Babbage was the father of the computer, then Ada, the Countess of Lovelace, was the first computer programmer.

H. L. Capron, *Computers*

Group 4

_____ a. As a group, for instance, Generation Xers try harder to work around employees' childcare needs by creating flexible schedules, and many encourage workers to bring their children—and even their pets—to the workplace for visits.

_____ b. Generation X entrepreneurs differ

_____ c. Generation X entrepreneurs are also more employee- and customer-centered than their elders.

Ronald Ebert and Ricky Griffin, *Business Essentials*

QUESTIONING FOR THE MAIN IDEA

To determine the main idea of a paragraph, an article, or a book, ask the three basic questions listed in the box opposite. The order of the questions may vary depending on your prior knowledge of the material. If the material is familiar, main idea construction may be automatic and thus a selection of significant details would follow. If the material is unfamiliar, as frequently occurs in textbook reading, identifying the details through key terms and concepts would come first and from them you would form a main idea statement.

> ► **READER'S TIP**   **Finding the Main Idea**
>
> ► *Establish the topic.* Who or what is this about? What general word or phrase names the subject? The topic should be broad enough to include all the ideas, yet restrictive enough to focus on the direction of the details. For example, identifying the topic of an article as "politics," "federal politics," or "corruption in federal politics" might all be correct, but the last may be the most descriptive of the actual contents.
>
> ► *Identify the key supporting terms.* What are the important details? Look at the details that seem to be significant to see if they point in a particular direction. What aspect of the subject do they address? What seems to be the common message? Details such as kickbacks to senators, overspending on congressional junkets, and lying to the voters could support the idea of "corruption in federal politics."
>
> ► *Focus on the message of the topic.* What is the main idea the author is trying to convey about the topic?
>
> This statement should be:
>   A complete sentence
>   Broad enough to include the important details
>   Focused enough to describe the author's slant
>
> The author's main idea about corruption in federal politics might be that voters need to ask for an investigation of seemingly corrupt practices by federal politicians.

Read the following example, and answer the questions for determining the main idea.

EXAMPLE   New high-speed machines also brought danger to the workplace. If a worker succumbed to boredom, fatigue, or simple miscalculation, disaster could strike. Each year of the late nineteenth century some 35,000 wage earners were killed by industrial accidents. In Pittsburgh iron and steel mills alone, in one year 195 men died from hot metal explosions, asphyxiation, and falls, some into pits of molten metal. Men and women working in textile mills were poisoned by the thick dust and fibers in the air; similar toxic atmospheres injured those working in anything from twine-making plants to embroidery factories. Railways, with their heavy equipment and unaccustomed speed, were especially dangerous. In Philadelphia over half the railroad workers who died between 1886 and 1890 were killed by accidents. For injury or death, workers and their families could expect no payment from employers, since the idea of worker's compensation was unknown.

James W. Davidson et al., *Nation of Nations*

1. Who or what is this about? _____

2. What are the major details? _____

3. What is the main idea the author is trying to convey about the topic?

_____

EXPLANATION   The passage is about injuries from machines. The major details are 35,000 killed, 195 died from explosions, etc., poisoned by dust, and half of rail workers killed. The main idea is that new high-speed machines brought danger to the workplace.

WHAT DO DETAILS DO?

Look at the details in the picture on the opposite page to decide what message the photographer is trying to communicate. Determine the topic of the picture, propose a main idea using your prior knowledge, and then list some of the significant details that support this point.

What is the topic? _____

_____

What are the significant supporting details? _____

_____

What is the point the photograph is trying to convey about the topic?

_____

The topic of this picture is a touchdown. The details show the football player in midair running with the ball. The spectators both in the foreground and the background are shouting for joy and raising their arms to show the touchdown signal. The details show a moment of victory and happiness. Photographers are catching the moment on film. The main idea of

this picture is very simply that the team has made a touchdown and the fans are rejoicing.

Details support, develop, and explain a main idea. Specific details can include reasons, incidents, facts, examples, steps, and definitions. The task of a reader is to recognize the major details and to pull them together into a main idea. Being able to pick out major details implies that the reader has some degree of prior knowledge on the subject and has probably already begun to form some notion of the main idea.

Textbooks are packed full of details, but fortunately all details are not of equal importance. Major details tend to support, explain, and describe main ideas, whereas minor details tend to support, explain, and describe the major details. Ask the following questions to determine which details are major in importance and which are not:

1. Which details logically develop the main idea?
2. Which details help you understand the main idea?
3. Which details make you think the main idea you have chosen is correct?

Noticing key words that form transitional links from one idea to another can sometimes help the reader distinguish between major and minor details.

> ▶ **READER'S TIP** **Signals for Significance**
>
> ▶ **Key words for major details:**
> one, first, another, furthermore, also, finally
> ▶ **Key words for minor details:**
> for example, to be specific, that is, this means

STATED AND UNSTATED MAIN IDEAS

Like paragraphs, pictures also suggest main ideas. Artists compose and select to communicate a message. Look at the picture below, and state the topic of the picture, the details that seem important, and the main idea that the artist is trying to convey.

What is the general topic of the picture? _____

_____

What details seem important? _____

_____

What is the main idea the artist is trying to convey about the topic?

_____

The topic is milk, or more specifically, a plea for people to drink milk. The details show actress Whoopi Goldberg with a glass of milk in her hand and a "milk mustache" over her upper lip. She directly aks the question, "Got milk?" The details in the picture suggest that Whoopi has indeed been drinking her milk, and that we should copy this noted comedian and do the same. Even without the captions, the main idea of the picture is clear. However, the captions add detail to further explain that Whoopi like many other people, is lactose-intolerant, yet she still found a type of milk that is "safe" for her to drink. Again, the main idea is a restatement of the question, "If I've got milk, you can get milk."

Now look at the picture below, which does not include a slogan or directly stated appeal. Again, state the topic of the picture, the important details, and the main idea the artist is trying to get across.

What is the general topic of the picture? _____

_____

What details seem important? _____

_____

What is the main idea the artist is trying to convey about the topic?

_____

The topic of the picture is the plight of refugees dropped in the middle of farm land without support facilities. The details show the two small and temporary Red Cross tents in the foreground. Hundreds of refugees are waiting for services, with military guards standing watch to maintain order. Notice that refugees in the background seem to have established minimum shelter with plastic covers. Prior knowledge would suggest that the people are from Kosovo, and the train in the background suggests that others may be arriving to this overburdened camp. The main idea of this picture is that masses of refugees are trapped in an open field without adequate support services and without hope. Although the point is unstated, do you sense the despair and the hardships of the refugees?

As in the pictures, an author's main point can either be directly stated in the material or it can be unstated. When the main idea is stated in a sentence, the statement is called a **topic sentence** or **thesis statement.** Such a general statement is helpful to the reader because it provides an overview of the material. It does not, however, always express the author's opinion of the subject. For that reason, although helpful in overviewing, the topic sentence may not always form a complete statement of the author's main point.

Frequency of Stated Main Idea. Research shows that students find passages easier to comprehend when the main idea is directly stated within the passage. How often do stated main ideas appear in college textbooks? Should the reader expect to find that most paragraphs have stated main ideas?

For psychology texts, the answer seems to be about half and half. In a recent study,[1] stated main ideas appeared in *only 58 percent* of the sampled paragraphs in introductory psychology textbooks. In one of the books, the main idea was directly stated in 81 percent of the sampled paragraphs, and the researchers noted that the text was particularly easy to read.

Given these findings, we should recognize the importance of being skilled in locating and, especially, in constructing main ideas. In pulling ideas together to construct a main idea, you will be looking at the big picture and not be bound to the text in search of any single suggestive sentence.

© 2000 Addison-Wesley Educational Publishers, Inc.

---

[1]B. Smith and N. Chase. "The Frequency and Placement of Main Idea Topic Sentences in College Psychology Textbooks." *Journal of College Reading and Learning* 24 (1991): 46–54.

Examples of Stated Main Idea

EXAMPLE

Managers can regain control over their time in several ways. One is by meeting whenever possible in someone else's office, so that they can leave as soon as their business is finished. Another is to start meetings on time without waiting for late-comers. The idea is to let late-comers adjust their schedules rather than everyone else adjusting theirs. A third is to set aside a block of time to work on an important project without interruption. This may require ignoring the telephone, being protected by an aggressive secretary, or hiding out. Whatever it takes is worth it.

Reitz and Jewell, *Managing*

1. Who or what is this about? _____

2. What are the major details? _____

3. What is the main idea the author is trying to convey about the topic?

_____

EXPLANATION The passage is about managers controlling their time. The major details are *meet in another office, start meetings on time,* and *block out time to work.* The main idea, stated in the first sentence, is that managers can do things to control their time.

Location of Stated Main Ideas. Should college readers wish for all passages in all textbooks to begin with stated main ideas? Indeed, research indicates that when the main idea is stated at the beginning of the passage, the text tends to be comprehended more easily. In their research, however, Smith and Chase found only 33 percent of the stated main ideas to be positioned as the first sentence of the paragraph.

Main idea statements can be positioned at the beginning, in the middle, or at the end of a paragraph. Both the beginning and concluding sentences of a passage can be combined for a main idea statement. The following examples and diagrams demonstrate the different possible positions for stated main ideas within paragraphs.

1. An introductory statement of the main idea is given at the beginning of the paragraph.

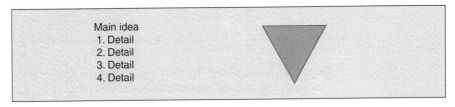

Main idea
1. Detail
2. Detail
3. Detail
4. Detail

EXAMPLE

Under hypnosis, people may recall things that they are unable to remember spontaneously. Some police departments employ hypnotists to probe for information that crime victims do not realize they have. In 1976, twenty-six young children were kidnapped from a school bus near Chowchilla, California. The driver of the bus caught a quick glimpse of the license plate of the van in which he and the children were driven away. However, he remembered only the first two digits. Under hypnosis, he recalled the other numbers and the van was traced to its owners.

David Dempsey and Philip Zimbardo, *Psychology and You*

2. A concluding statement of the main idea appears at the end of the paragraph.

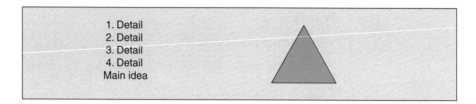

1. Detail
2. Detail
3. Detail
4. Detail
Main idea

EXAMPLE

Research is not a once-and-for-all-times job. Even sophisticated companies often waste the value of their research. One of the most common errors is not providing a basis for comparisons. A company may research its market, find a need for a new advertising campaign, conduct the campaign, and then neglect to research the results. Another may simply feel the need for a new campaign, conduct it, and research the results. Neither is getting the full benefit of the research. When you fail to research either the results or your position *prior* to the campaign, you cannot know the effects of the campaign. *For good evaluation you must have both before and after data.*

Edward Fox and Edward Wheatley, *Modern Marketing*

3. Details are placed at the beginning to arouse interest, followed by a statement of main idea in the middle of the paragraph.

1. Detail
2. Detail
Main idea
3. Detail
4. Detail

EXAMPLE

What happens when foreign materials do enter the body by breaking through the skin or epithelial linings of the digestive, circulatory, or respiratory systems and after the clotting process is complete? The next line of defense comes into action. Phagocytic cells (wandering and stationary) may engulf the foreign material and destroy it. But there is another and very complicated aspect of the process. *This is the production of specific antibody molecules. Antibodies may circulate in the blood as mentioned or they may be bound to cells;* less is known about these cell-bound antibodies. Antibodies inactivate or destroy the activity of antigens by combining with them. The reaction is a manifestation of the immune response, and the discipline primarily devoted to its study is immunology. Generally immunity is considered to be peculiar to the vertebrates, but recent evidence suggests that a form of immunity occurs in invertebrate animals also.

Willis H. Johnson et al., *Essentials of Biology*

4. Both the introductory and concluding sentences state the main idea.

Main idea
1. Detail
2. Detail
3. Detail
4. Detail
Main idea

EXAMPLE

A speech of tribute is designed to create in those who hear it a sense of appreciation for the traits or accomplishments of the person or group to whom tribute is paid. If you cause your audience to realize the essential worth or importance of the person or group, you will have succeeded. But you may go further than this. You may, by honoring a person, arouse deeper devotion to the cause he or she represents. Did this person give distinguished service to community or country? Then strive to enhance the audience's sense of patriotism and service. Was this individual a friend to young people? Then try to arouse the conviction that working to provide opportunities for the young deserves the audience's support. Create a desire in your listeners to emulate the person or persons honored. *Make them want to develop the same virtues, to demonstrate a like devotion.*

Douglas Ehninger et al., *Principles of Speech Communication*

Unfortunately, readers cannot always rely on a stated main idea being provided. For example, fiction writers rarely, if ever, use stated main ideas. The following is an example of a paragraph with an unstated main idea.

5. Details combine to make a point but the main idea is not directly stated.

1. Detail
2. Detail
3. Detail
4. Detail

EXAMPLE   This creature's career could produce but one result, and it speedily followed. Boy after boy managed to get on the river. The minister's son became an engineer. The doctor's sons became "mud clerks"; the wholesale liquor dealer's son became a bar-keeper on a boat; four sons of the chief merchant, and two sons of the county judge, became pilots. Pilot was the grandest position of all. The pilot, even in those days of trivial wages, had a princely salary—from a hundred and fifty to two hundred and fifty dollars a month, and no board to pay. Two months of his wages would pay a preacher's salary for a year. Now some of us were left disconsolate. We could not get on the river—at least our parents would not let us.

Mark Twain, *Life on the Mississippi*

EXPLANATION   Main idea: Young boys in the area have a strong desire to leave home and get a job on the prestigious Mississippi River.

EXERCISE 4.3   *Stated Main Ideas*

Read the following passages and use the three-question system to determine the author's main idea. For each passage in this exercise, the answer to the third question will be stated somewhere within the paragraph.

Passage A

Time is especially linked to status considerations, and the importance of being on time varies with the status of the individual you are visiting. If the person is extremely important, you had better be there on time or even early just in case he or she is able to see you before schedule. As the person's status decreases, so does the importance of being on time. Junior executives, for example, must be on time for conferences with senior executives, but it is even more important to be on time for the company president or the CEO. Senior executives, however, may be late for conferences with their juniors but not for conferences with the president. Within any hierarchy, similar unwritten rules are followed with respect to time. This is not to imply that these "rules" are just or fair; they simply exist.

Joseph DeVito, *Interpersonal Communication*

1. Who or what is this about? _____

2. What are the major details? _____

    _____

    _____

3. What is the main idea the author is trying to convey about the topic? Underline the main idea. _____

Passage B

Courting behavior in birds is also believed to be instinctive. In one experiment Daniel Lehrman of Rutgers University found that when a male blond ring dove was isolated from females, it soon began to bow and coo to a stuffed model of a female—a model that it had previously ignored. When the model was replaced by a rolled-up cloth, he began to court the cloth; and when this was removed the sex-crazed dove directed his attention to a corner of the cage, where it could at least focus its gaze. It seems that the threshold for release of the behavior pattern became increasingly lower as time went by without the sight of a live female dove. It is almost as though some specific "energy" for performing courting behavior were building up within the male ring dove.

Robert Wallace, *Biology: The World of Life*

1. Who or what is this about? _____

2. What are the major details? _____

   _____

   _____

3. What is the main idea the author is trying to convey about the topic?

   Underline the main idea. _____

Passage C

To retrieve a fact from a library of stored information, you need a way to gain access to it. In recognition tests, retrieval cues (such as photographs) provide reminders of information (classmates' names) we could not otherwise recall. Retrieval cues also guide us where to look. If you want to know what the pyramid on the back of a dollar bill signifies, you might look in *Collier's Encyclopedia* under "dollar," "currency," or "money." But your efforts would be futile. To get the information you want, you would have to look under "Great Seal of the United States." Like information stored in encyclopedias, memories are inaccessible unless we have cues for retrieving them. The more and better learned the retrieval cues, the more accessible the memory.

David G. Myers. *Psychology*

1. Who or what is this about? _____

2. What are the major details? _____

   _____

   _____

3. What is the main idea the author is trying to convey about the topic? Underline the main idea. _____

Passage D

Most of the Plains Indians believed that land could be utilized, but never owned. The idea of owning land was as absurd as owning the air people breathed. To some, the sacredness of the land made farming against their religion. Chief Somohalla of the Wanapaun explained why his people refused to farm. "You ask me to plow the ground! Shall I take a knife and tear my mother's bosom? . . . You ask me to cut grass and make hay and sell it, and be rich like white men! But how dare I cut off my mother's hair?"

James Kirby Martin et al., *America and Its People*

1. Who or what is this about? _____

   _____

2. What are the major details? _____

   _____

3. What is the main idea the author is trying to convey about the topic?

   Underline the main idea. _____

Passage E

A crab lives at the bottom of its ocean of water and looks upward at jelly-fish drifting above it. Similarly, we live at the bottom of our ocean of air and look upward at balloons drifting above us. A balloon is suspended in air and a jellyfish is suspended in water for the same reason: each is buoyed upward by a displaced weight of fluid equal to its own weight. In one case the displaced fluid is air, and in the other case it is water. In water, immersed objects are buoyed upward because the pressure acting up against the bottom of the object exceeds the pressure acting down against the top. Likewise, air pressure acting up against an object immersed in air is greater than the pressure above pushing down. The buoyancy in both cases is numerically equal to the weight of fluid displaced. **Archimedes' principle** holds for air just as it does for water: An object surrounded by air is buoyed up by a force equal to the weight of the air displaced.

Paul Hewitt, *Conceptual Physics*

1. Who or what is this about? _____

2. What are the major details? _____

   _____

   _____

3. What is the main idea the author is trying to convey about the topic?

   Underline the main idea. _____

Examples of Unstated Main Idea

EXAMPLE Michael Harner proposes an ecological interpretation of Aztec sacrifice and cannibalism. He holds that human sacrifice was a response to certain diet deficiencies in the population. In the Aztec environment, wild game was getting scarce, and the population was growing. Although the maize-beans combination of food that was the basis of the diet was usually adequate, these crops were subject to seasonal failure. Famine was frequent in the absence of edible domesticated animals. To meet essential protein requirements, cannibalism was the only solution. Although only the upper classes were allowed to consume human flesh, a commoner who distinguished himself in a war could also have the privilege of giving a cannibalistic feast. Thus, although it was the upper strata who benefited most from ritual cannibalism, members of the commoner class could also benefit. Furthermore, as Harner explains, the social mobility and cannibalistic privileges available to the commoners through warfare provided a strong motivation for the "aggressive war machine" that was such a prominent feature of the Aztec state.

Serena Nanda, *Cultural Anthropology*

1. Who or what is this about? _____

2. What are the major details? _____

3. What is the main idea the author is trying to convey about the topic?

_____

EXPLANATION The passage is about Aztec sacrifice and cannibalism. The major details are: *diet deficiencies occurred, animals were not available,* and *upper-class members and heroes could eat human flesh.* The main idea is that Aztec sacrifice and cannibalism met protein needs of the diet and motivated warriors to achieve.

> **EXERCISE 4.4** *Unstated Main Ideas*

Read the following passages and use the three-question system to determine the author's main idea. Pull the ideas together to state the main ideas in your own words.

Passage A

According to the U.S. Department of the Census, the demographic shift in the population will be "profound" in the next 50 years. By 2050, Hispanics will make up 24.5 percent of the population, up from 10.2 percent in 1996. The annual growth rate of the Hispanic population is expected to be 2 percent through the year 2030. To put this growth in perspective, consider the fact that even at the height of the baby boom explosion in the late 1940s and early 1950s, the country's annual population increase never reached 2 percent. Demographers, it seems, are alerting us to the enormous importance of such change. Says Gregory Spencer, Director of the Census Bureau's Population Projections Branch, "The world is not going to be the same in thirty years as it is now."

Ronald Ebert and Ricky Griffin, Business Essentials

1. Who or what is this about? _____

2. What are the major details? _____

   _____

   _____

3. What is the main idea the author is trying to convey about the topic?

   _____

   _____

Passage B

Prior to the time of Jan Baptiste van Helmont, a Belgian physician of the 17th century, it was commonly accepted that plants derived their matter from materials in the soil. (Probably, many people who haven't studied photosynthesis would go along with this today.) We aren't sure why, but van Helmont decided to test the idea. He carefully stripped a young willow sapling of all surrounding soil, weighed it, and planted it in a tub of soil that had also been carefully weighed. After five years of diligent watering (with rain water), van Helmont removed the greatly enlarged willow and again stripped away the soil and weighed it. The young tree had gained 164 pounds. Upon weighing the soil, van Helmont was amazed to learn that it had lost only 2 ounces.

Robert Wallace et al., Biology: The Science of Life, 3rd edition

1. Who or what is this about? _____

   _____

2. What are the major details? _____

   _____

   _____

3. What is the main idea the author is trying to convey about the topic?

   _____

   _____

Passage C

The Aswan High Dam, built in Egypt with Russian support, was supposed to provide hydroelectric power and to increase Egypt's food supply by controlling the unpredictable Nile River. The project meant that great art treasures were flooded as submerged land was drained for cultivation. However, only one-tenth of an acre of land was made available for each person added to Egypt's population during the period of construction. One result of the dam was that the Nile no longer flooded the delta farmlands annually. These annual floods served to restore the farmland fertility with deposited silt. This no longer the case, the quality of the farmland decreased. The dam also cut off the nutrients that had been washed to the Mediterranean Sea as a result of the annual floodings. Because of this, or the change in the salinity of the sea that the dam produced, the sardine catch dropped from 18,000 tons per year to 500 tons per year. The stable lake created by the dam allowed aquatic snails to flourish. The snails serve as an intermediate host to a blood fluke that bores into humans causing the dreaded disease, schistosomiasis. The construction of the dam had important political implications at the time.

Robert Wallace, *Biology: The World of Life*

1. Who or what is this about? _____

_____

2. What are the major details?   _____

_____

_____

_____

3. What is the main idea the author is trying to convey about the topic?

_____

_____

_____

Passage D

If using sunscreen, apply it at least 30–45 minutes before exposure, then reapply it periodically, especially after you swim or sweat. It is especially important to protect children. One or more severe sunburns with blisters in childhood or adolescence can double the risk of the skin cancer melanoma later in life. Additional protection can be provided by a wide-brimmed hat to protect your head and face, and opaque clothing to cover those body areas you wish to protect. Any fabric or material you can see through, including some beach umbrellas, does not give full protection. You should stay out of the sun between 10 A.M. and 2 P.M. when the rays are strongest.

Curtis O. Byer and Louis W. Shainberg, *Living Well*

1. Who or what is this about? _____

2. What are the major details?   _____

_____

_____

3. What is the main idea the author is trying to convey about the topic?

_____

_____

Passage E

In 1979 when University of Minnesota psychologist Thomas Bouchard read a newspaper account of the reuniting of 39-year-old twins who had been separated from infancy, he seized the opportunity and flew them to Minneapolis for extensive tests. Bouchard was looking for differences. What "the Jim twins," Jim Lewis and Jim Springer, presented were amazing similarities. Both had married women named Linda, divorced, and married women named Betty. One had a son James Alan, the other a son James Allan. Both had dogs named Toy, chainsmoked Salems, served as sheriff's deputies, drove Chevrolets, chewed their fingernails to the nub, enjoyed stock car racing, had basement workshops, and had built circular white benches around trees in their yards. They also had similar medical histories: Both gained 10 pounds at about the same time and then lost it; both suffered what they mistakenly believed were heart attacks, and both began having late-afternoon headaches at age 18.

Identical twins Oskar Stohr and Jack Yufe presented equally striking similarities. One was raised by his grandmother in Germany as a Catholic and a Nazi, while the other was raised by his father in the Caribbean as a Jew. Nevertheless, they share traits and habits galore. They like spicy foods and sweet liqueurs, have a habit of falling asleep in front of the television, flush the toilet before using it, store rubber bands on their wrists, and dip buttered toast in their coffee. Stohr is domineering toward women and yells at his wife, as did Yufe before he was separated.

David G. Myers, _Psychology_

1. Who or what is this about? _____

2. What are the major details? _____

_____

_____

_____

3. What is the main idea the author is trying to convey about the topic?

_____

_____

INTERPRETING LONGER SELECTIONS

Understanding the main idea of longer selections requires a little more thinking than finding the main idea of a single paragraph. Since longer selections such as articles or chapters involve more material, the challenge of tying the ideas together can be confusing and complicated. Each paragraph of a longer selection usually represents a new aspect of a supporting detail. In addition, several major ideas may contribute to developing the overall main idea. The reader, therefore, must fit the many pieces together under one central theme.

For longer selections, the reader needs to add an extra step between the two questions, "What is the topic?" and "What is the main idea the author is trying to convey?" The step involves organizing the material into manageable subunits and then relating those to the whole. Two additional questions to ask are, "Under what subsections can these ideas be grouped?" and "How do these subsections contribute to the whole?"

Use the suggestions in the box below to determine the main idea of longer selections. The techniques are similar to those used in previewing and skimming, two skills that also focus on the overall central theme.

© 2000 Addison-Wesley Educational Publishers, Inc.

READER'S TIP ▸ Getting the Main Idea of Longer Selections

▸ *Think about the significance of the title.* What does the title suggest about the topic?

▸ *Read the first paragraph or two for a statement of the topic or thesis.* What does the selection seem to be about?

▸ *Read the subheadings and, if necessary, glance at the first sentences of some of the paragraphs.* Based on these clues, what does the article seem to be about?

▸ *Look for clues that indicate how the material is organized.*

Is the purpose to define a term, to prove an opinion, or explain a concept, to describe a situation, or to persuade the reader toward a particular point of view?

Is the material organized into a list of examples, a time order or sequence, a comparison or contrast, or a cause-and-effect relationship?

▸ *As you read, organize the paragraphs into subsections.* Give each subsection a title. These become your significant supporting details.

▸ *Determine how the overall organization and subsections relate to the whole.* Answer the question, "What is the main idea the author is trying to convey in this selection?"

PATTERNS OF ORGANIZATION

The main idea and the pattern of organization chosen by a writer to deliver this idea are closely interwoven. Identifying one will often help identify the other, because the message can dictate the structure. A **pattern of organization** is a vehicle or structure for a message. Before beginning to write, an author must ask, "If this is what I want to say, what is the best way to organize my message?"

From a number of possible patterns, an author chooses the organizational structure that seems most appropriate. For example, if the intended main idea was that freshmen receive more support at junior colleges than at large universities, the author would probably organize the message through a pattern of comparison and contrast. On the other hand, if the writer wanted to explain that a college degree can lead to expanded opportunities, upward mobility within companies, later salary increases, and ultimately greater job satisfaction, the idea might best be communicated through a pattern of cause and effect, although words like *expanded* and *greater* also suggest a comparison.

Suppose you were writing an orientation article describing support services available at your own college. You could summarize the resources in a list pattern, or you could discuss them in the order in which a freshman is likely to need them. Within your article, you might use a separate paragraph to describe or define a relatively unknown service on campus, with examples of how it has helped others. Thus, one long article might have an overall list pattern of organization yet contain individual paragraphs which follow other patterns. The organizational pattern is a choice you make for structuring your message.

The importance of identifying organizational patterns is that they signal how facts will be presented. They are blueprints for you to use while reading. The number of details in a textbook can be overwhelming. Identifying the author's pattern can help you to master the complexities of the material by allowing you to predict the format of upcoming information.

Although key words can signal a particular pattern, the most important clue to the pattern is the main idea itself. In a single selection several patterns can be used. Your aim as a reader is to anticipate the overall pattern and place the supporting details into its broad perspective.

The following are examples of the patterns of organization that are found most frequently in textbooks.

Simple Listing

With a **simple listing,** items are randomly listed in a series of supporting facts or details. These supporting elements are of equal value, and the order in which they are presented is of no importance. Changing the order of the items does not change the meaning of the paragraph.

Signal words, often used as transitional words to link ideas in a paragraph with a pattern of simple listing, include *in addition, also, another, several, for example, a number of.*

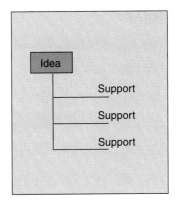

EXAMPLE

Work-related Stress

Work-related stress has increased significantly in the last few years. People are spending more hours at work and bringing more work home with them. Job security has decreased in almost every industry. Pay, for many, has failed to keep up with the cost of living. Women are subject to exceptionally high stress levels as they try to live up to all of the expectations placed upon them. Finally, many people feel that they are trapped in jobs they hate, but can't escape.

Curtis O. Byer and Louis W. Shainberg, *Living Well*

Definition

Frequently in a textbook, an entire paragraph is devoted to defining a complex term or idea. With **definition,** the concept is defined initially and then expanded with examples and restatements.

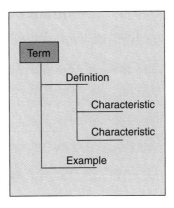

EXAMPLE

Ultrasound

Ultrasound is a relatively new technique that uses sound waves to produce an image that enables a physician to detect structural abnormalities. Useful pictures can be obtained as early as 7 weeks. Ultrasound is frequently used in conjunction with other techniques such as amniocentesis and fetoscopy.

John Dacey and John Travers, *Human Development*

Description

Description is like listing; the characteristics that make up a description are no more than a definition or a simple list of details.

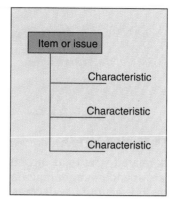

EXAMPLE

Caribbean

Caribbean America today is a land crowded with so many people that, as a region (encompassing the Greater and Lesser Antilles), it is the most densely populated part of the Americas. It is also a place of grinding poverty and, in all too many localities, unrelenting misery with little chance for escape.

H.J. De Blij and Peter O. Muller, *Geography*

Time Order or Sequence

Items are listed in the order in which they occurred or in a specifically planned order in which they must develop. In this case, the **time order** is important, and changing it would change the meaning.

Signal words that are often used for time order or sequence include *first, second, third, after, before, when, until, at last, next, later.*

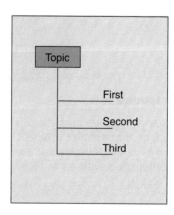

EXAMPLE

Napoleon

In May 1803, just two weeks after Napoleon sold Louisiana to the United States, France declared war on Britain. For the next 12 years, war engulfed Europe. In 1805 France defeated the armies of Austria and Russia at Austerlitz thereby winning control of much of the European continent. Napoleon then massed his troops and assembled a fleet of flat boats for an invasion of England.

James Kirby Martin et al., *America and Its People*

Comparison-Contrast

With **comparison-contrast,** items are presented according to similarities and differences among them. Signal words that are often used for comparison-contrast include *different, similar, on the other hand, but, however, bigger than, in the same way, parallels.*

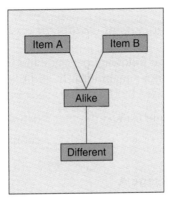

EXAMPLE

Oranges

An orange grown in Florida usually has a thin and tightly fitting skin, and it is also heavy with juice. Californians say that if you want to eat a Florida orange you have to get into a bathtub first. California oranges are light in weight and have thick skins that break easily and come off in hunks.

John McPhee, *Oranges*

Cause and Effect

With **cause and effect,** one element is shown as producing another element. One is the *cause* or the "happening" that stimulated the particular result or *effect.* Signal words that are often used for cause and effect include *for this reason, consequently, on that account, hence, because.*

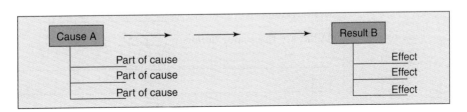

EXAMPLE   **Steroids**

There has been a great deal of discussion about "'roid rage," a kind of manic rage that has been reported by some steroid users. We should be careful on the basis of uncontrolled retrospective reports to attribute instances of violence to a drug, especially when the perpetrator of a violent crime may be looking for an excuse. However, there is a sufficient number of reports of violent feelings and actions among steroid users for us to be concerned and to await further research. According to Dr. William Taylor, a leading authority on anabolic steroids, "I've seen total personality changes. A passive, low-key guy goes on steroids for muscle enhancement, and the next thing you know, he's being arrested for assault or disorderly conduct."

Oakley Ray and Charles Ksir, *Drugs, Society, and Human Behavior*

EXERCISE 4.5   *Patterns of Organization and Main Idea*

Read the following passages and use the three-question system to determine the author's main idea. In addition, indicate the dominant pattern of organization used by the author. Select from the following list:

simple listing   definition   description

time order   comparison-contrast   cause and effect

Passage A

Let us follow the story of how rabbits were introduced into Australia. European rabbits reached Australia with the first European settlers in 1788 and repeated introductions followed. By the early 1800s rabbits were being kept in every large settlement and had been liberated many times. All the early rabbit introductions either died out or remained localized. No one knows why.

On Christmas Day, 1859, the brig HMS *Lightning* arrived at Melbourne with about a dozen wild European rabbits bound for an estate in western Victoria. Within three years rabbits had started to spread, after a bush fire destroyed the fences enclosing one colony. From a slow spread at first the colonization picked up speed during the 1870s, and by 1900 the European rabbit had spread 1000 miles to the north and west, changing the entire economy of nature in southeastern Australia.

Charles Krebs, *The Message of Ecology*

1. Who or what is this about? _____

2. What are the major details? _____

_____

_____

_____

_____

3. What is the overall pattern of organization? _____

4. What is the main idea the author is trying to convey about the topic?

_____

_____

Passage B

Sloppy people can't bear to part with anything. They give loving attention to every detail. When sloppy people say they're going to tackle the surface of a desk, they really mean it. Not a paper will go unturned; not a rubber band will go unboxed.

Neat people are bums and clods at heart. They have cavalier attitudes toward possessions, including family heirlooms. Everything is just another dust-catcher to them. If anything collects dust, it's got to go and that's that.

Suzanne Britt, *Neat People vs. Sloppy People*

1. Who or what is this about? _____

2. What are the major details? _____

_____

_____

3. What is the overall pattern of organization? _____

4. What is the main idea the author is trying to convey about the topic?

_____

_____

Passage C

The disadvantage faced by children who attempt morning schoolwork on an empty stomach appears to be at least partly due to hypoglycemia. The average child up to the age of ten or so needs to eat every four to six hours to maintain a blood glucose concentration high enough to support the activity of the brain and nervous system. A child's brain is as big as an adult's, and the brain is the body's chief glucose consumer. A child's liver is considerably smaller, and the liver is the organ responsible for storing glucose (as glycogen) and for releasing it into the blood as needed. The liver can't store more than about four hours' worth of glycogen; hence the need to eat fairly often. Teachers aware of the late-morning slump in their classrooms wisely request that a midmorning snack be provided; it improves classroom performance all the way to lunch time. But for the child who hasn't had breakfast, the morning may be lost altogether.

Eva May Nunnelley Hamilton et al., *Nutrition*

1. Who or what is this about? _____

2. What are the major details? _____

   _____

   _____

   _____

3. What is the overall pattern of organization? _____

4. What is the main idea the author is trying to convey about the topic?

   _____

   _____

Passage D

The media do influence public opinion to some degree. Their power comes largely from their role as gatekeepers—determining what information will be passed on to large numbers of people. There are at least five ways in which the media affect opinion. First, they *authenticate* information, making it more credible to the audience. A news item reported in the mass media often seems more believable than one passed by word of mouth. Second, the media *validate* private opinions, preferences, and values. If a famous commentator offers a view similar to our own, we are likely to feel more confident of our own opinion. Third, the media *legitimize* unconventional viewpoints. The wildest idea may eventually sound reasonable, or at least worth considering, if we read it repeatedly on the editorial pages of newspapers or hear it on the evening news. Fourth, the mass media *concretize* free-floating anxieties and ill-defined preferences. By supplying such labels as "population explosion," "the crime wave," and "the great racial divide," the media in effect create a world of objects against which feelings can be specifically expressed. Fifth, the mass media help *establish a hierarchy* of importance and prestige among persons, objects, and opinions. If the national media never interview the senators from your state, the public is not likely to consider them important, even if they are very influential among their colleagues in the Senate.

Alex Thio, *Sociology*

1. Who or what is this about? _____

2. What are the major details? _____

   _____

   _____

   _____

3. What is the overall pattern of organization? _____

4. What is the main idea the author is trying to convey about the topic?

_____

_____

Passage E

Intellectual property is created through a person's creative activities. Books, articles, songs, paintings, screenplays, and computer software are all intellectual property. The U.S. Constitution grants protection to intellectual property by means of copyrights, trademarks, and patents. Copyrights and patents apply to tangible expressions of an idea—not to the ideas themselves. Thus, you could not copyright the idea of cloning dinosaurs from fossil DNA. Michael Crichton could copyright his novel *Jurassic Park,* which is a tangible result of that idea, and sell the film rights to producer-director Steven Spielberg.

Ronald Ebert and Ricky Griffin, *Business Essentials*

1. Who or what is this about? _____

2. What are the major details? _____

_____

_____

3. What is the overall pattern of organization? _____

4. What is the main idea the author is trying to convey about the topic?

_____

_____

SUMMARY WRITING: A MAIN IDEA SKILL

A **summary** is a series of brief, concise statements in your own words of the main idea and the significant supporting details. The first sentence should state the main idea or thesis, and subsequent sentences should incorporate the significant details. Minor details and material irrelevant to the learner's purpose should be omitted. The summary should be in paragraph form and should always be shorter than the material being summarized.

Why Summarize?

Summaries can be used for textbook study and are particularly useful in anticipating answers for essay exam questions. For writing research papers, summarizing is an essential skill. Using your own words to put the essence of an article into concise sentences requires a thorough understanding of the material. As one researcher noted, "Since so much summarizing is necessary for writing papers, students should have the skill before starting work on research papers. How much plagiarism is the result of inadequate summarizing skills?"[2]

Writing a research paper may mean that you will have to read as many as thirty articles and four books over a period of a month or two. After each reading, you want to take enough notes so you can write your paper without returning to the library for another look at the original reference. Since you will be using so many different references, the notetaking should be done carefully. The complete sentences of a summary are more explicit than underscored text or the highlighted topic-phrase format of an outline. Your summary should demonstrate a synthesis of the information.

> **READER'S TIP**   **How to Summarize**
>
> ▶ *Keep in mind the purpose of your summary.* Your projected needs will determine which details are important and how many should be included.
>
> ▶ *Decide on the main idea the author is trying to convey.* Make this main idea the first sentence in your summary.
>
> ▶ *Decide on the major ideas and details that support the author's point.* Include in your summary the major ideas and as many of the significant supporting details as your purpose demands.
>
> ▶ *Do not include irrelevant or repeated information in your summary.*
>
> ▶ *Use appropriate transitional words and phrases to show relationships between points.*
>
> ▶ *Use paragraph form.*
>
> ▶ *Do not add your personal opinion as part of the summary.*

EXAMPLE   Read the following excerpt on political authority as if you were researching for a term paper and writing a summary on a notecard. Mark key terms that

---

[2]K. Taylor, "Can College Students Summarize?" *Journal of Reading* 26 (March 1983): 540–544.

you would include in your summary. Before reading the example provided, anticipate what you would include in your own summary.

Types of Authority

Where is the source of the state's authority? Weber described three possible sources of the right to command, which produce what he called traditional authority, charismatic authority, and legal authority.

Traditional Authority

In many societies, people have obeyed those in power because, in essence, "that is the way it has always been." Thus, kings, queens, feudal lords, and tribal chiefs did not need written rules in order to govern. Their authority was based on tradition, on long-standing customs, and it was handed down from parent to child, maintaining traditional authority from one generation to the next. Often, traditional authority has been justified by religious tradition. For example, medieval European kings were said to rule by divine right, and Japanese emperors were considered the embodiment of heaven.

Charismatic Authority

People may also submit to authority, not because of tradition, but because of the extraordinary attraction of an individual. Napoleon, Gandhi, Mao Tse-tung, and Ayatollah Khomeini all illustrate authority that derives its legitimacy from *charisma*—an exceptional personal quality popularly attributed to certain individuals. Their followers perceive charismatic leaders as persons of destiny endowed with remarkable vision, the power of a savior, or God's grace. Charismatic authority is inherently unstable. It cannot be transferred to another person.

Legal Authority

The political systems of industrial states are based largely on a third type of authority: legal authority, which Weber also called *rational authority*. These systems derive legitimacy from a set of explicit rules and procedures that spell out the ruler's rights and duties. Typically, the rules and procedures are put in writing. The people grant their obedience to "the law." It specifies procedures by which certain individuals hold offices of power, such as governor or president or prime minister. But the authority is vested in those offices, not in the individuals who temporarily hold the offices. Thus, a political system based on legal authority is often called a "government of laws, not of men." Individuals come and go, as American presidents have come and gone, but the office, "the presidency," remains. If individual officeholders overstep their authority, they may be forced out of office and replaced.

Alex Thio, *Sociology*

1. To begin your summary, what is the main point? _____

_____

2. What are the major areas of support? _____

_____

3. Should you include an example for each area? _____

_____

> EXPLANATION   Begin your summary with the main point, which is that
> Weber describes the three command sources as traditional, charismatic, and
> legal. Then define each of the three sources but do not include examples.
>   Read the summary and notice how closely it fits your own ideas.

Political Authority

Weber describes the three command sources as traditional, charismatic, and legal authority. Traditional authority is not written but based on long-standing custom such as the power of queens or tribal chiefs. Charismatic authority is based on the charm and vision of a leader such as Gandhi. Legal authority, such as that of American presidents, comes from written laws and is vested in the office rather than the person..

▶ EXERCISE 4.6   *Summarizing*

Read the following passages and mark the key terms. Begin your summary
with a statement of the main point and add the appropriate supporting details. Use your markings to help you write the summary. Be brief but include
the essential elements.

Passage A: Empathy

Perhaps the most difficult communication quality to achieve is the ability
to empathize with another person. The term *empathy* was derived from
Greek to translate the German word *Einfuhlung,* meaning "feeling with."
To empathize with someone is to feel as that person feels, to experience
what the other is experiencing from that person's point of view without
losing your own identity. To *sympathize,* in contrast, is to feel *for* the
person—to feel sorry for the person, for example. To empathize is to feel
as the person feels, to walk in the same shoes, to feel the same feelings
in the same way. Empathy, then, enables you to understand, emotionally
as well as intellectually, what another person is experiencing.

Animal researchers have argued that some animals show empathy.
For example, consider the male gorilla who watched a female try in vain
to get water that collected in an automobile tire and who then secured
the tire and brought it to the female. This gorilla, it has been argued,
demonstrated empathy; he felt the other gorilla's thirst (Angier 1995).
Similarly, the animal who cringes when another of its species gets hurt
seems also to be showing empathy.

To achieve empathy it is first necessary to be relatively calm and to
free yourself from your own intense emotions (Goleman 1995). If, for ex-

ample, you are angry, you'll be so caught up in your own anger that you'll be unable to feel or even hear the other person's perhaps equally justified anger or sadness or fear.

Should you wish to achieve empathy, your first step is to avoid evaluating the other person's behaviors. If you evaluate them as right or wrong, good or bad, you will see the behaviors through these labels and will fail to see a great deal more that might not be consistent with them. Therefore, resist the temptation to evaluate, to judge, to interpret, to criticize. Focus instead on understanding.

Second, learn as much as you can about the other person's desires, experiences, abilities, fears, and so on. The more you know about a person, the more you will be able to see what that person sees and feel what that person feels. Try to understand the reasons and the motivations for the person's feelings.

Third, try to experience emotionally what the other person is feeling from his or her point of view. Playing the role of the other person in your mind (or even out loud) can help you see the world a little more as the other person does.

Joseph DeVito, Interpersonal Communication

Use your marked text to write a summary.

Passage B: Suicide Among College Students

Compared to nonstudents of the same age, the suicide rate among college students is somewhat higher. Why is this so? For one thing, among the younger college students who commit suicide (ages 18–22), a common thread is the inability to separate themselves from their family and to solve problems on their own. College presents many of these younger students with the challenge of having to be independent in many ways while remaining dependent on family in other ways, such as financially and emotionally.

Several other characteristics of the college experience may relate to suicide. A great emphasis is put on attaining high grades and the significance of grades may be blown out of proportion. A student may come to perceive grades as a measurement of his or her total worth as a person, rather than just one of many ways a person can be evaluated. If a student is unable to achieve expected grades, there may be a total loss of self-esteem and loss of hope for any success in life.

In the college setting, where self-esteem can be tenuous, the end of a relationship can also be devastating. A student who has recently lost a close friend or lover can become so deeply depressed that suicide becomes an attractive alternative. The problem can be compounded when depression interferes with coursework and grades slip.

Curtis O. Byer and Louis W. Shainberg, Living Well

Use your marked text to write a summary.

Passage C: Making a Healthy Choice When It Comes to New Products

According to Charles M. Harper, chairman of ConAgra, Incorporated, the Healthy Choice line of frozen dinners began with his own heart attack, which had been brought on by years of "eating anything I could get my hands on." As he lay in the hospital recuperating, Harper imagined a line of healthy frozen foods that tasted good.

The Healthy Choice product line was carefully tested with consumers before being introduced to the general population. ConAgra's research and development staff spent a year working under the directive, "whatever the cost, don't sacrifice taste." The first test market results surprised even the ConAgra team. The low-sodium, low-fat, low-cholesterol frozen entrees sold much better than expected. According to the firm's vice president of marketing and sales, "We benefited from low expectations, [the products] were much better than people thought [they] would be." This finding supported ConAgra's decision to position the product against other high-quality frozen dinners rather than as a diet or health food.

The new product's brand name and packaging were an important part of the development process. The name *Healthy Choice* was chosen for the positive connotation it held for consumers. Because ConAgra felt the product would be an impulse purchase, it was important to make the items stand out in the freezer case. This was accomplished through the dark green packaging that not only differed from the competition but also suggested freshness and nutritive value.

Thomas C. Kinner et al., *Principles of Marketing*

Use your marked text to write a summary.

Summary Points

■ **What is a topic?**

The topic of a passage is the general term that forms an umbrella for the specific ideas presented.

■ **What is a main idea?**

The main idea is the point the author is trying to convey about the topic. In some passages the main idea is stated in a sentence, and in others it is unstated.

■ **What are significant details?**

Details support, develop, and explain the main idea. Some details are of major significance and others are only of minor significance in supporting the main idea.

■ **What is an organizational pattern?**

Organizational patterns for presenting details and developing ideas can vary, and anticipating the pattern can help the reader.

■ **What is a summary?**

Summaries condense material and include the main ideas and major details.

CONTEMPORARY FOCUS

Humans owe a debt to animals whose lives are manipulated and sacrificed for the sake of knowledge. Is there a line that marks the difference between when animal research is acceptable and when it is unethical?

BUILDING A BETTER MOUSE

Dennis Meredith

From *Meridian: Midway Airlines* August 1998, p. 29.

Masked, capped, gowned and gloved, Lin Allsbury plucks and places with practiced dexterity the wriggling pink baby mice from one clear plastic bin to another. Grasping each mouse gently with sterilized forceps, she zips them unerringly from old home to new, religiously following the intricate, weekly, cage-changing ritual. The technician allows no bare human hand ever to touch these tiny, priceless creatures. Mouse by squirming mouse, she lowers each onto a bed of pulverized corncobs heat-blasted to sterility in an autoclave. As each baby lands, the mother mouse busily nestles her brood into the cotton nesting material provided for new mothers. Transfer complete, Allsbury clamps down the germ-filtering lid on the micro-isolator cage. The mother mouse takes a quick sip of water treated with germ-killing hydrochloric acid, nibbles a bit of mouse chow, and nestles down into the fastidiously prepared cage.

These mice—among some 30,000 housed in Duke University's Transgenic Mouse Facility—live in such scrupulously sterile splendor because their altered genes harbor fundamental secrets that could help save millions of human lives. The tinkered-up DNA within the mice could yield a better understanding of cancer, genetic disorders, drug addiction, heart disease, or immune malfunctions—an incredible potential for such modest-looking creatures.

The scientific explosion of experiments with exotic mice is producing a population explosion of animals, requiring a multimillion-dollar investment by the university for new facilities to house the 60,000 mice needed within a decade. If the trend continues, 21st-century Duke could be home to more mice than humans.

Collaborate on responses to the following questions:

- What are the positive and negative arguments for a university conducting research on animals?
- What will probably be done to these mice with their tinkered-up DNA?
- Why are students invited to participate in research projects in psychology and education?

SKILL DEVELOPMENT—STAGE 1: PREVIEW

Preview the next selection to predict the purpose, organization, and your learning plan.

The author's main purpose is to describe the infant-mother relationship. Agree ☐   Disagree ☐

After reading this selection, I will need to know the meaning of contact comfort. Agree ☐   Disagree ☐

Activate Schema

Do parents who were abused as children later abuse their own children?

As a child, what did you use as a "security blanket"?

Learning Strategy

Explain the psychological needs of an infant monkey and the effect that depriva-tion of those needs can have on the whole pattern of psychological development.

Word Knowledge

What do you know about these words?

| surrogate | functional | anatomy | tentatively | novel |
| desensitized | ingenious | deprived | persisted | deficient |

Your instructor may give a true-false vocabulary review before or after reading.

STAGE 2: INTEGRATE KNOWLEDGE WHILE READING

Predict   Picture   Relate   Monitor   Correct

The baby monkey clings to the cloth surrogate mother.

MONKEY LOVE

From James V. McConnell, *Understanding Human Behavior*

The scientist who has conducted the best long-term laboratory ex-periments on love is surely Harry Harlow, a psychologist at the University of Wisconsin. Professor Harlow did not set out to study love—it happened by accident. Like many other psychologists, he was at first primarily interested in how organisms learn. Rather
5 than working with rats, Harlow chose to work with monkeys.

Since he needed a place to house and raise the monkeys, he built the Primate Laboratory at Wisconsin. Then he began to study the effects of

brain lesions on monkey learning. But he soon found that young animals
10   reacted somewhat differently to brain damage than did older monkeys, so
he and his wife Margaret devised a breeding program and tried various
ways of raising monkeys in the laboratory. They rapidly discovered that
monkey infants raised by their mothers often caught diseases from their
parents, so the Harlows began taking the infants away from their mothers
15   at birth and tried raising them by hand. The baby monkeys had been given
cheesecloth diapers to serve as baby blankets. Almost from the start, it became obvious to the Harlows that their little animals developed such
strong attachments to the blankets that, in the Harlows' own terms, it was
often hard to tell where the diaper ended and the baby began. Not only
20   this, but if the Harlows removed the "security" blanket in order to clean it,
the infant monkey often became greatly disturbed—just as if its own
mother had deserted it.

The Surrogate Mother

What the baby monkeys obviously needed was an artificial or *surrogate*
mother—something they could cling to as tightly as they typically clung to
25   their own mother's chest. The Harlows sketched out many different designs,
but none really appealed to them. Then, in 1957, while enjoying a champagne
flight high over the city of Detroit, Harry Harlow glanced out of the airplane
window and "saw" an image of an artificial monkey mother. It was a hollow
wire cylinder, wrapped with a terry-cloth bath towel, with a silly wooden
30   head at the top. The tiny monkey could cling to this "model mother" as closely
as to its real mother's body hair. This surrogate mother could be provided
with a functional breast simply by placing a milk bottle so that the nipple
stuck through the cloth at an appropriate place on the surrogate's anatomy.
The cloth mother could be heated or cooled; it could be rocked mechanically
35   or made to stand still; and, most important, it could be removed at will.

While still sipping his champagne, Harlow mentally outlined much of the
research that kept him, his wife, and their associates occupied for many years
to come. And without realizing it, Harlow had shifted from studying monkey
learning to monkey love.

Infant-Mother Love

40   The chimpanzee or monkey infant is much more developed at birth than the
human infant, and apes develop or mature much faster than we do. Almost
from the moment it is born, the monkey infant can move around and hold
tightly to its mother. During the first few days of its life the infant will approach and cling to almost any large, warm, and soft object in its environ-
45   ment, particularly if that object also gives it milk. After a week or so, however, the monkey infant begins to avoid newcomers and focuses its attentions
on "mother"—real or surrogate.

During the first two weeks of its life warmth is perhaps the most important
psychological thing that a monkey mother has to give to its baby. The Har-

50 lows discovered this fact by offering infant monkeys a choice of two types of mother-substitutes—one wrapped in terry cloth and one that was made of bare wire. If the two artificial mothers were both the same temperature, the little monkeys always preferred the cloth mother. However, if the wire model was heated, while the cloth model was cool, for the first two weeks after birth

55 the baby primates picked the warm wire mother-substitutes as their favorites. Thereafter they switched and spent most of their time on the more comfortable cloth mother.

Why is cloth preferable to bare wire? Something that the Harlows called *contact comfort* seems to be the answer, and a most powerful influence it is. In-

60 fant monkeys (and chimps too) spend much of their time rubbing against their mothers' skins, putting themselves in as close contact with the parent as they can. Whenever the young animal is frightened, disturbed, or annoyed, it typically rushes to its mother and rubs itself against her body. Wire doesn't "rub" as well as does soft cloth. Prolonged "contact comfort" with a surrogate

65 cloth mother appears to instill confidence in baby monkeys and is much more rewarding to them than is either warmth or milk. Infant monkeys also prefer a "rocking" surrogate to one that is stationary.

According to the Harlows, the basic quality of an infant's love for its mother is *trust*. If the infant is put into an unfamiliar playroom without its mother, the

70 infant ignores the toys no matter how interesting they might be. It *screeches* in terror and curls up into a furry little ball. If its cloth mother is now introduced into the playroom, the infant rushes to the surrogate and clings to it for dear life. After a few minutes of contact comfort, it apparently begins to feel more secure. It then climbs down from the mother-substitute and begins tentatively

75 to explore the toys, but often rushes back for a deep embrace as if to reassure itself that its mother is still there and that all is well. Bit by bit its fears of the novel environment are "desensitized" and it spends more and more time playing with the toys and less and less time clinging to its "mother."

Good Mothers and Bad

The Harlows found that, once a baby monkey has come to accept its mother

80 (real or surrogate), the mother can do almost no wrong. In one of their studies, the Harlows tried to create "monster mothers" whose behavior would be so abnormal that the infants would desert the mothers. Their purpose was to determine whether maternal rejection might cause abnormal behavior patterns in the infant monkeys similar to those responses found in human babies whose

85 mothers ignore or punish their children severely. The problem was—how can you get a terry-cloth mother to reject or punish its baby? Their solutions were ingenious—but most of them failed in their main purpose. Four types of "monster mothers" were tried, but none of them was apparently "evil" enough to

90 impart fear or loathing to the infant monkeys. One such "monster" occasionally blasted its babies with compressed air; a second shook so violently that the baby often fell off; a third contained a catapult that frequently flung the infant away from it. The most evil-appearing of all had a set of metal spikes buried

beneath the terry cloth; from time to time the spikes would poke through the
95 cloth making it impossible for the infant to cling to the surrogate.

The baby monkeys brought up on the "monster mothers" did show a brief
period of emotional disturbance when the "wicked" temperament of the surrogates first showed up. The infants would cry for a time when displaced from
their mothers, but as soon as the surrogates returned to normal, the infant
100 would return to the surrogate and continue clinging, as if all were forgiven. As
the Harlows tell the story, the only prolonged distress created by the experiment seemed to be that felt by the experimenters!

There was, however, one type of surrogate that uniformly "turned off" the
infant monkeys. S. J. Suomi, working with the Harlows, built a terry-cloth
105 mother with ice water in its veins. Newborn monkeys would attach themselves to this "cool momma" for a brief period of time, but then retreated to a
corner of the cage and rejected her forever.

From their many brilliant studies, the Harlows conclude that the love of
an infant for its mother is *primarily a response to certain stimuli the mother of-*
110 *fers.* Warmth is the most important stimulus for the first two weeks of the
monkey's life, then contact comfort becomes paramount. Contact comfort is
determined by the softness and "rub-ability" of the surface of the mother's
body—terry cloth is better than are satin and silk, but all such materials are
more effective in creative love and trust than bare metal is. Food and mild
115 "shaking" or "rocking" are important too, but less so than warmth and contact comfort. These needs—and the rather primitive responses the infant
makes in order to obtain their satisfaction—are programmed into the monkey's genetic blueprint. The growing infant's requirement for social and intellectual stimulation becomes critical only later in a monkey's life. And yet,
120 if the baby primate is deprived of contact with other young of its own
species, its whole pattern of development can be profoundly disturbed.

Mother-Infant Love

The Harlows were eventually able to find ways of getting female isolates pregnant, usually by confining them in a small cage for long periods of time with a
patient and highly experienced normal male. At times, however, the Harlows
125 were forced to help matters along by strapping the female to a piece of apparatus. When these isolated females gave birth to their first monkey baby, they
turned out to be the "monster mothers" the Harlows had tried to create with
mechanical surrogates. Having had no contact with other animals as they
grew up, they simply did not know what to do with the furry little strangers
130 that suddenly appeared on the scene. These motherless mothers at first totally
ignored their children, although if the infant persisted, the mothers occasionally gave in and provided the baby with some of the contact and comfort it
demanded.

Surprisingly enough, once these mothers learned how to handle a baby,
135 they did reasonably well. Then, when they were again impregnated and gave
birth to a second infant, they took care of this next baby fairly adequately.

Maternal affection was totally lacking in a few of the motherless monkeys, however. To them the newborn monkey was little more than an object to be abused the way a human child might abuse a doll or a toy train. These moth-
140 erless mothers stepped on their babies, crushed the infant's face into the floor of the cage, and once or twice chewed off their baby's feet and fingers before they could be stopped. The most terrible mother of all popped her infant's head into her mouth and crunched it like a potato chip.

We tend to think of most mothers—no matter what their species—as hav-
145 ing some kind of almost divine "maternal instinct" that makes them love their children and take care of them no matter what the cost or circumstance. While it is true that most females have built into their genetic blueprint the tendency to be interested in (and to care for) their offspring, this inborn tendency is always expressed in a given environment. The "maternal instinct" is
150 strongly influenced by the mother's past experiences. Humans seem to have weaker instincts of all kinds than do other animals—since our behavior patterns are more affected by learning than by our genes, we have greater flexibility in what we do and become. But we pay a sometimes severe price for this freedom from genetic control.

155 Normal monkey and chimpanzee mothers seldom appear to inflict real physical harm on their children; human mothers and fathers often do. Serapio R. Zalba, writing in a journal called *Trans-action*, estimated in 1971 that in the United States alone, perhaps 250,000 children suffer physical abuse by their parents each year. Of these "battered babies," almost 40,000 may be
160 very badly injured. The number of young boys and girls killed by their parents annually is not known, but Zalba suggests that the figure may run into the thousands. Parents have locked their children in tiny cages, raised them in dark closets, burned them, boiled them, slashed them with knives, shot them, and broken almost every bone in their bodies. How can we reconcile these
165 facts with the much-discussed maternal and paternal "instincts"?

The research by the Harlows on the "motherless mothers" perhaps gives us a clue. Mother monkeys who were themselves socially deprived or isolated when young seemed singularly lacking in affection for their infants. Zalba states that most of the abusive human parents that were studied turned out to
170 have been abused and neglected *themselves* as children. Like the isolated monkeys who seemed unable to control their aggressive impulses when put in contact with normal animals, the abusive parents seem to be greatly deficient in what psychologists call "impulse control." Most of these parents also were described as being socially isolated, as having troubles adjusting to marriage,
175 often deeply in debt, and as being unable to build up warm and loving relationships with other people—including their own children. Since they did not learn how to love from their own parents, these mothers and fathers simply did not acquire the social skills necessary for bringing up their own infants in a healthy fashion.

STAGE 3: RECALL

Stop to self-test, relate, and react.
Your instructor may choose to give you a true-false comprehension review.

 MONKEY LOVE

Explain and give examples of findings from Harlow's experiment that you believe are applicable to human infants.
Response Suggestion: Describe the experimental finding and use examples to relate it to the psychological needs of human infants.

Contemporary Link

Why would many people be more accepting of medical research on mice than of psychological research on monkeys? Give specific examples to support your statement.

SKILL DEVELOPMENT: SUMMARIZING

Using this selection as a source, summarize on index cards the information that you might want to include in a research paper entitled "Animal Rights: Do Scientists Go Too Far?"

SKILL DEVELOPMENT: MAIN IDEA

Answer with *T* (true) or *F* (false).

_____ 1. The main point of the first four paragraphs is that Harlow's shift to studying monkey love occurred by accident.

_____ 2. In the second section titled "Infant-Mother Love," the main point is that an infant monkey needs the "contact comfort" of the mother to give it a feeling of security while interacting with the environment.

_____ 3. In the beginning of the section titled "Good Mothers and Bad," the main point is that baby monkeys will reject monster mothers.

_____ 4. In the beginning of the section titled "Mother-Infant Love," the main point is that the maternal instinct is not influenced by the mother's past experiences.

_____ 5. The author's overall pattern of organization for this selection is comparison-contrast.

COMPREHENSION QUESTIONS

Main Idea   1. Who or what is the topic? _____

What is the main idea the author is trying to convey about the topic?

_____

_____

After reading the selection, answer the following questions with *a, b, c,* or *d.*

Inference   _____ 2. When Harry Harlow originally started his experiments with monkeys, his purpose was to study
a. love.
b. breeding.
c. learning.
d. disease.

Inference   _____ 3. The reason that the author mentions Harry Harlow's revelations on the airplane is to show
a. that he had extrasensory perception.
b. that he liked to travel.
c. that he was always thinking of his work.
d. in what an unexpected way brilliant work often starts.

Details   _____ 4. In his experiments Harlow used all of the following in designing his surrogate mothers except
a. a terry-cloth bath towel.
b. real body hair.
c. a rocking movement.
d. temperature controls.

Details   _____ 5. Harlow manipulated his experiments to show the early significance of warmth by
a. heating wire.
b. changing from satin to terry cloth.
c. equalizing temperature.
d. creating "monster mothers."

Inference   _____ 6. Harlow feels that for contact comfort the cloth mother was preferable to the wire mother for all of the following reasons except
a. the cloth mother instilled confidence.
b. the wire mother didn't "rub" as well.
c. the wire mother was stationary.
d. with the cloth mother, the infant felt a greater sense of security when upset.

Details _____ 7. Harlow's studies show that when abused by its mother, the infant will
   a. leave the mother.
   b. seek a new mother.
   c. return to the mother.
   d. fight with the mother.

Details _____ 8. For an infant to love its mother, Harlow's studies show that in the first two weeks the most important element is
   a. milk.
   b. warmth.
   c. contact comfort.
   d. love expressed by the mother.

Inference _____ 9. In Harlow's studies with motherless monkeys, he showed that the techniques of mothering are
   a. instinctive.
   b. learned.
   c. inborn.
   d. natural.

Inference _____ 10. The Harlows feel that child abuse is caused by all of the following problems except
   a. parents who were abused as children.
   b. socially isolated parents.
   c. parents who cannot control their impulses.
   d. parents who are instinctively evil.

Answer the following with *T* (true) or *F* (false).

_____ 11. The author feels that love in infant monkeys has a great deal of similarity to love in human children.
_____ 12. The author implies that isolated monkeys have difficulty engaging in normal peer relationships.
_____ 13. After learning how to handle the first baby, many motherless mothers became better parents with the second infant.
_____ 14. Zalba's studies support many of the findings of the Harlow studies.
_____ 15. Harlow had initially planned to perform drug experiments on the monkeys.

VOCABULARY

According to the way the italicized word was used in the selection, indicate *a*, *b*, *c*, or *d* for the word or phrase that gives the best definition.

_____ 1. "the *surrogate* mother" (23)
  a. mean
  b. thoughtless
  c. loving
  d. substitute

_____ 2. "a *functional* breast" (32)
  a. mechanical
  b. operational
  c. wholesome
  d. imitation

_____ 3. "on the surrogate's *anatomy*" (33)
  a. body
  b. head
  c. offspring
  d. personality

_____ 4. "begins *tentatively* to explore" (74–75)
  a. rapidly
  b. hesitantly
  c. aggressively
  d. readily

_____ 5. "fears of the *novel* environ-ment" (76–77)
  a. hostile
  b. literary
  c. dangerous
  d. new

_____ 6. "fears . . . are *desensitized*" (77)
  a. made less sensitive
  b. made more sensitive
  c. electrified
  d. communicated

_____ 7. "solutions were *ingenious*" (86–87)
  a. incorrect
  b. noble
  c. clever
  d. honest

_____ 8. "*deprived* of contact" (120)
  a. encouraged
  b. denied
  c. assured
  d. ordered into

_____ 9. "if the infant *persisted*" (131)
  a. stopped
  b. continued
  c. fought
  d. relaxed

_____ 10. "to be greatly *deficient*" (172)
  a. lacking
  b. supplied
  c. overwhelmed
  d. secretive

SEARCH THE NET

Conduct a search on the causes of child abuse. List some risk factors of children, parents, and the family environment that are related to child abuse. Reference your Websites.

Plan your own search or begin by trying the following:

http://www.os.dhhs.gov/

CONTEMPORARY FOCUS

Imagine being a successful black entrepreneur and feeling that you had to hide your identity in order to do business.

BLACK ENTREPRENEURS FACE A PERPLEXING ISSUE: HOW TO PITCH TO WHITES

Angelo B. Henderson

The Wall Street Journal, January 26, 1999, p. 1

When suburban clients close a deal with First Impressions Inc., they will probably shake hands with William Ashley or someone else who is white, although Eric Giles, who is African-American, did the client research, helped develop the sales strategy and made initial telephone contact for this restaurant and food-service employment agency.

"Unfortunately, in the end I can't send him out as the person who does the face-to-face and gets the deal signed," says Judy Y. Wiles, owner of Detroit-based First Impressions.

This might raise eyebrows about Ms. Wiles's own racial attitudes—except she is black herself. She says she has "unwavering confidence" in Mr. Giles. Ultimately, though, both worry that their success and even survival is based on what their company name suggests: first impressions. And in a business where restaurants, hotels and party givers can choose any number of white companies to supply bartenders, waiters, chefs and other restaurant personnel, First Impressions can't afford to lose a contract because some clients may hold preconceived notions about blacks.

Says Ms. Wiles, who is convinced that, over the years, she has lost as many as 20 jobs because of this very issue: "It's that fear that encourages me to use Bill or (another) front person."

The fear of this black entrepreneur, though some argue it is overblown, is one nonetheless often shared by other African-American businesspeople who cater to a largely white clientele. "I don't *have* to be seen," says La-Van Hawkins, a successful black Pizza Hut franchisee who, in the spirit of Ms. Wiles, uses a white alter ego to handle much of his suburban marketing.

Some think the times are changing, pointing to the phenomenal marketing success of basketball superstar Michael Jordan, who moves huge amounts of goods and services for white-owned companies, and, tangetially, the crossover appeal of black celebrities such as Will Smith and Denzel Washington with white audiences.

Collaborative Activity

Collaborate on responses to the following questions:

- What are the moral objections to concealing your ethnic identity in order to be successful in business?
- Would you be willing to give your company an ethnic portrayal that is not your own? Why or why not?
- What positive and negative aspects of civil rights issues does this dilemma of the black entrepreneurs suggest?

SKILL DEVELOPMENT—STAGE 1: PREVIEW

Preview the next selection to predict the purpose, organization, and your learning plan.

Who are some of the Civil Rights heroes mentioned?

When did the Civil Rights movement begin?

Activate Schema

How did Martin Luther King, Jr., die?

Who was Cesar Chavez and what was his cause?

Learning Strategy

Formulate a time line listing each leader's contribution to the Civil Rights Movement.

Word Knowledge

What do you know about these words?

ensuing	sprawling	acrimony	scathing	pacifists
revived	massive	futile	protracted	filibuster

Your instructor may give a true-false vocabulary review before or after reading.

STAGE 2: INTEGRATE KNOWLEDGE WHILE READING

Predict   Picture   Relate   Monitor   Correct

Rosa Parks receives the Presidential Medal of Freedom from Bill Clinton in 1996.

HEROES FOR CIVIL RIGHTS

From James Martin et al., *America and Its People*

On a cold afternoon in Montgomery, Alabama, Rosa Parks, a well-respected black seamstress, who was active in the NAACP, took a significant stride toward equality. She boarded a bus and sat in the first row of the "colored" section. The white section of the bus
5 quickly filled, and according to Jim Crow rules, blacks were expected to give up their seats rather than force whites—male or female—to stand. The time came for Mrs. Parks to give up her seat. She stayed seated. When told by the bus driver to get up or he would call the police, she said, "You may do that." Later she recalled that the act of defiance

10 was "just something I had to do." The bus stopped, the driver summoned the
police, and Rosa Parks was arrested.

Black Montgomery rallied to Mrs. Parks's side. Like her, they were tired of
riding in the back of the bus, tired of giving up their seats to whites, tired of
having their lives restricted by Jim Crow. Local black leaders decided to orga-
15 nize a boycott of Montgomery's white-owned and white-operated bus system. They hoped that economic pressure would force changes which court
decisions could not. For the next 381 days, more than ninety percent of
Montgomery's black citizens participated in an heroic and successful demonstration against racial segregation. The common black attitude toward the
20 protest was voiced by an elderly black woman when a black leader offered her
a ride. "No," she replied, "my feets is tired, but my soul is rested."

To lead the boycott, Montgomery blacks turned to the new minister of the
Dexter Avenue Baptist Church, a young man named Martin Luther King, Jr.
Reared in Atlanta, the son of a respected and financially secure minister, King
25 had been educated at Morehouse College, Crozier Seminary, and Boston Uni-
versity, from which he earned a doctorate in theology. King was an intellec-
tual, excited by ideas and deeply influenced by the philosophical writings of
Henry David Thoreau and Mahatma Gandhi as well as the teachings of
Christ. They believed in the power of nonviolent, direct action.
30 King's words as well as his ideas stirred people's souls. At the start of the
Montgomery boycott he told his followers:

> There comes a time when people get tired. We are here this evening to say to
> those who have mistreated us so long that we are tired—tired of being segregated
> and humiliated, tired of being kicked about by the brutal feet of oppression. . . .
> We've come here tonight to be saved from the patience that makes us patient
> with anything less than freedom and justice. . . . If you protest courageously and
> yet with dignity and Christian love, in the history books that are written in future
> generations, historians will have to pause and say "there lived a great people—a
> black people—who injected a new meaning and dignity into the veins of civilization."

Dr. Martin Luther King, Jr., gave voice to the new mood: "We're through
with tokenism and gradualism and see-how-far-you've-comeism. We're
through with we've-done-more-for-your-people-than-anyone-else-ism. We
35 can't wait any longer. Now is the time."

Sit-ins

On Monday, February 1, 1960, four black freshmen at North Carolina Agricultural and Technical College—Ezell Blair, Jr., Franklin McClain, Joseph McNeill,
and David Richmond—walked into the F. W. Woolworth store in Greensboro,
North Carolina, and sat down at the lunch counter. They asked for a cup of cof-
40 fee. A waitress told them that she would only serve them if they stood.

Instead of walking away, the four college freshmen stayed in their seats until the lunch counter closed. The next morning, the four college students
reappeared at Woolworth's accompanied by twenty-five fellow students. On

Wednesday, student protesters filled sixty-three of the lunch counter's sixty-
45 six seats. The sit-in movement had begun.

In April, 142 student sit-in leaders from eleven states met in Raleigh,
North Carolina, and voted to set up a new group to coordinate the sit-ins, the
Student Non-Violent Coordinating Committee (SNCC). Martin Luther King
told the students that their willingness to go to jail would "be the thing to
50 awaken the dozing conscience of many of our white brothers." The president
of Fisk University echoed King's judgment: "This is no student panty raid. It is
a dedicated universal effort, and it has cemented the Negro community as it
has never been cemented before."

College Registration

Civil rights activists' next major aim was to open state universities to black
55 students. Although many southern states opened their universities to black
students without incident, others were stiff-backed in their opposition to integration. A major breakthrough occurred in September 1962, when a federal
court ordered the state of Mississippi to admit James Meredith—a nine-year
veteran of the Air Force—to the University of Mississippi in Oxford. Ross Bar-
60 nett, the state's governor, promised on statewide television that he would "not
surrender to the evil and illegal forces of tyranny" and would go to jail rather
than permit Meredith to register for classes. Barnett flew into Oxford, named
himself special registrar of the university, and ordered the arrest of federal officials who tried to enforce the court order.

65 James Meredith refused to back down. A "man with a mission and a nervous
stomach," Meredith was determined to get a higher education. "I want to go to
the university," he said. "This is the life I want. Just to live and breathe—that isn't
life to me. There's got to be something more." Meredith arrived at the campus in
the company of police officers, federal marshals, and lawyers. Angry white stu-
70 dents waited, chanting, "Two, four, six, eight—we don't want to integrate."

Four times James Meredith tried unsuccessfully to register. He finally succeeded on the fifth try, escorted by several hundred federal marshals. The ensuing riot left two people dead and 375 injured, including 166 marshals. Ultimately, President Kennedy sent 16,000 troops to put down the violence.

"Boomingham"

75 It was in Birmingham, Alabama, that civil rights activists faced the most determined resistance. A sprawling steel town of 340,000 known as the "Pittsburgh of the South," Birmingham had a long history of racial acrimony.

Day after day, well dressed and neatly groomed men, women and children
marched against segregation—only to be jailed for demonstrating without a
80 permit. On April 12, King himself was arrested—and while in jail wrote a
scathing attack on those who asked black Americans to wait patiently for
equal rights. A group of white clergymen had publicly criticized King for stag-
ing "unwise and untimely" demonstrations.

© 2000 Addison-Wesley Educational Publishers, Inc.

For two weeks, all was quiet, but in early May demonstrations resumed with
85 renewed vigor. On May 2 and again on May 3, more than a thousand of Birmingham's black children marched for equal rights. In response, Birmingham's police
chief, Theophilus Eugene "Bull" Connor, unleashed police dogs on the children
and sprayed them with 700 pounds of water pressure—shocking the nation's conscience. Tension mounted as police arrested 2,543 blacks and whites between
90 May 2 and May 7, 1963. Under intense criticism, the Birmingham Chamber of
Commerce reached an agreement on May 9 with black leaders to desegregate
public facilities in ninety days, hire blacks as clerks and salespersons in sixty days,
and release demonstrators without bail in return for an end to the protests.

The March on Washington

The violence that erupted in Birmingham and elsewhere in 1961 and 1962
95 alarmed many veteran civil rights leaders. In December 1962, two veteran
fighters for civil rights—A. Philip Randolph and Bayard Rustin—met at the
office of the Brotherhood of Sleeping Car Porters in Harlem. Both men were
pacifists, eager to rededicate the civil rights movement to the principle of
nonviolence. Both men wanted to promote passage of Kennedy's civil rights
100 bill, school desegregation, federal job training programs, and a ban on job discrimination. Thirty-two years before, Randolph had threatened to lead a
march on Washington unless the federal government ended job discrimination against black workers in war industries. Now Rustin revived the idea of a
massive march for civil rights and jobs.
105   On August 28, 1963, more than 200,000 people gathered around the
Washington Monument and marched eight-tenths of a mile to the Lincoln
Memorial. As they walked, the marchers carried placards reading: "Effective
Civil Rights Laws—Now! Integrated Schools—Now! Decent Housing—
Now!" and sang the civil rights anthem, "We Shall Overcome."

The Civil Rights Act of 1964

110 For seven months, debate raged in the halls of Congress. In a futile effort to
delay the Civil Rights Bill's passage, opponents proposed more than 500
amendments and staged a protracted filibuster in the Senate. On July 2,
1964—a year and a day after President Kennedy had sent it to Congress—
the Civil Rights Act was enacted into law. As finally passed, the act prohib-
115 ited discrimination in voting, employment, and public facilities such as hotels and restaurants, and it established the Equal Employment Opportunity
Commission (EEOC) to prevent discrimination in employment on the basis of race, religion, or sex. Ironically, the provision barring sex discrimination had been added by opponents of the civil rights act in an attempt to
120 kill the bill.

STAGE 3: RECALL

Stop to self-test, relate, and react.

Your instructor may choose to give you a true-false comprehension review.

*Thinking
About*   HEROES FOR CIVIL RIGHTS

People and events in history are important for their cause-and-effect relationship to other people and other events. Explain the importance of three of the people or events in this selection in terms of historical cause-and-effect significance.

Contemporary Link

How do black entrepreneurs who conceal their identity differ philosophically from the civil rights heroes such as Rosa Parks and Dr. Martin Luther King, Jr.?

SKILL DEVELOPMENT: ORGANIZATION

Answer the following with *T* (true) or *F* (false).

_____ 1. The overall pattern or organization is comparison-contrast.

_____ 2. The main point of the section titled "Sit-ins" is that college students became involved in the integration of lunch counters.

_____ 3. By beginning the first paragraph with Rosa Parks, the author suggests that her actions precipitated the sequence of events.

_____ 4. The passage creates a cause-and-effect relationship for the Civil Rights Act of 1964.

_____ 5. The main idea of the section entitled "Boomingham" is that the city was known as the "Pittsburgh of the South."

Time line: Starting with Rosa Parks, make a time line of the major events and heroes leading to the Civil Rights Act of 1964.

COMPREHENSION QUESTIONS

After reading the selection, answer the following questions with *a, b, c,* or *d.*

Main Idea   _____ 1. The best statement of the main idea of this selection is
a. Rosa Parks began the Civil Rights movement.
b. Many heroes protested discrimination and fought for equality and civil rights.
c. The Civil Rights Act was passed by Congress in 1964.
d. Martin Luther King, Jr., began his career by leading the boycott in Montgomery, Alabama.

Detail   _____   2. Rosa Parks's protest was that
                               a. she would not get off the bus.
                               b. she sat in the section reserved for whites.
                               c. she would not give up her seat to a white.
                               d. she refused to sit down on the bus.

Inference   _____   3. The force that would ultimately make the boycott of the
                               Montgomery bus system successful was
                               a. economic pressure.
                               b. religious fervor.
                               c. the good will of the people of Alabama.
                               d. violence against oppressors.

Inference   _____   4. The purpose of the words quoted from the speech made by
                               Martin Luther King, Jr., at the beginning of the Mont-
                               gomery boycott was
                               a. to explain the nonviolent tactics of Gandhi.
                               b. to inspire the protesters with pride.
                               c. to honor Rosa Parks and other brave protesters.
                               d. to call for Congress to pass the Civil Rights Act.

Detail   _____   5. All of the following are true of the "sit-ins" except
                               a. they started in Greensboro, North Carolina.
                               b. the protesters were primarily students.
                               c. the protesters needed to be willing to go to jail.
                               d. the first protesters were freshmen at Fisk University.

Detail   _____   6. To prevent James Meredith from enrolling in the University
                               of Mississippi,
                               a. the President sent troops.
                               b. several hundred federal marshals escorted Meredith.
                               c. a federal court order was issued.
                               d. the state governor became registrar of the university.

Detail   _____   7. In Birmingham, civil rights activists were typically jailed for
                               a. disorderly conduct.
                               b. demonstrating without a permit.
                               c. trespassing on private property.
                               d. aggression against police.

Inference   _____   8. The author suggests that the protest that most shocked the
                               nation and ignited national support for civil rights was
                               a. the children's march in Birmingham.
                               b. the Woolworth's sit-in.
                               c. James Meredith's college registration.
                               d. the Montgomery bus boycott.

Detail   _____ 9. The Civil Rights Act of 1964 contained all of the following
                             except
                             a. equal employment opportunities for women.
                             b. integration of hotels.
                             c. prohibitions on voting discrimination.
                             d. higher wage guarantees for black workers.

Inference   _____ 10. The author suggests that the 1963 march on Washington
                             a. was a long and arduous walk through many southern
                                cities.
                             b. turned violent as the crowds swelled.
                             c. put pressure on Congress to pass civil rights legislation.
                             d. was attended by more whites than blacks.

               Answer the following with *T* (true) or *F* (false).

                  _____ 11. James Meredith was the first black student to attend a
                             southern university.
                  _____ 12. The Montgomery bus boycott lasted for over a year.
                  _____ 13. Bull Connor was governor of Alabama.
                  _____ 14. The author suggests that Kennedy was against the Civil
                             Rights Act.
                  _____ 15. The author suggests that Randolph and Rustin were southern-
                             ers who had previously participated in sit-in demonstrations.

VOCABULARY

According to the way the italicized word was used in the selection, select *a*, *b*,
c, or *d* for the word or phrase that gives the best definition.

_____ 1. "The *ensuing* riot" (72–73)
    a. brutal
    b. speedy
    c. resulting
    d. dangerous

_____ 4. "a *scathing* attack" (81)
    a. timely
    b. stinging
    c. lengthy
    d. publicized

_____ 2. "A *sprawling* town" (76)
    a. spread out
    b. ugly
    c. dirty
    d. unfriendly

_____ 5. "men were *pacifists*" (97–98)
    a. opponents of violence
    b. militants
    c. advocates for arms
    d. religious dissidents

_____ 3. "racial *acrimony*" (77)
    a. incidents
    b. alliances
    c. allegations
    d. animosity

_____ 6. "*revived* the idea" (103)
    a. created
    b. rekindled
    c. argued
    d. verified

_____ 7. "a *massive* march" (104)
    a. enormous
    b. forceful
    c. uncontrolled
    d. spontaneous

_____ 8. "In a *futile* effort" (110)
    a. last chance
    b. angry
    c. hopeful
    d. ineffectual

_____ 9. "a *protracted* filibuster" (112)
    a. short
    b. prolonged
    c. relentless
    d. merciless

_____ 10. "a protracted *filibuster*" (112)
    a. sit-in demonstration
    b. drama
    c. legislative delay tactic
    d. committee meeting

SEARCH THE NET

Conduct a search to find museums that house exhibits on heroes or events related to the Civil Rights movement. Describe the focus and central attraction of each museum. Reference your Websites.

    Plan your own search or begin by trying the following:

http://www.civilrightsmuseum.org   Civil Rights Museum

http://www.src.wl.com/index.htm   Southern Regional Council

CONTEMPORARY FOCUS

What happens when natural predators do not exist for animal and plants in an environment? What is needed to return balance to such an environment, and are we willing to pay the price?

DEATH IN VENISON

Geoffrey Norman

The American Spectator, February 1997, pp. 32–35

There's a Bambi crisis in America. White-tail deer are more numerous than ever before—so abundant, in fact, that they've become a suburban nuisance and a health hazard. Why can't the herd be thinned the old-fashioned way?

The small community of North Haven on Long Island is home to some 600–700 deer. The Department of Environmental Conservation estimates the optimum population at 60. The town has been browsed bare of vegetation, except where gardens and shrubs are protected by high fences. Drivers routinely collide with deer, and there are so many carcasses left by the side of the road that the town has made a deal with a local pet cemetery to collect and dispose of the bodies. Some people in the town have had two or three bouts of Lyme disease.

On the occasions when hunting has been tried, local animal-rights people have worked to secure injunctions against the hunts—and when that has failed, they stalked the hunters, banging on pots and pans to alert the deer. Town meetings called to discuss the problem inevitably dissolved into acrimony. The activists believe, simply, that the deer are not the problem.

Some communities have even discussed the possibility of bringing wolves back into the ecological mix. [That means] wolves, in the suburbs of Washington and New York? It is almost too wonderful not to try it. The wolves would kill deer, of course. They would also terrorize and kill dogs and cats which is not, one suspects, what the suburbanites have in mind.

For people who hunt, there is a kind of primitive joy in being the top predator. For those who despise hunting, there is a kind of wonderful righteousness in standing up for innocent life. These are views that are fundamentally, almost theologically, in opposition.

Collaborative Activity

Collaborate on responses to the following questions:

- What factors have contributed to the ecological problem of deer overpopulation?
- Do you believe in hunting and killing the deer?
- What suggestions would you have for solving the deer problem?

SKILL DEVELOPMENT—STAGE 1: PREVIEW

The author probably describes ecological problems. ☐ Agree ☐ Disagree

After reading this selection, I will need to know how to kill kudzu.

Agree ☐ Disagree ☐

Activate Schema

What do you recall about rabbits in Australia from a previous passage in this chapter?

What are your feelings about environmentalists obstructing development because of an endangered species?

Learning Strategy

Seek to understand the chain of events in each ecological example.

Word Knowledge

What do you know about these words?

extinct	precarious	disastrous	plummeted	warrens
fumigated	droves	herbivores	indiscriminate	exasperated

Your instructor may give a true-false vocabulary review before or after reading.

STAGE 2: INTEGRATE KNOWLEDGE WHILE READING

Predict   Picture   Relate   Monitor   Correct

NILE PERCH AND RABBITS AND KUDZU, OH MY!

From Cecie Starr and Ralph Taggart, *Biology: The Unity and Diversity of Life, 8th ed.*

Natives fish at the shore of Lake Victoria.

When you hear someone bubbling enthusiastically about an **exotic species**, you can safely bet the speaker is not an ecologist. This is a name for a resident of an established community that has moved from its home range and successfully taken up residence elsewhere. It makes 5 no difference whether the importation was deliberate or accidental. Unlike most imports, which cannot take hold outside their home range, an exotic species insinuates itself into the new community. Occasionally the addition is harmless and even has beneficial effects. However, of all the native species that are on rare or endangered lists or have already become extinct, *almost 70* 10 *percent owe their precarious existence or demise to displacement by exotic species.* Consider a few of the more spectacular cases.

Hello Victoria, Good-bye Cichlids

Finding better ways to manage our food supplies is essential, given the astounding growth rate of the human population. Such efforts are well intentioned, but they can have disastrous consequences when ecological principles
15   are not taken into account. For example, several years ago, someone thought it would be a great idea to introduce the Nile perch into Lake Victoria in East Africa. People had been using simple, traditional methods of fishing there for thousands of years. Now they were taking too many fish. Soon there would be too few fish to feed the local populations and no excess catches to sell for
20   profit. But Lake Victoria is a very big lake, and the Nile perch is a very big fish (more than 2 meters long). A big fish in a big lake seemed an ideal combination to attract commercial fishermen from the outside world, with their big, elaborate nets—right? Wrong.

Native fishermen had been harvesting native fishes called cichlids, which
25   eat mostly detritus and aquatic plants. The Nile perch eats other fish—including cichlids. Having had no prior evolutionary experience with the new predator, the 200 coexisting species of cichlids that were native to Lake Victoria had no defenses against it.

And so the Nile perch ate its way through the cichlid populations and de-
30   stroyed the lake's biodiversity. Dozens of cichlid species found nowhere else are extinct. Without the cichlids to clean up the lake bottom, levels of dissolved oxygen plummeted and contributed to frequent fish kills. By 1990, fishermen were catching mostly Nile perch. And now there are signs the Nile perch population is about to crash. By destroying its food source, the Nile
35   perch has undercut its own population growth. It has ceased to be a potentially large, exploitable food source for the people who live around the lake.

As if that weren't enough, the Nile perch is an oily fish. Unlike cichlids, which can be sun dried, the Nile perch must be preserved by smoking—and smoking requires firewood. The local people started cutting down more trees
40   in the local forests, and trees are not rapidly renewable resources. To add insult to injury, the people living near Lake Victoria never liked to eat Nile perch anyway. They prefer the flavor and texture of cichlids.

What is the lesson? A little knowledge and some simple experiments in a contained setting could have prevented the whole mess at Lake Victoria.

The Rabbits That Ate Australia

45   During the 1800s, British settlers in Australia just couldn't bond with koalas and kangaroos, so they started to import familiar animals from their homeland. In 1859, in what would be the start of a wholesale disaster, a landowner in northern Australia imported and released two dozen wild European rabbits (*Oryctolagus cuniculus*). Good food and good sport hunting, that was the idea.
50   An ideal rabbit habitat with no natural predators—that was the reality.

Six years later, the landowner had killed 20,000 rabbits and was besieged by 20,000 more. The rabbits displaced livestock, even the kangaroos. And

The fence did not prevent rabbits from destroying Australia's vegetation.

now Australia has 200 million to 300 million rabbits hippityhopping through the southern half of the country. They overgraze perennial grasses in good times and strip bark from shrubs and trees during droughts. You know where they've been; they transform grasslands and shrublands into eroded moonscapes or deserts.

Rabbits have been shot and poisoned. Their warrens have been plowed under, fumigated, and dynamited. Even when all-out assaults reduced their population size by 70 percent, the rapidly reproducing imports made a comeback in a year. And did the construction of a 2,000-mile-long fence protect western Australia? No. Rabbits made it to the other side before workers completed the fence.

In 1951, government researchers introduced the myxoma virus by way of mildly infected South American rabbits, its normal hosts. The virus causes *myxomatosis*. This disease has mild effects on the South American rabbits that coevolved with the virus, but it nearly always had lethal effects on *O. cuniculus*. Biting insects, mainly mosquitoes and fleas, quickly transmit the virus from host to host. With no coevolved defenses against the virus, the European rabbits died in droves.

As you might expect, however, natural selection has favored the rapid growth of *O. cuniculus* populations that are resistant to the virus.

In 1991, on an uninhabited island in Spencer Gulf, Australian researchers released a population of rabbits that they had injected with a calicivirus. The rabbits died quickly and relatively painlessly from blood clots in their lungs,

heart, and kidneys. In 1995, the test virus escaped from the island, maybe on insect vectors. It has been killing between 80 and 95 percent of the adult rabbits in various parts of Australia. At this writing, researchers are questioning whether the calicivirus should be used on a widespread scale, whether it can
80 jump boundaries and infect animals other than rabbits (such as humans), and what the long-term consequences will be.

Meanwhile, the Anti-Rabbit Research Foundation of Australia would very much like to get rid of the cult of the Easter Bunny. Their replacement candidate is the Easter Bilby, the bilby being a marsupial that evolved in Australia,
85 that does not reproduce nearly as rapidly as O. *cuniculus*, and that does not blitz the countryside.

The Plant That Ate Georgia

Imported animals and pathogens are not the only sources of ecological disaster. Consider the vine called kudzu (*Pueraria lobata*). Kudzu was deliberately brought over from Japan to the United States, where it faces no serious
90 threats from herbivores, pathogens, or competitor plants.

In temperate regions of Asia, kudzu is a well-behaved legume with a well-developed root system. Somehow, it *seemed* like a good idea to import it and use it for erosion control on hillsides and near highways in the southeastern United States. However, with nothing to stop it, kudzu's shoots
95 grow one-third of a meter (1 foot) per day. Vines now blanket streambanks, trees, telephone poles, houses, hills, and almost everything else in its path. Attempts to dig them up or burn them do no good. Grazing goats and herbicides can make a dent, but goats are indiscriminate eaters and herbicides can contaminate water supplies. Someone, obviously exasperated
100 with the menace, dubbed kudzu "the plant that ate Georgia." If the global temperature continues to rise, kudzu could reach the Great Lakes by the year 2040.

On the bright side, a Japanese firm is constructing a kudzu farm and processing plant in Alabama. Asians use a starch extract from kudzu in beverages,
105 candy, and herbal medicines. The idea is to export the starch to Asia, where the demand currently exceeds the supply. (And perhaps this gives new meaning to the expression, What comes around, goes around.) Also, kudzu might eventually help reduce the extent of logging operations. At the Georgia Institute of Technology, researchers have reported that kudzu may be useful as an
110 alternative source of paper.

STAGE 3: RECALL

Stop to self-test, relate, and react.

Your instructor may choose to give you a true-false comprehension review.

SKILL DEVELOPMENT: MAIN IDEA

Answer the following with *T* (true) or *F* (false).

    _____ 1. The main idea is stated in the first sentence of the passage.

    _____ 2. The overall organization of the selection is comparison and contrast.

    _____ 3. The information in each of the three sections, about the Nile perch, the rabbits, and the kudzu, is organized in a cause-and-effect pattern.

    _____ 4. The selection concludes with a summary sentence.

    _____ 5. The fact that Nile perch can grow more than 2 meters long is a major detail.

 NILE PERCH AND RABBITS AND KUDZU, OH MY!

Diagram the ecological chain of events that is described in the three examples in this selection: (1) the Nile perch in Lake Victoria, (2) the rabbits in Australia, and (3) the kudzu in the southeastern United States. Make a prediction of the next event in each case.

Contemporary Link

How do the origin and the psychological aspects of the solution to the white-tail deer dilemma differ from the origins and solutions to the perch, rabbits, and kudzu problems?

COMPREHENSION QUESTIONS

After reading the selection, answer the following questions with *a, b, c,* or *d.*

Main Idea   _____ 1. The best statement of the main idea of this selection is
a. an exotic species is the name for a resident of an established community that has been introduced into a new environment.
b. importing an exotic species into a new environment can produce disastrous consequences to the ecology of the area.
c. the introduction of the Nile perch into Lake Victoria destroyed the ecological balance of the lake.
d. animals that are taken out of their natural habitat are put in danger of extinction.

Detail _____ 2. The Nile perch was introduced into Lake Victoria
  a. to clean up the lake.
  b. to attract commercial fishermen.
  c. to control the growth of detritus.
  d. to discourage the use of nets for fishing.

Detail _____ 3. The introduction of the Nile perch into Lake Victoria
  caused the destruction of all of the following except
  a. cichlids.
  b. detritus.
  c. local forests.
  d. the oxygen balance of Lake Victoria.

Inference _____ 4. The author suggests that thus far the most promising
  method for reducing the rabbit population in Australia is
  a. fumigation.
  b. the 2,000-mile fence.
  c. the myxoma virus.
  d. the calicivirus.

Detail _____ 5. The initial difference between the South American rabbits
  and the O. *cuniculus* was that the South American rabbits
  a. did not reproduce nearly as quickly as O. *cuniculus*.
  b. could survive with the myxoma virus and O. *cuniculus*
     could not.
  c. were more susceptible to the calicivirus.
  d. coevolved with the myxoma virus after the O. *cuniculus*.

Inference _____ 6. In the sentence beginning with "Somehow, it *seemed* like a
  good idea to import it and use it for erosion . . ." the author
  suggests that
  a. plants rather than concrete should be used for erosion.
  b. the nation's worst erosion is in the southeastern United
     States.
  c. the southeastern United States is a temperate region simi-
     lar to Asia.
  d. it was a bad idea.

Inference _____ 7. The author suggests that kudzu is controlled in Asia by
  a. competitor plants.
  b. herbicides.
  c. temperature.
  d. pathogens.

Inference _____ 8. The author suggests that the primary position of the Anti-
  Rabbit Research Foundation on the myth of an Easter Bunny
  is that it
  a. glorifies a destructive pest.
  b. fails to consider the cultural diversity of Australia.

      c. slows the government research to control the rabbit
          population.
      d. contributes to the rapid reproduction rate of rabbits.

Inference   _____   9. An environmental problem that needed a solution was the
      primary purpose for the introduction of
      a. Nile perch in Lake Victoria.
      b. rabbits in Australia.
      c. kudzu in the South.
      d. both the Nile perch and the rabbits.

Detail   _____   10. All of the following are true about kudzu except
      a. it can be made into a starch extract.
      b. it grows up to 1 foot per day.
      c. it can be eradicated by burning the vegetation.
      d. goats will eat it.

Answer the following with *T* (true) or *F* (false).

Detail   _____ 11. The Nile perch destroyed the biodiversity of Lake Victoria
      by eating the cichlids that cleaned the lake bottom, thus
      maintaining a healthy level of dissolved oxygen.

Inference   _____ 12. The author suggests that oily fish need a more intense heat
      than sunshine for preserving.

Inference   _____ 13. The attitude of the author in this selection is both serious
      and humorous.

Detail   _____ 14. Rabbits injected with the calicivirus were taken by re-
      searchers from an island in Spencer Gulf and placed on the
      mainland to infect other rabbits.

Detail   _____ 15. Almost 70 percent of endangered species are classified as
      exotic.

VOCABULARY

According to the way the italicized word was used in the selection, select *a*, *b*,
c, or *d* for the word or phrase that gives the best definition.

_____ 1. "become *extinct*" (9)
     a. extinguished
     b. diseased
     c. sparse
     d. coevolving

_____ 2. "their *precarious* existence"
     (10)
     a. safe
     b. uncertain
     c. stable
     d. unknown

_____ 3. "*disastrou* consequences" (14)
    a. pred table
    b. har ful
    c. cc fusing
    d. v eventful

_____ 4. "dis olved oxygen *plummeted*" (3 -32)
    a divided
    . dropped
    c. rose
    d. equalized

_____ 5. "*warrens* have been plowed under" (58–59)
    a. bodies
    b. nests
    c. mates
    d. food storage places

_____ 6. "*fumigated* and dynamited" (59)
    a. to burn
    b. to treat chemically
    c. to inject
    d. to purify

_____ 7. "died in *droves*" (69–70)
    a. fits
    b. experiments
    c. agony
    d. herds

_____ 8. "threats from *herbivores*" (90)
    a. weed killer
    b. plant diseases
    c. plant eaters
    d. meat eaters

_____ 9. "*indiscriminate* eaters" (98)
    a. not choosy
    b. voracious
    c. ceaseless
    d. picky

_____10. "*exasperated* with the menace" (99–100)
    a. frightened
    b. angered
    c. repulsed
    d. euphoric

SEARCH THE NET

Conduct a search on exotic species and their impact on the environment. Choose from the following:

Describe two exotic invaders in your geographic region, or describe two exotic species introduced into the Great Lakes region. Explain the environmental consequences of each.

Describe the history of kudzu, the environmental consequences, and the future possibilities for the plant.

Plan your own search or begin by trying the following:

http://www.great-lakes.net

http://www.cptr.ua.edu/kudzu.htm

http://www.nbii.gov/invasive/org.html   Link page to National Organizations of Invasive Organisms

http://www.nbii.gov/index.html   National Biological Information Infrastructure

http://invader.dbs.umt.edu/   University of Montana Invaders Database System

Go Electronic!

For additional readings, exercises, and Internet activities, visit this book's Website at:
http://www.awlonline.com/smithBTG

For even more activities, visit the Longman English pages at:
http://longman.awl.com/englishpages

If you need a user name and password, please see your instructor.

Take a Road Trip to the Maine Woods, St. Louis Arch, and Ellis Island!

Be sure to visit the Main Idea, Supporting Details, and Patterns of Organization modules in your Reading Road Trip CD-ROM for multimedia tutorials, exercises, and tests.

READER'S JOURNAL

Name _____ Date _____

Chapter 4

Answer the following questions to reflect on your own learning and progress. Use the perforations to tear the assignment out for your instructor.

1. When trying to determine the author's point, why is it important to determine the topic first?

    _____

2. Why is prior knowledge important in stating the main idea?

    _____

3. Why should the main idea be stated in a complete sentence?

    _____

4. Which pattern of organization do you find most difficult to recognize? Why?

    _____

5. When you write a term paper, where do you usually state the main idea? Why?

    _____

6. What pattern of organization do you use most frequently in your papers?

    _____

7. For what purpose have you written a summary as part of your school work? What was difficult about writing it?

    _____

8. Reflect on the multiple-choice items in the longer selections. How were your errors similar to or different from your errors in the last chapter?

    _____

9. Compare your concentration on the history and psychology selections. Which did you feel more focused on and why?

    _____

10. How many of the thirty vocabulary items did you answer correctly?

    _____

Organizing Textbook Information

5

- What is study reading?
- What is annotating?
- What is the Cornell Method of notetaking?
- What is outlining?
- What is mapping?

Richard Shaw, House of Cards, *1998. Porcelain. Courtesy Nancy Margolis Gallery.*

THE DEMANDS OF COLLEGE STUDY

Your first assignment in most college courses will be to read Chapter 1 of the appointed textbook, at which time you will immediately discover that a textbook chapter contains an amazing amount of information. Your instructor will continue to make similar assignments designating the remaining chapters in rapid succession. Your task is to select the information that needs to be remembered, try to learn it, and organize it for future study for a midterm or final exam that is weeks or months away.

In a recent study, three college professors investigated the question, "What are the demands on students in introductory college history courses?"[1] They observed classes for a ten-week period and analyzed the actual reading demands, finding that students were asked to read an average of 825 pages in each class over the ten-week period. The average length of weekly assignments was over 80 pages, but the amount varied both with the professor and the topic. In one class, students had to read 287 pages in only ten days.

The college history professors expected students to be able to see relationships between parts and wholes, to place people and events into a historical context, and to retain facts. Professors spent 85 percent of the class time lecturing and 6 percent of the time testing. In short, the demands were high and students were expected to work independently to organize textbook material efficiently and effectively to prepare for that crucial 6 percent of test-taking time.

BUILDING KNOWLEDGE NETWORKS

The old notion of studying and learning is that studying is an information-gathering activity. Knowledge is the "product" and the student acquires "it" by transferring information from the text to memory. With this view, good learners locate important information, review it, and then transfer the information into long-term memory. The problem with this model is that review does not always guarantee recall, and rehearsal is not always enough to ensure that information is encoded into long-term memory.

More recent theories of studying and learning reflect the thinking of cognitive psychologists and focus on schemata, prior knowledge, and the learner's own goals. To understand and remember, the learner hooks new information

© 2000 Addison-Wesley Educational Publishers, Inc.

---

[1]J. G. Carson, N. D. Chase, S. U. Gibson, and M. F. Hargrove. "Literacy Demands of the Undergraduate Curriculum." *Reading, Research, and Instruction* 31 (1992): 25–30.

to already existing schemata, or networks of knowledge. As the reader's personal knowledge expands, new networks are created. The learner, not the professor, decides how much effort should be expended and adjusts studying according to the answers to questions such as "How much do I need to know?" "Will the test be multiple-choice or essay?" and "Do I want to remember this forever?" The learner makes judgments and selects the material to be remembered and integrated into knowledge networks.

METHODS OF ORGANIZING TEXTBOOK INFORMATION

This chapter will discuss four methods of organizing textbook information for future study: (1) annotating, (2) notetaking, (3) outlining, and (4) mapping. In a recent review of more than five hundred research studies on organizing textbook information, two college developmental reading professors concluded that "no one study strategy is appropriate for all students in all study situations."[2] They encourage students to develop a repertoire of skills. They feel that students need to know, for example, that underlining takes less time than notetaking, but notetaking or outlining produces better test results.

Your selection of a study strategy for organizing textbook material will vary according to the announced testing demands, the nature of the material, the amount of time you have to devote to study, and your preference for a particular strategy. Being familiar with all four strategies affords a repertoire of choices.

The following comments on organizing textbook and lecture materials come from college freshmen taking an introductory course in American history. These history students were coenrolled in a Learning Strategies for History course that focused on how to be a successful student. Their comments probably address some of your experiences in trying to rapidly organize large amounts of textbook material.

From a student who made an A in history:

Organization of my class notes is very important. The notes can be very easy to refer to if they are organized. This enables me to go back and fill in information and it also helps me to understand the cycle of events that is taking place. I generally try to outline my notes by creating sections. Sections help me to understand the main idea or add a description of a singular activity. I usually go back and number the sections to make them easy for reference.

Taking notes can be very difficult sometimes. In class, if my mind strays just a few times, I can easily lose track of where my notes were going. Then again, when I am reading my textbook, I may read without

[2]D. Caverly and V. Orlando, *Textbook Strategies in Teaching Reading and Study Strategies at the College Level* (Newark, NJ: International Reading Association, 1991), pp. 86–165.

even realizing what I just read. The difference in class and the textbook is that I can go back and reread the text.

It is very easy to overdo the notes that I take from the text. Originally, I tended to take too much information from the book, but now, as I read more, I can better grasp the main idea. Underlining also makes a big difference. When I underline, I can go back and reread the book.

From a student who made a B in history:

Taking notes is no longer something that you can just do and expect to have good and complete notes. I have learned that taking notes is a process of learning within itself.

From a student who made a C in history:

In starting college, I have made a few changes in how I take notes. For instance, I am leaving a lot more space in taking notes. I find that they are easier to read when they are spread out. I have also been using a highlighter and marking topics and definitions and people's names. I make checks near notes that will definitely be on a test so I can go over them.

When I am reading, I have begun to do a lot of underlining in the book, which I would never do before because my school would not take back books if they were marked. I have also started to note important parts with a little star and confusing parts with a question mark.

From a student who made an A in history:

I think that the best way to do it is to completely read the assignment and then go back over it to clear up any confusion. I would also recommend going over your lecture notes before starting your reading assignment, which is something I didn't do this past week. I also try to key in on words like "two significant changes" or "major factors." Sometimes you may go three or four pages without seeing anything like that. My question is, "What do you do then?" I think that you should write down the point or points that were repeated the most or stressed the most.

All of these students were successful in history, although the final grades vary. Each student's reflection offers sincere and sound advice. However you organize material—by annotating, notetaking, outlining, or mapping—seek to make meaning by making connections.

ANNOTATING

Which of the following would seem to indicate the most effective use of the textbook as a learning tool?

1. A text without a single mark—not even the owner's name has spoiled the sacred pages
2. A text ablaze with color—almost every line is adorned with a red, blue, yellow, and/or green colored marker

3. A text with a scattered variety of markings—highlighting, underlines, numbers, and stars are interspersed with circles, arrows, and short, written notes

Naturally, option three is the best. The rationale for the first is probably for a better book resale value, but usually used books resell for the same price whether they are marked or unmarked. The reason for the second is probably procrastination in decision making. Students who highlight everything rely on coming back later to figure out what is *really* important. Although selective highlighting in a light color such as yellow is a helpful strategy, highlighting everything is inefficient. The variety of markings in the third strategy enables you to pinpoint ideas for later study.

Why Annotate?

The textbook is a learning tool and should be used as such; it should not be preserved as a treasure. A college professor requires a particular text because it contains information vital to your understanding of the course material. The text places a vast body of knowledge in your hands, much more material than the professor could possibly give in class. It is your job to wade through this information, to make some sense out of it, and to select the important points that need to be remembered.

Annotating is a method of highlighting main ideas, significant supporting details, and key terms. The word *annotate* means to add marks. By using a system of symbols and notation and not just colored markers, you mark the text after the first reading so that a complete rereading will not be necessary. The markings indicate pertinent points to review for an exam. If you are running short on time, highlighting with a colored marker is better than not making any marks at all.

Marking in the textbook itself is frequently faster than summarizing, outlining, or notetaking. In addition, since your material and personal reactions are all in one place, you can view them at a glance for later study rather than referring to separate notebooks. Your textbook has become a workbook.

Students who annotate, however, will probably want to make a list of key terms and ideas on their own paper in order to have a reduced form of the information for review and self-testing.

When to Annotate

Annotations are best done after a unit of thought has been presented and the information can be viewed as a whole. This may mean marking after a single paragraph or after three pages; marking varies with the material. When you are first reading, every sentence seems of major importance as each new idea unfolds, and the tendency is to annotate too much. Overmarking serves no useful purpose and wastes both reading and review time. If you wait until a complete thought has been developed, the significant points will emerge from a background of lesser details. You will then have all the facts, and you can decide what you want to remember. At the end of the course your textbook should have that worn but well-organized look.

> ▶ **READER'S TIP**   **How to Annotate**
>
> Develop a system of notations. Use circles, stars, numbers, and whatever else helps you put the material visually into perspective. *Anything that makes sense to you is a correct notation.* Here is an example of one student's marking system:
>
> | | |
> |---|---|
> | Main idea | ( ) |
> | Supporting material | _____ |
> | Major trend or possible essay exam question | * |
> | Important smaller point to know for multiple-choice item | ✓ |
> | Word that you must be able to define | ⬭ |
> | Section of material to reread for review | { } |
> | Numbering of important details under a major issue | (1), (2), (3) |
> | Didn't understand and must seek advice | ? |
> | Notes in the margin | Ex., Def., Topic |
> | Questions in the margin | Why signif.? |
> | Indicating relationships | ∿ |
> | Related issue or idea | ← R |

EXAMPLE   The following passage is taken from a biology textbook. Notice how the notations have been used to highlight main ideas and significant supporting details. This same passage will be used throughout this chapter to demonstrate each of the five methods of organizing textbook material.

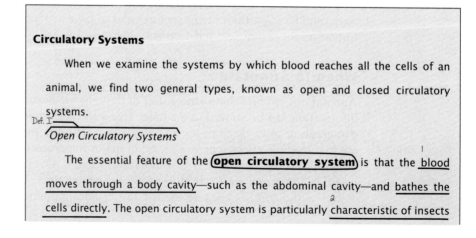

Circulatory Systems

When we examine the systems by which blood reaches all the cells of an animal, we find two general types, known as open and closed circulatory systems.

Def. I ‾‾‾

Open Circulatory Systems

The essential feature of the (**open circulatory system**) is that the blood moves through a body cavity—such as the abdominal cavity—and bathes the cells directly. The open circulatory system is particularly characteristic of insects and other arthropods, although it is also found in some other organisms. ^Ex.

In most insects the blood does not take a major part in oxygen transport. ^3 Oxygen enters the animal's body through a separate network of branching tubes that open to the atmosphere on the outside of the animal. (This type of respiratory system will be discussed in more detail in the next chapter.) ^4 Blood in an open circulatory system moves somewhat more slowly than in the average closed system. The slower system is adequate for insects because it does not have to supply the cells with oxygen.

Def. II
Closed Circulatory Systems

In a (closed circulatory system) the blood flows through a well-defined system of vessels with many branches. In the majority of closed systems the blood is responsible for oxygen transport. To supply all the body cells with sufficient oxygen, the blood must ^2 move quickly through the blood vessels. A closed circulatory system must therefore have an efficient ^3 pumping mechanism, or heart, to set the blood in motion and keep it moving briskly through the body.

Ex. 4
All vertebrates possess closed circulatory systems. Simple closed systems are also found in some invertebrates, including annelid worms. A good example of such a simple closed circulatory system can be seen in the earthworm. ^5

Ex. R ⟶ regeneration?

Victor A. Greulach and Vincent J. Chiapetta, eds. *Biology*

▶ **EXERCISE 5.1**   *Annotating*

Using a variety of notations, annotate the following passage as if you were preparing for a quiz on the material. Remember, do not underscore as you read, but wait until you finish a paragraph or a section and then mark the important points.

Stress Management

Each of us has our own optimum stress level, which is influenced by heredity and other factors. Some people thrive at stress levels that would quickly lead others to the state of exhaustion. How can we tell if we are stressed beyond our optimum level? Sometimes it is obvious; but, more often we fail to associate the symptoms we experience with their cause.

Different people respond to stress differently. For example, one person might gorge him- or herself with food while another might lose his or her appetite. One person might have trouble falling asleep at night while another person might sleep most of the time.

General Guidelines for Stress Management

Adopt a new way of looking at life. Stress management begins with adopting the philosophy that you, as an individual, are basically responsible for your own emotional and physical well-being. You can no longer allow other people to determine whether or not you are happy. You have little control over the behavior of anyone but yourself, and your emotional well-being is too important to trust to anyone but yourself. Your goal should be to develop such positive emotional wellness that nobody can ruin your day.

A positive outlook on life. This is absolutely essential to successful stress management. Your perception of events, not the events themselves, is what causes stress. Almost any life situation can be perceived as either stressful or nonstressful, depending on your interpretation. A negative view of life guarantees a high stress level. People who habitually view life negatively can recondition themselves to be more positive. One way is by applying a thought-stopping technique: Whenever you catch yourself thinking negatively, force yourself to think about the positive aspects of your situation. Eventually you will just automatically begin to see life more positively.

A regular exercise program. Exercise is an excellent tension reliever. In addition to the physical benefits, exercise is also good for the mind. Participating in at least three aerobic exercise sessions a week for at least 20 minutes each can greatly reduce stress. Daily stretching exercises provide relaxation and improve flexibility and posture. Participate in leisure activities that keep you physically active.

Be reasonably organized. Disorganization, sloppiness, chaos, and procrastination may seem very relaxed, but they are stressful. Set short-term, intermediate-term, and long-term goals for yourself. Every morning list the things you want and need to accomplish that day.

Learn to say no. Some people accept too many responsibilities. If you spread yourself too thin, not only will you be highly stressed, but important things will be done poorly or not at all. Know your limits and be assertive. If you don't have time to do something or simply don't want to do it, don't. Practice saying no effectively. Try, "I'm flattered that you've asked me, but given my commitments at this time, I won't be able to . . . ."

Learn to enjoy the process. Our culture is extremely goal oriented. Many of the things we do are directed toward achieving a goal, with no thought or expectation of enjoying the process. You may go to college for a degree, but you should enjoy the process of obtaining that degree. You may go to work for a paycheck, but you should enjoy your work. Happiness can seldom be achieved when pursued as a goal. It is usually a by-product of other activities. In whatever you do, focus on and enjoy the activity itself, rather than on how well you perform the activity or what the activity will bring you.

Don't be a perfectionist. Perfectionists set impossible goals for themselves, because perfection is unattainable. Learn to tolerate and forgive both yourself and others. Intolerance of your own imperfections leads to stress and low self-esteem. Intolerance of others leads to anger, blame, and poor relationships, all of which increase stress.

Look for the humor in life. Humor can be an effective part of stress management. Humor results in both psychological and physical changes. Its psychological effects include relief from anxiety, stress, and tension, an escape from reality, and a means of tolerating difficult life situations. Physically, laughter increases muscle activity, breathing rate, heart rate, and release of brain chemicals such as catecholamines and endorphins.

Practice altruism. **Altruism** is unselfishness, placing the well-being of others ahead of one's own. Altruism is one of the best roads to happiness, emotional health, and stress management. As soon as you start feeling concern for the needs of others, you immediately feel less stressed over the frustration of your own needs. Invariably, the most selfish people are the most highly stressed as they focus their attention on the complete fulfillment of their own needs, which can never happen.

Let go of the past. Everyone can list things in the past that he or she might have done differently. Other than learning through experience and trying not to make the same mistakes again, there is nothing to be gained by worrying about what you did or didn't do in the past. To focus on the past is nonproductive, stressful, and robs the present of its joy and vitality.

Eat a proper diet. How you eat affects your emotions and your ability to cope. When your diet is good you feel better and deal better with difficult situations. Try eating more carefully for two weeks and feel the difference it makes.

There is no unique stress-reduction diet, despite many claims to the contrary. The same diet that helps prevent heart disease, cancer, obesity, and diabetes (low in sugar, salt, fat, and total calories; adequate in vitamins, minerals, and protein) will also reduce stress.

Get adequate sleep. Sleep is essential for successfully managing stress and maintaining your health. People have varying sleep requirements, but most people function best with seven to eight hours of sleep per day. Some people simply don't allot enough time to sleep, while others find that stress makes it difficult for them to sleep.

Avoid alcohol and other drugs. The use of alcohol and other drugs in an effort to reduce stress levels actually contributes to stress in several ways. In the first place, it does *not* reduce the stress from a regularly occurring stressor such as an unpleasant job or relationship problems. Further, as alcohol and other drugs wear off, the rebound effect makes the user feel very uncomfortable and more stressed than before.

Don't overlook the possibility that excess caffeine intake is contributing to your stress. Caffeine is a powerful stimulant that, by itself, produces many of the physiological manifestations of stress. Plus, its effect of increased "nervous" energy contributes to more stressful, rushed behavior patterns. Remember that not only coffee and tea, but chocolate and many soft drinks contain caffeine.

Checkpoint

1. Why might two people in the same situation experience very different stress levels?

2. What is meant by "learn to enjoy the process"?
3. In what ways can being other-centered help reduce stress?

Curtis O. Boyer and Louis W. Shainberg, *Living Well*

Review your annotations. Have you sufficiently highlighted the main idea and the significant supporting details?

NOTETAKING

Many students prefer **notetaking,** or jotting down on their own paper brief sentence summaries of important textbook information. Margin space to the left of the summaries can be used to identify topics. Thus, topics of importance and explanations are side-by-side on notepaper for later study. In order to reduce notes for review, key terms can be further highlighted with a yellow marker to trigger thoughts for self-testing.

Why Take Textbook Notes?

Students who prefer this method say that working with a pencil and paper while reading keeps them involved with the material and thus improves concentration. Notetaking takes longer than annotating, but sometimes a student who has already annotated the text may feel the need, based on later testing demands, time, and the complexity of the material, to organize the information further into notes.

Although the following notetaking system recommends sentence summaries, writing short phrases can sometimes be more efficient and still adequately communicate the message for later study.

> **READER'S TIP**   **How to Take Notes**
>
> One of the most popular systems of notetaking is called the Cornell Method. The steps are as follows:
>
> 1. Draw a line down your paper two and one-half inches from the left side to create a two-and-one-half-inch margin for noting key words and a six-inch area on the right for sentence summaries.
>
> 2. After you have finished reading a section, tell yourself what you have read and jot down sentence summaries in the six-inch area on the right side of your paper. Use your own words and make sure you have included the main ideas and significant supporting details. Be brief, but use complete sentences.
>
> 3. Review your summary sentences and underline key words. Write these key words in the column on the left side of your paper. These words can be used to stimulate your memory of the material for later study.

The Cornell Method can be used for taking notes on classroom lectures. The chart shown on the following page, developed by Norman Stahl and James King, both explains the procedure and gives a visual display of the results. The example below applies the Cornell Method of notetaking to the biology passage on the circulatory system which you have already read. (See pages 192–193.)

Circulatory System	
Two types Open and closed	There are two types, the open and the closed, by which blood reaches the cells of an animal.
Open	In the open system, found mostly in insects and other arthropods, blood moves through the body and bathes the cells directly. The blood moves slower than in the closed system, and oxygen is supplied from the outside air through tubes.
Bathes cells	
Oxygen from outside	
Closed Blood vessels Blood carries oxygen Heart pumps	In the closed system, blood flows through a system of vessels, oxygen is carried by the blood so it must move quickly, and the heart serves as a pumping mechanism. All vertebrates, as well as earthworms, have closed systems.

Taking Class Notes: The Cornell Method

← 2½ INCHES →	←———————————— 6 INCHES ————————————→
REDUCE IDEAS TO CONCISE JOTTINGS AND SUMMARIES AS CUES FOR RECITING.	RECORD THE LECTURE AS FULLY AND AS MEANINGFULLY AS POSSIBLE.
Cornell Method	This sheet demonstrates the Cornell Method of taking classroom notes. It is recommended by experts from the Learning Center at Cornell University.
Line drawn down paper	You should draw a line down your notepage about 2½ inches from the left side. On the right side of the line simply record your classroom notes as you usually do. Be sure that you write legibly.
After the lecture	After the lecture you should read the notes, fill in materials that you missed, make your writing legible, and underline any important materials. Ask another classmate for help if you missed something during the lecture.
Use the recall column for key phrases	The recall column on the left will help you when you study for your tests. Jot down any important words or key phrases in the recall column. This activity forces you to rethink and summarize your notes. The key words should stick in your mind.
Five Rs	The Five Rs will help you take better notes based on the Cornell Method.
Record	1. Record any information given during the lecture which you believe will be important.
Reduce	2. When you reduce your information you are summarizing and listing key words/phrases in the recall column.
Recite	3. Cover the notes you took for your class. Test yourself on the words in the recall section. This is what we mean by recite.
Reflect	4. You should reflect on the information you received during the lecture. Determine how your ideas fit in with the information.
Review	5. If you review your notes you will remember a great deal more when you take your midterm.
Binder & paper	Remember it is a good idea to keep your notes in a standard-sized binder. Also you should use only full-sized binder paper. You will be able to add mimeographed materials easily to your binder.
Hints	Abbreviations and symbols should be used when possible. Abbrev. & sym. give you time when used automatically.

From N. A. Stahl and J. King, "A Language Experience Model for Teaching College Reading, Study and Survival" (Paper delivered at the twenty-fifth College Reading Association Annual Conference, Louisville, KY, October 20, 1981).

▶ **EXERCISE 5.2**   *Notetaking*

In college courses, you will usually take notes on lengthy chapters or entire books. For practice with notetaking here, use the passage, "Stress Management," which you have already annotated (pages 193–196). Prepare a two-columned sheet and take notes using the Cornell Method. ◀

OUTLINING

Outlining enables you to organize and highlight major points and subordinates items of lesser importance. In a glance the indentations, Roman numerals, numbers, and letters quickly show how one idea relates to another and how all aspects relate to the whole. The layout of the outline is simply a graphic display of main ideas and significant supporting details.

The following example is the picture-perfect version of the basic outline form. In practice your "working outline" would probably not be as detailed or as regular as this.

Use the tools of the outline format, *especially the indentations and numbers*, to devise your own system for organizing information.

Title
  I. First main idea
    A. Supporting idea
      1. Detail
      2. Detail
      3. Detail
        a. Minor detail
        b. Minor detail
    B. Supporting idea
      1. Detail
      2. Detail
    C. Supporting idea
  II. Second main idea
    A. Supporting idea
    B. Supporting idea

Why Outline?

Students who outline usually drop the preciseness of picture-perfect outlines, but make good use of the numbers, letters, indentations, and mixture of topics and phrases from the system to take notes and show levels of importance. A quick look to the far left of an outline indicates the topic with subordinate ideas indented underneath. The letters, numbers, and indentations form a visual display of the significance of the parts that make up the whole. Good outliners use plenty of paper so the levels of importance are evident at a glance.

Another use of the outline is to organize notes from class lectures. During class most professors try to add to the material in the textbook and put it into perspective for students. Since the notes taken in class represent a large percentage of the material you need to know in order to pass the course, they are extremely important. While listening to a class lecture, you must almost instantly receive, synthesize, and select material and, at the same time, record something on paper for future reference. The difficulty of the task demands order and decision making. Do not be so eager to copy down every detail that you miss the big picture. One of the most efficient methods of taking lecture notes is to use a modified outline form, a version with the addition of stars, circles, and underlines to emphasize further the levels of importance.

How to Outline

Professors say that they can walk around a classroom and look at the notes students have taken from the text or from a lecture and tell how well each has understood the lesson. The errors most frequently observed fall into the following categories:

1. Poor organization
2. Failure to show importance
3. Writing too much
4. Writing too little

<table>
<tr><td>► READER'S TIP</td><td>**Avoiding Pitfalls in Outlining**</td></tr>
</table>

The most important thing to remember when outlining is to ask yourself, *"What is my purpose?"* You don't need to include everything and you don't need a picture-perfect version for study notes. Include only what you believe you will need to remember later, and use a numbering system and indentations to show how one item relates to another. There are several other important guidelines to remember:

► **Get a general overview before you start.**

How many main topics do there seem to be?

► **Use phrases rather than sentences.**

Can you state it in a few short words?

► **Put it in your own words.**

If you cannot paraphrase it, do you really understand it?

► **Be selective.**

Are you highlighting or completely rewriting?

► **After outlining, indicate key terms with a yellow marker.**

Highlighting makes them highly visible for later review and self-testing.

EXAMPLE   Notice how numbers, letters, and indentations are used in the following outline to show levels of importance.

Circulatory System

I. Open circulatory system
 A. Blood moves through the body and bathes cells directly
 B. Examples—insects and other arthropods
 C. Oxygen supplied from outside air through tubes
 D. Slower blood movement since not supplying cells with oxygen
II. Closed circulatory system
 A. Blood flows through system of vessels
 B. Oxygen carried by blood so it must move quickly
 C. Heart serves as pumping mechanism
 D. Example—all vertebrates
 E. Example—earthworms

EXERCISE 5.3   *Outlining*

Outline the key ideas in the following selection as if you were planning to use
your notes to study for a quiz. You may want to annotate before you outline.

Reacting to Stress with Defense Mechanisms

Stress may occasionally promote positive outcomes. Motivated to overcome stress and the situations that produce it, we may learn new and
adaptive responses. It is also clear, however, that stress involves a very
unpleasant emotional component. **Anxiety** is a general feeling of tension
or apprehension that often accompanies a perceived threat to one's well-
being. It is this unpleasant emotional component that often prompts us
to learn new responses to rid ourselves of stress.

There are a number of techniques, essentially self-deception, that we
may employ to keep from feeling the unpleasantness associated with
stress. These techniques, or tricks we play on ourselves, are not adaptive
in the sense of helping us to get rid of anxiety by getting rid of the source
of stress. Rather, they are mechanisms that we can and do use to defend
ourselves against the *feelings* of stress. They are called **defense mechanisms.** Freud believed defense mechanisms to be the work of the unconscious mind. He claimed that they are ploys that our unconscious mind

uses to protect us (our *self* or *ego*) from stress and anxiety. Many psychologists take issue with Freud's interpretation of defense mechanisms and consider defense mechanisms in more general terms than did Freud, but few will deny that defense mechanisms exist. It *is* true that they are generally ineffective if consciously or purposively employed. The list of defense mechanisms is a long one. Here, we'll review some of the more common defense mechanisms, providing an example of each, to give you an idea of how they might serve as a reaction to stress.

Repression. The notion of **repression** came up earlier in our discussion of memory. In a way, it is the most basic of all the defense mechanisms. It is sometimes referred to as *motivated forgetting,* which gives us a good idea of what is involved. Repression is a matter of conveniently forgetting about some stressful, anxiety-producing event, conflict, or frustration. Paul had a teacher in high school he did not get along with at all. After spending an entire semester trying his best to do whatever was asked, Paul failed the course. The following summer, while walking with his girlfriend, Paul encountered this teacher. When he tried to introduce his girlfriend, Paul could not remember his teacher's name. He had repressed it. As a long-term reaction to stress, repressing the names of people we don't like or that we associate with unpleasant, stressful experiences is certainly not a very adaptive reaction. But at least it can protect us from dwelling on such unpleasantness.

Denial. **Denial** is a very basic mechanism of defense against stress. In denial, a person simply refuses to acknowledge the realities of a stressful situation. When a physician first tells a patient that he or she has a terminal illness, a common reaction is denial; the patient refuses to believe that there is anything seriously wrong.

Other less stressful events than serious illness sometimes evoke denial. Many smokers are intelligent individuals who are well aware of the data and the statistics that can readily convince them that they are slowly (or rapidly) killing themselves by continuing to smoke. But they deny the evidence. Somehow they are able to convince themselves that they aren't going to die from smoking; that's something that happens to other people, and besides, they *could* stop whenever they wanted.

Rationalization. **Rationalization** amounts to making excuses for our behaviors when facing the real reasons for our behaviors would be stressful. The real reason Kevin failed his psychology midterm is that he didn't study for it and has missed a number of classes. Kevin hates to admit, even to himself, that he could have been so stupid as to flunk that exam because of his own actions. As a result, he rationalizes: "It wasn't really *my* fault. I had a lousy instructor. We used a rotten text. The tests were grossly unfair. I've been fighting the darn flu all semester. And Marjorie had that big party the night before the exam." Now Susan, on the other hand, really did want to go to Marjorie's party, but she decided that she wouldn't go unless somebody asked her. As it happens, no one did. In short order, Susan rationalized that she "didn't want to go to that dumb party anyway"; she needed to "stay home and study."

Compensation. We might best think of **compensation** in the context of personal frustration. This defense mechanism is a matter of overemphasizing some positive trait or ability to counterbalance a shortcoming in some other trait or ability. If some particular goal-directed behavior becomes blocked, a person may compensate by putting extra effort and attention into some other aspect of behavior. For example, Karen, a seventh grader, wants to be popular. She's a reasonably bright and pleasant teenager, but isn't—in the judgment of her classmates—very pretty. Karen *may* compensate for her lack of good looks by studying very hard to be a good student, or by memorizing jokes and funny stories, or by becoming a good musician. Compensation is not just an attempt to be a well-rounded individual. It is a matter of expending *extra* energy and resources in one direction to offset shortcomings in other directions.

Fantasy. **Fantasy** is one of the more common defense mechanisms used by college students. It is often quite useful. Particularly after a hard day when stress levels are high, isn't it pleasant to sit in a comfortable chair, kick off your shoes, lie back, close your eyes, and daydream, perhaps about graduation day, picturing yourself walking across the stage to pick up your diploma—with honors.

When things are not going well for us, we may retreat into a world of fantasy where everything always goes well. Remember that to engage from time to time in fantasizing is a normal and acceptable response to stress. You should not get worried if you fantasize occasionally. On the other hand, you should realize that there are some potential dangers here. You need to be able to keep separate those activities that are real and those that occur in your fantasies. And you should realize that fantasy in itself will not solve whatever problem is causing you stress. Fantasizing about academic successes may help you feel better for a while, but it is not likely to make you a better student.

Projection. **Projection** is a matter of seeing in others those very traits and motives that cause us stress when we see them in ourselves. Under pressure to do well on an exam, Mark may want to cheat, but his conscience won't let him. Because of projection, he may think he sees cheating going on all around him.

Projection is a mechanism that is often used in conjunction with hostility and aggression. When people begin to feel uncomfortable about their own levels of hostility, they often project their aggressiveness onto others, coming to believe that others are "out to do me harm," and "I'm only defending myself."

Regression. To employ **regression** is to return to earlier, even childish, levels of behavior that were once productive or reinforced. Curiously enough, we often find regression in children. Imagine a four-year-old who until very recently was an only child. Now Mommy has returned from the hospital with a new baby sister. The four-year-old is no longer "the center of the universe," as her new little sister now gets parental attention. The four-year-old reverts to earlier behaviors and starts wetting the bed, screaming for a bottle of her own, and crawling on all fours in an attempt to get attention. She is regressing.

Many defense mechanisms can be seen on the golf course, including regression. After Doug knocks three golf balls into the lake, he throws a temper tantrum, stamps his feet, and tosses his three-iron in the lake. His childish regressive behavior won't help his score, but it may act as a release from the tension of his stress at the moment.

Displacement. The defense mechanism of **displacement** is usually discussed in the context of aggression. Your goal-directed behavior becomes blocked or thwarted. You are frustrated, under stress, and somewhat aggressive. You cannot vent your aggression directly at the source of the frustration, so you displace it to a safer outlet. Dorothy expects to get promoted at work, but someone else gets the new job she wanted. Her goal-directed behavior has been frustrated. She's upset and angry at her boss, but feels (perhaps correctly) that blowing her top at her boss will do more harm than good. She's still frustrated, so she displaces her hostility toward her husband, children, and/or the family cat.

Displacement doesn't have to involve hostility and aggression. A young couple discovers that having children is not going to be as easy as they thought. They want children badly, but there's an infertility problem that is causing considerable stress. Their motivation for love, sharing, and caring may be displaced toward a pet, nephews and nieces, or some neighborhood children—at least until their own goals can be realized with children of their own.

The list of defense mechanisms provided above is not an exhaustive one. These are among the most common, and this list gives you an idea of what defense mechanisms are like.

Josh Gerow, *Psychology: An Introduction*

EXERCISE 5.4   *Outlining*

For additional practice, outline the previous passage on "Stress Management" beginning on p. 193. Use your annotations and notes to help.

MAPPING

Mapping is a visual system of condensing material to show relationships and importance. A map is a diagram of the major points, with their significant subpoints, that support a topic. The purpose of mapping as an organizing strategy is to improve memory by grouping material in a highly visual way.

Why Map?

Proponents of popular learning style theories would say that mapping offers a visual organization that appeals to learners with a preference for spatial representation, as opposed to the linear mode offered by outlining and notetaking. A map provides a quick reference to overviewing an article or a chapter and can be used to reduce notes for later study.

Maps are not restricted to any one pattern, but can be formed in a variety of creative shapes, as the following diagrams illustrate:

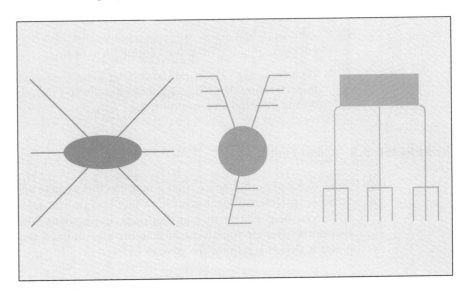

The following map highlights the biology passage on the circulatory system (see page 192–193). Notice how the visual display emphasizes the groups of ideas supporting the topic.

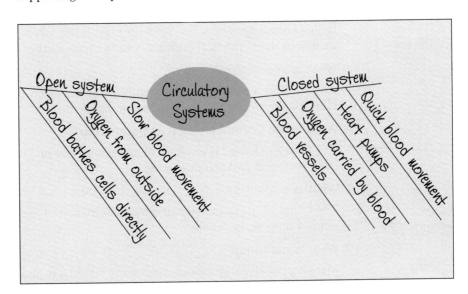

▶ READER'S TIP   How to Map

Use the following steps for mapping:

▶ *Draw a circle or a box* in the middle of a page and in it write the subject or topic of the material.

▶ *Determine the main ideas* that support the subject and write them on lines radiating from the central circle or box.

▶ *Determine the significant details* and write them on lines attached to each main idea. The number of details you include will depend on the material and your purpose.

▶ EXERCISE 5.5   *Mapping*

Refer to Exercise 5.3 and design a map for the passage entitled "Reacting to Stress with Defense Mechanisms," which you previously outlined. Use your outline to help you in making the map. Experiment with several different shapes for your map patterns on notebook or unlined paper. For additional practice, design a map for the passage in Exercise 5.1, page 193.

Summary Points

■ **What is study reading?**

Textbook reading is study reading. It is reading to learn and involves establishing knowledge networks. Students must select which textbook information to remember and organize it to facilitate further study.

■ **What is annotating?**

Annotating is a method of using symbols and notations to highlight main ideas, significant supporting details, and key terms.

■ **What is the Cornell Method of notetaking?**

The Cornell Method is a system of notetaking that includes writing summary sentences and marginal notes.

■ **What is outlining?**

The layout of the outline is a graphic presentation of main ideas and significant supporting details.

■ **What is mapping?**

Mapping is a visual system of condensing material to show relationships and importance.

C O N T E M P O R A R Y   F O C U S

The miracle of life becomes a double miracle with the advent of a new medical discovery. How can a fetus save the life of an adult?

UMBILICAL CORD BLOOD HELPS FIGHT CANCER

Renee Twombly

Duke Comprehensive Cancer Center Notes, Spring 1998

Gayle Serls didn't know she was dying until she woke up one day and discovered lumps everywhere. All her lymph nodes were grossly enlarged and she soon found out they were engorged with masses of sick immune cells rapidly dividing and multiplying. She went to the hospital in August 1995 and came home with a diagnosis: "Yesterday I was fine. Today I have cancer." What she specifically had was acute lymphocytic leukemia, which, true to Serls' words, comes on suddenly like a speeding train that might just run you over. The bone marrow cells that normally develop into immune system fighters called lymphocytes become cancerous and replace normal cells. These white blood cells had no place to go but clog up in her lymph nodes. Likely, some of the cancerous cells were released into the bloodstream and transported to vital organs. Serls faced immediate treatment with chemotherapy.

But there were more unpleasant surprises in store for this Durham mother of two. Although the disease went into a brief remission, doctors at Duke University Medical Center determined she had a particular set of genes, dubbed the "Philadelphia chromosome," resistant to chemotherapy used for the disease. That guaranteed a relapse.

Now Serls was faced with the last option available to her: a bone marrow transplant. In this procedure, all her cancerous white blood cells would be destroyed with high-dose chemotherapy and radiation. Her dead marrow would be removed, then replaced with marrow from a donor who had the same "immunity fingerprint" in the combination of HLA antigens that helps a body determine which is self and which is an invader. But another setback occurred. No donor marrow matched her profile, nor was there compatibility with her children's blood.

Serls then relapsed, massively. She was admitted to Duke Hospital, and underwent high-dose chemotherapy in an effort to buy time. She couldn't see, because inflammation swelled her eyes shut, and she was in terrible pain, for which she needed morphine. Her fatigue was profound. She made preparations for dying, such as a will and signing a power of attorney, but she didn't see death as "an option. It was totally incomprehensible. I continued to fight."

Duke physicians then turned to a procedure that had been successful with sick children, but was not tested in adult clinical trials. They decided to give Serls the marrow taken from a baby's umbilical cord, a small bag of fluid chock-full of new life. This placental blood is "friendly" to strangers—it can be used when HLA types are 50 percent matched, as Serls' was, or even less.

In May 1996, Serls underwent seven days of treatment with total body irradiation and three days of intense chemotherapy. When her lymph system was wiped clean, Serls received the baby blood. What followed was "real drama," she remembers, the time spent waiting in a "clean room," while microscopic predators normally held in check within the body went wild. But her white blood cell count began to creep up, and she let herself believe that a substance normally discarded after birth had saved her life.

Now, Serls can't help but think about the baby whose stem cells restored her. She says she has boy blood now. That's all she knows about the donor, and she playfully points out that different heritage. "My hair came back a lot darker and curlier at first," she said.

She said she believes the therapy is a simple "miracle," elegant use of blood that serves double-duty as a lifeline to a baby and then to a sick adult.

Collaborate on responses to the following questions:

■ According to published articles, umbilical cord blood can be harvested at birth for $1500 and stored for $100 a year. Would you do this for your child for biological insurance?

■ If you donated your child's umbilical cord blood, would you want to know the person who received it?

■ If you had cancer and were not near a major research hospital, what would you do to find out about new treatments?

STAGE 1: PREVIEW

Preview the next selection to predict its purpose and organization as well as your learning plan.

This selection is divided into how many sections? _____ After reading this selection, I will need to know _____

_____

Activate Schema

What hour of which day of the week were you born?

How much did you weigh?

Learning Strategy

Describe fetal growth in each trimester.

STAGE 2: INTEGRATE KNOWLEDGE WHILE READING

Predict   Picture   Relate   Monitor   Correct

Skill Development: Outlining

Outline or map the key ideas in each section as if you were planning to use your notes to study for a quiz.

A four-month-old fetus grows inside the mother's womb.

PREGNANCY AND BIRTH

From Robert Wallace, *Biology: The World of Life*[3]

Descriptions in bus-station novels notwithstanding, fertilization occurs with the mother-to-be totally unaware of the event. If

[3]From Robert A. Wallace, *Biology: The World of Life*, 3rd ed. Copyright © 1981 by Scott, Foresman and Company, HarperCollins College Publishers.

there are sperm cells thrashing around in the genital tract at any time within forty-eight hours before ovulation to about twelve hours after, the odds are
5 very good that pregnancy will occur. As soon as the egg is touched by the head of a sperm, it undergoes violent pulsating movements which unite the twenty-three chromosomes of the sperm with its own genetic complement. From this single cell, about 1/175 of an inch in diameter, a baby weighing several pounds and composed of trillions of cells will be delivered about 266 days
10 later.

For convenience, we will divide the 266 days, or nine months, into three periods of three months each. We can consider these *trimesters* separately, since each is characterized by different sorts of events.

The First Trimester

In the first trimester the embryo begins the delicate structural differentiations
15 that will lead to its final form. It is therefore particularly susceptible during this period to any number of factors that might influence its development. In fact the embryo often fails to survive this stage.

The first cell divisions result in cells that all look about alike and have roughly the same potentials. In other words, at this stage the cells are, theoreti-
20 cally anyway, interchangeable. Seventy-two hours after fertilization the embryo will consist of sixteen such cells. (So, how many divisions will have taken place?) Each cell will divide before it reaches the size of the cell that has produced it; hence the cells will become progressively smaller with each division. By the end of the first month the embryo will have reached a length of only $\frac{1}{8}$
25 inch, but it will consist of millions of cells.

In the second month the features of the embryo become more recognizable. Bone begins to form throughout the body, primarily in the jaw and shoulder areas. The head and brain are developing at a much faster rate than the rest of the body, so that at this point the ears appear and open, lidless eyes stare
30 blankly into the amniotic fluid. The circulatory system is developing and blood is pumped through the umbilical cord out to the chorion, where it receives life-sustaining nutrients and deposits the poisons it has removed from the developing embryo. The nitrogenous wastes and carbon dioxide filter into the mother's bloodstream, where they will be circulated to her own kidneys and
35 lungs for removal. At about day 46 the primordial reproductive organs begin to form, either as testes or ovaries, and it is now, for the first time, that the sex of the embryo becomes apparent. Near the end of the second month fingers and toes begin to appear on the flattened paddles which have formed from the limb buds. By this time the embryo is about two inches long and is more or less
40 human in appearance; it is now called a *fetus*. Growth and differentiation continue during the third month, but now the fetus begins to move. It breathes the amniotic fluid in and out of bulblike lungs and swallowing motions become distinct. At this point individual differences can be distinguished in the behavior of fetuses. The clearest differences are in their facial expressions. Some
45 frown a lot; others smile or grimace. It would be interesting to correlate this early behavior with the personality traits that develop after birth.

The Second Trimester

In the second trimester the fetus grows rapidly, and by the end of the sixth month it may be about a foot long, although it will weigh only about a pound
50 and a half. Whereas the predominant growth of the fetus during the first trimester was in the head and brain areas, during the second trimester the body grows at a much faster relative rate than the brain and begins to catch up in size with the head.

The fetus is by this time behaving more vigorously. It is able to move freely
55 within its sea of amniotic fluid and the delighted mother can feel it kicking and thrashing about. Interestingly, the fetus must sleep now, so there are periods when it is inactive. It is capable of reacting to more types of stimuli as time passes. For example, by the fifth month the eyes are sensitive to light, although there is still no sensitivity to sound. Other organs seem to be com-
60 plete, but remain nonfunctional. For example, the lungs are developed, but they cannot exchange oxygen. The digestive organs are present, but they cannot digest food. Even the skin is not prepared to cope with the temperature changes in the outside world. In fact, at the end of the fifth month the skin is covered by a protective cheesy paste consisting of wax and sweatlike secre-
65 tions mixed with loosened skin cells (*vernix caseosa*). The fetus is still incapable in nearly all instances of surviving alone.

By the sixth month the fetus is kicking and turning so constantly that the mother often must time her own sleep periods to coincide with her baby's. The distracting effect has been described as similar to being continually
70 tapped on the shoulder, but not exactly. The fetus moves with such vigor that its movements are not only felt from the inside, but can be seen clearly from the outside. To add to the mother's distraction, the fetus may even have periods of hiccups. By this stage it is so large and demanding that it places a tremendous drain on the mother's reserves.

75 At the end of the second trimester the fetus has the unmistakable appearance of a human baby (or a very old person, since its skin is loose and wrinkled at this stage). In the event of a premature birth around the end of this trimester, the fetus may be able to survive.

The Third Trimester

During the third trimester the fetus grows until it is no longer floating free in
80 its amniotic pool. It now fills the abdominal area of the mother. The fetus is crowded so tightly into the greatly enlarged uterus that its movement is restricted. In these last three months the mother's abdomen becomes greatly distended and heavy, and her posture and gait may be noticeably altered in response to the shift in her center of gravity. The mass of tissue and amniotic
85 fluid that accompanies the fetus ordinarily weighs almost twice as much as the fetus itself. Toward the end of this period, milk begins to form in the mother's mammary glands, which in the previous trimester have undergone a sudden surge of growth.

At this time, the mother is at a great disadvantage in several ways in terms
90 of her physical well-being. About 85 percent of the calcium she eats goes to
the fetal skeleton, and about the same percentage of her iron intake goes to
the fetal blood cells. Of the protein she eats, much of the nitrogen goes to the
brain and other nerve tissues of the fetus.

Some interesting questions arise here. If a woman is unable to afford ex-
95 pensive protein-rich foods during the third trimester, what is the probabil-
ity of a lowered I.Q. in her offspring? On the average the poorer people in
this country show lower I.Q. scores. Are they poor because their I.Q.'s are
low, or are I.Q.'s low because they are poor? Is there a self-perpetuating nature about either of these alternatives?

100 In the third trimester, the fetus is large. It requires increasingly greater
amounts of food, and each day it produces more poisonous wastes for the
mother's body to carry away. Her heart must work harder to provide food
and oxygen for two bodies. She must breathe, now, for two individuals. Her
blood pressure and heart rate rise. The fetus and the tissues maintaining it
105 form a large mass that crowds the internal organs of the mother. In fact, the
crowding of the fetus against the mother's diaphragm may make breathing
difficult for her in these months. Several weeks before delivery, however,
the fetus will change its position, dropping lower in the pelvis (called *"light-
ening"*) and thus relieve the pressure against the mother's lungs.

110 There are important changes occurring in the fetus in these last three
months, and some of these are not very well understood. The effects of these
changes, however, are reflected in the survival rate of babies delivered by
Caesarian section (an incision through the mother's side). In the seventh
month, only 10 percent survive; in the eighth month, 70 percent; and in the
115 ninth, 95 percent survive.

Interestingly, there is another change in the relationship of the fetus and
mother at this time. Whereas measles and certain other infectious diseases
would have affected the embryo during the first trimester of pregnancy, at
this stage the mother's antibodies confer an immunity to the fetus, a protec-
120 tion that may last through the first few weeks of infancy.

At some point about 255 to 265 days from the time of conception the life-sustaining placenta begins to break down. Certain parts shrink, the tissue structure
begins changing, and the capillaries begin to disintegrate. The result is a less hos-
pitable environment for the fetus, and premature births at this time are not un-
125 usual. At about this time the fetus slows its growth, and drops into position with
its head toward the bottom of the uterus. Meanwhile, the internal organs un-
dergo the final changes that will enable the newborn to survive in an entirely different kind of world. Its home has been warm, rather constant in its qualities, protected, and confining. It is not likely to encounter anything quite so secure again.

Birth

130 The signal that there will soon be a new member of the earth's most dominant species is the onset of *labor,* a series of uterine contractions that usually

begin at about half-hour intervals and gradually increase in frequency. Mean-while, the sphincter muscle around the cervix dilates, and as the periodic con-tractions become stronger, the baby's head pushes through the extended cer-
135 vical canal to the opening of the vagina. The infant is finally about to emerge into its new environment, one that, in time, may give it the chance to propel its own genes into the gene pool of the species.

Once the baby's head emerges, the pattern of uterine contractions changes. The contractions become milder and more frequent. After the head gradually
140 emerges through the vaginal opening, the smaller shoulders and the body ap-pear. Then with a rush the baby slips into a new world. As soon as the baby has emerged, the umbilicus by which it is attached to the placenta is tied off and cut. The placenta is expelled by further contractions as the *afterbirth*. The mother recovers surprisingly rapidly. In other species, which deliver their young
145 unaided, the mother immediately chews through the umbilicus and eats the af-terbirth so that it will not advertise to predators the presence of a helpless new-born. Fortunately, the behavior never became popular in our own species.

The cutting of the umbilicus stops the only source of oxygen the infant has known. There is a resulting rapid buildup of carbon dioxide in the blood,
150 which affects a breathing center in the brain. An impulse is fired to the di-aphragm, and the baby gasps its first breath. Its exhaling cry signals that it is breathing on its own.

In American hospitals the newborn is then given the first series of the many tests it will encounter during its lifetime. This one is called the *Apgar test series*,
155 in which muscle tone, breathing, reflexes, and heart rate are evaluated. The obstetrician then checks for skin lesions and evidence of hernias. If the infant is a boy, it is checked to see whether the testes have properly descended into the scrotum. A footprint is then recorded as a means of identification, since the new individual, despite the protestations of proud parents, does not yet have
160 many other distinctive features that would be apparent to the casual observer. And there have been more than a few cases of accidental baby-switching.

STAGE 3: RECALL

Stop to self-test, relate, and react.

Your instructor may choose to give you a true-false comprehension review.

 PREGNANCY AND BIRTH

Why it is important for pregnant women to get regular medical check ups, to avoid smoking, and to avoid consuming alcohol? Use information from the text to discuss your reasoning.

Contemporary Link

Should a company, parents, and/or a newborn baby make a profit from the sale of umbilical cord blood? If you were a new parent, what would you think are the ethical issues surrounding the donation or sale of this blood?

COMPREHENSION QUESTIONS

Mark each statement with *T* for true or *F* for false.

_____ 1. Babies are footprinted as a means of identification.
_____ 2. The fetus is most susceptible to measles during the last trimester.
_____ 3. During fertilization, the mother can feel the sperm and the egg touch.
_____ 4. During the first trimester, changes in the facial expression of the fetus occur.
_____ 5. During the second trimester, the fetus can have the hiccups.
_____ 6. During the third trimester, the fetus floats freely with room to move in the uterus.
_____ 7. The author implies that the mother's body works the hardest during the third trimester.
_____ 8. The baby is forced to breathe when the cervix dilates.
_____ 9. Sperm can live for several hours in the genital tract.
_____10. During the third trimester, the mother's antibodies confer immunity to the fetus.

SEARCH THE NET

Many difficulties and developmental disorders can occur during pregnancy. Conduct a search to investigate birth defects. Describe two birth defects, explain any preventive measures that can be taken to avoid these defects, and list a support group or Internet resource for each. Plan your own search or begin by trying the following:

http://www.birthdefects.prevention.org/birth.html

CONTEMPORARY FOCUS

Famous women in history were frequently controversial, receiving both sneers and cheers from contemporaries. Each in their own way changed both the image and the reality for all women.

EVITA STYLISH, THIEVING DIVA OF CULT POLITICS

Jim Pinkerton

USA Today, January 16, 1997, p. 13a

In 1940, Argentines enjoyed the eighth highest standard of living on the planet. A half century later, the country was thoroughly Third World.

The Perons, who took power in 1945, were catalysts for Argentina's decline. Juan Peron vastly expanded government spending, which endeared him to working class "descamisados," or the shirtless ones. "Give to the people, especially the workers, all that is possible," Peron said. "When it seems that already you are giving them too much, give them some more."

Such Robin Hood-like redistribution played well in the short run but in the long term was catastrophic. Investment dried up and gold reserves disappeared. When Peron kept spending by simply printing more pesos, hyperinflation wiped out savings and erased what remained of business confidence. As the economy fell still further, Peron suppressed civil liberties.

Of course, what separates Peron is his mythic wife. Born of humble origins, the star-quality Evita posed as the champion of the working class. As Madonna sings in the movie, "I've been unemployed and hate it too." But, as she trills to the masses, Peron is the answer: "I found my salvation" in him—and so will they.

Evita died of cancer in 1952. She was just 33, ensuring that her candle-in-the-rain legend would endure forever—much longer than her husband's regime, which was overthrown in 1955. Only then did the full extent of the couple's kleptocratic rule become apparent. According to a new biography, Eva's estate was found to have tucked away an Imelda Marcos-like hoard: $12 million in cash, 65 kilograms of gold and as much silver, "a 48-carat emerald, three platinum ingots, 1,650 diamonds, 120 gold bracelets, and 100 gold watches."

The bottom line is that cult-like politics are a function of the willingness to suspend disbelief and to follow one person—even over a cliff.

In the film, Madonna/Evita is described as "a diamond" in the "dull, gray lives" of ordinary Argentines. Maybe so, but Argentine history should convince us that too much glamor and excitement in politics is a lot more dangerous than too little.

Collaborative Activity

Collaborate on responses to the following questions:

■ Why do you suppose that the legend and fame of Evita, who was not the ruler, was greater than the reputation of leader Juan Peron?

- In the movie, Evita was portrayed in a positive manner. Who were the people that loved Evita and who were the people that hated her?
- How do you think power and political bias affect what is written about the Perons in Argentinian history textbooks?

STAGE 1: PREVIEW

Preview the next selection to predict its purpose and organization and your learning plan.

The pattern of organization in the first part of the selection is:

_____

After reading this selection, I will know Sojourner Truth's feelings on the weakness of women. Agree ☐   Disagree ☐

Activate Schema

Why did the Civil War throw women into many leadership roles?

Learning Strategy

Explain the contributions of individuals and groups toward changing the image of women.

Word Knowledge

What do you know about these words?

restrictive	detriment	defiant	communal	hecklers
pursue	hygiene	incessant	convalescent	naive

Your instructor may give a true-false vocabulary review before or after reading.

STAGE 2: INTEGRATE KNOWLEDGE WHILE READING

Predict   Picture   Relate   Monitor   Correct

Skill Development: Notetaking

Use the Cornell Method of notetaking to organize material in this selection for future study.

Clara Barton founded the American Red Cross.

WOMEN IN HISTORY

From Leonard Pitt, *We Americans*[4]

Three Radical Women

Amelia Bloomer (1818–1894) published the first newspaper issued expressly for women. She called it *The Lily*. Her fame, however, rests chiefly in dress reform. For six or eight years she wore an outfit composed of a knee-length skirt over full pants gathered at the
5 ankle, which were soon known everywhere as "bloomers." Wherever she went, this style created great excitement and brought her enormous audiences—including hecklers. She was trying to make the serious point that women's fashions, often designed by men to suit their own tastes, were too restrictive, often to the detriment of the health of those who wore them. Still, some of her con-
10 temporaries thought she did the feminist movement as much harm as good.

Very few feminists hoped to destroy marriage as such. Most of them had husbands and lived conventional, if hectic, lives. And many of the husbands supported their cause. Yet the feminists did challenge certain marital customs. When Lucy Stone married Henry Blackwell, she insisted on being
15 called "Mrs. Stone," a defiant gesture that brought her a lifetime of ridicule. Both she and her husband signed a marriage contract, vowing "to recognize the wife as an independent, rational being." They agreed to break any law which brought the husband "an injurious and unnatural superiority." But few of the radical feminists indulged in "free love" or joined communal marriage
20 experiments. The movement was intended mainly to help women gain control over their own property and earnings and gain better legal guardianship over their children. Voting also interested them, but women's suffrage did not become a central issue until later in the century.

Many black women were part of the movement, including the legendary
25 Sojourner Truth (1797–1883). Born a slave in New York and forced to marry a man approved by her owner, Sojourner Truth was freed when the state abolished slavery. After participating in religious revivals, she became an active abolitionist and feminist. In 1851 she saved the day at a women's rights convention in Ohio, silencing hecklers and replying to a man who had belit-
30 tled the weakness of women:

> The man over there says women need to be helped into carriages and lifted over ditches, and to have the best place everywhere. Nobody ever helps me into carriages or over puddles, or gives me the best place—and ain't I a woman? . . . Look at my arm! I have ploughed and planted and gathered into barns, and no man could head me—and ain't I a woman? I could work as much and eat as much as a

---

[4]From Leonard Pitt, *We Americans*. Copyright © 1987 Kendall/Hunt Publishing Company. Reprinted with permission.

man—when I could get it—and bear the lash as well! And ain't I a woman? I have borne thirteen children, and seen most of 'em sold into slavery, and when I cried out my mother's grief, none but Jesus heard me—and ain't I a woman?

Changing the Image and the Reality

The accomplishments of a few women who dared pursue professional careers had somewhat altered the image of the submissive and brainless child-woman. Maria Mitchell of Nantucket, whose father was an astronomer, discovered a comet at the age of twenty-eight. She became the first woman professor of as-
35 tronomy in the U.S. (at Vassar in 1865). Mitchell was also the first woman elected to the American Academy of Arts and Sciences and a founder of the Association for the Advancement of Women. Elizabeth Blackwell applied to twenty-nine medical schools before she was accepted. She attended all classes, even anatomy class, despite the sneers of some male students. As a physician,
40 she went on to make important contributions in sanitation and hygiene.

By about 1860 women had effected notable improvements in their status. Organized feminists had eliminated some of the worst legal disadvantages in fifteen states. The Civil War altered the role—and the image—of women even more drastically than the feminist movement did. As men
45 went off to fight, women flocked into government clerical jobs. And they were accepted in teaching jobs as never before. Tens of thousands of women ran farms and businesses while the men were gone. Anna Howard Shaw, whose mother ran a pioneer farm, recalled:

It was an incessant struggle to keep our land, to pay our taxes, and to live. Calico was selling at fifty cents a yard. Coffee was one dollar a pound. There were no men left to grind our corn, to get in our crops, or to care for our livestock; and all around us we saw our struggle reflected in the lives of our neighbors.

Women took part in crucial relief efforts. The Sanitary Commission, the
50 Union's volunteer nursing program and a forerunner of the Red Cross, owed much of its success to women. They raised millions of dollars for medicine, bandages, food, hospitals, relief camps, and convalescent homes.

North and South, black and white, many women served as nurses, some as spies and even as soldiers. Dorothea Dix, already famous as a reformer of
55 prisons and insane asylums, became head of the Union army nurse corps. Clara Barton and "Mother" Bickerdyke saved thousands of lives by working close behind the front lines at Antietam, Chancellorsville, and Fredericksburg. Harriet Tubman led a party up the Combahee River to rescue 756 slaves. Late in life she was recognized for her heroic act by being granted a
60 government pension of twenty dollars per month.

Southern white women suffered more from the disruptions of the Civil War than did their northern sisters. The proportion of men who went to war or were killed in battle was greater in the South. This made many women self-sufficient during the war. Still, there was hardly a whisper of feminism in the South.
65 The Civil War also brought women into the political limelight. Anna Dickson skyrocketed to fame as a Republican speaker, climaxing her career with an ad-

dress to the House of Representatives on abolition. Stanton and Anthony formed the National Woman's Loyal League to press for a constitutional amendment banning slavery. With Anthony's genius for organization, the League in 70 one year collected 400,000 signatures in favor of the Thirteenth Amendment.

Once abolition was finally assured in 1865, most feminists felt certain that suffrage would follow quickly. They believed that women had earned the vote by their patriotic wartime efforts. Besides, it appeared certain that black men would soon be allowed to vote. And once black men had the ballot in hand, 75 how could anyone justify keeping it from white women—or black women? Any feminist who had predicted in 1865 that women would have to wait another fifty-five years for suffrage would have been called politically naive.

STAGE 3: RECALL

Stop to self-test, relate, and react.

Your instructor may choose to give you a true-false comprehension review.

 WOMEN IN HISTORY

How did the actions of many early women "somewhat alter the image of the submissive and brainless child-woman"? List the women and discuss how each changed stereotypical thinking.

Contemporary Link

How do the sources of the power for Evita Peron and Sojourner Truth differ? Which woman do you admire more and why?

SKILL DEVELOPMENT: NOTETAKING

Review your notes before answering the following comprehension questions.

COMPREHENSION QUESTIONS

After reading the selection, answer the following questions with *a, b, c,* or *d.*

Main Idea   _____ 1. The best statement of the main point of this selection is that
   a. women made impressive gains because of their work during the Civil War.
   b. many women made early contributions toward changing the stereotypical image of the female role.

    c. Bloomer, Stone, and Truth changed a radical image into a reality.

    d. women were slow to get the right to vote despite their efforts.

Detail   _____ 2. In originating "bloomers," Amelia Bloomer's greatest concern was

    a. fashion.

    b. principle.

    c. expense.

    d. good taste.

Inference   _____ 3. The major purpose of Sojourner Truth's quoted speech was to

    a. prove that women are stronger than men.

    b. reprimand men for social courtesy.

    c. dramatize the strengths of women.

    d. praise childbearing as a womanly virtue.

Detail   _____ 4. Lucy Stone's major motive in retaining the name "Mrs. Stone" after marriage as to

    a. condone "free love" without marriage.

    b. de-emphasize the responsibilities of marriage.

    c. purchase property in her own name.

    d. be recognized as an independent person equal to her husband.

Detail   _____ 5. The article explicitly states that women worked during the Civil War in all of the following except

    a. farms and businesses.

    b. the military.

    c. government clerical jobs.

    d. the Red Cross.

Inference   _____ 6. The author implies that the eventual assumption of responsible roles by large numbers of women was primarily due to

    a. the feminist movement.

    b. the determination and accomplishments of female professionals.

    c. a desire to give women a chance.

    d. economic necessity.

Inference   _____ 7. The author believes that the Civil War showed southern women to be

    a. as capable but less vocal than northern women.

    b. more capable than their northern sisters.

    c. capable workers and eager feminists

    d. less able to assume responsible roles than northern women.

Inference   _____ 8. The author's main purpose in mentioning the accomplish-
                                    ments of Maria Mitchell is to point out that
                                    a. she discovered a comet.
                                    b. her professional achievements in astronomy were excep-
                                       tional and thus somewhat improved the image of women.
                                    c. she was the first woman professor of astronomy in the
                                       United States.
                                    d. she was a founder of the Association for the Advance-
                                       ment of Women.

Detail   _____ 9. The article states or implies that all of the following women
                                    worked to abolish slavery except
                                    a. Anna Howard Shaw.
                                    b. Harriet Tubman.
                                    c. Anna Dickson.
                                    d. Stanton and Anthony.

Inference   _____ 10. In the author's opinion, the long wait by women after the
                                    Civil War for suffrage
                                    a. was predictable in 1865.
                                    b. would not have been expected in 1865.
                                    c. was due to the vote of black men.
                                    d. was justified.

Answer the following with *T* (true) or *F* (false).

Detail   _____ 11. Women were granted the right to vote in 1920.
Detail   _____ 12. Sojourner Truth had been a southern slave.
Inference   _____ 13. The author implies that feminist leaders were more con-
                                    cerned with their own right to vote than with the abolition
                                    of slavery.
Detail   _____ 14. From the very beginning, the right to vote was the focal
                                    point of the women's movement.
Detail   _____ 15. Sojourner Truth had thirteen children.

VOCABULARY

According to the way the italicized word was used in the selection, indicate *a*,
b, *c*, or *d* for the word or phrase that gives the best definition.

_____ 1. "were too *restrictive*" (8)   _____ 2. "to the *detriment of*" (9)
            a. showy   a. harm
            b. expensive   b. anger
            c. complicated   c. apology
            d. confining   d. objection

3. "a *defiant* gesture" (15)
   a. unlucky
   b. resistive
   c. admirable
   d. ignorant

4. "*communal* marriage experiments" (19–20)
   a. permanent
   b. living together in groups
   c. illegal
   d. uncommon

5. "silencing *hecklers*" (29)
   a. soldiers
   b. rioters
   c. disciples
   d. verbal harassers

6. "*pursue* professional careers" (31)
   a. strive for
   b. abandon
   c. acknowledge
   d. indicate

7. "sanitation and *hygiene*" (40)
   a. garbage disposal
   b. biology
   c. health care
   d. mental disorders

8. "an *incessant* struggle" (line 1 of quote, p. 217)
   a. earlier
   b. final
   c. novel
   d. unceasing

9. "*convalescent* homes" (52)
   a. sanitary
   b. government
   c. reclaimed
   d. recuperating

10. "called politically *naive*" (77)
    a. unsophisticated
    b. well informed
    c. dishonest
    d. unfortunate

SEARCH THE NET

Conduct a search on the life of Sojourner Truth. Find her real name and describe her reasons for changing it. Reference your Websites. Plan your own search or begin by trying the following:

http://www.sojournertruth.org/ for the Sojourner Truth 200th Anniversary Committee

http://www.rr.gmcs.k12.nm.us/domagala.bhistory.htm for Black History Month Website

CONTEMPORARY FOCUS

Are the foods that taste the best always the worst for you? How can your knowledge of nutrition improve your performance and reduce stress?

BEST AND WORST CAFETERIA FOODS

Lisa M. Flores

From "Chow Line," College Student Survival Guide, *Muscle & Fitness*, May 1998, p. 130.

"There are no bad foods, only bad diets," says Keith Ayoob, EdD, RD. Even in a college dining hall, not-so-healthy foods are okay as long as you eat them in small portions and only every once in a while.

Beware

As a general rule, try to limit the amount of the following foods you consume:

- **Foods with cream sauces and gravy.** Cut down on extra fat by skipping smothered entrees.
- **Fried chicken.** If it's the only option, remove the skin.
- **Breaded meats.** Turkey cutlets and chicken patties are often breaded and thus more fattening.
- **French fries.** They may be offered at every meal, but eat them as a side only occasionally.

- **Desserts.** Avoid heavy desserts and choose frozen yogurt, chocolate milk or fruit instead.

Enjoy

The following foods are good-for-you cafeteria standbys:

- **Cereal.** Always available and a good choice when eaten with low- or nonfat milk and fresh fruit.
- **Fruit.** Get extra calories before a workout by loading up on fresh fruit.
- **Pasta.** Best when eaten plain or with meatless tomato sauce (or lean poultry or lean beef).
- **Skinless chicken.** Choose broiled or grilled chicken over fried.
- **Lean deli meats.** Sandwich meats such as roast beef, turkey breast and turkey bologna are usually available at lunch and dinner.

Collaborate on responses to the following questions:

■ Why should you limit fats in your diet?

■ What healthy food options do you regularly incorporate into your diet?

■ How can you "train your brain" through nutritional choices?

STAGE 1: PREVIEW

Preview the next selection to predict the purpose and organization as well as your learning plan.

After reading this selection, I would like to know:

_____

Activate Schema

What causes stress for you?

What is your typical response to stress?

Learning Strategy

Explain the scientific impact of nutrition, exercise, and stress on the body.

Word Knowledge

What do you know about these words?

attribute   crankiness   optimal   judiciously   mimic

aroused   prone   precursor   salient   euphoria

Your instructor may give a true-false vocabulary review before or after reading.

STAGE 2: INTEGRATE KNOWLEDGE WHILE READING

Predict   Picture   Relate   Monitor   Correct

Skill Development: Notetaking

Use an informal outline to take notes for later study.

NUTRITION, HEALTH, AND STRESS

From Barbara Brehm, *Stress Management*

A woman's crew team races on the Charles River in Cambridge, Massachusetts.

Nutrition and Stress: Running on Empty

Good nutrition and eating habits contribute significantly to good health and stress resistance. They are especially important during high-stress times, but these may be the times when we are least likely to eat well! The cupboard is bare, we have no time to plan a shopping list and no
5   money to go shopping, so we skip meals or grab whatever fast food is closest at hand. Sometimes we depend on a dining hall whose schedule doesn't match our own, or whose ideas of good nutrition and fine cuisine are limited

to meat, potatoes, and overcooked vegetables with lots of butter. Dessert is usually the high point of every meal.

Food and Energy: The Role of Blood Sugar

10 Everyone has experienced the fatigue and irritability that can result from being hungry. While many of the body's systems can make energy from fat, the central nervous system, including the brain, relies primarily on blood sugar, or glucose, for fuel. When blood sugar falls, these symptoms of fatigue result. Parents and people who work with children have observed the
15 hungry-cranky connection on many occasions. As adults, we tend to attribute our moods to external events and ignore our internal physiology, but hunger can cause crankiness in us just the same.

After you consume a meal, your blood glucose level rises as sugar enters the bloodstream from the digestive tract. A rising blood sugar level signals the
20 pancreas to release **insulin.** Insulin is a hormone that allows sugar to enter the cells and be used for energy. As the glucose gradually leaves the bloodstream, blood glucose levels begin to decrease.

Some people have more trouble regulating blood sugar than others and are prone to **hypoglycemia,** or low blood sugar, especially if they forget to eat or
25 when they participate in physical activity. Symptoms of hypoglycemia include hunger, shakiness, nervousness, dizziness, nausea, and disorientation.

The following are recommendations for keeping your blood sugar at a healthful level without peaks and dips.

Eat Regularly

Your body likes a regular schedule. Skipping meals means guaranteed hypo-
30 glycemia in people prone to this condition. Set up times for meals and snacks that are convenient for your schedule and stick to this routine as much as possible. This may mean planning ahead and carrying snacks with you if you are at work or out running errands. Many people, including those with hypoglycemia, find that eating five or six small meals or snacks each day helps
35 them feel more energetic than three large meals.

Include Protein Foods at Every Meal

Carbohydrate foods eaten without foods containing much protein are digested and enter the bloodstream quickly and are thus likely to challenge blood sugar regulatory processes in people prone to hypoglycemia. Protein slows digestion and allows blood sugar to rise more gradually. Protein servings
40 may be small: a slice or two of meat or cheese; a half-cup of cottage cheese, yogurt, or tuna salad; small servings of fish or shellfish; a dish made with lentils or other legumes; or soy products like tofu.

Avoid Sugar Overload

When you eat a large amount of carbohydrates, blood sugar rises quickly. A high blood sugar level calls forth a high insulin response, which in some

45 people causes a sort of rebound effect: glucose enters the cells, and the blood sugar level drops quickly, causing hypoglycemia. While you may feel energized for a short period of time after too much sugar, you may eventually begin to feel tired, irritable, and hungry.

Drink Plenty of Fluids

Many people fail to maintain optimal levels of hydration. The next time you
50 feel tired, try drinking a glass of water. Dehydration causes fatigue and irritability. Thirst is not an adequate indicator of dehydration; you become dehydrated before you get thirsty. Nutritionists advise drinking at least four cups of fluid each day, more with physical activity or hot weather. Caffeinated and alcoholic beverages don't count. Not only do they increase your
55 stress but they also dehydrate you and thus increase your fluid needs. Your urine will be pale if you are adequately hydrated; dark-colored urine is a sign of dehydration.

Limit Caffeine

Caffeine is a **sympathomimetic** substance, which means its effects mimic those of the sympathetic nervous system and thus cause the fight-or-flight re-
60 sponse. If you add caffeine to an already aroused sympathetic nervous system, the results can be stressful and produce high levels of anxiety, irritability, headache, and stress-related illness. Most caffeine drinks, including coffee, tea, and cola soft drinks, can also cause stomachaches and nausea, which often get worse under stress.

65 One or two caffeinated beverages consumed judiciously at appropriate times during the day appear to do no harm for most people. Indeed, a little caffeine can increase alertness. The problem with caffeine is that people are likely to overindulge in it when they are stressed. When summoning the energy necessary to get through the day feels like trying to squeeze water from a
70 rock, they reach for a shot of caffeine. Caffeine cannot substitute for a good night's sleep, however. When you are truly fatigued, caffeine does not help you concentrate; it simply leaves you wired, too jittery to sleep, and too tired to do anything productive.

Eating in Response to Stress: Feeding the Hungry Heart

Few people look on eating and food only in terms of hunger and nutrition.
75 Every culture in the world has evolved rituals around food and eating. Feasting and fasting carry layers of religious, cultural, and emotional overtones. As children, we learn to associate food with security, comfort, love, reward, punishment, anger, restraint. It's no wonder that we eat for many reasons other than hunger: because we're lonely, angry, sad, happy, nervous, or depressed.
80 Unlike alcohol, which we can give up if we are prone to a drinking problem, we must learn to live with food. If eating is the only way we take the time to nurture ourselves, we eat more than we are really hungry for. In extreme

cases, an inability to control eating can develop into an eating disorder known as **compulsive overeating,** that often gets worse under stress.

Food and Mood: The Role of Neurotransmitters

85 Most people feel relaxed and lazy after a big feast. For this reason many cultures have incorporated a siesta after the large midday meal, and professors who teach a class right after lunch or dinner rarely turn out the lights for a slide show. Why do we feel tired? Certainly our blood sugar should be adequate after eating all that food. Changes in brain biochemistry may be the rea-
90 son. The food we eat supplies the precursor molecules for manufacturing neurotransmitters that influence our emotions and mood. Some researchers believe that by selecting the right kinds of food we can encourage states of relaxation or alertness.

Big meals, especially those with a lot of fat, take a long time to digest, and
95 with a full stomach we feel like relaxing rather than working. On the other hand, smaller meals low in fat take less time and energy to digest and leave us feeling more energetic and alert.

Meals that are composed primarily of carbohydrates encourage production of the neurotransmitter *serotonin*, which makes us feel drowsy and relaxed.
100 High-carbohydrate meals are a prescription for relaxation and may be the reason some people overeat: it makes them feel good. A small, high-carbohydrate snack before bedtime can encourage sleep. Many people find that eating carbohydrates helps them feel less stressed and more relaxed. Some people find that a meal or snack with carbohydrate but little protein, especially in the
105 middle of the day, leaves them feeling tired.

Meals that include a small serving of protein foods, with or without carbohydrates, encourage alertness by favoring production of neurotransmitters such as *dopamine* and *norepinephrine*. A small lunch that includes protein foods is best for students who need to stay alert for a 1:00 class.

Physical Activity and Stress Resistance

110 Participation in regular physical activity is one of the most effective ways to increase your stress resistance. Countless studies comparing people with high and low levels of stress resistance have found exercise to be one of the most salient discriminators between these two groups. An important note is that the amount and intensity of exercise required to produce stress management benefits need
115 not be overwhelming. While many athletes enjoy extended periods of intense activity, other people find stress relief with a brisk walk, an hour of gardening, or a game of volleyball on the beach.

Exercise High: Endorphins, Hormones, and Neurotransmitters

In addition to canceling the negative effects of stress, exercise may induce some positive biochemical changes. Many exercisers report feelings of eupho-

120 ria and states of consciousness similar to those described by people using drugs such as heroin. Such accounts have led to use of the term *runner's high*, since these descriptions first came primarily from long-distance runners. These reports have intrigued both exercise scientists and the lay public and have suggested the possibility that certain types of exercise, particularly vigor-
125 ous exercise of long duration, may cause biochemical changes that mimic drug-induced euphoria.

As scientists have come to understand something of brain biochemistry, some interesting hypotheses have emerged. The most publicized of these has focused on a group of chemical messengers found in the central nervous sys-
130 tem (brain and spinal cord) called opioids, since they are similar in structure and function to the drugs that come from the poppy flower: opium, morphine, and heroin. **Beta-endorphins** belong to this group. They not only inhibit pain but also seem to have other roles in the brain as well, such as aiding in memory and learning and registering emotions. It is difficult for scientists to measure
135 opioid concentrations in the central nervous system of humans, but animal research has suggested that endogenous (produced by the body) opioid concentrations increase with level of exercise: more exercise, more opioids.

Rhythmic Exercise: Relaxed Brain Waves

Rhythmic exercises such as walking, running, rowing, and swimming increase **alpha-wave** activity in the brain. The electrical activity of the brain can be
140 monitored in the laboratory using an instrument called an **electroencephalograph (EEG)**. Alpha waves are associated with a calm mental state, such as that produced by meditation or chanting. The rhythmic breathing that occurs during some forms of exercise also contributes to an increase in alpha-wave activity. Rhythmic activity performed to music may be stress relieving in
145 other ways as well.

STAGE 3: RECALL

Stop to self-test, relate, and react.

Your instructor may choose to give you a true-false comprehension review.

 NUTRITION, HEALTH, AND STRESS

Explain how you can use the health and nutritional information in this selection to energize and stimulate your mental performance during exam week. Explain the purpose for each part of your plan and give specific examples.

Contemporary Link

The "Freshman 15" refers not to an athletic team but to the 15 pounds that students often gain during the first year of college. How do you plan to use this information about nutrition and cafeteria/fast food choices to avoid this weight gain?

COMPREHENSION QUESTIONS

After reading the selection, answer the following questions with *a*, *b*, *c*, or *d*.

Main Idea   _____ 1. The best statement of the main idea of this selection is
  a. a balanced diet is the most effective way to decrease stress.
  b. regular exercise and good eating habits contribute to stress reduction and both physical and emotional well being.
  c. stress negatively affects mental and physical performance.
  d. avoiding sugar overload and including protein at every meal help regulate blood sugar.

Detail   _____ 2. The pancreas is signaled to release insulin when
  a. protein is consumed.
  b. blood glucose levels rise.
  c. physical activity increases.
  d. blood sugar levels decrease.

Inference   _____ 3. By using the term "fine cuisine," the author suggests that
  a. "fine" meals include meat, potatoes, and vegetables.
  b. dessert is an important part of "fine dining."
  c. dining halls do not always serve good, nutritional meals.
  d. vegetables should be cooked without fats.

Detail   _____ 4. People who experience symptoms of hypoglycemia should do all of the following except
  a. eat three large meals per day and vary the times.
  b. combine proteins with carbohydrates.
  c. limit sugar intake.
  d. eat several small meals or snacks per day.

Inference   _____ 5. The implied similarity between drinking and eating problems is that
  a. many people who abuse alcohol are also prone to eating problems.
  b. compulsive eating is treated more easily than compulsive drinking.
  c. drinking alcohol and eating food sometimes are misguided responses to stress.
  d. the consumption of both food and alcohol releases endorphins, which reduce stress.

Detail _____ 6. The production of norepinephrine is stimulated by eating
   a. proteins.
   b. fats.
   c. carbohydrates.
   d. caffeine.

Detail _____ 7. The beta-endorphins believed to be released by exercise have all of the following benefits except
   a. inducing feelings of euphoria.
   b. inhibiting pain.
   c. regulating blood sugar.
   d. aiding memory.

Inference _____ 8. The activity most likely to increase alpha-wave activity in the brain would be
   a. playing a game of chess.
   b. jogging.
   c. lifting weights.
   d. playing baseball.

Inference _____ 9. For a midnight snack before bed, the author would most likely recommend
   a. a bagel.
   b. cappuccino.
   c. peanuts.
   d. a chicken leg.

Detail _____ 10. The author's attitude toward the use of caffeine by most people is that
   a. caffeine can be used to decrease fear because it arouses the fight-or-flight response.
   b. light amounts of caffeine appear harmless and can increase alertness.
   c. caffeine should be avoided because it causes stomachaches, nausea, headaches, and irritability.
   d. when a person is truly fatigued, caffeine can increase concentration.

Answer the following with *T* (true) or *F* (false).

Detail _____ 11. Glucose provides the primary fuel for the brain.

Detail _____ 12. Thirst is an adequate indicator of the body's optimal hydration level.

Inference _____ 13. The term *hungry heart* implies a need that food cannot satisfy.

Detail _____ 14. A glass of cola can be counted toward the number of cups of fluid the body needs each day.

Inference _____ 15. The author suggests that serotonin is more important for effective studying than dopamine and norepinephrine.

VOCABULARY

According to the way the italicized word was used in the selection, select *a, b, c,* or *d* for the word or phrase that gives the best definition.

_____ 1. "to *attribute* our moods" (15–16)
    a. to dissociate
    b. to credit
    c. to explain
    d. to reject

_____ 2. "can cause *crankiness*" (17)
    a. rage
    b. irritability
    c. drowsiness
    d. fatigue

_____ 3. "*optimal* levels" (49)
    a. medium
    b. low
    c. satisfactory
    d. regulatory

_____ 4. "its effects *mimic*" (58)
    a. distort
    b. imitate
    c. confuse
    d. falsify

_____ 5. "an already *aroused*" (60)
    a. excited
    b. not stimulated
    c. settled
    d. relaxed

_____ 6. "beverages consumed *judiciously*" (65)
    a. recklessly
    b. hastily
    c. cautiously
    d. carelessly

_____ 7. "we are *prone*" (80)
    a. damaged by
    b. inclined
    c. addicted
    d. connected

_____ 8. "the *precursor* molecules" (90)
    a. necessary
    b. final
    c. active
    d. forerunner

_____ 9. "*salient* discriminators" (112–113)
    a. noticeable
    b. instructive
    c. irrelevant
    d. damaging

_____ 10. "drug-induced *euphoria*" (126)
    a. insanity
    b. disorientation
    c. exhilaration
    d. serenity

SEARCH THE NET

Discover recommendations for an optimal diet and exercise plan by visiting health and nutrition sites. Submit your vital statistics for a plan tailored for you. Describe the recommendations and how you plan to use them. Reference your Websites. Plan your own search or begin by trying the following:

http://www.phys.com/b_nutrition/01self analysis/01home/self.htm

http://www.nutrition.miningco.com/

http://www.eatright.org/

http://www.caloriecontrol.org/caloriecontrol/cgi-bin/calorie calculator.cgi

Go Electronic!

For additional readings, exercises, and Internet activities, visit this book's Website at:
http://www.awlonline.com/smithBTG

For even more activities, visit the Longman English pages at:
http://longman.awl.com/englishpages

If you need a user name and password, please see your instructor.

Take a Road Trip to the Grand Canyon, Florida, and Seattle! Be sure to visit the Reading Textbooks, Outlining and Summarizing, and Note Taking and Textbook Highlighting modules in your Reading Road Trip CD-ROM for multimedia tutorials, exercises, and tests.

READER'S JOURNAL

Name _____ Date _____

Chapter 5

Answer the following questions to learn about your own learning and reflect on progress. Use the perforations to tear the assignment out for your instructor.

1. Why would you tend to learn more from notetaking than from annotating?

   _____

2. Why is it important to indent outlined notes?

   _____

3. Do you prefer the Cornell System of notetaking or outlining? Why?

   _____

4. When taking notes from a text, why do many students tend to write too much?

   _____

5. When you take lecture notes, do you tend to write too much or too little? Why?

   _____

6. Why is it more difficult to take notes on the selection on pregnancy than on the one about nutrition? _____

   _____

7. Why do experts recommend that you review class lecture notes within twenty-four hours after taking them? _____

   _____

8. How do the written critical thinking response questions enrich your understanding of the selection?

   _____

Inference

- What is an inference?
- What is the connotation of a word?
- What is figurative language?
- Why is prior knowledge needed for implied meaning?
- How does a reader draw conclusions?

Michael Melford/The Image Bank

WHAT IS AN INFERENCE?

The first and most basic level of reading is the *literal level*—that is, the level that presents the facts. In reacting to a literal comprehension question, you can actually point to the words on the page that answer the question. Reading, however, progresses beyond this initial stage. A second and more sophisticated level of reading deals with motives, feelings, and judgments; this is the *inferential level*. At this level you no longer can point to the answer, but instead must form the answer from suggestions within the selection. In a manner of speaking, you must read between the lines for the implied meaning.

With inference, rather than directly stating a fact, authors often subtly suggest and thus manipulate the reader. Suggestion can be a more effective method of getting the message across than a direct statement. Suggestion requires greater writing skill, and it is also usually more artistic, creative, and entertaining. The responsible reader searches beyond the printed word for insights into what was left unsaid.

For example, in cigarette advertisements the public is enticed through suggestion, not facts, into spending millions of dollars on a product that is stated to be unhealthful. Depending on the brand, smoking offers the refreshment of a mountain stream or the sophisticated elegance of the rich and famous. Never in the ads is smoking directly praised or pleasure promised; instead, the positive aspects are *implied*. A lawsuit for false advertising is avoided because nothing tangible has been put into print. The emotionalism of a full-page advertisement is so overwhelming that the consumer hardly notices the warning

Reprinted with special permission of King Features Syndicate.

peeking from the bottom of the page—"Warning: The Surgeon General Has Determined That Cigarette Smoking Is Dangerous to Your Health."

> **EXERCISE 6.1**   *Implied Meaning in Advertisements*

Look through magazines and newspapers to locate advertisements for cigarettes, alcoholic beverages, and fragrances. What characteristics do all three types of advertisements have in common? Select one advertisement for each product and answer the following questions about each.

1. What is directly stated about the product?
2. What does the advertisement say about the product?
3. Who seems to be the potential customer for the product?

Authors and advertisers have not invented a new comprehension skill; they are merely capitalizing on an already highly developed skill of daily life. When asked by a student in her class, "How do you like the new president of the college?" the professor might answer, "I think he wears nice suits and is always on time." rather than say, "I don't like the new president." A lack of approval has been suggested by an absence of information, and the professor has avoided making a direct negative statement. In everyday life, we make inferences about people by examining what people say, what they do, and what others say about them. The intuition of everyday life applied to the printed word is the inferential level of reading.

CONNOTATION OF WORDS

Notice the power of suggested meaning in responding to the following questions:

1. If you read an author's description of classmates, which student would you assume is smartest?
   a. A student annotating items on a computer printout
   b. A student with earphones listening to a CD
   c. A student talking with classmates about Seinfeld reruns
2. Which would you find described in a vintage small town of the 1960s?
   a. Movies
   b. Cinema
   c. Picture shows
3. Who probably earns the most money?
   a. A businessperson in a dark suit, white shirt, and tie
   b. A businessperson in slacks and a sport shirt
   c. A businessperson in a pale blue uniform

Can you prove your answers? It's not the same as proving when the Declaration of Independence was signed, yet you still have a feeling for how each question should be answered. Even though a right or wrong answer is difficult to explain in this type of question, certain answers can still be defended as most accurate—they are *a*, *c*, and *a*. The answers are based on feelings, attitudes, and knowledge commonly shared by members of society.

A seemingly innocent tool, word choice is the first key to implied meaning. For example, if a person is skinny, he is unattractive, but if he is slender or slim he must be attractive. All three words might refer to the same underweight person, but *skinny* communicates a negative feeling while *slender* or *slim* communicates a positive one. This feeling or emotionalism surrounding a word is called **connotation. Denotation** is the specific meaning of a word, but the connotative meaning goes beyond this to reflect certain attitudes and prejudices of society. Even though it may not seem premeditated, writers select words, just as advertisers select symbols and models, to manipulate the reader's opinions.

▶ **EXERCISE 6.2**   *Recognizing Connotation in Familiar Words*

In each of the following word pairs, write the letter of the word that connotes the more positive feeling:

_____	1. (a) guest	(b) boarder
_____	2. (a) surplus	(b) waste
_____	3. (a) conceited	(b) proud
_____	4. (a) buzzard	(b) robin
_____	5. (a) heavyset	(b) obese
_____	6. (a) explain	(b) brag
_____	7. (a) house	(b) mansion
_____	8. (a) song	(b) serenade
_____	9. (a) calculating	(b) clever
_____	10. (a) neglected	(b) deteriorated
_____	11. (a) colleague	(b) accomplice
_____	12. (a) ambition	(b) greed
_____	13. (a) kitten	(b) cat
_____	14. (a) courageous	(b) audacious
_____	15. (a) contrived	(b) designed
_____	16. (a) flower	(b) orchid
_____	17. (a) distinctive	(b) peculiar
_____	18. (a) baby	(b) kid
_____	19. (a) persuasion	(b) propaganda
_____	20. (a) gold	(b) tin
_____	21. (a) slump	(b) decline
_____	22. (a) lie	(b) misrepresentation
_____	23. (a) janitor	(b) custodian
_____	24. (a) offering	(b) collection
_____	25. (a) soldiers	(b) mercenaries

> **EXERCISE 6.3**   *Connotation in Textbooks*

For each of the underlined words in the following sentences, indicate the meaning of the word and reasons why the connotation is positive or negative. Note the following example:

EXAMPLE

While the unions fought mainly for better wages and hours, they also <u>championed</u> various social reforms.

Leonard Pitt, We Americans

championed: *means "supported"; suggests heroes and thus a positive cause*

1. The ad was part of the oil companies' program to sell their image rather than their product to the public. In the ad they <u>boasted</u> that they were re-seeding all the disrupted areas with a newly developed grass that grows five times faster than the grass that normally occurs there.

Robert Wallace, Biology: The World of Life

boasted: _____

2. John Adams won the election, despite <u>backstage maneuvering</u> by Alexander Hamilton against him.

James Kirby Martin et al., America and Its People

backstage maneuvering: _____

3. Tinbergen, like Lorenz and von Frisch, entered retirement by continuing to work. Tinbergen was a hyperactive child who, at school, was allowed to periodically dance on his desk to let off steam. So in "<u>retirement</u>" he entered a new arena, stimulating the use of ethological methods in autism.

Robert Wallace, Biology: The World of Life

"retirement": _____

4. The nation's capital is <u>crawling</u> with lawyers, lobbyists, registered foreign agents, public relations consultants, and others—more than 14,000 individuals representing nearly 12,000 organizations at last count—all seeking to influence Congress.

Robert Lineberry et al., Government in America

crawling: _____

5. Not since Wilson had tried to <u>ram</u> the League of Nations through the Senate had any president put more on the line.

Leonard Pitt, We Americans

ram: _____

FIGURATIVE LANGUAGE

Figurative language requires readers to make inferences about comparisons that are not literally true and sometimes not logically related. What does it mean to say, "She worked like a dog"? To most readers it means that she worked hard, but since few dogs work, the comparison is not literally true or particularly logical. **Figurative language** is, in a sense, another language because it is a different way of using "regular" words so that they take on new meaning. For example, "It was raining buckets" or "raining cats and dogs" are lively, figurative ways of describing a heavy rain. New speakers of English, however, who comprehend on a literal level, might look up in the sky for the descending pails or animals. The two expressions create an exaggerated, humorous effect, but on the literal level, they do not make sense.

Idioms

When first used, "works like a dog" and "raining cats and dogs" were probably very clever. Now the phrases have lost their freshness, but still convey meaning for those who are "in the know." Such phrases are called **idioms,** or expressions that do not make literal sense but have taken on a new generally accepted meaning over many years of use.

EXAMPLE   She tried to *keep a stiff upper lip* during the ordeal.

His eyes were *bigger than his stomach.*

EXPLANATION   The first means to maintain control and the second means to ask for more than you are able to eat.

EXAMPLE   What do the following idioms mean?

make up your mind _____

give me five _____

catch a cold _____

fit like a glove _____

EXPLANATION   *Make up your mind* means to decide, *give me five* means agreement, or "good job!", *catch a cold* means to get sick with a cold, and *fit like a glove* means to fit snugly.

Writers using figurative language try to move beyond familiar idioms and create original expressions. They use devices called similes, metaphors, personifications, and verbal irony to paint vivid images and to add zest, surprise, and beauty to the language. Readers may be caught off guard because such expressions are not literally true. Sophisticated readers use clues within the passage, as well as prior knowledge, to figure out meaning for these imaginative uses of language.

Similes

A **simile** is a comparison of two unlike things using the words *like* or *as*.

EXAMPLE

The spring flower pushed up its bloom *like a lighthouse* beckoning on a gloomy night.

And every soul, it passed me by,
Like the whizz of my crossbow!

Samuel Coleridge, *The Rime of the Ancient Mariner*

Metaphors

A **metaphor** is a direct comparison of two unlike things (without using *like* or *as*).

EXAMPLE

The corporate accountant is a computer from nine to five.

Miss Rosie was a wet brown bag of a woman who used to be the best looking gal in Georgia.

Lucille Clifton, *Good Times*

Personification

Personification is attributing human characteristics to nonhuman things.

EXAMPLE

The *birds speak* from the forest.
Time marches on.

Verbal Irony

Verbal **irony** is the use of words to express a meaning that is the opposite of what is literally said.[1] If the intent is to hurt, the irony is called **sarcasm.**

EXAMPLE

"What a great looking corporate outfit!" (said to someone wearing torn jeans)
"There is nothing like a sunny day for a picnic." (said to pouring rain)

▶ **EXERCISE 6.4**   *Figurative Language in Textbooks*

The figurative expressions in the following sentences are underlined. Identify the figurative type, define each expression, and suggest, if possible, the reason for its use. Follow this example:

---

[1]In situational irony, events occur contrary to what is expected, as if in a cruel twist of fate. For example, Juliet awakens and finds that Romeo has killed himself because he thought she was dead.

EXAMPLE

As a trained nurse working in the immigrant slums of New York, she knew that <u>table-top</u> abortions were common among poor women, and she had seen some of the tragic results.

Leonard Pitt, We Americans

It is a metaphor, which may now be an idiom, and means illegal. The connotation suggests the reality of where the operations probably occurred.

1. The War of 1812 was Tecumseh's final test. Although his alliance was incomplete, he recognized that the war was his last chance to prevail against the "Long Knives," as the Americans were called. He <u>cast his lot</u> with the British, who at one point gave him command over <u>a red coat army.</u>

Leonard Pitt, We Americans

cast his lot: _____

red coat army: _____

2. Everywhere one looked, the birds warbled and the dewdrops shone on the flowers like a rain of fiery pearls.

Eusebio Chacon, The Son of the Storm

like a rain of fiery pearls _____

3. Americans "<u>discovered</u>" the Spanish Southwest in the 1820s. Yankee settlers Moses and Stephen Austin took a party of settlers into Texas in 1821.

Leonard Pitt, We Americans

"discovered": _____

4. Then she screamed an extremely fierce "I said, preach it" and stepped up on the altar. The Reverend kept on throwing out phrases <u>like home-run balls</u> and Sister Monroe made a quick break and grasped for him. For just a second, everything and everyone in the church except Reverend Taylor and Sister Monroe hung loose <u>like stockings on a washline.</u>

Maya Angelou, "Sister Monroe"

like home-run balls: _____

like stockings on a washline: _____

5. The <u>Moving Finger</u> writes; and, having writ,
   Moves on; nor all <u>your Piety nor Wit</u>
   Shall lure it back <u>to cancel half a Line,</u>
   Nor all your <u>Tears wash out a Word of it.</u>

The Rubáiyát of Omar Khayyám

Moving Finger: _____

your Piety nor Wit: _____

to cancel half a Line: _____

Tears wash out a Word of it: _____

IMPLIED MEANING

Reading would be rather dull if the author stated every idea, never giving you a chance to figure things out for yourself. For example, in a mystery novel you carefully weigh each word, each action, each conversation, each description, and each fact in an effort to identify the villain and solve the crime before it is revealed at the end. Although textbook material may not have the Sherlock Holmes spirit of high adventure, authors use the same techniques to imply meaning.

Note the inferences in the following example:

EXAMPLE

Johnson in Action

Lyndon Johnson suffered from the inevitable comparison with his young and stylish predecessor. LBJ was acutely aware of his own lack of polish; he sought to surround himself with Kennedy advisers and insiders, hoping that their learning and sophistication would rub off on him. Johnson's assets were very real—an intimate knowledge of Congress, an incredible energy and determination to succeed, and a fierce ego. When a young marine officer tried to direct him to the proper helicopter, saying, "This one is yours," Johnson replied, "Son, they are all my helicopters."

LBJ's height and intensity gave him a powerful presence; he dominated any room he entered, and he delighted in using his physical power of persuasion. One Texas politician explained why he had given in to Johnson: "Lyndon got me by the lapels and put his face on top of mine and he talked and talked and talked. I figured it was either getting drowned or joining."

Robert A. Divine et al., *America Past and Present*

Answer the following with *T* (true) or *F* (false).

_____ 1. Johnson was haunted by the style and sophistication of John F. Kennedy.

_____ 2. Johnson could be both egotistical and arrogant about his presidential power.

_____ 3. Even if he did not mentally persuade, Johnson could physically overwhelm people into agreement.

EXPLANATION   The answer to question 1 is *True*. He "suffered from the inevitable comparison" and he went so far as to retain the Kennedy advisors. Question 2 is *True*. The anecdote about the helicopters proves that. Question 3 is *True*. His delight in "using his physical powers of persuasion" and the anecdote about the Texas politician support that.

In the following exercises, you can see how authors use suggestions. From the clues given, you can deduce the facts.

▶ EXERCISE 6.5   *Inference from Description*

Looking back on the Revolutionary War, one cannot say enough about Washington's leadership. While his military skills proved less than brilliant and he and his generals lost many battles, George Washington was the single most important figure of the colonial war effort. His original appointment was partly political, for the rebellion that had started in Massachusetts needed a commander from the South to give geographic balance to the cause. The choice fell to Washington, a wealthy and respectable Virginia planter with military experience dating back to the French and Indian War. He had been denied a commission in the English army and had never forgiven the English for the insult. During the war he shared the physical suffering of his men, rarely wavered on important questions, and always used his officers to good advantage. His correspondence with Congress to ask for sorely needed supplies was tireless and forceful. He recruited several new armies in a row, as short-term enlistments gave out.

Leonard Pitt, *We Americans*[2]

Answer the following with *T* (true) or *F* (false).

_____ 1. The author regards George Washington as the most brilliant military genius in American history.

_____ 2. A prime factor in Washington's becoming president of the United States was a need for geographic balance.

_____ 3. Washington resented the British for a past injustice.

_____ 4. The Revolutionary War started as a rebellion in the Northeast.

_____ 5. The author believes that Washington's leadership was courageous and persistent even though not infallible.

▶ EXERCISE 6.6   *Inference from Action*

When he came to the surface he was conscious of little but the noisy water. Afterward he saw his companions in the sea. The oiler was ahead in

[2]From Leonard Pitt, *We Americans*. Copyright © 1987 by Kendall Hunt Publishing Company. Reprinted with permission.

the race. He was swimming strongly and rapidly. Off to the correspondent's left, the cook's great white and corked back bulged out of the water, and in the rear the captain was hanging with his one good hand to the keel of the overturned dinghy.

There is a certain immovable quality to a shore, and the correspondent wondered at it amid the confusion of the sea.

Stephen Crane, *The Open Boat*

Answer the following with *a, b, c,* or *d.* Draw a map indicating the shore and the positions of the four people in the water to help you visualize the scene.

_____ 1. The reason that the people are in the water is because of
 a. a swimming race.
 b. an airplane crash.
 c. a capsized boat.
 d. a group decision.

_____ 2. In relation to his companions, the correspondent is
 a. closest to the shore.
 b. the second or third closest to the shore.
 c. farthest from the shore.
 d. in a position that is impossible to determine.

_____ 3. The member of the group that had probably suffered a previous injury is the
 a. oiler.
 b. correspondent.
 c. cook.
 d. captain.

_____ 4. The member of the group that the author seems to stereotype negatively as least physically fit is the
 a. oiler.
 b. correspondent.
 c. cook.
 d. captain.

_____ 5. The story is being told through the eyes of the
 a. oiler.
 b. correspondent.
 c. cook.
 d. captain.

EXERCISE 6.7   *Inference from Factual Material*

Except for some minor internal disturbances in the nineteenth century, Switzerland has been at peace inside stable boundaries since 1815. The basic factors underlying this long period of peace seem to have been (1)

Switzerland's position as a buffer between larger powers, (2) the comparative defensibility of much of the country's terrain, (3) the relatively small value of Swiss economic production to an aggressive state, (4) the country's value as an intermediary between belligerents in wartime, and (5) Switzerland's own policy of strict and heavily armed neutrality. The difficulties which a great power might encounter in attempting to conquer Switzerland have often been popularly exaggerated since the Swiss Plateau, the heart of the country, lies open to Germany and France, and even the Alps have frequently been traversed by strong military forces in past times. On the other hand, resistance in the mountains might well be hard to thoroughly extinguish. In World War II Switzerland was able to hold a club over the head of Germany by mining the tunnels through which Swiss rail lines avoid the crests of Alpine passes. Destruction of these tunnels would have been very costly to Germany, as well as to its military partner, Italy.

Jesse H. Wheeler et al., *Regional Geography of the World*

Answer the following with *T* (true) or *F* (false).

_____ 1. The author implies that Switzerland is rich with raw materials for economic production.

_____ 2. The most important economic area of Switzerland is protected from its neighbors by the Alps.

_____ 3. In World War II Germany did not invade Switzerland primarily because of the fear of the strong Swiss army.

_____ 4. The maintenance of a neutral Swiss position in World War II was due in part to a kind of international blackmail.

_____ 5. The Swiss have avoided international war on their soil for over one hundred years.

PRIOR KNOWLEDGE AND IMPLIED MEANING

Have you ever considered what makes a joke funny? Why is it no longer funny when you have to explain the meaning of a joke to someone who didn't understand it? The answer is that jokes are funny because of implied connections. The meaning that you may have to reluctantly explain is the inference or **implied meaning.** If the listener does not share the background knowledge to which the joke refers, your hilarious comic attempt will fall flat because the listener cannot understand the implied meaning. Listeners cannot connect with something they don't know, so you must choose the right joke for the right audience.

College reading may not be filled with comedy, but **prior knowledge** is expected and specifics are frequently implied rather than directly spelled out. For example, if a sentence began, "Previously wealthy investors were leaping from buildings in the financial district," you would know that the author was referring to the Stock Market Crash of 1929 on Wall Street in New York

City. The details fall into a already existing schema. Although the specifics are not directly stated, you have used prior knowledge and have "added up" the details that are meaningful to you to infer time and place.

© 2000 Addison-Wesley Educational Publishers, Inc.

> **EXERCISE 6.8**   *Inferring Time and Place*

Read the following passages and indicate *a, b,* or *c* for the suggested time or place. Use your prior knowledge of "anchor" dates in history to logically think about the possible responses. Underline the clues that helped you arrive at your answer.

Passage A

As women strove to maintain a semblance of home on the trail, they often experienced a profound sense of loss. The Sabbath, which had been ladies' day back home and an emblem of women's moral authority, was often spent working or traveling, especially once the going got rough. "Oh dear me I did not think we would have abused the sabbath in such a manner," wrote one guilt-stricken female emigrant. Women also felt the lack of close companions, to whom they could turn for comfort. One woman, whose husband separated their wagon from the train after a dispute, sadly watched the other wagons pull away: "I felt that indeed I had left all my friends to journey over the dreaded plains without one female acquaintance even for a companion—of course I wept and grieved about it but to no purpose."

James Davidson et al., *Nation of Nations*

_____ 1. The time when this takes place is probably in the
     a. 1920s.
     b. 1710s.
     c. 1840s.

_____ 2. The section of the United States is most likely the
     a. west.
     b. south.
     c. north.

        3. Underline the clues to your answers.

Passage B

There was an average of fifty storms a year. Cities kept their street lights on for twenty-four hours a day. Dust covered everything from food to bedspreads and piled up in dunes in city streets and barnyards. Thousands died of "dust pneumonia." One woman remembered what it was like at night: "A trip for water to rinse the grit from our lips, and then back to bed with washclothes over our noses, we try to lie still, because every turn stirs the dust on the blankets."

By the end of the decade three and a half million people had abandoned their farms and joined a massive migration to find a better life. Not all were forced out by the dust storms; some fell victim to large-scale agriculture, and many tenant farmers and hired hands were expendable during the depression. In most cases they not only lost their jobs, but they also were evicted from their houses.

Gary B. Nash et al., The American People

_____ 4. The time is probably in the
　　　　　　　　a. 1690s.
　　　　　　　　b. 1770s.
　　　　　　　　c. 1930s.

_____ 5. The place is most likely
　　　　　　　　a. New England.
　　　　　　　　b. the Great Plains.
　　　　　　　　c. the Deep South.

　　　　　　6. Underline the clues to your answer.

Passage C

On November 28 the first tea ship, the *Dartmouth,* docked. The local customs collectors fled to Fort Castle William, and the local committee of correspondence, headed by Samuel Adams and his associates, put guards on the *Dartmouth* and two other tea ships entering the port within the next few days. Repeatedly the popular rights faction insisted that the three tea ships be sent back to England. But Governor Hutchinson refused. Instead, he called upon Royal Naval vessels in the vicinity to block off the port's entrance.

James Martin et al., America and Its People

_____ 7. The time is probably in the
　　　　　　　　a. 1770s.
　　　　　　　　b. 1850s.
　　　　　　　　c. 1670s.

_____ 8. The place is probably in
　　　　　　　　a. Washington, D.C.
　　　　　　　　b. Boston.
　　　　　　　　c. New Orleans.

　　　　　　9. Underline the clues to your answers.

Expanding Prior Knowledge

Your response on these passages depends on your previous knowledge of history and your general knowledge. If you did not understand many of the inferences, you might ask, "How can I expand my prior knowledge?" The answer is not an easy formula or a quick fix. The answer is part of the reason that you are in college; it is a combination of broadening your horizons, reading more widely, and being an active participant in your own life. Expanding prior knowledge is a slow and steady daily process.

DRAWING CONCLUSIONS

To arrive at a conclusion, you must make a logical deduction from both stated and unstated ideas. Using the hints as well as the facts, you rely on prior knowledge and experience to interpret motives, actions, and outcomes. You draw conclusions on the basis of perceived evidence, but because perceptions differ, conclusions can vary from reader to reader. Generally, however, authors attempt to direct readers to preconceived conclusions. Read the following example and look for a basis for the stated conclusion.

EXAMPLE   **Underground Conductor**

Harriet Tubman was on a northbound train when she overheard her name spoken by a white passenger. He was reading aloud an ad which accused her of stealing $50,000 worth of property in slaves, and which offered a $5000 reward for her capture. She lowered her head so that the sunbonnet she was wearing hid her face. At the next station she slipped off the train and boarded another that was headed south, reasoning that no one would pay attention to a black woman traveling in that direction. She deserted the second train near her hometown in Maryland and bought two chickens as part of her disguise. With her back hunched over in imitation of an old woman, she drove the chickens down the dusty road, calling angrily and chasing them with her stick whenever she sensed danger. In this manner Harriet Tubman was passed by her former owner who did not even notice her. The reward continued to mount until it reached $40,000.

Leonard Pitt, *We Americans*

Conclusion: Harriet Tubman was a clever woman who became a severe irritant to white slave owners.

What is the basis for this conclusion?

_____

_____

EXPLANATION   Her disguise and subsequent escape from the train station provide evidence for her intelligence. The escalating amount of the reward, finally $40,000, proves the severity of the sentiment against her.

> **EXERCISE 6.9**   *Drawing Conclusions*

Read the following passages. For the first two passages indicate evidence for the conclusions that have been drawn. For the latter passages, write your own conclusion, as well as indicate evidence.

Passage A

A tragic counterpoint to the voluntary movement of American workers in search of jobs was the forced relocation of 120,000 Japanese-Americans from the West Coast. Responding to racial fears in California after Pearl Harbor, President Roosevelt approved an army order in February 1942 to move both the Issei (Japanese-Americans who had emigrated from Japan) and the Nisei (people of Japanese ancestry born in the United States and therefore American citizens) to concentration camps in the interior. Forced to sell their farms and businesses at distress prices, the Japanese-Americans lost not only their liberty but also most of their worldly goods. Herded into ten hastily built detention centers in seven western states, they lived as prisoners in tar-papered barracks behind barbed wire, guarded by armed troops.

Robert Divine et al., America Past and Present

Conclusion: After Pearl Harbor many Japanese-Americans were treated unfairly by the American government.

What is the basis for this conclusion?

_____

_____

Passage B

Pesticides are biologically rather interesting substances. They have no known counterpart in the natural world, and most of them didn't even exist thirty years ago. Today, however, a metabolic product of DDT, called DDE, may be the most common and widely distributed man-made chemical on earth. It has been found in the tissues of living things from the polar regions to the remotest parts of the oceans, forests, and mountains. Although the permissible level of DDT in cow's milk, set by the U.S. Food and Drug Administration, is 0.05 parts per million, it often occurs in human milk in concentrations as high as 5 parts per million and in human fat at levels of more than 12 parts per million.

Robert Wallace, Biology: The World of Life

Conclusion: DDT accumulates in the environment far beyond the areas where it was directly applied.

What is the basis for this conclusion?

_____

_____

Passage C

Writing is untidy and disconcerting. No successful ad company would want to market it. It's not fast, it's not predictable, it's not sweet. First we fantasize about that hushed moment when we'll be wonderfully alone with all our familiar, comforting writing implements at hand. I visualize a sunny room and my cup of tea. We savor the moment when, bulging with inspiration and wisdom, we at last lift our pen or start our computer and begin a new work. And work it is, though we forget that aspect in the amnesia necessary to bring us back to the blank page.

Pat Moro, "Universities" in *Nepantla*

Conclusion: _____

_____

What is the basis for this conclusion? _____

_____

Passage D

Panic attacks are not common, but they can be very debilitating for those who suffer them. They consist of sudden, irrational feelings of doom, sometimes accompanied by choking, sweating, and heart palpitations.

In an experiment conducted at NIMH laboratories in Maryland, a group of people who had previously suffered panic attacks were given 480 mg caffeine, equivalent to about 5 cups of brewed coffee. Panic attacks were precipitated in almost half of those people. In a group of 14 people who had never before experienced a panic attack, two suffered an attack after receiving 720 mg caffeine.

Oakley Ray and Charles Ksir, *Drugs, Society, and Human Behavior*

Conclusion: _____

_____

What is the basis for this conclusion? _____

_____

EXERCISE 6.10 *Building a Story with Inferences*

The following story unfolds as the reader uses the clues to predict and make inferences. To make sense out of the story, the reader is never told—but must figure out—who the main character is, what he is doing, and why he is doing it. Like a mystery, the story is fun to read because you are actively involved. Review the strategies for making inferences and then use your inferential skills to figure it out.

> **READER'S TIP**   **Making Inferences**
>
> ▶ Consider attitude in the choice of words.
>
> ▶ Unravel actions.
>
> ▶ Interpret motives.
>
> ▶ Use suggested meaning and facts to make assumptions.
>
> ▶ Draw on prior knowledge to make connections.
>
> ▶ Base conclusions on stated ideas and unstated assumptions.

Caged

Emphatically, Mr. Purcell did not believe in ghosts. Nevertheless, the man who bought the two doves, and his strange act immediately thereafter, left him with a distinct sense of the eerie.

Purcell was a small, fussy man; red cheeks and a tight, melon stomach. He owned a pet shop. He sold cats and dogs and monkeys; he dealt in fish food and bird seed, and prescribed remedies for ailing canaries. He considered himself something of a professional man.

There was a bell over the door that jangled whenever a customer entered. This morning, however, for the first time Mr. Purcell could recall, it failed to ring. Simply he glanced up, and there was the stranger, standing just inside the door, as if he had materialized out of thin air.

The storekeeper slid off his stool. From the first instant he knew instinctively, unreasonably, that the man hated him; but out of habit he rubbed his hands briskly together, smiled and nodded.

"Good morning," he beamed. "What can I do for you?"

The man's shiny shoes squeaked forward. His suit was cheap, ill-fitting, but obviously new. A gray pallor deadened his pinched features. He had a shuttling glance and close-cropped hair. He stared closely at Purcell and said, "I want something in a cage."

"Something in a cage?" Mr. Purcell was a bit confused. "You mean—some kind of pet?"

"I mean what I said!" snapped the man. "Something alive that's in a cage."

"I see," hastened the storekeeper, not at all certain that he did. "Now let me think. A white rat, perhaps."

"No!" said the man. "Not rats. Something with wings. Something that flies."

"A bird!" exclaimed Mr. Purcell.

"A bird's all right." The customer pointed suddenly to a suspended cage which contained two snowy birds. "Doves? How much for those?"

"Five-fifty. And a very reasonable price."

"Five-fifty?" The sallow man was obviously crestfallen. He hesitantly produced a five-dollar bill. "I'd like to have those birds. But this is all I got. Just five dollars."

Mentally, Mr. Purcell made a quick calculation, which told him that at a fifty-cent reduction he could still reap a tidy profit. He smiled magnanimously. "My dear man, if you want them that badly, you can certainly have them for five dollars."

"I'll take them." He laid his five dollars on the counter. Mr. Purcell teetered on tiptoe, unhooked the cage, and handed it to his customer. The man cocked his head to one side, listening to the constant chittering, the rushing scurry of the shop. "That noise?" he blurted. "Doesn't it get you? I mean all this caged stuff. Drives you crazy, doesn't it?"

Purcell drew back. Either the man was insane, or drunk.

"Listen." The staring eyes came closer. "How long d'you think it took me to make that five dollars?"

The merchant wanted to order him out of the shop. But he heard himself dutifully asking, "Why—why, how long *did* it take you?"

The other laughed. "Ten years! At hard labor. Ten years to earn five dollars. Fifty cents a year."

It was best, Purcell decided, to humor him. "My, my! Ten years—"

"They give you five dollars," laughed the man, "and a cheap suit, and tell you not to get caught again."

Mr. Purcell mopped his sweating brow. "Now, about the care and feeding of—"

"Bah!" The sallow man swung around, and stalked abruptly from the store.

Purcell sighed with sudden relief. He waddled to the window and stared out. Just outside, his peculiar customer had halted. He was holding the cage shoulder-high, staring at his purchase. Then, opening the cage, he reached inside and drew out one of the doves. He tossed it into the air. He drew out the second and tossed it after the first. They rose like wind-blown balls of fluff and were lost in the smoky grey of the wintry city. For an instant the liberator's silent and lifted gaze watched after them. Then he dropped the cage. A futile, suddenly forlorn figure, he shoved both hands deep in his trouser pockets, hunched down his head and shuffled away. . . .

The merchant's brow was puckered with perplexity. "Now why," Mr. Purcell muttered, "did he do that?" He felt vaguely insulted.

Lloyd Eric Reeve, Household Magazine

1. Where had the man been? _____

_____

2. How do you know for sure? Underline the clues.

_____

3. When did you figure it out? Circle the clincher. _____

_____

4. Why does he want to set the birds free? _____

_____

5. Why should the shopkeeper feel insulted? _____

_____

6. After freeing the birds, why is the stranger "a futile, suddenly forlorn figure," rather than happy and excited? _____

_____

Summary Points

■ **What is an inference?**

The inferential level of reading deals with motives, feelings, and judgments. The reader must read between the lines and look for the implied
meaning in words and actions.

■ **What is the connotation of a word?**

The feeling or emotionalism surrounding a word is its connotation. The
connotation reflects certain attitudes and prejudices of society that can be
positive or negative. The author's choice of words can manipulate the
reader.

■ **What is figurative language?**

Figurative language creates images to suggest attitudes. It is a different way
of using "regular" words so that the words take on a new meaning. A simile is a comparison of two unlike things using the words *like* or *as*, whereas
a metaphor is a directly stated comparison. Personification attributes human characteristics to nonhuman things. Verbal irony expresses a meaning
the opposite of what is literally said.

■ **Why is prior knowledge needed for implied meaning?**

The reader must have background knowledge in a subject in order to understand the suggested or implied meaning.

■ **How does a reader draw conclusions?**

The reader makes a logical deduction from hints, facts, and prior knowledge.

CONTEMPORARY FOCUS

Stressful circumstances can cause desperate reactions. The suffering and misery of war can cause a wide range of psychological responses, involving both soldiers and their loved ones at home.

TO MAKE A DRAMA OUT OF TRAUMA

Fokko De Vries

Lancet, May 23, 1998

The whole notion of an acute, chronic, or delayed post-traumatic stress disorder (PTSD) is, regrettably, a daily reality for millions of people. As a diagnostic concept, PTSD has been given, with universal validity, a well-deserved place in modern textbooks. Every modern textbook will tell you that PTSD has long been recognized in clinical psychiatry, but for which official recognition has been minimum, late in arriving, and long overdue.

Most of the mental problems present themselves much later, during "peacetime." In a war, all energy, or what is left of it, is focused on survival. In peacetime, an individual's horizon or perspective changes. The numbness is often replaced by intensive suffering once the individual realizes what has happened, and whom and what he or she has lost. About 60,000 Americans were killed in Vietnam. According to one estimate in 1985, more than 50,000 Vietnam veterans in the USA have killed themselves since their return, years after the war ended. How many of them already had mental problems during the war itself? Few, probably, compared with the numbers back home decades later. How many suicides could have been averted by early counseling?

Collaborate to respond to the following questions:

- What is post-traumatic stress disorder?
- Why do you suppose that post-traumatic stress disorder is frequently a delayed reaction?
- What countries today are in conflicts that could cause its citizens to suffer from post-traumatic stress disorder?

STAGE 1: PREVIEW

The author's main purpose is to tell a story.

Agree ☐   Disagree ☐

This selection is narrative rather than expository.

Agree ☐   Disagree ☐

Activate Schema

Have you read another short story by de Maupassant entitled "The Necklace"?

Word Knowledge

What do you know about these words?

cherish	unappeased	foraging	wiry	ferocious
perogative	atrocious	bellicose	devoured	reprisal

Your instructor may give a true-false vocabulary review before or after reading.

STAGE 2: INTEGRATE KNOWLEDGE WHILE READING

Predict   Picture   Relate   Monitor   Correct

This cottage is nestled in the woods of Provence, France.

MOTHER SAVAGE

From Guy de Maupassant, *Mademoiselle Fifi and Other Stories*

I had not been back to Virelogne for fifteen years. I returned there to do some shooting in the autumn, staying with my friend Serval, who had finally rebuilt his château, which had been destroyed by the Prussians.

5   I was terribly fond of that part of the country. There are some delightful places in this world which have a sensual charm for the eyes. One loves them with a physical love. We people who are attracted by the countryside cherish fond memories of certain springs, certain woods, certain ponds, certain hills, which have become familiar sights and can touch our

10   hearts like happy events. Sometimes indeed the memory goes back towards a forest glade, or a spot on a river bank, or an orchard in blossom, glimpsed only once on a happy day, but preserved in our heart like those pictures of women seen in the street on a spring morning, wearing gay, flimsy dresses, and which leave in our soul and flesh an unappeased, unforgettable desire, the feeling

15   that happiness has passed us by.

At Virelogne I loved the whole region, scattered with little woods and crossed by streams which ran through the ground like veins carrying blood to the earth. We fished in them for crayfish, trout and eels. What heavenly happiness we knew there! There were certain places where we could bathe, and

20   we often found snipe in the tall grass which grew on the banks of those narrow brooks.

© 2000 Addison-Wesley Educational Publishers, Inc.

I walked along, as light-footed as a goat, watching my two dogs foraging ahead of me. Serval, a hundred yards to my right, was beating a field of lucerne. I went round the bushes which mark the edge of Saudres woods, and

25 I noticed a cottage in ruins.

All of a sudden I remembered it as it had been the last time I had seen it, in 1869, neat, covered with vines, with chickens outside the door. What is sadder than a dead house, with nothing left standing but its skeleton, a sinister ruin?

I remembered too that a woman had given me a glass of wine inside the

30 house, one day when I was very tired, and that afterwards Serval had told me the story of the occupants. The father, an old poacher, had been killed by the gendarmes. The son, whom I had seen before, was a tall, wiry fellow who was likewise supposed to be a ferocious killer of game. People called the family the Savages.

35 Was it a name or a nickname?

I called out to Serval. He came over to me with his long lanky stride. I asked him: "What has become of the people who lived here?"

And he told me this story.

"When war was declared, the younger Savage, who was then thirty-three

40 years old, enlisted, leaving his mother alone at home. People didn't feel too sorry for the old woman, though, because they knew she had money.

"So she stayed all alone in this isolated house, far away from the village, on the edge of the woods. But she wasn't afraid, because she was made of the same stuff as her men, a tough, tall, thin old woman, who didn't laugh very

45 often and whom nobody joked with. Country women don't laugh much anyway. That's the men's business! They have sad, narrow souls, because they lead dull, dreary lives. The peasant learns a little noisy gaiety in the tavern, but his wife remains serious, forever wearing a stern expression. The muscles of her face have never learnt the motions of laughter.

50 "Mother Savage continued to lead her usual life in her cottage, which was soon covered with snow. She came to the village once a week to get bread and a little meat; then she returned to her cottage. As there was talk of wolves in the region, she went out with a gun slung over her shoulder, her son's gun, which was rusty, with the butt worn down by the rubbing of the hand. She

55 was a strange sight, the Savage woman, tall, rather bent, striding slowly through the snow, with the barrel of the gun showing above the tight black head-dress which imprisoned the white hair nobody had ever seen.

"One day the Prussians arrived. They were distributed among the local inhabitants according to the means and resources of each. The old woman, who

60 was known to be well off, had four soldiers billeted on her.

"They were four big young fellows with fair skins, fair beards and blue eyes, who had remained quite plump in spite of the hardships they had already endured, and good-natured even though they were in conquered territory. Alone with that old woman, they showed her every consideration, sparing her

65 fatigue and expense as best they could. All four were to be seen washing at the well every morning in their shirt-sleeves, splashing water, in the cold glare

of the snow, over their pink and white flesh, the flesh of men of the north, while Mother Savage went to and fro, cooking their soup. They could then be seen cleaning the kitchen, polishing the floor, chopping wood, peeling pota-
70 toes, washing the linen, and doing all the household jobs, just like four good sons helping their mother.

"But the old woman kept thinking all the time about her own son, her tall thin boy with his hooked nose, his brown eyes, and the bushy moustache which covered his upper lip with a roll of black hair. Every day she asked each
75 of the soldiers sitting around her hearth: 'Do you know where the French regiment has gone—the Twenty-third Infantry? My boy is in it.'

"They would reply: 'No, we don't know. We have no idea.'

"And, understanding her grief and anxiety, they, who had mothers of their own at home, performed countless little services for her. She for her part was
80 quite fond of her four enemies, for peasants scarcely ever feel patriotic hatred: that is the prerogative of the upper classes. The humble, those who pay the most because they are poor and because every new burden weighs heavily on them, those who are killed in droves, who form the real cannon-fodder because they are the most numerous, who, in a word, suffer the most from the
85 atrocious hardships of war because they are the weakest and most vulnerable, find it hard to understand those bellicose impulses, those touchy points of honour and those so-called political manoeuvres which exhaust two nations within six months, the victor as well as the vanquished.

"The people around here, speaking of Mother Savage's Germans, used to
90 say: 'Those four have found a cosy billet, and no mistake.'

"Now, one morning, when the old woman was alone in the house, she caught sight of a man a long way off on the plain coming towards her home. Soon she recognized him: it was the man whose job it was to deliver letters. He handed her a folded piece of paper, and she took the spectacles she used
95 for sewing out of their case. Then she read:

> Madame Savage, this is to give you some sad news. Your son Victor was killed yesterday by a cannon-ball which pretty well cut him in two. I was very close, seeing as we were side by side in the company, and he had asked me to let you know if anything happened to him.
>   I took his watch out of his pocket to bring it back to you when the war is over.
>   Best regards.
>   CÉSAIRE RIVOT,
>   Private in the 23rd Infantry.

"The letter was dated three weeks earlier.

"She didn't cry. She stood stock still, so shocked and dazed that she didn't even feel any grief yet. She thought to herself: 'Now it's Victor who's gone and got killed.' Then, little by little, the tears came into her eyes and grief
100 flooded into her heart. Ideas occurred to her one by one, horrible, agonizing ideas. She would never kiss him again, her big boy, never! The gendarmes had killed the father, the Prussians had killed the son. He had been cut in two by a cannon-ball. And it seemed to her that she could see the horrible thing hap-

pening: the head falling, the eyes wide open, while he was chewing the end of
105 his bushy moustache as he always did when he was angry.

"What had they done with his body afterwards? If only they had sent her
boy back to her, as they had sent back her husband, with the bullet in the
middle of his forehead!

"But then she heard the sound of voices. It was the Prussians coming back
110 from the village. She quickly hid the letter in her pocket and, having had time
to wipe her eyes, greeted them calmly, looking her usual self.

"All four of them were laughing with delight, for they had brought back a
fine rabbit, which had probably been stolen, and they made signs to the old
woman that they were going to eat something good.

115 "She set to work straight away getting dinner ready, but when it came to
killing the rabbit, her heart failed her. And it wasn't the first by any means!
One of the soldiers had to kill it with a punch behind the ears.

"Once the animal was dead she stripped the skin from the red body; but
the sight of the blood which she was touching, which covered her hands, the
120 warm blood which she could feel growing cold and congealing, made her
tremble from head to foot; and she kept seeing her big boy cut in two and red
all over, like the animal still quivering in her hands.

"She sat down to table with her Prussians, but she couldn't eat, not so
much as a mouthful. They devoured the rabbit without bothering about her.
125 She watched them on the sly, without speaking, thinking over an idea, her
face so expressionless that they noticed nothing.

"Suddenly she said: "We've been together a whole month now and I don't
even know your names."

"They understood, not without some difficulty, what she wanted, and gave
130 her their names. But that wasn't enough: she got them to write them down
for her on a piece of paper, with the addresses of their families; and, setting
her spectacles on her big nose, she inspected the unfamiliar script and then
folded the sheet of paper and put it in her pocket, with the letter which had
told her of the death of her son.

135 "When the meal was over, she said to the men: 'I'm going to do some
work for you.'

"And she started taking straw up to the loft in which they slept.

"They were puzzled by what she was doing. She explained to them that
the straw would keep them warmer, and they gave her a helping hand. They
140 piled the bundles of straw up to the roof and thus made themselves a sort of
big, warm, sweet-smelling room with four walls of forage, where they would
sleep wonderfully well.

"At supper one of them was upset to see that Mother Savage didn't eat
anything again. She said that she was suffering from cramps. Then she lit a
145 good fire to warm herself, and the four Germans climbed up to their room by
the ladder which they used every evening.

"As soon as the trap-door was closed, the old woman took away the ladder.
Then she quietly opened the outside door and went out to fetch some more
bundles of straw with which she filled the kitchen. She walked barefoot in the

150 snow, moving so quietly that the men heard nothing. Every now and then she listened to the loud, uneven snores of the four sleeping soldiers.

"When she decided her preparations were sufficient, she threw one of the bundles of straw into the hearth, and when it had caught fire she scattered it over the others. Then she went outside and watched.

155 "Within a few seconds a blinding glare lit up the whole inside of the cottage. Then it became a fearful brazier, a gigantic furnace, the light of which shone through the narrow window and fell on the snow in a dazzling ray.

"Then a great cry came from the top of the house, followed by a clamour of human screams, of heartrending shrieks of anguish and terror. Then, as the
160 trap-door collapsed inside the cottage, a whirlwind of fire shot into the loft, pierced the thatched roof, and rose into the sky like the flame of a huge torch; and the whole cottage went up in flames.

"Nothing more could be heard inside but the crackling of the flames, the crumbling of the walls and the crashing of the beams. All of a sudden the roof
165 fell in, and the glowing carcass of the house was hurled up into the air amid a cloud of smoke, a great fountain of sparks.

"The white countryside, lit up by fire, glistened like a cloth of silver tinted with red.

"In the distance a bell began ringing.

170 "Old Mother Savage remained standing in front of her burnt-out home, armed with her gun, her son's gun, for fear that one of the men should escape.

"When she saw that it was all over, she threw the weapon in the fire. An explosion rang out.

"People came running up, peasants and Prussians.

175 "They found the woman sitting on a tree trunk, calm and satisfied.

"A German officer, who spoke French like a Frenchman, asked her: 'Where are your soldiers?'

"She stretched out her thin arm towards the red heap of the dying fire, and replied in a loud voice: 'In there!'

180 "They crowded around her. The Prussian asked: 'How did the fire break out?'

"'I started it,' she said.

"They didn't believe her, thinking that the disaster had driven her mad all of a sudden. So, as everyone gathered around her to listen to her, she told the story from beginning to end, from the arrival of the letter to the last screams
185 of the men who had been burnt with her house. She didn't leave out a single detail of what she had felt or of what she had done.

"When she had finished, she took two pieces of paper out of her pocket, and, in order to tell them apart, put on her spectacles again. Then, showing one of them, she said: 'This one is Victor's death.'

190 "Showing the other, and nodding in the direction of the red ruins, she added: 'This one is their names so as you can write to their families.'

"She calmly held out the white sheet of paper to the officer, who was holding her by the shoulders, and went on: 'You must write to say what happened, and tell their parents that it was me that did it. Victoire Simon, the
195 Savage woman! Don't forget.'

"The officer shouted out some orders in German. She was seized and pushed against the walls of the house, which were still warm. Then twelve men lined up quickly facing her, at a distance of twenty yards. She didn't budge. She had understood, and stood there waiting.

200 "An order rang out, followed straight away by a long volley. A late shot went off by itself, after the others.

"The old woman didn't fall. She collapsed as if her legs had been chopped off.

"The Prussian officer came over to her. She had been practically cut in two, 205 and in her hand she was clutching her letter soaked in blood."

My friend Serval added: "It was by way of a reprisal that the Germans destroyed the local château, which belonged to me."

I for my part was thinking of the mothers of the four gentle boys burnt in there, and of the fearful heroism of that other mother, shot against that wall. 210 And I picked up a little stone, still blackened by the fire.

STAGE 3: RECALL

Stop to self-test, relate, and react.
Your instructor may choose to give you a true-false comprehension review.

Thinking About MOTHER SAVAGE

Explain Mother Savage's reasons for treating the soldiers as she did, both in the beginning and in the end.

Contemporary Link

Explain how a modern psychologist might describe Mother Savage's circumstances as post-traumatic stress disorder.

SKILL DEVELOPMENT: IMPLIED MEANING

According to the implied meaning in the selection, answer the following with *T* (true) or *F* (false).

_____ 1. The author begins the story by painting a picture to appeal to the reader's senses.

_____ 2. The story suggests that the pain of war spreads beyond the battleground.

_____ 3. The phrase, "fond memories . . . which have become familiar sights and can touch our hearts like happy events," contains personification.

_____ 4. The phrase, "streams which ran through the ground like veins carrying blood to the earth," contains a simile.

_____ 5. Mother Savage treated the soldiers kindly in the beginning because she knew she would kill them in the end.

COMPREHENSION QUESTIONS

After reading the selection, answer the following questions with *a, b, c,* or *d.*

Main Idea _____ 1. The best statement of the main idea of this selection is
a. soldiers pillage the land during war.
b. family members must become soldiers during war.
c. a mother takes revenge over the loss of her son.
d. a mother's love is stronger than a patriotic bond.

Inference _____ 2. The reader can conclude that the setting for this story is
a. England.
b. France.
c. Spain.
d. Prussia.

Detail _____ 3. Serval had to rebuild his house because of
a. Prussian revenge.
b. a military battle.
c. an accidental fire.
d. smoke and fire damage from the Savage house.

Inference _____ 4. Serval feels that "country women"
a. work too hard.
b. never learn to laugh.
c. are better at business than men.
d. spend more time in pubs than men.

Inference _____ 5. The author suggests that Mother Savage's treatment of the soldiers before the fire was regarded by her neighbors as
a. comfortable.
b. insensitive.
c. cruel.
d. humorous.

Inference _____ 6. The author suggests that the ones who suffer the most hardships from war are

a. the upper class.
b. the peasants.
c. politicians.
d. those who feel the most patriotic hatred.

Inference _____ 7. The author suggests that the four soldiers treated Mother Savage with
a. hatred.
b. ridicule.
c. respect.
d. laughter.

Inference _____ 8. The author suggests that Mother Savage put the straw in the loft in order to
a. make the soldiers more comfortable.
b. turn suspicion away from her actions.
c. fuel the fire.
d. make them warmer.

Inference _____ 9. The author suggests that Mother Savage
a. was the first person the soldiers suspected of setting the fire.
b. might have gone free if she had remained silent.
c. wanted to lie about the fire.
d. did not understand the consequences of what she had done.

Inference _____ 10. Mother Savage wanted the addresses of the soldiers primarily because
a. she wanted to show the police that she had planned the murders.
b. they had been kind to her.
c. the commander did not know the names of the soldiers.
d. she wanted their mothers to feel the same pain she had felt.

Answer the following with *T* (true) or *F* (false).

Detail _____ 11. The "I" in the story remembers Mother Savage for her kindness to him.

Detail _____ 12. Mother Savage's husband had been killed in a previous war.

Detail _____ 13. Mother Savage was forced to house more soldiers than others because of her money.

Detail _____ 14. The soldiers did little to help Mother Savage with the daily chores.

Detail _____ 15. The rabbit reminded Mother Savage of her son.

VOCABULARY

According to the way the italicized word was used in the selection, select *a*, *b*, *c*, or *d* for the word or phrase that gives the best definition.

_____ 1. "*cherish* fond memories" (8)
    a. choose
    b. relive
    c. glorify
    d. treasure

_____ 2. "*unappeased*, unforgettable desire" (14)
    a. sick
    b. unsatisfied
    c. selfish
    d. unnatural

_____ 3. "*foraging* ahead of me" (22–23)
    a. searching
    b. walking
    c. running
    d. barking

_____ 4. "tall, *wiry* fellow" (32)
    a. angry
    b. evil
    c. tense
    d. lanky

_____ 5. "*ferocious* killer of game" (33)
    a. fierce
    b. steady
    c. untrustworthy
    d. sneaky

_____ 6. "*prerogative* of the upper class" (81)
    a. curse
    b. fate
    c. privilege
    d. feeling

_____ 7. "*atrocious* hardships of war" (85)
    a. real
    b. horrible
    c. unavoidable
    d. shared

_____ 8. "*bellicose* impulses" (86)
    a. sudden
    b. quick
    c. calculated
    d. warlike

_____ 9. "*devoured* the rabbit" (124)
    a. removed
    b. gobbled
    c. cooked
    d. cut

_____ 10. "by way of a *reprisal*" (206)
    a. retaliation
    b. excuse
    c. resolution
    d. solution

SEARCH THE NET

Many of Guy deMaupassant's stories reflect the frustration of the French under Prussian occupation. His book, *Mademoiselle Fifi*, is a well-known piece of literature dealing with many of the same themes in "Mother Savage." The book was made into a movie in the 1940s. Conduct a search for information on *Mademoiselle Fifi*, either the movie or the book. Briefly summarize what you find, and include comments critiquing the work. Plan your own search or begin by trying the following:

    http://www.afionline.org/wise/films/mademoiselle_fifi/mf.html

    http://www.acm.vt.edu/~yousten/ul/fifi.html

    http://chomsky.acts.adelaide.edu.au/person/Dhart/Films/MlleFifi.html

CONTEMPORARY FOCUS

Do long words make ideas seem more important? If the purpose of language is to communicate, why replace a clear and simple term with a vague, embellished, and confusing phrase?

LANGUAGE IN THE DUMPS

John Leo

U.S. News and World Report, July 27, 1998

At my local recycling center, I always pause in wonderment at the bin marked "commingled containers." Whoever thought up that term could have taken the easy way out and just written "cans and bottles." But the goal apparently was to create a term that nobody would ever use in conversation, then slap it on every can-and-bottle bin in America to confuse as many people as possible.

The gold standard in governmentspeak is still "ground-mounted confirmatory route markers" (road signs), a traffic-control term used from coast to coast. In Oxford, England, city officials decided to "examine the feasibility of creating a structure in Hinksey Park from indigenous vegetation." They were talking about planting a tree to get some shade.

In Britain, the Plain English Campaign came up with these colorful examples of awful writing: "interoperable intermodal transport systems" (bus and train timetables) and a supermarket help-wanted ad for "an ambient replenishment assistant" (someone to stock shelves).

The Dialectic Society gave its 1996 award for buzzword of the year to "urban camper," a new term for "the homeless" or people who live on the street. Similar euphemisms have crept into the language: extramarital sex (adultery), "aggressive coalitionary behavior" (war games), "hypervigilance" (paranoia), and "wall artist" (tagger, graffiti sprayer).

Business is pumping a lot of gas into the language, too. We have "the social expression industry" (the greeting card business), "meal replacement" (junk food), "a new-car alternative" and "an experienced car" (a used car), "creative response conceptions" (damage control by public relations people), and "access controllers" (doormen). The federal government gave us "grain-consuming animal units" (the Agriculture Department's term for cows), "single-purpose agricultural facilities" (pigpens and chicken coops), and "post-consumer waste materials" (garbage). Better yet, let's make that commingled post-consumer processed units. The kind of stuff you find at a single-purpose nonrecycling center, formerly a dump.

Collaborate on responses to the following questions:

- Why do employees prefer complicated job titles rather than simple ones?
- Why does *extramarital sex* sound better than *adultery?*
- How does political correctness influence language changes?

STAGE 1: PREVIEW

Preview the next selection to predict its purpose and organization as well as your learning plan.

The author's purpose is to _____

_____

Activate Schema

Is it polite to say to a friend, "I'm sorry your grandmother died" or should you use the phrase *passed away*?

STAGE 2: INTEGRATE KNOWLEDGE WHILE READING

Predict   Picture   Relate   Monitor   Correct

Citizens offer differing views on a heated political issue.

DOUBTS ABOUT DOUBLESPEAK

William Lutz
From Gary Goshgarian, *Exploring Language*, 8th ed.

During the past year, we learned that we can shop at a "unique retail biosphere" instead of a farmers' market, where we can buy items made of "synthetic glass" instead of plastic, or purchase a "high velocity, multipurpose air circulator," or electric fan. A
5 "waste-water conveyance facility" may "exceed the odor threshold" from time to time due to the presence of "regulated human nutrients," but that is not to be confused with a sewage plant that stinks up the neighborhood with sewage sludge. Nor should we confuse a "resource development park" with a dump. Thus does doublespeak continue to spread.
10   Doublespeak is language which pretends to communicate but doesn't. It is language which makes the bad seem good, the negative seem positive, the unpleasant seem attractive, or at least tolerable. It is language which avoids, shifts or denies responsibility; language which is at variance with its real or purported meaning. It is language which conceals or prevents thought.
15   Doublespeak is all around us. We are asked to check our packages at the desk "for our convenience" when it's not for our convenience at all but for someone else's convenience. We see advertisements for "preowned," "experienced" or "previously distinguished" cars, not used cars and for "genuine imitation leather," "virgin vinyl" or "real counterfeit diamonds." Television offers
20 not reruns but "encore telecasts." There are no slums or ghettos, just the "inner city" or "substandard housing" where the "disadvantaged" or "economically nonaffluent" live and where there might be a problem with "substance

abuse." Nonprofit organizations don't make a profit, they have "negative deficits" or experience "revenue excesses." With doublespeak it's not dying
25 but "terminal living" or "negative patient care outcome."

There are four kinds of doublespeak. The first kind is the euphemism, a word or phrase designed to avoid a harsh or distasteful reality. Used to mislead or deceive, the euphemism becomes doublespeak. In 1984 the U.S. State Department's annual reports on the status of human rights around the world ceased us-
30 ing the word "killing." Instead the State Department used the phrase "unlawful or arbitrary deprivation of life," thus avoiding the embarrassing situation of government-sanctioned killing in countries supported by the United States.

A second kind of doublespeak is jargon, the specialized language of a trade, profession or similar group, such as doctors, lawyers, plumbers or car mechan-
35 ics. Legitimately used, jargon allows members of a group to communicate with each other clearly, efficiently and quickly. But when lawyers or tax accountants use unfamiliar terms to speak to others, then the jargon becomes doublespeak.

In 1978 a commercial 727 crashed on takeoff, killing three passengers, injuring 21 others and destroying the airplane. The insured value of the airplane
40 was greater than its book value, so the airline made a profit of $1.7 million, creating two problems: the airline didn't want to talk about one of its airplanes crashing, yet it had to account for that $1.7 million profit in its annual report to its stockholders. The airline solved both problems by inserting a footnote in its annual report which explained that the $1.7 million was due to
45 "the involuntary conversion of a 727."

A third kind of doublespeak is gobbledygook or bureaucratese. Such doublespeak is simply a matter of overwhelming the audience with words—the more the better. Alan Greenspan, a polished practitioner of bureaucratese, once testified before a Senate committee that "it is a tricky problem to find
50 the particular calibration in timing that would be appropriate to stem the acceleration in risk premiums created by falling incomes without prematurely aborting the decline in the inflation-generated risk premiums."

The fourth kind of doublespeak is inflated language, which is designed to make the ordinary seem extraordinary, to make everyday things seem impres-
55 sive, to give an air of importance to people or situations, to make the simple seem complex. Thus do car mechanics become "automotive internists," elevator operators become "members of the vertical transportation corps," grocery store checkout clerks become "career associate scanning professionals," and smelling something becomes "organoleptic analysis."
60 Doublespeak is not the product of careless language or sloppy thinking. Quite the opposite. Doublespeak is language carefully designed and constructed to appear to communicate when in fact it doesn't. It is language designed not to lead but mislead.

It's easy to laugh off doublespeak. After all, we all know what's going on,
65 so what's the harm? But we don't always know what's going on, and when that happens, doublespeak accomplishes its ends. It alters our perception of reality. It deprives us of the tools we need to develop, advance and preserve our society, our culture, our civilization. It breeds suspicion, cynicism, distrust and, ultimately, hostility. It delivers us into the hands of those who do

70 not have our interests at heart. As Samuel Johnson noted in 18th century
England, even the devils in hell do not lie to one another, since the society of
hell could not subsist without the truth, any more than any other society.

STAGE 3: RECALL

Stop to self-test, relate, and react.
Your instructor may choose to give you a true-false comprehension review.

Thinking About   ## DOUBTS ABOUT DOUBLESPEAK

Some critics say that doublespeak is rising rather than declining. What are the
factors in our society that seem to promote an increase in the use of doublespeak? Describe at least three factors, and explain the motivation for doublespeak in each.

Contemporary Link

Compare the attitude of the two authors, John Leo and William Lutz, on the
changes in our language. Use examples to support your points.

SKILL DEVELOPMENT: IMPLIED MEANING

Create an example for each of the four types of doublespeak as follows:

1. Create a euphemism for *disagreeable roommate*. _____

    _____

2. Create jargon for *heavy bookbags*. _____

    _____

3. Create bureaucratese for a notice that your car has been towed from an il-
    legal parking place. _____

    _____

4. Create inflated language for a title for yourself when you do your own
    laundry. _____

COMPREHENSION QUESTIONS

Answer the following with *T* (true) or *F* (false).

Detail _____ 1. The author uses the first paragraph to summarize the message of the essay.

Inference _____ 2. The author believes that doublespeak is a language of manipulation.

Inference _____ 3. The first two words in the phrase *genuine imitation leather* are contradictory.

Inference _____ 4. The author implies that the phrase *substance abuse* does not accurately describe the situation in the housing areas.

Detail _____ 5. In the example of the 727 crash, the airline made a profit of $1.7 million.

Inference _____ 6. The author implies that the doublespeak of jargon is more technical than that of euphemisms.

Inference _____ 7. The author implies that Alan Greenspan's sentence is incomprehensible.

Inference _____ 8. The author implies that the doublespeak of inflated language has the potential to transform a bank teller into a vice president of check exchanging.

Inference _____ 9. The author's attitude toward doublespeak is both serious and humorous.

Detail _____ 10. Samuel Johnson believed that truth is necessary for even the worst society to survive.

SEARCH THE NET

Politics is filled with spin doctors who master the art of doublespeak. Conduct a search for the information on the latest "spins" in government on the federal, state, or local level. Describe the spin and explain how doublespeak is used to further the aims of the politician or group. Plan your own search or begin by trying the following:

http://home.navisoft.com/alliance/afaweb/0697011.html

http://www.newhope.bc.ca/94-04-24.html

http://www.dt.org/html/doublespeak.html

http://www.hedweb.com/conserve.html

http://www.lies.com/cgi/lies_hn/get/ctt/9.html

CONTEMPORARY FOCUS

Arguments for and against bilingual education focus on two major questions, (1) What is best for the child? and (2) What is best for the country? Personal experiences and national desires shade the answers.

IF ONLY WE ALL SPOKE TWO LANGUAGES

Ariel Dorfman

New York Times, 24 June 1998, sect. A, p. 25

Ever since I came to settle in the United States 18 years ago, I have hoped that this nation might someday become truly multilingual, with everyone here speaking at least two languages.

I am aware, of course, that my dream is not shared by most Americans: if the outcome of California's referendum on bilingual education is any indication, the nation will continue to stubbornly prefer a monolingual country. California voters rejected the bilingual approach—teaching subjects like math and science in the student's native language and gradually introducing English. Instead, they approved what is known as the immersion method, which would give youngsters a year of intensive English, then put them in regular classrooms.

If people could realize that immigrant children are better off, and less scarred, by holding on to their first languages as they learn a second one, then perhaps Americans could accept a more drastic change. What if every English-speaking toddler were to start learning a foreign language at an early age, maybe in kindergarten? What if these children were to learn Spanish, for instance, the language already spoken by millions of American citizens, but also by so many neighbors to the South?

Most Americans would respond by asking why it is necessary at all to learn another language, given that the rest of the planet is rapidly turning English into the lingua franca of our time. Isn't it easier, most Americans would say, to have others speak to us in our words and with our grammar? Let them make the mistakes and miss the nuances and subtleties while we occupy the more powerful and secure linguistic ground in any exchange.

But that is a shortsighted strategy. If America doesn't change, it will find itself, let's say in a few hundred years, to be a monolingual nation in a world that has become gloriously multilingual. It will discover that acquiring a second language not only gives people an economic and political edge, but is also the best way to understand someone else's culture, the most stimulating way to open your life and transform yourself into a more complete member of the species.

No tengan miedo. Don't be afraid.

Your children won't be losing Shakespeare. They'll just be gaining Cervantes.

© 2000 Addison-Wesley Educational Publishers, Inc.

Collaborate on responses to the following questions:

■ What do you believe are the concrete and attitudinal advantages of learning a second language?

■ Do you agree that the prevailing American attitude has been monolingual? Why or why not?

■ Why has English evolved as the primary international language?

STAGE 1: PREVIEW

The author's main purpose is to change the school system.

Agree ☐   Disagree ☐

The overall pattern of organization is definition-example.

Agree ☐   Disagree ☐

After reading this selection, I will need to explain how to teach Spanish.

Agree ☐   Disagree ☐

Activate Schema

How do parents who speak English as a second language keep their first language alive for their children?

What is the national debate about English Only or English Plus?

Word Knowledge

What do you know about these words?

incongruity	tact	accentuated	trivial	profound
pried	effusive	garbled	menial	myth

Your instructor may give a true-false vocabulary review before or after reading.

STAGE 2: INTEGRATE KNOWLEDGE WHILE READING

Predict   Picture   Relate   Monitor   Correct

Bilingual students read directions in both Spanish and English.

BILINGUAL EDUCATION

From Richard Rodriguez, *Hunger of Memory*

I remember, to start with, that day in Sacramento, in a California now nearly thirty years past, when I first entered a classroom—able to understand about fifty stray English words. The third of four children, I had been preceded by my older brother and sister
5 to a neighborhood Roman Catholic school. But neither of them

had revealed very much about their classroom experiences. They left each morning and returned each afternoon, always together, speaking Spanish as they climbed the five steps to the porch. And their mysterious books, wrapped in brown shopping-bag paper, remained on the table next to the
10 door, closed firmly behind them.

An accident of geography sent me to a school where all my classmates were white and many were the children of doctors and lawyers and business executives. On that first day of school, my classmates must certainly have been uneasy to find themselves apart from their families, in the first institution of their
15 lives. But I was astonished. I was fated to be the "problem student" in class.

The nun said, in a friendly but oddly impersonal voice: "Boys and girls, this is Richard Rodriguez." (I heard her sound it out: *Rich-heard Road-ree-guess.*) It was the first time I had heard anyone say my name in English. "Richard," the nun repeated more slowly, writing my name down in her book. Quickly I
20 turned to see my mother's face dissolve in a watery blur behind the pebbled-glass door.

Supporters of Bilingual Education

Now, many years later, I hear of something called "bilingual education"—a scheme proposed in the late 1960s by Hispanic-American social activists, later endorsed by a congressional vote. It is a program that seeks to permit
25 non–English-speaking children (many from lower class homes) to use their "family language" as the language of school. Such, at least, is the aim its supporters announce. I hear them, and am forced to say no: It is not possible for a child, any child, ever to use his family's language in school. Not to understand this is to misunderstand the public uses of schooling and to trivialize the na-
30 ture of intimate life.

Supporters of bilingual education today imply that students like me miss a great deal by not being taught in their family's language. What they seem not to recognize is that, as a socially disadvantaged child, I considered Spanish to be a private language. What I needed to learn in school was that I had the
35 right—and the obligation—to speak the public language of *los gringos.*

My Education

Without question, it would have pleased me to hear my teachers address me in Spanish when I entered the classroom. I would have felt much less afraid. I would have trusted them and responded with ease. But I would have delayed—for how long postponed?—having to learn the language of public soci-
40 ety. I would have evaded—and for how long could I have afforded to delay?—learning the great lesson of school, that I had a public identity.

Fortunately, my teachers were unsentimental about their responsibility. What they understood was that I needed to speak a public language. So their voices would search me out, asking me questions. Each time I'd hear them,
45 I'd look up in surprise to see a nun's face frowning at me. I'd mumble, not re-

ally meaning to answer. The nun would persist, "Richard, stand up. Don't look at the floor. Speak up. Speak to the entire class, not just to me!" But I couldn't believe that the English language was mine to use.

Three months. Five. Half a year passed. Unsmiling, ever watchful, my
50 teachers noted my silence. They began to connect my behavior with the difficult progress my older sister and brother were making. Until one Saturday morning three nuns arrived at the house to talk to our parents. Stiffly, they sat on the blue living room sofa. From the doorway of another room, spying the visitors, I noted the incongruity—the clash of two worlds, the faces and voices
55 of school intruding upon the familiar setting of home. I overheard one voice gently wondering, "Do your children speak only Spanish at home, Mrs. Rodriguez?" While another voice added, "That Richard especially seems so timid and shy."

That Rich-heard!
60   With great tact the visitors continued, "Is it possible for you and your husband to encourage your children to practice their English when they are home?" Of course, my parents complied. What would they not do for their children's well-being? And how could they have questioned the Church's authority which those women represented? In an instant, they agreed to give up the language (the
65 sounds) that had revealed and accentuated our family's closeness. The moment after the visitors left, the change was observed. "*Ahora*, speak to us *en inglés*," my father and mother united to tell us.

English at Home

At first, it seemed a kind of game. After dinner each night, the family gathered to practice "our" English. (It was still then *inglés*, a language foreign to us,
70 so we felt drawn as strangers to it.) Laughing, we would try to define words we could not pronounce. We played with strange English sounds, often overanglicizing our pronunciations. And we filled the smiling gaps of our sentences with familiar Spanish sounds. But that was cheating, somebody shouted. Everyone laughed. In school, meanwhile, like my brother and sister,
75 I was required to attend a daily tutoring session. I needed a full year of special attention. I also needed my teachers to keep my attention from straying in class by calling out, *Rich-heard*—their English voices slowly prying loose my ties to my other name, its three notes, *Ri-car-do*. Most of all I needed to hear my mother and father speak to me in a moment of seriousness in broken—
80 suddenly heartbreaking—English. The scene was inevitable: One Saturday morning I entered the kitchen where my parents were talking in Spanish. I did not realize that they were talking in Spanish however until, at the moment they saw me, I heard their voices change to speak English. Those *gringo* sounds they uttered startled me. Pushed me away. In that moment of trivial
85 misunderstanding and profound insight, I felt my throat twisted by unsounded grief. I turned quickly and left the room. But I had no place to escape to with Spanish. (The spell was broken.) My brother and sisters were speaking English in another part of the house.

90 Again and again in the days following, increasingly angry, I was obliged to hear my mother and father: "Speak to us *en inglé.*" (*Speak.*) Only then did I determine to learn classroom English. Weeks after, it happened: One day in school I raised my hand to volunteer an answer. I spoke out in a loud voice. And I did not think it remarkable when the entire class understood. That day, I moved very far from the disadvantaged child I had been only days earlier.

95 The belief, the calming assurance that I belonged in public, had at last taken hold. Shortly after, I stopped hearing the high and loud sounds of *los gringos*. A more and more confident speaker of English, I didn't trouble to listen to *how* strangers sounded, speaking to me. And there simply were too many English-speaking people in my day for me to hear American accents anymore.

The Gain and the Loss

100 At last, seven years old, I came to believe what had been technically true since my birth: I was an American citizen.

But the special feeling of closeness at home was diminished by then. Gone was the desperate, urgent, intense feeling of being at home; rare was the experience of feeling myself individualized by family intimates. We remained a
105 loving family, but one greatly changed. No longer so close; no longer bound tight by the pleasing and troubling knowledge of our public separateness. Neither my older brother nor sister rushed home after school anymore. Nor did I. When I arrived home there would often be neighborhood kids in the house. Or the house would be empty of sounds.

110 Following the dramatic Americanization of their children, even my parents grew more publicly confident. Especially my mother. She learned the names of all the people on our block. And she decided we needed to have a telephone installed in the house. My father continued to use the word *gringo*. But it was no longer charged with the old bitterness or distrust. (Stripped of any
115 emotional content, the word simply became a name for those Americans not of Hispanic descent.) Hearing him, sometimes, I wasn't sure if he was pronouncing the Spanish word *gringo* or saying gringo in English.

Matching the silence I started hearing in public was a new quiet at home. The family's quiet was partly due to the fact that, as we children learned more
120 and more English, we shared fewer and fewer words with our parents. Sentences needed to be spoken slowly when a child addressed his mother or father. (Often the parent wouldn't understand.) The child would need to repeat himself. (Still the parent misunderstood.) The young voice, frustrated, would end up saying, "Never mind"—the subject was closed. Dinners would be noisy
125 with the clinking of knives and forks against dishes. My mother would smile softly between her remarks; my father at the other end of the table would chew and chew at his food, while he stared over the heads of his children.

My *mother!* My *father!* After English became my primary language, I no longer knew what words to use in addressing my parents. The old Spanish
130 words (those tender accents of sound) I had used earlier—*mamá* and *papá*—I couldn't use anymore. They would have been too painful reminders of how

© 2000 Addison-Wesley Educational Publishers, Inc.

much had changed in my life. On the other hand, the words I heard neighborhood kids call *their* parents seemed equally unsatisfactory. *Mother* and *Father*,
Ma, Papa, Pa, Dad, Pop (how I hated the all-American sound of that last
135 word especially)—all these terms I felt were unsuitable, not really terms of
address for *my* parents, As a result, I never used them at home. Whenever I'd
speak to my parents, I would try to get their attention with eye contact alone.
In public conversations, I'd refer to "my parents" or "my mother and father."

My mother and father, for their part, responded differently, as their children
140 spoke to them less. She grew restless, seemed troubled and anxious at the
scarcity of words exchanged in the house. It was she who would question me
about my day when I came home from school. She smiled at small talk. She
pried at the edges of my sentences to get me to say something more. (What?)
She'd join conversations she overheard, but her intrusions often stopped her chil-
145 dren's talking. By contrast, my father seemed reconciled to the new quiet.
Though his English improved somewhat, he retired into silence. At dinner he
spoke very little. One night his children and even his wife helplessly giggled at his
garbled English pronunciation of the Catholic Grace before Meals. Thereafter he
made his wife recite the prayer at the start of each meal, even on formal occa-
150 sions, when there were guests in the house. Hers became the public voice of the
family. On official business, it was she, not my father, one would usually hear on
the phone or in stores, talking to strangers. His children grew so accustomed to
his silence that, years later, they would speak routinely of his shyness. (My
mother would often try to explain: Both his parents died when he was eight. He
155 was raised by an uncle who treated him like little more than a menial servant. He
was never encouraged to speak. He grew up alone. A man of few words.) But my
father was not shy, I realized, when I'd watch him speaking Spanish with relatives. Using Spanish, he was quickly effusive. Especially when talking with other
men, his voice would spark, flicker, flare alive with sounds. In Spanish, he ex-
160 pressed ideas and feelings he rarely revealed in English. With firm Spanish
sounds, he conveyed confidence and authority English would never allow him.

I would have been happier about my public success had I not sometimes
recalled what it had been like earlier, when my family had conveyed its inti-
macy through a set of conveniently private sounds. Sometimes in public,
165 hearing a stranger, I'd hark back to my past. A Mexican farmworker approached me downtown to ask directions to somewhere. "*¿Hijito . . . ?*" he
said. And his voice summoned deep longing. Another time, standing beside
my mother in the visiting room of a Carmelite convent, before the dense
screen which rendered the nuns shadowy figures, I heard several Spanish-
170 speaking nuns—their busy, singsong overlapping voices—assure us that yes,
yes, we were remembered, all our family was remembered in their prayers.
(Their voices echoed faraway family sounds.)

A Private and a Public Individuality

Today I hear bilingual educators say that children lose a degree of "individuality" by becoming assimilated into public society. (Bilingual schooling was

175 popularized in the seventies, that decade when middle-class ethnics began to
resist the process of assimilation—the American melting pot.) But the bilingualists simplistically scorn the value and necessity of assimilation. They do
not seem to realize that there are *two* ways a person is individualized. So they
do not realize that while one suffers a diminished sense of *private* individual-
180 ity by becoming assimilated into public society, such assimilation makes possible the achievements of *public* individuality.

  The bilingualists insist that a student should be reminded of his difference
from others in mass society, his heritage. But they equate mere separateness
with individuality. The fact is that only in private—with intimates—is sepa-
185 rateness from the crowd a prerequisite for individuality. (An intimate draws
me apart, tells me that I am unique, unlike all others.) In public, by contrast,
full individuality is achieved, paradoxically, by those who are able to consider
themselves members of the crowd. Thus it happened for me: Only when I
was able to think of myself as an American, no longer an alien in *gringo* soci-
190 ety, could I seek the rights and opportunities necessary for full public individuality. The social and political advantages I enjoy as a man result from the day
that I came to believe that my name, indeed, is *Rich-heard Road-ree-guess.*

  I celebrate the day I acquired my new name.

  My awkward childhood does not prove the necessity of bilingual educa-
195 tion. My story discloses instead an essential myth of childhood—inevitable
pain. If I rehearse here the changes in my private life after my Americanization, it is finally to emphasize the public gain. The loss implies the gain: The
house I returned to each afternoon was quiet. Intimate sounds no longer
rushed to the door to greet me. There were other noises inside. The telephone
200 rang. Neighborhood kids ran past the door of the bedroom where I was reading my schoolbooks—covered with shopping-bag paper. Once I learned public language, it would never again be easy for me to hear intimate family
voices. More and more of my day was spent hearing words. But that may only
be a way of saying that the day I raised my hand in class and spoke loudly to
205 an entire roomful of faces, my childhood started to end.

STAGE 3: RECALL

  Stop to self-test, relate, and react.

  Your instructor may choose to give you a true-false comprehension review

BILINGUAL EDUCATION

  Describe Rodriguez's position on bilingual education, and explain your own
view on the issue.

Contemporary Link

How would Rodriguez's first year in school have been different if he had been taught by the bilingual approach or the immersion method? Describe how he would have been taught.

SKILL DEVELOPMENT: IMPLIED MEANING

According to the implied meaning in the selection, answer the following with *T* (true) or *F* (false).

_____ 1. The author feels a sense of loss along with the gain in his final victory over the English language.

_____ 2. The author suggests that constant happiness is a myth of childhood.

_____ 3. The author could understand spoken English before he could speak it himself.

_____ 4. The author believes that assimilation is necessary for success.

_____ 5. The author views the proponents of bilingual education as unrealistic.

COMPREHENSION QUESTIONS

Answer the following with *a, b, c,* or *d.*

Main Idea   _____ 1. The best statement of the main point of this selection is
a. children who speak another language are often mistreated by teachers.
b. bilingual education promotes self-confidence and family unity.
c. school children should be taught in the language of the school and not in the language of the family.
d. supporters of bilingual education fail to recognize the needs of the family.

Detail   _____ 2. The author is addressing the issue of bilingual education in American schools and is taking a position against
a. learning two languages.
b. speaking two languages at school.
c. using only English to teach Spanish-speaking students.
d. using only Spanish to teach Spanish-speaking students.

Inference   _____ 3. In looking back, the author believes that his teachers
a. should have taught him in Spanish.
b. were afraid to speak to him in Spanish.
c. did not know how to speak in Spanish.
d. were correct in not speaking to him in Spanish.

Inference   _____   4. The author's view of the nuns who came to his house is that
   a. they were wrong to intrude upon his family life.
   b. they were kind and ultimately changed his language perspective.
   c. they did not care about him or his family.
   d. they were too strict and demanding.

Inference   _____   5. When the author says, "I celebrate the day I acquired my new name," that "day" probably refers to
   a. the day the nuns came to his house.
   b. the day he started school.
   c. the day he first volunteered to answer a question in class.
   d. the day he felt the loss of Spanish in his home.

Detail   _____   6. After he learned to speak English in public, the author
   a. focused more on what was said rather than how it was said.
   b. listened to sounds to distinguish among different American accents.
   c. listened for the tone of voice that went with the words.
   d. noticed the high and low sounds of English as well as Spanish.

Inference   _____   7. Before his family began speaking English at home, the author believed the family shared a closeness that
   a. was a result of a separation they all felt in public.
   b. gave each of them a public identity.
   c. encouraged them to assimilate into the melting pot.
   d. eventually made him ashamed of his childhood.

Inference   _____   8. The author feels that his father was silent because
   a. his father was raised by an uncle after his parents died.
   b. his father lacked confidence with the English language.
   c. the children were frustrated at having to speak slowly to the parents.
   d. his mother became more assertive and dominated conversations.

Inference   _____   9. The author feels that those who support bilingual education
   a. do not realize the ultimate danger of the social isolation of language.
   b. do not sympathize with the disadvantaged.
   c. are not willing to resist the process of assimilation.
   d. do not recognize differences in heritage in a mass society.

Inference   _____   10. The author believes that in order to achieve "full individuality," a person must
   a. resist the characteristics that are common to the crowd.
   b. focus on differences rather than similarities.
   c. be comfortable as a member of the crowd.
   d. have a private rather than a public language.

Answer the following with *T* (true) or *F* (false).

Detail   _____ 11. The author was born in Mexico.

Detail   _____ 12. The author's father had been orphaned at an early age.

Detail   _____ 13. The author did not speak English as his public language until he was in fifth grade.

Detail   _____ 14. The author began to view English as a predominately public language because it was used in class to make oneself understood by others.

Detail   _____ 15. The author suggests that the authentic sounds of the Spanish language bring back warm memories of childhood.

VOCABULARY

According to the way the italicized word was used in the selection, indicate *a*, *b*, *c*, or *d* for the word or phrase that gives the best definition.

_____ 1. "noted the *incongruity*" (54)
    a. emotions
    b. lack of fit
    c. anger
    d. argument

_____ 2. "With great *tact*" (60)
    a. force
    b. conviction
    c. courage
    d. diplomacy

_____ 3. "*accentuated* our family's closeness" (65)
    a. emphasized
    b. denied
    c. aggravated
    d. controlled

_____ 4. "*trivial* misunderstanding" (84–85)
    a. honest
    b. petty
    c. important
    d. conflicting

_____ 5. "*profound* insight" (85)
    a. unhappy
    b. false
    c. deeply felt
    d. quick

_____ 6. "*pried* at the edges" (143)
    a. laughed
    b. stopped
    c. asked questions
    d. listened

_____ 7. "his *garbled* English" (147–148)
    a. slow
    b. confused
    c. confident
    d. abundant

_____ 8. "*menial* servant" (155)
    a. helpful
    b. loyal
    c. lowly
    d. honest

_____ 9. "was quickly *effusive*" (158)
    a. conservative
    b. bubbling
    c. aware
    d. nervous

_____ 10. "essential *myth* of childhood" (195)
    a. truth
    b. fictitious story
    c. concern
    d. difficult limitation

SEARCH THE NET

Use the Internet to visit the Amazon Bookstore, and search for a book by Richard Rodriguez entitled *Hunger of Memory*. Write a brief description of the book.

http://www.amazon.com/

Go Electronic!

For additional readings, exercises, and Internet activities, visit this book's Website at:
http://www.awlonline.com/smithBTG

For even more activities, visit the Longman English pages at:
http://longman.awl.com/englishpages

If you need a user name and password, please see your instructor.

Take a Road Trip to the Great Lakes! Be sure to visit the Inference module in your Reading Road Trip CD-ROM for multimedia tutorials, exercises, and tests.

READER'S JOURNAL

Name _____ Date _____

Chapter 6

Answer the following questions to learn about your own learning and reflect on your progress. Use the perforations to tear the assignment out for your instructor.

1. Why is it interesting to read material with many inferences?

   _____

2. Describe the inference of a "clean" joke that you know.

   _____

   _____

3. Why would literature tend to contain more inferences than a biology text?

   _____

4. "Reading between the lines" is an idiom. What does it mean?

   _____

   _____

5. What clues do you use to guess a person's age by his or her voice on the telephone?

   _____

6. What clues do you use to draw conclusions when you overhear conversations in public places?

   _____

7. On what do you base your assumptions when you first meet a new person?

   _____

8. Do you prefer to read fiction or nonfiction? Why?

   _____

   _____

9. Why are there no subheadings in works of fiction? _____

   _____

Point of View

- Is a textbook influenced by the author's point of view?
- What is the author's point of view?
- What is the reader's point of view?
- What is the difference between a fact and an opinion?
- What is the author's purpose?
- What is the author's tone?

M. C. Eschers "Symmetry Drawing E76"
© 1999 Cordon Art
B. V.-Baarn Holland.
All rights reserved.

IS A TEXTBOOK INFLUENCED BY THE AUTHOR'S POINT OF VIEW?

How many of the following statements are true?

_____ 1. Textbooks contain facts rather than opinions.

_____ 2. The historical account of an incident is based on fact and thus does not vary from one author to another.

_____ 3. Except for the author's writing style, freshman biology textbooks do not vary in their informational content.

_____ 4. The information presented in textbooks is supposed to be free from an author's interpretation.

Unfortunately, too many students tend to answer *"true"* to all of the above. Paying big money for a thick history book with lots of facts and an authoritative title does not mean, contrary to student belief, that the text is a cleansed chronicle of the nation's past. No purity rule applies to textbook writing. In the case of history, the author portrays the past from a uniquely personal perspective. The name of the first president of the United States does not vary from one text to another, but, depending on the point of view of the author, the emphasis on the importance of Washington's administration might vary.

In short, *everything you read is affected by the author's point of view, purpose, tone, and presentation of facts and opinions.*

WHAT IS THE AUTHOR'S POINT OF VIEW?

Authors of factual material, like authors of fiction, have opinions and theories that influence their presentation of the subject matter. For example, would a British professor's account of American history during the Revolutionary period be the same as a version written by a United States–born scholar from Philadelphia? Because of national loyalties and different biases in their own educational histories, the two scholars might look at the events from two different angles—the first as a colonial uprising on a distant continent and the second as a struggle for personal freedom and survival. Each of the two authors would write from a different **point of view** and express particular opinions because they have different ways of looking at the subject.

Recognizing the author's point of view is part of understanding what you read. Sophisticated readers seek to identify the beliefs of the author in order to "know where he or she is coming from." When the point of view is not directly stated, the author's choice of words and information provides clues for the reader.

© 1992, The Washington Post Writers Group. Reprinted with permission.

The terms *point of view* and *bias* are very similar and are sometimes used interchangeably. When facts are slanted, though not necessarily distorted, toward the author's personal beliefs, the written material is said to reflect the author's bias. Thus, a **bias** is simply an opinion or position on a subject. As commonly used, however, *bias* has a negative connotation suggesting narrow-mindedness and prejudice, whereas *point of view* suggests thoughtfulness and openness. Perhaps you would like to refer to your own opinion as point of view and to those of others, particularly if they disagree with you, as biases!

EXAMPLE   Read the following passage and use the choice of information and words to identify the author's point of view on whaling.

> Our own species is providing us with clear examples of how density-dependent regulation can fail. The great whales have been hunted to the brink of oblivion over the past few decades as modern whaling methods have reduced personal risk while increasing profits. Although there is nothing that whales provide that can't be obtained elsewhere, the demand for whale products (and their price) hasn't diminished, especially in Japan. Thus, instead of the human predators relaxing their pressure and allowing the whale population to recover, whaling fleets continue to exert their depressing effect on populations of the great mammals.... Then, as whales decrease in number, the price of whale products goes up, and the hunt becomes still more avid. If humans actually starved when they couldn't catch whales (which might once have been the case among the Eskimos) both populations might eventually stabilize (or cycle). But the current decline in whale numbers has had no effect on the growth of the human population.
>
> Robert Wallace et al., *Biology: Science of Life*

What is the author's point of view? Underline clues that suggest your answer.

EXPLANATION   The author is against commercial whaling because the whale population is severely declining. Whaling is for profit and seemingly unlimited greed and not for products that cannot be obtained elsewhere.

EXERCISE 7.1   *Comparing Authors' Points of View*

Read the following two descriptions of Mary of Scotland from two different history books. Although both include positive and negative comments, the second author obviously finds the subject more engaging and has chosen to include more positive details.

Passage A

Mary Stuart returned to Scotland in 1561 after her husband's death. She was a far more charming and romantic figure than her cousin Elizabeth, but she was no stateswoman. A convinced Catholic, she soon ran head-on into the granitelike opposition of Knox and the Kirk. In 1567 she was forced to abdicate, and in the following year she fled from Scotland and sought protection in England from Elizabeth. No visitor could have been more unwelcome.

Joseph R. Strayer et al., *The Mainstream of Civilization*

Passage B

Mary Stuart was an altogether remarkable young woman, about whom it is almost impossible to remain objectively impartial. Even when one discounts the flattery that crept into descriptions of her, one is inclined to accept the contemporary evidence that Mary was extraordinarily beautiful, though tall for a girl—perhaps over six feet. In addition to beauty, she had almost every other attractive attribute in high degree: courage, wit, resourcefulness, loyalty, and responsiveness, in short everything needful for worldly greatness save discretion in her relations with men and a willingness to compromise, if need be, on matters of religion. She was a thoroughgoing Roman Catholic, a good lover, and a magnificent hater.

Shepard B. Clough et al., *A History of the Western World*

1. How are the two descriptions alike? _____

   _____

2. How do the two descriptions differ? _____

   _____

3. Which do you like better, and why? _____

   _____

4. What clues signal that the author of the second description is more biased than the first? _____

   _____

5. What is the suggested meaning in the following phrases:

a. "no stateswoman" _____

b. "A convinced Catholic" _____

c. "granitelike opposition" _____

d. "more unwelcomed" _____

e. "save discretion in her relations with men" _____

f. "thoroughgoing Roman Catholic" _____

g. "magnificent hater" _____

_____

WHAT IS THE READER'S POINT OF VIEW?

To recognize a point of view, you have to know enough about the subject to realize that there is another opinion beyond the one being expressed. Thus, prior knowledge and a slightly suspicious nature open the mind to countless other views and alternative arguments.

On the other hand, prior knowledge can also lead to a closed mind and rigid thinking. Our existing opinions affect how much we accept or reject of what we read. If our beliefs are particularly strong, sometimes we refuse to hear what is said or we hear something that is not said. Research has shown that readers will actually "tune out" new material that is drastically different from their own views. For example, if you were reading that the AIDS virus should not be a concern for most middle-class Americans, would you be "tuned in" or "tuned out"?

EXAMPLE   Read the following passage on smoking first from the point of view of a non-smoker and second from the point of view of a smoker, and then answer the questions.

> Smoke can permanently paralyze the tiny cilia that sweep the breathing passages clean and can cause the lining of the respiratory tract to thicken irregularly. The body's attempt to rid itself of the smoking toxins may produce a deep, hacking cough in the person next to you at the lunch counter. Console yourself with the knowledge that these hackers are only trying to rid their bodies of nicotines, "tars," formaldehyde, hydrogen sulfide, resins, and who knows what. Just enjoy your meal.
>
> Robert Wallace, *Biology: The World of Life*

1. Is the author a smoker? Underline the clues suggesting your answer.

_____

2. What is your view on smoking? _____

_____

3. Reading this passage in the guise of a nonsmoker, what message is conveyed to you?_____

_____

4. Assuming the role of a smoker, what message is conveyed to you?

_____

5. What is the main point the author is trying to convey? _____

_____

EXPLANATION   Although it is possible that both the smoker and non-smoker would get exactly the same message, it is more likely that the non-smoker would be disgusted by the health risks, whereas the smoker would claim exaggeration and discrimination. The main point is that smoking causes permanent physical damage. The attitude suggests that the author is probably not a smoker.

EXERCISE 7.2   *Identifying Points of View*

Read the following passages and answer the questions about point of view.

Passage A: Columbus

On August 3, 1492, Columbus and some ninety mariners set sail from Palos, Spain, in the *Niña, Pinta,* and *Santa Maria.* Based on faulty calculations, the Admiral estimated Asia to be no more than 4500 miles to the west (the actual distance is closer to 12,000 miles). Some 3000 miles out, his crew became fearful and wanted to return home. But he convinced them to keep sailing west. Just two days later, on October 12, they landed on a small island in the Bahamas, which Columbus named San Salvador (holy savior).

A fearless explorer, Columbus turned out to be an ineffective administrator and a poor geographer. He ended up in debtor's prison, and to his dying day in 1506 he never admitted to locating a world unknown to Europeans. Geographers overlooked his contribution and named the Western continents after another mariner, Amerigo Vespucci, a merchant from Florence who participated in a Portuguese expedition to South America in 1501. In a widely reprinted letter, Vespucci claimed that a new world had been found, and it was his name that caught on.

James Martin et al., *America and Its People*

1. Which paragraph sounds more like the Columbus you learned about in elementary school? _____

_____

2. What is the author's position on Columbus? Underline clues for your answer?

_____

3. What is your view of Columbus? What has influenced your view?

_____

4. What is the main point the author is trying to convey? _____

_____

Passage B: Mexican Cession

The tragedy of the Mexican cession is that most Anglo-Americans have not accepted the fact that the United States committed an act of violence against the Mexican people when it took Mexico's northwestern territory. Violence was not limited to the taking of the land; Mexico's territory was invaded, her people murdered, her land raped, and her possessions plundered. Memory of this destruction generated a distrust and dislike that is still vivid in the minds of many Mexicans, for the violence of the United States left deep scars. And for Chicanos—Mexicans remaining within the boundaries of the new United States territories— aggression was even more insidious, for the outcome of the Texas and Mexican-American wars made them a conquered people. Anglo-Americans were the conquerors, and they evinced all the arrogance of military victors.

In material terms, in exchange for 12,000 lives and more than $100,000,000 the United States acquired a colony two and a half times as large as France, containing rich farm lands and natural resources such as gold, silver, zinc, copper, oil, and uranium which would make possible its unprecedented industrial boom. It acquired ports on the Pacific which generated further economic expansion across that ocean. Mexico was left with its shrunken resources to face the continued advances of the expanding capitalist force on its border.

Rodolfo Acuña, *Occupied America: A History of Chicanos*

1. What is the author's point of view? Underline clues. _____

_____

_____

2. How does this author's view differ from what you would expect in most American history texts? _____

_____

3. What is your point of view on the subject? _____

_____

4. What is the main point the author is trying to convey?

_____

_____

Passage C: Surviving in Vietnam

Vietnam ranks after World War II as America's second most expensive war. Between 1950 and 1975, the United States spent $123 billion on combat in Southeast Asia. More importantly, Vietnam ranks—after our Civil War and World Wars I and II—as the nation's fourth deadliest war, with 57,661 Americans killed in action.

Yet, when the last U.S. helicopter left Saigon, Americans suffered what historian George Herring terms "collective amnesia." Everyone, even those who had fought in 'Nam, seemed to want to forget Southeast Asia. It took nearly ten years for the government to erect a national monument to honor those who died in Vietnam.

Few who served in Vietnam survived unscathed, whether psychologically or physically. One of the 303,600 Americans wounded during the long war was 101st Airborne platoon leader James Bombard, first shot and then blown up by a mortar round during the bitter Tet fighting at Hue in February 1968. He describes his traumatic experience as

> feeling the bullet rip into your flesh, the shrapnel tear the flesh from your bones and the blood run down your leg. . . . To put your hand on your chest and to come away with your hand red with your own blood, and to feel it running out of your eyes and out of your mouth, and seeing it spurt out of your guts, realizing you were dying. . . . I was ripped open from the top of my head to the tip of my toes. I had forty-five holes in me.

Somehow Bombard survived Vietnam.

Withdrawing U.S. forces from Vietnam ended only the combat. Returning veterans fought government disclaimers concerning the toxicity of the defoliant Agent Orange. VA hospitals across the nation still contain thousands of para- and quadriplegic Vietnam veterans, as well as the maimed from earlier wars. Throughout America the "walking wounded" find themselves still embroiled in the psychological aftermath of Vietnam.

James Divine et al., *America: Past and Present*

1. What is the author's own view of the war? Underline clues for your answer.

_____

2. What is your own position on the Vietnam War? _____

_____

3. What is the purpose of Bombard's quotation? _____

_____

© 2000 Addison-Wesley Educational Publishers, Inc.

4. How do you feel about war after reading this passage?

_____

5. What is the main point the author is trying to convey? _____

_____

WHAT IS A FACT AND WHAT IS AN OPINION?

For both the reader and the writer, a point of view is a position or belief that logically evolves over time with knowledge and experience and is usually based on both facts and opinions. For example, what is your position on city curfews for youth, on helping the homeless, on abortion? Are your views on these issues supported solely by facts? Do you recognize the difference between the facts and the opinions used in your thinking?

Both facts and opinions are used persuasively to support positions. You have to determine which is which and then judge the issue accordingly. A fact is a statement based on actual evidence or personal observation. It can be checked objectively with empirical data and proved to be either true or false. By contrast, an opinion is a statement of personal feeling or a judgment. It reflects a belief or an interpretation rather than an accumulation of evidence, and it cannot be proved true or false. Adding the quoted opinion of a well-known authority to a few bits of evidence does not improve the data, yet this is an effective persuasive technique. Even though you may believe an opinion is valid, it is still an opinion.

EXAMPLE

Fact: Freud developed a theory of personality.
Fact: Freud believed that the personality is divided into three parts.

Opinion: Freud constructed the most complete theory of personality development.

Opinion: The personality is divided into three parts: the id, the ego, and the superego.

▶ **READER'S TIP**   **Questioning to Uncover Bias**

> ▶ What is your opinion on the subject?
>
> ▶ What is the author's opinion on the subject?
>
> ▶ What are the author's credentials for writing on the subject?
>
> ▶ What does the author have to gain?
>
> ▶ Does the author use facts or opinions as support?
>
> ▶ Are the facts selected and slanted to reflect the author's bias?

Authors mix facts and opinions, sometimes in the same sentence, in order to win you over to a particular point of view. Persuasive tricks include factually quoting sources who then voice opinions or hedging a statement with "It is a fact that" and attaching a disguised opinion. Recognize that both facts and opinions are valuable but be able to distinguish between the two.

> **EXERCISE 7.3**   *Fact or Opinion*

Read each of the following and indicate *F* for fact and O for opinion.

_____ 1. For women locked into socioeconomic situations that cannot promise financial independence, liberation is relatively meaningless and sometimes suggests the denial of femininity as a goal.

Reece McGee et al., Sociology: An Introduction

_____ 2. The territorial base from which Soviet ambitions proceed is the largest country area on the globe.

Jesse H. Wheeler, Jr., et al., Regional Geography of the World

_____ 3. Company sources attribute Coors' success to product quality, boasting that it "is the most expensively brewed beer in the world."

Louis Boone and David L. Kurtz, Contemporary Business

_____ 4. If you wish to "break the hunger habit" in order to gain better control over your own food intake, you might be wise to do so slowly—by putting yourself on a very irregular eating schedule.

James V. McConnell, Understanding Human Behavior

_____ 5. The first step in running for the nomination is to build a personal organization, because the party organization is supposed to stay neutral until the nomination is decided.

James M. Burns et al., Government by the People

_____ 6. It is true that American politics often rewards with power those who have proved that they can direct the large institutions of commerce and business, of banking, and of law, education, and philanthropy.

Kenneth Prewitt and Sidney Verba, An Introduction to American Government

_____ 7. Precipitation is not uniform, and neither is the distribution of population.

Robert J. Foster, Physical Geology

_____ 8. Massively built, with eyes so piercing they seemed like the headlights of an onrushing train, J. P. Morgan was the most powerful figure in American finance.

Robert Divine et al., American Past and Present

_____ 9. At least 10 percent of the world's available food is destroyed by pests, waste, and spoilage somewhere between the marketplace and the stomach of the consumer.

Robert Wallace, Biology: The World of Life

_____10. Woman, young girls, and even mere children were tortured by driving needles under their nails, roasting their feet in the fire, or crushing their legs under heavy weights until the marrow spurted from their bones, in order to force them to confess to filthy orgies with demons.

Edward M. Burns, Western Civilization

EXERCISE 7.4   _Fact and Opinion in Textbooks_

The following passage from a history text describes Franklin D. Roosevelt. Notice the mixture of facts and opinions in developing a view of Roosevelt. Mark the items that follow as fact (*F*) or opinion (*O*).

Franklin D. Roosevelt won the Democratic nomination in June 1932. At first glance he did not look like someone who could relate to suffering people; he had spent his entire life in the lap of luxury.

Handsome and outgoing, Roosevelt had a bright political future. Then disaster struck. In 1921, he developed polio. The disease left him paralyzed from the waist down and confined to a wheelchair for the rest of his life. Instead of retiring, however, Roosevelt threw himself into a rehabilitation program and labored diligently to return to the public life. "If you had spent two years in bed trying to wiggle your toe," he later observed, "after that anything would seem easy."

Few intellectuals had a high opinion of him. Walter Lippmann described Roosevelt as "a pleasant man who, without any important qualifications for the office, would very much like to be President."

The people saw Roosevelt differently. During the campaign, he calmed their fears and gave them hope. Even a member of Hoover's administration had to admit: "The people seem to be lifting eager faces to Franklin Roosevelt, having the impression that he is talking intimately to them." Charismatic and utterly charming, Roosevelt radiated confidence. He even managed to turn his lack of a blueprint into an asset. Instead of offering plans, he advocated the experimental method. "It is common sense to take a method and try it," he declared, "if it fails, admit it frankly and try another."

James Martin et al., America and Its People

_____ 1. Roosevelt won the Democratic nomination in June 1932.
_____ 2. He was handsome and outgoing.
_____ 3. He developed polio in 1921.
_____ 4. Few intellectuals thought highly of him.
_____ 5. Roosevelt radiated confidence.

WHAT IS THE AUTHOR'S PURPOSE?

Be aware that a textbook author can shift from an objective and factual explanation of a topic to a subjective and opinionated treatment of the facts. Recognizing the author's purpose does not mean that you won't buy the product; it just means that you are a more cautious, well-informed consumer.

An author always has a purpose in mind when putting words on paper. The reader of a textbook expects that the author's purpose will be to inform or explain objectively and, in general, this is true. At times, however, texts can slip from factual explanation to opinionated treatment of the facts, or persuasion. The sophisticated reader recognizes this shift in purpose and thus is more critical in evaluating the content. For example, a persuasive paragraph for or against more air quality control regulations should alert you to be more skeptical and less accepting than a paragraph explaining how air quality control works.

The author can have a single purpose or a combination of the following:

to inform	to argue	to entertain
to explain	to persuade	to narrate
to describe	to condemn	to describe
to enlighten	to ridicule	to shock

Read the following passage to determine the author's purpose.

EXAMPLE

love, *n.* A temporary insanity curable by marriage or by removal of the patient from the influences under which he incurred the disorder. This disease, like caries and many other ailments, is prevalent only among civilized races living under artificial conditions; barbarous nations breathing pure air and eating simple food enjoy immunity from its ravages. It is sometimes fatal, but more frequently to the physician than to the patient.

Ambrose Bierce, *The Devil's Dictionary*

EXPLANATION The author defines love in a humorous and exaggerated manner for the purpose of entertaining the reader.

EXERCISE 7.5   *Determining the Author's Purpose*

Read the following passage and answer the questions about the author's purpose.

Isabella Katz and the Holocaust: A Living Testimony

No statistics can adequately render the enormity of the Holocaust, and its human meaning can perhaps only be understood through the experience of a single human being who was cast into the nightmare of the Final Solution. Isabella Katz was the eldest of six children—Isabella, brother Philip,

5. What is Isabella's purpose in relating her story? _____

_____

6. Is the passage predominately developed through facts or opinions? Give an example of each._____

_____

7. How does the passage influence your thinking about the Holocaust?

_____◄

WHAT IS THE AUTHOR'S TONE?

The tone of an author's writing is similar to the tone of a speaker's voice. For listeners, it is fairly easy to tell the difference between an angry tone and a romantic tone by noticing the speaker's voice. Distinguishing among humor, sarcasm, and irony, however, may be more difficult. **Humorous** remarks are designed to be comical and amusing, while **sarcastic** remarks are designed to cut or give pain. As stated in the discussion of figurative language in Chapter 6, **ironic** remarks express something other than the literal meaning and are designed to show the incongruity between the actual and the expected. Making such precise distinctions requires more than just listening to sounds; it requires a careful evaluation of what is said. Because the sound of the voice is not heard in reading, clues to the tone must come from the writer's presentation of the message. Your job is to look for clues to answer the question "What is the author's attitude toward the topic?"

Try being the author yourself. Let's say that your friend is already a half-hour late for a meeting. You can wait no longer but you can leave a note. On your own paper, write your friend three different notes—one in a sympathetic tone, one in an angry tone, and one in a sarcastic tone. Notice in doing this how your tone reflects your purpose. Which note would you really leave and to which friend?

The following is a list of some of the words that can be used to describe the author's tone. Can you imagine an example for each:

angry	hateful	ironic	professional
bitter	hopeful	jovial	respectful
cynical	horrifying	lonely	sarcastic
defensive	hostile	loving	satirical
depressing	humorous	miserable	scornful
enthusiastic	hypocritical	nostalgic	subjective
fearful	hysterical	objective	sincere
gloomy	insulting	optimistic	sympathetic
happy	intellectual	pessimistic	threatening

EXAMPLE   Read the following passage and note that the overall tone is informative and educational. However, the author sees a certain aspect to the subject matter that brings out another tone. What is that tone?

> Some plants depend upon fire to maintain high densities. The most famous example is the giant sequoia (*Sequoiadendron giganteum*) of California. These magnificent trees are replaced by other conifers, but only in the absence of fire. Conservation attempts to protect the sequoia forests by stopping all forest fires have, in effect, almost doomed these trees to disappear, and attempts to restore fire to a useful place in forest management are currently under way in the National Parks Service of the United States.
>
> Large sequoia trees have a thick, fire-resistant bark and so they are not damaged by ground fires that are fatal to many other conifers, such as white fir and sugar pine. Sequoia seedlings also germinate best on bare mineral soil, and ground fires provide a good environment for seedling establishment by removing the litter on the forest floor. Thus organisms as different as blue grouse, moose, and sequoia trees may all depend upon habitat changes brought on by fire in order to keep their numbers high. Good habitats are not necessarily those that are never disturbed.
>
> Charles Krebs. *The Message of Ecology*

EXPLANATION   There is an underlying tone of irony as the author points out that fire, which is deadly to most, is essential for the life of the giant sequoias. Irony is the opposite of the expected. In fiction or life, it is the twist or surprise ending that no one anticipates. Irony can make us laugh, but usually it is a bittersweet and somewhat cruel chuckle.

> **EXERCISE 7.6**   *Determining the Author's Tone*

Read the following passages to determine the author's tone and attitude toward the subject.

Passage A: Water Pollution

In many locales the water is not safe to drink, as evidenced by the recent outbreaks of infectious hepatitis in the United States. Infectious hepatitis is believed to be caused by a virus carried in human waste, usually through a water supply that is contaminated by sewage. There is some disturbing evidence that this virus may be resistant to chlorine, especially in the presence of high levels of organic material. Despite our national pride in indoor plumbing and walk-in bathrooms, sewage treatment for many communities in the United States is grossly inadequate, and waste that has been only partially treated is discharged into waterways. Recently the news services carried a story announcing that the New Orleans water supply may be dangerous to drink. However, we have been assured that there is no cause for alarm—a committee has been appointed to study the problem!

Robert Wallace, *Biology: The World of Life*

1. What is the author's tone? _____

   _____

2. Circle the words and phrases that suggest this tone.

   _____

3. What is the author's point of view?

   _____

4. What is your own point of view on the subject?

   _____

5. What is the main point the author is trying to convey?_____

   _____

Passage B: The Redwoods

It is impossible to live in the redwood region without being profoundly affected by the massive destruction of this once-magnificent ecosystem. Miles and miles of clearcuts cover our bleeding hillsides. Ancient forests are being strip-logged to pay off corporate junk bonds. Log trucks fill our roads, heading to the sawmills with loads ranging from 1,000-year-old redwoods, one tree trunk filling an entire logging truck, to six-inch-diameter baby trees that are chipped for pulp.

Judi Bari, "The Feminization of Earth First!" reprinted by permission of *Ms* Magazine, © 1992.

1. What is the author's tone? _____

2. Circle the words and phrases that suggest this tone.

3. What is the author's point of view? _____

4. What is your own point of view on the subject? _____

5. What is the main point the author is trying to convey? _____

   _____

Passage C: The Injustice System

It's hard to change 3,000 years of attitudes, but parents and teachers, judges and lawmakers can help. We start by teaching little boys to respect the feelings—and words—of little girls. And what do we teach little girls?

I have two young daughters, and I want to protect them from harm just as my parents wanted to protect me. But the days are long gone when girls went directly from their father's house to their husband's.

I hope I can teach my daughters more than just how to avoid being alone with a man in an elevator. They will study karate as well as ballet. I want them to understand their own strength, the importance of knees and elbows, the power of a well-placed kick.

I'll teach them that the justice system can be unjust. They should use the system but not trust it, and work to reform it.

Patty Fisher, "The Injustice System." Reprinted with permission of the San Jose Mercury News, March 25, 1992.

1. What is the author's tone? _____

2. Circle the words and phrases that suggest this tone.

   _____

3. What is the author's point of view? _____

4. What is your own point of view on the subject? _____

5. What is the main point the author is trying to convey?

   _____

Passage D: The Comma

The commas are the most useful and usable of all the stops. It is highly important to put them in place as you go along. If you try to come back after doing a paragraph and stick them in the various spots that tempt you you will discover that they tend to swarm like minnows into all sorts of crevices whose existence you hadn't realized and before you know it the whole long sentence becomes immobilized and lashed up squirming in commas. Better to use them sparingly, and with affection, precisely when the need for each one arises, nicely, by itself.

Lewis Thomas, "Notes on Punctuation," from *The Medusa and the Snail* by Lewis Thomas, Copyright © 1979 by Lewis Thomas. Reprinted by permission of Viking Penguin, a division of Penguin Books USA Inc.

1. What is the author's tone? _____

2. Circle the words and phrases that suggest this tone.

3. What is the author's point of view? _____

4. What is your own point of view on the subject? _____

5. What is the main point the author is trying to convey?

   _____

© 2000 Addison-Wesley Educational Publishers, Inc.

EDITORIAL CARTOONS

Editorial cartoons vividly illustrate how an author or an artist can effectively communicate point of view without making a direct verbal statement. Through their drawings, cartoonists have great freedom to be extremely harsh and judgmental. For example, they take positions on local and national news events and frequently depict politicians as crooks, thieves, or even murderers. Because the accusations are implied rather than directly stated, the cartoonist communicates a point of view but is still safe from libel charges.

EXAMPLE   Study the cartoon below to determine what the cartoonist believes and is saying about the subject. Use the following steps to help you analyze the implied meaning and point of view.

Reprinted with special permission of King Features Syndicate.

1. Glance at the cartoon for an overview and read the signs.

2. Answer the question, "What is this about?" to determine the general topic.

   _____

3. Study the details for symbolism. Who is the man? What is he doing? What do the signs mean?

   _____

4. With all the information in mind, answer the question, "What is the main point the cartoonist is trying to get across?"

_____

5. Taking the message into consideration, answer "What is the cartoonist's purpose?" _____

_____

6. What is the tone of the cartoon?_____

_____

7. What is the cartoonist's point of view or position on the subject? What is your point of view? _____

_____

EXPLANATION To summarize, the cartoonist feels that America is a throwaway society. We are overwhelmed by stimulus of big businesses to consume more and more. Advertisers encourage us to dispose of the old and buy the new. In the cartoonist's view, recycling is a losing battle. Recycling amounts to an insignificant effort when confronting the vast amount of trash from avid consumerism. The tone is both sarcastic and pessimistic. The purpose is to heighten awareness, and the point of view of the cartoonist is in favor of recycling.

EXERCISE 7.7   *Interpreting an Editorial Cartoon*

Use the same steps to analyze the message and answer the questions in the cartoon shown on the opposite page.

1. What is the general topic of this cartoon? _____

_____

2. What do the people and objects represent? _____

_____

3. What is the main point the cartoonist is trying to convey? _____

_____

_____

© *S. C. Rawls*

4. What is the cartoonist's purpose? _____

5. What is the tone of the cartoon? _____

6. What is the cartoonist's point of view? _____

_____

7. What is your point of view on the subject? _____

   Cartoons are fun but challenging, because they require prior knowledge for interpretation. For current news cartoons, you have to be familiar with the latest happenings in order to make connections and understand the message. Look on the editorial page of your newspaper to enjoy world events from a cartoonist's point of view.

   As stated in the beginning of the chapter, even in college textbooks the author's attitudes and biases slip through. It is your responsibility as a reader to be alert for signs of manipulation and to be ready to question interpretations and conclusions. Sophisticated readers are aware and draw their own conclusions based on their own interpretation of the facts.

Summary Points

■ **Is a textbook influenced by the author's point of view?**

Authors have opinions, theories, and prejudices that influence their presentation of material. When facts are slanted, though not necessarily distorted, the material is biased toward the author's beliefs.

■ **What is the author's point of view?**

A bias is a prejudice, a mental leaning, or an inclination. The bias, in a sense, creates the point of view, the particular angle from which the author views the material.

■ **What is the reader's point of view?**

Students should not let their own viewpoints impede their understanding of the author's opinions and ideas.

■ **What is the difference between a fact and an opinion?**

Both facts and opinions are used persuasively to support positions. A fact is a statement that can be proved to be either true or false. An opinion is a statement of feeling or a judgment.

■ **What is the author's purpose?**

An author always has a purpose in mind, and a sophisticated reader should recognize that purpose in order to be a well-informed consumer. The author's purpose is usually informational, argumentative, or entertaining

■ **What is the author's tone?**

The tone of an author's writing is similar to the tone of a speaker's voice. The reader's job is to look for clues to determine the author's attitude about the subject.

CONTEMPORARY FOCUS

Family rituals bond family members together, just as cultural foods and traditions link citizens. We can learn an appreciation for humanity both from the family table and from the customs of a distant country.

THE NEW FAMILY DINNER

Carol Wallace

Parents, May, 1999, p. 106–110

Experts confirm that sharing regular meals as a family brings a banquet of benefits. Ben Silliman, Ph.D., a family-life specialist at the University of Wyoming's Cooperative Extension Service, says, "Children of all ages need to know that parents are accessible to them. One of the big messages that family dinner sends is 'You're important enough for me to spend this time with you.'"

"Mealtime is often the only time in the whole day when everybody's in the same room having a conversation," sasys William Doherty, Ph.D., author of *The Intentional Family* (Addison Wesley Longman, 1997), "so it's where the family's culture gets created." Even more impressive is the research suggesting that regular family meals can sharpen a child's intellect. Diane Beals Ed.D., of the University of Tulsa, and Patton Tabors, Ed.D., of Harvard, studied 80 preschoolers and found that mealtime conversation built vocabulary even more effectively than listening to stories being read aloud.

Indeed, the phrase "family dinner" has become almost a metaphor for a commitment to family—a commitment strong enough to survive the considerable odds against it. After all, in order to eat together, every family member must make it a priority.

"When my children were preteens," recounts Dr. Doherty, "we got into the habit of going out for pizza on Friday nights. We found we had more interesting conversations and far fewer fights. You haven't had to work to fix the meal, and you're out in public, so you behave a little better." The whole experience is just that much more pleasant.

Feeding a family is a big job, but it can be split into components that can easily be delegated: setting the table, making the salad, pouring the drinks, loading the dishwasher. "When kids are involved in preparing dinner," says Dr. Silliman, "they're invested in that time together." And, of course, you can always let your fingers do the walking and order takeout. After all, family meals will hardly stay enjoyable if one party resents the burden of putting on the show night after night.

Collaborate on responses to the following questions:

■ What are your "family dinner" rituals?

■ What traditions do you see in other families that you would like to have in your own?

■ Why and how do traditions hold families together?

STAGE 1: PREVIEW

Preview the next selection to predict its purpose and organization, as well as your learning plan.

The author will probably discuss _____.

Activate Schema

Why was the Vietnam War fought?

Why did many Vietnamese flee their country?

STAGE 2: INTEGRATE KNOWLEDGE WHILE READING

Predict   Picture   Relate   Monitor   Correct

Vietnamese family honor: Ta Thuc Phu, M.D., poses with his 92-year-old mother-in-law, Duong Thi Tri, and his wife, Hoang Thi Hanh.

ELDERLY PARENTS: A CULTURAL DUTY

From Ta Thuc Phu, *The Orlando Sentinel*, 2 May 1998, p. A-19.

A Vietnamese saying goes: "The father's creative work is as great as the Thai Son mountain; the mother's love is as large as the river flowing out to sea. Respect and love your parents from the bottom of your hearts. Achieve your duty of filial piety as a proper stan- 5 dard of well-behaved children."

I am pleased to answer the question, "How do you deal with your parents as they get older?" I want to relate some characteristics of the Vietnamese culture.

Living together with elderly parents under the same roof is one of 10 our national traditions. In fact, I am honored to have my 92-year-old mother-in-law living with me and my wife.

The family is the basic institution with which to perpetuate society and provide protection to individuals. Generally speaking, the family structure in Southeastern Asia is more complex than the American family structure.

15   In Vietnamese society, the father is the head of the family. However, the father shares with his wife and children collective responsibilities—legally, morally and spiritually—and these responsibilities continue, even after children are grown up and married. Always, the mother has the same status as the father. In addition, she is the embodiment of love and the spirit of self-denial and sacrifice.

20   Vietnamese parents consider the parent-child relationship their most important responsibility, and they train their children for a lifetime. In effect,

the family is the small school where children learn to follow rules of behavior and speaking. The cornerstone of the children's behavior in the family is filial piety. Filial piety consists of loving, respecting and obeying one's parents. As a
25 result, the obligation to obey parents does not end with the coming of age or marriage. Filial piety means solicitude and support of one's parents, chiefly in their old age. Vietnamese elders never live by themselves or in nursing homes. Instead, they live with one of their children, usually the eldest son. This is a family custom practiced in all Vietnamese homes.

30   We do not want to live far apart from our parents, regardless of whether they are young or old, healthy or infirm, because we want to take care of them at any time until their deaths. That is our concept of gratitude to our parents for their hard work and sacrifice throughout the years.

I recall that, when I was growing up, my mother was severely crippled.
35 When we walked together, she held on to my arm for balance. It was difficult to coordinate our steps. My wife and I took turns holding my mother when she cried, and we helped her to walk two hours a day to exercise her body.

By living with our aging parents under the same roof, we also have many occasions to demonstrate our respect for them in the solemn days of the lunar
40 year, such as New Year's Day (Tet), and to celebrate their anniversaries. Our children would present New Year's wishes and symbols of good luck, such as bright red ribbons, to their grandparents to represent prosperity and longevity.

Most important in the Vietnamese value system is undoubtedly our belief
45 that children ought to be grateful to parents for the debt of birth, rearing and education. Children are taught to think of parents first, even at their own expense, to make sacrifices for their parents' sake, to love and care for them in their old age. Unfortunately, that practice is denied now by the communist regime in Vietnam. Children have been taught to spy on their parents and re-
50 port to the Communist Party any subversive talk or irregular behavior.

Above all, since April 30, 1975, after the collapse of Saigon with the communist takeover of South Vietnam and the tragic exodus of more than 2 million refugees to all parts of the world in search of freedom and a better future, Vietnamese families still practice the custom of living with the parents
55 under the same roof. Deep feelings for families and ties to elders are still strong. These feelings and ties will endure despite these times of change. Even when our parents have been gone many years, we still think of them as living with us.

STAGE 3: RECALL

Stop to self-test, relate, and react.

Your instructor may choose to give you a true-false comprehension review.

ELDERLY PARENTS: A CULTURAL DUTY

Describe your family tradition and your philosophical view on the care of elderly parents. Also, describe your plan for the care of your own parents.

Contemporary Link

Just as family diiner traditions differ, why do you feel the typical American manner of caring for elderly parents differs from that of the Vietnamese?

SKILL DEVELOPMENT: EXPLORING POINT OF VIEW

Collaborative Activity

Form a collaborative group to discuss the following questions:

■ What is your view on nursing homes?

■ What do you feel is the government's responsibility in the care of the elderly?

■ If financial assistance is needed, who should pay for the care of the elderly?

■ Is the question of elder care only about money?

COMPREHENSION QUESTIONS

Answer the following with *T* (true) or *F* (false).

Inference   _____ 1. The author's primary purpose is to argue that Americans should have elderly parents living with them under the same roof.

Inference   _____ 2. The author's tone is objective.

Inference   _____ 3. The author feels both honored and happy to have an elderly parent living in his home.

Inference   _____ 4. The author implies that the Communists in Vietnam are undermining the traditional parent-child relationship.

Detail   _____ 5. According to the author, there are no nursing homes in Vietnam.

Inference   _____ 6. The author's statement that a mother "is the embodiment of love and the spirit of self-denial and sacrifice" is a statement of fact.

Detail   _____ 7. The author suggests that in Vietnamese culture, the mother is the actual head of the family.

Inference   _____ 8. The author suggests that Vietnamese refugees in America have begun to abandon the custom of living with parents under the same roof.

Inference   _____ 9. The author probably supported the Communist takeover of South Vietnam.

Inference   _____ 10. The author implies that family comes before business in the Vietnamese culture.

© 2000 Addison-Wesley Educational Publishers, Inc.

VOCABULARY

1. Define *filial* _____

2. Define *piety* _____

3. In your own words, define *filial piety* as used in the passage.

_____

SEARCH THE NET

The Internet can be a valuable resource for the elderly. Prepare a resource guide for an elderly friend or grandparent that includes Websites or links, or both, with useful information on retirement, healthcare, and homecare. Select at least four sites, and describe the information given in each. Plan your search or begin by trying the following:

http://www.caregiving.com

http://www.nahc.org

http://www.senior.com/

http://katesdrm.home.mindspring.com/

http://www.aahsa.org/

CONTEMPORARY FOCUS

When authors express their passion in their writings, we applaud their creativity. What happens when that same passion is expressed on the street where you live?

SAN ANTONIO JOURNAL: NOVELIST'S PURPLE PALETTE IS NOT TO EVERYONE'S TASTE

Sara Rimer

New York Times, July 13, 1998, sect. A, p. 14

Sandra Cisneros, the poet and novelist whose work explores the relationship between home and identity, did not want her own long-yearned-for house to be bland or timid or understated. The old coat of beige paint it had would not do. Ms. Cisneros found what she was looking for in Sherwin-Williams Corsican purple. Overnight, her bungalow became the Purple House.

It has become a kind of blank canvas, as well, layered with symbolism and inspiring intense passions and debate in this proudly Mexican-American city. Depending on who is looking at it, it is a work of art, a flagrant violation of the rules in Ms. Cisneros's historic neighborhood, a flag signifying Mexican-American pride, an embodiment of border culture, a symbol of freedom of expression, a sign of Ms. Cisneros's identification with her Mexican-American roots, a reflection of Ms. Cisneros's uppityness, a brilliant publicity stunt, a tourist attraction.

San Antonio has plenty of colorful buildings—the new library is enchilada red—and a purple house might not have created such a stir were it not for its being in the historic Victorian King William neighborhood. The city's Historic Design and Review Commission ruled that Corsican purple was historically incorrect—even if it was "exquisite," as Milton Babbitt, the architect in the group, called it—and had to be changed.

Elsa Calderone, 73, who lives a block away and is confined to her home because of poor health, insists on being driven by whenever she goes to the doctor. "It's like a fairy tale," said Mrs. Calderone, whose own house is white. "I belong to the King William Association and I agree with their standards, but once in a while you need something like that to brighten up your life."

One of seven children of a Mexican upholsterer and his Mexican-American wife, Ms. Cisneros, 43, grew up in Chicago but traveled often to Mexico City to visit her grandmother. "What the house is saying is, 'I'm very Mexican, and I'm proud of it,' and that it's another way of being American," the author said in a recent interview.

In "The House on Mango Street," the narrator, a young girl named Esperanza who lives in the Chicago barrio, is ashamed of her "sad red house, the house I belong but do not belong to." What she longs for: "A house all my own. With my porch and my pillow, my pretty purple petunias."

As for the exterior, both Ms. Cisneros and the city say they hope to reach a compromise. Ms. Cisneros, who has rejected such suggested colors as Plymouth green and Colonial-revival tan, has proposed repainting the roof terra cotta. The city has yet to respond.

"It's like a novel," said the author, who is finishing her second novel, "Caramelo," about a Mexican-American family. "You have to guess how it will end."

Collaborative Activity

Collaborate on responses to the following questions.

■ Why do some cities have design standards for the houses in certain neighborhoods?

■ Would you support keeping the purple color? Why or why not?

■ Why would some neighbors suggest that the purple house is a "brilliant publicity stunt"?

STAGE 1: PREVIEW

Preview the next selection to predict its purpose and organization, as well as your learning plan.

This story seems to be about _____

Activate Schema

Are the daughters and sons in your extended family treated equally by the parents?

STAGE 2: INTEGRATE KNOWLEDGE WHILE READING

Predict   Picture   Relate   Monitor   Correct

ONLY DAUGHTER

From Sandra Cisneros, *Women's Voices from Borderlands*

Sandra Cisneros poses in front of her home and proclaims that the colors celebrate the "Spirit of South Texas and Mexico."

Once, several years ago, when I was just starting out my writing career, I was asked to write my own contributor's note for an anthology I was part of. I wrote: "I am the only daughter in a family of six sons. *That* explains everything."

5 Well, I've thought about that ever since, and yes, it explains a lot to me, but for the reader's sake I should have written: "I am the only daughter in a *Mexican* family of six sons." Or even: "I am the only daughter of a Mexican father and a Mexican-American mother." Or: "I am the only daughter of a working-class family of nine." All of these had

10 everything to do with who I am today.

I was/am the only daughter and *only* a daughter. Being an only daughter in a family of six sons forced me by circumstance to spend a lot of time by myself because my brothers felt it beneath them to play with a *girl* in public. But that aloneness, that loneliness, was good for a would-be writer—it

15 allowed me time to think and think, to imagine, to read and prepare myself.

Being only a daughter for my father meant my destiny would lead me to become someone's wife. That's what he believed. But when I was in the fifth grade
and shared my plans for college with him, I was sure he understood. I remember
20 my father saying, "*Que bueno, mi'ja,* that's good." That meant a lot to me, especially since my brothers thought the idea hilarious. What I didn't realize was that
my father thought college was good for girls—good for finding a husband. After
four years in college and two more in graduate school, and still no husband, my
father shakes his head even now and says I wasted all that education.

25 In retrospect, I'm lucky my father believed daughters were meant for husbands. It meant it didn't matter if I majored in something silly like English.
After all, I'd find a nice professional eventually, right? This allowed me the
liberty to putter about embroidering my little poems and stories without my
father interrupting with so much as a "What's that you're writing?"

30 But the truth is, I wanted him to interrupt. I wanted my father to understand what it was I was scribbling, to introduce me as "My only daughter, the
writer." Not as "This is only my daughter. She teaches." *Es maestra*—teacher.
Not even *profesora.*

In a sense, everything I have ever written has been for him, to win his ap-
35 proval even though I know my father can't read English words, even though my
father's only reading includes the brown-ink *Esto* sports magazines from Mexico
City and the bloody *¡Alarma!* magazines that feature yet another sighting of *La
Virgen de Guadalupe* on a tortilla or a wife's revenge on her philandering husband by bashing his skull in with a *molcajete* (a kitchen mortar made of volcanic
40 rock). Or the *fotonovelas,* the little picture paperbacks with tragedy and trauma
erupting from the characters' mouths in bubbles.

My father represents, then, the public majority. A public who is disinterested in reading, and yet one whom I am writing about and for, and privately
trying to woo.

45 When we were growing up in Chicago, we moved a lot because of my father. He suffered bouts of nostalgia. Then we'd have to let go of our flat, store
the furniture with mother's relatives, load the station wagon with baggage
and bologna sandwiches and head south. To Mexico City.

We came back, of course. To yet another Chicago flat, another Chicago
50 neighborhood, another Catholic school. Each time, my father would seek out
the parish priest in order to get a tuition break, and complain or boast: "I have
seven sons."

He meant *siete hijos,* seven children, but he translated it as "sons." "I have
seven sons." To anyone who would listen. The Sears Roebuck employee who
55 sold us the washing machine. The short-order cook where my father ate his
ham-and-eggs breakfasts. "I have seven sons." As if he deserved a medal from
the state.

My papa. He didn't mean anything by that mistranslation, I'm sure. But
somehow I could feel myself being erased. I'd tug my father's sleeve and whis-
60 per: "Not seven sons. Six! and *one daughter.*"

When my oldest brother graduated from medical school, he fulfilled my father's dream that we study hard and use this—our heads, instead of this—our hands. Even now my father's hands are thick and yellow, stubbed by a history of hammer and nails and twine and coils and springs. "Use this," my father

65 said, tapping his head, "and not this," showing us those hands. He always looked tired when he said it.

Wasn't college an investment? And hadn't I spent all those years in college? And if I didn't marry, what was it all for? Why would anyone go to college and then choose to be poor? Especially someone who had always been poor.

70 Last year, after ten years of writing professionally, the financial rewards started to trickle in. My second National Endowment for the Arts Fellowship. A guest professorship at the University of California, Berkeley. My book, which sold to a major New York publishing house.

At Christmas, I flew home to Chicago. The house was throbbing, same as

75 always: hot tamales and sweet tamales hissing in my mother's pressure cooker, and everybody—my mother, six brothers, wives, babies, aunts, cousins—talking too loud and at the same time. Like in a Fellini film, because that's just how we are.

I went upstairs to my father's room. One of my stories had just been trans-

80 lated into Spanish and published in an anthology of Chicano writing and I wanted to show it to him. Ever since he recovered from a stroke two years ago, my father likes to spend his leisure hours horizontally. And that's how I found him, watching a Pedro Infante movie on Galavisión and eating rice pudding.

85 There was a glass filled with milk on the bedside table. There were several vials of pills and balled Kleenex. And on the floor, one black sock and a plastic urinal that I didn't want to look at but looked at anyway. Pedro Infante was about to burst into song, and my father was laughing.

I'm not sure if it was because my story was translated into Spanish, or be-

90 cause it was published in Mexico, or perhaps because the story dealt with Tepeyac, the *colonia* my father was raised in and the house he grew up in, but at any rate, my father punched the mute button on his remote control and read my story.

I sat on the bed next to my father and waited. He read it very slowly. As if

95 he were reading each line over and over. He laughed at all the right places and read lines he liked out loud. He pointed and asked questions: "Is this So-and-so?" "Yes," I said. He kept reading.

When he was finally finished, after what seemed like hours, my father looked up and asked: "Where can we get more copies of this for the relatives?"

100 Of all the wonderful things that happened to me last year, that was the most wonderful.

STAGE 3: RECALL

Stop to self-test, relate, and react.
Your instructor may choose to give you a true-false comprehension review.

 ONLY DAUGHTER

The author begins by saying that she did not fully express herself in stating that she is "the only daughter in a family of six sons." Why do you think she feels that she should have added that she was from a Mexican family, or that she had a Mexican father and a Mexican-American mother, or that it was a working-class family? Why does she feel that each of these three additional phrases should have been written for "the reader's sake"?

Contemporary Link

How do both her writings and the purple house make a bold statement of Sandra Cisneros's Mexican-American pride? Use examples to support your reasons.

Skill Development: Exploring Point of View

1. How does the author suggest two different opinions in the use of the word *only*. _____

2. How does the father's point of view on his daughter's attending college represent a generation gap? _____

   _____

3. How does the last sentence in the selection express the author's values?

   _____

   _____

4. As a college student, you are required to write in complete sentences, yet Cisneros, a prize-winning author, uses phrases in this selection that are not sentences. Use an example to explain her use of phrases. Why would this be accepted in her writing and not in yours?

   _____

© 2000 Addison-Wesley Educational Publishers, Inc.

COMPREHENSION QUESTIONS

Answer the following with *T* (true) or *F* (false).

_____ 1. The author has an optimistic attitude about the loneliness of a life with six brothers.

_____ 2. The author implies that her brothers encouraged her to go to college.

_____ 3. The author implies that her mother shared her father's "seven sons" perspective.

_____ 4. The author implies that her father reads religious magazines.

_____ 5. The author states that her father would uproot the family because he was homesick for Mexico.

_____ 6. The author gained recognition and success after ten years of writing.

_____ 7. The author italicizes the word *girl* in the third paragraph to emphasize a negative attitude rather than a positive one.

_____ 8. The author suggests that her father is temporarily rather than permanently ill.

_____ 9. The purpose of this selection is to criticize the father for his point of view.

_____ 10. The author suggests that her writing is based on fictional characters in imaginary settings.

SEARCH THE NET

Sandra Cisneros is one among the many voices of Mexican-American women. Conduct a search to learn more about her work or the work of other Hispanic female authors. Choose Cisneros or another author, and write a brief biographical sketch highlighting major accomplishments. List and briefly describe two of your author's books.

Plan your own search or begin by trying the following:

http://english.cla.umn.edu/lkd/vfg/ethnicity

http://www.utc.edu/~kswitala/feminism/chicana.html

http://www-lib.usc.edu/~retter/pitlatart.html

http://mail.igc.apc.org/women/activist/color.html

C O N T E M P O R A R Y   F O C U S

The threat of a lawsuit can prompt a company to be responsible and attend to the safety of the consumer. At what point, however, can a lawsuit work to the consumer's disadvantage?

TORT REFORM: EXCESSIVE LITIGATION BY TRIAL LAWYERS

Vital Speeches of the Day, vol. 64, no. 12 (April 1, 1998), pp. 362–365. Address delivered by William S. Stavropoulos, President and CEO of the Dow Chemical Company, to the Dallas Friday Group, Dallas, Texas, January 23, 1998

Today, I want to talk about a debate in which Texas is a national leader: civil justice reform. I want to talk not just of the threat that runaway lawsuits pose to business, but of the American way of justice, how juries operate, the important role judges play, and the influence of what happens in our courtrooms on democracy itself.

I don't pretend to be a disinterested party. You probably know that Dow Chemical has been hit with thousands of lawsuits for a product that we did not design, test, or manufacture . . . and that medical science says causes no harm.

Although I am concerned about the amount of money involved . . . money that is put to little productive use . . . I am more concerned with the violation of our basic rights, to be accused of wrongdoing when we did nothing wrong.

Tort costs in the United States are about two-and-a-half times the average of the other major industrial nations. In fact, tort costs comprise a shocking 2.2 percent of U.S. GDP; that's more money than our federal government spends on NASA, federal education programs, health care research, veterans benefits and services, and federal law enforcement combined.

In fact, in a typical year, American businesses spend about the same amount on legal services as we do on research and development. That means we spend as much money adjudicating the past as we do planning for growth in the future. One of our former presidents once claimed that "the business of America is business." Today, a more accurate statement would be, "the business of America is defending itself in court."

Why is the civil justice system out of control? Bluntly stated, we live in a lawsuit happy "blame someone else" culture that is encouraged and fostered by predatory trial lawyers . . . and, I might say, by our government itself. They prey on American business with two principal weapons of intimidation: mass, class-action lawsuits, and gigantic punitive awards. You might even call them weapons of mass destruction.

And in many class-action lawsuits, lawyers reap fortunes, while their clients are lucky to get a few dollars. In one case against a financial services company, the trial lawyers pocketed $8 million in legal fees, while their clients won $4 each.

When trial lawyers can win tens of millions, or even billions, of dollars in judgments, for minor infractions that cause little harm to people, they are being given the power to confiscate every legitimate business and dominate whole sectors this city depends on.

We don't need a second American Revolution to free our society from predatory trial lawyers. All we need to do is to restore the precepts of humanity, reason, and justice to our laws.

Collaborate on responses to the following questions:

■ What does the speaker seem to want from the audience?

■ Do you believe that trial lawyers are driven by greed or a desire for justice? Explain.

■ What are the compelling facts in this argument? Why?

STAGE 1: PREVIEW

Preview the next selection to predict its purpose and organization as well as your learning plan.

This passage probably defines issues concerning negligence and liability. Agree ☐   Disagree ☐

Activate Schema

How would you distinguish between a frivolous lawsuit and a legitimate one?

Word Knowledge What do you know about these words?

revenue	heeds	defray	willfully	skeptical
callous	scrutiny	pending	hinge	toxic

Your instructor may give a true-false vocabulary review before or after reading.

STAGE 2: INTEGRATE KNOWLEDGE WHILE READING

Predict   Picture   Relate   Monitor   Correct

UNDERSTANDING THE LEGAL CONTEXT OF BUSINESS

From Ricky Griffin and Ronald Ebert, *Business*, 4th ed.

McDonald's Brews Up a Lawsuit

McDonald's, the fast-food legend known for quality and service, runs more than 9,000 restaurants in the United States and serves up nearly a third of all hamburgers consumed by Americans. What's more, customers pause under the Golden Arches to buy a *billion* cups of McDonald's coffee each year. *Daily* revenue from coffee sales exceeds $1 million. Why does McDonald's sell so much coffee? For one thing, it serves its coffee the way most people like it: piping hot. For example, McDonald's heeds the recommendations of industry groups that

coffee tastes best when brewed with water heated to 195 degrees and served at
about 180 degrees. Temperatures that hot, of course, can cause serious burns,
10 and in 1992, 81-year-old Stella Liebeck was scalded when she tried to remove the
lid of a cup of coffee that she had purchased at the drive-through window of a
McDonald's restaurant in Albuquerque, New Mexico. After McDonald's rejected Mrs. Liebeck's request for $800 to defray the cost of medical treatment,
the injured woman hired a lawyer and sued. To the amazement of many ob-
15 servers, a jury sided with Mrs. Liebeck and awarded her considerably more than
$800—$2.9 million, in fact.

   Should burns from a 49-cent cup of coffee justify an award of that size?
Liebeck's attorneys pointed out that her injuries were quite serious: She suffered third-degree burns and was hospitalized for seven days while undergoing
20 skin grafts. After leaving the hospital and receiving no satisfaction from Mc-
Donald's, Liebeck met attorney Reed Morgan. Morgan had been involved in a
1986 lawsuit involving McDonald's coffee. Although that case had been settled for $27,500, Morgan remained convinced that McDonald's was willfully
serving coffee at a temperature that was both unnecessary and dangerous.
25   On Liebeck's behalf, Morgan filed a lawsuit contending that McDonald's coffee was "defective" because it was too hot. Originally, Morgan was willing to settle the case for $300,000, but McDonald's legal team refused the offer. Instead,
it chose to defend the company's practice of brewing and serving piping-hot coffee. In fact, the defense team denied liability for Liebeck's injuries even after its
30 own investigators had gathered data on coffee temperatures in other Albuquerque restaurants: McDonald's was indeed the hottest by a good margin.

   As the trial opened, some jurors seemed skeptical about the merits of the
suit. Then, however, they began to hear the evidence. Jurors were informed, for
example, that McDonald's had received hundreds of complaints about coffee
35 burns—and had in fact already paid more than $500,000 in settlements. In addi-
tion, the testimony of *defense* witnesses did little to help McDonald's cause. For
example, a quality-assurance manager at the company admitted that McDonald's had never consulted burn experts about the possible dangers of extremely
hot coffee. "There are," he explained, "more serious dangers in restaurants." An-
40 other expert witness called by the defense reported that, after all, the number of
severe coffee scaldings was statistically insignificant in comparison to annual
sales of a billion cups of coffee. Gradually, said one juror after the trial, it began
to appear that McDonald's had, as the plaintiff charged, showed "a callous disregard for the safety of the people." The jury finally awarded $160,000 in com-
45 pensatory damages and $2.7 million in punitive damages.

   Although a New Mexico state court judge later reduced the punitive damages to $480,000, the parties ultimately settled out of court. For McDonald's,
of course, the episode was costly not only in dollars but in negative publicity.
For many U.S. firms—both large and small—it also serves as an object lesson
50 on the possible impact of the legal system on business practices. The McDonald's case, however, has also focused the attention of many legal-system critics.
In the fall of 1994, for example, the Republican "Contract with America"
brought the U.S. legal system—especially negligence and product liability

law—under close and official Congressional scrutiny. The size of the Liebeck
award (indeed, the lawsuit itself) was cited to support the call for a "common
sense" overhaul of personal-injury litigation. Business and trade associations
have stepped up lobbying efforts for reform, and in May 1995, the U.S. Senate
voted in favor of a bill that would apply a new formula for determining punitive damages: $250,000 or twice the combined amount of money awarded for
pain and suffering, lost wages, and medical bills—whichever is greater.

Lining up against reform are consumer groups and the Association of Trial
Lawyers. In reality, argue opponents of the pending legislation, juries seldom
make outlandish personal-injury awards. Moreover, they point out, only one
in four cases ever goes to trial; the vast majority are settled out of court. Finally, they contend that no new formulas are needed because many judges—
like the one who adjusted the final Liebeck award—already adhere to a "three
times compensatory" formula (that is, punitive awards that are no more than
triple damages paid for injuries actually suffered).

As this episode shows, even well-established businesses with good reputa-
tions can find themselves in court. Indeed, the activities of many U.S. businesses—both large and small—are increasingly being constrained by laws and
court verdicts. We have laws, for example, requiring that children's clothing
be fireproof, that food producers use no cancer-causing chemicals, and that
automobiles be fuel-efficient.

Firms face serious financial penalties, and may even fail, when managers
misunderstand—or ignore, or violate—the law.

Tort Law

Tort law applies to most business relationships *not governed by contracts*. A
tort is a *civil*—that is, noncriminal—injury to people, property, or reputation
for which compensation must be paid.

Negligence Torts

Ninety percent of tort suits involve charges of **negligence**: conduct falling below legal standards for protecting others against unreasonable risk. If a company installs a pollution-control system that fails to protect a community's
water supply, it may later be sued by an individual who gets sick from drinking the water. Negligence torts may also result from employee actions. For example, if a janitor fails to post a sign warning about a wet floor, the employer
might be sued by a customer who slips and breaks a leg. If a company's delivery driver runs a red light and strikes a pedestrian, both driver and employer
may be sued for negligence.

Juries Target Gun Merchants. For example, should a retail store be held
liable when it sells a gun that is used to kill or injure someone? In at least one
case, the answer is yes. In 1993, a jury ordered Kmart to pay Deborah
Kitchen $12.5 million in damages for recklessly selling a firearm to her ex-
boyfriend, who used the weapon to shoot her at point-blank range. Kitchen,
who was shot in the neck, is now a quadriplegic.

Testimony showed that on December 14, 1987, Thomas Knapp bought a
95 .22 caliber rifle at Kmart. He had drunk a case of beer and a fifth of whiskey
and could not legibly fill out the form required by federal law on all gun purchases. The Kmart clerk obliged by copying the information on a new form
and had Knapp sign it. The case, however, did not hinge on Knapp's drunken-
ness: The key was the clerk's lack of knowledge about firearm sales. "It was
100 not so much that [Knapp] was drunk," reported the jury foreman. "There was
negligence on Kmart's part for not training the salesperson."

Kmart, of course, defended itself: The retailer, claims the company's director
of corporate communications, "always has taken very seriously the responsibility that goes along with the selling of firearms. We require training in firearms-
105 law procedures at the local, state and federal level." However, inspectors for the
Bureau of Alcohol, Tobacco, and Firearms have repeatedly cited Kmart stores
for violations of firearms laws. For example, during a routine check at a store in
Oxon Hill, Maryland, BATF inspectors found that federal forms were not filled
out and that clerks failed to require customers to show identification. In fact,
110 the store did not even have a current, valid state firearms license. "The problem," explains the sporting goods manager at the Oxon Hill store, "is not with
the written policies but with the people who are not following them."

Product Liability Torts

In cases of **product liability,** a company may be held responsible for injuries caused
by its products. For example, product liability is an issue in the following situation:

> Toy manufacturers have been successfully sued when children swallowed
> small parts. Plaintiffs charged that labeling should have been clearer when toys
> were designed for older children. (Whenever McDonald's offers toys as pro-
> motions, it now substitutes toys with fewer small parts for younger children.)

115 According to a special government panel on product liability, about 33 million people are injured and 28,000 killed by consumer products each year.
Moreover, the effects of liability cases can be far-reaching and expensive.

Strict Product Liability.   Since the early 1960s, businesses have faced a
number of legal actions based on the relatively new principle of **strict product**
120 **liability:** the principle that liability can result not from a producer's negligence
but from a *defect in the product itself.* An injured party need show only that

1. The product was defective,
2. The defect was the cause of injury, and
3. The defect caused the product to be unreasonably dangerous.

Many recent cases in strict product liability have focused on injuries or ill-
nesses attributable to toxic wastes or other hazardous substances that were
legally disposed of. Because plaintiffs need not demonstrate negligence or
125 fault, these suits frequently succeed. Not surprisingly, the number of such
suits promises to increase.

STAGE 3: RECALL

Stop to self-test, relate, and react.

Your instructor may choose to give you a true-false comprehension review.

Thinking About ── UNDERSTANDING THE LEGAL CONCEPT OF BUSINESS

Describe and give examples of the advantages and disadvantages of tort laws from the consumer's perspective.

Contemporary Link

What would William Stavropoulos, the president and CEO of Dow Chemical, think of the "Contract with America"?

SKILL DEVELOPMENT: POINT OF VIEW

Explain how and why the point of view of each of the following differs on the negligence and liability laws:

Business _____

Consumers _____

Association of Trial Lawyers _____

Congress _____

COMPREHENSION QUESTIONS

After reading the selection, answer the following questions with *a, b, c,* or *d.*

Main Idea _____ 1. The best statement of the main idea of this selection is
   a. McDonald's was punished by the courts for negligence.
   b. tort and liability laws create a system of compensation for injury.
   c. businesses are constrained by laws and financial penalties that protect the consumers.
   d. the temperature of the coffee served at McDonald's was dangerous to consumers.

Inference   _____ 2. The author suggests all of the following except
                             a. the Liebeck case could have been settled quickly for only
                                $800.
                             b. Liebeck was not seriously hurt and the case was frivolous.
                             c. McDonald's had been sued several times before for coffee
                                burns.
                             d. Liebeck's attorney had experience in conducting a suc-
                                cessful suit against McDonald's.

Detail   _____ 3. The final amount of money that Stella Liebeck received
                                from McDonald's was
                             a. $2.9 million.
                             b. $2,860,000.
                             c. $640,000.
                             d. not mentioned in the selection because it was settled out
                                of court.

Inference   _____ 4. In describing the Liebeck trial, the author italicized the
                                word "defense" because
                             a. the witnesses ironically did not support the side of the
                                case for which they were called.
                             b. the witnesses were called to testify by the plaintiff.
                             c. one of the witnesses was a quality-assurance manager.
                             d. the defense was able to benefit from the plaintiff's wit-
                                ness by using sarcasm.

Inference   _____ 5. The purpose of the Congressional efforts to change personal-
                                injury litigation is
                             a. to encourage the settlement of cases without going to
                                trial.
                             b. to increase the compensatory damages.
                             c. to limit punitive damages.
                             d. to increase the power of judging in determining punitive
                                damages.

Inference   _____ 6. In Liebeck's case against McDonald's, the author suggests that
                             a. the punitive damages should not have been reduced by
                                the state court judge.
                             b. the initial damage award was in line with the new for-
                                mula proposed by Congress.
                             c. the jury adhered to the "common sense" suggestion in the
                                "Contract with America."
                             d. at the beginning of the trial, the jury seemed to favor Mc-
                                Donald's rather than Liebeck.

Detail   _____ 7. In the case of Knapp against Kmart, the author suggests that
                                the winning legal issue was
                             a. the severity of Kitchen's injuries.
                             b. the intoxication of Knapp.

c. the lack of employee training by Kmart.
d. the legibility of the form required by federal law.

Inference   _____ 8. We can conclude that a tort law would apply to all of the
following except
a. the loss of money through the failure of an employee to
honor a signed contract.
b. the loss of a job because of slanderous written statements.
c. the loss of personal property due to the explosion of a defective gas line explosion.
d. personal injury from a traffic accident.

Inference   _____ 9. The tone of this selection is
a. subjective.
b. objective.
c. sarcastic.
d. angry.

Detail   _____ 10. The difference between *product liability* and *strict product liability* is that the company is not only responsible for injury
from the product but also for injury from
a. negligence in the use of the product.
b. the improper use of the product.
c. danger and damages from the correct use of the product.
d. product defects without the proof of negligence.

Answer the following with *T* (true) or *F* (false).

Detail   _____ 11. The author suggests that the temperature was a primary factor in the popularity of McDonald's coffee.

Inference   _____ 12. The author suggests that the McDonald's defense team was
not as hot as the McDonald's coffee.

Inference   _____ 13. The reform legislation on liability laws would benefit businesses more than consumers.

Inference   _____ 14. The author's purpose in relating the McDonald's case was to
give an example of tort law before defining it.

Detail   _____ 15. The majority of liability cases are settled out of court.

VOCABULARY

According to the way the italicized word was used in the selection, select *a, b,
c,* or *d* for the word or phrase that gives the best definition.

_____ 1. "*revenue* from coffee sales" (4–5)   _____ 2. "*heeds* the recommendation" (7)
   a.   income   a.   avoids
   b.   cost to the company   b.   listens to
   c.   expenses   c.   questions
   d.   wholesale price   d.   debates

_____ 3. "*defray* the costs (13)
a. repay
b. calculate
c. manage
d. debate

_____ 4. "was *willfully* serving (23–24)
a. mistakenly
b. knowingly
c. illegally
d. recklessly

_____ 5. "jurors seemed *skeptical*" (32)
a. unconcerned
b. thoughtful
c. disbelieving
d. narrow minded

_____ 6. "*callous* disregard" (43–44)
a. accidental
b. unwholesome
c. steadfast
d. hardened in feeling

_____ 7. "Congressional *scrutiny*" (54)
a. authority
b. management
c. close examination
d. jurisdiction

_____ 8. "*pending* legislation" (62)
a. new
b. waiting
c. unpopular
d. supported

_____ 9. "did not *hinge* on" (98)
a. rely
b. open
c. close
d. finish

_____ 10. "*toxic* wastes" (123)
a. dirty
b. distasteful
c. poisonous
d. unsightly

SEARCH THE NET

You have been injured because of a defect in a new product manufactured by a major American company. You are looking for a lawyer to represent you. Conduct a search to select several attorneys located in your area that you would consider calling. Next to or beneath each lawyer's name, list at least three qualifications that led you to consider the person. Plan your search and reference your Websites.

Go Electronic!
For additional readings, exercises, and Internet activities, visit this book's Website at:
http://www.awlonline.com/smithBTG
For even more activities, visit the Longman English pages at:
http://longman.awl.com/englishpages
If you need a user name and password, please see your instructor.
Take a Road Trip to the Getty Museum! Be sure to visit the Purpose and Tone module in your Reading Road Trip CD-ROM for multimedia tutorials, exercises, and tests.

READER'S JOURNAL

Name _____ Date _____

Chapter 7

Answer the following questions to learn about your own learning and reflect on your progress. Use the perforations to tear the assignment out for your instructor.

1. How can your point of view cloud your understanding of material you read? _____

    _____

    _____

2. Select a current and controversial news issue and describe your position.

    _____

    _____

    _____

3. When you read for pleasure, what type of material do you enjoy? What tends to be the author's main purpose in that material? _____

    _____

4. Define the following tones and give an example:

    sarcastic _____

    _____

    skeptical _____

    _____

    cynical _____

    _____

5. How is multiculturalism connected to point of view? _____

    _____

    _____

6. How can education give us greater appreciation for different cultural views?

    _____

    _____

Critical Thinking

- ■ What is critical thinking?
- ■ What are the characteristics of critical thinkers?
- ■ What are the barriers to critical thinking?
- ■ Why do critical thinkers have power?
- ■ How do critical thinkers analyze an argument?
- ■ What is the difference between inductive and deductive reasoners?
- ■ What does creative thinking add to critical thinking?

René Margritte, 1898–1967. La Grande Famille, 1947. Oil on canvas. Private collection © 2000 C. Herscovici/Artists Rights Society (ARS), New York. Herscovici/Art Resource, NY.

WHAT IS CRITICAL THINKING?

Do you accept the thinking of others or do you think for yourself? Do you examine and judge? Can you identify important questions and systematically search for answers? Can you justify what you believe? If so, you are thinking critically. For example, if each of the following represented a textbook portrayal of Christopher Columbus, which would you tend to accept most readily and why?

Was he a courageous hero?

Was he a despot who enslaved the Indians?

Was he a hapless explorer who failed to find India or gold?

Rather than answer immediately, most students would say, "I need more information. I want to consider the arguments, weigh the facts, and draw my own conclusions."

Thinking critically means deliberating in a purposeful, organized manner in order to assess the value of information, both old and new. Critical thinkers search, compare, analyze, clarify, evaluate, and conclude. Critical thinkers do not start from scratch; they build on previous knowledge or schemata to forge new relationships. They recognize both sides of an issue and evaluate the reasons and evidence in support of each.

Some professors speak of critical thinking as if it were a special discipline rather than an application of many known skills. Frank Smith, an educator who has written eleven books on thinking, says that thinking critically refers simply to the manner in which thinking is done.[1] It is merely an approach to thinking, in the same sense that thinking impulsively or thinking seriously are approaches, and the approach can be practiced and learned.

APPLYING SKILLS TO MEET COLLEGE GOALS

Many colleges cite the ability to think critically as one of the essential academic outcome goals for students graduating after four years of college work. An educated person is expected to think systematically, to evaluate, and to draw conclusions based on logic. At your college, an emphasis on critical thinking probably crosses the curriculum, and thus becomes a part of every college course. When an instructor returns a paper to you and comments, "Good logic" or "Not enough support," the comments are referring to critical thinking. The same is true if you make a class presentation and are told either that your thesis is very convincing or that you are missing vital support.

[1] Frank Smith, *To Think* (New York: Teachers' College Press, 1990).

© 2000 Addison-Wesley Educational Publishers, Inc.

Critical thinking is thus not a new skill; it is the systematic application of many well-learned skills. These include identifying details, inferences, and point of view. In this chapter we will also discuss a few new techniques for evaluating the support for an argument or thesis.

Critical thinking instruction has its own specialized vocabulary, often using seemingly complex terms for simple ideas. As you work through this chapter, you will become familiar with the critical thinking application of the following terminology:

analogy	argument	assertion	believability	conclusion	consistency
deduction	fallacy	induction	premise	relevance	reliability

▶ **READER'S TIP**   **How to Think Critically**

- ▶ **Be willing to plan.** Think first and write later. Don't be impulsive. Develop a habit of planning.
- ▶ **Be flexible.** Be open to new ideas. Consider new solutions for old problems.
- ▶ **Be persistent.** Continue to work even when you are tired and discouraged. Good thinking is hard work.
- ▶ **Be willing to self-correct.** Don't be defensive about errors. Figure out what went wrong and learn from your mistakes.

Barriers to Critical Thinking

Some people will not allow themselves to think critically. They are mired in their own belief system and do not want to change or be challenged. They are gullible and thus easily persuaded by a slick presentation or an illogical argument. In their book *Invitation to Critical Thinking*.[2] Joel Rudinow and Vincent E. Barry identified the following barriers to critical thinking:

1. *Frame of reference:* Each of us has an existing belief system that influences the way we deal with incoming information. We interpret new experiences according to what we already believe. We are culturally conditioned to resist change and feel that our own way is best. We refuse to look at the merits of something our belief system rejects, such as the advantages of legalizing drugs, for example.
2. *Wishful thinking:* We talk ourselves into believing things that we know are not true because we want them to be true. We irrationally deceive ourselves and engage in self-denial. For example, we might refuse to believe well-founded claims of moral corruption leveled at our favored politician or relative.

---

[2]J. Rudinow and V. E. Barry, *Invitation to Critical Thinking*, New York: Harcourt Brace College Publishers, 1994, pp. 11–19.

3. *Hasty moral judgments:* We tend to evaluate someone or something as good or bad, right or wrong, and remain fixed in this thinking. Such judgments are often prejudiced, intolerant, emotional, and self-righteous. An example of such a barrier to thinking critically would be the statement, "Abortion should never be legal."

4. *Reliance on authority:* An authority such as a clergy member, a doctor, or a teacher is an expert source of information. We give authorities and institutions such as church or government the power to think for us and thus block our own ability to question and reason.

5. *Labels:* Labels ignore individual differences and lump people and things into categories. Labels oversimplify, distort the truth, and usually incite anger and rejection. To say, "People who love America and people who do not," forces others to take sides as a knee-jerk reaction.

EXERCISE 8.1   *Identify Types of Barriers*

Read the numbered statements below and identify with *a, b, c,* or *d* the type of barrier the statement best represents:

    a. Wishful thinking
    b. Frame of reference or hasty moral judgments
    c. Reliance on authority
    d. Labels

EXAMPLE   The new drug will not be helpful because the FDA has not yet approved it.

EXPLANATION   The answer is *c*, reliance on authority, which in this case is a government agency. A critical thinker might argue that the FDA is slow to test and respond to new drugs, and that many drugs are used safely and successfully in other countries before the FDA grants approval for Americans.

_____ 1. My son was not involved in the robbery because he could not do such a horrible thing.

_____ 2. In some countries people eat horse meat and dog meat, but it is wrong to do so because these animals are friends of humans.

_____ 3. Our country is divided into two groups of people: those who work and those who don't work.

_____ 4. Polygamy and polyandry should be legalized.

POWER OF CRITICAL THINKING

Critical thinkers are willing to hold their own opinions up to scrutiny and to consider over and over again, "Is this position worth holding?" They drive to the heart of issues and assess reasons for opposing views. They solve problems and gain knowledge. They do not feel the need to persuade or to argue for right or wrong, but they are not afraid of questions. As a result of logical thinking and the ability to justify their own positions, critical thinkers gain confidence.

Courtroom Analogy

Jurors use critical thinking in deciding court cases. The judge defines the issue and clever lawyers argue "conflicting versions of the truth" before the jury. Each presents reasons and selected evidence to support the case of the client. Needless to say, in the summation to the jury, each attorney interprets the truth in the client's best interest. The jury is left to weigh the validity of the evidence, to reflect on what might be missing, and to decide between two logical arguments. Through the critical thinking process, the jurors systematically answer the following questions:

1. What is the issue?
2. What are the arguments?
3. What is the evidence?
4. What is the verdict?

College students can adapt the jury's critical thinking approach to textbook reading. The same four questions are as relevant in weighing information about Christopher Columbus, genetic engineering, or manic depression as they are to making life-or-death courtroom decisions.

RECOGNIZING AN ARGUMENT

We often make statements that are not arguments. Assertions such as "I like milk" or "We had a huge overnight snowfall, and my car is covered" are not meant to trigger extensive thought, provoke questions, and lead to analysis. These are nonargumentative statements that are intended to inform or explain. An argument, on the other hand, is an assertion or set of assertions that supports a conclusion and is intended to persuade.

The basic difference between an argument and a nonargumentative statement is the intent or purpose. Nonargumentative statements do not question truth but simply offer information to explain and thereby help us understand. For example, the statement, "The grass is wet because it rained last night" is an explanation, not an argument. To say, however, "You should water the grass tonight because rain is not predicted for several days" constitutes an argument. In the latter case, the conclusion of watering the grass is based on a "fact," the forecast, and the intent is to persuade by appealing to reason. To identify arguments we must use inferential skills and recognize the underlying purpose or intent of the author.

EXERCISE 8.2   *Identify the Argument*

Practice recognizing arguments by identifying each of the following statements with *A* for argument or *N* for a nonargumentative statement of information.

EXAMPLE   The foods in salad bars sometimes contain preservatives to keep them looking fresh and appealing.

> **EXPLANATION**   This is not an argument. It is not intended to move you to action. It is a statement of fact similar to "It sometimes snows at night."

_____ 1. Food preservatives can cause cancer and thus you should avoid eating food that contains them.

_____ 2. According to the verification of a famed Nobel laureate, take Vitamin C regularly in order to prevent colds.

_____ 3. Contaminated water can cause many serious, life-threatening diseases.

_____ 4. Parrots talk because people have taught them how to speak and to understand.

STEPS IN CRITICAL THINKING

Analyzing an argument through critical thinking and evaluation combines the use of most of the skills that have been taught in this text. The amount of analysis depends on the complexity of the argument. Some arguments are simple, while others are lengthy and complicated. The following is a four-step procedure that can be used as a format to guide your critical thinking:

1. Identify the issue.
2. Identify the support for the argument.
3. Evaluate the support.
4. Evaluate the argument.

Step 1: Identify the Issue

In the courtroom, the judge instructs the jury on the issue and the lawyers provide the arguments. In reading, however, the issues may not be as obvious or clearly defined. The reader must cut through the verbiage to recognize underlying issues as well as to identify support.

Good readers are "tuned in" to look for issues that have opposing points of view. Writers strive to convince readers but are under no obligation to explain, or even to admit persuasion. Knowledgeable readers, however, sense possible biases; they look for the hidden agendas. Good readers constantly ask, "How am I being manipulated or persuaded?" to detect an argument and then ask, "What is the debatable question or central issue in this argument?"

In a college course on critical thinking or logic, the parts of an argument that you would be asked to identify would probably be called the *conclusion* and the *premises*. The conclusion is an assertion or position statement. It is what the author is trying to convince you to believe or to do. For example, in the statement "You should water the grass because rain is not in the forecast," the conclusion is "You should water the grass." The premise, or support, is "because rain is not in the forecast." In the terminology of this textbook, the conclusion also could be viewed as a statement of the main point.

To identify the issue or conclusion in persuasive writing, use your main-idea reading skills. First ask yourself, "What is the passage primarily about?" to determine the topic. Then ask, "What is the main point the author is trying to convey about the topic?" Your answer will be a statement of the issue that is being argued, which could also be called the main point, the thesis, or the conclusion.

Begin by reading the material all the way through. Do not allow your own beliefs to cloud your thinking. Set aside your own urge to agree or disagree, but be alert to the bias of the author. Be aware of the barriers to critical thinking that include limited frame of reference, wishful thinking, hasty moral judgments, reliance on authority, and labeling. Be sensitive to emotional language and the connotation of words. Cut through the rhetoric and get to the heart of the matter.

EXAMPLE   Read the following passage and identify the issue that is being argued.

> The technology for television has far exceeded the programming. Viewers are recipients of crystal clear junk. Network programming appeals to the masses for ratings and advertising money and offers little creative or stimulating entertainment.

EXPLANATION   Several debatable issues about television are suggested by this passage. They include the abundance of technological advancement, the power of ratings, and the importance of advertising money. The central issue, however, concerns the quality of network programming. Although it is not directly stated, the argument or central issue is "Network television programming is not any good."

Recognizing Analogies as a Familiar Pattern in Issues. George Polya, a pioneer in mathematical problem solving, said we cannot imagine or solve a problem that is totally new and absolutely unlike any problem we have ever known.[3] We seek connections and look for similarities to previous experiences. Such comparisons are called **analogies.**

Analogies are most easily made on a personal level. We think about how the issue has affected or could affect us or someone we know. For example, if high school principals were seeking your input on the issue of declining mathematics scores, you would first relate the problem to your own experience. How did you score in math? Why do you think you did or did not do well? What about your friends? From your memory of high school, what would you identify as the key reasons for the declining scores? The problem now has a personal meaning and is linked to prior knowledge.

Linking new knowledge with personal and expanded comparisons applies past experience to new situations. Two researchers tested the importance of analogies by asking students to read technical passages with and without

---

[3]G. Polya, *How to Solve It*, 2nd ed. (Princeton, N.J.: Princeton University Press, 1957).

analogies to familiar topics.[4] The students who read the material containing the analogies scored higher on tests of comprehension and recall than students who did not have the benefit of the familiar comparisons.

Referring back to the previous example on television programming, what analogies could you draw from your own personal experience? What television programs do you consider junk? Are they all junk? What network programs do you feel are high-quality entertainment?

Identifying the Issue Through Signal Words. The central issue may be stated as the thesis or main point at the beginning of an argument, it may be embedded within the passage, or it may be stated at the end as a conclusion. The following key words are sometimes used to signal the central issue being argued:

as a result	finally	in summary	therefore
consequently	for these reasons	it follows that	thus

EXAMPLE   What is the central issue that is being argued in the following passage?

> A year in a United States prison costs more than a year at Harvard; however, almost no one is rehabilitated. Prisoners meet and share information with other hardened criminals to refine their skills. It seems reasonable, therefore, to conclude that prisons in the U.S. are societal failures.

EXPLANATION   The central issue in this argument is directly stated in the last sentence. Note the inclusion of the signal word *therefore*.

EXERCISE 8.3   *Identify the Issue*

Read the following sentence groups and underline or state in a sentence the central issue that is being argued in each.

1. Weekly television comedies frequently show parents in an unflattering light. The parents are usually bettered by the kids, who are portrayed as smarter. The kids win laughs with rude and sarcastic comments directed at the parents.
2. The price of oil, gas, and electricity continues to rise for heating and cooling homes. This rise could lead to renewed interest in solar heating. If the price of installing solar heating panels declined, the result could be that more people would use solar energy as a source for home heating and cooling.

---

[4]C. C. Hansen and D. F. Halpern *Using Analogies to Improve Comprehension and Recall of Scientific Passages."* Paper presented at the annual meeting of Psychonomic Society, Seattle, WA. 1987.

3. Shoplifting raises the price of what we purchase by more than 2 percent. Medicare fraud costs the average taxpayer several hundred dollars each year. The costs of exaggerated insurance claims is passed along to all policy holders in increased premiums. For these reasons it follows that when we cheat corporations, we cheat ourselves and our friends.

4. Censorship is difficult to enforce. A major problem concerns who will do the enforcing. A second issue involves what works will be censored. As a result of these complexities, censorship is unacceptable.

5. Multiple-choice questions measure recognition rather than recall. They do not encourage students to study "the big picture," and thus they should not be used in college classes.

Step 2: Identify Support for the Argument

In a college logic course, after identifying the central issue of an argument, you would be asked to identify and number the premises. In the example presented earlier about watering the grass, only one premise, "because rain is not in the forecast," was offered. Other premises such as "the grass will die without water" and "water is plentiful right now" would have added further evidence in support of the conclusion. In reality, the identification of premises is simply the identification of significant supporting details for the main point.

Identifying Supporting Reasons through Signal Words. Supporting reasons may be directly stated or may be signaled. The key words that signal support for an argument are in some cases the same as those that signal significant supporting details. They include the following:

> because
>
> since
>
> if
>
> first . . . second . . . finally
>
> assuming that
>
> given that

EXAMPLE   In the previous passage about U.S. prisons, signal words can be used to introduce supporting details:

> One can conclude that prisons in the United States are failures. First, almost no one is rehabilitated. Second, prisoners meet and share information with other hardened criminals to refine their skills. Taxpayers should also consider that a year in prison costs more than a year at Harvard.

EXPLANATION The argument is the same with or without the signal words. In a longer passage the signal words usually make it easier to identify the significant supporting details or reasons.

EXERCISE 8.4   *Identify the Parts of an Argument*

Read the following sentence groups and identify the central issue that is being argued and the supporting reasons. Place the letter *I* before sentences containing the central issue and the letter *S* before those containing supporting reasons.

1. The shad or any fish that runs upstream is an excellent choice for sea ranching. Such fish use their own energies to swim and grow in open waters and then swim back to be harvested.

2. Major game reserves in Africa such as the Ngorongoro Crater are in protected areas, but many lie adjacent to large tracts of land with no conservation status. Animals who migrate off the reserves compete with humans for food and are endangered. Thus, clear boundaries between areas for animals and people would minimize friction.

3. Advertisements can be misleading. Their major purpose is to sell something. They use suggestion rather than logic to be convincing.

4. A visit to a doctor's office is a lesson in humility for the patient. First, you see the receptionist who tells you to fill out forms and wait your turn. Next, the nurse takes your blood pressure and extracts blood while you look at the diplomas on the wall. Finally, you are led into a bare room to strip down and wait still longer for the doctor to appear for a few expensive minutes of consultation.

5. In most companies, college graduates get higher-paying jobs than those who do not attend college. As the years go by in a company, promotions and their accompanying raises tend to go primarily to the college graduates. Thus, it can be concluded that a college degree is worth money.

Identifying Types of Supporting Reasons. As support for arguments, readers would probably prefer the simplicity of a smoking gun with fingerprints on it, but such conclusive evidence is usually hard to find. Evidence comes in many different forms, and may be tainted with opinion. The box below contains some categories of "evidence" typically used as supporting reasons in an argument. Each type, however, has its pitfalls and should be immediately tested with an evaluative question.

> **READER'S TIP** **Categories of Support for Arguments**
>
> ▶ **Facts:** objective truths
> Ask: How were the facts gathered? Are they true?
>
> ▶ **Examples:** anecdotes to demonstrate the truth
> Ask: Are the examples true and relevant?
>
> ▶ **Analogies:** comparisons to similar cases
> Ask: Are the analogies accurate and relevant?
>
> ▶ **Authority:** words from a recognized expert
> Ask: What are the credentials and biases of the expert?
>
> ▶ **Causal relationship:** saying one thing caused another
> Ask: Is it an actual cause or merely an association?
>
> ▶ **Common knowledge claim:** assertion of wide acceptance
> Ask: Is it relevant? Does everyone really believe it?
>
> ▶ **Statistics:** numerical data
> Ask: Do the numbers accurately describe the population?
>
> ▶ **Personal experiences:** personal anecdotes
> Ask: Is the experience applicable to other situations?

Step 3: Evaluate the Support

As a reader, you will decide to accept or reject the author's conclusion based on the strength and acceptability of the reasons and evidence. Strong arguments are logically supported by well-crafted reasons and evidence, but clever arguments can be supported by the crafty use of reason and evidence.

In evaluating the support for an argument, teachers of logic warn students to beware of fallacies. A **fallacy** is an inference that appears to be reasonable at first glance, but closer inspection proves it to be unrelated, unreliable, or illogical. For example, to say that something is right because everybody is doing it is not a convincing reason for accepting an idea. Such "reasoning," however, can be compelling and is so frequently used that it is labeled a *bandwagon fallacy.*

Logicians have categorized, labeled, and defined over 200 types of fallacies or tricks of persuasion. The emphasis for the critical thinker should not be on memorizing a long list of fallacy types but rather on understanding how such irrelevant reasoning techniques can manipulate logical thinking. Fallacies are tools employed in constructing a weak argument that critical thinkers should spot. In a court of law, the opposing attorney would shout "Irrelevant, Your Honor!" to alert the jury to the introduction of fallacious evidence.

Evaluate the support for an argument according to three areas of reasoning: (1) relevance, (2) believability, and (3) consistency. The following list of fallacies common to each area can sensitize you to the "tools" of constructing a weak argument.

1. Relevance Fallacies: Is the support related to the conclusion?

Ad hominem: an attack on the person rather than the issue in hopes that if the person is opposed, the idea will be opposed
Example: Do not listen to Mr. Hite's views on education because he is a banker.

Bandwagon: the idea that everybody is doing it and you will be left out if you do not quickly join the crowd
Example: Everybody around the world is drinking Coke® so you should too.

Misleading analogy: a comparison of two things suggesting that they are similar when they are in fact distinctly different
Example: College students are just like elementary school students; they need to be taught self-discipline.

Straw person: a setup in which a distorted or exaggerated form of the opponent's argument is introduced and knocked down as if to represent a totally weak opposition
Example: When a teen-aged daughter is told she cannot go out on the weeknight before a test, she replies with "That's unreasonable to say that I can never go out on a weeknight."

Testimonials: opinions of agreement from respected celebrities who are not actually experts
Example: A famous actor endorses a headache pill.

Transfer: an association with a positively or negatively regarded person or thing in order to lend the same association to the argument (also guilt or virtue by association)
Example: A local politician quotes President Lincoln in a speech as if Lincoln would have agreed with and voted for the candidate.

2. Believability Fallacies: Is the support believable or highly suspicious?

Incomplete facts *or* **card stacking:** omission of factual details in order to misrepresent reality

Example: Buy stock in this particular restaurant chain because it is under new management and people eat out a lot.

Misinterpreted statistics: numerical data misapplied to unrelated populations which they were never intended to represent
Example: Over 20 percent of people exercise daily and thus do not need fitness training.

Overgeneralizations: examples and anecdotes asserted to apply to all cases rather than a select few
Example: High school students do little work during their senior year and thus are overwhelmed at college.

Questionable authority: testimonial suggesting authority from people who are not experts
Example: Dr. Lee, a university sociology professor, testified that the DNA reports were 100 percent accurate.

3. Consistency Fallacies: Does the support hold together or does it fall apart and contradict itself?

Appeals to emotions: highly charged language used for emotional manipulation
Example: Give money to our organization to help the children who are starving orphans in desperate need of medical attention.

Appeals to pity: pleas to support the underdog, the person or issue that needs your help
Example: Please give me an A for the course because I need it to get into law school.

Signe Wilkerson/Cartoonists and Writers Syndicate

Begging the question *or* **circular reasoning:** support for the conclusion which is merely a restatement of it
Example: Drugs should not be legalized because it should be against the law to take illegal drugs.

Oversimplification: reduction of an issue to two simple choices, without consideration of other alternatives or "gray areas" in between
Example: The choices are very simple in supporting our foreign-policy decision to send troops. You are either for America or against it.

Slippery slope: Objecting to something because it will lead to greater evil and disastrous consequences
Example: Support for assisting the suicide of a terminally ill patient will lead to the ultimate disposal of the marginally sick and elderly.

EXERCISE 8.5   *Identify the Fallacy*

Identify the type of fallacy in each of the following statements by indicating *a*, *b*, or *c*.

_____ 1. Hollywood movie stars and rock musicians are not experts on the environment and should not be dictating our environmental policy.
   a. testimonial
   b. *ad hominem*
   c. bandwagon

_____ 2. Michael Jordan says, "I always wear this brand of athletic shoes. They are the best."
   a. *ad hominem*
   b. misleading analogy
   c. testimonial

_____ 3. The fight for equal rights is designed to force men out of jobs and encourage women to leave their young children alone at home.
   a. bandwagon
   b. questionable authority
   c. straw person

_____ 4. People should give blood because it is important to give blood.
   a. begging the question
   b. appeal to pity
   c. appeal to emotion

_____ 5. Prayer in the schools is like cereal for breakfast. They both get the morning off to a good start.

a. circular reasoning
b. appeal to emotions
c. misleading analogy

_____ 6. The advocate for rezoning of the property concluded by saying, "George Washington was also concerned about land and
freedom."
a. transfer
b. *ad hominem*
c. straw person

_____ 7. The explanation for the distribution of grades is simple. College students either study or they do not study.
a. misinterpreted statistics
b. oversimplification
c. appeal to pity

_____ 8. Your written agreement with my position will enable me to
keep my job.
a. misinterpreted statistics
b. appeal to pity
c. card stacking

_____ 9. Everyone in the neighborhood has worked on the new park
design and agreed to it. Now we need your signature of
support.
a. bandwagon
b. appeal to emotion
c. begging the question

_____ 10. Democrats go to Washington to spend money with no regard for the hard-working taxpayer.
a. circular reasoning
b. bandwagon
c. overgeneralization

_____ 11. The suicide rate is highest over the Christmas holidays,
which means that Thanksgiving is a safe and happy holiday.
a. misinterpreted statistics
b. card stacking
c. questionable authority

_____ 12. The workers' fingers were swollen and infected, insects
walked on their exposed skin, and their red eyes begged for
mercy and relief. We all must join their effort.
a. oversimplification
b. appeal to emotions
c. overgeneralization

_____13. Our minister, Dr. Johnson, assured the family that our cousin's cancer was a slow-growing one so that a brief delay in treatment would not be detrimental.
   a. transfer
   b. straw person
   c. questionable authority

_____14. Crime in this city has been successfully addressed by increasing the number of police officers, seeking neighborhood support against drug dealers, and keeping teenagers off the streets at night. The city is to be commended.
   a. misleading analogy
   b. incomplete facts
   c. misinterpreted statistics

_____15. A biology professor cannot possibly advise the swim coach on the placement of swimmers in the different races.
   a. *ad hominem*
   b. testimonial
   c. transfer

Determining What Support Is Missing. Arguments are written to persuade, and thus include the proponent's version of the convincing reasons. Writers do not usually supply the reader with any more than one or two weak points that could be made by the other side. In analyzing an argument, ask yourself, "What is left out?" Be an advocate for the opposing point of view and guess at the evidence that would be presented. Decide if evidence was consciously omitted because of its adverse effect on the conclusion. For example, a businessperson arguing for an increased monthly service fee might neglect to mention how much of the cost is administrative overhead and profit.

Step 4: Evaluate the Argument

Important decisions are rarely quick or easy. A span of incubation time is often needed for deliberating among alternatives. Allow yourself time to go over arguments, weighing the support, and looking at the issues from different perspectives. Good critical thinkers are persistent in seeking solutions.

Diane Halpern expresses the difficulty of decision making by saying, "There is never just one war fought. Each side has its own version, and rarely do they agree."[5] The reader must consider carefully in seeking the truth. Halpern uses a picture of a table and compares the legs of the table to four different degrees of support.

1. Unrelated reasons give no support.
2. A few weak reasons do not adequately support.
3. Many weak reasons can support.
4. Strong related reasons provide support.

---

[5]Halpern, *Thought and Knowledge*, 2nd ed. (Hillsdale, N.J.: Lawrence Erlbaum, 1989), p. 191.

Remember, in critical thinking there is no "I'm right, and you are wrong." There are, however, strong and weak arguments. Strong relevant, believable, and consistent reasons build a good argument.

EXERCISE 8.6　*Evaluate Your Own Decision Making*

Now that you are familiar with the critical thinking process, analyze your own thinking in making an important recent decision of where to attend college. No college is perfect; many factors must be considered. The issue or conclusion is that you have decided to attend the college where you are now enrolled. List relevant reasons and/or evidence that supported your decision. Evaluate the strength of your reasoning. Are any of your reasons fallacies?

1. _____

2. _____

3. _____

4. _____

5. _____

How would you evaluate your own critical thinking in making a choice of colleges? Perhaps you relied heavily on information from others. Were those sources credible?

INDUCTIVE AND DEDUCTIVE REASONING

In choosing a college, did you follow an inductive or deductive reasoning process? Did you collect extensive information on several colleges and then weigh the advantages and disadvantages of each? **Inductive reasoners** start by gathering data, and then, after considering all available material, they formulate a conclusion. Textbooks written in this manner give details first and lead you into the main idea or conclusion. They strive to put the parts into a logical whole and thus reason "up" from particular details to a broad generalization.

Deductive reasoners, on the other hand, follow the opposite pattern. They start with the conclusion of a previous experience and apply it to a new situation. Perhaps your college choice is a family tradition; your parents are alumni, and you have always expected to attend. Although your thinking may have begun with this premise for your choice, you may have since discovered many reasons why the college is right for you. When writers use a deductive pattern, they first give a general statement and then enumerate the reasons.

Despite this formal distinction between inductive and deductive reasoning, in real life we switch back and forth as we think. Our everyday observations lead to conclusions that we then reuse and modify to form new conclusions.

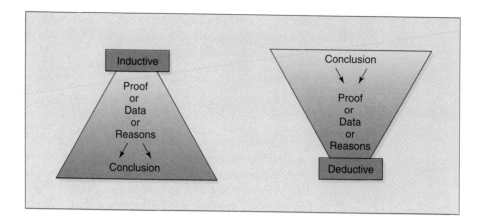

Applying the Critical Thinking Steps 1–4: An Example

The following is an example of how the four-step format can be used to evaluate an argument. Read the argument, analyze according to the directions for each step, and then read the explanation of how the critical thinking process was applied.

The Argument: Extraterrestrial Life

Surely life exists elsewhere in the universe. After all, most space scientists today admit the possibility that life has evolved on other planets. Besides, other planets in our solar system are strikingly like Earth. They revolve around the sun, they borrow light from the sun, and several are known to revolve on their axes, and to be subject to the same laws of gravitation as earth. What's more, aren't those who make light of extraterrestrial life soft-headed fundamentalists clinging to the foolish notion that life is unique to their planet?

Joel Rudinow and Vincent Barry, *Invitation to Critical Thinking*

■ Step 1: Identify the issue: What is the topic of this argument and what is the main point the writer is trying to convey? Although many ideas may be included, what is the central concern that is being discussed and supported? Underline the central issue if it is directly stated or write it above the passage if it is implied.

■ Step 2: Identify the support for the argument: What are the significant supporting details that support the central issue that is being argued? Put brackets at the beginning and end of each assertion of support and number the assertions separately and consecutively. Do not number background information or examples that merely illustrate a point.

■ Step 3: Evaluate the support: Examine each supporting assertion separately for relevance, believability, and consistency. Can you identify any as fallacies that are intended to sell a weak argument? Also list the type of supporting information that you feel is missing.

1. _____

2. _____

3. _____

What is missing? _____

■ Step 4: Evaluate the argument: What is your overall evaluation of the argument? Is the argument convincing? Does the argument provide good reasons and/or evidence for believing the thesis?

Explanation of the Steps

■ Step 1: Identify the issue: The central issue, assertion, thesis, main point, or conclusion is directly stated in the first sentence. Good critical thinkers would note, however, that "life" is not clearly defined as plant, animal, or human.

■ Step 2: Identify the support for the argument: This argument contains the three main premises or significant supporting details, which can be numbered as follows:

1. Space scientists admit the possibility that life has evolved from other planets.
2. Other planets in our solar system are strikingly like Earth.
3. Those who make light of extraterrestrial life are soft-headed fundamentalists clinging to the foolish notion that life is unique to this planet.

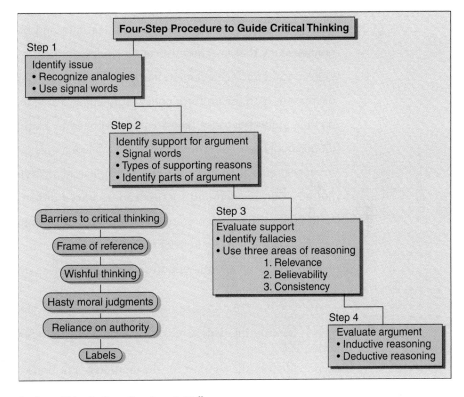

Professor Helen R. Carr, San Antonio College.

■ Step 3: Evaluate the support: The first supporting detail is a vague appeal to authority that does not reveal who "most space scientists" are. Do the scientists work for NASA? The second statement is also vague and presented as a misleading comparison. Other planets may be round, but they have different temperatures and different atmospheres. The third statement is an oversimplified, personal attack on those who may not agree with the argument. Scientific support for this argument seems to be missing.

■ Step 4: Evaluate the Argument: This is not a good argument. There may be good reasons to believe that life exists on other planets, but this argument fails to provide them. The possibility of extraterrestrial life might be argued through statistics from astronomy and a specific definition of "life."

▶ **EXERCISE 8.7**   *Apply the Steps*

Read the following three arguments and apply the four-step format for evaluation. Identify the issue and the support, then evaluate the support and the argument.

Argument 1: School Uniforms

A review of the evidence shows that a mandatory school uniform policy can be a solution to many high school learning and behavior problems. Studies show that in schools recently implementing a mandatory uniform policy, academic achievement has gone up and discipline problems have decreased. With the uniform policy, students are able to spend more time on their studies because they are not distracted by clothing choices. In addition, students who learn to respect and follow a dress code will also learn to respect other institutional rules. The principal of Taylor High School reported, "Our newly found success can be traced directly back to our uniform policy. The students enjoy and appreciate the opportunity to wear our school uniform." In light of this evidence, one can only conclude that denying our students the opportunity for uniforms is denying them academic success.

Joel Rudinow and Vincent E. Barry, *Invitation to Critical Thinking*

■ Step 1: Identify the issue: State or underline the main point or issue the author is arguing.

■ Step 2: Identify the support for the argument: Put brackets at the beginning and end of each major assertion of support and letter the assertions.

■ Step 3: Evaluate the support: Examine each supporting assertion for relevance, believability, and consistency. Identify and label any fallacies. List missing support.

_____

_____

_____

_____

_____

_____

■ Step 4: Evaluate the argument: What is your overall evaluation and why?

_____

_____

_____

Argument 2: Invasion of Privacy

When you call 911 in an emergency, some police departments have a way of telling your telephone number and address without your saying a word. The chief value of this, say the police, is that if the caller is unable to communicate for any reason, the dispatcher knows where to send help. But don't be duped by such paternalistic explanations. This technology is a despicable invasion of privacy, for callers may be unaware of the insidious device. Even if they are, some persons who wish anonymity may be reluctant to call for emergency help. Remember that the names of complainants and witnesses are recorded in many communities' criminal justice systems. A fairer and more effective system seemingly would include an auxiliary number for callers who wish anonymity.

Joel Rudinow and Vincent E. Barry, _Invitation to Critical Thinking_

■ Step 1: Identify the issue: State or underline the main point or issue the author is arguing.
■ Step 2: Identify the support for the argument: Put brackets at the beginning and end of each major assertion of support and letter the assertions.

■ Step 3: Evaluate the support: Examine each supporting assertion for relevance, believability, and consistency. Identify and label any fallacies. List missing support.

■ Step 4: Evaluate the argument: What is your overall evaluation and why?

Argument 3: Against Legalizing Euthanasia

The Karen Ann Quinlan case once again has raised the issue of euthanasia. A number of voices have been heard advocating the legalization of voluntary euthanasia. While the agonizing plight of many of our terminally ill makes this proposal understandable, there are good reasons to resist liberalizing our euthanasia laws.

First of all, no matter how you look at it, euthanasia is killing and thus is wrong. The Bible is clear on that point, and our society has always forbidden it.

Second, it is questionable whether a terminally ill patient can make a voluntary decision to begin with. Those who advocate voluntary euthanasia believe that patients should be allowed to die on request when they've developed a tolerance to narcotics. But exactly when are those patients to decide? When they're drugged? If so, then surely their choices can't be considered voluntary. And if they're to decide after the drugs have been withdrawn, this decision can't be voluntary either. Anyone who's had a simple toothache knows how much pain can distort judgment and leave us almost crazy. Imagine how much more irrational we'd likely be if we were suffering from some dreadful terminal disease and suddenly had our ration of morphine discontinued.

But even if such a decision could be completely voluntary, isn't it really unwise to offer such a choice to the gravely ill? I remember how, before she died of stomach cancer, my mother became obsessed with the idea that she was an emotional and financial burden on her family. She actually kept apologizing to us that she went on living! Had she had the option of euthanasia, she might have taken it—not because she was tired of living but because she felt guilty about living!

I shudder to think of the stress that such a choice would have put on us, her family. Surely we would have been divided. Some of us would have said, "Yes, let mother die," while others would have resisted out of a sense of love or devotion or gratitude, or even guilt.

Then there's the whole question of mistaken diagnoses. Doctors aren't infallible. Even the best of them errs. The story is told of the brilliant diagnostician Richard Cabot who, when he was retiring, was given the complete medical histories and results of careful examinations of two patients. The patients had died and only the pathologist who'd seen the descriptions of their postmortems knew their exact diagnoses. The pathologist asked Cabot for his diagnoses. The eminent Dr. Cabot muffed both of them! If a brilliant diagnostician can make a mistake, what about a less accomplished doctor? Let's face it: There's always the possibility of a wrong diagnosis.

But suppose we could be sure of diagnoses. Even so, there's always the chance that some new pain-relieving drug, or even a cure, is just around the corner. Many years ago, the President of the American Public Health Association made this point forcefully when he said, "No one can say today what will be incurable tomorrow. No one can predict what disease will be fatal or permanently incurable until medicine becomes stationary and sterile."

But what frightens me the most about legalizing voluntary euthanasia is that it will open the door for the legalization of *involuntary* euthanasia. If we allow people to play God and decide when and how they'll die, then it won't be long before society will be deciding when and how defective infants, the old and senile, and the hopelessly insane will die as well.

Joel Rudinow and Vincent E. Barry, *Invitation to Critical Thinking*

■ Step 1: Identify the issue: State or underline the main point or issue the author is arguing.

_____

■ Step 2: Identify the support for the argument: Put brackets at the beginning and end of each major assertion of support and letter the assertions.

■ Step 3: Evaluate the support: Examine each supporting assertion for relevance, believability, and consistency. Identify and label any fallacies. List missing support.

_____

_____

_____

_____

_____

■ Step 4: Evaluate the argument: What is your overall evaluation and why?

_____

_____

_____

CREATIVE AND CRITICAL THINKING

A chapter on critical thinking would not be complete without an appeal for creative thinking. You may ask, "Are critical thinking and creative thinking different?" Creative thinking refers to the ability to generate many possible solutions to a problem, whereas critical thinking refers to the examination of those solutions for the selection of the best of all possibilities. Both ways of thinking are essential for good problem solving.

Diane Halpern uses the following story to illustrate creative thinking:[6]

> Many years ago when a person who owed money could be thrown into jail, a merchant in London had the misfortune to owe a huge sum to a money-lender. The money-lender, who was old and ugly, fancied the merchant's beautiful teenage daughter. He proposed a bargain. He said he would cancel the merchant's debt if he could have the girl instead.

_____

[6]Halpern, *Thought and Knowledge*, p. 408.

Both the merchant and his daughter were horrified at the proposal. So the cunning money-lender proposed that they let Providence decide the matter. He told them that he would put a black pebble and a white pebble into an empty money-bag and then the girl would have to pick out one of the pebbles. If she chose the black pebble she would become his wife and her father's debt would be cancelled. If she chose the white pebble she would stay with her father and the debt would still be cancelled. But if she refused to pick out a pebble her father would be thrown into jail and she would starve.

Reluctantly the merchant agreed. They were standing on a pebble-strewn path in the merchant's garden as they talked and the money-lender stooped down to pick up two pebbles. As he picked up the pebbles the girl, sharp-eyed with fright, noticed that he picked up two black pebbles and put them into the money-bag. He then asked the girl to pick out the pebble that was to decide her fate and that of her father.

If you were the girl, what would you do? Think creatively, and, without evaluating your thoughts, list at least five possible solutions. Next think critically to evaluate and then circle your final choice.

1. _____
2. _____
3. _____
4. _____
5. _____

In discussing the possible solutions to the problem, Halpern talks about two kinds of creative thinking, vertical thinking and lateral thinking. **Vertical thinking** is a straightforward and logical way of thinking that would typically result in a solution like, "Call his hand and expose the money-lender as a crook." The disadvantage of this solution is that the merchant is still in debt so the original problem has still not been solved. **Lateral thinking,** on the other hand, is a way of thinking *around* a problem or even redefining the problem. DeBono[7] suggests that a lateral thinker might redefine the problem from "What happens when I get the black pebble?" to "How can I avoid the black pebble?" Using this new definition of the problem and other seemingly irrelevant information, DeBono's lateral thinker came up with a winning solution. When the girl reaches into the bag, she should fumble and drop one of the stones on the "pebble-strewn path." The color of the pebble she dropped could then be determined by looking at the one left in the bag. Since the remaining pebble is black, the dropped one that is now mingled in the path must have been white. Any other admission would expose the money-lender as a crook. Probably the heroine thought of many alternatives, but thanks to her ability ultimately to generate a novel solution and evaluate its effectiveness, the daughter and the merchant lived happily free of debt.

---

[7]E. DeBono. *New Think: The Use of Lateral Thinking in the Generation of New Ideas* (New York: Basic Books, 1968), p. 195.

DeBono defines vertical thinking as "digging the same hole deeper" and lateral thinking as "digging the hole somewhere else."[8] For example, after many years of researching a cure for smallpox, Dr. Edward Jenner stopped focusing on patients who were sick with the disease and instead began studying groups of people who never seemed to get the smallpox. Shortly thereafter, using this different perspective, Dr. Jenner discovered the clues that led him to the smallpox vaccine.

Creative and critical thinking enable us to see new relationships. We blend knowledge and see new similarities and differences, a new sequence of events, or a new solution for an old problem. We create new knowledge by using old learning differently.

Summary Points

■ **What is critical thinking?**

Thinking critically means deliberating in a purposeful, organized manner in order to assess the value of information, both old and new.

■ **What are the characteristics of critical thinkers?**

Critical thinkers are flexible, persistent, and willing to plan and self-correct.

■ **What are the barriers to critical thinking?**

Some people do not allow themselves to think critically because of their frame of reference or because of wishful thinking, hasty moral judgments, reliance on authority, and labeling.

■ **Why do critical thinkers have power?**

Critical thinkers have power because they accept scrutiny and are willing to question and reconsider their opinions.

■ **How do critical thinkers analyze an argument?**

Critical thinkers can use a four-step plan for analyzing an argument: (1) identify the issue; (2) identify the support for the argument; (3) evaluate the support; and (4) evaluate the argument.

■ **What is the difference between inductive and deductive reasoners?**

Inductive reasoners start by gathering data; deductive reasoners start with the conclusion and apply it to a new situation.

■ **What does creative thinking add to critical thinking?**

Creative thinking involves both vertical and lateral thinking.

[8]E. DeBono, "Information Processing and New Ideas—Lateral and Vertical Thinking," in S. J. Parnes, R. B. Noller, and A. M. Biondi, eds., *Guide to Creative Action: Revised Edition of Creative Behavior Guidebook* (New York: Scribner's, 1977).

CONTEMPORARY FOCUS

Watching film, either television or movies, can be a waste of time, or it can be enriching. What makes the difference? Under what circumstances can film add educational value, and when does it become mindless?

SCREEN: END OF THE WORD?

Colin MacCabe

The Guardian (London), 10 July 1998, p. 14.

At the level of higher education, it is impossible to study twentieth-century literature without studying film. The decision in the seventies to set up separate departments of film in universities makes no sense in cultural or educational terms. The situation in schools is even more disastrous. Media studies without literature is a contradiction.

My joint concern for traditional literacy and the study of the new media led me to formulate two years ago the hypothesis that audio-visual media could be used to improve print literacy. The School of Education at King's College, London, was interested enough to join forces with the British Film Institute to test the hypothesis, which was tested in different ways at the primary and secondary level.

The primary project concentrated on integrating the making of an animated cartoon with the reading of Roald Dahl's *Fantastic Mr Fox*. A control class simply read the book. The emphasis in the experimental class was the necessity of using reading and writing in the making of the cartoon. One part of the class would produce a summary treatment which would then be used by another part of the class to storyboard. This, in turn, would lead to further writing exercises until the final images were decided on. At the secondary level, our pilot put the emphasis on adaptation. The pilot class was taught *Oliver Twist* with both David Lean's version and Lionel Bart's musical. The control class studied Dickens's novel on its own. I used an old-fashioned comprehension test taken from a part of the novel that was not in either film version in order to compare the two classes. The results were almost unbelievable—in seven weeks, the children in the experimental class improved their reading by almost two years against the control class.

Collaborative Activity

Collaborate on responses to the following questions:

- Explain the two different experiments in the passage.
- When have you used film to enhance text?
- Why do you think reading a book first adds to or detracts from seeing the movie based on the book?

STAGE 1: PREVIEW

The author seems to be against watching TV. Agree ☐   Disagree ☐

Activate Schema

What books would you like to read?

STAGE 2: INTEGRATE KNOWLEDGE WHILE READING

Predict   Picture   Relate   Monitor   Correct

© Malcolm Hancock

HAS TELEVISION KILLED OFF READING—AND IF SO, SO WHAT?

From Carole Wade and Carol Tavris, *Psychology*, 5th ed.

You find yourself with a free evening, and you decide to spend it at home. A novel beckons from the book-shelf. The TV listings tempt you with a new sitcom. Which do you pick—the book or the tube? A growing number of academics,
5   writers, and social commentators think you'll make the wrong choice.

Reading, the critics say, appears to be going out of fashion. More books are being published than ever before, but many are sold as gifts and are not neces-sarily read or even skimmed. More and more people are reading no books at all, and fewer and fewer people read a newspaper. Writer Katha Pollitt (1991)
10 has observed that debates on college campuses about which books students should be required to read miss the point: If students don't read *on their own*, they won't like reading and will forget the books on the required reading list the minute they finish them, no matter what the books are. "While we have been arguing so fiercely about which books make the best medicine," Pollitt
15 writes, "the patient has been slipping deeper and deeper into a coma."

One reason that people are reading less these days is that they are watching TV, typically for 20 to 30 hours a week. The problem, say critics, is not just tele-vision's content, which is often mindless, but the medium itself, which creates mindlessness. We watch TV primarily to amuse ourselves, but in fact television
20 has a negative impact on both mood and alertness. Although television relaxes people while they are watching, afterward viewers are likely to feel more tense,

bored, irritable, and lonely than they did before, as well as less able to concentrate. In contrast, reading tends to leave people more relaxed, in a better mood, and with improved ability to concentrate (Kubey and Csikszentmihalyi, 1990).

25 Because television supplies the viewer with readymade visual images, it may also discourage the development of imagination and novel ideas (Valkenburg and van der Voort, 1994). In one experiment, children *remembered* more of a story when they saw it on TV than when they heard it on radio (because visual images are memorable), but their thinking became more *imaginative* when they heard

30 the story on the radio (because they had to imagine what the characters looked like and what they were doing). The researchers concluded that children who are raised on a mental diet limited to television "may have more information but be less imaginative, less verbally precise, and less mentally active" than earlier generations who grew up listening to the radio (Greenfield and Beagles-Roos, 1988).

35 The replacement of reading by television watching may be contributing to a growing inability of young people to use dialectical reasoning and reflective judgment, and an unwillingness to spend time searching for answers to intellectual problems (Suedfeld et al., 1986). Because television lumps serious issues with silly ones, sells politicians the way it sells cereal, and relies on a for-

40 mat of quick cuts and hot music, its critics fear that it discourages sustained, serious thought (Postman, 1985). In contrast, reading requires us to sit still and follow extended arguments. It encourages us to think in terms of abstract principles and not just personal experience. It gives us the opportunity to examine connections among statements and to spot contradictions. As writer

45 Mitchell Stephens (1991) put it, "All television demands is our gaze."

STAGE 3: RECALL

Stop to self-test, relate, and react.

SKILL DEVELOPMENT: CRITICAL THINKING

Apply the four-step format for evaluating the argument. Use the perforations to tear out and hand this page to your instructor.

■ Step 1: Identify the issue: State the main point or issue the author is arguing.

■ Step 2: Identify the support for the argument: List and letter each major assertion of support.

_____

_____

_____

■ Step 3: Evaluate the support: Comment on weaknesses in relevance, believability, and consistency for the assertions listed above. Label the fallacies.

_____

_____

_____

_____

What support do you feel is missing? _____

_____

■ Step 4: Evaluate the argument: What is your overall evaluation and why?

_____

_____

What is your opinion on the issue?

_____

Thinking About

HAS TELEVISION KILLED OFF READING— AND IF SO, SO WHAT?

Describe how and why you feel college students misuse television, and then suggest several types of programming that you feel would be intellectually stimulating and entertaining for a college television network.

COMPREHENSION QUESTIONS

Answer the following questions about the selection.

1. What does Katha Pollitt mean by this statement: "While we have been arguing so fiercely about which books make the best medicine, the patient has been slipping deeper and deeper into a coma."

_____

_____

2. What is the research of Csikszentmihalyi that you previously encountered in this textbook?

_____

_____

3. What additional meaning is suggested by writing the following in italics in the selection?

on their own _____

remembered _____

imaginative _____

4. To what extent do you control TV and does TV control you? Explain.

_____

_____

SEARCH THE NET

 Do you think television has a positive or negative effect on childhood reading? Does television discourage children from reading, or do programs like *Sesame Street* promote reading? Conduct a search to explore this issue. State your opinion and explain how a particular Website supports or influences your attitude.
    Plan your own search or begin by trying the following:

http://childrenstv.minigco.com/mbropage.htm	Link Page
http://www.fcc.gov/	FCC Home Page
http://www.education.unesco.org/	United Nations Educational, Scientific and Cultural Organization (UNESCO)
http://www.cep.org/	Center for Educational Priorities
http://www.ira.org/	International Reading Association

CONTEMPORARY FOCUS

Students are taught to express their opinions on topics and issues even before the ideas are fully explored and developed. Is this method of teaching ultimately helpful or harmful to society? Why is it important to have knowledge before you have an opinion?

THE SOUND AND FURY OF IGNORANCE

Peter Cochrane

The Daily Telegraph, 20 August 1998, p. 10.

All humans have the right to freely voice their views, concerns and opinions on any topic, and have them represented. We are all passengers on spaceship earth and have a vested interest in sustaining life. But who would consult an Amazonian witch doctor when his car needed repairing? No one. So why are the media increasingly full of people who clearly know nothing, pontificating about the dangers of scientific and engineering developments? Why do politicians, members of the cloth and others with irrelevant titles, education and experience see fit to alarm the public on the basis of no knowledge and unbridled ignorance?

In the latest round of noise and panic, we have genetic engineering in the sights of these modern witch doctors and seers. Genetic engineering is thousands of years old—our species has been modifying strains of plant and animal life to its advantage for aeons—so why the sudden interest and panic? And why all the statements about this being the realm of God, forbidden to us? Scientists and engineers choose to publicize and inform society of the amazing advances they are making on our behalf. Cheaper, fresher, longer-lasting, and disease-free food do seem to warrant a mention. But listen to the roar of protest. There is a plethora of important matters that society needs to address, but it requires informed and intelligent debate, not panic reactions.

With greater knowledge comes greater responsibility, and the primary responsibility is to understand. This is not a time for witchdoctors—it is a time for understanding.

Collaborate on responses to the following questions:

- What area seems to be the author's primary concern about opinionated ignorance?
- Give some examples of recent encounters with people who voiced opinions without knowledge.
- Do you have an opinion on cloning? Why or why not?

STAGE 1: PREVIEW

The author seems to be giving his opinion. Agree ☐   Disagree ☐

Activate Schema

Have you ever written a letter to an author?

STAGE 2: INTEGRATE KNOWLEDGE WHILE READING

Predict   Picture   Relate   Monitor   Correct

STUDENTS LED TO BELIEVE OPINIONS MORE IMPORTANT THAN KNOWLEDGE

Thomas Sowell
The Arizona Republic, August 18, 1998

Thomas Sowell is a senior fellow at Stanford University's Hoover Institution.

Reaching the public also means that the public reaches you. My mail ranges from fan mail to hate mail. But there is a special kind of letter that bothers me more than the most idiotic obscenities. That is the letter from some teenager (or younger) who is writing
5 because his school has led him to believe that he ought to have opinions on some **issue** or other—and ought to express those opinions to strangers he has read about and expect those strangers to take up their time discussing his opinions.

A single word in a recent letter from a 15-year-old boy epitomized what is
10 so wrong with such premature presumption. He said that American military leaders "over-estimated" the casualties that would have resulted from an invasion of Japan in World War II, so that we were unjustified in dropping the atomic bomb instead.

This particular issue is not the point. The point is that people expect to
15 have their opinions taken seriously just because these are their opinions.

Here is someone with no military training or experience, much less achievements, blithely second-guessing General Douglas MacArthur, who served in the military more than twice as long as this kid has been in the world. Here is someone in the safety and comfort of a classroom issuing pro-
20 nouncements about assessments made by someone who fought on the battlefields of two world wars and left a record of stunning victories with low casualties that have caused him to be ranked among the great military minds in history.

If this were just one kid who has gotten too big for his britches, then it
25 would only be a small part of the passing parade of human foibles. But schoolchildren all across the country are being encouraged or assigned to engage in letter-writing campaigns, taking up the time of people ranging from journal-

ists to congressmen and presidents. Worse, these pupils are led to believe that having opinions is more important than knowing what you are talking about.

30   Few things are more dangerous than articulate superficiality. Glib demagogues have been the curse of the twentieth century and tens of millions of human beings have paid with their lives for the heady visions and clever talk of political egotists. Yet the danger is not that a particular child will follow in the footsteps of Lenin, Hitler, or Mao. The danger is that great numbers of

35   people will never know what it is to know, as distinguished from sounding off.
They will be sitting ducks for the demagogues of their times.

If our so-called educators cannot be bothered to teach our children knowledge and logic, they can at least refrain from undermining the importance of knowledge and logic by leading students to believe that how you feel and ex-

40   press yourself are what matter.

It takes considerable knowledge just to realize the extent of your own ignorance. Back in 1982, when I began an international study of peoples and cultures, I planned to write a chapter on India. It was only after reading books about India, visiting India twice and talking with Indian scholars, officials,

45   businessmen, and journalists that I realized what a monumental job it would be to write about this vast and complex society.

Although my study took 15 years and resulted in three books, there was no chapter on India. I realized that I didn't know enough to write one.

Assigning students to write letters and papers on vast topics is training them

50   in irresponsibility. It is putting the cart before the horse. There will never be a shortage of ignorant audacity. What is always scarce is thorough knowledge and carefully reasoned analysis, systematically checked against factual evidence.

Our education-is-fun approach is setting up the next generation to be patsies for any political manipulator who knows how to take advantage of their

55   weaknesses. Educators who are constantly chirping about how this or that is "exciting" ignore the reality that education is not about how you feel at the moment but how well the young are being prepared for future responsibilities.

Classroom letter-writing assignments are not just silliness. They are a dangerous betrayal of the young and an abdication of adult responsibility by self-

60   indulgent teachers.

STAGE 3: RECALL

Stop to self-test, relate, and react.

SKILL DEVELOPMENT: CRITICAL THINKING

Apply the four-step format for evaluating the argument. Use the perforations to tear out and hand page 359 to your instructor.

■ Step 1: Identify the issue: State the main point or issue the author is arguing.

_____

_____

■ Step 2: Identify the support for the argument: List and letter each major assertion of support.

_____

_____

_____

_____

_____

■ Step 3: Evaluate the support: Comment on weaknesses in relevance, believ-ability, and consistency for the assertions listed above. Label the fallacies.

_____

_____

_____

_____

What support do you feel is missing?

_____

■ Step 4: Evaluate the argument: What is your overall evaluation and why?

_____

_____

What is your opinion on the issue?_____

Contemporary Link

Read the editorial page of your local or school newspaper, and find an example in an editorial or in a letter to the editor of someone who is giving an opinion without having adequate knowledge. Explain the issue, the opinion, and what you believe is the void in knowledge.

COMPREHENSION QUESTIONS

Answer the following questions about the selection.

1. What prompted the writing of this editorial?

   _____

   _____

2. What does the author mean by "They will be sitting ducks for the demagogues of their times."

   _____

   _____

3. Why does the author feel letter-writing assignments are "a dangerous betrayal of the young"?

   _____

   _____

4. Would you describe the author's views as liberal or conservative? Explain.

   _____

   _____

5. Define the following phrases as used by the author:

   idiotic obscenities _____

   epitomized what is so wrong _____

   blithely second-guessing _____

   human foibles _____

   articulate superficiality _____

   glib demagogues _____

   ignorant audacity _____

© 2000 Addison-Wesley Educational Publishers, Inc.

SEARCH THE NET

Thomas Sowell is a syndicated columnist whose editorials appear in many newspapers around the country. Conduct a search to find out more about his work.

- List the title and briefly describe the contents of one of his books.
- Locate and read another of his editorials. Briefly summarize his message.

CONTEMPORARY FOCUS

If law-abiding citizens were allowed to carry registered concealed weapons, do you think crime would increase or decrease? In many states, gun control advocates have argued effectively against permitting concealed weapons, but the mood of the country may be changing.

SHOULD YOU CARRY A GUN?

Romesh Patnesar

Time, July 6, 1998

Is a gun-carrying nation a safer nation? Fearful of being victimized by indiscriminate violence, many Americans are gnawed by a dilemma: Should I or shouldn't I carry a gun? The question is a real one for a growing number of Americans because the tally of states with "right to carry" laws has gone from eight to 31 since 1985. These states will issue a concealed-weapon permit to any citizen without a criminal record who wants one—no questions asked.

The author of a new book, *More Guns, Less Crime: Understanding Crime and Gun Control Laws*, has analyzed crime rates in the 10 states that passed right-to-carry laws from 1977 to 1992. He contends that after more relaxed concealed-carry laws were enacted, murders fell an average of 8%, rapes 5% and aggravated assaults 7%. (For the same period in the entire country, the number of murders went up 24%, and rapes 71%. Assaults more than doubled.) The purported reason: would-be criminals were deterred from choosing victims who just might have a pistol tucked in their purse. Increases in accidental deaths by handguns—on the whole relatively rare—were barely noticeable, fewer than one death a year. With the National Rifle Association flacking the book to members, it sold out its first printing in three weeks.

More Guns, Less Crime has touched off furious protests from gun-control lobbyists and criminologists, who call the book's research spurious, its statistics suspect and its conclusion—that "allowing law-abiding citizens to carry concealed handguns will save lives"—dangerous. Part of what's threatening about the book is its author: John Lott, a wonkish University of Chicago economist who has never been an N.R.A. member and prior to writing the book did not own a gun. (He has since bought a .38-cal. pistol.) "If I had really strong views about guns," he says, "I wouldn't have waited until I was 40 to write this."

Collaborate on responses to the following questions:

■ Why is Professor Lott's argument compelling?

■ How can concealed weapons be a danger to children?

■ If weapons were permitted, in what situations would you like to carry a gun?

STAGE 1: PREVIEW

The editorial is based on a news story. Agree ☐ Disagree ☐

Activate Schema

Do you have a gun in your house?

STAGE 2: INTEGRATE KNOWLEDGE WHILE READING

Predict   Picture   Relate   Monitor   Correct

© Tribune Media Services, Inc. All Rights Reserved. Reprinted with permission.

SHOOTING HOLES IN GUN LAWS

From Mike Royko, *Tribune Media Services*

It was just a short news story, tucked away in the back pages, but it caused me to slightly alter my views on gun control laws.

The story was about a young woman who lives on the South Side of Chicago. A few nights ago, she was waiting for a bus. She had been visiting a
5 friend, and it was after midnight.

Instead of a bus, a car pulled up. A man got out. He was holding a knife. He told the woman to get into the car or he would cut her. She got into the car. The man drove to an alley and spent the next two hours raping her.

Then he drove her a few blocks from her home and dumped her out of the
10 car. She began walking home, intending to call the police.

But before she got home, another man walked up to her. He, too, had a knife. He walked her to an abandoned building, where he raped her. After he finally let her go, she made it to a friend's house, the police were called, and she was hospitalized.

15 Now, we've all heard of gang rapes, and of women being held prisoner and raped by whichever two-legged animal happens to wander along.

But this is the first case I've come across of a woman being yanked off the street and raped by two different men within a matter of hours.

So what does this have to do with my views on gun controls?

20   If that woman had a pistol in her purse or coat pocket, knew how to use it, and was alert to danger, it's doubtful that the first rapist would have been able to get her into his car.

As soon as he got out of his car and approached her with his knife, she could have had the gun out, pointed it at his chest, and said something like:
25   "Go away or die." My guess is that his libido would have quickly cooled. But if it didn't, he would have had a new hole in his anatomy.

Of course, if the woman had a gun in her purse, she would have been violating the law that forbids carrying a concealed weapon. That's a part of the gun laws that I think should be changed.

30   I still believe all guns should be registered. I'm against the selling of the mini-machine guns that allow deranged people to blow away kids in school-yards or their former co-workers. I also believe in cooling-off periods before guns are sold and background checks of those who want to buy guns.

But I think the law concerning carrying a concealed weapon should be
35   amended so that a woman who has no serious criminal background or history of mental disorders and lives or works in or near a high-crime area of a city should be able to legally tote a pistol in her purse or pocket.

As long as gun ownership is legal in our society, it doesn't make much sense that I should be able to keep a couple of fully loaded pump-action shot-
40   guns in my home, but a woman on a dark street in a dangerous neighborhood is forbidden by law to carry a pistol in her purse.

Who is in greater danger? Me, with my doors double-locked, my dog, and my shotguns? Or a woman in a neighborhood where rape and other assaults are almost as common as church pancake parties in small towns?

45   I'm not saying that a gun in a purse would put an end to all of it. But I don't doubt that after a few mugs suddenly find they have an extra navel, those of similar inclinations might ponder what that lady coming down the street might have in her purse.

Of course, I don't really expect the gun laws to be changed to permit
50   women to protect themselves.

So I have another suggestion for females. Get a gun and carry it in your purse anyway. If you put a hole in some thug who pops out of a doorway or a car with a knife, I doubt if a judge will do more than deliver a lecture.

These days, there's always a good chance that the same judge put the guy
55   with the knife back out on the street in the first place.

STAGE 3: RECALL

Stop to self-test, relate, and react.

SKILL DEVELOPMENT: CRITICAL THINKING

Apply the four-step format for evaluating the argument. Use the perforations to tear out and hand this page to your instructor.

■ Step 1: Identify the issue: State the main point or issue the author is arguing.

_____

■ Step 2: Identify the support for the argument: List and letter each major assertion of support.

_____

_____

_____

_____

_____

_____

■ Step 3: Evaluate the support: Comment on weaknesses in relevance, believability, and consistency for the assertions listed above. Label the fallacies.

_____

_____

_____

_____

What support do you feel is missing? _____

_____

■ Step 4: Evaluate the argument: What is your overall evaluation and why?

_____

_____

What is your opinion on the issue? _____

_____

Contemporary Link

In your opinion, which of the two articles advocating concealed weapons is more convincing? Use details from the selections to explain your answer.

COMPREHENSION QUESTIONS

Answer the following questions about the selection.

1. Do you believe this story is true? Why or why not?

   _____

   _____

2. What do you like or dislike about the author's style of writing?

   _____

3. What was the author's purpose in writing this editorial?

   _____

4. What does the author insinuate about judges?

   _____

SEARCH THE NET

Gun control is a complex issue about which people tend to be firmly for or against. Decide on your position, and write an argument advocating your view. Use material in support of your argument that does not appear in the two articles. Conduct a search to borrow from the arguments used by major organizations such as those listed below. Expect the information to be biased. Support your argument with both facts and opinions. Plan your own search or begin by trying the following:

http://www.gunfire.org/csgu/csgusumm.htm   Coalition to Stop Gun Violence (CSGU)

http://www.nra.org/   National Rifle Association (NRA)

http://www.afa.ca/   National Firearms Association (NFA)

Go Electronic!

For additional readings, exercises, and Internet activities, visit this book's Website at:
http://www.awlonline.com/smithBTG

For even more activities, visit the Longman English pages at:
http://longman.awl.com/englishpages

If you need a user name and password, please see your instructor.

Take a Road Trip to the American Southwest! Be sure to visit the Critical Thinking module in your Reading Road Trip CD-ROM for multimedia turorials, exercises, and tests.

READER'S JOURNAL

Name _____ Date _____

Chapter 8

Answer the following questions to learn about your own learning and reflect on your progress. Use the perforations to tear the assignment out for your instructor.

1. Before reading this chapter, what was your definition of critical thinking?

   _____

   _____

2. How has your definition changed? _____

   _____

   _____

3. Would you like to be a lawyer or to be on a college debating team? Why or why not? _____

   _____

   _____

4. Recall a recent conversation in which a position was supported with fallacious thinking. What was the fallacy that was most used?

   _____

   _____

   _____

5. How do you think you will use critical thinking when you have graduated from college? Give an example at work and an example in your personal life.

   _____

   _____

   _____

6. What fallacies do you use the most when you argue with your parents?

   _____

7. What is your strongest barrier to critical thinking? Explain.

   _____

Graphic Illustrations

- What do graphics do?
- What is a diagram?
- What does a table do?
- What is most helpful on a typical map?
- What does a pie graph represent?
- How do you read a bar graph?
- What is a line graph?
- What information does a flowchart convey?

Steve DiBenedetto, Confused by Choice, 1987. Acrylic and spray on. Courtesy Tony Shafrazi Gallery.

WHAT GRAPHICS DO

If a picture is worth a thousand words, a graphic illustration is worth at least several pages of facts and figures. Graphics express complex interrelationships in simplified form. Instead of plodding through repetitious data, you can glance at a chart, a map, or a graph and immediately see how everything fits together as well as how one part compares with another. Instead of reading several lengthy paragraphs and trying to visualize comparisons, you can study an organized design. The graphic illustration is a logically constructed aid for understanding many small bits of information.

Graphic illustrations are generally used for the following reasons:

1. **To condense.** Pages of repetitious, detailed information can be organized into one explanatory design.
2. **To clarify.** Processes and interrelationships can be more clearly defined through visual representations.
3. **To convince.** Developing trends and gross inequities can be forcefully dramatized.

There are five kinds of graphic illustrations: (1) diagrams, (2) tables, (3) maps, (4) graphs, and (5) flowcharts. All are used in textbooks, and the choice of which is best to use depends on the type of material presented. This chapter contains explanations and exercises for five types of graphic illustration. Read the explanations, study the illustrations, and respond to the questions as instructed.

►EXERCISE 9.1   *Diagrams*

A *diagram* is an outline drawing or picture of an object or a process. It shows the labeled parts of a complicated form such as the muscles of the human body, the organizational makeup of a company's management and production teams, or the directional flow of a natural ecological system.

The diagrams shown on the opposite page display the arrangement of teeth in the human mouth and show the anatomy of a single tooth.

Refer to the diagrams to respond to the following items with *T* (true), *F* (false), or *CT* (can't tell).

_____ 1. The mouth contains eight incisors.
_____ 2. The last three teeth in each jaw are molars.

Tooth Arrangement and Anatomy

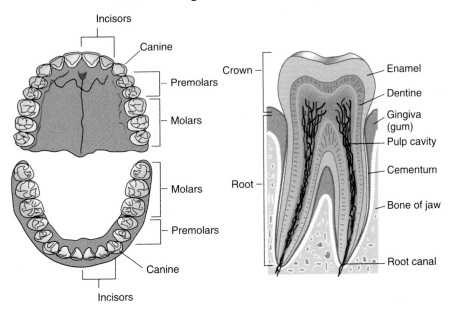

Tooth Arrangement in the Human Mouth   Anatomy of a Single Tooth

From Carl E. Rischer and Thomas A. Easton, Focus on Human Biology

_____ 3. Because of overcrowding, many adults have had their molars removed.

_____ 4. The upper jaw contains more premolars than the lower jaw.

_____ 5. The lower jaw contains two canine teeth.

_____ 6. The crown of a tooth extends above the gum.

_____ 7. The outer layer of a tooth is the dentine.

_____ 8. The root of the tooth extends into the bone of the jaw.

_____ 9. The pulp cavity contains the root canal.

_____10. Plaque attacks a tooth and is a precursor of tooth decay.

11. The purpose of each diagram is _____

_____

▶ **EXERCISE 9.2**   *Tables*

A *table* is a listing of facts and figures in columns and rows for quick and easy reference. The information in the columns and rows is usually labeled in two

> READER'S TIP

How to Read Graphic Material

▶ **Read the title to get an overview.** What is it about?

▶ **Look for footnotes and read italicized introductory material.**

Identify the who, where, and how.
How and when were the data collected?
Who collected the data?
How many persons were included in the survey?
Do the researchers seem to have been objective or biased?
Considering the above information, does the study seem valid?

▶ **Read the labels.**

What do the vertical columns and the horizontal rows represent?
Are the numbers in thousands or millions?
What does the legend represent?

▶ **Notice the trends and find the extremes.**

What are the highest and lowest rates?
What is the average rate?
How do the extremes compare with the total?
What is the percentage of increase or decrease?

▶ **Draw conclusions and formulate future exam questions.**

What does the information mean?
What needs to be done with the information?
What wasn't included?
Where do we go from here?

different directions. First read the title for the topic and then read the footnotes to judge the source. Determine what each column represents and how they interact.

Refer to the tables shown on page 371 to respond to the following with *T* (true), *F* (false), or *CT* (can't tell). Note the amounts being compared, the average, and the range.

_____ 1. Decaffeinated brewed coffee contains no caffeine.

_____ 2. Imported brands of brewed tea can range higher in caffeine than U.S. brands.

_____ 3. The amount of iced tea measured for caffeine was the same as the amount of brewed tea.

_____ 4. On the average, two ounces of dark chocolate contains more caffeine than two ounces of milk chocolate.

_____ 5. A twelve-ounce serving of Coca-Cola has more caffeine than an equal serving of Pepsi.

CAFFEINE IN BEVERAGES AND FOODS

Item	Caffeine (mg)	
	Average	Range
Coffee (5-oz. cup)		
Brewed, drip method	115	60–180
Brewed, percolator	80	40–170
Instant	65	30–120
Decaffeinated, brewed	3	2–5
Decaffeinated, instant	2	1–5
Tea (5-oz.cup)		
Brewed, major U.S. brands	40	20–90
Brewed, imported brands	60	25–110
Instant	30	25–50
Iced (12-oz. glass)	70	67–76
Cocoa beverage (5-oz. cup)	4	2–20
Chocolate milk beverage (8-oz. glass)	5	2–7
Milk chocolate (1 oz.)	6	1–15
Dark chocolate, semisweet (1 oz.)	20	5–35
Baker's chocolate (1 oz.)	26	26
Chocolate-flavored syrup (1 oz.)	4	4

CAFFEINE IN POPULAR SOFT DRINKS

Brand	Caffeine (mg)*
Sugar-Free Mr. Pibb®	58.8
Mountain Dew®	54.0
Mello Yello®	52.8
Tab®	46.8
Coca-Cola®	45.6
Diet Coke®	45.6
Shasta Cola®	44.4
Mr. Pibb®	40.8
Dr. Pepper®	39.6
Big Red®	38.4
Pepsi-Cola®	38.4
Diet Pepsi®	36.0
Pepsi Light®	36.0
RC Cola®	36.0
Diet Rite®	36.0
Canada Dry Jamaica Cola®	30.0
Canada Dry Diet Cola®	1.2

Per 12-oz. serving

From Oakley Ray and Charles Ksir, Drugs, Society, and Human Behavior

_____ 6. On the average, iced tea has more caffeine than an equal amount of Coca-Cola®.

_____ 7. In equal amounts, brewed coffee has over twice as much caffeine as a Canada Dry Jamaica Cola®.

_____ 8. The caffeine is easier to put in dark drinks and food as opposed to lighter ones.

_____ 9. On the average, instant tea and coffee contain less caffeine than their brewed counterparts.

_____ 10. Mello Yello® is light in color and thus most people assume that is does not contain caffeine.

11. The purpose of each table is _____

_____

EXERCISE 9.3   *Maps*

A *map* shows a geographic area. I⁺ can show differences in physical terrain or variations over specified areas. The legend of a map, which usually appears in a corner box, explains the meanings of symbols and shading.

Use the legend on the map shown on the opposite page to help you respond to the following with *T* (true), *F* (false) or *CT* (can't tell).

_____ 1. Arizona and New Mexico have no hazardous waste sites within either state.

_____ 2. California has 41 or more hazardous waste sites.

_____ 3. The state of Washington has more hazardous waste sites than Tennessee.

_____ 4. Maine is too far north and too cold to have hazardous waste sites.

_____ 5. Florida has more hazardous waste sites than Alabama and Georgia combined.

_____ 6. New York and Pennsylvania have the same number of hazardous waste sites.

_____ 7. California and New York have a high number of hazardous waste sites because the population of each state is high.

_____ 8. North Carolina and South Carolina are both within the same range on the number of hazardous waste sites located within each state.

_____ 9. The states along the East Coast have more hazardous waste sites in each state than any of the states along the West Coast.

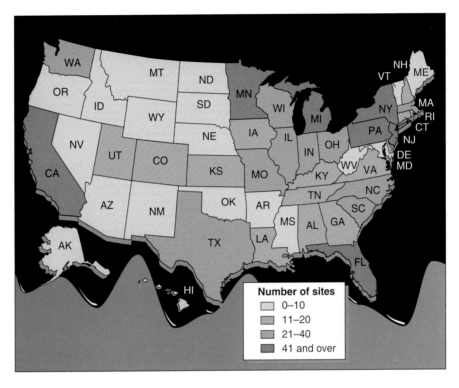

From U.S. Department of the Interior.

_____ 10. Delaware is a small state but it has more hazardous waste sites than New Jersey.

11. The purpose of this map is _____

_____

Geographic Review

Use the map on page 374 to test your knowledge of world geography.

Citizens of the World Show Little Knowledge of Geography

In the spring of 1988, twelve thousand people in ten nations were asked to identify sixteen places on the following world map. The average citizen in the United States could identify barely more than half. Believe it or not, 14 percent of Americans tested could not even find their own country on the map. Despite years of fighting in Vietnam, 68 percent could not locate this Southeast Asian country. Such lack of basic geographic knowledge is quite common throughout the world. Here is the average score for each of the ten countries in which the test was administered.

Country	Average Score
1 Sweden	11.6
2 West Germany	11.2
3 Japan	9.7
4 France	9.3
5 Canada	9.2
6 United States	8.6
7 Great Britain	8.5
8 Italy	7.6
9 Mexico	7.4
10 Soviet Union	7.4

How would you do? To take the test yourself, match the numbers on the map to the places listed.

Robert L. Lineberry et al., *Government in America*

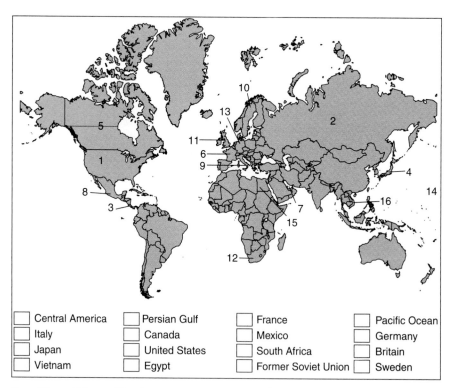

☐ Central America	☐ Persian Gulf	☐ France	☐ Pacific Ocean
☐ Italy	☐ Canada	☐ Mexico	☐ Germany
☐ Japan	☐ United States	☐ South Africa	☐ Britain
☐ Vietnam	☐ Egypt	☐ Former Soviet Union	☐ Sweden

From Warren E. Leary. "Two Superpowers' Citizens Do Badly in Geography." New York Times, *November 9, 1989, A6.*

> **EXERCISE 9.4**   *Pie Graphs*

A *pie graph* is a circle that is divided into wedge-shaped slices. The complete pie or circle represents a total, or 100 percent. Each slice is a percent or fraction of that whole. Budgets, such as the annual expenditure of the federal or state governments, are frequently illustrated by pie graphs.

Refer to the pie graphs below to respond to the following statements with *T* (true), *F* (false), or *CT* (can't tell).

American Pet Ownership

In 1993 the American Veterinary Medical Association reported that 34, 600,000 American households had dogs as pets. The following graph describes those households by family size and income.

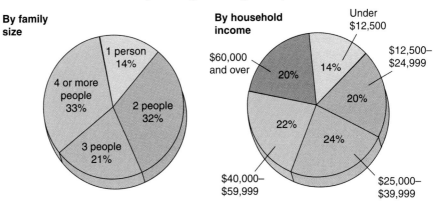

Who Owns Dogs?
(Percentage of all dog owners)

From The Macmillan Visual Almanac, *Bruce Glassman, ed.*

_____ 1. Over half of the dog-owning households had an income of more than $25,000.

_____ 2. The households with higher incomes tended to have more than one dog.

_____ 3. Households with only one person made up the smallest percentage of dog owners.

_____ 4. Households with an income of $60,000 and over made up the largest percentage of dog owners.

_____ 5. The graph indicates that 33% of the households has three or more dogs.

_____ 6. The number of dog owners in America exceeds the number of cat owners.

_____ 7. More than half of the dogs in America exist in households with three or more people.

_____ 8. Approximately 27,680,000 of the dog-owning households have an income of $60,000 or more.

_____ 9. Approximately 4,844,000 single people have dogs.

_____ 10. The percentage of dog ownership steadily increases as the number of family members increases.

11. The purpose of each pie graph is to _____

_____

_____

EXERCISE 9.5   *Bar Graphs*

A *bar graph* is a series of horizontal or vertical bars in which the length of each bar represents a particular amount or number of what is being discussed. A series of different items can be quickly compared by noting the different bar lengths.

Refer to the bar graph on the opposite page to respond to the following with *T* (true), *F* (false), or *CT* (can't tell).

_____ 1. In each age group and educational group, the percentage of men who smoke is higher than the percentage of women who smoke.

_____ 2. Approximately 10% of the women who smoke are 75 years of age and older.

_____ 3. Approximately 71% of the men between ages 45 to 64 do not smoke.

_____ 4. From 18 to 75 years of age, the percentage of smokers in each age group steadily declines.

_____ 5. The 25–44 age group has the highest percentage of smokers.

_____ 6. The percentage of smokers by educational group shows a steady decline as the amount of formal education increases.

_____ 7. The percentage of smokers who are 75 years of age and older is lower than for other groups because this age group has seen more people die of lung cancer from smoking.

_____ 8. The difference in the percentage of men and women smokers with high school diplomas is approximately 15%.

_____ 9. The percentage of smokers with a college degree is less than half the percentage of smokers with only high school diplomas.

_____ 10. The difference between the percentage of smokers without a high school diploma and with a high-school diploma only is greater for men than for women.

Profile of Adult U.S. Cigarette Smokers
(Percentage by selected characteristics)

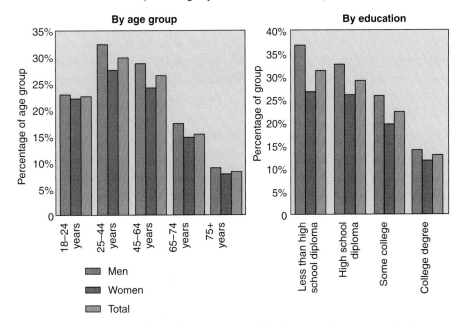

From U.S. Department of Health and Human Services, U.S. Centers for Disease Control in The MacMillan Visual Almanac, Bruce Glassman, ed.

11. The purpose of the bar graph is to _____

_____

> ## EXERCISE 9.6   *Line Graphs*

A *line graph* is a continuous curve or frequency distribution. The horizontal scale measures one aspect of the data and the vertical line measures another aspect. As the data fluctuate, the line will change direction and, with extreme differences, will become very jagged.

In the graph shown on page 378, notice that the horizontal side measures age and the vertical side measures the arrest rate per 100,000 persons. Also, notice that one line indicates property crime arrests and the other indicates violent crime arrests.

Refer to the line graph to respond to the following with *T* (true), *F* (false), or *CT* (can't tell).

_____ 1. Violent crime arrests and property crime arrests do not peak at the same age.

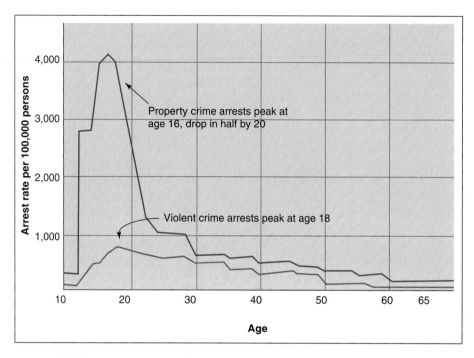

From FBI, Uniform Crime Report, 1995, pp. 218–219, in Larry Siegel, Criminology (NewYork: Wadsworth, 1998), p. 53.

_____ 2. At age 20, over twice as many people are arrested for property crimes as are arrested for violent crimes.

_____ 3. At age 30, approximately 500 out of every 100,000 people are arrested for violent crimes.

_____ 4. No arrest rate in any age group is as high as the property crime arrests for teenagers.

_____ 5. The violent crime and property crime arrest rate is lower for people over 40 because they are not as physically able to perpetrate the crimes as younger people.

6. The purpose of the line graph is to _____

_____.

© 2000 Addison-Wesley Educational Publishers, Inc.

EXERCISE 9.7   *Flowcharts*

Flowcharts provide a diagram of the relationships and sequence of elements. They were first used in computer programming. Key ideas are stated in boxes,

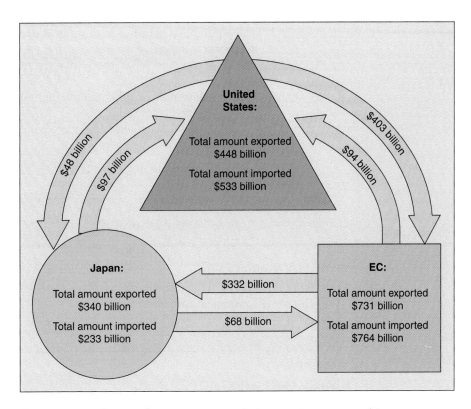

From International Financial Statistics, Japan Trade Center, U.S. Department of Commerce, O.E.C.D. data, and Eurostat, External Trade and Balance of Payments, 1993, in Thomas C. Kinnear et al., Principles of Marketing *(New York: HarperCollins, 1985), source of quote below.*

along with supporting ideas that are linked by arrows. In the flowchart above, arrows pointing toward an area indicate money coming into the economy and arrows pointing away from an area indicate money leaving the economy.

In 1993 American companies exported goods worth approximately $448 billion, the European Economic Community nations exported goods worth $731 billion (including trade among EC members), and Japan exported about $340 billion in goods. By comparison, the United States imported $533 billion worth of goods, the EC imported $764 billion worth of goods, and Japan imported $233 billion worth. The difference between the values of a country's exports and imports is called its **balance of trade.** If exports exceed imports, there is a **trade surplus;** if imports exceed exports, there is a **trade deficit.**

Refer to the explanation and the flowchart to respond to the following with *T* (true), *F* (false), or *CT* (can't tell).

_____ 1. The United States exports more to the EC than it exports to Japan.

_____ 2. The United States imports from Japan over twice as much as it exports to Japan.

_____ 3. The EC exports to Japan more than ten times as much as it imports.

_____ 4. Japanese automobiles make up the highest percentage of goods exported from Japan.

_____ 5. Of the three leading world traders, Japan is the only one that exports more than it imports.

6. The purpose of the flowchart is _____

Summary Points

■ **What do graphics do?**

Graphic illustrations condense, clarify, and convince. They express complex interrelationships in simplified form.

■ **What is a diagram?**

A diagram is an outline drawing or picture of an object or a process with labeled parts.

■ **What does a table do?**

A table lists facts and figures in columns for quick and easy reference. You must determine what the columns represent and how they interact.

■ **What is most helpful on a typical map?**

The legend on a map of a geographic area explains the symbols and shading used to convey information.

■ **What does a pie graph represent?**

A pie graph depicts a total, or 100 percent, divided into wedge-shaped slices.

■ **How do you read a bar graph?**

You must determine what is represented by the length of a series of horizontal or vertical bars.

■ **What is a line graph?**

A line graph is a frequency distribution. You must identify what is measured by the horizontal and vertical scales in order to read a point on the continuous line.

■ **What information does a flowchart convey?**

A flowchart provides a diagram of the relationship and sequence of events of a group of elements. The key ideas usually appear in boxes and arrows are used to connect the elements.

C O N T E M P O R A R Y   F O C U S

Most colleges offer programs to educate students about drinking, hoping that knowledge about how alcohol is processed by the body will influence student alcohol consumption decisions. Do you think such educational programs can have any impact on ritual drinking? Should colleges offer other options in order to respect the rights of nondrinkers?

HIGHER EDUCATION: CROCKED ON CAMPUS

Christine Gorman

Time, 19 December 1994.

Neal, a 21-year-old college student, knows he had a good time last September when he attended a costume party in suburban Los Angeles. He just can't remember it. After downing a dozen hits of vodka and cranberry juice, the University of Southern California senior staggered outside and passed out on a nearby lawn. At 3 A.M., two strangers drove him back to campus. He fell over a bike rack, passed out again, then woke up to find one of L.A.'s finest snapping handcuffs on him. The police did not press charges, and the officer handed Neal over to a campus security guard, who had to drive him home at 5 A.M. Today, the young man has no remorse over anything about the evening—except the '70s-style disco clothes he was wearing. "I was dressed like a complete moron," Neal recalls. "I wasn't really embarrassed about the rest."

Remorseless drinking has long been as much a ritual of university life as football, final exams, and frat parties. Almost every college graduate can spin at least a few tales about a boisterous night of carousing that culminated in slugging shots of tequila at sunrise or tossing drained kegs into the president's pool.

Enforcing strict rules on university turf seemed to push the parties off campus. Raising the legal drinking age from 18 to 21 in the 1980s merely triggered a boom in the business of creating fake ID cards.

Now there may be a new force for change. Students who are tired of paying $20,000 a year to have someone throw up on their shoes have launched a growing backlash against their inebriated peers. Not just freshmen, prodded by overanxious parents, but upperclassmen as well are demanding alcohol- and drug-free living and study environments.

Still small and somewhat timid, the campus temperance movement has taken its cue from antismoking campaigns. Restrictions on public smoking gained momentum after nonsmokers learned about the dangers of secondhand smoke.

The movement got a major boost from a study published by researchers at the Harvard School of Public Health. Appearing in the Journal of the American Medical Association, the report contains the first scientifically reliable national survey that documents not only the astonishing prevalence of undergraduate drinking but also the effect that drinkers have on other students. Based on the responses of 17,592 students at 140 campuses, the researchers declared that nearly half of collegians are binge drinkers who cause all sorts of trouble, from vandalism to attacks on classmates. At the schools where drinking was most popular, more than two-thirds of students had had their sleep or study interrupted by drunken peers. More than half had been forced to care for an inebriated friend, and at least a fourth had suffered an unwanted sexual advance. Alcohol plays a role in 90% of rapes and almost all violent crime on campus.

Collaborate on responses to the following questions:

- How does college drinking adversely affect you?
- Why do you suppose some college students have a remorseless attitude about drinking?
- What can realistically be done to limit college drinking?

STAGE 1: PREVIEW

The author's main purpose is to condemn alcohol.

Agree ☐   Disagree ☐

The different sections describe the cause-and-effect relationship of alcohol on the body.   Agree ☐   Disagree ☐

After reading this selection, I will need to know how alcohol affects the brain.   Agree ☐   Disagree ☐

Activate Schema

What is the legal limit for driving a car on a breathalyzer test?

Word Knowledge

What do you know about these words?

counterparts	diffuse	sedating	lethal	toxic
enhanced	prudent	ruefully	abstinence	devastates

STAGE 2: INTEGRATE KNOWLEDGE WHILE READING

Predict   Picture   Relate   Monitor   Correct

The liver can process only one drink per hour.

ALCOHOL AND NUTRITION

From Eva May Nunnelley Hamilton et al., *Nutrition*

People naturally congregate to enjoy conversation and companionship, and it is natural, too, to offer beverages to companions. All beverages ease conversation whether or not they contain alcohol. Still, some people choose alcohol over cola, milk, or coffee, and
5   they should know a few things about alcohol's short term and long term effects on health. One consideration is energy—alcohol

yields energy to the body, and many alcoholic drinks are much more fattening than their nonalcoholic counterparts. Additionally, alcohol has a tremendous impact on the overall well-being of the body.

10   People consume alcohol in servings they call "a drink." However, the serving that some people consider one drink may not be the same as the standard drink that delivers $\frac{1}{2}$ ounce pure ethanol:

> 3 to 4 ounces wine
> 10 ounces wine cooler
> 12 ounces beer
> 1 ounce hard liquor (whiskey, gin, brandy, rum, vodka)

The percentage of alcohol in distilled liquor is stated as *proof:* 100-proof liquor is 50 percent alcohol; 90-proof is 45 percent, and so forth. Compared
15   with hard liquor, beer and wine have a relatively low percentage of alcohol.

Alcohol Enters the Body

From the moment an alcoholic beverage is swallowed, the body confers special status on it. Unlike foods, which require digestion, the tiny alcohol molecules are all ready to be absorbed; they can diffuse right through the walls of an empty stomach and reach the brain within a minute. A person can be-
20   come intoxicated almost immediately when drinking, especially if the person's stomach is empty. When the stomach is full of food, molecules of alcohol have less chance of touching the walls and diffusing through, so alcohol affects the brain a little less immediately. (By the time the stomach contents are emptied into the small intestine, it doesn't matter that food is mixed
25   with the alcohol. The alcohol is absorbed rapidly anyway.)

A practical pointer derives from this information. If a person wants to drink socially and not become intoxicated, the person should eat the snacks provided by the host (avoid the salty ones; they make you thirstier). Carbohydrate snacks are best suited for slowing alcohol absorption. High-fat snacks
30   help too because they slow peristalsis, keeping the alcohol in the stomach longer.

If one drinks slowly enough, the alcohol, after absorption, will be collected into the liver and processed without much affecting other parts of the body. If one drinks more rapidly, however, some of the alcohol bypasses the liver and
35   flows for a while through the rest of the body and the brain.

Alcohol Arrives in the Brain

People use alcohol today as a kind of social anesthetic to help them relax or to relieve anxiety. One drink relieves inhibitions, and this gives people the impression that alcohol is a stimulant. Actually the way it does this is by sedating *inhibitory* nerves, allowing excitatory nerves to take over. This is temporary.
40   Ultimately alcohol acts as a depressant and sedates all the nerve cells. Figure R1 describes alcohol's effects on the brain.

© 2000 Addison-Wesley Educational Publishers, Inc.

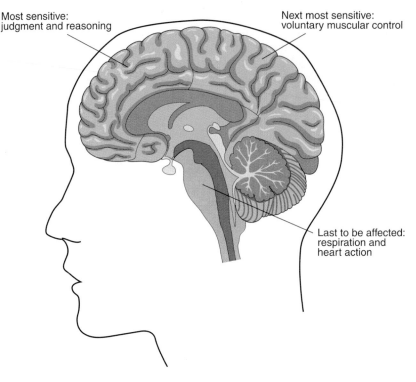

Most sensitive:
judgment and reasoning

Next most sensitive:
voluntary muscular control

Last to be affected:
respiration and
heart action

Figure R1
Alcohol's Effects on the Brain

It is lucky that the brain centers respond to elevating blood alcohol in the order described in Figure R1 because a person usually passes out before managing to drink a lethal dose. It is possible, though, for a person to drink fast
45 enough so that the effects of alcohol continue to accelerate after the person has gone to sleep. The occasional death that takes place during a drinking contest is attributed to this effect. The drinker drinks fast enough, before passing out, to receive a lethal dose. Table R1 shows the blood alcohol levels that correspond with progressively greater intoxication and Table R2 shows the brain
50 responses that occur at these blood levels.

Brain cells are particularly sensitive to excessive exposure to alcohol. The brain shrinks, even in people who drink only moderately. The extent of the shrinkage is proportional to the amount drunk. Abstinence, together with good nutrition, reverses some of the brain damage—possibly all of it if heavy
55 drinking has not continued for more than a few years—but prolonged drinking beyond an individual's capacity to recover can cause severe and irreversible effects on vision, memory, learning ability, and other functions.

Anyone who has had an alcoholic drink knows that alcohol increases urine output. This is because alcohol depresses the brain's production of **antidi-**
60 **uretic hormone.** Loss of body water leads to thirst. The only fluid that will relieve dehydration is water, but if alcohol is the only drink available, the thirsty

Table R1   **Alcohol Doses and Blood Levels**

Number of Drinks[a]	Percent Blood Alcohol by Body Weight				
	100 lb	120 lb	150 lb	180 lb	200 lb
2	0.08	0.06	0.05	0.04	0.04
4	0.15	0.13	0.10	0.08	0.08
6	0.23	0.19	0.15	0.13	0.11
8	0.30	0.25	0.20	0.17	0.15
12	0.45	0.36	0.30	0.25	0.23
14	0.52	0.42	0.35	0.34	0.27

[a]Taken within an hour or so.

Table R2   **Alcohol Blood Levels and Brain Responses**

Blood Level (%)	Brain Response
0.05	Judgment impaired
0.10	Emotional control impaired
0.15	Muscle coordination and reflexes impaired
0.20	Vision impaired
0.30	Drunk, totally out of control
0.35	Stupor
0.50–0.60	Total loss of consciousness, finally death

person may choose another alcoholic beverage and worsen the problem. The smart drinker, then, alternates alcoholic beverages with nonalcoholic choices and when thirsty chooses the latter.

65   The water loss caused by hormone depression involves loss of more than just water. The water takes with it important minerals, such as magnesium, potassium, calcium, and zinc, depleting the body's reserves. These minerals are vital to the maintenance of fluid balance and to nerve and muscle action and coordination.

Alcohol Arrives in the Liver

70 The capillaries that surround the digestive tract merge into veins that carry the alcohol-laden blood to the liver. Here the veins branch and rebranch into capil-

laries that touch every liver cell. The liver cells make nearly all of the body's al-
cohol-processing machinery, and the routing of blood through the liver allows
the cells to go right to work on the alcohol. The liver's location at this point
75 along the circulatory system guarantees that it gets the chance to remove toxic
substances before they reach other body organs such as the heart and brain.

The liver makes and maintains two sets of equipment for metabolizing alcohol. One is an enzyme that removes hydrogens from alcohol to break it
down; the name almost says what it does—**alcohol dehydrogenase (ADH).**[1]
80 This handles about 80 percent or more of body alcohol. The other alcohol-
metabolizing equipment is a chain of enzymes (known as the **MEOS**) thought
to handle about 10 to 20 percent of body alcohol. With high blood alcohol
concentrations, the MEOS activity is enhanced, as will be shown later. But let
us look at the ADH system first.

85 The amount of alcohol a person's body can process in a given time is limited by the number of ADH enzymes that reside in the liver.[2] If more molecules of alcohol arrive at the liver cells than the enzymes can handle, the extra
alcohol must wait. It enters the general circulation and is carried to all parts of
the body, circulating again and again through the liver until enzymes are
90 available to degrade it.

The number of ADH enzymes present is affected by whether or not a person eats. Fasting for as little as a day causes degradation of body proteins, including the ADH enzymes in the liver, and this can reduce the rate of alcohol
metabolism by half. Prudent drinkers drink slowly, with food in their stom-
95 achs, to allow the alcohol molecules to move to the liver cells gradually
enough for the enzymes to handle the load. It takes about an hour and a half to
metabolize one drink, depending on a person's body size, on previous drinking
experience, on how recently the person has eaten, and on general health at the
time. The liver is the only organ that can dispose of significant quantities of al-
100 cohol, and its maximum rate of alcohol clearance is fixed. This explains why
only time will restore sobriety. Walking will not; muscles cannot metabolize
alcohol. Nor will it help to drink a cup of coffee. Caffeine is a stimulant, but it
won't speed up the metabolism of alcohol. The police say ruefully that a cup
of coffee will only make a sleepy drunk into a wide-awake drunk.

105 As the ADH enzymes break alcohol down, they produce hydrogen ions
(acid), which must be picked up by a compound that contains the B vitamin
niacin as part of its structure. Normally this acid is disposed of through a metabolic pathway, but when alcohol is present in the system, this pathway shuts
down. The niacin-containing compound remains loaded with hydrogens that it
110 cannot get rid of and so becomes unavailable for a multitude of other vital body
processes for which it is required.

---

[1] There are actually two ADH enzymes, each for a specific task in alcohol breakdown. Enzyme 1, alcohol dehydrogenase, converts alcohol to acetaldehyde. Enzyme 2, acetaldehyde dehydrogenase, converts acetaldehyde to a common body compound, acetyl CoA, identical to that derived from carbohydrate and fat during their breakdown.
[2] Some ADH enzymes reside in the stomach, offering a protective barrier against alcohol entering the blood. Research shows that alcoholics make less stomach ADH, and so do women. Women may absorb about one-third
more alcohol than men, even when they are the same size and drink the same amount of alcoholic beverage.

The synthesis of fatty acids also accelerates as a result of the liver's exposure to alcohol. Fat accumulation can be seen in the liver after a single night of heavy drinking. **Fatty liver,** the first stage of liver deterioration seen in heavy drinkers, interferes with the distribution of nutrients and oxygen to the liver cells. If the condition lasts long enough, the liver cells die, and fibrous scar tissue invades the area—the second stage of liver deterioration called **fibrosis.** Fibrosis is reversible with good nutrition and abstinence from alcohol, but the next (last) stage—**cirrhosis**—is not. All of this points to the importance of moderation in the use of alcohol.

The presence of alcohol alters amino acid metabolism in the liver cells. Synthesis of some proteins important in the immune system slows down, weakening the body's defenses against infection. Synthesis of lipoproteins speeds up, increasing blood triglyceride levels. In addition, excessive alcohol increases the body's acid burden and interferes with normal uric acid metabolism, causing symptoms like those of **gout.**

Liver metabolism clears most of the alcohol from the blood. However, about 10 percent is excreted through the breath and in the urine. This fact is the basis for the breathalyzer test that law enforcement officers administer when they suspect someone of driving under the influence of alcohol.

Alcohol's Long-Term Effects

By far the longest term effects of alcohol are those felt by the child of a woman who drinks during pregnancy. Pregnant women should not drink at all. For nonpregnant adults, however, what are the effects of alcohol over the long term?

A couple of drinks set in motion many destructive processes in the body, but the next day's abstinence reverses them. As long as the doses taken are moderate, time between them is ample, and nutrition is adequate meanwhile, recovery is probably complete.

If the doses of alcohol are heavy and the time between them is short, complete recovery cannot take place, and repeated onslaughts of alcohol gradually take a toll on the body. For example, alcohol is directly toxic to skeletal and cardiac muscle, causing weakness and deterioration in a dose-related manner. Alcoholism makes heart disease more likely probably because alcohol in high doses raises the blood pressure. Cirrhosis can develop after 10 to 20 years from the additive effects of frequent heavy drinking episodes. Alcohol abuse also increases a person's risk of cancer of the mouth, throat, esophagus, rectum, and lungs. Women who drink even moderately may run an increased risk of developing breast cancer. Although some dispute these findings, a reliable source tentatively ranks daily human exposure to ethanol as high in relation to other possible carcinogenic hazards. Other long-terms effects of alcohol abuse include:

Ulcers of the stomach and intestines
Psychological depression
Kidney damage, bladder damage, prostate gland damage, pancreas damage

Skin rashes and sores

Impaired immune response

Deterioration in the testicles and adrenal glands, leading to feminization and sexual impotence in men

Central nervous system damage

Malnutrition

Increased risk of violent death

This list is by no means all inclusive. Alcohol has direct toxic effects, independent of the effect of malnutrition, on all body organs.

155 The more alcohol a person drinks, the less likely that he or she will eat enough food to obtain adequate nutrients. Alcohol is empty calories, like pure sugar and pure fat; it displaces nutrients. In a sense, each time you drink 150 calories of alcohol, you are spending those calories on a luxury item and getting no nutritional value in return. The more calories you spend this way, the fewer you have left to spend on nutritious foods. Table R3 shows the calorie 160 amounts of typical alcoholic beverages.

Alcohol abuse not only displaces nutrients from the diet but also affects every tissue's metabolism of nutrients. Alcohol causes stomach cells to oversecrete both acid and an agent of the immune system, histamine, that produces inflammation. These changes make the stomach and esophagus linings 165 vulnerable to ulcer formation. Intestinal cells fail to absorb thiamin, folate, and vitamin B_{12}. Liver cells lose efficiency in activating vitamin D and alter their production and excretion of bile. Rod cells in the retina, which normally process vitamin A alcohol (retinol) to the form needed in vision, find themselves processing drinking alcohol instead. The kidneys excrete magnesium, 170 calcium, potassium, and zinc.

© 2000 Addison-Wesley Educational Publishers, Inc.

Table R3   **Calories in Alcoholic Beverages and Mixers**

Beverage	Amount (oz)	Energy (cal)
Beer	12	150
Light beer	12	100
Gin, rum, vodka, whiskey (86 proof)	1 ½	105
Dessert wine	3 ½	140
Table wine	3 ½	85
Tonic, ginger ale, other sweetened carbonated waters	8	80
Cola, root beer	8	100
Fruit-flavored soda, Tom Collins mix	8	115
Club soda, plain seltzer, diet drinks	8	1

Alcohol's intermediate products interfere with metabolism too. They dislodge vitamin B_6 from its protective binding protein so that it is destroyed, causing a vitamin B_6 deficiency and thereby lowered production of red blood cells.

Most dramatic is alcohol's effect on folate. When alcohol is present, it is as
175 though the body were actively trying to expel folate from all its sites of action and storage. The liver, which normally contains enough folate to meet all needs, leaks folate into the blood. As the blood folate concentration rises, the kidneys are deceived into excreting it, as though it were in excess. The intestine normally releases and retrieves folate continuously, but it becomes damaged by fo-
180 late deficiency and alcohol toxicity; so it fails to retrieve its own folate and misses out on any that may trickle in from food as well. Alcohol also interferes with the action of what little folate is left, and this inhibits the production of new cells, especially the rapidly dividing cells of the intestine and the blood. Alcohol abuse causes a folate deficiency that devastates digestive system function.

185 Nutrient deficiencies are thus a virtually inevitable consequence of alcohol abuse, not only because alcohol displaces food but also because alcohol directly interferes with the body's use of nutrients, making them ineffective even if they are present. Over a lifetime, excessive drinking, whether or not accompanied by attention to nutrition, brings about deficits of all the nutri-
190 ents mentioned in this discussion and many more besides.

Alcohol and Drugs

The liver's reaction to alcohol affects its handling of drugs as well as nutrients. In addition to the ADH enzymes, the liver possesses an enzyme system that metabolizes *both* alcohol and drugs—any compounds that have certain chemical features in common. As mentioned earlier, at low blood alcohol concen-
195 trations, the MEOS handles about 10 to 20 percent of the alcohol consumed. However, at high blood alcohol concentrations, or if repeatedly exposed to alcohol, the MEOS is enhanced.

As a person's blood alcohol concentration rises, the alcohol competes with—and wins out over—other drugs whose metabolism relies on the
200 MEOS. If a person drinks and uses another drug at the same time, the drug will be metabolized more slowly and so will be much more potent. The MEOS is busy disposing of alcohol, so the drug cannot be handled until later; the dose may build up to where its effects are greatly amplified—sometimes to the point of killing the user.

205 In contrast, once a heavy drinker stops drinking and alcohol is not present to compete with other drugs, the enhanced MEOS metabolizes those drugs much faster than before. This can make it confusing and tricky to work out the correct dosages of medications. The doctor who prescribes sedatives every four hours, for example, unaware that the person has recently gone from be-
210 ing a heavy drinker to an abstainer, expects the MEOS to dispose of the drug at a certain predicted rate. The MEOS is adapted to metabolizing large quantities of alcohol, however. It therefore metabolizes the drug extra fast. The drug's effects wear off unexpectedly fast, leaving the client undersedated.

215 Imagine the doctor's alarm should a patient wake up on the table during an operation! A skilled anesthesiologist always asks the patient about his drinking pattern before putting him to sleep.

This discussion has touched on some of the ways alcohol affects health and nutrition. Despite some possible benefits of moderate alcohol consumption, the potential for harm is great, especially with excessive alcohol consumption. 220 Consider that over 50 percent of all fatal auto accidents are alcohol related. Translated to human lives, more than 25,000 people die each year in alcohol-related traffic accidents. The best way to avoid the harmful effects of alcohol is, of course, to avoid alcohol altogether. If you do drink, do so with care—for yourself and for others—and in moderation.

STAGE 3: RECALL

Stop to self-test, relate, and react.

Your instructor may choose to give you a true-false comprehension review.

 ## ALCOHOL AND NUTRITION

Use the information in this selection to write a letter to a friend who drinks and drives. In a scientific manner explain to your friend why driving after having a few drinks is dangerous.

Contemporary Link

Use your own knowledge and the information in this selection to explain why binge drinking can kill you.

SKILL DEVELOPMENT: READING GRAPHICS

Refer to the designated graphic and answer the following items with *T* (true) or *F* (false).

_____ 1. According to Figure R1, alcohol first affects muscular control.

_____ 2. According to Table R1, a person who has two drinks and weighs 120 pounds would have 13 percent blood alcohol level.

_____ 3. According to Table R2, a blood alcohol level of 0.35 will cause a stupor.

_____ 4. According to Tables R1 and R2, a person weighing 150 pounds who has eight drinks would have impaired vision.

_____ 5. According to Table R3, vodka has more calories than rum.

COMPREHENSION QUESTIONS

After reading the selection, answer the following questions with *a*, *b*, *c*, or *d*.

Main Idea _____ 1. The best statement of the main idea of this selection is
   a. alcohol is involved in over half of the fatal auto accidents each year.
   b. alcohol is processed by the liver.
   c. alcohol is a drug rather than a food.
   d. alcohol is a drug that has a complex and interrelated impact on the body.

Detail _____ 2. When the stomach is full of food, alcohol
   a. goes directly to the liver.
   b. bypasses the liver for the bloodstream.
   c. affects the brain less immediately.
   d. rapidly diffuses through the walls of the stomach.

Detail _____ 3. The brain responds to elevated blood alcohol in all of the following ways except
   a. loss of consciousness.
   b. shrinking.
   c. sedating nerve cells.
   d. increasing production of antidiuretic hormones.

Detail _____ 4. Most of the body's processing of alcohol is done by the
   a. liver.
   b. brain.
   c. stomach.
   d. blood.

Detail _____ 5. Alcohol reaches the liver through
   a. direct absorption.
   b. veins and capillaries.
   c. the intestines.
   d. loss of body water.

Detail _____ 6. When enzymes are not available to degrade the total amount of alcohol consumed, this extra alcohol that cannot be immediately processed by the liver
   a. waits in the liver for enzymes to become available.
   b. circulates to all parts of the body.
   c. is metabolized by the MEOS.
   d. is sent to the stomach for storage.

Detail _____ 7. All of the following are true about ADH except
   a. its production can be accelerated to meet increased demand.
   b. it removes hydrogen from the alcohol.
   c. the number of ADH enzymes is affected by the presence of food in the stomach.
   d. ADH enzymes can reside in the stomach.

Detail

_____ 8. The destruction of vitamin B_6 by alcohol results in
  a. the excretion of bile.
  b. a reduction in the number of red blood cells.
  c. the oversecretion of acid and histamine.
  d. loss of retinol by the rod cells in the eye.

Detail

_____ 9. The negative influence of alcohol on production of new cells is due to
  a. folate excretion.
  b. ulcer formation.
  c. esophagus inflammation.
  d. carcinogenic hazards.

Detail

_____ 10. If a doctor knows that a patient has recently progressed from being a heavy drinker to an abstainer, the doctor should expect that prescribed drugs will be metabolized
  a. at a normal rate.
  b. slower than normal.
  c. faster than normal.
  d. only when the MEOS has returned to normal.

Answer the following with _T_ (true) or _F_ (false).

Inference

_____ 11. The sentence in the first paragraph, "All beverages case conversation whether or not they contain alcohol" is a statement of fact.

Detail

_____ 12. Carbohydrate snacks slow alcohol absorption.

Detail

_____ 13. Alcohol can bypass the liver and flow directly to the brain.

Detail

_____ 14. High doses of alcohol can raise blood pressure.

Detail

_____ 15. Men absorb alcohol faster than women.

VOCABULARY

According to the way the italicized word was used in the selection, indicate _a_, _b_, _c_, or _d_ for the word or phrase that gives the best definition.

_____ 1. "their nonalcoholic _counterparts_" (8)
  a. duplicates
  b. sugars
  c. energy sources
  d. stimulants

_____ 2. "_diffuse_ right through the walls" (18)
  a. disappear
  b. weaken
  c. stick together
  d. spread widely

_____ 3. "_sedating_ inhibitory nerves" (38–39)
  a. soothing
  b. connecting
  c. closing
  d. exciting

_____ 4. "receive a _lethal_ dose" (48)
  a. complete
  b. large
  c. legal
  d. deadly

_____ 5. "remove *toxic* substances"
(75–76)
a. inhibiting
b. foreign
c. poisonous
d. digestive

_____ 6. "MEOS activity is *enhanced*" (83)
a. increased
b. condensed
c. redirected
d. consolidated

_____ 7. "*Prudent* drinkers" (94)
a. older
b. wise
c. experienced
d. addicted

_____ 8. "police say *ruefully*" (103)
a. happily
b. angrily
c. mournfully
d. humorously

_____ 9. "next day's *abstinence*" (136)
a. headache
b. sickness
c. repentance
d. giving up drinking

_____ 10. "*devastates* digestive system"
(184)
a. destroys
b. divides
c. follows
d. loosens

SEARCH THE NET

A friend of yours has a young relative with fetal alcohol syndrome (FAS). There are several groups and associations that offer information, services, and support. Conduct a search to find a Website for such an organization, by E-mail write to your friend describing the services it has to offer. Plan your own search or begin by trying the following:

http://www.nofas.org/whatnofa.htm   National Organization on Fetal
                                      Alcohol Syndrome

http://thearc.org/misc/faslist.html   The Arc's Fetal Alcohol Syndrome
                                      Resource and Materials Guide

READER'S JOURNAL

Name _____   Date _____

Chapter 9

Answer the following to learn about your own learning and reflect on your progress. Use the perforations to tear the assignment out for your instructor.

1. Which of the graphic illustrations did you find easiest to understand? Why?

   _____

   _____

2. When would you use a pie graph rather than a bar graph?

   _____

   _____

3. When would you use a flowchart rather than a table?

   _____

   _____

4. When would you use a bar graph rather than a line graph?

   _____

   _____

5. Why were almost all of the questions on the alcohol selection detail rather than inference questions? _____

6. How did the complex, technical nature of the material affect your comprehension?

   _____

   _____

7. How did your background in science help you with the selection?

   _____

   _____

Rate Flexibility

■ What is your reading rate?

■ How fast should you read?

■ How do faster readers maintain a better reading rate?

■ What are some techniques for faster reading?

■ What happens during regression?

■ Why skim?

■ What is scanning?

Steeplechasing, ex. 1935 by Sybil Andrews/Drewcatt Neate Fine Art Auctioneers, Newbury, Berkshire, UK/Bridgeman Art Library, London/New York.

WHY IS RATE IMPORTANT?

Professors of college reading are far more concerned with comprehension than with a student's rate of reading. They would say that you should not attempt to "speed read" textbooks, and they would be right.

However, when students are asked what they would like to change about their reading, most will say, "I read too slowly. I would like to improve my reading speed." Whether or not this perception is accurate, rate is definitely a concern of college students. Whether you are reading a magazine or a textbook, reading 150 words per minute takes twice as long as reading 300 words per minute. Understanding the factors that contribute to rate can both quell anxiety and help increase reading efficiency.

WHAT IS YOUR READING RATE?

How many words do you read on the average each minute? To find out, read the following selection at your usual reading rate, just as you would have read it before you started thinking about speed. Time your reading of the selection so that you can calculate your rate. Read carefully enough to answer the ten comprehension questions that follow the selection.

▶ **EXERCISE 10.1** *Assessing Rate*

Directions: Time your reading of this selection so that you can compute your words-per-minute rate. To make the calculations easier, try to begin reading on the exact minute, with zero seconds. In other words, begin when the second hand points to twelve. Record your starting and finishing times in minutes and seconds. Then answer the questions that follow. Remember, read the selection at your normal rate.

Starting time: _____ minutes _____ seconds

Sea Lions

"Hey, you guys, hurry up? They're gonna feed the seals!" No visit to the zoo or the circus would be complete without the playful antics of the trained "seal." However, the noisy animal that barks enthusiastically while balancing a ball on its nose is not really a seal at all. In reality, it is a small species of sea lion.

Like all mammals, sea lions are air breathers. Nevertheless, they spend most of their lives in the ocean and are skilled and graceful swimmers. Two species live off the Pacific coast of North America. The California sea lion is the smaller and more southerly. This is the circus "seal." An adult male may measure over seven feet in length and weigh more than 500 pounds. Females are considerably smaller, with a length of six feet and a weight of 200 pounds.

The larger northern, or Steller, sea lion lives off the Alaskan shore in summer and off the California coast in winter. Bulls may weigh over a ton and reach a length of more than eleven feet. Cows weigh some 750 pounds and are about nine feet long. The northern sea lion is generally not as noisy as the California sea lion, but it can bellow loudly when it wants to make its presence known.

At one time, sea lions were hunted almost to extinction for their hides, meat, and oil. Eskimos even stored the valuable oil in pouches made from the sea lion's stomach. Today, sea lions are protected by law, but many fall prey to their natural enemies, the shark and the killer whale. Sea lions are often disliked and sometimes killed by fishermen who accuse them of eating valuable fish and damaging nets. For the most part, the accusations are untrue. The northern sea lion eats mostly "trash fish," which are of little commercial value. The California sea lion prefers squid. Although sea lions do eat salmon, they also eat lampreys, a snake-like parasitic fish that devours salmon in great numbers. By controlling the lamprey population, the sea lion probably saves more salmon than it eats.

Sea lions come ashore in early summer to give birth and to mate. First to arrive are the bulls, which immediately stake out individual territories along the beach. The cows follow and soon give birth to the single pup that each has been carrying since the previous summer. The newborn pup has about a dozen teeth. Its big blue eyes are open from birth and will turn brown after a few weeks.

The pup is born into a tumultuous world of huge, bellowing adults, and it must mature quickly to avoid being trampled by the teeming mob around it. It can move about within an hour, and can be seen scrambling nimbly among its elders within a few days. It doubles its weight in the first month or two. The quick weight gain is largely attributable to the extremely rich milk of the sea lion mother. Low in water and high in protein, the milk is almost 50 percent fat, whereas cow's milk is about 4 percent fat. Zookeepers have found it difficult to provide sea lion pups with adequate nourishment in the absence of the mother. At Marineland of the Pacific, an orphaned pup was successfully raised on a diet of whipping cream, liquified mackerel muscle, calcium caseinate, and a multivitamin syrup. Not a very delectable-sounding menu, perhaps, but the pup loved it.

Throw a human infant into the ocean and it would drown. So would a sea lion baby. The only mammals that are known to swim from birth are whales and manatees. Although it will spend most of its twenty-year life in the ocean, the sea lion pup is at first terrified of water. The mother must spend about two months teaching it to swim.

Mating is no quiet affair among the sea lions. Almost immediately after the birth of the pups the huge bulls begin to wage bloody battles, trying to keep control of their harems of about a dozen cows. Using their long canine teeth as weapons, they fight with great ferocity for possession of the females. Fighting and mating consume so much of the bulls' time and energy during this period that little time is left for sleeping or eating.

At the end of the summer, the sea lions return to the ocean. The bulls, thin and scarred after a busy breeding season, regain their lost weight with several months of active feeding. As the weather grows colder, the huge northern sea lions begin their southward migration; leaving deserted the northern beaches which in warm weather were covered with their massive dark bodies.

The sea lion has to adapt to a considerable range of climate conditions. Its thick blubber and rapid metabolism are assets in the cold northern waters. But the California sea lion ranges as far south as the Galápagos Islands off the coast of South America. How does it adapt to a hot and dry environment?

The most important thing that the sea lion does to stay cool is to sleep in the daytime and take care of business during the cooler night hours. Sea lions in warm climates spend a great deal of time sleeping on the wet sand. Their bodies are designed in such a way that a large surface of the torso comes in contact with the cool ground when the animal lies down. About 10 percent of body heat can be lost in this way. Furthermore, the animal produces nearly 25 percent less heat while it sleeps than it does when awake and active.

Unfortunately, none of the sea lion's cooling mechanisms are highly effective. Ultimately, the animal relies on immersion in the ocean to keep itself cool.

Victor A. Greulach and ᵕincent J. Chiappetta, Biology

958 Words

Finishing time: _____ minutes _____ seconds

Reading time in seconds _____

Words per minute _____ (see chart on page 399)

Comprehension (% correct) _____ %

Mark each statement with *T* for true or *F* for false.

_____ 1. The author focuses mainly on the sea lion's insatiable appetite for high-protein food.

_____ 2. The larger northern sea lion is the circus "seal."

_____ 3. Sea lions eat lampreys, which eat salmon.

_____ 4. Sea lions both give birth and get pregnant in the summer.

Time (Min.)	Words per Minute	Time (Min.)	Words per Minute
3:00	319	5:10	185
3:10	303	5:20	180
3:20	287	5:30	174
3:30	274	5:40	169
3:40	261	5:50	164
3:50	250	6:00	160
4:00	240	6:10	155
4:10	230	6:20	151
4:20	221	6:30	147
4:30	213	6:40	144
4:40	205	6:50	140
4:50	198	7:00	137
5:00	190		

_____ 5. Sea lion milk contains a higher percentage of fat than cow's milk.

_____ 6. Baby sea lions, like whales and manatees, are natural swimmers.

_____ 7. Male sea lions mate with more than one female.

_____ 8. The cool ground provides the sea lion with a greater release of body heat than the ocean water.

_____ 9. In warm climates sea lions sleep more at night than during the day.

_____ 10. Sea lions are able to stay under water because they have gills.

HOW FAST SHOULD YOU READ?

Reading specialists say that the average adult reading speed on relatively easy material is approximately 250 words per minute at 70 percent comprehension. The rate for college students tends to be a little higher, averaging about 300 words per minute on the same type of material with 70 percent comprehension. However, these figures are misleading for a number of reasons.

Anyone who says to you, "My reading rate is 500 words per minute" is not telling the whole story. The question that immediately comes to mind is, "Is that the rate for reading the newspaper or for a physics textbook?" For an efficient reader, no one reading rate serves for all purposes for all materials. Efficient readers demonstrate their flexibility by varying their rate according to their own purpose for reading or according to their prior knowledge of the material being read.

Rate Varies According to Prior Knowledge

One reason textbooks usually require slower reading than newspapers is that the sentences are longer, the language is more formal, the vocabulary and ideas are new, and prior knowledge is limited. If you already have a lot of knowledge on a topic, you can usually read about it at a faster rate than if you are exploring a totally new subject. For example, a student who is already involved in the field of advertising will probably be able to work through the advertising chapter in a business textbook at a faster rate than would be likely with a chapter on a less familiar topic, like supply-side economics. The student may need to slow to a crawl at the beginning of the economics chapter in order to understand the new concepts, but as the new ideas become more familiar, the student can perhaps read at a faster rate toward the end of the chapter.

The "difficulty level" of a textbook is primarily measured by you according to your own prior knowledge of the subject. Another measure combines the length of the sentences and the number of syllables in the words. The longer sentences and words indicate a more difficult level of reading. Freshman textbooks vary greatly in difficulty from field to field and from book to book. Some are written at levels as high as 16th grade level (senior in college), whereas others may be on the 11th or 12th grade level. Even within a single textbook the levels vary from one section or paragraph to another. Unfamiliar technical vocabulary can bring a reader to a complete stop. Complex sentences are more difficult to read than simple, concise statements. Sometimes the difficulty is caused by the complexity of the ideas expressed and sometimes, perhaps unnecessarily, by the formality of the author's writing style.

Before starting on the first word and moving automatically on to the second, third, and fourth at the same pace, take a minute to ask yourself, "Why am I reading this material?" and, based on your answer, vary your speed according to your purpose. Do you want 100 percent, 70 percent, or 50 percent comprehension? In other words, figure out what you want to know when you finish and read accordingly. If you are studying for an examination, you probably need to read slowly and carefully, taking time to monitor your comprehension as you progress. Because 100 percent comprehension is not always your goal, be willing to switch gears and move faster over low-priority material even though you may sacrifice a few details. If you are reading only to get an overview or to verify a particular detail, read as rapidly as possible to achieve your specific purpose.

TECHNIQUES FOR FASTER READING

Concentrate

Fast readers, like fast race car drivers, concentrate on what they are doing; they try to think quickly while they take in the important aspects of the course before them. Although we use our eyes, we actually read with our minds. If our attention is veering off course, we lose some of that cutting-edge quickness necessary for success. Slow readers tend to become bored because ideas are coming too slowly to keep their minds alert. Fast readers are curious to learn, mentally alert, and motivated to achieve.

Distractions that interfere with concentration, as mentioned in Chapter 1, fall into two categories: external and internal. External distractions, the physical happenings around you, are fairly easy to control with a little assertiveness. You can turn the television off or get up and go to another room. You can ask people not to interrupt or choose a place to read where interruptions will be at a minimum. Through prior planning, set yourself up for success and create a physical environment over which you have control.

Internal distractions, the irrelevant ideas that pop into your head while reading, are more difficult to control. As mentioned in Chapter 1, a to-do list will help. Write down your nagging concerns as a reminder for action. Spend less time worrying and more time doing, and you will clear your head for success. Visualize as you read so that you will become wrapped up in the material.

Stop Regressing

During your initial reading of material, have you ever realized halfway down the page that you have no idea what you have read? Your eyes were engaged, but your mind was wandering. Do you ever go back and reread sentences or paragraphs? Were you rereading because the material was difficult to understand, because you were tired and not concentrating, or because you were daydreaming? This type of rereading is called a **regression.**

Regression can be a crutch that allows you to make up for wasted time. If this is a problem for you, analyze when and why you are regressing. If you discern that your regression is due to thinking of something else, start denying yourself the privilege in order to break the habit. Say, "OK, I missed that paragraph because I was thinking of something else, but I'm going to keep going and start paying close attention."

Rereading because you did not understand is a legitimate correction strategy used by good readers who monitor their own comprehension. Rereading because your mind was asleep is a waste of time and a habit of many slow readers.

Daydreaming is a habit caused by lack of involvement with the material. Be demanding on yourself and expect 100 percent attention to the task. Visualize the incoming ideas, and relate the new material to what you already know. Don't just read the words; think the ideas.

Expand Fixations

Your eyes must stop in order to read. These stops, called **fixations,** last a fraction of a second. On the average, 5 to 10 percent of reading time is spent on fixations. Thus, reading more than one word per fixation will reduce your total reading time.

Research on vision shows that the eye is able to see about one-half inch on either side of a fixation point. This means that a reader can see two or possibly three words per fixation. To illustrate, read the following phrase.

in the car

Did you make three fixations, two, or one? Now read the following word.

entertainment

You can read this word automatically with one fixation. As a beginning reader, however, you probably stopped for each syllable for a total of four fixations. If you can read *entertainment*, which has thirteen letters, with one fixation, you can certainly read the eight-letter phrase *in the car* with only one fixation.

Use your peripheral vision on either side of the fixation point to help you read two or three words per fixation. In expanding your fixations, take in phrases or thought units that seem to go together automatically. To illustrate, the following sentence has been grouped into thought units with fixation points.

After lunch,   I studied   in the library   at a table.

By expanding your fixations, the sentence can easily be read with four fixations rather than ten and thus reduce your total reading time.

Monitor Subvocalization

Subvocalization is the little voice in your head that reads for you. Some experts say that subvocalization is necessary for difficult materials, and others say that fast readers are totally visual and do not need to hear the words. Good college readers will probably experience some of both. With easy reading tasks you may find yourself speeding up to the point that you are not hearing every word, particularly the unimportant "filler" phrases. However, with more difficult textbook readings, your inner voice may speak every word. The voice seems to add another sensory dimension to help you comprehend. Because experts say that the inner voice can read up to about 400 words per minute, many college students can make a considerable improvement in speed while still experiencing the inner voice.

Vocalizers, on the other hand, move their lips while reading to pronounce each word. This is an immature habit that should be stopped. Putting a slip of paper or a pencil in your mouth while reading will alert you to lip movement and inspire you to stop.

Preview

Size up your reading assignment before you get started. If it is a chapter, glance through the pages and read the subheadings. Look at the pictures and notice the italicized words and boldface print. Make predictions about what you think the chapter will cover. Activate your schema or prior knowledge on the subject. Pull out your mental computer chip and prepare to bring something to the printed page.

Use Your Pen as a Pacer

The technique of using your pen or fingers as a pacer means pointing under the words in a smooth, flowing motion, moving back and forth from line to line. Although as a child you were probably told never to point to words, it is a very effective technique for improving reading speed. The technique seems to have several benefits. After you overcome the initial distraction, the physical act of pointing tends to improve concentration by drawing your attention directly to the words. The forward motion of your pen tends to keep you from regressing because rereading would interrupt your established rhythm. By pulling your eyes down the page, the pen movement helps set a rapid, steady pace for reading and tends to shift you out of word-by-word reading and move you automatically into phrase reading. Obviously, you cannot read a whole book using your pen as a pacer, but you can start out with this technique. Later, if you feel yourself slowing down, use your pen again to get back on track.

The technique is demonstrated in the following passage. Your pen moves in a *Z* pattern from one side of the column to the other. Because you are trying to read several words at each fixation, your pen does not have to go to the extreme end of either side of the column.

> Rapid reading requires quick thinking
> and intense concentration. The reader
> must be alert and aggressive. Being
> interested in the subject helps improve speed.

As you begin to read faster and become more proficient with the *Z* pattern, you will notice the corners starting to round into an *S*. The *Z* pattern is turning into a more relaxed *S* swirl. When you get to the point of using the *S* swirl, you will be reading for ideas and not be reading every word. You are reading actively and aggressively, with good concentration. Use the *Z* pattern until you find your pen or hand movement has automatically turned into an *S*. The illustration below compares the two.

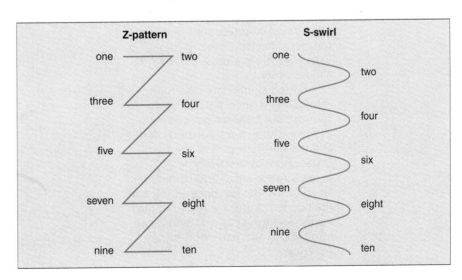

Push and Pace

Be alert and aggressive and try to read faster. Sit up straight and attack the text. Get uncomfortable and force yourself to hurry. Changing old habits is difficult. You will never read faster unless you try to read faster.

Set goals and pace yourself. Count the number of pages in your homework assignments and estimate according to your reading rate how many pages you can read in thirty minutes. Use a paper clip or a sticky note to mark the page you are trying to reach. Push yourself to achieve your goal.

EXERCISE 10.2   *Pacing*

The following passages are written in columns with approximately six words on each line. Using your pen as a pacer, read each passage, and try to make only two fixations per line. A dashed line has been placed down the middle of the column to help you with the fixations. Record your time for reading each passage and then answer the comprehension questions.

Determine your rate from the rate chart at the end of the passage. Before reading, use the title and any clues in the passage to predict organization: Is it definition or description? _____

Skunks

Skunks are small, omnivorous animals found throughout most of the United States. Striped skunks are at home in practically every habitat in every state, living in dens and often beneath abandoned buildings. They can be seen wandering around on cloudy days and at sunset. They eat a variety of fruits, berries, insects, earthworms, other small invertebrates, and some rodents. They sport many color variations, from almost black to almost white.

Spotted skunks are also found throughout a good portion of the country, but they are not common in some of the more northerly states and the northern part of the East Coast. They eat a variety of invertebrates, eggs, and sometimes small birds. The hognose skunk and the hooded skunk are found in the Pacific Southwest and extend down into Mexico and parts of Central America.

In a country where millions of dollars are spent every year on human deodorants, it is not to be wondered that the skunk is not favored. Then, too, the animal can carry rabies. Thus removal procedures are the order of the day when skunks invade suburban areas or campgrounds in large numbers. They can be kept away from buildings by repellents—moth balls (paradichlorobenzene) are effective. Screens can prevent them from getting under buildings. Proper fencing will keep them from chicken coops or apiaries (skunks like honeybees). Removal of insects from golf-course grasses is useful.

Despite their bad reputation, skunks do help keep small rodent and insect populations in check.

Stanley Anderson, *Managing Our Wildlife Resources*

245 words

Time _____

Time (Min.)	Words per Minute	Time (Min.)	Words per Minute
0:30	490	1:10	210
0:40	368	1:20	184
0:50	294	1:30	163
1:00	245	1:40	147

Words per minute _____

Mark each statement with *T* for true or *F* for false.

_____ 1. Skunks eat rats and insects.
_____ 2. Skunks are repelled by moth balls.

EXERCISE 10.3   *Pacing*

Predict organization: Is it time order or definition and example? _____

Cultural Time

Attitudes toward time vary from one culture to another. In one study, for example, the accuracy of clocks was measured in six cultures— Japanese, Indonesian, Italian, English, Taiwanese, and North American (U.S.). The Japanese had the most accurate and Indonesians had the least accurate clocks. A measure of the speed at which people in these six cultures walked, found that the Japanese walked the fastest, the Indonesians the slowest. Another very interesting aspect of cultural time is your "social clock." Your culture and your more specific society maintain a time schedule for the right time to do a variety of important things—for example, the right time to start dating, to finish college, to buy your own home, to have a child. And you no doubt learned about this clock as you were growing up. Based on this social clock you then evaluate your own social and professional development. If you are on time with the rest of your peers —for example, you all started dating at around the same age or you're all finishing college at around the same age —then you will feel well adjusted, competent, and a part of the group. If you are late ("Everyone I graduated with is settled down and well into a career and here I am still waiting tables, waiting for my big break"), you will probably experience feelings of dissatisfaction.

Joseph DeVito, *Messages*

229 words

Time _____

Time (Min.)	Words per Minute	Time (Min.)	Words per Minute
0:30	458	1:10	196
0:40	344	1:20	171
0:50	275	1:30	153
1:00	229	1:40	137

Words per minute _____

Mark each statement with *T* for true or *F* for false.

_____ 1. In the study of cultures, the Indonesians walked the fastest.

_____ 2. According to the author, your position on your social clock is probably connected with your self-satisfaction.

EXERCISE 10.4   *Pacing*

Predict organization: Is it definition and example or simple listing? _____

Breaking Habits

Perhaps the best known of Guthrie's applications are his methods for changing a bad habit. The methods depend on finding out what stimuli evoke the undesirable response and then finding a way of making some other response occur in the presence of those stimuli. This other response should then occur again the next time the stimuli are presented. The emphasis is on the exact stimulus and the exact response that are connected.

Guthrie gives the example of a 10-year-old girl who, whenever she came in the door of her house, threw her hat and coat on the floor. Time and again her mother scolded her and made her go back and hang them up, but to no avail. Finally, the mother realized that the stimulus for the girl to hang up her wraps was the mother's nagging. The next time the girl threw down her wraps, her mother insisted that she put them on again, go outside, come in the door again, and hang up her coat and hat at once. After a few trials of this procedure the girl learned to hang up her wraps. The desired response had been attached to the stimuli of coming in the door and the habit of throwing down the wraps had thus been replaced by the habit of hanging them up. This procedure worked where the previous nagging had failed because this time the mother saw to it that the girl hung up her wraps in the presence of the particular stimuli (those resulting from having just come through the door) that had previously led to the response of throwing the wraps down.

Winfred Hill, *Learning: A Survey of Psychological Interpretations*

271 words

Time _____

Time (Min.)	Words per Minute	Time (Min.)	Words per Minute
0:30	542	1:10	232
0:40	407	1:20	203
0:50	325	1:30	181
1:00	271	1:40	163

Words per minute _____

Mark each statement with *T* for true or *F* for false.

_____ 1. To break the child's habit, the mother had to stop nagging.

_____ 2. The child had to put the coat back on before she could learn to hang it up.

EXERCISE 10.5   *Pacing*

Predict organization: Is it simple listing or description? _____

Shy People

The shy person does not seem to take full advantage of social opportunities to meet new persons and cultivate friendships. In public, shy persons are usually silent. They avoid eye contact and speak quietly when they speak at all. They avoid others whenever possible and take refuge in a private project such as reading.

Privately, shy persons are supersensitive about what other people think about them. They worry about unpleasant aspects of social situations and about leaving others with a negative impression. Increased pulse rate, blushing, perspiration, and rapid heart rate are pronounced in people who are shy in public. But the major problem for shy persons, which distinguishes them from others who have only occasional bouts of shyness, is that they label themselves as being shy. If persons believe they are shy, then they are likely to be especially sensitive to social situations that might produce shyness.

Probably the key to overcoming shyness involves practicing new forms of behavior designed to provide the person with rewarding experiences when meeting others. The chronically shy person has developed a self-defeating pattern of behavior: "I am a shy person, so I am going to be silent and

withdrawn when I meet other people. I meet other
people and keep silent, and no one talks to me.
Therefore, I must be odd and basically shy."

Valerian J. Derlega and Louis H. Janda, *Personal Adjustment*

222 words

Time _____

Time (Min.)	Words per Minute	Time (Min.)	Words per Minute
0:30	444	1:10	190
0:40	333	1:20	167
0:50	266	1:30	148
1:00	222	1:40	133

Words per minute _____

SKIMMING

Skimming is a technique of selectively reading for the main idea. Because it involves processing material at rates of around 900 words per minute, it is not defined by some experts as reading. Skimming involves skipping words, sentences, paragraphs, and even pages. It is a method of quickly overviewing material to answer the question, "What is this about?"

Skimming and previewing are very similar in that both involve getting an overview. Previewing sets the stage for later careful reading, whereas skimming is a substitute for a complete reading. Skimming is useful for material that you want to know about but don't have the time to read. For example, you might want to skim some supplemental articles that have been placed on reserve in the library because your professor expects you only to understand the main idea of each article and a complete reading would be unnecessary. Or you may want to pick up a book and just "get the idea" but not read it completely. Skimming is a useful tool. The technique is presented in the box on page 410.

SCANNING

Because **scanning** is a process of searching for a single bit of information, it is more of a locating skill than a reading skill. A common use of scanning is looking up a number in a telephone book. When scanning for information, you do not need to understand the meaning of the material, but instead you merely need to pinpoint a specific detail. For example, you might find that after reading a chapter on pricing in your marketing textbook, you cannot recall the definition of *price lining*. To locate the information, you would not reread, but

> ## ► READER'S TIP — Techniques for Skimming
>
> ► Read the title and subheadings as well as words in italics and bold-face print to get an idea of what the material is about.
>
> ► Try to get an insight into the organization of the material as discussed in a previous chapter to help you anticipate where the important points will be located. Look for certain organizational patterns and understand their functions:
>
> Listing: Explains items of equal value.
>
> Definition and examples: Defines a term and gives examples to help the reader understand the term.
>
> Time order or sequence: Presents items in chronological order.
>
> Comparison-contrast: Compares similarities and differences of items.
>
> Description: Explains characteristics of an item.
>
> Cause and effect: Shows how one item has produced another.
>
> Problem-solution: Explains the problem, causes, and effects and also suggests a solution.
>
> Opinion-proof: Gives an opinion and then supports it with proof.
>
> ► If the first paragraph is introductory, read it. If not, skip to a paragraph that seems to introduce the topic.
>
> ► Move rapidly, letting your eyes float over the words. Try to grasp the main ideas and the significant supporting details.
>
> ► Notice first sentences in paragraphs and read them if they seem to be summary statements.
>
> ► Skip words that seem to have little meaning, like *a, an,* and *the.*
>
> ► Skip sentences or sections that seem to contain the following:
>
> Familiar ideas
>
> Unnecessary details
>
> Superfluous examples
>
> Restatements or unneeded summaries
>
> Material irrelevant to your purpose
>
> ► If the last paragraph of a section is a summary, read it if you need to check your understanding.

scan the chapter to find the key phrase *price lining* and then review the definition. This same scanning technique works well when using a glossary or an index or when doing on-line research on the Internet.

Researchers use a combination of skimming and scanning. If you are working on a research paper on paranoia, you might have a list of thirty books and articles to read. A complete reading of each reference is probably unnecessary. Instead, you can scan to locate the information relevant to your topic and skim to get the main idea.

> ▶ **READER'S TIP** | **Techniques for Scanning**

> ▶ Figure out the organization of the material. Get an overview of which section will probably contain the information you are looking for.

> ▶ Know specifically what you are looking for. Decide on a key expression that will signal your information, but be ready to switch to a related idea if that doesn't work.

> ▶ Repeat the phrase and hold the image in your mind. Concentrate on the image so that you will recognize it when it comes into view.

> ▶ Move quickly and aggressively. Remember, you are scanning, not reading.

> ▶ Verify through careful reading. After locating your information, read carefully to make sure you have really found it.

Summary Points

■ **What is your reading rate?**

Your individual reading rate can be calculated if you know your total reading time and the total number of words read during that time.

■ **How fast should you read?**

The average adult reading speed on relatively easy material is approximately 250 words per minute at 70 percent comprehension.

■ **How do faster readers maintain a better reading rate?**

Faster readers concentrate, are curious to learn, stay mentally alert, and are motivated to achieve.

■ **What are some techniques for faster reading?**

Before reading, faster readers make predictions, anticipate organization, and activate schemata. Using the pen as a pacer is an important technique that can improve both concentration and rate.

■ **What happens during regression?**

With regression, you must go back and reread material because of inattention. Regression thus wastes time.

■ **Why skim?**

Skimming is a technique that allows you to get a quick overview of the material.

■ **What is scanning?**

Scanning is the process of searching for a single bit of information.

SELECTION 1 ALLIED HEALTH

SKILL DEVELOPMENT: SKIMMING

Skim to find the definition of asthma, which is _____.

SKILL DEVELOPMENT: SCANNING

Scan to find the likely number of passive smoke lung cancer deaths each year as reported by the 1993 EPA report. _____ deaths per year

SKILL DEVELOPMENT: RATE

Now read the selection in order to answer five true-false items. Use your pen as a pacer and time your reading.

Starting time: _____ minutes _____ seconds

Concern over second-hand smoke places limits on smokers

Secondhand smoke harm's a child's health.

PASSIVE SMOKING

From Curtis Byer and Louis Shainberg, *Living Well*

The right of nonsmokers to a smoke-free environment has become an emotional issue. The controversy centers around how seriously the nonsmoker is threatened by **passive smoke,** also called "second-hand" or "side-stream" smoke.

5 Studies have shown that the danger from passive smoking is very real. The smoke rising from a burning cigarette resting in an ashtray or in a smoker's hand is *not* the same as the smoker is inhaling. The smoker is inhaling smoke that has been filtered through the tobacco along the length of the cigarette (and usually by its filter) while the 10 nonsmoker is inhaling smoke that is totally unfiltered. Of course, the smoker also inhales this unfiltered smoke. Unfiltered "side-stream" smoke contains 50 times the amounts of carcinogens, is twice as high in tar and nicotine, has 5 times the carbon monoxide, and has 50 times as much ammonia as smoke inhaled through the 15 cigarette. Although the nonsmoker does not usually inhale side-stream smoke in the concentration that the smoker inhales the **mainstream smoke,** the concentration inhaled still amounts to, for the average person in the United States, the equivalent of smoking one cigarette per day. For people working in very smoky places, 20 such as a bar or office, passive smoking can reach the equivalent of 14 cigarettes per day.

412

Cancer Affecting Passive Smokers

In January 1993, a long-awaited Environmental Protection Agency (EPA) report classified passive cigarette smoke as a human carcinogen that causes lung cancer in nonsmokers. According to the report, passive smoking causes
25 somewhere between 700 and 7000 lung cancer deaths a year in the United States. The agency said that the most likely number is about 3000 deaths a year. This report is expected to result in additional limits on smoking in public places and federal regulations on smoking in the workplace. Predictably, the tobacco industry said that the report was based on inadequate
30 scientific data.

Other Effects

Passive tobacco smoke is a major lung irritant. At the very least, breathing second-hand smoke causes discomfort and coughing. Research has demonstrated that children raised in homes of smokers show early signs of conditions known to lead to heart disease in adulthood. For example, they show in-
35 creased stiffness of the arteries, thickened walls of the heart chambers, and an unfavorable change in the blood's ratio of high-density lipoprotein to low-density lipoprotein.

For people susceptible to **asthma** (attacks of difficult breathing caused by narrowing of the bronchioles), passive smoking can bring on a full-blown
40 asthma attack. This is especially true for children. The incidence of asthma is higher among children who live in homes where someone smokes than among those from homes in which no one smokes. One estimate is that passive smoking may cause up to 100,000 new cases of childhood asthma in the United States each year. Further, asthmatic children from homes in which someone
45 smokes are likely to be in poorer health than asthmatic children from homes where no one smokes. Infants living in homes with smokers also experience twice as many respiratory infections as other infants.

Societal Issues

Many people do not enjoy the smell of burning tobacco, do not want to have the taste of their dinner spoiled by the smell of smoke, do not want their
50 clothing or hair contaminated with the smell of stale smoke, and consider it very rude to be subjected to these intrusions.

Conversely, many smokers are addicted to nicotine and are thus uncomfortable if required to forgo smoking for extended periods. Many have tried to quit smoking without success. To be denied the right to smoke in public
55 places makes it difficult or impossible for them to enjoy restaurant dining and other activities. As long as there are both smokers and nonsmokers we can expect to see conflicts regarding the rights of each group.

629 words

Finishing time: _____ minutes _____ seconds

Calculate Your Reading Rate

Subtract your starting time from your finishing time and then use the time chart to find your rate in words per minute.

Time (Min.)	Words per Minute	Time (Min.)	Words per Minute	Time (Min.)	Words per Minute
1:00	629	2:10	290	3:20	189
1:10	539	2:20	270	3:30	180
1:20	471	2:30	252	3:40	175
1:30	419	2:40	236	3:50	164
1:40	377	2:50	222	4:00	157
1:50	343	3:00	210	4:10	151
2:00	314	3:10	199	4:20	145

Words per minute _____

© 2000 Addison-Wesley Educational Publishers, Inc.

COMPREHENSION QUESTIONS

Mark each statement with *T* for true or *F* for false.

Detail   _____ 1. Side-stream smoke contains 50 times the carcinogens as smoke inhaled through a cigarette.

Detail   _____ 2. The smoker inhales passive smoke and the observer inhales mainstream smoke.

Detail   _____ 3. A nonsmoker in an environment with smokers can inhale the equivalent of 14 cigarettes per day.

Inference   _____ 4. The author suggests that the rate of lung cancer deaths and the incidence of asthma are higher among nonsmokers than among smokers.

Inference   _____ 5. The author suggests that government regulations eventually will solve most of the problems between smokers and nonsmokers.

Thinking About   PASSIVE SMOKING

Why are nonsmokers sometimes reluctant to ask others not to smoke? Why should they not be reluctant?

SKILL DEVELOPMENT: SKIMMING

Skim the first paragraph to find the definition of demographics, which is _____.

SKILL DEVELOPMENT: SCANNING

Scan to find the years the Generation Xers were born. Between _____ and _____

SKILL DEVELOPMENT: RATE

Now read the selection in order to answer five true-false items. Use your pen as a pacer and time your reading.

Starting time: _____ minutes _____ seconds

An Xer produces in a nontraditional work-place.

THE BABY BOOMERS AND THE GENERATION XERS

From Philip Kotler and Gary Armstrong, *Principles of Marketing*

Demographics involve people, and people make up markets. Thus, marketers track demographic trends and groups carefully. Two of today's most important demographic groups are the so-called *baby boomers* and the *generation Xers*.

The Baby Boomers

5 The postwar baby boom, which began in 1946 and ran through 1964, produced 75 million babies. Since then, the baby boomers have become one of the biggest forces shaping the marketing environment. The boomers have presented a moving target, creating new markets as they grew through infancy to preadolescent, teenage, young-adult, and now middle-age years.

10 The baby boomers account for a third of the population but make up 40 percent of the work force and earn over half of all personal income. Today, the aging boomers are moving to the suburbs, settling into home ownership, and raising families. They are also reaching their peak earning and spending years. Thus, they constitute a lucrative market for housing, furniture and ap-

15 pliances, children's products, low-calorie foods and beverages, physical fitness products, high-priced cars, convenience products, and financial services.

The older boomers are now in their fifties; the youngest are in their thirties. Thus, the boomers are evolving from the "youthquake generation" to the "backache generation." They're slowing up, having children, and settling down. They're experiencing the pangs of midlife and rethinking the purpose and value of their work, responsibilities, and relationships. The maturing boomers are approaching life with a new stability and reasonableness in the way they live, think, eat, and spend. The boomers have shifted their focus from the outside world to the inside world. Community and family values have become more important, and staying home with the family has become their favorite way to spend an evening. The upscale boomers still exert their affluence, but they indulge themselves in more subtle and sensible ways.

The Generation Xers

Some marketers think that focusing on the boomers has caused companies to overlook other important segments, especially younger consumers. Focus has shifted in recent years to a new group, those born between 1965 and 1976. Author Douglas Coupland calls them "Generation X," because they lie in the shadow of the boomers and lack obvious distinguishing characteristics. Others call them baby busters, or twentysomethings, or Yiffies—young, individualistic, freedom-minded, few.

Unlike the boomers, the Xers do not share dramatic and wrenching experiences, such as the Vietnam War and Watergate, that might have unified their subculture and lifestyle. However, they do share a different set of influences. Increasing divorce rates and higher employment for mothers have made them the first generation of latchkey kids. Whereas the boomers created a sexual revolution, the Xers have lived in the age of AIDS. Having grown up during times of recession and corporate downsizing, they have developed a pessimistic economic outlook. This outlook is aggravated by problems in finding good jobs—the management ranks already are well stocked with boomers who won't retire for another 20 years or more.

As a result, the Xers are a more skeptical bunch, cynical of frivolous marketing pitches that promise easy success. They know better. The Xers buy lots of products, such as sweaters, boots, cosmetics, electronics, cars, fast food, beer, computers, and mountain bikes. However, their cynicism makes them more savvy shoppers. Because they often did much of the family shopping when growing up, they are experienced shoppers. Their financial pressures make them value conscious, and they like lower prices and a more functional look. The Generation Xers respond to honesty in advertising, as exemplified by Nike ads that focus on fitness and a healthy lifestyle instead of hyping shoes. They like irreverence and sass and ads that mock the traditional advertising approach.

Generation Xers share new cultural concerns. They care about the environment and respond favorably to companies such as The Body Shop and Ben & Jerry's, which have proven records of environmentally and socially responsible actions. Although they seek success, the Xers are less materialistic. They want better quality of life and are more interested in job satisfaction than in sacrificing personal happiness and growth for promotion. They prize experience, not acquisition.

The Generation Xers will have a big impact on the work place and market-place of the future. There are now 40 million of them poised to displace the lifestyles, culture, and materialistic values of the baby boomers. By the year 2010, they will have overtaken the baby boomers as a primary market for al-
65 most every product category.

733 Words

Finishing time: _____ minutes _____ seconds

Calculate Your Reading Rate

Subtract your starting time from your finishing time and then use the time chart to find your rate in words per minute.

Time (Min.)	Words per Minute	Time (Min.)	Words per Minute	Time (Min.)	Words per Minute	Time (Min.)	Words per Minute
1:00	733	2:00	366	3:00	244	4:00	183
1:10	628	2:10	338	3:10	231	4:10	176
1:20	550	2:20	314	3:20	220	4:20	169
1:30	489	2:30	293	3:30	209	4:30	163
1:40	440	2:40	275	3:40	200	4:40	157
1:50	398	2:50	259	3:50	191	4:50	152
						5:00	147

Words per minute _____

COMPREHENSION QUESTIONS

Mark each statement with *T* for true or *F* for false.

_____ 1. Market trends indicate that maturing baby boomers are find-ing family values and home life increasingly more important.

_____ 2. The author suggests that the shared experiences of the Viet-nam War and Watergate may have psychologically unified the baby boom generation.

_____ 3. Some of the Generation Xers are in their thirties today.

_____ 4. The author suggests that the Generation Xers are more cost conscious when spending their money than the baby boomers.

_____ 5. The author suggests that the Generation Xers value prestige and power more than the baby boomers.

 Thinking About THE BABY BOOMERS AND THE GENERATION XERS

Why are generation Xers not pursuing the same goals as the baby boomers?

SKILL DEVELOPMENT: SKIMMING

Skim the selection and mark the following statements with *T* for true or *F* for false.

_____1. The author is expressing her opinion.

_____2. The author is telling about her own experience in the school.

SKILL DEVELOPMENT: SCANNING

Scan to find each of the following details.

1. What was the number of her classroom?
2. What was her teacher's name?

SKILL DEVELOPMENT: RATE

Now read the selection in order to answer ten true-false items. Use your pen as a pacer and time your reading.

Starting time: _____ minutes _____ seconds

A child in California intently concentrates on coloring with a red crayon.

THE SANCTUARY OF SCHOOL[1]

Lynda Barry

I was 7 years old the first time I snuck out of the house in the dark. It was winter and my parents had been fighting all night. They were short on money and long on relatives who kept "temporarily" moving into our house because they had nowhere else to go.

5 My brother and I were used to giving up our bedroom. We slept on the couch, something we actually liked because it put us that much closer to the light of our lives, our television.

At night when everyone was asleep, we lay on our pillows watching it with the sound off. We watched Steve Allen's mouth moving. We watched Johnny

10 Carson's mouth moving. We watched movies filled with gangsters shooting machine guns into packed rooms, dying soldiers hurling a last grenade and beautiful women crying at windows. Then the sign-off finally came and we tried to sleep.

---

[1]"The Sanctuary of School" appeared in *Education Life*, a special feature in *The New York Times*, on January 5, 1992.

15 The morning I snuck out, I woke up filled with a panic about needing to get to school. The sun wasn't quite up yet but my anxiety was so fierce that I just got dressed, walked quietly across the kitchen, and let myself out the back door.

It was quiet outside. Stars were still out. Nothing moved and no one was in the street. It was as if someone had turned the sound off on the world.

I walked the alley, breaking thin ice over the puddles with my shoes. I didn't
20 know why I was walking to school in the dark. I didn't think about it. All I knew was the feeling of panic, like the panic that strikes kids when they realize they are lost.

That feeling eased the moment I turned the corner and saw the dark outline of my school at the top of the hill. My school was made up of about 15
25 nondescript portable classrooms set down on a fenced concrete lot in a run-down Seattle neighborhood, but it had the most beautiful view of the Cascade Mountains. You could see them from anywhere on the playfield and you could see them from the windows of my classroom—Room 2.

I walked over to the monkey bars and hooked my arms around the cold
30 metal. I stood for a long time just looking across Rainier Valley. The sky was beginning to whiten and I could hear a few birds.

In a perfect world my absence at home would not have gone unnoticed. I would have had two parents in a panic to locate me, instead of two parents in a panic to locate an answer to the hard question of survival during a deep fi-
35 nancial and emotional crisis.

But in an overcrowded and unhappy home, it's incredibly easy for any child to slip away. The high levels of frustration, depression, and anger in my house made my brother and me invisible. We were children with the sound turned off. And for us, as for the steadily increasing number of neglected chil-
40 dren in this country, the only place where we could count on being noticed was at school.

"Hey there, young lady. Did you forget to go home last night?" It was Mr. Gunderson, our janitor, whom we all loved. He was nice and he was funny and he was old with white hair, thick glasses, and an unbelievable number of
45 keys. I could hear them jingling as he walked across the playfield. I felt incredibly happy to see him.

He let me push his wheeled garbage can between the different portables as he unlocked each room. He let me turn on the lights and raise the window shades and I saw my school slowly come to life. I saw Mrs. Holman, our
50 school secretary, walk into the office without her orange lipstick on yet. She waved.

I saw the fifth-grade teacher, Mr. Cunningham, walking under the breezeway eating a hard roll. He waved.

And I saw my teacher, Mrs. Clair LeSane, walking toward us in a red coat
55 and calling my name in a very happy and surprised way, and suddenly my throat got tight and my eyes stung and I ran toward her crying. It was something that surprised both of us.

It's only thinking about it now, 28 years later, that I realize I was crying from relief, I was with my teacher, and in a while I was going to sit at my

60 desk, with my crayons and pencils and books and classmates all around me, and for the next six hours I was going to enjoy a thoroughly secure, warm, and stable world. It was a world I absolutely relied on. Without it, I don't know where I would have gone that morning.

Mrs. LeSane asked me what was wrong and when I said "Nothing," she 65 seemingly left it at that. But she asked me if I would carry her purse for her, an honor above all honors, and she asked if I wanted to come into Room 2 early and paint.

She believed in the natural healing power of painting and drawing for troubled children. In the back of her room there was always a drawing table 70 and an easel with plenty of supplies, and sometimes during the day she would come up to you for what seemed like no good reason and quietly ask if you wanted to go to the back table and "make some pictures for Mrs. LeSane." We all had a chance at it—to sit apart from the class for a while to paint, draw, and silently work out impossible problems on 11×17 sheets of 75 newsprint.

Drawing came to mean everything to me. At the back table in Room 2, I learned to build myself a life preserver that I could carry into my home.

We all know that a good education system saves lives, but the people of this country are still told that cutting the budget for public schools is neces- 80 sary, that poor salaries for teachers are all we can manage and that art, music, and all creative activities must be the first to go when times are lean.

Before- and after-school programs are cut and we are told that public schools were not made for baby-sitting children. If parents are neglectful temporarily or permanently, for whatever reason, it's certainly sad, but their un- 85 lucky children must fend for themselves. Or slip through the cracks. Or wander in a dark night alone.

We are told in a thousand ways that not only are public schools not important, but that the children who attend them, the children who need them most, are not important either. We leave them to learn from the blind eye of 90 television, or to the mercy of "a thousand points of light" that can be as far away as the stars.

I was lucky. I had Mrs. LeSane. I had Mr. Gunderson. I had an abundance of art supplies. And I had a particular brand of neglect in my home that allowed me to slip away and get to them. But what about the rest of the kids 95 who weren't as lucky? What happened to them?

By the time the bell rang that morning I had finished my drawing and Mrs. LeSane pinned it up on the special bulletin board she reserved for drawings from the back table. It was the same picture I always drew—a sun in the corner of a blue sky over a nice house with flowers all around it.

100 Mrs. LeSane asked us to please stand, face the flag, place our right hands over our hearts and say the Pledge of Allegiance. Children across the country do it faithfully. I wonder now when the country will face its children and say a pledge right back.

1300 words

Finishing time: _____ minutes _____ seconds

Calculate Your Reading Rate

Subtract your starting time from your finishing time and then use the time chart to find your rate in words per minute.

Time (Min.)	Words per Minute	Time (Min.)	Words per Minute	Time (Min.)	Words per Minute	Time (Min.)	Words per Minute
1:00	1300	4:00	325	5:20	244	6:40	195
2:00	650	4:10	312	5:30	236	6:50	190
3:00	434	4:20	300	5:40	230	7:00	186
3:10	410	4:30	289	5:50	223	7:10	181
3:20	390	4:40	279	6:00	217	7:20	177
3:30	371	4:50	269	6:10	211	7:30	173
3:40	355	5:00	260	6:20	205	7:40	170
3:50	339	5:10	252	6:30	200	7:50	165

Words per minute _____

 THE SANCTUARY OF SCHOOL

Why are fewer college students today pursing teaching careers?

COMPREHENSION QUESTIONS

Mark each statement with *T* for true or *F* for false.

_____ 1. The author uses the word *sanctuary* to mean a place of protection.

_____ 2. She and her brother slept on the couch because the house had only one bedroom.

_____ 3. The story the author tells of leaving for school in the dark occurred in the winter.

_____ 4. The school was made up of portable classrooms.

_____ 5. The author's parents were in a panic to locate her when she left for school that morning alone.

_____ 6. The author recognizes art as a kind of therapy.

_____ 7. The author told Mrs. LeSane about her problems at home.

_____ 8. The author uses an anecdote to support an argument.

_____ 9. The author suggests that her picture reflected her dreams.

_____ 10. The author feels that the government does not do enough to support the children who are falling through the cracks.

READER'S JOURNAL

Name _____ Date _____

Chapter 10

Answer the following to reflect on your own learning and progress. Use the perforations to tear the assignment out for your instructor.

1. How would you describe your concentration on different reading materials? Give at least two examples.

   _____

2. When your mind wanders as you read, what are you usually thinking about?

   _____

3. If your rate of reading is a concern for you, how would you describe the problem?

   _____

4. Did the timed exercises help you read faster? Why or why not?

   _____

5. Will you continue to use your pen as a pacer to speed up your reading? Why or why not?

   _____

6. How much did your reading speed increase as you worked through this chapter?

   _____

   _____

7. How did your increased speed affect your comprehension?

   _____

   _____

8. On what type of reading materials will you try to practice and increase your speed?

   _____

   _____

Test Taking

- Can testwiseness help?
- How should you prepare before a test?
- What should you notice during a test?
- What strategies should you use to read a comprehension passage?
- What are the major question types?
- What hints help with multiple-choice items?
- How do you answer an essay question?

Alfred Jensen (American, 1903–1981). Beginning Study for Changes and Communications (Detail), 1978. Oil on Canvas. The Baltimore Museum of Art. Bequest of Saidie A. May, by exchange.

CAN TESTWISENESS HELP?

Receiving a passing grade on a test should not be the result of a trick; your grade should be a genuine assessment of the mastery of a skill or the understanding of a body of information. High scores, therefore, should depend on preparation, both mental and physical, and not on schemes involving length of responses or the likelihood of *b* or *c* being the right answer. Research has proven many such gimmicks don't work.[1] Tricks will not get you through college. For a well-constructed examination, the only magic formula is mastery of the skill and an understanding of the material being tested.

Insight into test construction and the testing situation, however, will help you achieve at your highest potential. You will perhaps discover answers that you know but didn't think you knew.

The purpose of this chapter is to help you gain points by being aware. You can improve your score by understanding how tests are constructed and what is needed for maximum performance. Study the following and do everything you can both mentally and physically to gain an edge.

STRATEGIES FOR MENTAL AND PHYSICAL AWARENESS

Before Taking a Test

Get Plenty of Sleep the Night Before. How alert can you be with inadequate sleep? Would you want a physician operating on you who had had only a few hours of sleep the night before? The mental alertness that comes from a good night's sleep could add two, four, or even six points to your score and might mean the difference between passing or failing. Why take a chance by staying up late and gambling at such high stakes?

Arrive Five or Ten Minutes Early and Get Settled. If you run in flustered at the last second, you will spend the first five minutes of the test calming yourself rather than getting immediately to work. Do your nerves a favor and arrive early. Find a seat, get settled with pen or pencil and paper, and relax with a classmate by making small talk.

Know What to Expect on the Test. Check beforehand to see if the test will be essay or multiple choice so that you can anticipate the format. Research

---

[1] W. G. Brozo, R. V. Schmelzer, and H. A. Spires, "A Study of Test-Wiseness Clues in College and University Teacher-Made Tests with Implications for Academic Assistance Centers," *College Reading and Learning Assistance*, Technical Report 84-01 (ERIC, 1984), ED 240928.

has shown that studying for both types should stress main ideas, and that it is as difficult to get a good grade on one as it is on another.[2]

Have Confidence in Your Abilities. The best way to achieve self-confidence is to be well prepared. Be optimistic, and approach the test with a positive mental attitude. Lack of preparation breeds anxiety, but positive testing experiences tend to breed confidence. Research shows that students who have frequent quizzes during a course tend to do better on the final exam.[3]

Know How the Test Will Be Scored. If the test has several sections, be very clear on how many points can be earned from each section so that you can set priorities on your time and effort.

Find out if there is a penalty for guessing and, if so, what it is. Because most test scores are based on answering all of the questions, you are usually better off guessing than leaving items unanswered. Research shows that guessing can add points to your score.[4] Know the answers to the following questions and act accordingly:

Are some items worth more points than others?

Will the items omitted count against you?

Is there a penalty for guessing?

Plan Your Attack. At least a week before the test, take an inventory of what needs to be done and make plans to achieve your goals. Preparation can make a difference for both standardized tests and with content area exams. (See the box on page 426.)

During the Test

Concentrate. Tune out both internal and external distractions and focus your attention on the material on the test. Visualize and integrate old and new knowledge as you work. Read with curiosity and an eagerness to learn something new. If you become anxious or distracted, close your eyes and take a few deep breaths to relax and get yourself back on track.

On a teacher-made test, you may have a few thoughts that you want to jot down immediately on the back of the test so that you don't forget them. Do so, and proceed with confidence.

Read and Follow Directions. Find out what you are supposed to do by reading the directions. On a multiple-choice test, perhaps more than one answer is needed. Perhaps on an essay exam you are to respond to only three of five questions. Find out what to do, and then do it.

---

[2]P. M. Clark, "Examination Performance and Examination Set," in D. M. Wark, ed., *Fifth Yearbook of the North Central Reading Association* (Minneapolis: Central Reading Association, 1968), pp. 114–22.
[3]M. L. Fitch, A. J. Drucker, and J. A. Norton, "Frequent Testing as a Motivating Factor in Large Lecture Classes," *Journal of Educational Psychology* 42 (1951): 1–20.
[4]R. C. Preston, "Ability of Students to Identify Correct Responses Before Reading," *Journal of Educational Research* 58 (1964): 181–83.

► READER'S TIP   **Preparing for a Test**

Professors report that students gain awareness before content exams from truthfully writing answers to questions like the following:

► **How will the test look?**

How many parts to the test? What kind of questions will be asked? How will points be counted?

► **What material will be covered?**

What textbook pages are covered? What lecture notes are included? Is outside reading significant?

► **How will you study?**

Have you made a checklist or study guide? Have you read all the material? Will you study notes or annotations from your textbook? Will you write down answers to potential essay questions? Will you include time to study with a classmate?

► **When will you study?**

What is your schedule the week before the test? How long will you need to study? How much of the material do you plan to cover each day? What are your projected study hours?

► **What grade are you honestly working to achieve?**

Are you willing to work for an A, or are you actually trying to earn a B or C?

© 2000 Addison-Wesley Educational Publishers, Inc.

Schedule Your Time. Wear a watch and plan to use it. When you receive your copy of the test, look it over, size up the task, and allocate your time. Determine the number of sections to be covered and organize your time accordingly. As you work through the test, periodically check to see if you are meeting your time goals.

On teacher-made tests, the number of points for each item may vary. Do the easy items first, but spend the most time on the items that will yield the most points.

Work Rapidly. Every minute counts. Do not waste the time that you may need later by pondering at length over an especially difficult item. Mark the item with a check or a dot and move on to the rest of the test. If you have a few minutes at the end of the test, return to the marked items for further study.

Think. Use knowledge, logic, and common sense in responding to the items. Be aggressive and alert in moving through the test.

If you are unsure, use a process of elimination to narrow down the options. Double-check your paper to make sure you have answered every item.

Don't Be Intimidated by Students Who Finish Early. Early departures draw attention and can create anxiety for those still working, but calm yourself with knowing that students who finish early do not necessarily make the highest scores. Even though some students work more rapidly than others, fast workers do not necessarily work more accurately. If you have time, review areas of the test where you felt a weakness. If your careful rethinking indicates another response, change your answer to agree with your new thoughts. Research shows that scores can be improved by making such changes.[5]

After the Test

Analyze Your Preparation. Question yourself after the test, and learn from the experience. Did you study the right material? Do you wish you had spent more time studying any particular topic? Were you mentally and physically alert enough to function at your full capacity?

Analyze the Test. Decide if the test was what you expected. If not, what was unexpected? Did the professor describe the test accurately or were there a few surprises? Why were you surprised? Use your memory of the test to predict the patterns of future tests.

Analyze Your Performance. Most standardized tests are not returned, but you do receive scores and subscores. What do these scores tell you about your strengths and weaknesses? What can you do to improve?

Content area exams are usually returned and reviewed in class. Ask questions and seek a clear understanding of your errors. Find out why any weak responses that were not wrong did not receive full credit. Do you see any patterns in your performance? What are your strengths and weaknesses? Plan to use what you learn to make an even higher grade on the perpetual "next test."

Meet with your professor if you are confused or disappointed. Ask the professor to analyze your performance and suggest means of improvement. Find out if tutorial sessions or study groups are available for you to join. Ask to see an "A" paper. Formulate a plan with your professor for improved performance on the next test.

---

[5]F. K. Berrien, "Are Scores Increased on Objective Tests by Changing the Initial Decision?," *Journal of Educational Psychology* 31 (1940): 64–67.

STRATEGIES FOR STANDARDIZED READING TESTS

Read to Comprehend the Passage as a Whole

While discussing test-taking strategies a student will usually ask, "Should I read the questions first and then read the passage?" Although the answer to this is subject to some debate, most reading experts would advise reading the passage first and then answering the questions. The reasoning behind this position is convincingly logical. Examining the questions first arms the reader with a confusing collection of key words and phrases. Rather than reading to comprehend the author's message, the reader instead searches for many bits of information. Reading becomes fragmented and lacks focus. Few people are capable of reading with five or six purposes in mind. Not only is this method confusing, but it is also detail-oriented and does not prepare the reader for more general questions concerning the main idea and implied meanings.

Too many students muddle through test passages with only the high hopes that they will later be able to recognize answers. In other words, they passively watch the words go by with their fingers crossed for good luck. Avoid this by being aggressive. Attack the passage to get the message. Predict the topic and activate your schema. Interact with the material as you read, and use the thinking strategies of good readers. Monitor and self-correct. Function on a metacognitive level and expect success. Apply what you already know about the reading process to each test passage.

Read to understand the passage as a whole. Each passage has a central theme. Find it. If you understand the central theme or main idea, the rest of the ideas fall into place. The central theme may have several divisions that are developed in the different paragraphs. Attempt to understand what each paragraph contributes to the central theme. Don't worry about the details, other than understanding how they contribute to the central theme. If you find later that a minor detail is needed to answer a question, you can quickly use a key word to locate and reread for accuracy the sentence in which it appears.

Anticipate What Is Coming Next

Most test passages are untitled and thus offer no initial clue for content. Before reading, glance at the passage for a repeated word, name, or date. In other words, look for any quick clue to let you know whether the passage is about Queen Victoria, pit bulls, or chromosome reproduction.

Do not rush through the first sentence. The first sentence further activates your computer chip and sets the stage for what is to come. In some cases, the first sentence may give an overview or even state the central theme. Other times, it may simply pique your curiosity or stimulate your imagination. In any case, the first sentence starts you thinking, wondering, and anticipating. You begin to guess what will come next and how it will be stated.

Anticipating and guessing continue throughout the passage. Some guesses are proven correct and others are proven wrong. When necessary, glance back in the passage to double-check a date, fact, or event that emerges differently than expected. Looking back does not signal weak memory but instead indicates skill in monitoring one's own comprehension.

Read Rapidly, But Don't Allow Yourself to Feel Rushed

Use your pen as a pacer to direct your attention both mentally and physically to the printed page. Using your pen will help you focus your attention, particularly at the times of the test when you feel more rushed.

That uneasy, rushed feeling tends to be with you at the beginning of the test when you have not yet fixed your concentration and become mentally involved with the work. During the middle of the test, you may feel anxious again if you look at your watch and discover you are only half finished and half of your time is gone (which is where you should be). Toward the end of the test, when the first person finishes, you will again feel rushed if you have not yet finished. Check your time, keep your cool, and use your pen as a pacer. Continue working with control and confidence.

Read with Involvement to Learn and Enjoy

Reading a passage to answer five or six questions is reading with an artificial purpose. Usually you read to learn and enjoy, not for the sole purpose of quickly answering questions. Most test passages can be fairly interesting to a receptive reader. Try changing your attitude about reading the passages. Use the thinking strategies of a good reader to become involved in the material. Picture what you read and relate the ideas to what you already know. Think, learn, and enjoy—or at least, fake it.

Self-Test for the Main Idea

Pull it together before pulling it apart. At the end of a passage, self-test for the main idea. This is a final monitoring step that should be seen as part of the reading process. Work efficiently, with purpose and determination. Actively seek meaning rather than waiting for the questions to prod you. Take perhaps ten or fifteen seconds to pinpoint the focus of the passage and to tell yourself the point that the author is trying to make. Again, if you understand the main point, the rest of the passage will fall into place.

Pretend that the passage on the next page is part of a reading comprehension test. Read it using the above suggestions. Note the handwritten reminders to make you aware of a few aspects of your thinking.

Certainly your reading of the passage contained many more thoughts than those indicated on the page. The gossip at the beginning of the passage humanizes the empress and makes it easier for the reader to relate emotionally

Practice Passage A

[Handwritten annotations in margins:]

No title, so glance for key words. Dates? Names?

Great image

Surprise!

Will he be tsar?

What is she planning?

Did she kill him?

Ironic, since she's not Russian

Unusual term

Did she kill them?

Now moving from personal info to accomplishments

Double check years—not long

So, she did little toward human progress

In January 1744 a coach from Berlin bumped its way eastward over ditches and mud toward Russia. It carried Sophia, a young German princess, on a bridal journey. At the Russian border she was met with pomp, appropriate for one chosen to be married to Peter, heir to the Russian throne. The wedding was celebrated in August 1745 with gaiety and ceremony. *Why wait 1½ years?*

For Sophia the marriage was anything but happy because the seventeen-year-old heir was "physically less than a man and mentally little more than a child." The "moronic booby" played with dolls and toy soldiers in his leisure time. He neglected his wife and was constantly in a drunken stupor. Moreover, Peter was strongly pro-German and made no secret of his contempt for the Russian people, intensifying the unhappiness of his ambitious young wife. This dreary period lasted for seventeen years, but Sophia used the time wisely. She set about "russifying" herself. She mastered the Russian language and avidly embraced the Russian faith; on joining the Orthodox church, she was renamed Catherine. She devoted herself to study, reading widely the works of Montesquieu, Voltaire, and other Western intellectuals. *What is that? How?*

When Peter became tsar in January 1762, Catherine immediately began plotting his downfall. Supported by the army, she seized power in July 1762 and tacitly consented to Peter's murder. It was announced that he died of "hemorrhoidal colic." Quickly taking over the conduct of governmental affairs, Catherine reveled in her new power. For the next thirty-four years the Russian people were dazzled by their ruler's political skill and cunning and her superb conduct of tortuous diplomacy. Perhaps even more, they were intrigued by gossip concerning her private life. *What gossip? Lovers?*

Long before she became empress, Catherine was involved with a number of male favorites referred to as her house pets. At first her affairs were clandestine, but soon she displayed her lovers as French kings paraded their mistresses. Once a young man was chosen, he was showered with lavish gifts; when the empress tired of him, he was given a lavish going-away present.

Catherine is usually regarded as an enlightened despot. She formed the Imperial Academy of Art, began the first college of pharmacy, and imported foreign physicians. Her interest in architecture led to the construction of a number of fine palaces, villas, and public buildings and the first part of the Hermitage in Saint Petersburg. Attracted to Western culture, she carried on correspondence with the French *philosophes* and sought their flattery by seeming to champion liberal causes. The empress played especially on Voltaire's vanity, sending him copious praise about his literary endeavors. In turn this *philosophe* became her most ardent admirer. Yet while Catherine discussed liberty and equality before the law, her liberalism and dalliance with the Enlightenment was largely a pose—eloquent in theory, lacking in practice. The lot of serfs actually worsened, leading to a bloody uprising in 1773. This revolt brought an end to all talk of reform. And after the French Revolution, strict censorship was imposed. *Changes to foreign policy accomplishments*

In her conduct of foreign policy, the empress was ruthless and successful. She annexed a large part of Poland and, realizing that Turkey was in decline, waged two wars against this ailing power. As a result of force and diplomacy, Russian frontiers reached the Black Sea, the Caspian, and the Baltic. Well could this shrewd practitioner of power tell her adopted people, "I came to Russia a poor girl. Russia has dowered me richly, but I have paid her back with Azov, the Crimea, and Poland." *What was the point?*

T. Walter Wallbank et al., *Civilization Past and Present*

to the historic figure. Did you anticipate Peter's downfall and Catherine's subsequent relationships? Did you note the shift from gossip to accomplishments, both national and then international? The shift signals the alert reader to a change in style, purpose, and structure.

Take a few seconds to regroup and think about what you have read before proceeding to the questions that follow a passage. Self-test by pulling the material together before you tear it apart. Think about the focus of the passage and then proceed to the questions.

RECOGNIZING THE MAJOR QUESTION TYPES

Learn to recognize the types of questions asked on reading comprehension tests. Although the phraseology may vary slightly, most tests will include one or more of each of the following types of comprehension questions.

Main Idea

Main idea questions test your ability to find the central theme, central focus, gist, controlling idea, main point, or thesis. The terms are largely interchangeable in asking the reader to identify the main point of the passage. Main idea items are stated in any of the following forms:

> The best statement of the main idea is . . . .
>
> The best title for this passage is . . . .
>
> The author is primarily concerned with . . . .
>
> The central theme of the passage is . . . .

Incorrect responses to main idea items tend to fall into two categories. Some responses will be too general and express more ideas than are actually included in the passage. Other incorrect items will be details within the passage that support the main idea. The details may be attention-getting and interesting, but they do not describe the central focus of the passage. If you are having difficulty with the main idea, reread the first and last sentences of the passage. Sometimes, though not always, one of the two sentences will give you an overview or focus.

The following main idea items apply to the passage on Catherine the Great. Notice the handwritten remarks reflecting the thinking involved in judging a correct or incorrect response.

_____ The best statement of the main idea of this passage is
a. Peter lost his country through ignorance and drink. *(Important detail, but focus is on her)*
b. Gossip of Catherine's affairs intrigued the Russian people. *(Very interesting, but a detail)*

    c. Progress for the Russian people was slow to come. *(Too broad and general, or not really covered)*

    d. Catherine came to Russia as a poor girl but emerged as a powerful empress and a shrewd politician. *(Yes, sounds great)*

_____ The best title for this passage is:

    a. Catherine Changes Her Name. *(Detail)*

    b. Peter Against Catherine. *(Only part of the story, so detail)*

    c. Catherine the Great, Empress of Russia. *(Sounds best)*

    d. Success of Women in Russia. *(Too broad—this is only about one woman)*

Details

Detail questions check your ability to locate and understand explicitly stated material. Such items can frequently be answered correctly without a thorough understanding of the passage. To find the answer to such an item, note a key word in the question and then scan the passage for the word or a synonym. When you locate the term, reread the sentence to double-check your answer. Stems for detail questions fall into the following patterns:

> The author states that . . . .
>
> According to the author . . . .
>
> According to the passage . . . .
>
> All of the following are true except . . . .
>
> A person, term, or place is . . . .

Incorrect answers to detail questions tend to be false statements. Sometimes the test maker will trick the unsophisticated reader by using a pompous or catchy phrase from the passage as a distractor. The phrase may indeed appear in the passage and sound authoritative, but on close inspection it means nothing. Read the detail question on Catherine the Great and note the handwritten remarks.

_____ Catherine changed all of the following except *(Look for the only false item as the answer.)*

    a. her religion. *(True, she joined the Orthodox church)*

    b. her name. *(True, from Sophia to Catherine)*

    c. Russia's borders. *(True, she gained seaports)*

    d. the poverty of the serfs. *(The serfs were worse off, but still in poverty, so this is the best answer.)*

Implied Meaning

Questions concerning implied meaning test your ability to look beyond what is directly stated and your understanding of the suggested meaning.

Items testing implied meaning deal with attitudes and feelings, sarcastic comments, snide remarks, the motivation of characters, favorable and unfavorable descriptions, and a host of other hints, clues, and ultimate assumptions. Stems for such items include the following:

> The author believes (or feels or implies). . . .
> It can be inferred from the passage . . . .
> The passage or author suggests . . . .
> It can be concluded from the passage that . . . .

To answer inference items correctly, look for clues to help you develop logical assumptions. Base your conclusions on what is known and what is suggested. Incorrect inference items tend to be false statements. Study the following question.

_____ The author implies that Catherine
   a. did not practice the enlightenment she professed. *(Yes, "eloquent in theory but lacking practice")*
   b. preferred French over Russian architecture. *(not suggested)*
   c. took Voltaire as her lover. *(not suggested)*
   d. came to Russia knowing her marriage would be unhappy. *(not suggested)*

Purpose

The purpose of a reading passage is not usually stated; it is implied. In a sense, the purpose is part of the main idea; you probably need to understand the main idea to understand the purpose. Generally, however, reading comprehension tests include three basic types of passages, and each type tends to dictate its own purpose. Study the following three types.

1. **Factual**

   Identification: gives the facts about science, history, or other subjects

   Strategy: If complex, do not try to understand each detail before going to the questions. Remember, you can look back.

   Example: textbook

   Purposes: to inform, to explain, to describe, or to enlighten

2. **Opinion**

   Identification: puts forth a particular point of view

   Strategy: The author states opinions and then refutes them. Sort out the opinions of the author and the opinions of the opposition.

   Example: newspaper editorial

   Purposes: to argue, to persuade, to condemn, or to ridicule

3. Fiction

Identification: tells a story

Strategy: Read slowly to understand the motivation and interrelationships of characters.

Example: novel or short story

Purposes: to entertain, to narrate, to describe, or to shock

_____ The purpose of the passage on Catherine is
   a. to argue. *(No side is taken)*
   b. to explain. *(Yes, because it is factual material)*
   c. to condemn. *(Not judgmental)*
   d. to persuade. *(No opinion is pushed)*

Vocabulary

Vocabulary items test your general word knowledge as well as your ability to use context to figure out word meaning. The stem of most vocabulary items on reading comprehension tests is as follows:

As used in the passage, the best definition of _____ is _____

Note that both word knowledge and context are necessary for a correct response. The item is qualified by "As used in the passage," and thus you must go back and reread the sentence (context) in which the word appears to be sure you are not misled by a multiple meaning. To illustrate, the word *sports* means *athletics* as well as *offshoots from trees*. As a test taker you would need to double-check the context to see which meaning appears in your test passage. In addition, if you knew only one definition of the word *sport*, rereading the sentence would perhaps suggest the alternate meaning to you and help you get the item correct. Note the following example.

_____ As used in the passage, the best definition of dreary is *(2nd paragraph)*
   a. sad. *(Yes, unhappiness is used in the previous sentence)*
   b. commonplace. *(Possible, but not right in the sentence)*
   c. stupid. *(Not right in the sentence)*
   d. neglected. *(True, but not the definition of the word)*

STRATEGIES FOR MULTIPLE-CHOICE ITEMS

Consider All Alternatives Before Choosing an Answer

Read all the options. Do not rush to record an answer without considering all the alternatives. Be careful, not careless, in considering each option. Multiple-choice test items usually ask for the best choice for an answer, not any choice that is reasonable.

_____ Peter was most likely called a "moronic booby" because
  a. he neglected Catherine.
  b. he drank too much.
  c. he disliked German customs.
  d. he played with dolls and toys.

Although the first three answers are true and reasonable, the last answer seems to be most directly related to that particular name.

Anticipate the Answer and Look for Something Close to It

As you read the beginning of a multiple-choice item, anticipate what you would write for a correct response. Develop an answer in your mind before you read the options, and then look for a response that corroborates your thinking.

_____ The author suggests that Catherine probably converted to the Russian Orthodox church because ... *she wanted to rule the country and wanted the people to think of her as Russian, rather than German.*
  a. she was a very religious person.
  b. Peter wanted her to convert.
  c. she was no longer in Germany.
  d. she wanted to appear thoroughly Russian to the Russian people.

The last answer most closely matches the kind of answer you were anticipating.

Avoid Answers with 100 Percent Words

All and *never* mean 100 percent, without exceptions. A response containing either word is seldom correct. Rarely can a statement be so definitely inclusive or exclusive. Other 100 percent words to avoid are:

no	none	only
every	always	must

_____ Catherine the Great was beloved by all the Russian people.

Answer with *true* or *false*.

All means 100 percent and thus is too inclusive. Surely one or two Russians did not like Catherine, so the answer must be false.

Consider Answers with Qualifying Words

Words like *sometimes* and *seldom* suggest frequency but do not go so far as to say *all* or *none*. Such qualifying words can mean more than *none* and less than *all*. By being so indefinite, the words are difficult to dispute. Therefore, qualifiers are more likely to be included in a correct response. Other qualifiers are:

few	much	often	may
many	some	perhaps	generally

_____ Catherine was beloved by many of the Russian people.

Answer with *true* or *false*.

The statement is difficult to dispute, given Catherine's popularity. An uprising against her occurred, but it was put down, and she maintained the support of many of the Russian people. Thus the answer would be *true*.

Choose the Intended Answer Without Overanalyzing

Try to follow logically the thinking of the test writer rather than overanalyzing minute points. Don't make the question harder than it is. Use your common sense and answer what you think was intended.

_____ Catherine was responsible for Peter's murder.

Answer with *true* or *false*.

This is false in that Catherine did not personally murder Peter. On the other hand, she did "tacitly consent" to his murder, which suggests responsibility. After seizing power, it was certainly in her best interest to get rid of Peter permanently. Perhaps without Catherine, Peter would still be playing with his toys, so the intended answer is *true*.

True Statements Must Be True Without Exception

A statement is either totally true or it is incorrect. Adding an incorrect *and, but,* or *because* phrase to a true statement makes the statement false and thus an unacceptable answer. If a statement is half true and half false, mark it false.

_____ Catherine was an enlightened despot who did her best to improve the lot of all her people.

Answer with *true* or *false*.

It is true that Catherine was considered an enlightened despot, but she did very little to improve the lot of the serfs. In fact, conditions for the serfs worsened. The statement is half true and half false, so it must be answered *false*.

If Two Options Are Synonymous, Eliminate Both

If *both* is not a possible answer and two items say basically the same thing, then neither can be correct. Eliminate the two and spend your time on the others.

_____ The purpose of this passage is
a. to argue.
b. to persuade.
c. to inform.
d. to entertain.

Because *argue* and *persuade* are basically synonymous, you can eliminate both and move to the other options.

Study Similar Options to Determine the Differences

If two similar options appear, frequently one of them will be correct. Study the options to see the subtle difference intended by the test maker.

_____ Catherine was
a. unpopular during her reign.
b. beloved by all of the Russian people.
c. beloved by many of the Russian people.
d. considered selfish and arrogant by the Russians.

The first and last answers are untrue. Close inspection shows that the 100 percent *all* is the difference between the second and third answer that makes the second answer untrue. Thus, the third answer with the qualifying word is the correct response.

Use Logical Reasoning If Two Answers Are Correct

Some tests include the options *all of the above* and *none of the above*. If you see that two of the options are correct and you are unsure about a third choice, then *all of the above* would be a logical response.

_____ Catherine started
a. the Imperial Academy of Art.
b. the first college of pharmacy.
c. the Hermitage.
d. all of the above.

If you remembered that Catherine started the first two but were not sure about the Hermitage, *all of the above* would be your logical option because you know that two of the above *are* correct.

Look Suspiciously at Directly Quoted Pompous Phrases

In searching for distractors, test makers sometimes quote a pompous phrase from the passage that doesn't make much sense. Students read the phrase and think, "Oh yes, I saw that in the passage. It sounds good, so it must be right." Beware of such repetitions and make sure they make sense before choosing them.

_____ In her country Catherine enacted
   a. few of the progressive ideas she championed.
   b. the liberalism of the Enlightenment.
   c. laws for liberty and equality.
   d. the liberal areas of the philosophers.

The first response is correct because Catherine talked about progress but did little about it. The other three answers sound impressive and are quoted from the text, but are totally incorrect.

Simplify Double Negatives by Canceling Out Both

Double negatives are confusing to unravel and, in addition, time consuming to think through. Simplify a double negative statement by first canceling out both negatives. Then reread the statement without the confusion of the two negatives, which at this point have canceled each other out, and decide on the accuracy of the statement.

_____ Catherine's view of herself was not that of an unenlightened ruler.

Answer with *true* or *false*.

Cancel out the two negatives, the *not* and the *un* in the word *unenlightened*. Reread the sentence without the negatives and decide on its accuracy: Catherine's view of herself was that of an enlightened ruler. The statement is correct so the answer is *true*.

Use Can't-Tell Responses If Clues Are Insufficient

Mark an item *can't tell* only if you are not given clues on which to base an assumption. In other words, there is no evidence to indicate the statement is either true or false.

_____ Catherine the Great had no children.

From the information in this passage, which is the information on which your reading test is based, you do not have any clues to indicate whether she did or did not have children. Thus, the answer must be *can't tell*.

Validate True Responses on "All of the Following Except"

In this type of question, you must recognize several responses as correct and find the one that is incorrect. Corroborate each response and, by the process of elimination, find the one that does not fit.

Note Oversights on Hastily Constructed Tests

Reading tests developed by professional test writers are usually well constructed and do not contain obvious clues to the correct answers. However, some teacher-made tests are hastily constructed and contain errors in test making that can help a student find the correct answer. Do not, however, rely on these flaws to make a big difference in your score because they should not occur in a well-constructed test.

Grammar. Eliminate responses that do not have subject-verb agreement. The tense of the verb as well as modifiers such as *a* or *an* can also give clues to the correct response.

_____ Because of his described habits, it is possible that Peter was an
a. hemophiliac.
b. alcoholic.
c. Catholic.
d. barbarian.

The *an* suggests an answer that starts with a vowel. Thus *alcoholic* is the only possibility.

Clues from Other Parts of the Test. Because the test was hastily constructed, information in one part of the test may help you with an uncertain answer.

_____ Not only was Peter childlike and neglectful, but he was also frequently
a. abusive.
b. drunk.
c. dangerous.
d. out of the country.

The previous question gives this answer away by stating that he was possibly an alcoholic.

Length. On poorly constructed tests, longer answers are more frequently correct.

_____ The word *cunning* used in describing Catherine suggests that she was
a. evil
b. dishonest.
c. untrustworthy.
d. crafty and sly in managing affairs.

In an effort to be totally correct without question, the test maker has made the last answer so complete that its length gives it away.

Absurd Ideas and Emotional Words. Avoid distractors with absurd ideas or emotional words. The test maker probably got tired of thinking of distractors and in a moment of weakness included nonsense.

_____ As used in the passage, the term *house pets* refers to
a. Peter's toys.
b. Catherine's favorite lovers.
c. the dogs and cats in the palace.
d. trained seals that performed for the empress.

Yes, the test maker has, indeed, become weary. The question itself has very little depth, and the last two answers are particularly flippant.

▶ EXERCISE 11.1   *Reading with Understanding*

Pretend that the following selection is a passage on a reading comprehension test. Use what you have learned to read with understanding and answer the questions.

It seems odd that one of the most famous figures of antiquity—the founder of a philosophical movement—was a vagrant with a criminal record. Diogenes the Cynic began life as the son of a rich banker. This fact may not seem so strange when one remembers the rebellious young people of the late 1960s in America, many of whom also came from affluent families.

The turning point in Diogenes' life came when his father, Hikesios, treasurer of the flourishing Greek commercial city of Sinope in Asia Minor, was found guilty of "altering the currency." Since Hikesios was a sound money man concerned about maintaining the high quality of the Sinopean coinage, this was obviously a miscarriage of justice. The Persian governor of nearby Cappadocia had issued inferior imitations of the Sinopean currency, and Hikesios, who realized that this currency was undermining the credit of Sinope, ordered the false coins to be defaced in order to put them out of circulation. But a faction of Sinopean citizens—it is not clear whether for economic or political reasons—successfully prosecuted Hikesios. Hikesios was imprisoned, and Diogenes, who was his father's assistant, was exiled. He eventually settled in Athens.

The shock of this experience caused Diogenes to become a rebel against society—to continue "altering the currency," but in a different way. He decided to stop the circulation of all false values, customs, and conventions. To achieve this goal, he adopted the tactics that made him notorious—complete freedom in speaking out on any subject and a type of outrageous behavior that he called "shamelessness."

Diogenes called free speech "the most beautiful thing in the world" because it was so effective a weapon. He shocked his contemporaries with such statements as "Most men are so nearly mad that a finger's breadth would make the difference." He advocated free love, "recognizing no other union than that of the man who persuades with the woman who consents." He insisted that "the love of money is the mother of all evils"; when some temple officials caught someone stealing a bowl from a temple, he said, "The great thieves are leading away the little thief." He liked to point out that truly valuable things cost little, and vice versa. "A statue sells for three thousand drachmas, while a quart of flour is sold for two copper coins." And when he was asked what was the right time to marry, he replied, "For a young man not yet; for an old man never at all."

Diogenes' "shamelessness"—his eccentric behavior—was his second weapon against the artificiality of conventional behavior as well as his means of promoting what he called "life in accordance with nature," or self-sufficiency. He believed that gods are truly self-sufficient and that people should emulate them: "It is the privilege of the gods to want nothing, and of men who are most like gods to want but little." It was said that he "discovered the means of adapting himself to circumstances through watching a mouse running about, not looking for a place to lie down, not afraid of the dark, not seeking any of the things that are considered dainties." And he got the idea for living in a large pottery jar—his most famous exploit—from seeing a snail carrying its own shell. Above all, Diogenes admired and emulated the life-style of dogs because of their habit of "doing everything in public." For this reason he was called *Kynos*, "the Dog," and his disciples were called Cynics.

"We live in perfect peace," one Cynic wrote, "having been made free from every evil by the Sinopean Diogenes." Eventually the citizens of Sinope also came to honor their eccentric exile with an inscription in bronze:

Even bronze grows old with time, but your fame, Diogenes, not all eternity shall take away. For you alone did point out to mortals the lesson of self-sufficiency, and the easiest path of life.

T. Walter Wallbank et al., Civilization Past and Present

Identify each question type and answer with *a, b, c,* or *d.* Explain what is wrong with the incorrect distractors.

_____ 1. The best statement of the main idea of this passage is

(Question type _____)   (Explain errors)

   a. the turning point in the life of Diogenes
      was the imprisonment of his father.   _____

   b. the eccentric Diogenes founded a phil-
      osophy and promoted self-sufficiency.   _____

   c. Diogenes became famous for living
      the life of a dog.   _____

   d. the Greek way of life and thought changed
      under the influence of Diogenes.   _____

_____ 2. The best title for this passage is

(Question type _____)   (Explain errors)

   a. Diogenes Shocks Athens.   _____
   b. Great Greek Philosophers.   _____
   c. The Eccentric Behavior of a Philosopher.   _____
   d. Diogenes, the Self-Sufficient Cynic.   _____

_____ 3. Diogenes's father

(Question type _____)   (Explain errors)

a. was exiled from Athens.   _____

b. destroyed counterfeit money.   __ _____

c. stole from the treasury.   __ _____

d. was treasurer of Sinope and Cappadocia. _____

_____ 4. The author believes that Diogenes was all of the following except

(Question type _____)   (Explain errors)

a. uninhibited by tradition.   _____

b. insincere in not practicing what he preached.   _____

c. angered by his father's persecution.   _____

d. vocal in advocating free speech.   _____

_____ 5. The author's purpose is to

(Question type _____)   (Explain errors)

a. argue.   _____

b. inform.   __ _____ __

c. ridicule.   __ _____ __

d. persuade.   _____

_____ 6. As used in the passage, the best definition of *affluent* is

(Question type _____)   (Explain errors)

a. wealthy.   _____

b. close-knit.   _____

c. loving.   _____

d. politically prominent.   _____

STRATEGIES FOR CONTENT AREA EXAMS

Almost all professors would say that the number one strategy for scoring high on content exams is to study the material. Although this advice is certainly on target, there are other suggestions that can help you gain an edge.

Multiple-Choice Items

Multiple-choice, true-false, or matching items on content area exams are written to evaluate the following three categories: factual knowledge, conceptual comprehension, and application skill. Factual questions tap your knowledge of names, definitions, dates, events, and theories. Conceptual comprehension questions evaluate your ability to see relationships, notice similarities and differences, and combine information from different parts of a chapter. Application questions provide the opportunity to generalize from a theory to a real-life illustration, and they are particularly popular in psychology and sociology. The following is an example of an application question from psychology.

_____ An illustration of obsessive-compulsive behavior is
    a. Maria goes to the movies most Friday nights.
    b. Leon washes his hands over a hundred times a day.
    c. Pepe wants to buy a car.
    d. Sue eats more fish than red meat.

The second response is obviously correct, but such questions can be tricky if you have not prepared for them. To study for a multiple-choice test, make lists of key terms, facts, and concepts. Quiz yourself on recognition and general knowledge. Make connections and be sure you know similarities and differences. Lastly, invent scenarios that depict principles and concepts. Use your own knowledge, plus the previous suggestions for multiple-choice tests, to separate answers from distractors.

Short-Answer Items

Professors ask short-answer questions because they want you to use your own words to describe or identify. For such questions, be sure that you understand exactly what the professor is asking you to say. You do not want to waste time writing more than is needed, but on the other hand, you do not want to lose points for not writing enough. Study for short-answer items by making lists and self-testing, just as you do when studying for multiple-choice items.

Essay Questions

Essay answers demand more effort and energy from the test taker than multiple-choice items. Rather than simply recognizing correct answers, you must recall, create, and organize. On a multiple-choice test, all the correct answers are somewhere before you. On an essay exam, however, the only thing in front of you is a question and a blank sheet of paper. This blank sheet of paper can be intimidating to many students. Your job is to recall appropriate ideas for a response and pull them together under the central theme designated in the question. The following suggestions can help you respond effectively.

Translate the Question. Frequently the "question" is not a question at all. It may be a statement that you must first turn into a question. Read and reread this statement that is called a *question*. Be sure you understand it and then reword it into a question. Even if you begin with a question, translate it into your own words. Simplify the question into straight terms that you can understand. Break the question into its parts.

Convert the translated parts of the questions into the approach that you will need to use to answer the question. Will you define, describe, explain, or compare? State what you will do to answer. In a sense, this is a behavioral statement. The following example demonstrates the process.

Statement to Support: It is both appropriate and ironic to refer to Catherine as one of the great rulers of Russia.

Question: Why is it both appropriate and ironic to refer to Catherine as one of the great rulers of Russia?

Translation: The question has two parts:

1. What did Catherine do that was really great?
2. What did she do that was the opposite of what you would expect (irony) of a great Russian ruler?

Response Approach: List what Catherine did that was great and list what she did that was the opposite of what you would expect of a great Russian ruler. Relate her actions to the question. (See page 430.)

Answer the Question. Your answer should be in response to the question that is asked and not a summary of everything you know about a particular subject. Write with purpose so that the reader can understand your views and relate your points to the subject. Padding your answer by repeating the same idea or including irrelevant information is obvious to graders and seldom appreciated.

Example: An inappropriate answer to the question "Why is it both appropriate and ironic to refer to Catherine as one of the great rulers of Russia?"

> Catherine was born in Germany and came to Russia as a young girl to marry Peter. It was an unhappy marriage that lasted seventeen years. She . . .

(This response does not answer the question: it is a summary.)

Organize Your Response. Do not write the first thing to pop into your head. Take a few minutes to brainstorm and jot down ideas. Number the ideas in the order that you wish to present them and use this plan as your outline for writing.

In your first sentence, establish the purpose and direction of your response. Then list specific details that support, explain, prove, and develop your point. Reemphasize the points in a concluding sentence and restate your purpose. Whenever possible, use numbers or subheadings to simplify your message for the reader. If time runs short, use an outline or a diagram to express your remaining ideas.

Example: To answer the previous question, think about the selection on Catherine and jot down the ideas that you would include in a response.

Use an Appropriate Style. Your audience for this response is not your best friend or buckaroo but your learned professor who is going to give you a grade. Be respectful. Do not use slang. Do not use phrases like "as you know" or "well." They may be appropriate in conversation, but they are not appropriate in formal writing.

I. <u>Appropriate</u>
1. Acquired land
2. Art, medicine, buildings
3. 34 years
4. Political skill & foreign diplomacy

II. <u>Ironic (opposite)</u>
1. Not Russian
2. Killed Peter
3. Serfs very poor
4. Revolt against her

Avoid empty words and thoughts. Words like *good, interesting,* and *nice* say very little. Be more direct and descriptive in your writing.

State your thesis, supply proof, and use transitional phrases to tie your ideas together. Words like *first, second,* and *finally* help to organize enumerations. Terms like *however* and *on the other hand* show a shift in thought. Remember, you are pulling ideas together, so use phrases and words to help the reader see relationships.

Study this response to the question for organization, transition, and style.

Catherine was a very good ruler of Russia. She tried to be Russian but she was from Germany. Catherine was a good politician and got Russia seaports on the Baltic, Caspian, and Black Sea. She had many boyfriends and there was gossip about her. She did very little for the Serfs because they remained very poor for a long time. She built nice buildings and got doctors to help people. She was not as awesome as she pretended to be.

(Note the total lack of organization, the weak language, inappropriate phrases, and the failure to use traditional words.)

Be Aware of Appearance. Research has shown that, on the average, essays written in a clear, legible hand receive a grade level higher score than essays written somewhat illegibly.[6] Be particular about appearance and considerate of the reader. Proofread for correct grammar, punctuation, and spelling.

Predict and Practice. Predict possible essay items by using the table of contents and subheadings of your text to form questions. Practice brainstorming to answer these questions. Review old exams for an insight both into the questions and the kinds of answers that received good marks. Outline answers to possible exam questions. Do as much thinking as possible to prepare yourself to take the test before you sit down to begin writing.

View Your Response Objectively for Evaluation Points. Respond to get points. Some students feel that filling up the page deserves a passing grade. They do not understand how a whole page written on the subject of Catherine could receive no points.

Although essay exams seem totally subjective, they cannot be. Students need to know that a professor who gives an essay exam grades answers according to an objective scoring system. The professor examines the paper for certain relevant points that should be made. The student's grade reflects the quantity, quality, and clarity of these relevant points.

Unfortunately, essay exams are shrouded in mystery. The hardest part of answering an item is to figure out what the professor wants. Ask yourself, "What do I need to say to get enough points to pass or to make an *A?*"

Do not add personal experiences or extraneous examples unless they are requested. You may be wasting your time by including information that will give you no points. Stick to the subject and the material. Demonstrate to the professor that you know the material by selectively using it in your response.

The professor scoring the response to the question about Catherine used the following checklist for evaluation.

Appropriate	Ironic
1. Acquired land	1. Not Russian
2. Art, medicine, buildings	2. Killed Peter
3. 34 years	3. Serfs very poor
4. Political skill and foreign diplomacy	4. Revolt against her

The professor determined that an *A* paper should contain all of the items. In order to pass, a student should give 5 of the 8 categories covered. Listing and explaining less than five would not produce enough points to pass. Naturally, the professor would expect clarity and elaboration in each category.

---

[6]H. W. James, "The Effect of Handwriting upon Grading," *English Journal* 16 (1927): 180–85.

© 2000 Addison-Wesley Educational Publishers, Inc.

> ## READER'S TIP · Key Words in Essay Questions
>
> The following key words of instruction appear in essay questions.
>
> ► *Compare:* List the similarities between things.
>
> ► *Contrast:* Note the differences between things.
>
> ► *Criticize:* State your opinion and stress the weaknesses.
>
> ► *Define:* State the meaning so that the term is understood, and use examples.
>
> ► *Describe:* State the characteristics so that the image is vivid.
>
> ► *Diagram:* Make a drawing that demonstrates relationships.
>
> ► *Discuss:* Define the issue and elaborate on the advantages and disadvantages.
>
> ► *Evaluate:* State positive and negative views and make a judgment.
>
> ► *Explain:* Show cause and effect and give reasons.
>
> ► *Illustrate:* Provide examples.
>
> ► *Interpret:* Explain your own understanding of a topic that includes your opinions.
>
> ► *Justify:* Give proof or reasons to support an opinion.
>
> ► *List:* Record a series of numbered items.
>
> ► *Outline:* Sketch out the main points with their significant supporting details.
>
> ► *Prove:* Use facts as evidence in support of an opinion.
>
> ► *Relate:* Connect items and show how one influences another.
>
> ► *Review:* Write an overview with a summary.
>
> ► *Summarize:* Retell the main points.
>
> ► *Trace:* Move sequentially from one event to another.

After the Test, Read an **A** ***Paper.*** Maybe the *A* paper will be yours. If so, share it with others. If not, ask to read an *A* paper so that you will have a model from which to learn. Ask your classmates or ask the professor. You can learn a lot from reading a good paper; you can see what you should and could have done.

When your professor returns a multiple-choice exam, you can reread items and analyze your mistakes to figure out what you did wrong. However, you cannot review essay exams so easily. You may get back a C paper with only a word or two of comment and never know what you should have done.

Ideally, essay exams should be returned with an example of what would have been a perfect *A* response so that students can study and learn from a perfect model and not make the same mistakes on the next test, but this is seldom, if ever, done. Your best bet is to ask to see an *A* paper.

Study the following response to the previous question. The paper received an *A*.

> To call Catherine one of the great rulers of Russia is both appropriate and ironic. It is appropriate because she expanded the borders of Russia. Through her cunning, Russia annexed part of Poland and expanded the frontier to the Black Sea, Caspian, and Baltic. Catherine professed to be enlightened and formed an art academy, a college of pharmacy, and imported foreign physicians. She built many architecturally significant buildings, including the Hermitage. For thirty-four years she amazed the Russian people with her political skill and diplomacy.
>
> On the other hand, Catherine was not a great Russian, nor was she an enlightened leader of all the people. First, she was not Russian; she was German, but she had worked hard to "russify" herself during the early years of her unhappy marriage. Secondly and ironically, she murdered the legitimate ruler of Russia. When she seized power, she made sure the tsar quickly died of "hemorrhoidal colic." Third, she did nothing to improve the lot of the poor serfs and after a bloody uprising in 1773, she became even more despotic. Yet, Catherine was an engaging character who, through her cunning and intellect, has become known to the world in history books as "Catherine the Great."

(Note the organization, logical thinking, and use of transitions in this response.)

LOCUS OF CONTROL

Have you ever heard students say, "I do better when I don't study," or "No matter how much I study, I still get a C"? According to Julian Rotter, a learning theory psychologist who believes that people develop attitudes about control of their lives, such comments reflect an external locus of control regarding test taking.[7] Such "externalizers" feel that fate, luck, or others control what happens to them. Since they feel they can do little to avoid what befalls them, they do not face matters directly and thus do not take responsibility for failure or credit for success.

People who have an internal locus of control, on the other hand, feel that they, rather than "fate," have control over what happens to them. Such students might evaluate test performance by saying, "I didn't study enough" or "I should have spent more time organizing my essay response." "Internalizers" feel their rewards are due to their own actions, and thus they take steps to be sure they receive those rewards. When it comes to test taking, be an "internalizer," take control, and accept the credit for your success.

---

[7]J. Rotter, "External Control and Internal Control," *Psychology Today*, 5(1) (1971): 37–42.

Summary Points

- ### Can testwiseness help?

  Test taking is a serious part of the business of being a college student. Preparation and practice can lead to improved scores on both standardized reading tests and content area exams.

- ### How should you prepare before a test?

  Study according to the type of test you are taking. Plan your study times so that you are not cramming. Arrive rested and alert.

- ### What should you notice during a test?

  Read the directions and keep up with the time.

- ### What strategies should you use to read a comprehension passage?

  Items on standardized reading tests tend to follow a predictable pattern and include five major questions types. Learn to recognize these types and the skills needed for answering each.

- ### What are the major question types?

  They are (1) main idea, (2) details, (3) inference, (4) purpose, and (5) vocabulary.

- ### What hints help with multiple-choice items?

  Be careful, not careless; consider all options; notice key words; and use logical reasoning.

- ### How do you answer an essay question?

  Be sure you understand the question, brainstorm your response, organize your thoughts, and write in paragraphs with specific examples.

Go Electronic!

For additional readings, exercises, and Internet activities, visit this book's Website at:
http://www.awlonline.com/smithBTG

For even more activities, visit the Longman English pages at:
http://longman.awl.com/englishpages

If you need a user name and password, please see your instructor.

Take a Road Trip to Hollywood! Be sure to visit the Test Taking module in your Reading Road Trip CD-ROM for multimedia tutorials, exercises, and tests.

READER'S JOURNAL

Name _____ Date _____

Chapter 11

Answer the following to learn about your own learning and reflect on your and progress. Use the perforations to tear the assignment out for your instructor.

1. How were you or were you not physically prepared for your last test?

   _____

2. How did you divide your time on the last test?

   _____

3. In what subjects do you have test anxiety? Why?

   _____

4. Are you anxious about public speaking? Why or why not?

   _____

5. Review your correct and incorrect responses to the comprehension questions in this text. What type of question seems to be most difficult for you?

   _____

6. What type of question do you usually get correct?

   _____

   _____

7. How would you diagnose your problems on multiple-choice tests?

   _____

   _____

8. How would you describe the difference in your preparation for a multiple-choice or an essay exam in history?

   _____

   _____

9. Do you score higher on multiple-choice or essay exams? Why?

   _____

   _____

Textbook Application

- Can you transfer your reading skills?
- Can you plan your attack?
- Can you succeed?

Giuseppe Arcimboldo (1527–1593). The Librarian, 1566. Oil on canvas. Slott, Skokloster, Sweden. Erich Lessing/Art Resource, NY.

MEETING THE CHALLENGE

Your ultimate challenge is to apply the reading skills and learning strategies in this text to the many reading assignments in the college courses in your curriculum. In order to practice this transfer of skills, this last chapter of *Bridging the Gap* contains a selection entitled "Race and Ethnicity" adapted from a popular textbook that combines both history and sociology. The selection begins with examples to heighten curiosity and sensitize the reader. Words such as *race, minority,* and *ethnicity* are defined from the perspective of a sociologist, and different forms of acceptance and rejection are also explained. The selection concludes with a history of six different ethnic groups written from a sociological perspective.

Take the initiative with this chapter and coordinate your own reading and studying. Study strategy suggestions and questions are inserted, but they do not constitute all that is needed for you to master this material. Two tests have been prepared in the *Instructor's Manual* for this chapter. One is a multiple-choice test, and the other is an essay exam. Systematically work through the chapter using the skills you have learned.

> ## READER'S TIP Organizing Your Study
>
> ▶ **Preview**
> Read the table of contents.
> Overview the pages and selectively read subheadings.
> Predict topics, set a purpose, and set goals.
> Brainstorm to activate your schema on the subject.
>
> ▶ **Integrate knowledge using the five thinking strategies**
>   Predict   Picture   Relate   Monitor   Correct
> Identify and connect major ideas.
> Annotate for later study.
> Take notes using a system that works for you.
>
> ▶ **Recall**
> Explain the major issues.
> Make connections by linking similarities and differences.
> Study your notes and memorize essentials.
> Predict questions and practice essay responses.

CONTEMPORARY FOCUS

As we become more accepting of other cultures, are we losing our moral judgment? Are you willing to say, despite the cultural differences, that some behaviors are just plain wrong? How can we appreciate diversity, and still maintain standards of civility?

A NO-FAULT HOLOCAUST

by John Leo

U. S. News and World Report, July 21, 1997

In 20 years of college teaching, Professor Robert Simon has never met a student who denied that the Holocaust happened. What he sees quite often, though, is worse: students who acknowledge the fact of the Holocaust but can't bring themselves to say that killing millions of people is wrong. Simon reports that 10 to 20 percent of his students think this way. Usually they deplore what the Nazis did, but their disapproval is expressed as a matter of taste or personal preference, not moral judgment. "Of course I dislike the Nazis," one student told Simon, "but who is to say they are morally wrong?"

Overdosing on nonjudgmentalism is a growing problem in the schools. Articles in the *Chronicle of Higher Education* say that some students are unwilling to oppose large moral horrors, including human sacrifice, ethnic cleansing, and slavery, because they think that no one has the right to criticize the moral views of another group or culture.

Kay Haugaard, a freelance writer who teaches creative writing at Pasadena City College in California writes that her current students have a lot of trouble expressing any moral reservations or objections about human sacrifice. The subject came up when she taught her class Shirley Jackson's *The Lottery*, a short story about a small American farm town where one person is killed each year to make the crops grow. In the tale, a woman is ritually stoned to death by her husband, her 12-year-old daughter, and her 4-year-old son.

Haugaard has been teaching since 1970. Until recently, she says, "Jackson's message about blind conformity always spoke to my students' sense of right and wrong." No longer, apparently. A class discussion of human sacrifice yielded no moral comments, even under Haugaard's persistent questioning. One male said the ritual killing in *The Lottery* "almost seems a need." Asked if she believed in human sacrifice, a woman said, "I really don't know."

Writers believe multiculturalism has played a role in spreading the vapors of nonjudgmentalism.

Christina Hoff Sommers, author and professor of philosophy at Clark University in Massachusetts, points beyond multiculturalism to a general problem of so many students coming to college "dogmatically committed to a moral relativism that offers them no grounds to think" about cheating, stealing, and other moral issues. Simon calls this "absolutophobia"—the unwillingness to say that some behavior is just plain wrong.

Collaborative Activity

Collaborate on responses to the following questions.
- What was the Holocaust?
- How are multiculturalism and nonjudgmentalism linked?
- How can "absolutophobia" be dangerous to society?

STAGE 1: PREVIEW

Use the outline and the subheadings to preview the following chapter to predict purpose, organization, and your learning plan.

The focus of the chapter will probably be _____.

Activate Schema

Why did different ethnic groups come to America?

How have immigrants strengthened America?

STAGE 2: INTEGRATE KNOWLEDGE WHILE READING

Predict   Picture   Relate   Monitor   Correct

In the largest naturalization event in history, nearly 10,000 people become citizens at the Orange Bowl.

RACE AND ETHNICITY

From Alex Thio, *Sociology: A Brief Introduction*

Chapter Contents

Introduction

Identifying Minorities

    Race

    Ethnicity

    Minority

Racial and Ethnic Relations

    Functionalist Perspective

    Conflict Perspective

Race and Ethnicity in the United States

    Native Americans

    African Americans

    Hispanic Americans

    Asian Americans

    Jewish Americans

    European Americans

Conclusion

Myths and Realities

MYTH: *When people move from one country to another their racial characteristics, such as skin color and facial features, do not change. Therefore, if African Americans go to another country, they will be considered blacks there, as in the United States.*

REALITY: It is true that people's physical features do not change when they move to another country. But their racial identification as blacks or whites may change. Most African Americans in the United States, for example, would be considered whites in some Latin American countries.

MYTH: *As "model Americans," Asian Americans are more economically successful than other groups, including whites.*

REALITY: The family income is higher for Asians than whites, but this is because the average Asian family is larger and more members of the family work, compared with the average white family. Individual income is lower for Asians than for whites.

MYTH: *Since Jewish Americans as a whole are prosperous, they tend to be conservative or to vote Republican, like other prosperous U.S. citizens.*

REALITY: On the contrary, they tend more to be liberal, supporting welfare, civil rights, women's rights, and the like. They are also more likely to vote Democratic.

Introduction

In this chapter, we will examine the criteria for identifying minorities and the nature of prejudice and discrimination against them. Then we will analyze the alternative ways in which a society may reject or accept a minority group. Finally, we will find out how various racial and ethnic groups have fared in the
5 United States.

What are the major organizational sections of this chapter?

What is the purpose of each section?

*How can you divide your reading
and notetaking on this chapter?*

In the summer of 1992 a deluge of horror stories about human cruelties shocked the world. They poured out of newly independent Bosnia and Herzegovina, the most ethnically diverse republic of what used to be Yugoslavia. The Serbs were reported to engage in an "ethnic cleansing" campaign by "dri-
10 ving Muslims and Croats from their homes, torturing and killing some of them, and abusing and terrorizing the rest." In a northern Bosnian town, armed Serbs, after rounding up 100 prisoners for a move from one detention

camp to another, pulled out about 30 of them and shot them. At a camp, the
family of one starving prisoner tried to bring him some food, but the guards
15 took it away and then beat the prisoner in front of his relatives. In a town
called Doboj, the Serbs sprayed insecticide on loaves of bread, which they fed
to Muslim boys, making them violently ill. Near Tuzla in eastern Bosnia,
three Muslim girls were stripped and chained to a fence "for all to use." After
being raped for three days, they were doused with gasoline and set on fire.
20 Other Muslim and Croatian girls had been used as sex slaves for months, and
if they became pregnant they were set free to "have Serbian babies." While
most reports focused on Serbian cruelties, some Muslims and Croats struck
back with atrocities of their own in areas where they predominate.

Mistreatment of minorities does not, however, take place in Bosnia alone.
25 In other parts of Eastern Europe, minorities—such as the Slovaks in Czecho-
slovakia, ethnic Albanians in Yugoslavia, ethnic Hungarians in Romania, and
ethnic Turks in Bulgaria—also suffer. In Western Europe, too, Pakistanis,
Turks, Algerians, and other non-European minorities are often subjected to
random insults and hostile stares, which sometimes escalate into gang attacks
30 or firebombs thrown from the streets. In Japan, the Koreans, Burakumin
(sometimes called *Eta*, meaning "much filth"), and Konketsuji (American-
Japanese mixed bloods) are also targets of considerable prejudice and discrimination. These are only a few of the countless cases of mistreatment suffered
by minorities in various countries.

Identifying Minorities

35 Americans are accustomed to thinking of a minority as a category of people
who are physically different and who make up a small percentage of the population. But the popular identification of minorities is often misleading. The
Jews in China do not "look Jewish"—they look like other Chinese. Similarly,
the Jews in the United States look like other white Americans. Jews cannot be
40 differentiated from the dominant group on the basis of their physical characteristics, but they are considered a minority. In South Africa, blacks are a minority group, even though they make up a majority of the population. Neither physical traits nor numbers alone determine whether people constitute a
minority group. To get a clearer idea of what a minority is, we need first to see
45 what races and ethnic groups are.

Should you annotate and then take notes on this material?

*Before reading what sociologists believe, how would you
define race, ethnicity, and minorities?*

Should you list an example to illustrate each definition?

Race

As a biological concept, race refers to a large category of people who share
certain inherited physical characteristics. These characteristics may include

particular skin color, head shape, hair type, nasal shape, lip form, or blood type. One common classification of human races recognizes three groups:
50 Caucasoid, Mongoloid, and Negroid. Caucasoids have light skin, Mongoloids yellowish skin, and Negroids dark skin—and other physical differences exist among the three groups.

There are, however, at least two important problems with such a classification of races. First, some groups fit into none of these categories. Natives of
55 India and Pakistan have Caucasoid facial features but dark skin. The Polynesians of Pacific Islands have a mixture of Caucasoid, Mongoloid, and Negroid characteristics.

Another problem with the biological classification of races is that there are no "pure" races. People in these groups have been interbreeding for centuries.
60 In the United States, for example, about 70 percent of blacks have some white ancestry and approximately 20 percent of whites have at least one black ancestor. Biologists have also determined that all current populations originate from one common genetic pool—one single group of humans that evolved about 30,000 years ago, most likely in Africa. As humans migrated all
65 over the planet, different populations developed different physical characteristics in adapting to particular physical environments. Thus, the Eskimos' relatively thick layer of fat under the skin of their eyes, faces, and other parts of the body provides good insulation against the icy cold of Arctic regions. The Africans' dark skin offers protection from the burning sun of tropical regions.
70 Yet there has not developed a significant genetic difference among the "races." As genetic research has indicated, about 95 percent of the DNA molecules (which make up the gene) are the same for all humans, and only the remaining 5 percent are responsible for all the differences in appearance. Even these outward differences are meaningless because the differences among members
75 of the same "race" are greater than the average differences between two racial groups. Some American blacks, for example, have lighter skins than many whites, and some whites are darker than many blacks.

Since there are no clear-cut biological distinctions—in physical characteristics or genetic makeup—between racial groups, sociologists prefer to define
80 race as a social rather than biological phenomenon. Defined sociologically, a **race** is a group of people who are *perceived* by a given society as biologically different from others. People are assigned to one race or another, not necessarily on the basis of logic or fact but by public opinion, which, in turn, is molded by society's dominant group. Consider an American boy whose fa-
85 ther has 100 percent white ancestry and whose mother is the daughter of a white man and black woman. This youngster is considered "black" in our society, although he is actually more white than black because of his 75 percent white and 25 percent black ancestry. In many Latin American countries, however, this same child would be considered "white." In fact, according to
90 Brazil's popular perception of a black as "a person of African descent who has no white ancestry at all," about three-fourths of all American blacks would *not* be considered blacks. They would be considered white because they have some white ancestry.

© 2000 Addison-Wesley Educational Publishers, Inc.

What is a race?

To what extent do we all share the same genetic pool?

Ethnicity

Jews have often been called a race. But they have the same racial origins as
95 Arabs—both being Semites—and through the centuries Jews and non-Jews
have interbred extensively. As a result, as we noted earlier, Jews are often
physically indistinguishable from non-Jews. Besides, a person can become a
Jew by choice—by conversion to Judaism. Jews do not constitute a race. Instead, they are a religious group or, more broadly, an ethnic group.
100   Whereas race is based on popularly perceived physical traits, ethnicity is
based on cultural characteristics. An **ethnic group** is a collection of people
who share a distinctive cultural heritage and a consciousness of their common
bond. Members of an ethnic group may share a language, accent, religion, history, philosophy, national origin, or life-style. They always share a feeling that
105 they are a distinct people. In the United States, members of an ethnic group
typically have the same national origin. As a result, they are named after the
countries from which they or their ancestors came. Thus, they are Polish
Americans, Italian Americans, Irish Americans, and so on.
       For the most part, ethnicity is culturally learned. People learn the lifestyles,
110 cooking, language, values, and other characteristics of their ethnic group. Yet
members of an ethnic group are usually born into it. The cultural traits of the
group are passed from one generation to another, and ethnicity is not always a
matter of choice. A person may be classified by others as a member of some ethnic group, for example, on the basis of appearance or accent. In fact, racial and
115 ethnic groups sometimes overlap, as in the case of African or Asian Americans.
Like race, ethnicity can be an ascribed status.

How does ethnicity differ from race?

Whom do you know who has dropped their ethnicity?

Who has maintained their ethnicity?

Minority

A **minority** is a racial or ethnic group that is subjected to prejudice and discrimination. The essence of a minority group is its experience of prejudice
and discrimination. **Prejudice** is a negative attitude toward members of a mi-
120 nority. It includes ideas and beliefs, feelings, and predispositions to act in a
certain way. For example, whites prejudiced against blacks might fear meeting a black man on the street at night. They might resent blacks who are successful. They might plan to sell their houses if a black family moves into the
neighborhood.
125   Whereas prejudice is an attitude, **discrimination** is an act. More specifically, it is unequal treatment of people because they are members of some
group. When a landlord will not rent an apartment to a family because they
are African-American or Hispanic, that is discrimination.

What is a minority?

What is prejudice?

What is discrimination?

Are you a member of a minority?

*Why do sociologists define race as a social rather
than a physical phenomenon?*

*What is ethnicity, and why do sociologists prefer to use this
concept to explain the diverse behavior of minorities?*

When does a racial or ethnic group become a minority group?

Racial and Ethnic Relations

Racial and ethnic relations appear in different forms, from violent conflict to
130 peaceful coexistence. The functionalist perspective emphasizes peaceful coexistence and other positive forms of intergroup relations because they are
functional to society, contributing to social order and stability. In contrast, the
conflict perspective focuses on violent conflict and other negative aspects of
intergroup relations, in which the powerful, dominant group mistreats power-
135 less minorities. Alternatively, the symbolic interactionist perspective focuses
on how perceptions influence intergroup interactions and vice versa.

What is the focus of this section?

What is the pattern of organization under each subheading?

What will you need to know after reading this section?

How are the boldface words connected?

Functionalist Perspective

According to the functionalist perspective, various racial and ethnic groups
contribute to social order through assimilation, amalgamation, or cultural pluralism. **Assimilation** is the process by which a minority adopts the dominant
140 group's culture as the culture of the larger society. **Amalgamation** is the
process by which the subcultures of various groups are blended together,
forming a new culture. **Cultural pluralism** is the peaceful coexistence of various racial and ethnic groups, each retaining its own subculture.

Assimilation. Assimilation can be expressed as $A + B + C = A$, where mi-
145 norities B and C lose their subcultural traits and become indistinguishable
from the dominant group A. There are two kinds of assimilation: The first is
behavioral assimilation, the social situation in which the minority adopts the
dominant group's language, values, and behavioral patterns. Behavioral assimilation, however, does not guarantee **structural assimilation,** the social condi-
150 tion in which the minority is accepted on equal terms with the rest of society.

A white Russian immigrant who speaks halting English may find it relatively easy to get structurally assimilated in the United States, but this is less the case with a black middle-class American. Nevertheless, most members of the disadvantaged minorities look upon assimilation as necessary to get ahead—
155 economically and socially—in the United States.

What is behavioral assimilation? Name a personal example.

What is structural assimilation? Name a personal example.

What factors encourage and prevent behavioral and structural assimilation?

Amalgamation.   In a society that encourages assimilation, there is little respect for the distinctive traits of minority groups. By contrast, a society that seeks amalgamation as an ideal has a greater appreciation for the equal worth of various subcultures. Amalgamation is popularly compared to a "melting
160 pot," in which many subcultures are blended together to produce a new culture, one that differs from any of its components. It can be described as A + B + C = D, where A, B, and C represent different groups jointly producing a new culture—D—unlike any of its original components.

More than 80 years ago, a British-Jewish dramatist portrayed the United
165 States as an amalgamation of subcultures. "There she lies," he wrote, "the great melting pot—listen! . . . Ah, what a stirring and seething—Celt and Latin, Slav and Teuton, Greek and Syrian, Black and Yellow—Jew and Gentile." Indeed, to some extent the United States is a melting pot. In popular music and slang you can find elements of many subcultures. And there has been considerable inter-
170 marriage among some groups, particularly among those of English, German, Irish, Italian, and other European backgrounds. But such amalgamation is less likely to involve white and nonwhite groups.

What is amalgamation?

How does amalgamation differ from assimilation?

Cultural Pluralism.   Switzerland provides an example of yet a third way in which ethnic groups may live together. In Switzerland, three major groups—Ger-
175 mans, French, and Italians—retain their own languages while living together in peace. They are neither assimilated nor amalgamated. Instead, these diverse groups retain their distinctive subcultures while coexisting peacefully. Unlike either assimilation or amalgamation, cultural pluralism encourages each group to take pride in its distinctiveness, to be conscious of its heritage, and to retain its identity. Such plu-
180 ralism can be shown as A + B + C = A + B + C, where various groups continue to keep their subcultures while living together in the same society. To some extent, the United States has long been marked by cultural pluralism. This can be seen in the Chinatowns, Little Italies, and Polish neighborhoods of many U.S. cities.

What is cultural pluralism?

What are the dangers of cultural pluralism?

Toward Multiculturalism? Multiculturalism is the belief that all racial and ethnic cultures in the United States should be equally respected and cultivated. But according to its advocates, the United States has failed to practice multiculturalism, even though we are the most racially and ethnically diverse country in the world. Multiculturalists urge that American students study African, Asian, and Latin American civilizations as much as Western civilization.

Most Americans, including nonwhites, continue to accept Western civilization (such as the English language, Western legal system, and Western history and literature) as the dominant feature of American culture, though with less enthusiasm than before. Therefore, despite the inevitable increase in ethnic conflict, the United States still remains the most successful, stable large multiethnic nation in the world. This may be traced to the core of American culture, namely, the unique tolerance for diversity and conflict, which apparently is the product of a long history of being a plural nation.

What is multiculturalism?

Conflict Perspective

To conflict theorists, racial and ethnic relations can be negative, marked by **racism,** the belief that one's own race or ethnicity is superior to that of others. Racism tends to cause the dominating group to *segregate, expel,* and *exterminate* minorities.

Segregation. Segregation means more than spatial and social separation of the dominant and minority groups. It means that minority groups, because they are believed inferior, are compelled to live separately, and in inferior conditions. The neighborhoods, schools, and other public facilities for the dominant group are both separate from and superior to those of the minorities.

The compulsion that underlies segregation is not necessarily official, or acknowledged. In the United States, for example, segregation is officially outlawed, yet it persists. In other words, **de jure segregation**— segregation sanctioned by law—is gone, but **de facto segregation**—segregation resulting from tradition and custom—remains. This is particularly the case with regard to housing for African Americans. Like the United States, most nations no longer practice de jure segregation. Even South Africa finally ended its official policy of *apartheid*—racial separation in housing, jobs, and political opportunities—in 1992. But apartheid has become so entrenched that it will continue in the form of de facto segregation for many years to come.

What is de jure *segregation?*

What is de facto *segregation?*

Expulsion. In some cases, the dominant group has expelled a minority from certain areas or even out of the country entirely. During the nineteenth century, Czarist Russia drove out millions of Jews, and the U.S. government forced the Cherokee to travel from their homes in Georgia and the Carolinas to reservations in Oklahoma. About 4000 Cherokee died on this "Trail of Tears." During the 1970s, Uganda expelled more than 40,000 Asians—many of them Ugandan citizens—and Vietnam forced 700,000 Chinese to leave the country.

What are examples of rejection by expulsion?

Can you add examples of others not mentioned?

Extermination. The most drastic action against minorities is to kill them. **Genocide,** the wholesale killing of a racial or ethnic group, has been attempted in various countries. During the nineteenth century, Dutch settlers in South Africa exterminated the native Khoikhoin, or "Hottentots." During the pioneer days of the United States, white settlers slaughtered Native Americans. On the island of Tasmania, near Australia, British settlers killed the entire native population, whom they hunted like wild animals. Between 1933 and 1945, the Nazis systematically murdered six million Jews. More recently, in 1992, the Serbs in Bosnia killed and tortured numerous Muslims and Croats as part of their campaign of "ethnic cleansing." In 1993 and 1994, thousands of minority members were massacred in the African country of Rwanda.

What is genocide?

What are examples of genocide?

In what different ways can the majority group accept members of a minority group?

What can happen when a dominant group decides to reject a racial or ethnic minority?

Race and Ethnicity in the United States

The United States is a nation of immigrants. The earliest immigrants were the American Indians, who arrived from Asia more than 20,000 years ago. Long after the Indians settled as Native Americans, other immigrants began to pour in from Europe and later from Africa, Asia, and Latin America. They came as explorers, adventurers, slaves, or refugees—most hoping to fulfill a dream of success and happiness. The English were the earliest of these immigrants and, on the whole, the most successful in fulfilling that dream. They became the dominant group. Eventually, they founded a government dedicated to the democratic ideal of equality, but they kept African Americans as slaves and discriminated against other racial and ethnic groups. This "American dilemma"—the discrepancy between the ideal of equality and the reality of discrimination—still exists, though to a lesser degree than in the past. Let us look at how the major minority groups have fared under the burden of the American dilemma.

Ancestry of U.S. Population

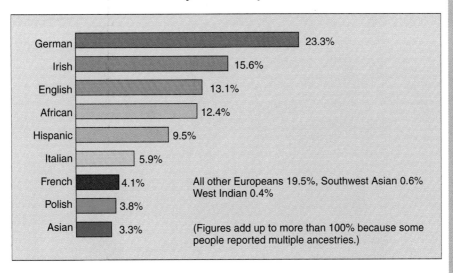

German — 23.3%
Irish — 15.6%
English — 13.1%
African — 12.4%
Hispanic — 9.5%
Italian — 5.9%
French — 4.1%
Polish — 3.8%
Asian — 3.3%

All other Europeans 19.5%, Southwest Asian 0.6%
West Indian 0.4%

(Figures add up to more than 100% because some people reported multiple ancestries.)

Data from Statistical Abstract of the United States, 1994.

What is the focus of this section?

What major groups are discussed?

What seems to be the pattern of organization for the discussion of each group?

How detailed should your notes be?

How much will you need to know for the test?

What do you already know about the Native Americans?

How have the Native Americans fared in their own country?

Native Americans

Native Americans have long been called Indians—one result of Columbus's mistaken belief that he had landed in India. The explorer's successors passed
255 down many other distorted descriptions of the Native Americans. They were described as savages, although it was whites who slaughtered hundreds of thousands of them. They were portrayed as scalp hunters, although it was the white government that offered large sums to whites for the scalps of Indians. They were stereotyped as lazy, although it was whites who forced them to give up
260 their traditional occupations. These false conceptions of Native Americans were reinforced by the contrasting pictures whites painted of themselves. The white settlers were known as pioneers rather than invaders and marauders; their taking of the Native Americans' land was called homesteading, not robbery.

Native Americans attend the movie premiere of Pocahontas *in New York City.*

When Columbus "discovered" America, there were more than 300 Native
265 American tribes, with a total population exceeding a million. Of those he encountered around the Caribbean, Columbus wrote: "Of anything they have, if
it be asked for, they never say no, but do rather invite the person to accept it,
and show as much lovingness as though they would give their hearts." In
North America, too, the earliest white settlers were often aided by friendly
270 Native Americans.

The Changing Status. As the white settlers increased in numbers and
moved westward, however, Native Americans resisted them. But the native
population was decimated by outright killing, by destruction of their food
sources, and by diseases brought by whites, such as smallpox and influenza.
275 With their greater numbers and superior military technology, the whites pre-
vailed. Sometimes they took land by treaty rather than by outright force. The
treaties required the U.S. government to provide Native Americans with "foreign aid," such as helping them maintain a reasonable level of education and
health and protecting their resources. But the treaties have often been vio-
280 lated even to this day.

By 1995, there were about two million Native Americans. Slightly more
than half lived on 278 reservations, mostly in the Southwest, the rest in urban
areas. After more than two centuries of colonial subjugation, Native Americans today find themselves at the bottom of the socioeconomic ladder—the
285 poorest minority in the United States. Their unemployment and poverty rates
are much higher than those among other Americans, and their family income

is also considerably lower. Moreover, they suffer from much higher rates of pneumonia, influenza, diabetes, tuberculosis, suicide, alcoholism, and car accidents, compared with the general U.S. population.

290 Under constant pressure by Native Americans, the U.S. government has since 1988 instituted a policy "to promote tribal economic development, tribal self-sufficiency, and strong tribal government." Today, on some reservations Native Americans are exempted from paying taxes and, further, are allowed to sell gasoline, cigarettes, and other items tax-free to non-Indians.

295 About 59 percent of the reservations are also permitted to run highly profitable gambling operations that cater to non-Indians. At least seven tribes have recently been allowed to govern themselves virtually as sovereign nations. These tribes may set their own budgets, run their own programs, and negotiate directly with the federal government for services, functions that have long

300 been performed by the U.S. Bureau of Indian Affairs.

Cultural Pride. All this has sparked a national movement to recapture traditions, to make Native Americans feel proud of their cultural heritage. Virtually every tribe places a heavy emphasis on teaching the younger generation its native language, crafts, tribal history, and religious ceremonies. There used

305 to be a lack of unity among the 300 tribes, but today intertribal visiting and marriage are common occurrences. Moreover, in the last 15 years, many Native American men and women have successfully established themselves in business, law, and other professions. Of course, the majority of Native Americans still have a long way to go. Without a viable economic base to draw on,

310 they still find themselves powerless, mired in high unemployment, deep poverty, and other problems. The last 15 years have not been long enough to overcome two centuries of government oppression.

How did government policies devastate Native Americans?

How has cultural pride been reasserted?

*How have Native Americans been accepted
and rejected by society?*

African Americans

There are more than 31 million African Americans, constituting about 12 percent of the U.S. population. They are the largest minority in the nation. In

315 fact, there are more blacks in the United States than in any single African nation except Nigeria.

Their ancestors first came from Africa to North America as indentured servants in 1619. Soon after that they were brought here as slaves. Most lived in the South, where they worked on cotton, tobacco, or sugar-cane plantations.

320 Slavery ended during the Civil War in 1865. But soon after federal troops withdrew from the South, white supremacy returned. Many **Jim Crow laws** were enacted to segregate blacks from whites in all kinds of public and private facilities—from restrooms to schools. A more basic tactic to control blacks was terror. If an African American man was suspected of killing a white or of

325 raping a white woman, he might be lynched, beaten to death, or burned at
the stake.

Lynchings occurred in the North, too. Still, the North did offer more opportunities to African Americans. Since the early 1900s, as southern farms
were mechanized and as the demand for workers in northern industrial centers
330 rose during the two World Wars, many southern African Americans migrated
north. When the wars ended and the demand for workers decreased, however,
they were often the first to be fired. Even in the North, where there were no
Jim Crow laws, African Americans faced discrimination and segregation.

Desegregation.   A turning point in U.S. race relations came in 1954 when
335 the U.S. Supreme Court ordered that public schools be desegregated. The order gave momentum to the long-standing campaign against racial discrimination. In the late 1950s and 1960s, the civil rights movement launched
marches, sit-ins, and boycotts. The price was high: many civil rights workers
were beaten and jailed; some were killed. Eventually Congress passed the
340 landmark Civil Rights Act of 1964, prohibiting segregation and discrimination
in virtually all areas of social life, such as public facilities, schools, housing,
and employment.

In the last 30 years, the Civil Rights Act has put an end to many forms of
segregation and paved the way for some improvement in the position of
345 African Americans. Various studies have shown a significant decline in white
opposition to such issues as school integration, integrated housing, interracial
marriage, and voting for an African American president. The number of
African Americans elected to various public offices has sharply increased since
1980. The proportion of African Americans with college degrees has also
350 grown significantly. An affluent middle class has emerged among African
Americans.

Full equality, however, is still far from being achieved. Most evident is the
continuing large economic gap between blacks and whites. The latest figures
on median family income are $21,161 for blacks and $38,909 for whites—
355 with blacks earning only about 54 percent of the amount made by whites, a
decline from 57 percent in 1980. Over 33 percent of blacks live in poverty,
compared with less than 12 percent of whites. More glaring racial inequality
shows up in housing. Over the last decade there has been some decline in residential segregation, especially in relatively small metropolitan areas with ac-
360 tive housing construction in the South and West. But the decline has been
very modest; most blacks continue to reside in segregated neighborhoods and
are more likely than whites with similar incomes to live in overcrowded and
substandard housing.

In sum, progress has been significant in education and politics, but not in
365 housing and economic conditions. The economic situation is a little complicated, though. Unemployment and poverty have soared in the black working
class, primarily because of numerous plant shutdowns caused by the shift
from a manufacturing to a service economy in the face of increased global
competition. On the other hand, the black middle class has become more

Colin Powell leads a Veteran's Day parade in Chicago. He was a leader in many public opinion polls as a presidential contender before he decided not to run in the 1996 contest.

370 prosperous, largely because of their advanced education and skills required by the technological changes in the U.S. economy. Still, it is difficult for middle-class blacks to enjoy the rewards of their success. They are often outraged at being treated like the "black underclass," which involves being stopped and questioned as crime suspects by police, getting bad—or no—service in shops
375 and restaurants, having difficulty flagging down a taxi, or being falsely charged with shoplifting.

What were Jim Crow laws and what were the effects?

How have African Americans been accepted and rejected by society?

Hispanic Americans

In 1848 the United States either won in war or bought from Mexico land that would become Texas, California, Nevada, Utah, Arizona, New Mexico, and Colorado. Many Mexicans consequently found themselves living in U.S. terri-
380 tories as U.S. citizens. The vast majority of today's Mexican Americans, how-ever, are the result of immigration from Mexico since the turn of the century.

At first immigrants came largely to work in the farmlands of California and to build the railroads of the Southwest. Later a steady stream of Mexicans began to pour into the United States, driven by Mexico's population pressures and
385 economic problems and attracted by U.S. industry's need for low-paid, unskilled labor.

In 1898 the United States added Puerto Rico to its territory by defeating Spain in the Spanish-American War. In 1917 Congress granted all Puerto Ricans citizenship, but they may not vote in presidential elections and are not rep-
390 resented in Congress. Over the years, especially since the early 1950s, many Puerto Ricans, lured by job opportunities and the cheap plane service between New York City and San Juan, have migrated to the mainland. In the last two decades, though, more have returned to Puerto Rico than have come here.

Thus, a new minority group has emerged in the United States—Hispanic
395 Americans, also called Latinos. Today the category actually includes several groups. Besides Mexican Americans and Puerto Ricans, there are Cuban immigrants who began to flock to the Miami area when their country became communist in 1959. There are also the "other Hispanics"—immigrants from other Central and South American countries who have come here as political refugees
400 and job seekers. By 1992, the members of all these groups totaled about 24 million, constituting over 9 percent of the U.S. population, the second largest minority. Because of high birth rates and the continuing influx of immigrants, Hispanic Americans may outnumber African Americans in the next decade.

The Spanish language is the unifying factor among Hispanic Americans.
405 Another source of common identity is religion: at least 85 percent of them are Roman Catholic. There is an increasing friction, though, between Mexican Americans and the newly arrived immigrants from Mexico. Many Mexican Americans blame illegal aliens for lower salaries, loss of jobs, overcrowding of schools and health clinics, and deterioration of neighborhoods. According to
410 one survey, for example, 66 percent of Mexican Americans accused illegal immigrants of taking jobs from American citizens.

Differences in Hispanic Groups.   There are, however, significant differences within the Hispanic community. Mexican Americans are by far the largest group, accounting for 61 percent of the Hispanics. They are heavily
415 concentrated in the Southwest and West. Puerto Ricans make up 15 percent and live mostly in the Northeast, especially in New York City. As a group, they are the poorest among the Hispanics, which may explain why many have gone back to Puerto Rico. Those born in the United States, however, are more successful economically than their parents from Puerto Rico. The Cubans, who
420 constitute 7 percent of the Hispanic population, are the most affluent. They therefore show the greatest tendency toward integration with "Anglos"—white Americans. The remaining Hispanics are a diverse group, ranging from uneducated, unskilled laborers to highly trained professionals.

As a whole, Hispanics are younger than the general population. The me-
425 dian age is 23 for Hispanics, compared with 30 for other Americans. The youthfulness of the Hispanic population is due to relatively high fertility

Hispanic author Richard Rodriguez has received critical acclaim for his literary works.

and heavy immigration of young adults. This is particularly the case with Mexican Americans, who have the most children and are the youngest of all Hispanic groups. At the other extreme are Cubans, who have even
430 fewer children and are older than non-Hispanic Americans, with a median age of 41.

Hispanics in general lag behind both whites and blacks in educational attainment. Among those age 25 or older, only 9 percent have completed college, compared with 23 percent for whites and 12 percent for blacks. But
435 some Hispanic groups are more educated than others. Cubans are the best educated, primarily because most of the early refugees fleeing communist Cuba were middle-class and professional people. Mexican Americans and Puerto Ricans are less educated because they consist of many recent immigrants with much less schooling. The young, U.S.-born Hispanics usually have more edu-
440 cation. Lack of proficiency in English has slowed the recent Hispanic immigrants' educational progress. As many as 25 percent of Hispanics in public schools speak little or no English, which has resulted in higher dropout rates than those for non-Hispanic students.

In short, Hispanics as a group are still trailing behind the general popula-
445 tion in social and economic well-being. However, the higher educational achievement of young Hispanics provides hope that more Hispanics—not just Cubans—will be joining the higher paid white-collar work force in the future.

As shown by recent research, if Hispanics speak English fluently and have at least graduated from high school, their occupational achievement is close to
450 that of non-Hispanics with similar English fluency and schooling. According to another study, the huge Latino population in Los Angeles is thriving, thanks to its traditionally stable families and community spirit. Nationwide, Hispanics are also already a growing force in American politics. They now have more members of Congress, more state governors, and more mayors of
455 large cities than before. Most important, the states with the largest concentration of Hispanics—California, Texas, New York, and Florida—are highly significant for both state and national elections. It is no wonder that Hispanics were eagerly courted by both parties in the last two presidential elections. Interestingly, though, while most Hispanic leaders describe themselves as pri-
460 marily liberal, the majority of ordinary Hispanics consider themselves moderate to conservative.

What commonalities unite Hispanics?

What are the different Hispanic groups?

How do the different Hispanic groups differ in their economic status in America?

Asian Americans

Since 1980, Asian Americans have been the fastest growing minority. Their population has increased by 108 percent, far higher than the next highest increase rate of 53 percent among Hispanics. (For even sharper contrast, the
465 U.S. population as a whole has grown only 10 percent.) Nevertheless, Asian Americans remain a much smaller minority—3 percent of the U.S. population—than Hispanics and African Americans. There is tremendous diversity among Asian Americans, whose ancestry can be traced to over 20 different countries. Filipinos are the most numerous, followed by Chinese, Viet-
470 namese, Koreans, and Japanese. But it is the second and fifth largest groups— Chinese and Japanese—that are the best-known in the United States because before 1980 they had for a long time been the largest Asian-American groups.

The Chinese first came during the gold rush on the West Coast in 1849, pulled by better economic conditions in America and pushed by economic
475 problems and local rebellions in China. Soon huge numbers of Chinese were imported to work for low wages, digging mines and building railroads. After these projects were completed, jobs became scarce, and white workers feared competition from the Chinese. As a result, special taxes were imposed on the Chinese, and they were prohibited from attending school, seeking employ-
480 ment, owning property, and bearing witness in court. In 1882 the Chinese Exclusion Act restricted Chinese immigration to the United States, and it stopped all Chinese immigration from 1904 to 1943. Many returned to their homeland.

Immigrants from Japan met similar hostility. They began to come to the
485 West Coast somewhat later than the Chinese, also in search of better eco-

nomic opportunities. At first they were welcomed as a source of cheap labor. But soon they began to operate small shops, and anti-Japanese activity grew. In 1906 San Francisco forbade Asian children to attend white schools. In re-
490 sponse, the Japanese government negotiated an agreement whereby the Japanese agreed to stop emigration to the United States, and President Theodore Roosevelt agreed to end harassment of the Japanese who were already here. But when the Japanese began to buy their own farms, they met new opposition. In 1913 California prohibited foreign-born Japanese from
495 owning or leasing lands; other Western states followed suit. In 1922 the U.S. Supreme Court ruled that foreign-born Japanese could not become American citizens.

World War II. Worse events occurred during World War II. All the Japanese, aliens and citizens, were rounded up from the West Coast and
500 confined in concentration camps set up in isolated areas. They were forced to sell their homes and properties; the average family lost $10,000. The action was condoned even by the Supreme Court as a legitimate way of ensuring that the Japanese Americans would not help Japan defeat the United States. Racism, however, was the real source of such treatment. After all,
505 there was no evidence of any espionage or sabotage by a Japanese American. Besides, German Americans were not sent to concentration camps, although Germany was at war with the United States and there *were* instances of subversion by German Americans. In 1976, though, President Ford proclaimed that the wartime detention of Japanese Americans had
510 been a mistake, calling it "a sad day in American history." In 1983 a congressional commission recommended that each surviving evacuee be paid $20,000. In 1987, when the survivors sued the government for billions of dollars in compensation, the solicitor general acknowledged that the detention was "frankly racist" and "deplorable." And in 1988 the Senate voted
515 overwhelmingly to give $20,000 and an apology to each of the surviving internees.

Educational and Economic Success. Despite this history of discrimination, the Asians *seem* to be educationally and economically among the most successful minorities in the United States today. As the graph shows, a higher
520 percentage of Asians than whites have college degrees and annual family incomes of $50,000 or more. But the same figure indicates more poverty among Asians than whites. Moreover, the Asians' higher family income is misleading for two reasons: First, the average Asian family is larger and more members of the family work, compared with the average white family. *Individual* income
525 is actually lower for Asians than for whites. Second, most Asians live in California, Hawaii, and New York, where the cost of living is higher than the national average. Contrary to popular belief, then, Asian Americans still have not attained real income equality with whites, even though they have more education.

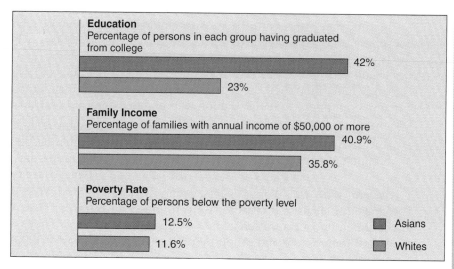

How Asian Americans Fare

Education
Percentage of persons in each group having graduated from college
42%
23%

Family Income
Percentage of families with annual income of $50,000 or more
40.9%
35.8%

Poverty Rate
Percentage of persons below the poverty level
12.5%
11.6%

Asians
Whites

Data from U.S. Census Bureau, 1994.

530   Discrimination against Asians is subtle. Many well-educated Asian Americans can get work as professionals and technicians, but they rarely become officials and managers. White bosses often cite language deficiencies as an excuse for denying promotions. Privately, they stereotype the Asians as weak and incapable of handling people, although Japanese-managed companies are
535 well known for outperforming U.S. companies. It is assumed that Asian talent can flourish in the classroom or laboratory but not in senior management. The Asians are in effect victims of the **glass ceiling,** the prejudiced belief that keeps minority professionals from holding high, leadership positions in organizations. Thus, many Asian professionals are prevented from joining the top
540 ranks of corporations.

    The stereotype of Asians as a "model minority" also hurts. It implies that virtually all Asians do well, which of course is not true because there is still much poverty among, for example, Filipinos and Chinatown residents. By suggesting that Asian Americans are not victims of discrimination, the model-mi-
545 nority stereotype further shuts Asians out of affirmative action programs. The stereotype is similarly used against Hispanics and African Americans. They are told directly or indirectly that they do not need racial preferences because "the Asians have made it, so why can't you?" This provokes resentment and even hostility against Asians, as blacks have shown against Korean stores in some
550 cities. Finally, the model-minority stereotype puts undue pressure on young Asian Americans to succeed in school, particularly in mathematics and science classes, which may lead to mental health problems and even teen suicide.

What laws were passed against Asian Americans?

How do Asian Americans fare educationally and economically?

Jewish Americans

The first Jews came here from Brazil in 1654; their ancestors had been expelled from Spain and Portugal. Then other Jews arrived directly from Europe. Their numbers were very small, however, until the 1880s, when large numbers of Jewish immigrants began to arrive, first from Germany, then from Russia and other Eastern European countries. Here they were safe from the *pogroms* (massacres) they had faced in Europe, but not from prejudice and discrimination.

During the 1870s, many colleges in the United States refused to admit Jewish Americans. At the turn of the century, Jews often encountered discrimination when they applied for white-collar jobs. During the 1920s and 1930s, they were accused of being part of an international conspiracy to take over U.S. business and government, and **anti-Semitism**—prejudice or discrimination against Jews—became more widespread and overt. The president of Harvard University proposed restrictive quotas for Jewish Americans. Large real estate companies in New Jersey, New York, Georgia, and Florida refused to sell property to Jews. The Chamber of Commerce of St. Petersburg, Florida, announced its intention to make St. Petersburg "a 100 percent American gentile city." Many country clubs and other social and business organizations barred Jewish Americans from membership.

But since the 1960s anti-Semitism has declined sharply. Today Jewish Americans are widely recognized as hard-working, family-oriented, religious, and friendly. Their contributions to U.S. cultural life are appreciated. Vandalism and violence against Jewish Americans are rare; the membership of anti-Semitic hate groups is extremely small; economic and social discrimination against Jews has practically disappeared; and non-Jews have elected a growing number of Jews to high public office.

Jewish Americans are so highly regarded largely because they have become the most successful minority. Their levels of education, occupation, and income are higher than those of any other group. Their success may stem from the emphasis Jewish culture gives to education, from a self-image as God's chosen people, and from parental pressure to succeed. Not all Jews are successful, though. There is still significant poverty in their midst. Being rich or poor has much to do with the recentness of arrival to the United States. Most of the poor Jews are Orthodox, the most recent immigrants in the United States. The more successful are Conservative Jews, who have been in this country longer. The wealthiest are Reform Jews, who have been here the longest.

Although Jewish Americans as a whole are prosperous, they are not conservative or inclined to vote Republican, as other prosperous U.S. citizens are. Instead, they tend more to be liberal—supporting welfare, civil rights, women's rights, civil liberties, and the like—and to vote Democratic. Perhaps this reflects their ability to identify with the dispossessed and oppressed. It also reflects the impact of Jewish norms underlying *tzedakah* (pronounced si-DOCK-ah, meaning "righteousness"), which requires the fortunate and the well-to-do to help individuals and communities in difficulty.

© 2000 Addison-Wesley Educational Publishers, Inc.

Physicist Albert Einstein was one of the large number of Jewish immigrants who left Germany with the rise of fascism in that country in the 1930s.

Jewish Americans, however, are in danger of losing their traditional identity. Today, about half of all Jewish Americans are not affiliated with a
600   synagogue, and only a small minority (about 20 percent) attend synagogue regularly. Marriage with non-Jews has increased greatly; over half of all Jewish marriages involve a non-Jew, and most children from such marriages are brought up as non-Jews. The Jewish birth rate has also declined. All this has caused consternation among some rabbis and Jewish communal
605   workers. But Jewish sociologists point out that, despite all those changes in their lives, Jews "have been able to maintain a stronger sense of group identity than most other ethnic groups" in the United States. A major reason is that Jewish cohesion does not derive from traditional Jewish values but rather from occupational and residential concentration. By sharing sim-
610   ilar neighborhoods, schools, occupations, organizations, and friends, Jewish Americans have been and continue to be able to maintain the highest level of cohesion.

What is anti-Semitism?

How have Jews been assimilated into society?

European Americans

The majority of the U.S. population is descended from immigrants from Europe.

WASPs and Other Western and Northern European Americans.

Western and northern European Americans make up the dominant group in
615 the United States. This group includes WASPs (white Anglo-Saxon Protestants), Germans, Irish, and others whose ancestors came from western and
northern Europe. Most WASPs are English, and a few are Scottish and Welsh.
With the exception of Native Americans, WASPs have a longer history in the
United States than any other racial or ethnic group. However, since 1990
620 WASPs have been outnumbered by Germans and Irish.

White Ethnics: Southern and Eastern European Americans.

Toward the
end of the nineteenth century a new wave of immigrants came from southern
and eastern Europe. Many native-born citizens thought these new immigrants to
be inferior people and treated them as such. This belief was reflected in the National Origins Act of 1924, which set quotas that greatly restricted immigration
625 from southern and eastern Europe—a policy that was not altered until 1965.

Today, the descendants of those immigrants are called **white ethnics**,
Americans of eastern and southern European origins. Although they have
made their mark in education, business, profession, and politics, they are often stereotyped as ultraconservative, uneducated blue-collar workers. In fact,
630 there are more middle-class people among white ethnics than other minorities, and about half have attended college, the same proportion as other European Americans. According to several surveys, white ethnics largely favor
liberal policies, such as welfare programs, antipollution laws, and guaranteed
wages. They are also relatively free of racial prejudice, perhaps because they
635 can easily identify with African Americans since, like blacks, many have held
low-paying manual jobs and been subjected to discrimination.

White ethnics by and large no longer speak their immigrant parents' language,
no longer live in ethnic neighborhoods, and routinely marry into the dominant
640 group. They have become such an integral part of mainstream U.S. society that
it is difficult to tell them apart. Traces of prejudice toward some white ethnics
still exist, though. Italian Americans, for example, continue to be associated with
organized crime, although people of Italian background make up less than 1 percent of the 500,000 individuals involved in such activities. In general, the young
645 and highly educated white ethnics are particularly sensitive to ethnic stereotypes, because they identify themselves strongly with their ethnicity.

What are the white ethnic groups?

What tends to be the economic status of white ethnics?

Conclusion

Put in perspective, the status of all the minorities is generally better today
than before. Getting closest to the American dream of success are Jews,

650 Asians, and white ethnics, followed by blacks and Hispanics. Ironically, the original owners of this land—Native Americans—have experienced the least improvement in their lives. Of course, we still have considerable prejudice and discrimination. But it is less than before, especially less than in a country like South Africa, where racism has until recently been an official policy.

655 It is also less serious than in Bosnia, Rwanda, and other countries, where a single incident of ethnic conflict often takes hundreds or thousands of lives. Therefore, as black sociologist Orlando Patterson notes, "The sociological truths are that America, while still flawed in its race relations, is now the least racist white-majority society in the world; has a better record of legal protection of minorities than any other society, white or black; offers more opportunities to a greater 660 number of black persons than any other society, including all those of Africa; and has gone through a dramatic change in its attitude toward miscegenation [interracial marriage or sexual relations] over the last 25 years."

QUESTIONS FOR DISCUSSION AND REVIEW

1. What different policies has the government adopted toward Native Americans, and why have they often been resisted?
2. Why are large numbers of African Americans still not fully equal?
3. Who are the different groups of Hispanic Americans, and what factors unify all of them?
4. Why have Asian Americans gained more educational and professional success than other minority groups?
5. How have the experiences of Jewish Americans differed from those of other white ethnic groups?
6. Does the "American Dilemma" still exist, or have American intergroup relations improved?

Thinking About   RACE AND ETHNICITY

For at least four of the ethnic groups described, discuss a situation that you feel is just plain wrong.

STUDY STRATEGIES

1. Recall the focus of each section of this chapter.
2. Make a study sheet including words like "race," "assimilation," and "anti-Semitic." Define them and give examples.
3. Create scenarios with fictional characters to illustrate a list of words like "cultural pluralism" and "expulsion" in preparation for application questions.

4. Connect your new knowledge by discussing recent articles that deal with some of the same issues in this chapter.
5. Brainstorm possible essay questions that connect the different sections of the chapter. Practice by writing answers to your questions.
6. Plan your attack by answering the following questions:

How will the test look?

What material will be covered?

How will you study?

When will you study?

What grade are you honestly working to achieve?

Study for success!

SEARCH THE NET

Amnesty International and the Anti-Defamation League are two international organizations working to oppose racial violence and genocide. Visit their Web sites and select a recent article on these issues to read and summarize. In your summary, identify the source of conflict, the ethnic groups, the nationalities, and the governments or leaders involved.

http://www.amnesty.org/	Amnesty International
http://www.adl.org	Anti-Defamation League
Key search words:	*genocide, racial Violence, ethnic Violence, hate Crimes*

Go Electronic!

For additional readings, exercises, and Internet activities, visit this book's Website at:
http://www.awlonline.com/smithBTG

For even more activities, visit the Longman English pages at:
http://longman.awl.com/englishpages

If you need a user name and password, please see your instructor.

Take a Road Trip to the Grand Canyon! Be sure to visit the Reading Textbooks module in your Reading Road Trip CD-ROM for multimedia tutorials, exercises, and tests.

Glossary

analogy A comparison showing connections with and similarities to previous experiences.

annotating A method of using symbols and notations to highlight textbook material for future study.

argument Assertions that support a conclusion with the intention of persuading.

assertion A declarative statement.

attention Uninterrupted mental focus.

bar graph An arrangement of horizontal or vertical bars in which the length of each represents an amount or number.

believability Support that is not suspicious but is believable.

bias An opinion or position on a subject recognized through facts slanted toward an author's personal beliefs.

cause and effect A pattern of organization in which one item is shown as having produced another.

chronological order A pattern of organization in which items are listed in time order or sequence.

cognitive psychology A body of knowledge that describes how the mind works or is believed to work.

comparison-contrast A pattern of organization in which similarities and differences are presented.

concentration The focusing of full attention on a task.

conclusion Interpretation based on evidence and suggested meaning.

connotation The feeling associated with the definition of a word.

consistency Support that holds together and does not contradict itself.

context clues Hints within a sentence that help unlock the meaning of an unknown word.

Cornell method A system of note taking that involves writing sentence summaries on the right side of the page with key words and topics indicated on the left.

creative thinking Generating many possible solutions to a problem.

critical thinking Deliberating in a purposeful, organized manner to assess the value of information or argument.

deductive reasoning Thinking that starts with a previously learned conclusion and applies it to a new situation.

definition A pattern of organization devoted to defining an idea and further explaining it with examples.

denotation The dictionary definition of a word.

description A pattern of organization, listing characteristics of a person, place, or thing, as in a simple listing.

details Information that supports, describes, and explains the main idea.

diagram A drawing of an object showing labeled parts.

external distractors Temptations of the physical world that divert the attention from a task.

fact A statement that can be proven true or false.

fallacy An inference that first appears reasonable, but closer inspection proves it to be unrelated, unreliable, or illogical.

figurative language Words used to create images that take on a new meaning.

fixation A stop the eyes make while reading.

flowchart A diagram showing how ideas are related, with boxes and arrows indicating levels of importance and movement.

habit Repetitious act almost unconciously performed.

humorous Comical or amusing.

idiom A figurative expression that does not make literal sense but communicates a generally accepted meaning.

imagery Mental pictures created by figurative language.

implied meaning Suggested rather than directly stated meaning.

inductive reasoning Thinking based on the collection of data and the formulation of a conclusion based on it.

inference Subtle suggestions expressed without direct statement.

internal distractions Concerns that come repeatedly to mind and disturb concentration.

irony A twist or surprise ending that is the opposite of what is expected and elicits a bittersweet, cruel chuckle.

knowledge network A cluster of knowledge about a subject; a schema.

lateral thinking A way of creatively thinking around a problem or redefining it to seek new solutions.

learning style A preference for a particular manner of presenting material to be learned.

line graph A frequency distribution in which the horizontal scale measures time and the vertical scale measures amount.

main idea A statement of the particular focus of the topic in a passage.

map A graphic designation or distribution.

mapping A method of graphically displaying material to show relationships and importance for later study.

metacognition Knowledge of how to read as well as the ability to regulate and direct the process.

metaphor A figure of speech that directly compares two unlike things (without using the words *like* or *as*).

mnemonics A technique using images, numbers, rhymes, or letters to improve memory.

note taking A method of writing down short phrases and summaries to record textbook material for future study.

opinion A statement of a personal view or judgment.

outlining A method of using indentations, Roman numerals, numbers, and letters to organize textbook material for future study.

pattern of organization The structure or framework for presenting the details in a passage.

personification Attributing human characteristics to nonhuman things.

pie graph A circle divided into wedge-shaped slices to show portions totaling 100 percent.

point of view A position or opinion on a subject.

premise The thesis or main point of an argument.

previewing A method of predicting what reading passage is about in order to assess knowledge and need.

prior knowledge Previous learning about a subject.

propaganda A systematic and deliberate attempt to persuade others to a particular doctrine or point of view.

purpose The author's underlying reason or intent for writing.

rate Reading pace described in number of words per minute.

recall Reviewing what was included and learned after reading material.

regression Rereading material because of a lack of understanding.

relevance Support that is related to the conclusion.

sarcasm A tone that is witty, usually saying the opposite of what is true, but with the purpose of undermining or ridiculing someone.

scanning Searching to locate single bits of information in reading material.

schema A skeleton or network of knowledge about a subject.

simile A comparison of two things using the words *like* or *as*.

simple listing A pattern of organization that lists items in a series.

skimming A technique for selectively reading for the gist or main idea.

study system A plan for working through stages to read and learn textbook material.

subvocalization The inaudible inner voice in the head that enables you to read and comprehend words.

summary A concise statement of the main idea and significant supporting details.

table A listing of facts and figures in columns for quick reference.

tone The author's attitude toward the subject.

topics A word or phrase that labels the subject of a paragraph.

vertical thinking A straightforward and logical way of thinking that searches for a solution to the stated problem.

Credits

Photo

Page 1: Ed Malitsky/Liaison Agency Inc.; **20:** Shahn Kermani/Liaison Agency Inc.; **34:** Nina Leen, Life Magazine, Copyright © Time Inc.; **43:** Mark Wallinger, *Q3*, 1994. Acrylic on canvas. Private Collection. Copyright © Mark Wallinger, Courtesy Anthony Reynolds Gallery, London; **71:** Winslow Homer, 1836–1910, United States. *Sunlight and Shadow,* 1872. Oil on canvas. Cooper-Hewitt, National Design Museum, Smithsonian Institution/Art Resource, NY. Gift of Charles Savage Homer, Jr., 1917-14-7. Cooper-Hewitt, National Design Museum, Smithsonian Institution/Art Resource, NY; **91 TL:** Copyright © Monkmeyer/Hiller; **91 TR:** Copyright © Myrleen Ferguson/PhotoEdit; **91 ML:** Copyright © SuperStock, Inc.; **91 MR:** Esbin-Anderson/The Image Works; **91 BL:** Color Day Productions/The Image Bank; **91 BR:** David De Lossy/The Image Bank; **94:** Copyright © The New Yorker Collection 1992 Mike Twohy from cartoonbank.com. All Rights Reserved; **101:** James Schnepf/Liaison Agency Inc.; **111:** Fabian Falco/Stock Boston; **121:** Georges Seurat, *Le Cirque,* 1890–1891. Oil on canvas. Musee d'Orsay, Paris. Erich Lessing/Art Resource, NY; **129:** Sichov Sipa Press; **130:** Courtesy of the National Fluid Milk Processor Promotion; **131:** Duomo/Al Tielemans; **158:** Harlow Primate Laboratory, University of Wisconsin; **168:** Stephen Jaffe/Liaison Agency Inc.; **177:** Neil Cooper/Panos Pictures; **179:** Medford Taylor/NGS Image Collection; **187:** Richard Shaw, *House of Cards,* 1998. Porcelain. Courtesy Nancy Margolis Gallery; **208:** Guigoz/Petit Format, Science Source/Photo Researchers; **216:** Corbis/Bettmann; **223:** James Lemass/Liaison Agency Inc.; **233:** Michael Melford/The Image Bank; **234:** Reprinted with special permission of Kings Feature Syndicate; **254:** Copyright © Ric Ergenbright; **264:** Bob Daemmrich/The Image Works; **269:** Copyright © Ulrike Welsch/PhotoEdit; **281:** M.C. Eschers *"Symmetry Drawing E76"* Copyright ©1999 Cordon Art B.V.-Baarn Holland. All rights reserved; **283:** ©1993, The Washington Post Writers Group. Reprinted with permission; **299:** Reprinted with special permission of Kings Feature Syndicate; **301:** © S.C. Rawls; **304:** Copyright © Angela Peterson/The Orlando Sentinel; **309:** AP/Wide World Photos, Inc.; **325:** René Magritte, 1898–1967. *La Grande Famille,* 1947. Oil on canvas. Private Collection © 2000 C. Herscovici/Artists Rights Society (ARS), New York. Herscovici/Art Resource, NY.; **338:** Signe Wilkerson/Cartoonists and Writers Syndicate; **352:** © Malcolm Hancock; **357:** James D. Wilson/Liaison Agency Inc.; **362:** ©Tribune Media Services, Inc. All Rights Reserved. Reprinted with permission; **367:** Steve DiBenedetto, *Confused by Choice,* 1987. Acrylic and spray on. Courtesy Tony Shafrazi Gallery; **382:** Copyright © Telegraph Colour Library/FPG International LLC; **395:** *Steeplechasing,* ex. 1935 by Sybil Andrews/Drewcatt Neate Fine Art Auctioneers, Newbury, Berkshire, UK/Bridgeman Art Library, London/New York; **412T:** Noel Quidu/Liaison Agency Inc.; **412B:** Copyright © David Young-Wolff/PhotoEdit; **415:** Corbis; **418:** Copyright © Tom McCarthy/PhotoEdit; **423:** Alfred Jensen (American, 1903–1981). *Beginning Study for Changes and Communications* (Detail), 1978. Oil on canvas. The Baltimore Museum of Art.; **451:** Giuseppe Arcimboldo (1527–1593). *The Librarian,* 1566. Oil on canvas. Slott, Skokloster, Sweden. Erich Lessing/Art Resource, NY.; **454:** Corbis/Bettmann-UPI; **464:** Remi Benalti/Liaison Agency Inc.; **467:** Loren Santow/Impact Visuals; **469:** John Chiasson/Liaison Agency Inc.; **474:** AP/Wide World Photos, Inc.

Text

"Net Addiction" from Oracle Service Humor Mailing List (oracle-humor-subscribe@lyris.oracle-humor.com) (Website: www. oraclehumor.com). Compiled by Sarah Lindsay and Mickey McLean.

"Motorcyclists in Cross-Hairs" by Jim Jensen. Copyright © 1998 *Denver Rocky Mountain News*, June 26, 1998. Reprinted by permission.

"The Story of Harley-Davidson Motorcycles" from *Principles of Marketing*, Fourth Edition by Thomas C. Kinnear, Kenneth Bernhardt, Kathleen Krentler. Copyright © 1995 by HarperCollins Publishers. Reprinted by permission of HarperCollins College Publishers.

"It's What You Say and Do That Will Make an Impression" and "Become Accustomed to Customs of International Clients," by Marcia H. Pounds. *Sun-Sentinel*, March 14 and March 21, 1997. Copyright © 1997. Reprinted by permission from the Sun-Sentinel, Fort Lauderdale, FL.

"Unity in Diversity" from *Sociology*, Fourth Edition by Donald Light, Jr. and Suzanne Keller. Copyright © 1986 McGraw-Hill, Inc. Reproduced by permission of McGraw-Hill, Inc.

Excerpts from *The American People: Creating a Nation and a Society*, Third Edition by Gary B. Nash, et al., general editors. Copyright © 1994 by HarperCollins College Publishers. Reprinted by permission of HarperCollins College Publishers.

Excerpts from *Nation of Nations: A Narrative History of the American Republic Volume II: Since 1965* by James West Davidson et al. Copyright © 1990 by McGraw-Hill, Inc. Reprinted by permission of McGraw-Hill, Inc.

Excerpts from *Business Essentials*, Second Edition by Ronald J. Ebert and Ricky W. Griffin. Copyright © 1998 Prentice Hall, Inc. Reprinted by permission of Prentice-Hall, Inc., Upper Saddle River, NJ.

Excerpts from *Managing* by Joseph Reitz and Linda N. Jewell. Copyright © 1985 Scott, Foresman and Company, HarperCollinsCollege Publishers.

Excerpts from *Principles of Speech Communication* by Bruce E. Gronbeck, Kathleen German, Douglas Ehninger and Alan H. Monroe. Copyright © 1997 Addison Wesley Longman, Inc.

Excerpts from *Interpersonal Communication*, Sixth Edition by Joseph DeVito. Copyright © 1998 Addison Wesley Longman, Inc.

Excerpts from *America and Its People* by James Kirby Martin, et al. Copyright © 1989, 1997 James Kirby Martin, Randy Roberts, Steven Mintz, Linda O. McMurry, and James H. Jones. Published by HarperCollins Publishers, Inc., Addison Wesley Longman, Inc.

Excerpts from *Conceptual Physics*, Eighth Edition by Paul Hewitt. Copyright © 1998 Addison Wesley Longman, Inc.

Excerpts from *Cultural Anthropology*, Fourth Edition by Serena Nanda. Copyright © 1991 by Wadsworth, Inc. Reprinted by permission of Wadsworth Publishing Company, Inc.

Excerpts from *Business*, Fourth Edition by Ronald Ebert and Ricky Griffen. Copyright © 1996 Prentice-Hall, Inc. Prentice-Hall, Inc., Reprinted by permission of Prentice-Hall, Inc., Upper Saddle River, NJ.

Excerpts from *Living Well: Health in Your Hands*, Second Edition by Curtis O. Byer and Louis W. Shainberg. Copyright © 1995 by HarperCollins College Publishers. Reprinted by permission of HarperCollins College Publishers.

Excerpts from *Human Development*, Second Edition by John Dacey and John Travers. Copyright © 1994 WCB Brown & Benchmark.

Excerpts from *Geography: Realms, Regions and Concepts*, Seventh Edition by H.J. DeBlij and Peter O. Muller. Copyright © 1994 by John Wiley & Sons, Inc. Reprinted by permission of John Wiley & Sons, Inc.

Excerpts from *Oranges* by John McPhee. Copyright © 1966, 1967 by John McPhee. Reprinted by permission of Farrar, Straus & Giroux, Inc.

Excerpts from *Drugs, Society and Human Behavior*, Sixth Edition by Oakley Ray, Ph.D. and Charles Ksir, Ph.D. Copyright © 1993 by Mosby-Year Book, Inc. Reprinted with permission.

From "Neat People vs. Sloppy People" by Suzanne Britt. *Show and Tell*, 1992.

"Mother Savage" from *Mademoiselle Fifi and Other Stories* by Guy de Maupassant, translated by Roger Colet. Copyright © Roger Colet, 1971. Published by Penguin Classics. Reproduced by permission of Penguin Books Limited.

"Language in the Dumps" by John Leo. In: *U.S. News & World Report*, July 27, 1998. Copyright © July 27, 1998, U.S. News & World Report. Reprinted by permission.

"Doubts About Doublespeak" by William Lutz. In: *State Government News*. Reprinted by permission.

"If Only We All Spoke Two Languages" by Ariel Dorfman. In: *The New York Times*, June 24, 1998. Copyright © 1998 by The New York Times Company. Reprinted by permission.

"Bilingual Education" from *Hunger of Memory* by Richard Rodriguez. Copyright © 1982 by Richard Rodriguez. Reprinted by permission of David R. Godine, Publisher, Inc.

Excerpt from "Legacy of Hate: The Myth of a Peaceful Belligerent" by Rodolfo Acuna. From *Myth and the American Experience, Volume One*, Third Edition, edited by Nicholas Cords and Patrick Gerater. Copyright © 1991. New York: HarperCollins Publishers.

Excerpt from "Mary Queen of Scots" in *The Mainstream of Civilization*, Fourth Edition by Joseph R. Strayer and Hans W. Gatzke. Harcourt Brace Jovanovich, Inc.

Excerpts from *Contemporary Business* by Louis E. Boone and David L. Kurtz. Copyright © 1976 by The Dryden Press.

Excerpt from *Understanding Human Behavior: An Introduction to Psychology* by James V. McConnell. Copyright © 1974 by Holt, Rinehart and Winston, Inc. Reprinted by permission of the publisher.

Excerpts from *Western Civilization* by Edward M. Burns.

Excerpts from *The Devil's Dictionary* by Ambrose Bierce.

Excerpt from *Civilizations of the World: The Human Adventure* by Richard L. Greaves. Copyright © 1990 by Harper & Row, Publishers, Inc. Reprinted by permission of HarperCollins Publishers.

Excerpt from "The Feminization of Earth First!" by Judi Bari. Ms., 1992. Copyright © 1992. Reprinted by permission of *Ms.* magazine

Excerpt from "The Injustice System" by Patty Fisher. *San Jose Mercury News*, March 25, 1992.

Excerpt from "Notes on Punctuation" in *The Medusa and the Snail* by Lewis Thomas. Copyright © 1979 by Lewis Thomas. Used by permission of Viking Penguin, a division of Penguin Books USA Inc.

"Elderly Parents: A Cultural Duty" from "Vietnamese: A Lifetime Commitment" by Ta Thuc Phu. *Orlando Sentinel*, May 2, 1998. Copyright © 1998. Reprinted by permission of Ta Thuc Phu.

"San Antonio Journal: Novelist's Purple Palette Is Not to Everyone's Taste" by Sara Rimer. *New York Times*, July 13, 1998. Copyright © 1998 by The New York Times Co. Reprinted by permission.

"Only Daughter" by Sandra Cisneros. Copyright © 1990 by Sandra Cisneros. First published in *Glamour*, November 1990. Reprinted by permission of Susan Bergholz Literary Services, New York. All rights reserved.

"Tort Reform: Excessive Litigation by Trial Lawyers." Address delivered by William Stavropoulos, CEO Dow Chemical Company to the Dallas Friday Group, Dallas, TX, January 23, 1998. Reprinted by permission of William Stavropoulos.

"Understanding the Legal Context of Business" from *Business*, Fourth Edition by Ronald Ebert and Ricky Griffen. Copyright © 1996 Prentice-Hall, Inc. Prentice-Hall, Inc., Reprinted by permission of Prentice-Hall, Inc., Upper Saddle River, NJ.

Excerpts from *Invitation to Critical Thinking*, Third Edition by Vincent E. Barry and Joel Rudinow. Copyright © 1994 by Holt, Rinehart and Winston, Inc. Reprinted by permission of the publisher.

Index

"A No-Fault Holocaust," from *U.S. News and World Report*, by John Leo, 453

Acronyms, 66–67

Active learning, 1–42

"Alcohol and Nutrition," from *Nutrition*, Eva May Nunnelley by Hamilton et al, 382–390

Analogies, 64–65, 331–332

Annotating, 190–196

Argument, 329–330

Attention, 2–4

Bar graphs, 376–377

Barriers to critical thinking, 327–328

Barry, Lynda, "The Sanctuary of School," from *The New York Times*, 418–421

"Best and Worst Cafeteria Foods," from *Muscle & Fitness*, by Lisa Flores, 222

Bias, 283

"Bilingual Education," from *Hunger of Memory*, by Richard Rodriguez, 269–274

"Black Entrepreneurs Face a Perplexing Issue: How to Pitch to Whites," from *The Wall Street Journal*, by Angelo Henderson, 167

Brehm, Barbara, "Nutrition and Stress: Running on Empty" from *Stress Management*, 223–227

"Building a Better Mouse," from *Meridian: Midway Airlines*, by Dennis Meredith, 157

Byer, Curtis and Louis Shainberg, "Passive Smoking," from *Living Well*, 412–413

Capron, H. L. from *Computeres:Tools for an Information Age*, "The Internet," 20–23

Cartoons, 299–301

Cause and effect, 147–148

Cisneros, Sandra, "Only Daughter,", from *Women's Voices from Borderlands*, 309–311

Cochrane, Peter, "The Sound and Fury of Ignorance," from *The Daily Telegraph*, 356

Cognitive psychology, 2

Cognitive styles, 5–6

Comparison-contrast, 147

Concentration, 6–10

Concept cards, 45

Conclusions, 247–252

Connotation, 235–237

Content area exams, 442–448

Context clues, 46–52

Cox, Daniel, "Maternal Instincts," from *Life*, 33

Creative thinking, 348–350

"Critical-Period Hypothesis," from *Understanding Human Behavior*, by James McConnell 34–37

Critical thinking, 325–367

Csikszentmihalyi, Mihaly, "Finding the Flow," from *Psychology Today*, 89

"Death in Venison," from *The American Spectator*, by Geoffrey Norman, 176

Deductive reasoning, 341–342

Definition, 145–146

Denotation, 236

Description, 146

Details, 128–130, 432–433

de Maupassant, Guy "Mother Savage," from *Mademoiselle Fifi and Other Stories*, 254–259

De Vries, Fokko, "To Make a Drama Out of Trauma," from *Lancet*, 253

Diagrams, 368–370

Dictionary usage, 57–59

Dorfman, Ariel "If Only We All Spoke Two Languages," from *New York Times*, 268

"Doubts about Doublespeak," from *Exploring Language*, by William Lutz," 264–266

Drawing conclusions, 247–252

Easily confused words, 65–66

Editorial Cartoons, 299–301

"Elderly Parents: A Cultural Duty," from *The Orlando Sentinel* by TaThuc Phu, 304–305

External distractions, 7–9

"Evita Stylish, Thieving Diva of Cult Politics," from *USA TODAY* by Jim Pinkerton, 214

Fact, determining, 289–291

Fallacies, 335–340

Figurative language, 238–241

"Finding the Flow," by Mihaly Csikszentmihalyi from *Psychology Today*, 89

Fixations, 401–402

Flores, Lisa, "Best and Worst Cafeteria Foods," from *Muscle & Fitness*, 222

Flowcharts, 378–380

Glossary, 61–62,

Glossary for this book, 479–482

Gorman, Christine, "Higher Education: Crocked on Campus," in *Time*, 381

Graphic illustrations, 367–394

Griffin, Ricky and Ronald Ebert, "Understanding the Legal Context of Business," from *Business*, 315–318

"Has Television Killed Off Reading—and If So, So What?" from *Psychology*, by Carole Wade and Carol Tavris, 352–353

Hamilton, Eva May Nunnelley et al. "Alcohol and Nutrition," from *Nutrition*, 382–390

Henderson, Angelo, "Black Entrepreneurs Face a Perplexing Issue: How to Pitch to Whites," from *The Wall Street Journal*, 167

"Heroes for Civil Rights," from America and Its People, by James Martin et al, 168–171

"Higher Education: Crocked on Campus," by Christine Gorman in *Time*, 381

Idioms, 238

"If Only We All Spoke Two Languages," from *New York Times* by Ariel Dorfman, 268

Implied meaning, 241–247

Inductive reasoning, 341–343

Inference, 233–280

Integrate knowledge, 72, 77–84

Internal distractions, 9–12

"It's What You Say and Do," from *Sun Sentinel* by Marcia Pounds, 110

"Jensen, Jim, "Motorcyclists in Cross–Hairs," from *Rocky Mountain News*, 100

Keirsey Temperament Sorter II, 6

Kinnear, Thomas, Kenneth Bernhardt, and Kathleen Krentler, "The Story of Harley–Davidson Motorcycles," from *Principles of Marketing*, 101–105

Kotler, Philip and Gary Armstrong, "The Baby Boomers and the Generation Xers," from *Principles of Marketing*, 415–417

"Language in the Dumps," from *U.S. News and World Report*, by John Leo, 263

Left–brain dominance, 6

Leo, John, "A No–Fault Holocaust," from *U.S. News and World Report*, 453

Leo, John "Language in the Dumps," from *U.S. News and World Report*, 263

Light, Jr., Donald and Suzanne Keller, "Unity in Diversity," from *Sociology*, 111–115

Line graphs, 377–378

Locus of control, 448–449

Lutz , William "Doubts about Doublespeak," from *Exploring Language*," 264–266

MacCabe, Colin Screen: End of the Word?" from *The Guardian*, 351

Main idea, 121–186, 431–432

Mapping, 204–206

Maps, 372–375

Martin, James et al, "Heroes for Civil Rights," from *America and Its People*, 168–171

"Maternal Instincts," from *Life*, by Daniel Cox, 33

McConnell, James, "Critical-Period Hypothesis," from *Understanding Human Behavior*, 34–37

McConnell, James, "Monkey Love," from *Understanding Human Behavior*, 158–162

Meredith, Dennis, "Building a Better Mouse," from *Meridian: Midway Airlines*, 157

Metacognition, 78–84

Metaphors, 239

"Monkey Love," from *Understanding Human Behavior*, by James V. McConnell, 158–162

"Mother Savage," from *Mademoiselle Fifi and Other Stories*, by Guy de Maupasant 254–259

"Motorcyclists in Cross–Hairs," from *Rocky Mountain News*, by Jim Jensen, 100

Multiple–choice items, 434–442

Multiple meanings, 52

Myers, David, "The Effects of Facial Expressions," from *Psychology*, 5th ed., 91–96

Myers-Briggs Type Indicator, 5–6

"Net Addition," from *Sky: Delta Air Lines*, 19

"Nile Perch and Rabbits and Kudzu, Oh My!" from *Biology: The Unity and Diversity of Life*, 8th ed., by Cecie Starr and Ralph Taggart, 177–180

Norman, Geoffrey, "Death in Venison," from *The American Spectator*, 176

Notetaking, 196–199

"Nutrition and Stress: Running on Empty" from *Stress Management*, by Barbara Brehm 223–227

"Only Daughter," by Sandra Cisneros from *Women's Voices from Borderlands*, 309–311

Opinion, 289–291

Oracle Service Humor, "Net Addiction," 19

Organizing textbook information, 187–232

Outlining 199–204

"Passive Smoking," from *Living Well*, by Curtis Byer and Louis Shainberg, 412–413

Patnesar, Romesh, "Should You Carry a Gun?" from *Time*, 361

Patterns of organization, 144–151

Pen as pacer, 403–409

Personification, 239

Phu, Ta Thuc "Elderly Parents: A Cultural Duty," from *The Orlando Sentinel*, 304–305

Pie graphs, 375–376

Pinkerton, Jim, "Evita Stylish, Thieving Diva of Cult Politics," from *USA TODAY*, 214

Pitt, Leonard, "Women in History," from *We Americans*, 216–218

Point of view, 281–323

Pounds, Marcia "It's What You Say and Do," from *Sun Sentinel*, 110

Prefixes, 54–56

"Pregnancy and Birth," from *Biology: The World of Life*, by Robert Wallace, 208–212

Preview, 72–76

Prior knowledge, 122–123, 400

Purpose, 291–295, 433–434

"Race and Ethnicity," from *Sociology: A Brief Introduction*, by Alex Thio, 454–476

Rate flexibility, 395–422

Reader's Journal, 42, 70, 120, 186, 232, 279, 323, 366, 394, 422, 450

Reading Rate, 399–409

Reading and Study Strategies, 71–120

Recall, 72, 84–87

Regressions, 401

Right-brain dominance, 6

Rimer, Sara "San Antonio Journal: Novelist's Purple Palette Is Not to Everyone's Taste," from *New York Times*, 308

Rodriguez, Richard "Bilingual Education," from *Hunger of Memory*, 269–274

Roots, 54–56

Royko, Mike "Shooting Holes in Gun Laws," from *Tribune Media Services*, 362–363

"San Antonio Journal: Novelist's Purple Palette Is Not to Everyone's Taste," from *New York Times*, by Sara Rimer, 308

Scanning, 409–411

Schedule for weekly activities, 8

Schemata, 76

"Screen: End of the Word?" from *The Guardian*, by Colin MacCabe, 351

Search the Net, 32, 41, 69, 99, 109, 118–119, 166, 175, 184, 213, 221, 230, 262, 276, 278, 313, 322, 355, 360, 365, 393

Searching the Net, 27–32

Sequence, 146–147

"Shooting Holes in Gun Laws," from *Tribune Media Services*, by Mike Royko 362–363

"Should You Carry a Gun?" by Romesh Patnesar from *Time*, 361

Similes, 239

Simple listing, 144–145

Skimming, 409–410

Sky: Delta Air Lines, "Net Addition," 19

Sowell, Thomas, "Students Led to Believe Opinions More Important than Knowledge," from *The Arizona Republic*, 357–358

Standardized reading tests, 428–431

Starr, Cecie and Ralph Taggart "Nile Perch and Rabbits and Kudzu, Oh My!" from *Biology: The Unity and Diversity of Life*, 8th ed., 177–180

Stavropoulos, William, "Tort Reform: Excessive Litigation by Trial Lawyers," from *Vital Speeches of the Day*, 314

"Students Led to Believe Opinions More Important than Knowledge," from *The Arizona Republic*, by Thomas Sowell 357–358

Study system, 72–73

Structure, 53–56

Subvocalization, 402

Suffixes, 54–56

Summary, 151–156

Summary Points, 18, 68, 88, 156, 206, 252, 302, 350, 380, 411, 449

Syllabus, 15–18

Tables, 370–372

Test taking 423–451

Textbook application, 451–477

"The Baby Boomers and the Generation Xers," from *Principles of Marketing*, by Philip Kotler and Gary Armstrong 415–417

"The Effects of Facial Expressions," from *Psychology*, 5th ed., by David Myers 91–96

"The Internet," from *Computeres: Tools for an Information Age*, by H. L. Capron, 20–23

"The New Family Dinner," from *Parents* by Carol Wallace, 303

"The Sanctuary of School," from *The New York Times*, by Lynda Barry, 418–420

"The Sound and Fury of Ignorance," from *The Daily Telegraph*, by Peter Cochrane, 356

"The Story of Harley–Davidson Motorcycles," from *Principles of Marketing* by Thomas Kinnear, Kenneth Bernhardt, and

Kathleen Krentler, 101–105

Thesaurus, 62–63

"To Make a Drama Out of Trauma," from *Lancet*, by Fokko De Vries, 253

Thio, Alex, "Race and Ethnicity," from *Sociology: A Brief Introduction*, 454–476

Time order, 146–147

Tone, 295–299

Topics, 124–128

"Tort Reform: Excessive Litigation by Trial Lawyers," from *Vital Speeches of the Day*, by William Stavropoulos, 314

Transitional words, 67–68

Twombly, Renee, "Umbilical Cord blood Helps Fight Cancer," from *Duke Comprehensive Cancer Center Notes*, 207

"Umbilical Cord blood Helps Fight Cancer," from *Duke Comprehensive Cancer Center Notes*, by Renee Twombly, 207

"Understanding the Legal Context of Business," from *Business*, by Ricky Griffin and Ronald Ebert, 315–318

"Unity in Diversity," from *Sociology* by Donald Light, Jr. and Suzanne Keller, 111–115

Vocabulary, 43–70, 434

Verbal irony, 239

Wade, Carole and Carol Tavris, "Has Television Killed Off Reading—and If So, So What?" from *Psychology*, 352–353

Wallace, Carol, "The New Family Dinner," from *Parents*, 303

"Women in History," from *We Americans* by Leonard Pitt, 216–218

Word origins, 60–61

PAIRED READINGS IN *BRIDGING THE GAP*, 6TH EDITION

This edition of *Bridging the Gap* features paired readings at the end of each chapter. Each reading selection begins with a "contemporary focus" reading drawn from a popular source, such as a newspaper or magazine, that demonstrates the relevance of the following textbook selection to the world beyond college. A complete listing of the longer end-of-chapter academic readings, along with their accompanying contemporary focus articles, appears below.

	Title/Source of End-of-Chapter Textbook or Academic Selection	Title/Source of Accompanying Contemporary Focus Article
Chapter 1 **Active** **Learning**	"The Internet," by H. L. Capron, *Computers: Tools for an Information Age*	"Net Addiction," from *Oracle Service: Humor Mailing List* (oracle-humor-subscribe@lyris.oraclehumor.com)
	"Critical-Period Hypothesis," by James V. McConnell, *Understanding Human Behavior*	"Maternal Instincts," by Daniel J. Cox, *Life*
Chapter 3 **Reading and** **Study Strategies**	"Expressing Emotion," by David Myers, *Psychology, fifth edition*	"Finding the Flow," by Mihaly Csikszentmihalyi, *Psychology Today*
	"The Story of Harley-Davidson Motorcycles," from Thomas C. Kinnear et al., *Principles of Marketing*	"Motorcyclists in Cross-Hairs," by Jim Jensen, *Rocky Mountain News*
	"Unity in Diversity," by Donald Light, Jr., and Suzanne Keller, *Sociology, fourth edition*	"It's What You Say and Do," by Marcia Pounds, *Sun Sentinel*
Chapter 4 **Main Idea**	"Monkey Love," by James V. McConnell, *Understanding Human Behavior*	"Building a Better Mouse," by Dennis Meredith, *Meridian: Midway Airlines*
	"Heroes for Civil Rights," by James Martin et al., *America and Its People*	"Black Entrepreneurs Face a Perplexing Issue: How to Pitch to Whites," by Angelo B. Henderson, *The Wall Street Journal*
	"Nile Perch and Rabbits and Kudzu, Oh My!" by Cecie Starr and Ralph Taggart, *Biology: The Unity and Diversity of Life, eighth edition*	"Death in Venison," by Geoffrey Norman, *The American Spectator*
Chapter 5 **Organizing** **Textbook** **Information**	"Pregnancy and Birth," by Robert Wallace, *Biology: The World of Life*	"Umbilical Cord Blood Helps Fight Cancer," by Renee Twombly, *Duke Comprehensive Cancer Center Notes*
	"Women in History," by Leonard Pitt, *We Americans*	"Evita Stylish, Thieving Diva of Cult Politics," by Jim Pinkerton, *USA Today*
	"Nutrition, Health, and Stress," by Barbara Brehm, *Stress Management*	"Best and Worst Cafeteria Foods," by Lisa M. Flores, *Muscle & Fitness*

MEMORY
MUSIC

JAMES LANDRY

First edition, 2014.

Library of Congress Cataloging-in Publication Data Available on Request

Landry, James P.

Memory Music/James P. Landry. 1st Ed.

ISBN 978-0-9798992-5-6 (Paperback)

ISBN 978-0-9798992-6-3 (E-Book)

1. Arts & Photography   2. Blog

CONTENTS

INTRODUCTION   1

2006   4

2007   18

2008   46

2009   72

2010   116

ABOUT THE ARTIST   151

MUSIC

MEMORY

INTRODUCTION

In January 2005, Jim Landry began publishing a photoblog, MusicFromTheFilm. For the next eight years, he published a photograph and commentary or story several times a week, creating a work of over 1,000 photographs and stories.

For the text, Jim took his inspiration from the photograph itself or his past experiences or those of people he knew. He also tapped into overheard conversations on the Green and Red Line Metro or on downtown D.C. streets on his way to and from his job at SCIENCE magazine. He took his camera and photographed wherever he went: Washington, D.C., the Eastern Shore of Maryland, Britain, Iceland, Spain, Hawaii. Jim was a master of using "found art," as these photographs and stories attest.

Jim published new blog entries in MusicFromTheFilm until February 2012, when he felt that he had finished it. Two years later, he continues to post photos and commentary on Facebook and repost past entries from the vast archive of MusicFromTheFilm. What's old is new. Jim's art and artful living continue to inspire his friends and family to live and create using the materials at hand.

NICOLE BURTON, *Riverdale Park, Maryland*
April 2014

MUSIC

MEMORY

2006

TUESDAY, JULY 4, 2006

There are moments in a life that define what that life becomes from that point on. Sometimes they are simple things that become more important over time. Sometimes they are major events that suddenly shift a life into a place it would never otherwise be. For me, one of those moments happened in high school, in shop class, probably in 10th grade. It seemed every boy ended u p either in shop class or in automotive restoration, which meant taking a junker and turning it into a hot rod. Shop class was where you learned to build a small bookcase, but you started out with building a simple wooden lamp.

The first day of class was chaotic as the shop teacher tried to figure out who was who and where they would sit and who would be the dud and who would build a world-class bookcase. While all of this was going on, we were allowed to explore the classroom, which was filled with wood and power tools, including saws. A kid I barely knew but recognized as a troublemaker turned on the band saw and found a block of walnut that he proceeded to make progressively smaller. I was standing behind him, observing. As a piano student, I didn't want to be the first to "handle" a saw blade. As it turned out, this was a very good strategy and eventually offered the teacher a teaching moment, because the bored band saw chopper momentarily lost track of where his fingers and the wood were. Perhaps he was distracted by a noise or by looking for a pal to witness his walnut-sawing abilities. All I know is that he turned to face me, holding his right hand up. His index finger was missing. There was just a stump of a finger there. But, at least for a moment, there was no blood, so I wasn't too concerned. I thought maybe it was a trick. But, no, the blood came out in a gush and everyone started screaming. I must have been one of the screamers, I don't remember.

The walnut-sawing kid was rushed to the nurse's office by the teacher, who came back to look for the sawed-off finger shortly after. We were ordered to sit at our tables and the electricity to the tools was turned off. At that moment, I knew I would never be a carpenter and that I would avoid power tools for the rest of my life. The lamp I made in class was glued together, not nailed, and my bookcase fell apart.

FRIDAY, AUGUST 4, 2006

Tallulah Bankhead is buried not too far from this angel, in a cemetery on Maryland's Eastern Shore. She was, by all accounts, a woman of outrageous appetites. She is quoted as saying: "If I had to do it over again, I'd make the same mistakes, only sooner." And my favorite: "My mother told me all about whiskey and men, but she never said anything about cocaine and women."

"If I had to do it over again,
I'd make the same mistakes,
only sooner."

MONDAY, AUGUST 21, 2006

She always wanted to feel beautiful. She wanted other people to think of her as elegant and carefree; to be the kind of person who could drag a mink coat behind her across the floor and not think anything of it. She wanted to be glamorous, like a movie star, to have many lovers and to pay no mind to where the money went. If she wanted it, she bought it.

After the accident, however, she began to change. Maybe it was enough just to be alive, even though each day she awoke to pain. Everyone said that she was lucky, and she thought that she probably was. But, somewhere inside of her, she missed that carefree person who was a little reckless, but who made people turn their heads as she went by. She always wanted to feel beautiful.

WEDNESDAY, SEPTEMBER 6, 2006

In high school there was a lot of enthusiasm about the concept of "pep." "Pep" was something you were supposed to have along with things such as hair, limbs, and a quest for knowledge. Leaders had "pep"; losers did not. "Pep" was what got you through or got you over, along with a sunny disposition and a positive attitude. I can't say that I possessed this attribute. I certainly don't have much "pep" now, even after a Grande Espresso with an extra shot. But, from the perspective of 2006, "pep" doesn't seem such a bad thing. The person pictured above most certainly has it, and it looks pretty good.

"Pep" something you were supposed to have along with things such as hair, limbs, and a quest for knowledge.

FRIDAY, OCTOBER 20, 2006

Sometimes, chaos falls together in a pleasing way that allows you to see the hand of God, if that is your inclination. Different and seemingly unconnected pieces of the fabric of life twist together in such a manner that some new version of reality is, for a moment, visible. Then, just as suddenly as it appears, it is gone and the random sounds and rhythms return to their meaningless pulse.

MONDAY, DECEMBER 18, 2006

think that religions are what their followers do. On that basis, I've never been happy with the religions out there, except for the vapor that is Zen. I like the idea of nothing-ness, of passing like a vapor, a low hum, a breeze. When I walk down the street, I try to become the other people, the buildings, the sound of traffic; to be the sky and the clouds, the things I see as I turn my head, the sounds that wash over me and are gone. I try to be the moment that turns into another moment and then another, losing myself in the surround, becoming a part of the wheel that turns.

I like the idea
of nothingness, of
passing like a vapor,
a low hum, a breeze.

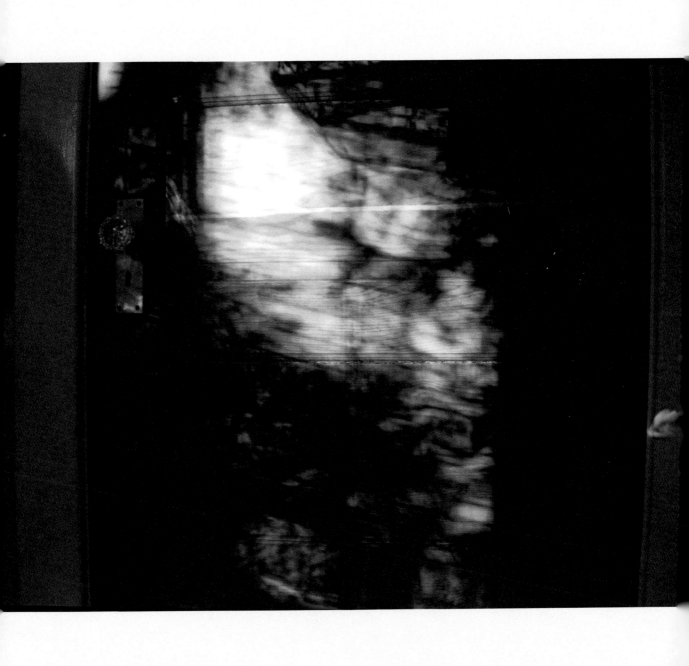

MUSIC

MEMORY

2007

WEDNESDAY, JANUARY 24, 2007

She said, "I had this dream where I was free, truly free, uncaged at last. It was wonderful to be free of worry, fear, lies, the dread I've felt since he was sent off to fight. It was like being released from prison and seeing the sky without looking through steel bars. My heart was uncaged, free to fly anywhere it wanted to go. Oh, it was wonderful. After I awoke, I just lay there enjoying the feelings I had experienced, knowing they wouldn't last the day or the morning or even till the alarm went off. I felt this dream was a message that he wouldn't die there alone, that he'd be coming home in one piece."

FRIDAY, FEBRUARY 23, 2007

At age 80, my Dad decided that what he really wanted to do was to be a cowboy. So, he bought some land in Tidewater, Virginia, and populated it with six cows and a bull, chickens, geese, peahens, peacocks, and a dog. And he is happier than I have ever known him to be. There's not much of anything where he is, but he doesn't seem to care. He's got his cows and a tractor and the land. And I wonder what power took him by the hand and directed him to that place and that purpose. His choice seems so different from the ones I am compelled to make. There must be a spirit guide for each of us when it is time to make a change, attuned to our needs and somehow knowing the right thing to do. Some, I think, accept that destiny; they are the ones at peace. Others either don't hear the call or fight it; they are the ones who are weary with pain.

TUESDAY, FEBRUARY 13, 2007

He said: "She asked me my name and I said, 'Smoke.' I was once lost in the water and smoke showed me how to save myself, so I took it as my name. Smoke is a relative of fire. Smoke travels on the air but is part of the earth, too. Smoke is a relative of mine. All that is sacred to us can be changed into smoke without much trouble. We must take care that this does not happen. Smoke, like me, is first here and then gone."

All that is sacred to us can be changed into smoke without much trouble.

THURSDAY, MARCH 22, 2007

He said: "Trains have a very different meaning, depending on your heritage and history. Trains mean one thing to European Jews and something completely different to African Americans. Trains meant a visit to Grandma to me when I was growing up. For friends living in San Francisco in 1978 after the Jonestown massacre, there was a long, long wait for family or friends to be shipped home on a train from Delaware, where all the victims were sent from Guyana. I love the "Chunnel" train that painlessly connects Britain with France, and my son's friend is looking forward to riding the "Bullet Train" in Tokyo this summer. We must all ride on different trains to get to our ultimate destinations. We always have trains in common."

TUESDAY, MARCH 6, 2007

I sat next to a man on the subway who asked me how I was. I told him that I didn't know yet. He replied, "Well, Jesus loves you," to which I answered, "This I know" and smiled at him. I hoped that at any moment the two of us would begin singing classic gospel songs and maybe the entire carload of people would join in and we'd be riding the train bound for glory instead of work. Instead, we both turned to our inner thoughts. He put his hands in his coat pockets because it was cold. I read a magazine article about three Mexican fishermen who survived nine months at sea. One of the fishermen was named Jesus.

WEDNESDAY, MAY 23, 2007

What would it mean to be a part of everything around us instead of just casual observers, remote engines, taking in selected pieces and over-looking everything else? What would it be like to participate in full instead of being detached and lost in some interior monologue? Maybe it would be too overwhelming, too much information coming at us too fast to understand. I'd like to know what it would be like anyway. I'd like to know what it would have felt like to have been among the first to experience the garden in full, to be in a place where everything was always new, always different in subtle ways, always amazing and sublime.

"I'd like to know what it would have felt like to have been amongt he first to experience a garden in full . . ."

MONDAY, JULY 23, 2007

As long as she could remember, she had been able to hear music. It wasn't music that just anyone could hear because it emanated from inside her head. Sometimes it sounded like an orchestra tuning up; sometimes the orchestra played long passages of subtle key changes that slowly evolved into a beautiful crashing wave of sound. At other times the music sounded like an avant-garde jazz ensemble honking away into the tiny hours before daybreak. As a teenager, she assumed that everyone could hear what she was hearing. It was only later that she realized this was not the case.

In her early 20s, the music began and ended with pain. The headaches would almost knock her down, and when she felt them coming on, she had only about three minutes to find a place to lie down. The music and the pain were then accompanied by nausea and blindness. As the orchestral sounds reached a climax, her vision would fail and change from color to a world of white. The music in her head devolved into random chaos, with the horn section waging a war against the strings and percussion edging them both out in the final chord. She finally sought medical care, and with the saxophone player taking a solo behind a stride piano and the circular brushes of the drummer keeping time, the doctor told her there was an inoperable tumor pressing on part of her brain. She would begin chemo and radiation next week. As she slowly put this information together and attempted to make it understandable, the piano player shifted to a minor key and played a slow, soft solo.

FRIDAY, JULY 20, 2007

Everything changes all of the time, without warning and usually beyond expectation. The air we breathe, the sounds we hear, the smells and tastes, the vibrations and textures of each moment evolve into memory and then fade into darkness. It has always been this way. We pass through our days like smoke in the air. We are our own camera, watching the film before us, trying to follow the story, waiting for the punch line before the credits roll.

MONDAY, JULY 9, 2007

She knew exactly where she was going and that was away, as far and fast as she could get there. She had some money she'd taken from her Mom's sugar bowl and a small bag of clothes, and she was going to get away. Beyond that, she had no plans and wasn't sure where she'd go. There had been a fight. Her Mom yelled, and she had yelled back. Her Mom hit her, and she hit her Mom back. Her Mom fell to the floor, and she ran for her room and slammed the door and began to throw some clothes into a bag. She grabbed the money that her Mom hid and left without saying "goodbye," "I'm sorry," or anything else. She was gone and she wasn't ever coming back!

THURSDAY, JULY 5, 2007

This is what we know: Police officers found the individual's car Sunday morning before 7 a.m. The doors were locked, and the keys hung visibly from the ignition. There was an envelope with a letter inside on the driver's side dashboard. The contents of this letter have not been made public at this time. The individual's wife reported that a small-caliber handgun was routinely kept in the glove compartment. The gun was not found in the initial search of the car. Fingerprints were taken from the interior and exterior of the vehicle. Results from these tests have not been made public. The vehicle was tested for bloodstains, and none were found. At this time, additional tests of materials found in the vehicle are being performed at a police laboratory in the area and officers are continuing to search for the vehicle's owner, described as a middle-aged white male, 5 feet, 10 inches tall, 165 pounds, with a scar across his left-hand index finger. The public has been asked to report any information concerning this individual to local police. Thank you.

FRIDAY, OCTOBER 12, 2007

One of the many things that define us as individuals is the ratio of what we keep to what we throw away. Some, for reasons of their own, keep everything: old letters, billing receipts from a dozen or more years, broken coffee cups, the tears of angels or saints, regrets and disappointments. Others keep hardly anything, preferring to travel light. Some keep only what they value, things like love and loyalty and the closeness of friends. There must be, at the end, some ideal ratio that will bestow the highest value on us, some ideal weight that reflects our character based on what we kept and what we gave away.

"Some, for reasons of their own, keep everything. . . . Others keep hardly anything . . . "

MONDAY, DECEMBER 31, 2007

She knew as a matter of faith that in Heaven there wouldn't be any lines and all the latest stuff would be readily available. In Heaven you could get anything without the hassles that you had to put up with here. And there wouldn't be any problem with returns. If you decided after a month or so that you didn't like the stuff you bought in Heaven, they would take it back with no questions or attitude. Heaven would have all the sizes, not just the extra-large sizes that you had to pick through here, and you could order anything in any color. This is just one of the things that make Heaven, Heaven: It's a shopper's paradise.

THURSDAY, DECEMBER 20, 2007

The more he talked, the faster his words were used and gone. Into the silence fell his fears, and with his fears went desire. With desire gone, there was no longer hunger. With hunger gone, there developed in time a kind of peace that he never imagined could exist. He smiled and became still, and in a heartbeat he was gone.

MUSIC

MEMORY

2008

TUESDAY, JANUARY 8, 2008

He thought about all the people he'd seen in movies who know somehow that they will die, but don't know that the movie will end. That's what Hell must be like, he said, to have salvation just around the corner without the realization that it's there for you like an emergency door or a get-out-of-jail-free card. To see the horror around you, knowing that you are a part of it, but not knowing that there is an end where the Director cries "Cut! That's a wrap." An end where the actors take up their real lives, removing the makeup and the doomed clothing that doesn't belong to them but to some character created to move a story line forward, and then meet up with the people they love to have a drink or a meal or just relax against each other in a darkened movie theater.

"That's what Hell must be like, he said, to have salvation just around the corner without the realization that it's there for you . . ."

TUESDAY, MARCH 4, 2008

On the train, headed home on a Friday, he had a vision. This vision told him that all of the stories he knew were true: the stories of valor; the ones where good overcame evil; the stories of love and betrayal and revenge and the ones that resulted in redemption and forgiveness; the stories where one person's sacrifice made all the difference and the ones that told of universal truths being revealed to someone suffering; the stories that ended happily; and the ones that led to other stories that informed the listener and soothed them to a magical state of acceptance. Before he came to his stop, he knew with clarity that stories lead to larger truths and that these truths lead to a deeper understanding of where the stories would end.

WEDNESDAY, APRIL 9, 2008

He said: "I was born after the war and before the bounty that followed it, which placed me advantageously to experience the late 1960s as I came of age. I witnessed the murders of John Kennedy and Bobby and Martin Luther King and others whose only crime was to have a compassionate heart. I also saw what burned: children in Vietnam and homes and storefronts here in the USA. Things are different now. The divide is just as wide and the anger just as strong, but now we don't expect it to be different. We're used to the pain now and don't feel it much anymore, even though it's still there. It's still very much there."

"We're used to the pain now and don't feel it much anymore, even though it's still there."

THURSDAY, JUNE 12, 2008

THE PLENITUDE: CABS

He said: "This is what I think: If you are rich, as we are, and you die, as we must someday, your wealth will influence the future beyond your natural lifetime. Wealth is a way to be immortal. Just as money has an effect on how we live, it will have an effect on how we die. Wealth is a way to live beyond the grave."

FRIDAY, SEPTEMBER 19, 2008

It wasn't fear that he felt, but a lightness of being: a terminus. He knew that what he was doing was dangerous. He was still in bondage as the elders had been in bondage before him. He had traveled far and wanted nothing more than to lay down his body and rest. But he knew that would come later, much later. There was the river yet to cross and the fields beyond to cross after that, but only at night. These were the days of shadow and the nights of frost.

TUESDAY, SEPTEMBER 2, 2008

She said: "William Faulkner said that the past is not dead; in fact, it's not even past. I know for a fact that he is correct. Everything that I have seen and everything that I have felt or experienced or have been told about by friends or family is still with me, living in me every day. Some parts make me stronger. I have known sorrow. I have known horror. But I have also known kindness and courage. Each day is another link in a chain that feeds me and informs me and gives me the strength to take another breath."

MONDAY, OCTOBER 27, 2008

She said: "We had a neighbor named Vivian, who was 90 years old and vigorous. She still used a wringer washing machine in her basement because the house was built around it and the washer couldn't be taken out or another brought in. She mostly ate meat patties that she prepared herself and boiled potatoes. She'd walk to the grocery store and bring home a five-pound bag of potatoes in a wheeled cart. She was an artist, so her house was filled with her artwork. In the fall of every year she would walk into the woods and select the most vivid leaves and bring them home. She'd spend hours picking out the most beautiful ones. One year shortly before she died, I asked: 'Vivian, what do you do with those lovely leaves I see you pluck from the trees at the beginning of November each year?' And she told me that she sent them to her nieces and nephews. I thought it was so sweet of her. It took me a little while to do the math, but a few days later it struck me: Oh, my God! Her nieces and nephews must be in their 60s or 70s! She must have sent them autumn leaves for 50 or more years! Some of those nieces and nephews may have even passed on during this time. What could they possibly think of their annual mail from Aunt Vivian? And then I thought that it didn't really matter. It was still a very sweet thing to do. I would love to have someone mail me beautiful fall leaves every year."

WEDNESDAY, OCTOBER 15, 2008

He said: "I was brought up by the Roman Catholic nuns. That was my education when I was coming up. It was the same for everybody. This was not our religion; it was somebody else's religion. The nuns were strict, boy. They were a tough bunch, and I guess they had to be. But I fell away from the Church as I got older. I don't know many of the stories now and couldn't tell them to you from memory. My people's religion means more to me now. We have our festivals where we come together to remember where we came from and how we fit together as a people. I don't know too much about the Catholic church. If you asked me about God, I wouldn't know what to say. My God is up there. My God is in the sky."

WEDNESDAY, NOVEMBER 26, 2008

She said: "He escaped early, the oldest of eight sons on a farm during what was later known as the Great Depression. Lied about his age, joined the Army, and ended up somewhere in Nevada along with a bunch of other recruits waiting for the Big Bang. They spent the night digging trenches in the darkness out in the desert. All they knew was that they would wait until they were told to put on their darkened goggles and stand up. Shortly afterward, they would see a bright flash from something 15 miles away and wait for the wind that would follow. The wind would blow sand into their faces and bury it deep in their clothing. They would open their arms to embrace the nuclear wind that would enfold them with unseen radiation, entering them in ways more intimate than anything living ever could have. They were the beginning of what would shortly be the end."

"The wind would blow sand into their faces and bury it deep in their clothing."

MONDAY, NOVEMBER 17, 2008

He said: "Oh, yes, we marched. We marched all over the country, or at least it felt like it sometimes. We marched in the Jim Crow South; we marched in the icy North. We marched against segregation and against the war, any number of them, and we marched for each other. Didn't seem like it made any difference sometimes. Seemed like nothing was ever gonna change, one way or the other. We marched for the young people who might follow us and we marched for ourselves and for each other because sometimes that was all we had. Some went home on their own two legs and some had to be shipped home in a plain pine box. Those were hard times, let me tell you; real hard times. I still can't bear the sight of them German dogs. But, anyway, we're OK now. Now it seems like somehow it all worked out the way we wanted it to. Now it seems like our prayers got answered a little bit. I'm still keeping my fingers crossed, though. Be a fool not to. But I'm hoping we don't have to march no more."

WEDNESDAY, DECEMBER 24, 2008

He said: "It was very difficult to leave everything behind us, everything we had built and the life that we had made for ourselves. But we knew we had to leave. We had to go because if we did not, they would come and kill us. They told us so. They sent letters saying, 'You and your family will die,' 'You are cowards and collaborators,' 'You will be slaughtered like sheep,' and so on. So, there was not another way. We wanted to live.

"I had a cousin in Chicago. That is where we went. We knew nothing when we got there. I could speak only a little English; my family, none. We had the clothes we came with, nothing more. We had no furniture, no bedding, no food, no jobs. My cousin helped us get started with this new, strange life. It is OK. It will be OK. We are alive and we are together and that is the most important thing. We don't have to be afraid all the time now. We can breathe here. It will be all right. It will be OK."

MONDAY, DECEMBER 15, 2008

She said: "He was a funny guy, but I liked him, even with all of the quirks in his personality. There is one story about a trip he took to the East Coast that I just love to tell. You see, he wasn't that crazy about airplanes. Even in the best of conditions, he wasn't a good flyer. Even in first class. He didn't like to be in small spaces, smashed up against other people. He didn't like the air inside the airplane cabin; he didn't like airplane food; he just plain didn't like to fly. That was the heart of the matter. He just didn't like flying. But he did it anyway. So, he had to fly to the East Coast for some reason and I took him to the airport. We were early, the way he liked to be. As we were waiting for the flight to New York to be called, I noticed that he was getting more and more nervous. He was looking around at everyone; really looking at them. I noticed, but didn't pay it any mind. The longer we waited, the more nervous he became, until he finally got up and told me we had to go. 'Go? Go where?' I asked him. 'Home,' he said. 'Why? What's the matter?' I asked him. 'We just have to go.' So, we went. I took him back home, and he missed the flight.

"The next day, I asked him to explain why he wouldn't get on the flight. He told me, 'They were doomed.' He told me the people waiting for that flight to New York looked like doomed people to him and that's why he left. He felt the flight was a doomed flight and all of the people waiting to board looked like doomed people and he didn't want to die with them and that's why he wouldn't board. They were all doomed."

MUSIC

MEMORY

2009

MONDAY, DECEMBER 15, 2008

She said: "Well, I guess I had to give up a lot, but I never thought about it in those terms. I just did what I had to do. I mean, I couldn't just stand back and watch what was going on. Nothing would've changed if I did that. They were killing the water, killing the land, killing the birds and the other animals that depend on the Gulf. They already hated me because I was a woman, so I never really thought about what they would do to me that they hadn't already done. I was never one of those people that could watch something terrible happen and just walk away. I had to do something.

"So, I set my boat on fire to block the entrance to the commercial water lanes. That was the beginning of my protest. Now, mind you, my boat was my whole life. Without my boat, I couldn't make a living. But with my wreck of a boat sitting right in the middle of the shipping lane, they couldn't deliver their poisons to the Gulf. It's surprising how quickly a body can get used to being put in jail. It got to be just a regular part of my life. 'Course, being a woman in South Texas isn't much better than being in jail anyway."

WEDNESDAY, APRIL 15, 2009

He said: "I have a disease that will eventually kill me. I'm not afraid, because this disease is slow in working its wonder. It isn't written on my face so sharply that anyone would know that I am ill. I walk among healthy people who do not give me a second look or a second thought. I am a little bit sicker each day, yet I am the only one who knows. Me, and the doctors who attempt, vainly, to cure me. I am becoming comfortable with the idea of death. Maybe it will be a welcome relief when it comes. But, for the moment, for today, I am as well as I can be and that is a gift. Looking at your smile is a gift. The touch of your hand is a gift. This breath that I breathe is a gift. The comfort of friends is a gift. Even remembering is a gift now. I am ill, but I possess many gifts and as long as you grant me that, I will be a lucky man."

"I walk among healthy people who do not give me a second look or a second thought."

THURSDAY, APRIL 9, 2009

She said: "This is what I am not: I am not a gender, I am not a color, I am not a race, I am not an authority on anything. This is what I am: I am a voice, I am a whisper, I am a curtain set in motion by a summer breeze, I am the air that brushes against your skin when day is done and the sun has almost set, I am the thing you are looking for but will not easily find because you do not yet know where to look."

TUESDAY, JUNE 16, 2009

He said: "I never thought about money. There wasn't a lot to think about, I guess. It was always there for me. I never had to work for it or do anything to make money be there. It was always just there, like dust or water. I never had a budget like other people do. I never saved anything. Why would I? It would be like saving fingernail clippings. Whatever I wanted, I got. I just paid the bill and left. There wasn't any magic or mystery; I didn't even think we were rich or anything. I took it all for granted, in my stride, as they say. I thought it was like this for almost everyone. At least everyone we knew and socialized with. Money is like air or like water; it is essential to life on earth. It you don't have money, gosh, I can't even imagine it. It would be so foreign. What do people do without money? And where do they go?"

"It you don't have money, gosh, I can't even imagine it. It would be so foreign. What do people do without money?

TUESDAY, JUNE 9, 2009

He said: "I can remember our first car very clearly. I say 'our' because it was meant to benefit everyone in the family: Mom, who didn't know how to drive yet but would soon learn, and Dad, whose machine it really was since he picked it out and paid for it. But it would eventually be for my older brother, Hank, since he had just come home from the war and a car quickly became essential if you wanted to impress women. I was only 11 when the car came into our family, but I remember the excitement when Dad pulled into the drive with his Ford. It was all black and had two doors. The seats in the front folded back to let Hank and me get in. Mom and Dad sat up front, of course. The car had this great feature, which I think Dad paid extra for: a metal stick that stuck out of the sides of the car up front, near where the wheels were, and made a scratching noise on the curb if you got too close. I suppose this was meant to guide you when you were parking on the street so that you didn't mess up the paint on the side of the car. Other than that, the car had no extras: no radio, no ashtray, nothing, but that didn't really matter. It was our first car ever.

"America was on the move and soon everyone would have a car, but we were the first on our street and that counted for something back then. Who would have guessed that it would lead to where we are now with global warming and oil getting scarce and many families having a car for everyone in the family, sometimes extras that no one really drives? It's so crazy now. It used to be that you drove the car to get someplace far away, like to the beach or a trip to Baltimore to visit Grandma. Now you need a car to do anything. People drive a mile to buy a pack of cigarettes and then drive home. It used to be that the car was a kind of freedom. Now it's a kind of jail."

WEDNESDAY, JUNE 3, 2009

She said: "I am an artist. That is what I am, and it could never be any other way. I describe things that are not there and define things that have no boundaries. When I am successful, I create a world that has not yet existed and populate it with dreams and tears and love and memories. Once I bring this world to life, I forget everything and start all over again. It is an endless process, and when I am done there will be others to take up the task and start again. It is a process that is never complete, not even in death. It is not a 'calling' because it is not something that is brought to you, but something that has always been there, waiting for you to find it, embrace it, and then be swallowed whole."

"Once I bring this world to life,
I forget everything and start
all over again."

THURSDAY, JULY 30, 2009

He said: "I met him twice when I was a student in Connecticut. He was an imposing man with his beard and glasses and his chanting and the way that people were attracted to his calmness and his center. He wanted peace, just like we all wanted peace then. He would come to some of the protests at the university, and his presence would attract other people to come as well. He would play a kind of squeezebox with his feet and sing along. He would remind people to pick up trash before they left: to 'do your kitchen yoga' as he called it. I was amazed that he would come all the way from the city to spend time with young people. He was, after all, quite famous for various things. We had read his poetry and knew that he had helped create a whole new kind of writing years before we were aware of him.

"I was always struck by the book about his mother, who was ill and committed to institutions, and who died in one. I remember his telling about a letter she sent to him in the last few days of her life. She told him where she was going and where she would be and where he could find hope and the strength within him to carry on without her, because it was time for her to leave. She told him that the key was in the window of their apartment in New York. The key was in the window, in the sunlight of the window, and would always be there for him or anyone who needed it. That was her gift to him and also to me, who she didn't even know existed."

MONDAY, JULY 27, 2009

He said: "I dreamed that I had two lives that were completely different from each other, and yet were lived at the same time. In one life I was an elderly and frail man of letters who was being abused by the caretaker who was supposed to look after my health and my affairs. I lived in a large stone house in the countryside and had only an estranged daughter left to help me. In my other life, I lived in a large city and was young, just starting my life. I had many friends of both genders whose company I enjoyed. I was an artist living in a rundown neigh-borhood where other artists and musicians also lived because of the inexpensive rental rates. Both these people were aware of their other half. For the old man, the young man was his future; for the young man, the old man was his past."

TUESDAY, JULY 21, 2009

He said: "I don't know what the big deal is about memory. Why do I have to remember everything? Why is a good memory such a favored attribute? Remember what? Why do I have to remember death or pain or hate? What does it matter if I don't remember how old you are or what your late father's middle name was? Of what use are the names of everyone I went to first grade with now that I am nearing the ending of this life? Shouldn't I only recall what is of use to me? It is not an effort to remember your face and the number of times that I have kissed it. I have no problem remembering the way you smell after a bath, or the gentle way you touch me as I awaken, or the way you look when you talk about our lives together. I can remember every time we made love and I can remember the way a full moon lights up the night and the way that certain flowers smell and the taste of chocolate. Isn't that enough? I remember the day. I remember passion. I remember joy. I remember the look of freshly fallen snow. I remember the taste of fresh air in the fall and I remember why I'm here. Everything is not important."

"I remember the taste of
fresh air in the fall and
I remember why I'm here."

TUESDAY, AUGUST 25, 2009

She said: "You are a part of it whether you know it or not. You didn't have to fill out any paperwork; you didn't have to practice or memorize anything, or pledge anything, or even do anything in particular. You are a part of it just by being here. Wasn't that easy? It should be easy because there's nothing hard about it at all. You just have to be here along with the rest of us. You just have to look up and see what there is to see, feel it, smell it if you want to, then hold it and take it into your being. Then, and this is really the only difficult part, you have to follow it where it's going to take you."

not limo

Do n

FRIDAY, AUGUST 14, 2009

She said: "He wasn't a cowboy, but he was from the farm. He had grown up with animals and knew how to ride a horse, but never had a horse of his own. He grew up fast and left the farm and joined the Army and made a life out of that until he couldn't take it any more and started a business in real estate and sold and later built houses. He smoked cigarettes from the earliest times he could remember. He went through a couple of brands, but ended up smoking the cowboy brand. I never liked the smell of smoke on a man, but he had other attributes that made up for the stink. I guess I loved him, at least at one time I did. I was with him up until the last moments in the hospital. He died while I was out, taking a break. He was under a lot of different medications, so we didn't talk too much. I just held his hand mostly. I don't even really know if he knew I was there most of the time. I sure wish I could have been there to hold his hand when he passed. I miss him now. But I wish I could have been there when he died."

MONDAY, AUGUST 10, 2009

He said: "There is a peace beyond peace and a solitude beyond solitude and a quiet so silent that it suspends time and place. This place is not difficult to find. One can find it in the blink of an eye or in the breath taken at dusk as the light fades and we all return to the sleep that is our selves."

MONDAY, AUGUST 3, 2009

He said: "It's amazing, isn't it? Life goes on somehow, in spite of everything that seeks to kill it once and for all. Wars happen, and life goes on; plagues happen, and life goes on; floods happen, famine happens, all kinds of horror. Somehow we are still here, getting up each morning and getting dressed, opening the window, and breathing the fresh air. Then whatever is waiting for us on the other side of the hill notices that we are here; that we are fragile and weak; that we can be crushed, destroyed like a snowflake, and utterly erased from history. Yet we survive and tell our children how we did it. Somehow, in spite of everything, life goes on."

"Somehow we are still here, getting up each morning and getting dressed, opening the window, and breathing the fresh air."

TUESDAY, SEPTEMBER 8, 2009

He said: "Oh, Hell! They're still touring? I can't believe it. Why? Surely they have enough money. It can't be for the money. They made millions in the 60s and 70s. Millions! Why on earth would they want to get back on the road? What do they have to prove? Nothing!

"I just don't get it. I was, and still am, one of their biggest fans. When I was young, I followed them around the country when they toured, which was like always. I loved everything they did. They could play all night and all day without any real break, forever. It was the closest thing I could think of to being a gypsy. If I ever had a fantasy of being in a band, it was their band. But, dude, that was a long time ago. I just can't believe they're on the road again. I hope they don't die."

FRIDAY, SEPTEMBER 4, 2009

She said: "Oh, she was such a fine vocalist. When she sang, my heart bled; I swear it did. She sang from her very center, her soul, and when she sang, it was like she was singing just for me. I went to see her perform as often as I could. If I couldn't get someone to take me, I took myself. She was one of the reasons I put up with living in the city. If I had to drive to the city every time I wanted to do something, I would have gone crazy by now. Oh, I can see her now in my mind's eye. If I'm at home, I have the Hi-Fi on and she is right there with me. She kept me whole, I'm telling you. She had everything: a voice that could melt ice or burn down the house. She was beautiful: dark but not too dark, with that sultry look that men liked so much. The only thing she could have done better was to stay away from drugs. If she could have done that, she would have lived longer and there would have been more of her music to hear, and to cry over in the cold night, and to put me down to sleep."

TUESDAY, OCTOBER 6, 2009

He said: "I am a metaphor. That is, I am something other than what I am. I am the thing you struggle to understand. I am the currents that swirl around you and the wind that brushes against your back. I am the stand-in, the thing you are waiting to remember, the taste that remembers your mouth. I am the seasons that change each day and I am the things that fall away, perish, and become something new again. I am the walk in the woods."

MONDAY, NOVEMBER 30, 2009

He said: "To all the vets of all the wars, I say 'Welcome home'; to those bleeding now across an ocean, 'Welcome home.' For the brothers and sisters who marched for us, 'Welcome home.' For those who stood up and raised their voices demanding justice and who risked their lives for who we are today, 'Welcome home.' For the men and women who love each other and who, in turn, love themselves because we are all spirits of the light, 'Welcome home.' For the ghosts guiding us through the passage, for those who are loved and those who love, for the ones who will not be forgotten, 'Welcome home and Amen!'"

SATURDAY, NOVEMBER 14, 2009

He said: "When I was 16 years old I swore that I would never set foot in Alabama or Mississippi. I don't know why I didn't include Florida or Georgia or the Carolinas; it was just Alabama and Mississippi. For me, those two states symbolized the South and its torture, misery, injustice, "strange fruit," burning churches, and shots in the night. Everything about those places was frightening and repulsive to me, so I swore that I would remove them from my world, even though I knew that wasn't an option to the people who lived there. For them, it was a twisted history that went back as far as time and showed no chance of changing before the pastor said the last words over their caskets. But I made up my mind early, before the marches, the dogs, the water cannons, and the prayers, and to this day I have held fast to my younger self's pledge. I haven't gone to Mississippi or Alabama, and I never will. I just feel like I can't go there. Even now, I can't go there."

MONDAY, NOVEMBER 2, 2009

He said: "I realized one morning that what I had was not enough. It seemed to me that my life wasn't as rich or varied or lyrical as other people's, and this made me sad. I wanted to have the life and dreams that other people had, but try as I might, I was powerless to change my life. It continued as it always had. So, I worked harder. I observed more closely, listened more intensely, lingered where other people gathered, and learned from them. I began to change slowly. Realizing that, I worked harder and over time my life began to change radically. I became another person, and my secret was simple: I have successfully made other people's memories my own. I have found the way to a meaningful life. I take the dreams of others and make them my own."

FRIDAY, DECEMBER 18, 2009

He said: "I guess you would call her a radical, but I didn't think of her that way. I met her because of a note tacked on a campus billboard about tutoring kids in the projects. We both volunteered. It didn't last long because the program was being run by the Panthers, and word came back from Oakland that the movement didn't need any white people. So, that was that. She left eventually and moved to San Francisco and I, after a time, moved there myself and wanted to see her, so she gave me directions on where to meet.

"The place turned out to be a church in the Haight that was packed with people. A band was playing and people were testifying, and eventually she came onstage to tell how the spirit had helped her kick drugs and how the Reverend was helping the poor people in the city regain their health. We met later, she introduced me to the Reverend Jones, we talked, and then she was gone. I later found out that she and the whole church had moved to South America. I didn't hear about her again until after the murders in the jungle. Several hundred church members died: young, old, and babes in arms. She was at a house in town when it happened instead of at the jungle compound and survived the killings. I often think about her, but I don't think we'll see each other again. Sometimes, things just end permanently."

THURSDAY, DECEMBER 17, 2009

She said: "The first things you notice about him are his hands. They are hands that have lasted a lifetime making objects of beauty. When I first saw him and he took my hand in his in greeting, I almost lost it. At close to 90, he still looks strong. His hands are still strong and he still works every day. His studio is amazing. There was artwork everywhere I looked. Every corner, every inch of the floor, and every table and chair had works in progress on it. The only free space was the small area where he set down his coffee cup. We talked a lot about what he was currently doing. He didn't want to talk about the past. He said that it didn't mean anything to him; he was happy every day, so the past and the present were all one for him. It was such an honor to meet him for the article. He has lived such a large life in his art. We got some good footage and video and the film will be good, I'm sure, but the thing that I took away with me was the image of his hands."

MUSIC

MEMORY

2010

SUNDAY, JANUARY 31, 2010

She said: "My name is 'Cherished Treasure.' That's not first name, 'Cherished,' second name, 'Treasure,' but 'Cherished Treasure' all together. As you might guess, my parents were hippies. I often wonder what they could have been thinking to have given a helpless child this name. I guess they were probably stoned and not thinking right. But, truth to tell, the farm where we lived had a lot of strangely named people. I wasn't the only one, and I didn't think anything of my name until I had to go to a real school after the commune broke up. My name in that school got lots of laughs, as you can imagine, and it got to the point that I hated to have my name called out in class, because they always got it wrong and when they got it right, the other kids giggled and made me feel weird. When I was 18, I had my name changed. I was mostly on my own by that time and it was a hassle and a bother, but I finally was able to legally change my name to Cheryl Anne. (That's first name, 'Cheryl,' and middle name, 'Anne.') I think it suits me better, and everyone thinks it's normal."

THURSDAY, JANUARY 28, 2010

She said: "We must work harder to make the past present. I want you to take me down to the river; to the river of light; to the river of love, the river of faith and of hope. And when you have taken me there, leave me so that I can be lifted up by the tides and sent to where we all belong in the end. I cannot get there by myself. I will need you to give me courage and leave me so that I can be washed up on the mountain where I will make my peace."

"We must work harder to make the past present."

TUESDAY, JANUARY 26, 2010

He said: "Assassinate your beliefs! They will not help you. Strangle your doubts. They will only hold you back. We must struggle to free our minds and bodies and make ourselves ready for our miraculous and divine destiny. Our strengths will bear us away to another place unknown to us. We will fly. We will fly away in wonder."

THURSDAY, FEBRUARY 4, 2010

She said: "Let me tell you, they didn't let too many women come on up to that place. It was sure enough a man's world up there. They let me come up because I could sing and I could scat and I could play piano. Mostly, though, they let me come up because I could put up with them and I could drink any of them under the table, and I didn't mind the mice and the bugs and the drugs. Only squares showed up before 1 a.m., and often we didn't leave till the sun came up, whenever that was. The music changed every night, depending on who came to play. Man, we had us some WILD times. I remember Monk the best, but there was a whole bunch of players that you would probably never have heard about. The walls rocked! There wasn't any complaints from neighbors because in that part of the city there wasn't much in the way of anything, especially neighbors. We didn't have heat. We didn't have a toilet. We sure enough didn't have no refrigerator, and you couldn't even see out the windows. That's how dirty they were. But we sure enough had ourselves a good time and we sure did learn a whole bunch from the people who played that sweet, sweet way on into the night!"

MONDAY, MARCH 22, 2010

He said: "I had a cousin named Charles but called Chuck. It wasn't a very Jewish name, but then it wasn't a time to have a Jewish name. Anyway, he drowned at the New Jersey shore in 1956 at the age of six. His mother told him to go and wash his hands in the surf before getting an ice cream and a freak wave came and took him away. When my mother got the news, she screamed and then fainted. I was seven when this happened. We were living in Germany after the war. Chuck was always, from then on, the missing person at family reunions. He was there, but he was not. The grownups talked about him in whispers. He was the only family member to drown and, of course, he was so young and being taken at such a young age was awful, truly awful. Anyway, the years went on and Chuck continued to be the drowned cousin. I only have dim pictures of him in my head because I didn't know him very well. The thing that really got me, though, was the fact that he never got older. He was always a child. I'm now more than 60 years old, but Chuck, or Charles, is still only six and he is still just trying to wash the sand off his hands at the beach."

FRIDAY, MARCH 12, 2010

He said: "I wish that I knew a way to make it better, but I don't. I wish the pain would lessen, but I know that it won't. I wish that every day could be another in a long chain of wonderful days full of warmth and joy and fulfilled expectations. I wish that I knew what to say, but I don't. And I wish that I knew how to say it, but I don't. It all comes down to one thing in the end: whatever you live, is life."

FRIDAY, APRIL 2, 2010

She said: "There is a kind of pain that can't be felt but only seen. There is a kind of ache that keeps you up at night but is gone with the first sunlight. There is a kind of ending that leaves no room for new beginnings, and there are tastes that foul the mouth so that the ire cannot be swallowed. We all live with different diseases. There is the disease of neglect. There is the disease of faithlessness. There is the disease of waiting for it all to pass. We are each silently reaching for the moment of peace when all the pain collects so that it can be forever put away, locked away in a dark place from which there is no return."

"There is a kind of ache that keeps you up at night but is gone with the first sunlight."

129

TUESDAY, MAY 25, 2010

She said: "These are the words I will give to you: patience so that you can know the gentle passing of time; understanding, so that you can trust what you hear and be strong enough to say so; faith, so that you can know where you came from and where you will eventually stay; strength to get you through each day, no matter how difficult; love, so that you can give back what was so generously given to you; mercy, so that you will always know that anything can happen at any time, to anyone. The last word I give you is hope, which is the strongest word and the one you must guard by pressing it to your heart. Without hope, you have nothing that will stay with you. Hope is the strongest word of all. Be certain to keep hope with you always."

TUESDAY, JUNE 1, 2010

He said: "A small package of great worth will come to you. It will contain everything that you desire at this moment. You must open it at noon, for it is at noon when desire is strongest. This package is being sent to you as a gift. That is the only way it can be transferred. Once it is yours, you will have it forever. This is a great responsibility as well as a great gift. You must never know who sent it to you. It is enough to know that someone, somewhere, thinks that you have the courage to open the package and make it your own."

SUNDAY, AUGUST 15, 2010

He said: "She was the oldest daughter of emigrants and married the oldest son of emigrants. She gave him two sons and a daughter and carried the dishes and the curtains each time they moved to another foreign place. Her right hip was injured at birth and she always walked with a limp that she tried to hide, but couldn't. She held on to a slight accent from living among people who had to relearn a language to speak. She had small hands and big feet. She smoked a lot and loved to cut pats of butter and eat each of them on a small piece of bread. Sometimes she didn't even bother with the bread. Her husband had other wives but no other children. She sat down one night to watch Walter Cronkite give the days' news and never got up. She had a heart attack and died before the first commercial, never really knowing what it was like not to be an emigrant."

MONDAY, AUGUST 2, 2010

She said: "She was old. No one really wanted her. She was sick a lot, and nobody wants to be around sick old people. And she was always forgetting stuff, like her cell phone number and where she put the keys. I mean, how hard is it to not lose your keys? I told her over and over to just put the darn keys in one place, but she could never remember to do that. And her clothes were smelly. She was always going to the doctor. You'd think they were having an affair or something. Gross! And she had to take all these pills and stuff. All she really did was watch TV and cook. That's all. I guess most of her girlfriends were either dead, or in a home somewhere, so I tried to be nice to her, but she didn't have a whole lot to say that was interesting. So, anyway, she was old, she died, and then I got my old room back."

WEDNESDAY, SEPTEMBER 22, 2010

He said: "I wasn't running away. I was running toward something. I was reaching out and hoping that someone would see me before I drowned. It seemed like I was always running. I ran by the church choir singing their hearts out for Jesus. I ran up the stairs and out the door. I ran away from the war that will never end and I ran from the heat and hatred of Mississippi and Georgia. I ran from the parents who didn't know who I was. I ran from the towns and over the mountains. I ran to the beat of my heart and with a tear in my eye from the dust on the road. I saw others, like myself, who ran until they could not run anymore. I followed the sun and the moon and the stars and my own compass and my own time. I ran and then stopped when I could not run anymore. I stopped and waited on the side of the road for my brothers and my friends so that they could find me somehow and take me back home."

"I ran to the beat of my heart
and with a tear in my eye
from the dust on the road."

TUESDAY, SEPTEMBER 7, 2010

He said: "I remember the times we had together back then when we were young, footloose, and a little bit crazy. Science now tells us, of course, that when all that stuff was happening, our brains were still developing and that's why we did the things we did: because we only had three-fourths of what would, in adulthood, be our brains. Damn, we had good times though. I remember racing around the quad at 3 a.m. wearing nothing but a grin. I wasn't doing much grinning the next morning, as I recall. Of course, we probably wouldn't have had to spend a creepy weekend in lockup if we had had a brain then. And then there was the driving: I drove us into New York City and for the whole ride I wasn't really sure where the roadway was. I guess, looking back, that it's amazing we're still here to testify how stupid young men can be. I know what you're going to say and it's correct: 'That was a long time ago.' It was, that's for sure. It was a different era with different ways to get into trouble. But it doesn't really feel that long ago. Not really. Not when you think back. It seems just like it was yesterday."

SATURDAY, SEPTEMBER 4, 2010

She said: "It wasn't always easy for us, the women among all those men. The men were the ones in charge; the woman did whatever the men said. They had us running around doing this and shining that, doing, basically, what was called 'women's work.' I didn't mind so much, though. That was what got me out of New Jersey and into the world. I would not have been able to do what I did and see what I saw without the war and everything that came with it. I couldn't have become the person that I am today if not for the war and the death and stink and smoke that was our days. I learned a lot. I learned how not to weep for the dead; I learned how to deal with one moment at a time. I became a stronger person because of the war and because I was a woman in that war. I guess you could say that was the price I had to pay to become me."

"I couldn't have become the person that I am today if not for the war and the death and stink and smoke that was our days."

WEDNESDAY, SEPTEMBER 1, 2010

He said: "There are so many things that need to be connected. We are always looking for the connection that is waiting to be found. We are a tribe. We are a nexus. We are swimming upstream in our attempt to find home. What happened to 'home'? How could we have strayed so far and become so lost? We look for our brothers and our sisters. It is too late now for our parents. We lost them a long time ago. They just spun away, and we did not follow. We have our own road to travel and our own stories to tell. There will be peace someday. I know this to be true. There will be peace and we will sit down with our brothers and tell the stories of our people and we will hear the stories of the others and we will be sustained."

FRIDAY, DECEMBER 24, 2010

He said: "At least now I know. Before now, I didn't know. I thought that it was just me and that this was just part of the way I am. I never could spell well and was never good with names, so this new thing didn't mean anything, not really. But, now, everything is different. My family is upstairs asleep and I am down here, crying and cursing God for the joke he has played on me. It's not fair, but then again, I guess there is a lot in life that isn't fair. I'm not happy about what happened, but there you go. It will get worse over time. I will forget where I am. I will forget where I'm going. I will forget who you are. I will forget what you just said to me. I will forget to eat and I will forget that I have slept. I will forget who you are and that will be the worst part of all. I will forget that I loved you."

WEDNESDAY, DECEMBER 1, 2010

She said: "It was the end of an era that was fun and filled with excitement. As you may remember, we were creating a new way of life for a new decade. We were accused of the foulest scandals! I have to say that most of the accusations were true. We wanted to burn down the bridges and then cross over on them. We had plans. Our vision reached far and wide and included new musical forms, new ways to think, new visions for dancers and writers and artists. We were the bomb thrown into the room while no one was watching. But that was then and this is now. Things have calmed down to a great extent. No one is that excited about anything anymore. The paintings now look dated. The music is tiresome after the first few minutes. We stopped dyeing our hair and no longer wear outrageous clothes. It was the end of an era of everything being over the top. It was the end of a Grand Experiment. It was the end of a generation; the end of aluminum underwear."

MUSIC

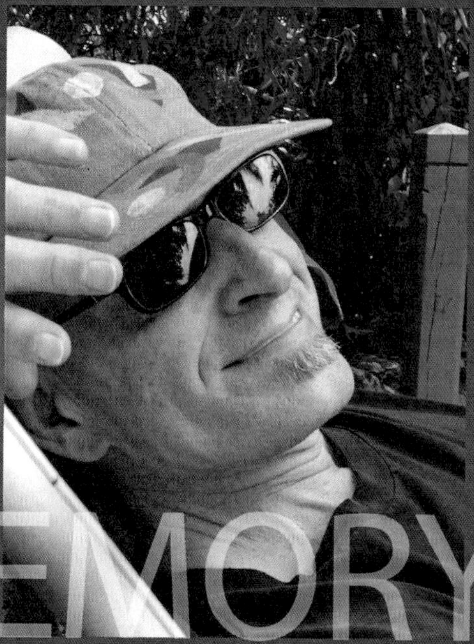

MEMORY

ARTIST's STATEMENT

ARTISTIC STATEMENT

I always wanted to "do" things: take pictures, make music, construct paintings. For me, these activities all seemed like the same thing. I'm a photographer, painter, musician (keyboards), blogger, poet, performer, husband, and father.

After obtaining a B.A. in English and film from the University of Bridgeport in Connecticut, I moved to San Francisco for a year. There I got my first "real" camera, a Nikon, and learned to process film and make black-and-white prints. In 1972, I moved back to the Washington, D.C. area where I grew up, and eventually started a band, Acrylix. We toured the East Coast from New York to Miami. In 1985, the band reorganized as Shocko Bottom, named after a neighborhood in Richmond, VA. In 1988, I married Nicole Burton, a playwright, and we moved to Riverdale Park, MD. I've been a member of the Hyattsville Community Artists Alliance since 1990.

My art, whether acrylic paintings, black-and-white photo prints, color photographs, or collaborations with poets, keeps me engaged and leads me to the next project I need to start. The works seem to create themselves in a circle, and we know that a circle has no end.

PHOTO BLOGGING

From 2005 to 2011, I created a photo blog, http://www.musicfromthefilm.blogspot.com/, combining photographs with stream-of-consciousness and "found" narrative. The site has received thousands of worldwide hits and includes over 1,000 of my photographs.

ART AND PHOTOGRAPHY SHOWS

The Cars, JEMS Optical, Washington, D.C. (October 2013–present)

Pixelated Portraits and Boy Toys, Joe's Movement Emporium, Mt. Rainier, MD (March–May 2013)

Memories From All Directions, Government House, Annapolis, MD (January 2012)

Franklin's Restaurant Gallery, Hyattsville, MD (2000–2013)

Man Made, Solo Show, Maryland-National Capital Park and Planning Commission (August 2010)

Pixelated Portraits, Solo Show, Greenbelt Arts Center (April 2010)

Art-o-matic, Paintings and Photography, Washington, D.C. (summer 2008 and 2009)

Multicultural Artists Exhibition, Marlboro Gallery, Largo, MD (November 2005)

Façades, HNTB Gallery, Washington, D.C. (April 2002)

Seeing is Believing, Montpelier Gallery, Laurel, MD (November 2002)

Artspin Gallery, Hyattsville, MD (Representation 2002–2003)

The Artists at Riversdale, Riversdale Mansion, Riverdale Park, MD (October 2000)

Snap Shot, Contemporary Museum, Baltimore, MD (June 2000)

New Themes, Market 5 Gallery, Washington, D.C. (September 1999)

Works by Contemporary Maryland Artists, Government House, Annapolis, MD (April 1999)

Boy Toys, Solo Show, The Gallery, Greenbelt Library, Greenbelt, MD (1997)

ART SERIES

Boy Toys—Greatly enlarged color photos of small plastic toys from my son's collection, exploring the strange world of a child's imagination.

Urban Landscapes—Large 36" x 48" acrylic paintings based on my color landscape photographs.
Pixel Series—Still lifes and portraits made of one-inch square "pixels." Close up, these images are hard to recognize, but they reveal themselves at a distance.

The Shadow Series—Twenty black-and-white prints in which the primary subject is not what's seen but what's not seen. These works include shadows of people projected on landscapes, and shadows of landscapes projected on urban architecture.

The Bed Series—Seventeen black-and-white portraits of friends and neighbors posed on their beds. The bed is the most private furniture in anyone's life, a place of dreams, rest, and lovemaking. Its inclusion in these photos affected the way the subjects posed and prepared themselves for the photograph.

PUBLISHING AND PERFORMANCE PROJECTS

How to Catch a Moving Train (2012)—I wrote, scored, and performed this one-hour multimedia performance piece, which contains music and narrative about a cross-country train trip I took in 1980 during which I made one crucial mistake. I performed *Train* at the Takoma Park Community Auditorium.

A Natural History of My Husband's Cars (2011)—My wife, Nicole Burton, and I wrote, scored, and performed this one-hour multimedia performance piece, which contains music, car photographs, social history, and a narrative of the nine cars I've owned in my life. We performed *Cars* at the Takoma Park Community Auditorium and the Kennedy Center in Washington, D.C.

The Body (2009–2011)—With Anne Becker, friend and Poet Laureate of Takoma Park, MD, I collaborated to create a handmade book of poetry and photographs entitled *The Body*. I made over 900 photographs of nature and human still lifes. Many have been displayed as part of *The Body Project*, a community dance, poetry, and musical performance event. *The Body Project* premiered at the Takoma Park Community Auditorium.

Random Reports (2009)—Collaborating with Barbara Henry, a poet and expert in traditional typesetting, we created a limited edition book of poems and photographs called *Random Reports*. Ms. Henry created the poems from words and phrases taken solely from the front page of Sunday editions of *The New York Times*. She set the type by hand and printed the books on handmade paper on a printing press located in her Jersey City home. I provided counterpoint photographs and coffee. *Random Reports* is part of the permanent collection at the Ransom Center of the University of Texas at Austin, and in the British Museum in London.

SCIENCE magazine (1986–2010)—In fall 2010, I retired as Production Director of *SCIENCE* magazine, the journal published by The American Association for the Advancement of Science. I had a great time working there with the people who make the news about anything involving science. They were all smarter than me but were kind enough never to let on that I knew that.